THE
Salmagundi
READER

THE Salmagundi READER

Edited by

Robert Boyers and Peggy Boyers

INDIANA UNIVERSITY PRESS
Bloomington

In Memory of Leslie H. Farber
and for
Anne Farber

Manufactured in the United States of America

Library of Congress Cataloging in Publication Data
Main entry under title:

The Salmagundi reader.

1. Social sciences—Addresses, essays, lectures.
2. Humanities—Addresses, essays, lectures. I. Boyers, Robert. II. Boyers, Peggy, 1952– .
H35.S2564 1983 300 82-49294
ISBN 0-253-35060-3
1 2 3 4 5 87 86 85 84 83

CONTENTS

II. Literature and Literary Theory

Foreword

BY DENIS DONOGHUE

The name, first. The O.E.D. says that salmagundi means "a dish composed of chopped meat, anchovies, eggs, onions with oil and condiments". Also sallad-magundy, connected in some way with Solomon Gundy. If you like that kind of food, you enjoy its variety, delighting as W. King did (1709) in "hodge-podge, gallimaufries, forced meats, jussels, and salmagundies". If you don't, you think it a mess, as the *Westminster Review* (January 1833) scorned some indecorous document, "a kind of salmagundi of law, literature, joke, and blunder". Not necessarily more to the point: Washington Irving edited, early in his career, a magazine called *Salmagundi*. I assume that our editors, Robert Boyers and Peggy Boyers, want to emphasize in the name the variety of their interests and, in the same breath, to mark some degree of continuity with earlier American ventures. Variety: there are magazines which don't particularly want it, they have a cause in view and they mean to serve it. I think of *Diacritics* in that respect: to read it consistently one must subscribe to the cause, it is a place for insiders, the elect of Deconstruction. A magazine attracts those readers, few or many, who appreciate its offering: a particular direction of interests, a recognisable idiolect, or some other indication that a cell has been formed. I am not opposed to the formation of cells, provided I am free not to join. Besides, it is a mark of our culture that, in default of a general audience, it sustains many smaller groups, constituencies defined by more occult interests than those which would sustain a general audience or readership. But I am pleased that *Salmagundi* has maintained a preference for variety, and for the tolerance which attends the preference. It is a 'little magazine', no doubt; it is unlikely to engage the interests of the many. But it does not take undue pride in its littleness, or insist on its exclusiveness.

As for its character, "a quarterly of the humanities and social sciences", I have some difficulty with the little preposition. 'Of', as readers of Wallace Stevens's poems have cause to know, is the most irritating word in the language. Sometimes it may be replaced by 'about', as if

Salmagundi were merely to claim that it discusses or reviews events in the humanities and social sciences. As indeed it does. But the little preposition also implies, and sometimes enforces the point, that far more is involved than discussion or commentary. A magazine of the humanities might claim to participate in them, in some degree to constitute them, and to provide a portion of the substance upon which comment may be made. *Salmagundi* could make that claim, too. It publishes new poems and fictions, including several which find their way into notable collections. A short list of its poems would include work by Robert Penn Warren, Robert Lowell, W. D. Snodgrass, Howard Nemerov, Louise Glück, Ben Belitt. I emphasize this commitment to poems and fictions because the present book has been obliged to omit them. Even in a large book, the inclusion of a decently representative selection of poems and stories would crowd out the essays. I regret the omission; but I admit that many of the poems one would like to read again here are easily available in the gatherings of a poet's work which make up a current volume or a *Selected Poems*. A short story or a novella—and *Salmagundi* is cordial to the longer form—is often harder to retrieve; here again the considerations of space were severe. But there is this much to be said: essays, the conditions of publishing being what they are, are very hard to recover. Few critics are famous enough to have their current essays gathered into a book. Publishers take on the publishing of essays as a dismal chore or, at best, as the good deed they are occasionally impelled to do in a naughty world. I don't think the present book provides sinister evidence that there is a warmer welcome for discursiveness than for creation; for commentary rather than the poetic text. But an ideal reader would retain, while engaged with the book, a sense of the other forms of imaginative work *Salmagundi* publishes.

Our understanding of the function of little magazines is largely indebted to Lionel Trilling. His essay on the subject in *The Liberal Imagination* was first published in 1946 at a time when little magazines—he had *Partisan Review* chiefly but not solely in view—were trying to establish the decency of their aims and to gather their energies together. Trilling associated the work of such magazines with 'the educated class,' his phrase for "those people who value their ability to live some part of their lives with serious ideas." He identified *Partisan Review* with "the impulse to insist that the activity of politics be united with the imagination under the aspect of mind".

No one doubts the seriousness with which Trilling proposed a relation between politics, ideas, imagination, and mind; or the nobility of an enterprise which would take due care of such considerations. A magazine which would take such care would be meritorious indeed. But the circumstances under which a little magazine is published today differ from those Trilling had in view. The status of ideas is not what it was in 1946. Some people still live part of their lives with serious ideas, but their sense of such ideas is likely to be far more rueful, more dispirited, than it was for their parents. It is almost necessary to say that the only accredited relation to ideas at present is a diagnostic relation, and that it is likely to be held with an ironic if not sceptical demeanour. We are living at a time chiefly characterised by the speed with which, in the public world, one idea is superseded by another. Many of the essays in *The Salmagundi Reader* reflect a sense of the obsolescence of the ideas which, yesterday or the day before, were accepted as wise. Group encounter: primal scream; self-actualization; the counterculture: it is hardly possible to utter these phrases today without adding quotation marks to indicate that the reference is nostalgic or otherwise retrospective. It is difficult to refer to ideas as boldly as Trilling did; or to invoke with his degree of security the educated class which is supposed to care for them. It would be excessive to say that Watergate and Vietnam invalidated politics; but it is hard to propose a political consideration which takes for granted the seriousness of politics as such.

My sense of this change is ambivalent. I feel some hesitation in referring to ideas in the spontaneously favorable tone so characteristic of Trilling's relation to them. Ideas are formulated at a late stage in the development of one's experience: they often seem congealed in their character, as if they had lost connexion with the feelings that produced them. At that stage they become institutions, so long as they last, and they exemplify "the imbalance of institutions over men", which Adorno has described in his essay on "Society". Adorno's theme is the preponderance of social institutions over the people who inhabit them; so that people come little by little to be the incapacitated products of the institutions. Perhaps Trilling had more confidence than we are likely to have in the critical force of mind when it is directed upon ideas: he may have felt that the exercise of mind is always strong enough to keep ideas responsive and mobile. Or so he hoped, mostly against hope. In his later essays, especially in "Mind in the Modern World", he pondered the widespread loss of confidence in the mind; the revulsion against its criteria, especially evident in the young who demanded an immediate relation to experience and knew that mind could not provide it. Trilling's urbanity did not allow him to express a sense of outrage, but the loss of confidence in mind distressed him. I recall arguing the issue with him. I maintained that by bringing to bear upon contemporary society the considerations entailed by mind, reason, and order, he could hardly fail to reach dispiriting conclusions. Wouldn't it make a congenial difference if he were to invoke rather the criteria entailed by reference to imagination, vision, and creativity? Trilling was prepared to accept the question as a question; he didn't think it merely evasive or otherwise crass. But he insisted that eventually, after due allowance had been made for the terms of imagination, one would still have to assess the evidence by the criteria of mind.

Trilling was alive to the change he regretted; but I am not sure that he foresaw how far it would go. Did he foresee the gap between theory and practice which now troubles us; or the displacement of interest from ideas to language? Trilling assumed that language was an instrument of thought, and that it was possible to separate the two. But he hardly anticipated the fetichization of Language which is so widely practised today. Or the forms of Textuality which undermine knowledge by treating its ostensible objects as texts to be read and thereby reduce all objects of attention to the equal status of being textual.

I have glanced at these matters mainly to suggest that our sense of the function of a little magazine can hardly coincide at all points with Trilling's. He could take much for granted. He didn't feel obliged to establish every large concept before invoking it. The authority of those concepts was still available. Besides, he believed that he could establish them afresh if they were challenged. A word or a concept might be put under some stress, but no Derridean erasure was required. It was normally possible not only to define a concept but to describe, with some confidence, the sentiments generally attached to it.

But before going any further, I should explain why my own relation to ideas—or rather to the form in which they receive public recognition as ideas—is ambivalent. The situation is odd. I have mentioned that the textualist inclination would reduce the status of objects. How could we award any privilege to a few objects of attention if every such object is equally textual? On the other hand, ideas are publicly received in a reified form; they are characterized as if they were things. Even though the Cartesian-empiricist tradition insists that ideas are such as to stand over against the objective world, nevertheless they are deemed to stand in such a relation to the world as to constitute, each of them, a rival object. The idea may be questioned in its various relations, but not in its status as an object-like idea. Fredric Jameson, referring to the mind's tendency toward illusions of its autonomy, describes a moment in which "there comes into being an illusion of transparency, in which the mind looks like the world, and we stare at concepts as though they were things." This is what I had in mind when I compared ideas to institutions. To the extent to which they can be invoked in something like a public character, they have the presence and often the force of an institution; and they are just as likely to exert similar pressure upon people. But on the other hand I can hardly be content to find ideas treated as if they were merely constituents of ideologies, corruptible by any social or political force that plans to use them. Trilling believed that a critical intelligence acting upon ideas would keep them alive and mobile; perhaps by projecting its own life, its own mobility, upon them. But in the scene of suspicion—the place of contemporary thought—it is common to find critical intelligence insisting upon its ineptitude; and asserting that the engagement of the mind with ideas is spurious, or at best self-deceived.

One is tempted to shout "stinking fish;" or "stinking sophistry." With at least this justification: that even a disinterested account of the Sophists makes them sound very like ourselves. E. M. Cioran has an essay on style in his *The Temptation to Exist* in which he maintains that 'reality' is not a sophist's concern: "he knows that it depends on the signs which express it and which must, simply, be mastered." In the life of the mind, he remarks, "there occurs a moment when style, transforming itself into an autonomous principle, becomes fate: it is then that the Word, as much in philosophical speculations as in literary productions, reveals both its vigor and its void". Aren't we too supposed to give ourselves, like the Sophists, to "a purely verbal art of thinking"? Aren't we supposed to be French, in Cioran's characterization of France: "Dubious of our possibilities of knowing, she is not so of our possibilities of formulating our doubts, so that she identifies our truths with the mode of translating our mistrust of them"?

Several writers in *The Salmagundi Reader* seem to me to be burdened by these considerations, even when they have evidently taken a decision—I am thinking of John Bayley's review of *Mr. Sammler's Planet*—to let them alone. Of course it is possible to let them alone. The philosophy of 'as if' should be useful to us now if ever: the secular form of Anselm's formula, *fides quaerens intellectum*. Or, like Mr. Sammler himself, we could accept the secondariness of our projects without losing sleep over it: as in a meditation about originality and belatedness he concludes that it is better "to accept the inevitability of imitation and then to imitate good things". Make peace therefore, he urges, with intermediacy and representation, "but choose higher representations". Why should I be grovelled with doubt merely because I am told—and do believe—that doubt is incorrigible? Why give up interpreting merely because its results are undecideable? I don't see why we should force ourselves, by excess of scruple, into anxieties which could be evaded by saying: let ABC be a triangle. Let it be.

Still, if we were really free we wouldn't have to proclaim our freedom.

Some of the essays in the *Reader* meet these issues directly; Lentricchia on Derrida, for instance. Or Jameson, when he proposes dialectical thinking as "an attempt to think self-consciously about our own thought while we are in the act of thinking about some object, to be both conscious and self-conscious at the same time". Some essays look at the issues aslant, and retain them as a shadow in their concern for other matters. William H. Gass maintains that "facts are not so stubborn as we sometimes like to think", and that "we can often talk things into being only what we want to say about them"; and he talks several things into being, or appearing to be for the duration of the paragraph, what he wants to say about them. *Salmagundi* itself is alert to the pervasiveness of these questions, but hasn't thought it necessary to decide which of them must be acted upon and which can safely be left to resolve themselves in time. What is decisive is the editorial determination to intervene on selected issues.

I am thinking especially of the symposia, which presumably arise from an editorial decision that this, rather than that, is a far-reaching question and must be examined. What then can we deduce from the fact that the *Reader* has reprinted—either in their entirety or in substantial excerpts—the symposia on Bellow, Trilling's *Sincerity and Authenticity,* Philip Rieff's *Fellow Teachers* and Christopher Lasch's *The Culture of Narcissism?* None of these provides any major interrogation of the theories most in favor among contemporary intellectuals. Each of them proposes certain reflections on the present character of our society; and prompts us to ask whether the reflections are, on the whole, true or false. Indeed, the symposia proceed on the assumption that a public context is still available; that it is still possible to debate a substantial issue without much concern for theory. Variety of judgment, it is supposed, will do the clarifying work of theory and, in addition, will maintain the politics of diversity: many voices in one room.

The symposium is, in that sense, an act of faith. Few of them, in my experience, live up to the generosity of the hope that proposed them. Even so, the genre itself is so admirable that it would be worth retaining even if its results were not so satisfying as they have often been in *Salmagundi.* The same hope and the same generosity take another opportunity for themselves in the interview. I assume that *Salmagundi* favors the interview as a genre for some obvious reasons and some remote ones. The obvious ones are: the occasion the interview offers for informality, or at least for the appearance of informality: the possibility that a writer will reveal more of his personality than he has chosen to reveal in his books, preoccupied as he has been with method, form, style, and a demanding rhetoric: the hope that a writer may be charmed or irritated out of his normal demeanour by a lively conversation. Is V. S. Naipaul as tetchy in his informal hours as in his discursive books? Answer: yes. Consult the interview herein for evidence. So much is obvious. Why Naipaul, Bellow and—outside the scope of this volume—Carlos Fuentes or Susan Sontag or Foucault? Why not? But the more remote reasons, I think, have to do with voice: the desirability of hearing a voice at a time when, if you believed what some people are telling you, you would regard voice as a metaphysical mystification, and your attention to it as flagrantly nostalgic. There may be a further reason. Television has accustomed us to the chat-show, in which the form itself is far more significant than anything said under its auspices. Wouldn't it then be a fine thing to retain the form, as an interview, and achieve the novelty of a conversation worth attending to? In any case, there is evidence that *Salmagundi* has a particular ear for voices, and likes whatever companionship the occasion allows.

But there is another consideration which brings us back to the question of society or shows that we have never left it. R. P. Blackmur deduced from *The Liberal Imagination* that Trilling "cultivates a mind never entirely his own, a mind always deliberately to some extent what he understands to be the mind of society". Blackmur was not at all sure that there was such a mind, or that it could be drawn over, if it existed, in support of one's own; so he nearly always insisted on using a mind as if it were entirely his own. I'm not sure whether or not the situation has changed; mainly because I don't know what would constitute evidence, either way. But I read the interviews and symposia in the *Reader* as an editorial act of faith in the "mind of society," or at least in its mere existence regardless of further quality. If you talk to someone, if four or five people sit around a table talking about *Sincerity and Authenticity,* each is forced to acknowledge a context in an obvious sense public rather than a function of his isolation. Whatever sentiments the notion of discourse may incite in Foucault's breast, he has to accept the conventions of discourse when he talks to someone. Interviews and symposia force their participants to agree upon the fundamental genre, conversation as such, before disagreeing upon the issue at hand.

There remains the essay, the third form of discursiveness. The essayist accepts some of the conventions which apply to interviews and symposia, but only in a desultory manner; he takes freedoms which an interview would not permit. He has his own sense of 'the mind of society', but is not intimidated by it. Kermode, Fiedler, Pachter, Domenach, and Barthes may be taken as observing the decencies of discourse, but it would not require much in the way of practical criticism to show that their observances differ. Kermode does not run to the *O altitudo* effects favored by some of Fiedler's paragraphs. And so on. Decorum is maintained, but variously, as befits the magazine we are reading.

Essay, interview, and symposium represent, then, different relations to the mind of society, if such a mind be assumed. They are all different forms of intervention. *Salmagundi* itself is another form, and it has its typical moment: when a cultural force has reached the stage of appearing to settle into an orthodoxy. Then the magazine intervenes, presumably in the hope—which is still practised in something like Trilling's spirit—of disturbing the orthodoxy, unsettling it. I think of the symposium on R. D. Laing as such an intervention. Or the one on Lasch's book.

But an intervention on whose behalf? *Salmagundi* doesn't have a political axe to grind. Most of the people who write for it are to be found at various points between the Far Left and the Near Right. If the magazine has a position in religion or metaphysics, I don't know what it is. If it has a mandate, it can only be some notion of an intelligentsia and its proper range of interests. On this matter it is useful to think of Gramsci's account of the intelligentsia in a Marxist context; especially of his distinction between traditional intellectuals and organic intellectuals. Traditional intellectuals are those who claim to speak for historical continuity uninterrupted by political formations or social events. Gramsci would regard them as claiming to see the truth of human life *sub specie aeternitatis,* and he would give the word 'traditional' a force entirely negative. It is the function of intellectuals, he maintained, to develop in the masses a critical consciousness, so that change—the proper revolutionary change—may come about. This work is to be done by organic intellectuals, who identify themselves with the class or group from which they have derived or whose purposes they espouse.

Gramsci's distinction between traditional and organic intellectuals is good enough for any Marxist purpose. If an intellectual is not part of the solution, he's part of the problem. But in a context not specifically Marxist, if Marxist at all, the distinction is not sufficient. Nor is Edward Said's recent project for 'oppositional criticism' much better: it seems to me to be the liberal imagination at the desperate stage of deciding that it must fight ideology with the weapons and tactics of ideology. Perhaps the liberal imagination is enough, if we hold to an undesperate form of its activity. But if we need another phrase, comparable in lucidity to Gramsci's traditional and organic intellectuals, I suggest 'heuristic intellectual', with only the dictionary's authority. The O.E.D. cites Caird's commentary on Kant (1877): "The ideas of reason are heuristic, not ostensive: they enable us to ask a question, not to give the answer". The small dictionary defines heuristic as: 'serving to find out or discover'. In any case, an heuristic criticism would be projective rather than expository, it would be turned toward a future in which its questions might be answered. To give it a further character: let me recall the passage in the second chapter of *The Middle of the Journey* in which John Laskell "lay through the day, drinking in the light that filled the room, and experienced something just short of an emotion. It had great delicacy and simplicity, as if the circulation of his blood had approached the threshold of his consciousness and was just about to become an idea. It was as if being had become a sensation". An heuristic criticism could be regarded as having its 'moment' somewhere between the different stages of sentience represented by a sensation and an idea; after the one, and just short of the other. The question would have been proposed, but the answer or the solution would have to remain implicit, as if companioned by scruple.

Is this the kind of reader *Salmagundi* proposes to attract? I have no authority to commit the magazine, or to represent anything but my sense of it as a reader. But I envisage such a reader, approaching these essays on film, poetry, fiction, government, morality, psychiatry, psychoanalysis, history, science, religion, and other matters. He is unlikely to be equally informed on all these subjects. Perhaps one of them has his professional commitment, and the others must be ancillary. In his professional capacity he must be expert, but as a reader of this magazine he does well to have free interests; a minister without portfolio, ready to take a responsible interest in nearly everything and more particular care of the issues, few or many, which engage his intensity.

THE
Salmagundi
READER

PART ONE
Culture and Politics

The City under Attack

BY GEORGE STEINER

1. In Fragment 114 of Heraklitus we read: "if a man would speak rationally, he must strengthen himself with that which is comprehensive, which is common to all as is a city with the law." Like much of Heraklitus, this injunction is opaque. But a number of radical motifs, of conceptions rooted in the inception of western thought, are here at work and congruent. The possibility of rational human discourse hinges on a common foundation of understanding, on a consensus of the limits of articulacy (this will be the Cartesian axiom). But this enabling commonalty of reason is no mere common denominator. It is a universal aggregate of meaning, an ordering fabric of the universe from which man selects and structures both his individual and his communal codes. Heraklitus' implicit picture is at once central and complex. Hence the importance of the simile: rational discourse in man relates to this universal commonwealth of ordered reality as does a city to the law. Observe how many key terms are interacting: discourse, reason, universality, the city and the law. After two thousand five-hundred years they are interactive still in the meshing of a triad of words which we do not, often enough, register as originally inter-woven: 'communion', 'communication' and 'community'. Moreover, though each of these terms and their immensely ramified fields of connotation has obviously changed in the course of western history, much of their core and of the life of relation between them remain Greek.

Greek thought bears constantly on the notion of the city *(polis)*. It is the locale where the density, the specific gravity of discourse are greatest. Speech which, in classic sensibility, very nearly defines the excellence as well as the tragic singularity of man, relates functionally to urban needs and spaces: in the matrices of commerce, of political debate, of rhetorical and dramatic presentation and, principally, of the philosophic dialectic. Repeatedly, the opening sections of Plato's Dialogues tell of a meeting in the city between Socrates and his companions, between Socrates and a visiting luminary such as Parmenides or Protagoras. The contest of minds is joined in the city square, under the temple porch, in the colonades of the academy. The city is, literally, the framing context or scene of the mind when it is in a condition of elucidative, exploratory motion. It is, tautologically, the setting for politics: the semantics of *polis,* politics, policy, police are indivisible. A subtle, finely detailed vision of the political ideals and limitations of the human species underlies the Aristotelian prescription that no city should have a circumference exceeding that in which a cry for help, wherever uttered, can be clearly heard at the outer gates. Only urban man is qualified, indeed compelled, to participate in the administration and judgment of public business. Women, children and slaves are excluded from this activity which is simultaneously fundamental and expressive of maturity. He who shuns politics, who wilfully encloses his house in privacy is, in Greek terminology, an 'idiot'. He who is of a city can, must be, a citizen. (Notice that our own idiom, though in an age of nation-states and even of supra-national forms, retains the antique identification between citizenship and urban centre.)

The *polis* is the place of art. Here again we find in Greek philosophic thought and in Greek mythology intimations that go back to the very sources of western feeling. The magus, the poet who, like Orpheus and Arion is also a supreme sage, can make stones of music. One version of the myth has it that the walls of Thebes were built of song, the poet's voice and harmonious learning summoning brute matter into stately civic form. The implicit metaphors are far-reaching: the 'numbers' of music and of poetry are cognate with the proportionate use and division of matter and of space; the poem and the built city are exemplars both of the outward, living shapes of reason. And only in the city can the poet, the dramatist, the architect find an audience sufficiently compact, sufficiently informed to yield him adequate echo. Etymology preserves the link between 'public', in the sense of the literary or theatrical public, and the 'republic' meaning the assembly of men in the space and governance of the city.

Having exalted the city, having almost identified urbanity with the realisation of man's philosophic, political and artistic genius, Greek consciousness was correspondingly haunted by the vulnerability of cities. No body of myths, no literature, no school of historical writing is more deeply possessed by the image of the destroyed city. We do not know precisely when or even where the laying waste of Troy occurred. But the drama and desolation of that ruin, the spectacle of the "topless towers of Ilium" perishing in a single night of divine malice and betrayal, has never lost its grip on the western mind. The *Odyssey* tells of a man wandering cityless. Again we suspect, but cannot prove, that a large complex of historical fact lies behind the legend, the remembrance of a period, in c. the 12th and 11th centuries B.C. when barbarian incursions and internecine warfare made ancient Mediterranean cultures homeless and drove unhoused men to wander an enemy earth.

The terror of such occasions, of the dawn in which there is only smoke where a city was, shrills through the plays of Euripides, through the *Andromache* and the *Trojan Women*. To be without a city is to be naked. We feel the same terror, analysed, in Thucydides' account of the Peloponnesian Wars, in his reflections on the destruction of Miletus and on the possible fate awaiting Athens as exhaustion and defeat draw near. When plague comes to Athens the bonds and sinews of man's humanity loosen fatally. Thomas Hobbes, who had thought much about the organic meaning of the city and who knew the nightmare of pestilence, translates admirably:

> And the laws which they formerly used touching funerals were all now broken, every one burying where he could find room. And many for want of things necessary, after so many deaths before, were forced to become impudent in the funerals of their friends. For when one had made a funeral pile, another getting before him would throw on his dead and give it fire. And when one was in burning, another would come and, having cast thereon him whom he carried, go his way again.

The ancient panic, the images of urban devastation which obsessed the Greeks are with us still. Hauptmann's version of *Agamemnon* was staged in Germany shortly after the end of the Second World War. At the point when the Herald speaks of the destruction of Troy a greatly enlarged aerial photograph descended on the stage. It showed the skeleton of Dresden after the fire-storm. "Woe to the destroyed city," says the Aeschylaean chorus, but "woe also to the destroyer of cities". Both are the mark of the folly, of the rage of self-mutilation in man.

2. The Hebraic tradition is radically different. Man's origin, his first and all-determining rendez-vous with God are set in a garden. All locations after that garden are the desperate or the next-best thing. The teleology of history, the fundamental impulse of man's normal existence is a nostalgic passion for return, for re-entry into Eden. The high moments of spiritual meaning after the fall come to pass in the desert or in the mountains. The first reference to a municipal construction made in the Bible is that to the fatal enterprise at Babel. The earliest cities to mark Biblical history are the city Cain built for Enoch and Sodom and Gomorrah. This is, obviously, no accident. The early Jews are a nomadic people coming to uneasy terms with the settled existence of agriculture. For a long spell their shrines are mobile or set on the high rocky places. Architecture on the large scale, the confining order of cities have on them the brand of Egypt. When he journeys to Jerusalem at high holidays, the Judaean shepherd, the wine-grower from Galilee is uneasily aware of the tension between the original tenor and image-world of his faith and its new fixed, urban setting in the citadel of David and courtyard of Solomon.

This tension vibrates through prophetic literature. From Hosea to

Malachi, the texts are shrill with vituperation against the whoredom of cities. The relations of Jeremiah to Jerusalem are perhaps the most intense of which we have record in the history of man and city. His vision of urban ruin is so graphic that one senses brick and mortar loosening under the hammer of the prophet's speech:

> And I will smite the inhabitants of this city, both man and beast: they shall die of a great pestilence. . . . He that abideth in this city shall die by the sword, and by famine and by the pestilence. . . . And many nations shall pass by this city, and they shall say everyman to his neighbour, Wherefore has the Lord done this unto this great city?

But when disaster has struck, Jeremiah's lament has the same utter desolation as that of the Trojan women in Euripides howling like homeless dogs under the charred walls of Ilium:

> How doth the city sit solitary, that was full of people! how is she become as a widow! she that was great among the nations, and princess among the provinces, how is she become tributary!
>
> She weepeth sore in the night, and her tears are on her cheeks: among all her lovers she hath none to comfort her: all her friends have dealt treacherously with her, they are become her enemies.

Yet observe the crucial difference. In the Greek vision the agony lies in the destruction of a particular material city, in the devastation of its secular beauty and political power. For Jeremiah Jerusalem is only the outward garb of Israel. It is not, as is Athens for Pericles, a manifestation of man's creative genius, but merely the tent of stone, as it were, in which the Covenant lodges. Hence the vehement personalization, indeed femininization of Jeremiah's mode of address. The city is a widow when God is absent. The literal existence of Jerusalem is no more than a function of Israel's relation to God.

A pagan city is doubly damned. Its apparent solidity, its arrogant opulence, conceal spiritual emptiness and pollution. After more than two millennia the very names of Babylon, of Nineveh, of Tyre have come down to us charged with malediction. We feel the lineaments of Babylon in the stress and sensual occasions of every great urban centre. The curse over Nineveh is heard each time a great city is gutted by economic crisis or damaged by war. After the Great Fire of London, when Chicago had burned, in the wake of the conflagration of Paris during the Commune, the vocabulary of description, of polemic, of didactic remorse was always scriptural. "The cleansing flame has purged Babylon" proclaimed Russian mystics after the ruin of Moscow in 1812. Communion with God lies in the wilderness. The Redeemer comes from the hills and silent places; Satan is on the boulevard.

This polarity gives a paradoxical character to the actual history of Judaism. After the destruction of the Temple, the Jew becomes an urban creature. The life of the Diaspora is that of great cities: Alexandria, Damascus, Toledo, Salonika, Frankfurt, Prague, New York. The *ghetto* is a city within a city, concentrating both the intellectual resources and physical restraints of urban ways. The typical pursuits of the Jew—economic, scholarly, juridical—are metropolitan. The cobbled or asphalt street, the coffee house, the bourse, are his ecology. Though born of the Central European cities, Zionism is a pastoral vision, a summons to the barren places and open skies of Israel. Nothing is more striking in the Zionist accomplishment than the retransformation, the mutation backward, of urban exile into rural homecoming. Though Tel Aviv is built and Jerusalem reconquered, the root ideal is that of the kibbutz and the Negev. Ben Gurion resides not in Jerusalem but in the solitary frontier settlement at Arad. Suspicion of the city, the conviction that man must replant the garden from which he was exiled into the darkness of history, remain a deep element in Judaism, in the dialogue of human ideals which opposes Athens and Jerusalem.

3. So far as western history goes—this may be its distinctive but also isolating characteristic—the Attic vision prevailed. The major portion of our political, social, intellectual and artistic history is that of the great cities from Rome and Byzantium to Leningrad and New York. The urban centrality of the Roman model of empire modulates readily into Christianity. The Augustine sense of the human condition is crystallized not in the holy mountain of God, not in the desert of His burning bush, but in *The City of God (De civitate Dei)*. We segment our image of historical epochs—medieval, renaissance, baroque—according to the rise and fall of representative cities. The medieval university (has there ever been a prouder claim implicit in the title of any institution?) shifts the active nerve-centres of mental life away from the monasteries, often isolated and rural. Henceforth the city is the generator and store-house of knowledge. It is around the personalities, local features, and social chronicles of Rome, Florence, Milan, Venice, that we organize our understanding of the development of political theory, monetary practises, manufacture and the sciences. The primacy of the city, both material and symbolic, fully survives the shift from the city-state to the nation-state. It is in London, in Paris, in Berlin, that the political-social history of the respective nation-states is concentrated. The result is a profound, possibly myopic bias in our entire western notion of past reality: almost to a man, we record and picture historical events in their metropolitan setting. To all but the specialist, the rural world, where the numerical bulk of humanity in fact conducted its physical and emotional existence, is a timeless blur. In this essentially unrecorded terrain, the 'eternal cycle of the seasons', 'the immemorial cadence of plant and

animal life' (phrases charged with dismissive inference) replace the drama of conscious, rapidly-changing history as it is made and experienced by urban man. The suggestion of a rural 'historicity', of complex historical evolution also amid the inarticulate mass of the peasantry did not, so far as I can make out, arise before well into the 19th century. It may well be the uniqueness of Chinese institutions, of the Chinese categories of high culture that they were, and have to a striking degree remained, land- and not city-based.

Note the literal inherence of the city in the crucial semantic clustres of the western vocabulary of culture. The word-family which comprises 'civic', 'civil', 'civility', 'civilization' itself, is one of the most value-charged in our idiom. As early as 1533 'civility' connotes a liberal education of the kind only available in the city *(civitatem);* in the 1550's and 60's the range of the term broadens to include those modes of polished discourse and social encounter which differentiate 'civilized' men and women from rustic barbarism. To us the word 'urbane' has a debilitated, faintly suspect resonance. For most of its linguistic career, however, it carried strong, positive entailments. From the 1530's on, it signified courtesy and ease in society, an art of life such as only the city *(urbs)* could foster. Dryden aptly associates moral doctrine with "urbane or well-mannered wit", i.e. with the kind of perception founded on the confident bearing of the 'city man'. The strength of the old usage endures, surprisingly, in Wordsworth when he evokes a three-step advance of humanity from "savage life to rustic and rustic to urbane". Indeed, though the romantic movement has clouded the point, poets in western literature were praisers of the city to a far greater extent and long before they became singers of landscape, William Dunbar's

> London, thou art the flower of cities all!
> Gemme of all joy, jasper of jocunditie,

Charles Péguy's hymn to Paris *"ville des villes, capitale des capitales"*, or Carl Sandburg's celebration of Chicago—

> Come and show me another city with lifted head singing
> so proud to be alive and coarse and strong and cunning—

are a part of a long, immensely prolific tradition of homage and delight. When Dr. Johnson decreed that a man who is tired of London is tired of life, he was only being lapidary about a commonplace of classic sensibility. In Chekhov's *Three Sisters* the reiterated adjuration "if only we could get to Moscow" or "when at last we live in Moscow" stand for the elusive sum of human fulfillment, for that just realisation of a man or woman's vital chance which solely the great city can provide. This entire world-view, ultimately inherited from Periclean Athens, is perhaps most pointedly summarized at the close of Molière's *Le Misanthrope*. Outraged by the mendacities of fashionable convention, Alceste will flee to the "desert" *(mon désert)*. The context leaves us in doubt as to his exact intention: he is going a few miles out of Paris.

4. The counter-current was, of course, always present. The poetry of Horace is of such importance for the western idiom just because it is the first to localize and exploit the tensions between urbanity and the rustic ideal. Horatian man is steeped in the values of the imperial capital but he feels the magnetism of a contrary mode, of a retreat to the calm vine or the silent cottage. In the early church this magnetism assumes a radical, often apocalyptic force. There is a church of the desert and the cave which looks with darkening misgiving on the urbanity of the evolving episcopate. The stylite, the hermit, the monk or mendicant of the open road are not only in retreat from the bureaucracy and mundane functions of the metropolitan church. They are drastic critics of a worldly *ecclesia,* of a faith which has literally immersed itself in the civic structure of Rome, Alexandria or Byzantium and thus reneged on its original genius of agrarian populism and meditative solitude. The Adamite and chiliastic movements of the middle ages, with their culmination in the ferocious peasant wars of the 15th and 16th centuries, are directly related to this polarity. In the visionary despair of the *jacqueries* and agrarian uprisings we find, over and again, the image of an archaic church, freed from the pomp of the great towns, freed from the control of bishop and burgher in the whoredom and political ruthlessness of the city.

These deep impulses of Edenic return have their secular analogue. The subject of pastoral art and literature is so large that I can do no more than allude to it. Originating in a complex amalgam of Theocritus, of the Latin eclogue, of Hellenistic romance and, unquestionably, of Christian primitivism and fable, the tradition of pastoral is one of the small number of archetypes, of dominant recursive genres, in our culture. It is as central to Ronsard and Tasso as it is to Keats and Lamartine; it relates Herrick to Wallace Stevens. Allegoric painting turns on it, as does so very much of music from Monteverdi's laments of nymphs and shepherds to Debussy's evocations of fawns and arcadian pipes. Our gardens, our public parks and grottoes, are deliberate versions of pastoral. The pendulum cadence of middle-class life between work in town and leisure in the country implies the pastoral mode. But the crucial point is this: in its classic vein, the pastoral vision holds no threat to urbanity. On the contrary: the renaissance image of Arcadia, the *bergerie* or model dairy of the *ancien régime,* the cottage or sylvan manse of the romantics and Victorians, are projections of urban tastes and ideals on to the countryside. The summer guest mimes rusticity, he 'roughs it' by deliberate, playful choice. The straw hats and parasols bob up and down amid the corn-flowers; the picnic-basket lies snug on the fell. Proust gazed at the white hawthorne blossoms, of which he was to be the incomparable recorder, through the closed windows of a car. Undoubtedly the pastoral style, particularly in the 17th century, had elements of a critique of court and city life. But this critique came from within the urban value-system. It was little more than a safety-valve, coloured by the unreality of arcadian romance and decorative mythology. When shepherds pipe on oaten straws

> And merry larks are ploughmen's clocks,
> When turtles tread, and rooks, and daws,
> And maidens bleach their summer smocks,

all is well and under control in the vacation-Eden of city-man *(le citadin)*.

The dialectic turn does not, I think, come before Rousseau. Rousseau's own 'naturalism' is in large part a variant on the classic pastoral (consider his idyllic poems and successful opera, *Le Devin du village*). But there is something very new and potentially menacing, a strain of 'anti-civility' sprung, perhaps, of Rousseau's Calvinist background and of the acidity of his own genius. In his famous essay on the corruption of manners, Rousseau posits the thesis that civilization is tantamount with human decay, that so-called civilized man is fallen utterly from the estate of happiness and moral clarity which marked his primitive existence. If Geneva is to remain morally habitable, it must ban all theatre and rid itself of the luxuries and cultural institutions which were the pride of classic urbanity. But it is improbable that urban man can be saved. From Sodom there is no avenue but flight. Rousseau is playing no literary game here; he does not see nature as an extension to the city park. His return to nature is an advance to radical utopia. His acute, though sometimes hysterical critique of mundanity contains an unmistakable summons to destruction. Rousseau's rhetoric of primitivism builds a bridge between the anti-urban tirades of the Prophets and the cold menace of Brecht—"nothing shall remain of the great cities except the winds that blew through them".

With the landscape of the early Brecht, in which Chicago plays so decisive a symbolic role, we have come full circle. I do not know who first evoked "the jungle of the cities". The buried metaphor or oxymoron is latent in Dickens's description, in *Hard Times,* of the great serpents of smoke coiling from factory chimneys, of machinery in the mills pounding up and down like crazed elephants, of urban gutters garish with industrial dies brighter, more poisonous than Amazonian flora. Engels, Zola, Dreiser familiarize the imagination with the comparison between the blind savageries of economic struggle in the city of capital and slum, and the similar, but innocent savageries in the primaeval forests of Darwinian ethology. Soon—witness *Green Mansions* or the magical day-dreams of Douanier Rousseau's jungle-paintings—there is an ironic reversal. It is not the real jungle which is cruel and full of blood-lust. It is the industrial metropolis. Baudelaire's rag-picker, tapping his way along the pavement in the Parisian dawn, picks up remnants of lust, abjection and even murder such as no hunter would find in darkest Africa. Nature, preferrably untouched by western man, is now the authentic locale of civility. The city is 'red in tooth and claw'. The subtlest equivocation, summarizing the traditional tension between urban and primitive, but showing how that tension was no longer under control, occurs at the beginning of Conrad's *Heart of Darkness*. The actual narration is set on the glittering Thames, majestic and orderly at the centre of imperial London. But the tide and the river itself run inexorably towards the corruption, the terror which Conrad's narrator discovers in the exploited heart of the jungle. The attack on the city, which marks so much of the political mood today, was gathering impetus.

5. It developed on several fronts. In so far as the city was the crystallization and perpetuating instrument of mature capitalism, it became the express target of socialist, Marxist and anarchist dissent. It was in the big city, as Engels showed memorably in his study of Manchester, that the contrasts between rich and poor, between west end and slum, were most inhuman. Such dichotomies had always existed; but the new landscape of technology, of industrial filth and over-crowding had given the distinction a terrible intensity. The city was no longer a community, an aggrandized village with a coherent flow of life. Capitalism and the technologies of mass production had made of it a congeries of hostile camps. The successive reconstructions of Paris after the revolutions of 1830, 1848 and 1871 gave brutal, cynical expression to the clairvoyance of the bourgeoisie. Around the *beaux quartiers* ran the open boulevards and adroit vistas needed by the gunners.

The radical critique of urban conditions—in which novelists such as Dickens, Dostoevski and Zola played so major a part—was obviously just. We owe to the detailed testimony, to the angry statistics of social reformers what improvements there have been in the hygiene, in the standards of construction, in the allocation of space in the modern metropolis. The suggestion that men and women have a right to decent housing whatever their economic status was a piece of red terror when first put forward. It is now a platitude (though far, still, from any complete realisation). Yet if the critique was valid and long overdue, it is fair also to say that the actual coming of socialist or Marxist societies has nowhere brought with it a genuine mutation in the urban fabric. The

19th century dream of the new phalanstery, of the "cities of light", remains just that, a bright chapter in the history of utopia. The Bolshevik revolution was made by urban men. All bureaucracies build bureaus. Again China may be the one challenging exception.

Hence the more extreme, the more total critique of the city by what I would call 'the new millennarians' or ecologists. Man must quit the doomed Nineveh in which, whether he will or not, all existence depends on the exploitation of fellow-man. In virtue of its physical structure, of its parasitic status with regard to the production of food and raw material, of its mountainous waste-products, the technocratic city is the dynamo of pollution. It embodies, at their dramatic nadir, all the false values of superfluity, private hypocrisy and blind greed which have made of modern western man the enemy of the natural world. The city zoo mocks the innumerable species he has reduced to extinction; the city arboretum is a ghostly parody of the forests he has pulped. Salvation lies on the open road, in the rural commune or in the far places of a promised Asia.

The rhetoric of the flower-child has traditional roots: in primitive Christianity and chiliasm, in pastoralism and Rousseau. It is, characteristically, the idiom of a rebellion born *inside* the city. Its vision of pastoral innocence is almost grotesquely uninformed concerning the complicated, often ugly realities of agrarian life and history. But it draws on at least two novel, interrelated sources of panic. Albeit replete with cheap slogans and naivetés, the debate over the environment is about something. Rightly or not we are frightened; the possibility that our abuse of the organic world is already beyond repair cannot be ruled out. We have laid waste our inheritance as if in subconscious vengeance on the garden from which we were expelled. In this sense of a crisis of environment, the cancerous, seemingly uncontrollable rapacities of urban life play an acute role. The air above the metropolis is unbreathable; the waters around and beneath it are a cess-pit. To a large extent (or so current radical orthodoxy would have it) the spoiler has been the white man, the predator and technological exploiter from Europe and the United States. This is the second, closely related motif of the new apocalyptics. Far from being the principal generator of human excellence, the begetter and trustee of the main evolutionary thrust, the civilization of Plato and Newton, of Leonardo and of Mozart, has been a leprosy on the natural earth and mere enslaver of more innocent races. It matters little whether this reading of history is masochistic idiocy, whether it is only the spurious breast-beating of academic illiterates. It possessed wide psychological and even political appeal. Inherent in it is a hatred of the *polis*. Through its libraries and museums, through its academies and monuments, the western city is the insolent incarnation of a long record of sanguinary domination over its own oppressed classes and over the underdeveloped world. There must be retribution for so much guilt. Or to use an image which turns up, ominously, around the 1850's, when the European and Anglo-Saxon hegemony stood at its confident zenith, "let the day come when Tartar horses slake their long thirst in the ruined fountains of the Tuileries".

6. These ideological and symbolic attacks (I make no apology for having quoted often from poets and novelists: they saw furthest) have found a vulnerable target. The contemporary metropolis hardly inspires the celebration and confidence which were expressed from the 16th to the earlier decades of the 20th century. My remarks here focus mainly on the United States, but what is true of America today is very largely bound to be the case in Europe, the U.S.S.R. and Japan tomorrow. There has been a flight from the urban middle to the suburbs and semi-rural zones in commuter belts. The phenomenology of the suburb is exceedingly complex and by no means perfectly understood. At one level it constitutes a repudiation of urban ideals, a pastoral artifice with its own very peculiar rhythm of bucolic time—a temporal fiction absurdly removed from the realities of actual rural existence. The suburbanite who works in the core-city assumes a contrasting persona at evening and on weekends. In the northeastern United States and around Chicago, areas in which the suburban mode is most consciously developed, winter-weather can bring on a counter-motion, an irruption of authentic rural conditions (snow-drifts, blocked roads, even isolation) into what is most other times a fictitious landscape. But observe the tangled paradox: the very suburbs and commuter townships which were intended to inhibit the engulfing march of the city, which were meant to provide a life away from urbanism, are becoming an agent of even greater urbanization. I refer, of course, to Jean Gottman's seminal concept of 'megalopolis', to the insight, since confirmed by actual growth and projective analysis, that ever more closely-woven filaments and networks of suburbs and commuter-belts will soon fuse to gigantic urban galaxies. Such 'mega-cities' already stretch across the middle of Japan and will soon span the final gaps of open country between Boston and Washington, D.C.

We are now, it would seem, in a phase of transition or unstable equilibrium. There is evidence, though it is difficult to gauge, that the exodus to the suburbs is being halted and even reversed. The advantages of mock-pastoral no longer outweigh the handicaps imposed by the wide-spread chaos of bankrupt public transportation. Nevertheless, there is a real dilemma of emptiness at the heart of the night-time metropolis. The slow, highly diverse process of transformation from the medieval and renaissance condition in which home and place of business were in the same edifice to modern 'downtown' has culminated in a dangerous anomaly. For one half of the weekday and during all of weekends and holidays, the economic and, in certain cases, the physical heart of the city is inert. To walk on Wall Street or Threadneedle Street after seven in the evening is to confront a hollow stage-set. The vital continuity between place of abode and locale of maximalized intellectual and nervous energy is broken. The consequent physical and psychological dissociation has undoubtedly impaired not only the structural rationale of the city but the identification between it and its inhabitants.

The anomaly of emptiness, furthermore, is now being experienced in residential areas as well. Several factors are involved: among them the cost and uncertainty of transport, the availability, through television and long-playing records, of top-flight entertainment right in the home, and the sheer nervous-bodily exhaustion of the man who has had difficult distances to cover to and from work. More spectacularly, there is the matter of violence in the city streets. On this garish topic a little perspective is needed. Bodies floated quite regularly under the elegant bridges of 16th-century Paris or Florence; the street-gangs of Augustan London made many nights a terror; no modern witness has ever seen the blind frenzy of urban mobs on the go as they were during the Gordon Riots; the bully-boys of early 19th-century New York were legend. Crime and physical danger have been endemic to cities throughout history. Our presumption of safety derives from an extremely short period, less than one hundred years, of middle-class power and stable, subservient social or ethnic castes. But in social attitudes facts count for less than one's feeling of facts. Whether history or statistics bear us out, we do feel threatened as never before when we walk the filth-strewn pavements of American cities. Theft, mugging and worse seem routine in even the centre of Manhattan or San Francisco. Each unlit hallway, each empty elevator holds menace. The great parks no longer provide the safe solitude of an organized pastoral; their emptiness is that of fear. Under these circumstances intimations that cities are ungovernable when they reach dimensions such as those of New York or Tokyo, that the survival of urban existence as we have known it is now doubtful, have spread even to responsible quarters. More and more often one hears, only partly in jest, the cry: 'we must begin all over again'.

7. We cannot, of course. And cities are stubborn: Jericho is c. 8000 years old, Damascus not very much less. What we must do is to think through the functions of the city in the quickly changing emotional, political and ecological framework of the current crisis. I am in no way competent to do so. Let me restrict my concluding remarks to two possible areas of discussion.

It is becoming clear that the 'information revolution', the revolution in the storage, processing and communication of knowledge through electronic means will be at least as fundamental in its effects on daily life as was the industrial revolution. Data-banks, the cybernetics of feed-back, the modes of learning and analysis made available by on-line computers, are far more than electronic devices merely accelerating or rationalizing traditional procedures. They entail radically new ways of thinking about and using the past (i.e. the accumulation of previous data) and of analyzing future alternatives. Many facets of our lives will be subject to programming and to investigatory models which are bound to modify essential habits of thought and feeling. The present instinct—for reasons that have to do with the costing of space, with military security, with freedom from vibration or electric interference—is to locate the great new complexes of information-storage, retrieval and analysis away from the older urban centres. This is, I think, short-sighted. It is one of our vital jobs, as beings with historical consciousness, to relate the new modes to the old. This relation has its physical correlate. Even after the transfer to magnetic tape of the great corpus of extant print, even after the substitution of electronic retrieval techniques for traditional bibliographies and means of reference, a major library will have a very important part to play. It will, as it were, embody the margins for error, the solicitations to waste motion (the hand moving along the shelf and finding the book it did not look for) on which the autonomous, discontinuous process of creation depend. In short: it may prove of the utmost importance to associate the new technologies of the intellect with the more traditional locale of civilization. It is speculative, to be sure, but not irresponsible, to envisage future cities as complex data-banks, as synapses—perhaps with specialized functions, such as Magnitogisk, the Siberian 'Science City'—in a global network or cortex of information processing. (It may be worth noting, in this connection, that a number of countries, notably the United Kingdom, are having second thoughts about the location of universities. The impulse to ruralism or small-town tranquility, which characterized the foundation of many post-war universities and technical colleges, is rapidly fading. Even with their nightmares of crowding and distraction, great cities are proving to be the more rational matrix for active intellectual pursuit.)

My second point is equally tentative. (It is only a naive reflection.) There are indices, though variously read, that television, the long-playing record and other means of indirect presentment, are losing ground. There is a growing hunger for immediate encounter with the arts and the performing artist. Only the city provides a natural milieu for the world of drama, of opera, of symphonic performance, of the major art exhibit. The immensely problematic 'leisure-crisis' will soon be on us. A four-day work-week is no longer a utopian fantasy or threat (depending on one's point of view). The organization of leisure along lines which are more or less positive, which enrich rather than diminish the reserves of human understanding and self-respect, will tax our social policies to the utmost. In this organization the cities, and the city-centres—now abandoned and unfunctional in the evenings—could prove decisive. The closure to all but pedestrian traffic after sundown and on week-ends of central districts in Amsterdam, Basel and Bonn is an example of what I have in mind. Here concentrated urban areas are treated as an explicit setting for leisure and culture. The failure, until now, of the Lincoln Center in Manhattan seems to me to hinge precisely on the absence of the necessary context; nothing was done to prepare the adjoining areas of the city for the opportunities and demands of this resplendent but fragile hub. The day may not be far off when we do not scurry to the surburbs and Westchesters come Friday afternoon, but prepare to return to the city-centres for our leisure and stimulation. Both in regard to the information revolution and to the continuation of the arts, the city is the only format in which the past moves constantly into the new.

These are only tentative, inevitably superficial approaches to the vast problem of the survival and future of the western or Japanese megalopolis. There are instances where it may already be too late. Some of the leviathan conurbations—a word as ugly as the thing itself—may break up. Conceivably cities have an optimal dimension, say somewhere between Toledo and Leningrad, beyond which they are in constant danger of fission. But it is difficult to believe that the *polis* will not be with us for a very long time to come or that the sequence of benediction *urbi et orbi*—the city coming first—will not continue to symbolize an indispensable reality in our culture. What I have sought to suggest is that the two notions are inseparable, that civilization and city are cognate *at* as well as *in* their roots of meaning. Heraklitus began by relating discourse to understanding and city to law. There is, he adduced, no communication of reason without community, without the organic web of mutual cognizance and responsibility that makes for the grammar of speech and for the law-abiding *polis*. Reason and law are live shapes of order. So, when it is true to itself, is the city of man. It is now under attack. But where else should he lodge?

From "Fellow Teachers"—

BY PHILIP RIEFF

EDITORS' NOTE: On March 26, 1971, Philip Rieff came to Skidmore College to submit to an extensive public interview conducted by the two of us. An edited transcript of that interview was to be published in Salmagundi, but for a variety of reasons the document did not turn out to be as substantial, as illuminating, as Professor Rieff had hoped, though surely satisfactory from our point of view. He decided to write in place of the interview the altogether extraordinary document that he calls "Fellow Teachers." It is an impassioned and beautifully reasoned essay, polemic, letter—one is at a loss to describe it precisely—addressed to us, two younger men clearly committed to Philip Rieff's work and anxious to pursue researches of a sort he has so brilliantly extended in his books. Many of the questions he examines were recommended to him by us in correspondence preliminary to the actual interview at Skidmore, while others emerged in the course of subsequent exchanges. The issues were, of course, suggested to us by careful and devoted readings of Freud: The Mind Of The Moralist *and* The Triumph Of The Therapeutic *and of Professor Rieff's scattered essays and prefaces, as well as by comparisons these brought to mind with the works of others who have engaged comparable issues. Philip Rieff's response to the questions and issues we raised is, we think, a major cultural document of the greatest significance. What appears in this reader is part one of that document.*

—Robert Boyers and Robert Orrill

Fellow teachers,

Is it possible that my invitation to come to Skidmore on 26th March 1971, to be publicly interviewed, was based upon a happy misunderstanding? Did you imagine that I am a herald of the therapeutic? I am neither for nor against my ideal type. Nor am I Freudian or anti-Freudian, Marxist or anti-Marxist, Weberian or anti-Weberian. I am a scholar-teacher of sociological theory; as such, I try to help myself and my students to see not only what the theorist has seen, but through him to see what is at stake in his vision. Anyone who knows how to make his way toward the light will find himself in shadows. For example: there are long shadows, of Jew-hatred, cast by Marx on the Jewish Question. Even so, some of my Jewish students resolutely prefer the shadows; they come away from their lessons confirmed in their self-hatred. For more general reasons I shall try to explain later, I cannot resolve that self-hatred. My job, as I understand it, is to convey the highly specialized objectivity that derives, not from some impersonal methodological gimmick, but from attempting to get inside the theoretical work of my predecessors, and of their objects of understanding. Once inside structures of thought not necessarily obvious to their authors, exploring the interior space opened up and shaped by the work and its objects, my students and I sometimes find ourselves earning further entry into that space, a little way deeper into it than the author may have imagined—always within the discipline and for exercise in the classroom, which is a rather small part of life. The real test of a good college class is what its teacher learns from it. Students, alas, too often come away with the impression that they have learned something when, in fact, they have been entertained or excited or directed. Preaching is not teaching.

As teachers in the humane studies, our sacred world must remain the book. But we recognize that the profane world regularly refuses to become a text analogue. Living between those two worlds, respecting both, our vocation is to make interpretations that will not collapse one into the other. An interminable making of interpretations is the duty of the teacher; in this duty he is freer than most other citizens. That unique condition can only exist if academics do not try to destroy it by a frequent taking of sides, as auxiliaries in the ever-changing struggle for power. The university has been only grudgingly exempted from full and immediate participation in those many-sided struggles. If we teachers understood those struggles, we would stay out of them; battle lines are not to be trusted. Fighting attitudes do not mix well with analytic. Criticism is not superior to advocacy. Neither describes that close, personal and positionless understanding which constitutes the true objectivity of the scholar-teacher. Our task is to understand all sides, to analyze all reasons—including reasons of state. Trust only that the sides will change faster than we can or should change our minds. Our duty is to hang back, always a little behind the times. Our objectivity, always from within our culture, has nothing whatever to do with the cant of 'value-neutrality'; we cannot derive our insights from that ideological slogan of the positivist movement. Rather, one of our tasks is to analyze all insights as they derive from movements, including those that derive from the Marxist.

As a teacher, positionless, I had no business allowing myself to be interviewed; this was to yield too obviously to the marketing of positions. Yet even here I can do little else. The medium is fit only for messages. But messages and positions are the death of true teaching. As scholars and teachers, we have a duty to fight against our own positions. If the university is still to be the temple of the intellect, then its high priests can only worship the intellect, which does not worship itself. The enforcement of intellect, upon ourselves and reluctant students—that is our one force; it is to that force that we have a duty, uniquely unchangeable. Because the university must be the temple of the intellect, uniquely unchangeable in that respect, it is a sacred institution, the last in our culture. If the university is not the temple of the intellect, then it is not a university.

In my profession, as a teacher of sociological theory, I do what I can, in practice to defend the university against becoming a training center for technicians, equipped with print-out formulae and/or quantified slogans; I am equally opposed to the teaching of my subject as a high moralizing entertainment, with the professor recast as guru, dispensing world-historical or psycho-political nostrums to over-eager young activists who have discovered that they are guilty of merely thinking about the world when what it so obviously needs are the changes by which innocence will be achieved, at last. In their own way facile as the profit-making problem-solvers they profess to despise, the gurus are profaners of our sacred precinct. How can we outwit these profaners if we ourselves aim at positioning our students, by being popular and direct in our teachings?

Yet here I am obliged to say something that will respond directly, unmediated by books, and despite the limits of our distant acquaintance, to your special interest in my published work. We shall not escape the theatricality of our situation. Our exchange cannot be disciplined, objective, personal—a complex of indirections, set by close attention to the work of our predecessors. We have no continuing intellectual relation; without this continuity, there can be no successive generations of privileged knowers. On the contrary, we professors of the present become minor actor-managers in more or less provincial road-shows; students and townsfolk never know how right they are when they tell us, after such shows as we gave on 26th March 1971, how much they 'enjoyed' it; I cringe at the thought of my performance, and at their evident pleasure in it.

How seriously these audiences take their pursuits of pleasures is evident in the commercial success of an astonishing number of value change actor-managers, who parallel in a minor, less profitable way, the managerial entrepreneurs of the research grant industry. In relation to their audiences (most corrupt of all when transferred to a classroom), the quick value change professors of the college circuit are not much different from the managers of Big Science, who direct the operations of an ever-expanding horde of dependent technicians. The managers of the knowledge industry produce whatever facts are needed, while, in the new division of labor, the actor-managers of our culture crisis produce value-criticism—and, nowadays, what is worse, rude personifications of those criticisms. More and more, orchestrating youth protest, the value managers feel they must act out their criticisms. To do good is to put on a bad show; thus the value managers surpass their critical apostle-genius forebears. If Nietzsche ever acted out, then at least he did truth—which is repression successfully, though never finally, achieved—the honor of going mad. Acting out the eccentricities of prophets does not make a prophet. Elijah was not who he was because he ate dung. By their play-acting at the prophetic role, the actor-managers of total criticism have reduced our exquisite traditions of prophecy, including the Nietzschean, to primitive rudenesses. Now primitive rudeness is honored with a sociological rubric: 'counter culture.'

No primitive was rude. Our college-trained primitives have been charmed by the idea that rudeness of manner, speech and thought is criticism personified. They express not criticism but hostility to culture in any form. Their chorused obscenities and temper tantrums are the debased liturgical form taken, nowadays, by the high nineteenth century religion of criticism, about which they have not the slightest knowledge. Only projects—inputs and outputs, quickly made—really interest them. But the feeling intellect is a long-term project, which would be blessed by less capital funding for Research and far less publicity. Meanwhile, the apparent enemies of the gurus, the bagmen of a commercial technological culture, are learning how to ape everything, including Revolution, for which there is a market. Attracted to the university by the new money and status in it since 1946, the bagmen and the gurus between them, are destroying our sacred institution. Both sides are equally ready to make over the temple of the intellect into whatever it cannot be: Research and Development Center, political camp, college of therapists.

Teachers cannot be therapists. Our god-terms are no parody godheads. Because those in therapy take their pleasures too seriously, they can only take their god-terms too lightly. The order to which we teachers belong is authoritative and commands its members to prepare for long mindful devotions to the understanding of god-terms and their social organization. The academy does not exist as a place from which to depart; it is not therapeutic. Our colleges cannot be made over into orders for order-hoppers; the rapid turnover of our students mocks the tenacious concentration necessary for study. We scholar-teachers are the university. Yet, in our hurry to get somewhere, to some conclusion that will not hold, we have helped make over the university into a therapeutic institution. Nothing more desecrating has ever been introduced into the temple of the intellect than the present dominant alliance: between political theatre, by demagogues of Eros; and data-management, by entrepreneurs of the knowledge industry. Do not despair. Even together, the gurus and the entrepreneurs have not quite wiped out that transference, in disciplined and specialized intensities, of a privileged knowledge which can only be in the personal gift of modest masters to patient students.

Returning to the question of our public interview: if (I say, only, *if*) our personal knowledge is privileged, not readily or publicly available, then how can we transfer it, by public interview, among almost total strangers? Privileged knowledge—the most objective, closest, personal understandings—can only be conveyed by the art of concealment. We teachers are called to represent the god-terms, in all their marvelous indirections, inhibiting what otherwise might be too easily done. Even Christ, as he revealed, precisely in order to reveal, concealed. Concealment is the most necessary pedagogic art, without which there are no revelations. If I have written anything worth rereading, then it is necessary and right that you should misunderstand me. I write as I teach, with extreme caution; indeed, I am a rewriter. If you read in order to conclude, for or against, then read at your peril. There is nothing conclusive here.

Misunderstanding may be the highest form of prudence. But there are better reasons why a concealing transfer of privileged knowledge is the unchangeable work of teachers: in the first place, being mere interpreters of interpreters, not ourselves prophets, we are authorized only by the greatness that has preceded us, from which we make knowledge our own. You will now understand why my students are rarely allowed to read, under my indirections, living authors. Plato, Beethoven, Weber, Haydn, Freud: all our greatest teachers are always dead. Yet God enlivens their minds in us. Except for us, their scores become too settled; they need constant performance in order to be realized. Our task is to perform them, in order to see what lives. When, prepared slowly enough, a student can make his own sudden plunge through the words, into the interior space shaped by those words, then he inherits his share in the living authority of our great predecessors. So, and only so, students, like their teachers, may acquire personal authority; so, together, we come into possession of, and are possessed by, our inheritance—and may even improve upon it. That improving possession—slow, never certain, not always practical or with a happiness-output—constitutes the activity peculiar to life in a university. As a work of art shapes its audience, so a book shapes its readers. In both cases, audience and reader are so active that they find themselves reshaping the work. So they become the true objects of the work.

Anyone who is possessed by the objectivity of close and personal understandings must run the risk of that possession: the risk is in destroying one's own position. Before this risk, some flee. Others violently disagree, all the more violently when they discover that agreements and disagreements, in the temple of the intellect, could not matter less. Some insist that their teachers function as gurus, supplying mini social orders and, at the same time, the intellectualized emotional dexterities with which to hop from one mini order to another. As teachers, we must be at war with the cultic life style, with the endless order-hopping of the questing young, often formatively encouraged by their still questing parents, for whom the quest is an escape from the untaught authority of their own pasts.

To be a scholar-teacher, neither guru nor entrepreneur, is only to continue the life of study; at best, a scholar-teacher is a virtuoso student. There are alternatives: to play the virtuoso of prophetic views, plugged into Criticism; to be the friendly manager of your local databank, plugged into Method; both are easy roles nowadays. But the rhythms of teaching and learning are slow and unpredictable; the progress we teachers achieve is hard to couple with the advance of any social movement. Henry James offers one splendid example of complex, unprogressive teaching, unaddicted precisely to ideas. In Eliot's description of James's genius, we may take a hint of the perfect teacher: "most tellingly in his mastery over, his baffling escape from ideas; a mastery and an escape which are perhaps the last test of a superior intelligence. He had a mind so fine that no idea could violate it. . . ."[1] Here is the trouble with us, and with the masses we educate: our minds are too easily violated by ideas. We paste ideas on our foreheads, in order to follow them. It is not simply that a little learning is a dangerous thing, or that virtue cannot be taught. The case is more desperate. In the age of universal higher education, we excite minds that are never given time enough, or the inner strength, to learn how to avoid immediate

1. Both James and Eliot were writers of supreme intellect. By 'idea,' Eliot meant ideology, I think: those ideas that excited minds acquire when they are released from patient thought—for example, the 'idea' that American culture is 'repressive.' No artist was ever more thoughtful than James. No novelist thought through his fictions more carefully. In his famous excoriation of a Trollope novel, James wrote: "Our great objection to 'The Belton Estate' is that we seem to be reading a work written for children, a work prepared for minds unable to think, a work below the apprehension of the average man or woman. 'The Belton Estate' is a *stupid* book . . . essentially, organically stupid. It is without a single idea. It is utterly incompetent to the *primary function of a book of whatever nature, to suggest thought.*" (My italics.) Perfectly said. Much of what passes for 'Liberation' writing and chat, nowadays, is below the apprehension of the average man or woman, intended for the expanding market of educated fools, the Sniffpecks of our anti-culture.

violation by ideas; Weber, using Simmel's phrase, refers to the 'romanticism of the intellectually interesting.' There are students who are defenseless before any idea, or phrase, that excites their interest; they apply what they cannot understand. By this thinly intellectualized acting out, the young betray their own impatience with both ideas and life, as if each were a recalcitrant parent, unwilling to yield to their demands. How shall we cope with a universally critical style? Popular criticism is so unprepared, so unprivileged, so swiftly acquired that it possesses no intelligence disciplined enough to master and escape the violence done by its own popularity. Paranoid styles flourish.

This critical idea-mongering is one understandable result of all the banausic non-teaching to which students are subjected, the learning of formulae—all sloganizings, expressionist or scientist. It remains our pedagogic duty to oppose the orgiasts of criticism and their counterparts, the entrepreneurs of programmed Reason; research gimmicks are the entrepreneureal parallels of the latest Experience bag. Methodized reason, like orgiastic experience, consumes culture. Memory-data banks and retrieval systems are what Culture[2] is not. Our data banks and exciting ideas have no authority; they cannot compel us to indebted thought, as can a presiding intellectual presence, a Plato or a Freud. But to preside is not to rule; here is the hairline that makes all the difference in the world between culture and politics.

You asked, early during our performance, within what *tradition* I taught. That is easy to say: my tradition is the one that would draw hermeneutic circles if it could. In my teaching tradition, I am one link in a long chain of interpreters. That chain has been broken in many places. It may be beyond repair. The tactics of interpretation grow more treacherous as interpretation itself is trapped within final and resolutive rather than tentative and reproductive modes. Our pedagogic task remains to repair the old and forge new links, not to continue breaking old ones already so broken that our students have scarcely done more than hear rumors of their existence. Without links to intellectual authority, our students cannot know what they are criticizing, nor respect the complexity of all true criticism. (I shudder at the simple-mindedness of my Fanonist students, who do not respect Fanon enough to read him closely; indeed, few students know how to read a book and fewer come out of families blessed still with oral traditions, upon which abilities to read build up.) How do you teach totally unprepared students? The American universities are now producing tens of thousands of failed intellectuals and artists of life; this mass production may lead to the destruction of culture in any received sense.

To teach is to conserve the related benefits and penalties of our in-

2. A term to cover the death of our great traditions first made, for consumption by high-minded professional audiences, by Arnold the younger.

herited existence, beyond earlier transferred observations of what is not to be done; and to sharpen our observations of what exceptions there may be to rules that constitute no game, no scenario, no psycho-drama, no third kingdom, no movement of natural or historical forces. To act out, in the classroom, our one and only role, is to teach in defense of the privileged knowledge that must be constantly reconstructed from acute constructions already made—and for us to remake. How dare we dismiss the authority of the past as if we understood it? The academic tradition in which I act is aristocratic, open to talent, exegetical, not least to discipline our ignorant passion for originality.

The transference of theory, our hermeneutic art rightly worked, resists its own ambition. In all effortful theory, there is the danger of asserting itself as practice; such assertions show a failure to respect the limits theory itself teaches. The triumphs of our art are confined to our art; too readily transferred to life, those triumphs have always mocked the teacher's vision. Were there ever more obvious mockeries of Platonism than in Plato's practice? Marxist Russia under Lenin, Trotsky and Stalin? The psychoanalytic professionals of Freud? Let me know if you can think of any mockeries more obvious. Our presiding presences are better after we respectfully digest them, at the sacramental feast of learning.

As theorists, and as critics of other theories, our first responsibility is to cultivate a modest sense of the different spheres of life. For the safety of our own souls, to prevent the mental disease of praxis, we teachers of various theories have to imagine truths still to be stable old men, never fickle young women ever itchy to bed down with the latest winners in a perpetual intellectual-political style show. This means our temples of the intellect can never be put into the service of any politics and that we abjure prophecy. We are not problem-solvers; most real social problems are not solvable by any method that can be taught in the classroom—or taught on any rational model. For us, in our priestly roles, everything there is is there to be interpreted; outside the temple, we are not priests. We have no objectivity. The closeness of our personal understandings are removed by life itself. Who among us can live as he teaches? It is a monstrous possibility. Because it is not for us to organize any methodical conduct of life, outside the temple, those to whom we make our interpretations cannot be a large or unprepared or remote public. It is our duty, as teachers, not to be public men; as public men, we cannot teach. Societies are not vast academies. They are vast public networks by which secret lives are linked one to another, and yet at a distance remote enough for each life to remain as it is, inviolate, secret from all others. Publicity, calling itself democratic or scientific, more and more exposes the secret life, as if under some mandate to ruin the only life worth living, which is one not too well known, or necessarily too well liked, by others.

Yet through these crowded streets, we teachers are asked, even commanded, to be guides. How shall we be guides and yet not in power? The classical answer was to become the uneasy advisor of those in power. Every political world exists in its own right only when it can justify itself. There is no justice without reverence. This is the principle of order without which there can be no law, as Protagoras rightly teaches. Our higher schools have the burden of teaching the art of critical interpretation; but they cannot, at the same time, serve as bases for thrusts of power against established power. The arts of criticism can only remain true when they are unarmed. Otherwise, all god-terms die and men are free to become demons. Armed criticism will defend its own establishment soon enough and prevent mind from entering those interior spaces opened and shaped by our continuous interpretative sciences, in institutions reserved to that end. Our schools must be powerless institutions of the political orders in which they exist; otherwise, they cannot be schools. Falsely positioned in any struggle for power, the school reserves its autonomy as an institution of authority so long as its task remains to draw circles of interpretation around all those capable of doing more than adjusting to power as it is. The relation between political power and pedagogic authority can never be simple, direct or straightforward. No domination can be simple and direct without becoming brutal, inartistic.

Even as he practices the art of critical concealments, not fit for all to learn, a practitioner in the academic order needs to resign himself to the treachery his interpretative activity must create within the political order. In return for the indirectness of this treachery, those who administer the political order must allow them; so long as they are not directly political, they are inseparable from academic freedom. Academic freedom is the historic compromise between sophisticated academy and philistine state. The state need not worry overmuch about academic freedom. To inhibit its treachery, every successful interpretation is bound to develop its own defensive cadre; without defensive cadres, interpretations run wild and impose themselves too immediately upon life. No public should be too quickly ready for Change. Such readiness indicates a breakdown of culture. Interpretative efforts gain their inner strength from continuities of their preparation, outside the world of fashionable ideas; the life of study is inherently cautious and cannot be rightly politicized. Only as links in a chain of interpreters, keeping a cautious distance from the political order, as from a vicious animal, more than apologists, more than critics, can we teachers achieve our necessarily privileged and dangerous knowledge, favored neither by officialdom nor revolutionaries (defined as an officialdom not yet taken office).

To be inwardly and institutionally distant from every political order is not to ride loose to all symbolics, outside every constraining hermeneutic circle. We teachers are not free to hop from one circle to another. That critical style, more than any other, has blunted our inherited acute constructional senses, substituting a crude animus against culture in any form. Such an animus is likely to serve the immediate needs of those struggling for power without authority. We can only represent an authority which is not reducible to power. Such authority can help to inhibit all sides in the struggle for power. Indeed, a true intellectual neutrality, in service to no side, would be inhibiting. The greatest teachers are deep inhibitors of the latest conclusions and final solutions of power and its justifications.

On various sides, presently in the endless struggle for power, are two apparently opposing cadres: 1) rationalizers of technological reason; 2) orgiasts of revolutionary sensuality; these cadres converge in the cult of violence. By *cult of violence* I mean that critical openness to possibility in which nothing remains true; in this original of all cults, all oppositions are welcomed as if life could be an endless experience of political, technological or interpretative breakthroughs, against orders recognized only for purposes of disestablishment. Both cadres are hostile to culture in any form and transmit this hostility under apparently opposed means: as rationalizing science or scientific irrationalizing. Politically, this double condition of modern life expresses itself in the resolution of all authority as the triumph of power and what follows from power—the freedom to pursue pleasures. That freedom exists only at the very top and bottom of power structures, which is why top and bottom, potentates and plebes, find themselves allies against all autonomous or independent centers of both power and authority. The regressiveness of the sensualists is as dangerous as the progressiveness of the technologists: both implicitly assume that the authority of truth inhibits the endlessness of power. I suppose that assumption to be correct. No theorist of power can maintain the authority of truth. As a theorist of power, Lenin tried to break the inhibiting character of authority when he remarked, following Engels, that nothing is more authoritative than a revolution.

To oppose the double movement of modernity—technological-political and sensual-political hostilities to culture in any form—is not, however, to become a pietist of culture; such pietists continue to represent the condition of the high culture just before our own, when the pursuit of pleasure needed a Kruezer sonata to blame for the mendacious games our educated classes have learned to play in order to raise their consciousness of possibility. Tolstoy correctly grasped the tension between a work of art and the pursuit of pleasure. A work of art is a moralizing form; moved as we are by it, no work of art can be neutral in the eternal war of culture. Art is the most subtle form of social direction. Either a work of art deepens the thrust of culture into character, creating ever greater loyalties to the godheads alive in (and only in) that order; or, as in its present extremity, art subverts that order, murders its own godheads, or merely mocks its own use of god-terms. It is interior space that is first reshaped, preliminary to the reshaping of social order. Plato first taught us to understand the necessarily and mutually endangering relation between art and social order. In our own uniquely revolutionary time, not only an alternative space but so many spaces have been opened up that even the least cultivated are aware of the vast emptiness inside; all our symbolics are manufactured for instant use; none are constraining; all oppose constraint, which is itself the main conceptual term of opposition to the revolutionary opening up of new interior space, within which humans get a different sense of themselves and others.

The 'Everything New' syndrome, a constantly redefined spaciousness, is ready-made for eternally youthful order-hoppers. In this formula of Change is one predicative cultural condition from which we have, coming to us, our future unremarkable absence of soul, an endlessly developing Self, mocking, by its consumption of them, all constraints. Against this coming pliancy, Culture has proved helpless to maintain the constraints integral to its business of soul-making. Cultural piety cannot make itself functional as the equivalent of a godhead and so conserve human beings in their particular orders; too often, we pietists of culture have become professional curators, guides for masses of tourists intent only on hurrying through our museums so to declare that they have been there and had it. Cultural pietists are no better than any other among all the putative guides who disclaim authority as they conduct tours among artifacts that are not authoritative but only valuable. If a past has no authority, then it is dead, however expensive its artifacts. There can be no culture without living authority, right and proper demands superior to competing immediacies, not reducible to them, nor identical with power, which is the successful assertion of one's own immediacy over another's.

Weber identified authority with service to ends, and ends with faith. But his faiths—"rational, humanitarian, social, ethical, cultural, worldly, or religious"—are a functionalized psychology of motive. Faith, as an 'end' to be served, is not a concept that carries the slightest particularizing resistance of truth against immediacy in it. Weber's ends, the *causes* there to be served, are means of acting. To say "some kind of faith must always exist," as Weber said, is to implicate *therapy*, the great conceptual term for the justification of all immediacies, the great procedure of release from the authority of the past. Weber knew that a variety of faiths suited the variety of human occasions; yet it is the purpose of one variety to reduce all others. That reduction is what 'world rejection' means. Not Weber, not any theorist of my acquaintance, knows how to escape this modern functionalization of faith into therapy. No therapy can be world-rejecting. A 'world-rejecting' therapy merely parodies world rejection in order to defeat it.

Faith is one word for the most privileged knowledge: of the ways in which humans justify their behavior. Faith is the horrified suspicion of justification. Because this suspicion is horrifying, no justification worth calling to mind has ever satisfied its user; look at old Calvin's ravaged face, or read Luther's table talk. Yet to act without justification is more terrible. Few have been able to tolerate their acts unjustified. Mind begs to be violated by ideas. To be a professional student of violating ideas is to know what bizarre justifications there have been, and with what bêtise the human animal flocks after them.

Every genuine community has been credal; men love to conceal their acts, specially the most violent, which challenge justification, in an order of justifications. Perversely, it is thought that the most violent actions seal justification as if the latter serves on behalf of the former. Ideas are falsely sanctioned in blood. The tension inherent in every community between the life of the mind and its disordering violations makes it imperative that teachers, if they must be guides, exercise a passion for good manners, grace, wit, decorum—whatever will keep the life of the mind and its enacted violations a little distant from one another, away from the taste of blood. Without taste and tact, theorists, who can see for themselves only when they see through theorists preceding them, grow ugly and hateful in each other's company. Gurus sanctify; teachers educate. If we must have him as a unifying figure, then let Eros wear heavy, concealing dress and eat modest rations of his followers. Let Eros be an old man. With enough taste and tact, we professional interpreters will know enough not to produce new justifications where some old and tried one already found wanting enough to be tolerated, will do. The hardest job for intellectuals is to prevent themselves from over-intellectualizing, not least on their own behalf, which is tantamount to demagogy. Too often we teachers become arrivistes; to be intellectually fashionable is to produce ever more justifying violations of mind, most often nowadays in the name of criticism or progress. Scientists produce new facts; orgiasts produce new experiences. We teachers should produce nothing new, no breakthroughs, until we produce, first in ourselves, those protections of older wisdom which may help stave off arrogant stupidities parading as originality, modernization, revolution, etc. Respect for what is long known is not charismatic. We have no business making over our students into followers, least of all by offering them breakthroughs as if they were gifted with genius or prophecy. Privileged knowledge is rarely revolutionary. On the contrary, our privilege is to know in detail how slow deep down things are to change, and equally to know what superficiality and blaséness is encouraged by mystiques of change.

The greatest theorist of therapy was neither superficial nor blasé.

Freud indulged no mystique of change. On the contrary, he grasped "the slowness with which profound changes in the mind bring themselves about." One of the mysteries of Western spiritual history is how, specially in America, Freudian ideas were misused to violate the slowness with which profound changes took place in the mind. Freud accepted the constraints of privileged knowledge. His analytic couch was not the world. The therapeutic relation was not a social order. Despite some lapses, as in the case of Dora, what is moral remained to Freud, as he said, self-evident. The last thing in the world this interpreter of interpretations would become is an impresario of his own endless expressional quest. His first masterpiece, *The Interpretation of Dreams,* is masterly not least in its self-concealments. One task of the third force we need to construct in defense of culture, neither technological nor sensualist, but a cadre of teaching interpreters, is to keep a close watch on what is being done by our impresarios, under the entitlements of Science and Self. We are subjected to endless breakthroughs, by hosts of mini-charismatics, intruding on our private selves, demanding that we abolish them. Against these breakthroughs, and their celebrants, revolutionary and regressive, we need a science of limits; our primal feeling, if only we could reconstruct it, must be for what we have long known is not to be done.

Our cause is not hopeless. An old American alliance, between technological radicalism and cultural conservatism, appears broken. Battlelines are being redrawn. The technological radicals will merge with the cultural radicals. 'Counter-Culture' is a purchasable gimmick. As the sides merge, strategic opportunities wait to be exploited. But our third force seems weaker than ever before, precisely in the universities. We can scarcely make ourselves heard; there is tumult even in our classrooms. If we are realists about our own limits, then our weakness would not be so alarming as it may sound, for we can only work to confirm and disconfirm authority, not to originate it. Old authority cannot begin to make its next right and proper claim upon our capacity for obedience through teaching in the classroom. Teaching begins long before a student reaches the classroom. Until there are vast numbers of true parents, we cannot expect vast numbers of true teachers—or true students. How can we teachers expect to achieve disciplines of the feeling intellect so late in the student day, and in a cultureless society—one that divorces us from the interdicts? Moreover, we teachers now easily accept, so long as our jobs and affluence are not threatened, that same cultureless society into which our students have been born. Affluence is becoming only for restrained people. We Americans have never learned to reject enough new things; absence of restraint is the key to our affluence and to our populist inclinations. Very American, we teachers have no cause for complaint about our students. We are up on the latest and have become ex-somethings—ex-Marxists, ex-Jews, ex-bourgeois, ex-straights. How can we complain that the chain of interpretation has been broken? All new links must appear as forgeries if only the self is authentic. Our acceptances of experience are thought to be most satisfying when they are without precedent. We have no stable old ruling ideas and, therefore, can have no stable old presiding class.

We cannot simply dismiss the argument that the struggle for power, revealed for all to see, makes our kind of work at best irrelevant. It has been argued, as I have said, that our transferable interpretations are now so contradictory that they can never again prepare for soul making and ethics, but only generate neuroses. New scientific interpreters, marching out behind their quotation marks, as if they were shibboleths, aim to acquire an inner freedom to act—any role; this freedom renews the most ancient dexterity, the liveliness with which a human can step aside, as if no particular act represented the responsible I in the middle of his head. Putting all the god-terms and their necessary enemies, the transgressions—'defilement,' 'impurity,' 'lust,' 'untruth,' whatever breaks through—between quotation marks, the new interpreters, improving upon both science and democracy, have made ambiguous and entirely problematic all orders in which we might conceivably live. Our feasts of commitment grow more and more swiftly movable; eternally young and unsettled, we teachers ourselves engage in the most acrobatic hopping from one order to another. Yeats was mistaken: all centers hold equally well. To be radically contemporaneous, to be sprung loose from every particular culture, is to achieve a conclusive, unanswerable failure of historical memory. This is the uniquely modern achievement. Barbarians have never before existed. At the end of this tremendous cultural development, we moderns shall arrive at barbarism. Barbarians are people without historical memory. Barbarism is the real meaning of radical contemporaneity. Released from all authoritative pasts, we progress towards barbarism, not away from it.

Barbarism means more than radical contemporaneity; it is a playing at being 'Man,' or 'Human'; barbarism means the universality of those educated out of membership in the binding particularities of their culture and, being able to entertain all, inhibited by no new god-terms. One clever, radically contemporary reviewer of a recent non-book of oracles[3] backed me accurately into my historical corner, along with others:

> Philip Rieff . . . comes over with a touching nostalgia for the educated man who once could place himself in a usable tradition. Now, the barbarians are taking over—the barbarians being classically defined as people without a history, and dwelling most naturally in America, a country dominated by 'an ingenuous will to transform, without regard to what is being destroyed and what is being constructed.' The source of the trouble is the

3. See *New Statesman*, 11 February 1972, p. 182: "Conference Smog."

> revolutionary activity of the bourgeoisie, for the bourgeoisie is both greedy and rational, reckoning that neither God nor nature nor human nature set any limits to what it might do with the world. Against this Gadarene Rush, intellectuals are powerless: Rieff mentions in an aside that history is only stopped by 'prophecy,' but that dark saying is left unilluminated.
>
> Indeed, even under some pressure from their interviewers, the contributors who are asked for prophecy invariably back away. Werner Heisenberg talks some calm good sense about the silliness of the demand for 'new values' and about the idea that science can or ought to provide them. He is plainly right.

Another reviewer of those same sayings[4] hints further our strategic opportunity:

> Herr Werner Heisenberg, the eminent German physicist, points out that utility is no longer a sufficient justification for new inventions or new applications of technology. Some broader, more socially responsible criteria are required. The point is reinforced separately and elegantly by the American sociologist, Mr. Philip Rieff, from a perspective closer to politics, when he points out that technology carries no interior controls.

Here is the negative point at which we teachers in the humane studies might realize our vocations. A science of limits, an interdictory order, cannot come from the scientists. If we teachers wish to make any sort of new beginning at that one necessary old science, then we can begin only by recognizing that our barbaric enlightenments have deinhibited the agency of inhibition: super-ego. That agency made too active in any cause, modern criminals and would-be revolutionaries are not creatures of 'impulse,' as in the 19th century imagination,[5] but more and more often, I suspect, driven creatures of high principle, militants of this immediacy and that. Rapists grow didactic. Apostles of the body flaunt their principles. Who is not to have his say and express himself fully? Is it a resolutive contradiction in terms for the super-ego to express itself chiefly in transgressive activity. Such activists of easy principle are one price we are paying for packaging authority entirely inside quotation marks; inside those quotes our principles no longer bring home to us the tragic sense of danger inseparable from all their enactments. Pseudo-sensibility develops into the finest art. How pompous our cultural revolutionaries are about their morality, in all its preachments of honesty, lightness and play. Our academic world is full of Sniffpecks, who are full of abject snobberies about their effortful liberations from the morality of self-concealment. These Sniffpecks issue more vile sayings than our latest novels; precepts for a liberated Humanity are handed out like leaflets on a gusty day. Such revolutionaries must end each as a patriot

4. See *The Economist,* 12 February 1972: "Doomchat."
5. The new 'black' is the old 'dangerous classes,' colored and caste, with middle class white empathy for his transgressive action.

for himself, trying to pose as The People. Sniffpecks are talkers of terror. How have we circled back to those exhibitions of personality, indignant as a revolutionary act, that that most scientific revolutionary, Dr. Marx, so distrusted? I do not know. I do know Marx is rightly served, hoist on his own praxis. With the ethical functionalized out of existence, under the concept of ideology, Marx could get no scientific grip on the fact that any aggressive action (e.g., class exploitation) must be transgressive and not a movement of the historical forces of production.

By our own time, post-Marxist in the light of Lenin and Stalin, we know that transgressiveness knows no political boundaries, neither Right nor Left. Making a revolution (in the Marxist sense) is obsolete—along with revolution in its original meaning, as a return—except return to the orgiastic as original action. Against this originality, every artifice of culture, if it works, recreates us as obedient persons. A truth of resistance is not to impulse, but to transgressive behavior. Countercultural revolutionaries institutionalize transgressive behavior in spheres slightly different from those of their political enemies; but the difference is one of content rather than form. Business is business. Sex is sex. Politics is politics. Enter these different spheres and we witness different transgressions. Who now preaches a faith that will subject these differences, and their spheres, to a uniform set of interdicts? At least since Durkheim, we sociologists have known that modern societies are too complex for a catholic faith, including a catholic Science—that fantasy of Durkheim's positivist forebears in which he himself could no longer believe. For Durkheim, science was to function as a check on the dynamics of all faiths; he had little hope in the dynamics of science itself as a basis for some new catholic social organization, as his predecessors, Saint-Simon and Comte, had hoped. Science and technology fizzled out, as a collective effervescence, in the century of their triumph, the twentieth.

It is out of a highly differentiated society, spheres of action separate, none subject to the same interdicts, and all to fewer, that the therapeutic has been born. This ideal type is free, in the first place, because he can live his life among authorities so long divided that none can assert themselves strongly even in their own sphere—quite the contrary of Durkheim's quasi-syndicalist hope. There is, however, something new about the therapeutic: a conclusive freedom, all interdicts evaginated, so highly surfaced that none can survive. Why should the therapeutic feel anything deeply when he can exhibit his sensibilities? Living on his surfaces, as he does, the therapeutic is an acutely sensitive man; it is only deep down that he has learned to be less vulnerable. I was struggling toward this point in a passage from *The Triumph of the Therapeutic* of which you reminded me during our public interview:

> With Freud, the individual took a great and final step toward that mature and calm feeling which comes from having nothing to hide. To live on the surface prevents deep hurts.

It takes a certain genius to survive the deepest hurts. Freud favored asking less of people, most of whom are not moral geniuses or any other kind. Most of us cannot transform our hurts into anything that does not hurt (ourselves or others) more. A true culture imposes certain limits on itself; it does not ask ordinary men to make extraordinary renunciations. But in a true culture, a genius is not considered a criminal, nor is criminality honored as genius. Life is not confused with Art. Terribilita should remain an aesthetic, not a political, capacity; it rightly belonged to Beethoven and Michelangelo, in their work, not to the conditierri, or Hitler, in theirs. An extraordinarily rare talent does not emerge in transgressions; rather, in works of art, or science, that control their own spheres with full interdictory force, called 'form.' Confusing spheres, modern aspirants to freedom from all authority have produced a parody terribilita in all spheres. Our educated classes, rich consumers of everything available, are scarcely competent to perform the most elementary decencies—yet they are urged to fulfill themselves, as if each were a Beethoven, perhaps a little deaf to his own music and in need of some third ear hygiene. The therapeutic teaching of transgressive behavior confuses art and life, rare genius and common culture, public life and private. Encounter-group teachings, for example, mainly by therapists of the revolutionary rich, follow the precedent set by the technological radicalism of those same rich in their earlier scramble: for more. That the opposing sides of the American scene, deviants and straights, are both suspicious of authority, is mainly the fault of what passes for authority in our nation; the authority figures themselves are so often inferior persons that their offices cannot conceal the absence of any reference beyond themselves to a presiding presence. Modern revolt has no authority and is all the more dangerous because there is no authority against which to revolt; we are reducing politics to a mere struggle for power and more power.

Presences have never been encouraged to preside—now less than ever before, I think. The therapeutic has no presence. It is impossible to revolt against him, for all genuine revolution has been understood, heretofore, as against authority, giving rise to a new presiding presence, without which authority cannot exist—as, for example, the Jews cannot exist without the Mosaic presence, as Freud understood, in his attempt at a resolutive interpretation of the Jewish historical character. Suppose, however, there is no authority—only power and its theatrical affects? How can there be a crisis of authority? Among our reflexive sorts, there is much fashionable talk of crisis, of our times of trouble. I doubt the crisis; the time seems to me less greatly troubled than others. What can 'trouble' mean if our society is growing cultureless, without presiding presences and a public order of meaning? Guilt is much overestimated as a working force in the new society, usable mainly as a tactic toward its continuing dissolution. During a year in Germany, I met precious few guilty people. My German friends were having an authentically good time. My American friends seem equally guiltless, although they throw up their hands regularly as if aghast at their sense of guilt. I think they are playing games. To feel guilt takes a certain submission to authority. There can be no transgressive sense without someone to transgress.

We professors of the present have in stock a large supply of god-terms and can conjure orders galore, all from the grab-bag of things past, passing and to come. Precisely in the age of Science, all the dead gods have risen from their graves. Our god-terms mock their ancestors, the gods, in one special respect: no god-term worth using can be merely heuristic, a device for extending intellectual reach. God-terms must have binding authority, compelling not merely intellectual interest but also suspicion of that interest. Our god can only reveal as he conceals himself; ask that, concealment with every revelation, and you have understood why the major questions must always continue as if unanswered. It is when the god-terms lose their inhibiting dynamic that they become protean. ('Protean man' does not descend from the god Proteus. He has no descent, and therefore no existence.) The barbarian who is emerging, stuffed with tactical advice culled from the ages, can hop from order to order, committing himself, as in modern marriage, to a serial monogamy that is massively polygamous. To say this barbarian is universally faithless is only to say that no character becomes authoritative in him. Only cultureless societies can exist without presiding presences. No presence can preside when all are subject to abandonments quick as their adoptions. Our passionate truths are so provisional, they move so quickly with the electrified times, that none can prepare us to receive them deeply into ourselves, as character; they do not become compelling in their interdicts but endlessly attractive in their remissions. Where creeds were, there therapies will be. Our way is an unlearning. What, then, have we to teach?

It is as the typical creature of a cultureless society that I have imagined the therapeutic. I do not imagine him as a serious man. Seriousness is a state of possession by god-terms, even to the negation of justified violence in their defense. Serious attacks on authority must breed new authority. In the therapeutic, I imagined someone who takes nothing seriously. Of course, a therapeutic can resonate empty militancies that signal an acceptance of their emptiness. Opposing this experimental life, in which all god-terms can be taken lightly, rather as heuristic devices, there can be only a culture of militant, opposing truths—god-terms that are interdictory before they are remissive and thus to be taken seriously because humans will oppose the interdicts with all their wits. (To take a god-term seriously, however, is not to be without a sense of humor; on the contrary, as I have said, no justification worth calling to mind ever sets it at rest. What may be taken lightly is not the god-term, but oneself. Luther called this the joy of the faithful.) A culture of truth opposing self—what culture is, understood sociologically—abides experimental lives only in its own service; thus, for example, monasticism, which opposed the corporate self-glorification of the church, served culture. Except through institutional services, before they harden into further glorifications and false self-sacrifice, experiment belongs in the laboratory and to art, most rarely to publicized individuality. Our continuous publicity for experimental living predicates that totalitarian disorder of which fascist movements gave one premonitory flash. I shall return, below,* to the important point that, as Mussolini declared, fascism is not a creed but an opportunity.

Now I am in position to answer your question (perhaps the result of our happy misunderstanding) whether the coming of the therapeutic is to be welcomed insofar as he is free from any need of corporate faith. With this emergent type, you ask, will we be delivered from the nightmare history of the last half-century, and spared the kinds of mass brutality of the last fifty years? No; I suspect we will not be spared. Violence is the therapy of therapies, as Dr. Fanon suggests. There is less and less to inhibit this final therapy, least where the most progressively educated classes seem ready to go beyond their old hope of deliverance, from violence as the last desperate disciplinary means built into the interdicts as punishment, to violence as a means toward a saving indiscipline, as self-expression. Geniuses of this saving indiscipline roam the college circuit, selling their guidance toward a cultureless society, without interdicts deeply installed. Which cadre of putative guides to the new freedom will you follow: our rationalizing functionaries or our functional irrationalizers? Never mind: they will meet at the end of their roads. The functional irrationalizers are well on their way to becoming our next rationalizing functionaries. Both cadres will produce endless therapies. With the end of authority, no violence will be illegitimate. Rather, as they destroy the civilities basic to cultured society, the brutalities of direct action will be differently understood. Victims are being taught their complicity, their role, in brutal acts. Let every actor play his variable part, without indignation—except when indignation promotes the part. The new society already has the look, both in America and in the Soviet Union, of a hospital-theatre—in con-

*The portion of *"Fellow Teachers"* to which Rieff refers is not included in this excerpt.

trast to the old society, which had the look of a church. The successor to our failed credal organizations will not be another credal one, not even Marxist, which names the last major credal effort to reorganize western society; we shall be dominated by anti-creeds and think ourselves free.

I am no advocate of some earlier credal organization. In particular, I have not the slightest affection for the dead church civilization of the West. I am a Jew. No Jew in his right mind can long for some variant of that civilization. Its one enduring quality is its transgressive energy against the Jew of culture; those transgressions have been built so deeply into the church-organized interdicts that they survive even now, after the main interdictory motifs of Christendom are dead. Christian transgressions are still so vital that the recent well-publicized statements of Christian remorse are likely to be a condition of further transgression, as the Jews continue to resist their assigned roles and, worst gall, refuse to disappear into the universalist future 'Man.' The gospels were not good news; the ungospelled present has its supremely pleasant feature, the death of the church—or, less pleasant, its conversion into naively therapeutic institutions, hawking a few antique graces to ornament our triumphant gracelessness. A contentless faith in 'faith' is but one of the rather noisy rhetorics of commitment to movement—any movement—that characterize the superego turned against itself, against inhibition and for action.

I, for one, am not keen on being where the action is; there brutality and the horror of total politics, uninhibited by any presiding presence will be. One necessary thing that we inactivists, we academic men, suspicious of all politics, have to teach our students is how not to invest in all the nostrums of direct action now being hawked. It is our duty to protect and nurture, in our academies, a few enclaves within which to practice an inhibiting subtlety, to think in something like late Jamesean sentences.[5a] If we are not allowed these indirections, if we must serve some program, one side or another, then the academy has no unique service; it is least fit, of all institutions, to take stands or rationalize them. The more directly political it becomes, the more certain the university must commit itself to shifting positions, in the endless war for advantage, and so destroy its intellectual integrity. To resist endless politicizing is made more difficult when politics and therapy merge in fancies of a student culture opposed to study. Yet, despite the erotic incitements on campus, some of our students remain ardent to be students.

The threat to study is double: not only from masses of students who cannot study, but from faculty who will not teach. By their gurus and Research paymasters, the collegiate young are being re-educated before

5a. Then, after James, we may graduate to Proust, who grasped Chardin, the master of still-life.

they have been educated. From our collegiate ranks, the therapeutic will appear a re-educated man, one who can conquer even his subtler inhibitions; his final know-how will be to irrationalize his rationality and play games, however intellectualized, with all god-terms in order to be ruled by none. In their moral modesty, therapeutics will be capable of anything; they will know that everything is possible because they will not be deeply inhibited by any truth. Far more destructively than earlier interdict-burdened character types, the therapeutic will be the warring state writ small; he may be even cannier, less sentimental, stronger in ego, shifting about his principles and his impulses like so many stage props.

Of one condition the therapeutic, conqueror of his feeling intellect, is likely to be incapable: *inwardness,* the quality of self-concealment. That has become, as Kierkegaard predicted, an aberration. A student once revealed to me the new untruth: that "we are all going to be—we all have to be—'up front.'" I gleaned from her the idea of a human who exposes himself completely and reveals nothing. She was training to be a therapist—welfare work and all that—mainly with clients released from psychiatric hospitals. Almost all her clients were already 'up front,' she said. How glad I was for her; she had found her vocation—not as a director of souls, but as a semi-official supervisor of soullessness. My one-time student, who scarcely understood a word I said or wrote, could be easily imagined as a functionary, herself in permanent therapy, in the coming total welfare state.[6] After all, what every state can best use are empty people, without the gift of self-concealment. Beyond the concealed life, opposing it as once our souls (and then our historical neuroses) opposed therapy, lies the kind of naked life in which everything is exposed and nothing revealed. How we moderns love to undress. So I imagine the political order of therapeutics, for whom all uniforms will fit perfectly and none are to be reverenced. My ideal type is no idolator, not even when standing in front of the mirror. Rather, there he will appear in his most revealing disguise, as a comic figure.

6. Nietzsche wrote, in 1886, of my student and her social welfare teachers: "It is almost always a symptom of what is lacking in himself when a thinker senses in every 'causal connection' and 'psychological necessity' something of constraint, need, compulsion to obey, pressure, and unfreedom; it is suspicious to have such feelings—the person betrays himself." How have we Americans lost our suspicion of this type? How have we developed our tremendous apologetics for those who "do not wish to be answerable for anything, or blamed for anything, and owing to an inward self-contempt, seek to *lay the blame for themselves somewhere else*"? How well Nietzsche understood the intellectualized varieties of this type, with their contempt for inwardness. "When they write books, [they] are in the habit today of taking the side of criminals; a sort of socialist pity is their most attractive disguise." *Beyond Good and Evil* (New York, 1966, Kaufmann tr.), p. 29. Here is prophecy, which most often takes the form of forewarning. The type Nietzsche imagined, rare in 1886, is common today in our universities and bureaucracies.

Rieff's "Fellow Teachers"

BY NORMAN O. BROWN

Editor's Note: In April and May of 1973 Norman O. Brown had occasion to spend some time in Saratoga Springs. He had shortly before read and very much admired Philip Rieff's long essay "Fellow Teachers" in the Summer–Fall 1972 issue of SALMAGUNDI, and had determined to make some public observations on Rieff's text. To this end, Robert Orrill and I met with Norman O. Brown in the television studios of the N.Y. State Education Department in Albany, N.Y., under circumstances arranged by Empire State College. Our purpose was to discuss "Fellow Teachers" in a video-tape that would subsequently be used by students in a variety of disciplines. What follows is an edited transcript of a more or less extemporaneous address made by Norman O. Brown, at the start of that taping session, with the assistance of note-cards and various other jottings. The text we've put together speaks for itself, of course, but I might say that it does engage issues raised by Rieff in a way we had not ourselves considered, and should interest readers of SALMAGUNDI for a variety of other reasons as well.—Robert Boyers.

I met Philip Rieff a long time ago: at Herbert Marcuse's wedding to Inge Neumann, in fact. Around the year 1959 there were three books published on the subject of Freud, all of them attempts to get at the social implications of psychoanalysis. One was Herbert Marcuse's *Eros and Civilization,* another was Philip Rieff's *Freud: The Mind of the Moralist,* and a third was the one I wrote called *Life Against Death.* Since then we've gone separate ways. But I'm reminded of the philosopher Heraklitus: the unseen harmony is stronger than the seen. In fact I find myself now greatly impressed and deeply stirred by Rieff's latest piece, addressed to "Fellow Teachers." The publication this fall (1973) in book form of *Fellow Teachers* will coincide with the publica-

This text is published with the permission of Empire State College and the State University of New York.

tion of a new book of mine called *Closing Time*. Perhaps my reaction to his piece as it appeared in SALMAGUNDI in the fall of 1972 will throw light both on his work and on mine, and on the question to which we are both addressing ourselves, namely, what time is it?

What time is it? The title of my book, *Closing Time,* is symbolic of what time I think it is. I take the structure of the book from a philosopher of history whom, strangely enough, Philip Rieff does not mention—Vico. To oversimplify the Viconian system of thought beside which I want to place Rieff's, let me say that Vico in a great panoramic view says the history of the world goes through four stages. First there is the age of the gods, then there is the age of the heroes, then there is the age of men. This is followed by an interlude of dissolution into barbarism, followed by a cyclical renewal and a return of the age of the gods.

The first thing to be said about "Fellow Teachers" is that it anticipates the return of the gods: Rieff rediscovers the necessity for the category of the sacred. As is appropriate, the gods make their presence felt in mysterious and ambiguous language. He says: "Only cultureless societies can exist without presiding presences."* And, then, just in case you might think "presiding presences" are things like Presidents of the United States, he says in another passage, "In our authority figures, the absence of any reference beyond themselves to a presiding presence is fatally weakening to their position as authority figures." These presiding presences are referred to later on as "God-terms," God-terms "that will not be treated as mere heuristic devices," "God-terms that must have binding authority."

In Rieff, as in Vico, the great historical process in a long-range view is a process of secularization, or profanation. He sees America "edging nearer and nearer to a condition of life entirely free from the sacred and its prohibitions." This is what (in Rieff's terms) the triumph of the therapeutic means: instead of souls we have neuroses, instead of sacraments we have shows. There is an almost Viconian summary of the process of secularization: "Therapy is that form which degrades all contents, for use by those who will succeed the late 19th and early 20th century psychologizers, themselves successors to moralizers, themselves regular successor types to all primitive spiritualizers." In the beginning there was primitive spiritualization—Vico's age of the gods.

In his meditations on the process of secularization, Rieff makes some very interesting observations about Marxism. He describes Marxism as "the last major credal effort to reorganize western society," the last

*All quotations from Philip Rieff's "Fellow Teachers" included in this essay by Norman O. Brown are drawn from the text published in *Salmagundi* (Summer–Fall 1972, pp. 5–85). They do not make reference to the later, revised and much expanded book version which was not yet available in the spring of 1973.

major effort to draw on its religious roots, to transform or transcend itself: Stalin is seen as putting an end to that last major effort by transforming credal discipline into organizational discipline. The final obituary is given in the form of a quotation from Hannah Arendt: "The consistent elimination of conviction as a motive for action Hannah Arendt considered a matter of record, since the great terror under Stalin." It would be interesting to ask Rieff to comment now upon Maoism in this context.

But this piece of Rieff's is addressed to fellow teachers. What does he have to say to us? There are some confusing and irrelevant invocations of traditional notions of the highly specialized objectivity of the professor. There are contradictions in Rieff: he says for instance that teachers are not preachers; but he preaches. The real preachment, the real position, though, is that the university is the temple of intellect, the last sacred institution in our culture; if a university is not the temple of the intellect then it is not a university at all. In the university we teachers are called upon to represent the god-terms, and Rieff does not hesitate to call our role priestly. Also, as in Vico, our priestly role is inherently aristocratic—we are a priestly elite. All knowledge, the kind of knowledge we can pass on, is privileged. What Rieff sees around him is the destruction of all aristocracies of feeling intellect.

The priesthood of professors has two main functions: the restoration of the authority of the past and the reinstatement of the law: "The role of the professor is to be an interpreter of the interpreter, and thus to form a great link in the chain of interpretations by which higher culture is held together." We are not ourselves prophets, we should produce nothing new, no breakthroughs—breakthroughs are seen as destructive. We can only work to confirm or disconfirm but not to originate. Originality in thought—he has a phrase which he repeats, "the endless expressional quest"—is in his categories both transgressive and orgiastic. The maintenance of the tradition, the authority of the past, is our primary sacred responsibility; the act of teaching becomes interpretation, and the interpretation of preceding interpretations, thus forming that great link which is a tradition.

Against those breakthroughs that have characterized the "intellectual rhapsodes," as he calls them, of modern times, against these breakthroughs and their celebrants, revolutionary enthusiasts, we need a science of limits, or what Rieff calls an interdictory order. Interdicts are the main constituents of god-terms; to go back to the Old Testament, God said "No" before He said "Let there be light." God's first word was "No." Against our democratic orgiasts, Philip Rieff calls for a revival of a severe code of laws. These interdictory restraints are integral to the reinstatement of the process of soul-making, and to the rediscovery of that sense of guilt without which, says Philip Rieff, there can be no culture.

Thus the teacher, in Rieff's presentation, emerges finally as the equivalent of Dostoyevski's Grand Inquisitor. I am fully aware of what I'm saying and how terrible that vision is. According to Rieff our duty as teachers is "the enforcement of intellect on ourselves and reluctant students." We must be masters of guilt and of the knowledge of guilt, he says. Commenting on the novelist John Barth, he writes that "All giftedness, like Barth's, signifies guilt—although all guilt does not signify giftedness, for to become gifted, guilt must take on the form of privileged knowledge. This is to say: our guilt must be instructed. For a true culture, there must be masters of the knowledge of guilt." The stern severity with which he pursues the logic of the Grand Inquisitor is shown in another passage: "The human being is born a criminal. To praise the infantile is to praise criminality. You and I, fellow teachers, are the real police, whether we like it or not. No culture can survive without police of our sort—priests and teachers." The deeper chords of Rieff's meaning are struck when he says "fear is not a bad teacher of certain elementary lessons." *Principium sapientiae timor dei*—the beginning of wisdom is the fear of the Lord. (So also Vico.)

Although Rieff explicitly abjures prophecy, he's a great apocalyptic prophet in this piece. He sees the return of barbarism which is the final stage of the Viconian cycle. He begins and ends where George Steiner begins and ends his book *Bluebeard's Castle:* with T. S. Eliot's *Notes Towards The Definition of Culture*. All these men see the phenomenon of hostility to culture in any form—I think correctly—as a distinctly modern phenomenon. Rieff's elaborations of this theme are full of insight, showing the many ways in which we are experiencing the return of barbarism: "Our desire for permanent revolution is for a permanent barbarism." By permanent revolution he means the cult of innovation in all spheres of culture, not just in politics. For example, science is not forgotten, perhaps the most energetic barbarizing activity in our culture. "Without a science of limits"—rooted in godheads—"the domination of science implies a cultureless society; we are bound to become the world's first barbarians."

In the same spirit he has sharp remarks to make about what is journalistically called the counter culture, and to which many of us teachers, in touch with the young, have mixed or even sympathetic feelings. Among the paradoxical and extreme formulations which he risks in this piece you find the following: "Immediately behind the hippies stand the thugs"; "transgressive succeeds remissive." I think he's very suggestive, perhaps just plain right, on the complicity of art and intellect and politics in the spread of violence. Let me just refer you to his basic definition of the cult of violence: "By *cult of violence* I mean that critical openness to possibility in which nothing remains true; in this original of all cults, all oppositions are welcomed as if life could be an endless experience of political, technological or interpretative breakthroughs, against orders recognized only for purposes of disestablishment." Now anyone who lives in a university would have to say that critical openness to possibility has been recognized or even praised as the proper atmosphere. What a variety of types (including myself) are linked in common responsibility for the cult of violence by such a formula as this: "What destructiveness is implied in our desire to make life extraordinary."

Rieff has insights and aphorisms probing the interchangeability between terror as an artistic phenomenon and terror as a political phenomenon. Burckhardt in his praise of the Renaissance used the term "terribilita," as something that could be applied equally to the sculpture of Michelangelo and the politics of Cesare Borgia. Philip Rieff looks at Hitler and sees some further consequences, some further twisted horrors down that path. Hitler he calls the failed artist or the armed bohemian, and this is exactly what the American university is turning out in excessive quantities: "The American universities are now producing tens of thousands of failed intellectuals and artists of life; this mass production may lead to the destruction of culture in any received sense."

Now the return of barbarism is not a subject to joke about. In my book *Closing Time* I try to face the truth that Rieff here has painted with such dazzling darkness, and yet situate our time in a different perspective. Engels, in *The Origin of the Family, Private Property and The State*—one of the Marxist classics which I consider relevant to our time—is quoted in *Closing Time* as saying: "Only barbarians are capable of rejuvenating a world laboring under the death-throes of unnerved civilization." Engels may have had only the limited political idea that the socialist revolution that he and Marx expected would not come from the advanced industrial civilization of the west but from some barbarians further to the east instead: the Russians for example, or from some barbarians even further east. My guide Vico has a more fundamental and necessary affirmation of the principle of the necessary renewal through barbarism. In the Viconian cycle we go from the age of gods to the age of heroes to the age of men, and then into a second barbarism. But only barbarians are simple-minded enough to recognize gods. That is to say, only barbarians can acquire that second innocence which is necessary for the return of the gods. Let me read from section 1106 of Vico's *New Science,* which is strange to put beside Philip Rieff, and leaves much to think about that I cannot spell out. Vico contemplates the return to barbarism as he sees it in his own age, which is 1740, and he speaks as follows: "But if the people are rotting in that ultimate civil disease and cannot agree on a monarch from without, and are not conquered and preserved by better nations from without, then providence for their extreme ill has its extreme remedy at hand. For such peoples, like so many beasts, have fallen into the custom of each man thinking only of his own private interests, and have reached the extreme of delicacy, or better, of pride, in which like wild animals they bristle and lash out at the slightest displeasure. Thus, no matter how great the throng and press of their bodies, they live like wild beasts in a deep solitude of spirit and will, scarcely any two being able to agree, since each follows his own pleasure or caprice.

"By reason of all this, Providence decrees that, through obstinate factions and desperate civil wars, they shall turn their cities into forests and their forests into dens and lairs of men. In this way, through long centuries of barbarism, rust will consume the misbegotten subtleties of malicious wits that have turned them into beasts made more inhuman by the barbarism of reflection than the first men had been made by the barbarism of sense. For the latter displayed a generous savagery, against which one could defend oneself or take flight or be on one's guard; but the former, with a base savagery, under soft words and embraces, plots against the life and fortunes of friends and intimates. Hence peoples who have reached this point of premeditated malice, when they receive this last remedy of providence and are thereby stunned and brutalized, are sensible no longer of comforts, delicacies, pleasures, and pomp, but only of the sheer necessities of life. And the few survivors, in the midst of an abundance of the things necessary for life naturally become sociable and, returning to the primitive simplicity of the first world of people, are again religious, truthful and faithful. Thus providence brings back among them the piety, faith, and truth which are the natural foundations of justice as well as the graces and beauties of the eternal order of God."

There is a difference in time perspective between me and Philip Rieff: how close we are, how far apart we are. We share a feeling of the barbarism of our present interlude, but Vico's cycle moves forward to a fresh beginning with a fresh age of the gods, which Rieff cannot see. And so Rieff has to draw back into the posture of restoration—restoring the authority of the past, reinstating the old law. To Philip Rieff I have to say that it is later than he thinks. If the university is our last sacred institution, we who are in it know that the temple is in ruins. The leopards have broken into the temple and drunk of the sacred chalice. Let us say it openly—Western civilization is over. Rieff himself says it openly: "In particular, I have not the slightest affection for the dead church civilization of the West. I am a Jew. No Jew in his right mind can long for some variant of that civilization." But there is a very strange fellow walking through the pages of Rieff's paper; he appears in the next sentence as "the Jew of Culture." In another strange passage Rieff tries to align what he calls "the proud elitist culture of Israel" on the side of Nietzsche and against the democratic, rancorous tendencies which he derives from Hellenism, and against the Christian principle of love. This principle he sharply caricatures: "Nothings would be instant everythings by imposing a love that was entirely mendacious." And Rieff's Jew of Culture turns out to have a strange symbiotic identity with Western culture as a whole—at the end of the essay he is finally revealed as "Lionel Trilling, superior teacher and leading American Jew of Culture." Now Rieff speaks sharply and clearly about religion, and we too have to speak sharply and clearly. Lionel Trilling, the Jew of culture, is the Jew whose Moses is Matthew Arnold. Rieff, who is very self-aware, immediately recognizes the ironies of the position he has drawn: "For us pedagogically inclined Jews of culture, England was Zion, the fantasy fatherland; perhaps it was only the Pax Britannica, seen from the top of Magdalen tower." With the same ambiguous irony he signs this whole message as written from the Codrington Library, All Souls College, Oxford.

We are talking seriously about religion, and we must take seriously Rieff's involvement with Judaism. Rieff's sense of Moses as the presiding presence of Judaism is very strong, omnipresent throughout the essay: "Jews cannot exist without that Mosaic presence." He picks up and repeats what he has learned from his life-long study and interpretation of Freud as the 20th century Jew: "The Mosaic revolution is the formative event in Freud's primal history." Therefore he can now come forward with that final appreciation of the tragic and overpowering significance of Freud's book *Moses and Monotheism:* "It is in Freud's last testament to his own prototypical history, *Moses and Monotheism,* that we discover the ultimate murderer of Moses, Freud himself." Freud himself, who has been in *The Triumph of the Therapeutic* ambiguously distinguished from the therapeutic tendencies which succeeded him, is here seen as the father of the therapeutic and the murderer of Moses.

It is no surprise, if you remember his picture of the teacher as Grand Inquisitor, that the Moses of Rieff is the Moses of the Ten Commandments only, "a supreme interdictory figure." Moses at no point appears as the Moses who led the children of Israel out of bondage in Egypt, Moses the liberator. He is simply the author of the Ten Commandments, an interdictory figure. Even Jesus—we are still speaking of Jews—even Jesus is transformed by Rieff into an interdictory figure: "Jesus is a tremendous reviver of the interdicts. He came explicitly to deepen the law, not to abolish it." There is, from my point of view, a misquotation here, a mistranslation. The word in the New Testament text says that Jesus came to fulfill the law; Christian theology interprets the passage as meaning that by fulfilling the law, ultimately by the crucifixion, he paid off in full the debt owing to the angry father figure, and thus liberated the sons from the angry father figure and the Grand

Inquisitor. In an uncanny moment in Rieff's address he amends the seven last words of Jesus on the cross as truthfully he says a Freudian would have heard them spoken, not as a Jew of culture would hear them spoken: "father, father, why have we forsaken thee?" From the Christian point of view we must return from this blasphemous alteration of the text to the original "father, father, why hast thou forsaken me?" It is his moment of liberation.

Whereas Rieff says we should be grateful for our sense of guilt, Jesus came to preach forgiveness. There is no forgiveness in Rieff that I can see. Jesus preached remission of sins, but Rieff uses the word remissive as if it were permissive, anarchic, orgiastic, a bad word. I do note a qualification at one point; Rieff has been speaking of the necessity of no's and thou shalt nots, and he says: "*No* has to be studied and interpreted almost without break, although it too must exist in a sense heavily qualified, under the sabbath rule of remissions." I would like to hear more from Rieff about the sabbath rule of remissions. To speak as sharply as he speaks, there is no forgiveness in Rieff. In my view he stands condemned out of his own mouth. There are a number of passages in which he rejects American civilization as rancour: "our rancorous civic religion"; "a culture organized by contempt and rancour." One has to register that Philip Rieff's address to fellow teachers is rife with rancour.

Rieff's Judaism has no Messiah. I guess the first appearance of the Messiah in Judaism is in that Moses who led the children of Israel out of Egypt into the promised land. Christians have always seen Christ as some kind of reincarnation of that Moses. We need a new Moses to lead us in a new exodus, an exodus out of western civilization into that world civilization that has been promised to us. There is no world to be preserved; there is a world to be made or to be remade. As James Joyce says in *Finnegans Wake:* "We are once amore as babes awondering in a wold made fresh where with the hen in the storyaboot we start from scratch."

For me it comes to a collision between Rieff and *Finnegans Wake*. In my book *Closing Time* I have tried to compress Vico's *New Science* and Joyce's book, asking those two authors the same question—what time is it?—and making a collage of their answers. Joyce's answer is as different from Rieff's as Vico's is: as Rieff calls us to a return to tragedy, Joyce announces and enacts a return to the satyr play, that original goat-story out of which those siamixed twins, as Joyce calls them, tragedy and comedy, by separation arose; you know the word tragedy in Greek just means goat song. For Rieff, "the most original figure of lightness and play is the satyr, who opposes the Jew of culture." I should like to ask Philip Rieff what he thinks of this quotation from Nietzsche's *Ecce Homo:* "What does that synthesis of god and goat in the satyr mean? I estimate the value of human beings as races according to how necessarily they cannot understand the god apart from the satyr." Rieff should have discussed in "Fellow Teachers" not Barth's *End of the Road* but *Giles Goat-Boy* where you have precisely an obscene reincarnation of a satyr born from a goat mother and sired by a computer father. Barth over-elaborates his ideas, but this work does include a marvelous parody of Sophocles' *Oedipus the King,* transformed into farce taking place on an academic campus. From *Finnegans Wake*—I'm still an interpreter of texts—I get the message to go back, back, back to a time before Moses and before Jesus, when gods were appearing in the form of beasts. Earlier we mentioned Rieff's solemn contrast between the Jew of culture and the satyr. But marvelous inconsistencies crop up in Rieff; there is an extraordinary passage in "Fellow Teachers" which is straight out of a satyr play. It reads: "This reminds me of a little book for humans, titled *My Thoughts,* written down by my wife and myself at the command of our Dandie Dinmont terrier, Darcy, that unfailing, decent and comic representative of what a presiding presence must have been like. You are aware of what *dog* is, spelt backwards." Such madness is only given to Dionysian spirits. One of Rieff's strengths is his knowledge of Nietzsche, who recognized his own style of exaggeration and aphorism as the style of decadence and destruction. I don't know whether Rieff knows how deeply he has been bitten.

It is perhaps another way of saying the same thing to say that we have to reconsider another key religious term in Rieff's analysis—orgy. In Rieff, orgy is the enemy against which all interdicts are directed. "Orgiasts produce new experiences," he tells us. "Note that orgy is the one, only and original totally democratic institution." Ezra Pound has a line somewhere in the *Cantos* where he says, confusion, source of renewal. Mircea Eliade in his studies of comparative religion has taught us to see in the orgy the form in which over-rigid structures have to be periodically dissolved in order to be renewed. In Freud's *Group Psychology and the Analysis of the Ego* there is a passage in which he recognizes the possibility that the separateness of the separate ego must be periodically dissolved in ritual orgy or saturnalia, festival orgy, so that it can be renewed or emerge again restored. Freud says: "It is quite conceivable that the separation of the ego ideal and the ego cannot be borne for long, and this is indeed shown by the institution of festivals which in origin are nothing more than excesses provided by law and which owe their cheerful character to the release they bring." Freud mentions the saturnalia of the Romans and the essential feature of their festivals as their ending in debaucheries of every kind, in transgressions of what were at other times the most sacred commandments. Thus, he says, as a result of the abrogation of the ideals—Rieff's interdicts—the orgy may be regarded as a magnificent festival for the ego. It is possible that we have to extend the notion of orgy from being an institution which individuals need to being also an institution which history needs. That is to say, great historical periods may end, or have to end, in that orgy out of which they can be reborn.

Perhaps I speak as a Christian when at this point I use the category of rebirth, or second birth. The category was introduced into psychoanalysis by Erikson in his book *Young Man Luther,* where he drew on William James' distinction between the once-born and the twice-born. The chosen young man like young man Luther—notice the analogy between the chosen young man and the Jews as the chosen people—who has suffered catastrophic loss of objective identity and total alienation from the roles in which he finds himself, may have to go through a regression which in Freudian terms would take you back to birth, or before birth, in order to be reborn. I give you a summary of this idea not from Erikson but from a more orthodox psychoanalyst, H. Lichtenstein: "Thus the danger arises that instead of maintaining a sense of identity, that the reaction to a depersonalized social role may empty the sense of identity and create the danger of alienation. Under such circumstances a return to earlier mirroring narcissistic experiences will again become necessary, leading even to a temporary object loss. At other times it may indicate a second birth in the sense in which Erikson, following William James, has used this term." I have the feeling that second birth is precisely what is happening to Philip Rieff. Hence the violence: as I said in *Love's Body,* birth is bursting, and it is a knife that cuts open the womb. I feel in the whole text of "Fellow Teachers" a shaking of the foundations taking place in Rieff's mind; one says, as Shakespeare says in such moments, is it a birth, is it a death? This piece of writing feels as if it were an explosive birth of a nova, a new star which sheds light all over the place. What will come of it?

I'd like to end with the question of language. Vico had those three stages of history—the age of the gods, of the heroes, of men—and he had three correlative languages—of gods, heroes, and men. With the return to the age of the gods we would return to the language of the gods. What that could mean is a question which I think we clerks, we professors of humanities, who have a particular responsibility to the language, should ask ourselves. What can we do to prepare for the return of the gods to the language of the gods? Rieff acknowledges, to me very movingly, the way his language and himself are trapped in the language of critical intellect. Some of his more formal didactic statements are quite terrifying. At one point he says that he rarely allows his students to read living authors. Students advance under his tutelage to "something like late Jamesean sentences." Then they advance possibly to Proust and "to Chardin and still life." I say that still life is still born.

Vico is never tired of pointing out that language began with the poets; that the word poet means maker; that poets are makers and creators through being makers of language and thus of culture and humanity. I think we must turn from the philosophers to the poets—or at least turn philosophy, in the manner of the late Heidegger, to listen to the poets, as Heidegger listens to Hölderlin, waiting for the return of the gods. In this spirit I'm releasing not a book but a set of tapes—it's possible that the spoken or rather the singing word is closer to the language of the gods than the written—tapes entitled *To Greet the Return of the Gods*. They will appear simultaneously with my book *Closing Time*. The presiding presences are not so far away. The spirit stalks us. Inspiration lies waiting for us. We need a new language, to greet the return of the gods.

Society

BY T. W. ADORNO

THE IDEA of society confirms Nietzsche's insight that concepts "which are basically short-hand for process" elude verbal definition. For society is essentially process; its laws of movement tell more about it than whatever invariables might be deduced. Attempts to fix its limits end up with the same result. If one for instance defines society simply as mankind, including all the sub-groups into which it breaks down, out of which it is constructed, or if one, more simply still, calls it the totality of all human beings living in a given period, one misses thereby all the subtler implications of the concept. Such a formal definition presupposes that society is already a society of human beings, that society is itself already human, is immediately one with its subjects; as though the specifically social did not consist precisely in the imbalance of institutions over men, the latter coming little by little to be the incapacitated products of the former. In bygone ages, when things were perhaps different—in the stone age, for instance—the word society would scarcely have had the same meaning as it does under advanced capitalism. Over a century ago, the legal historian J. C. Bluntschli characterized "society" as a "concept of the third estate." It is that, and not only on account of the egalitarian tendencies which have worked their way down into it, distinguishing it from the feudal or absolutistic idea of "fine" or "high" society, but also because in its very structure this idea follows the model of middle-class society.

In particular it is not a classificatory concept, not for instance the highest abstraction of sociology under which all lesser social forms would be ranged. In this type of thinking one tends to confuse the current scientific ideal of a continuous and hierarchical ordering of categories with the very object of knowledge itself. The object meant by the concept society is not in itself rationally continuous. Nor is it to its elements as a universal to particulars; it is not merely a dynamic category, it is a functional one as well. And to this first, still quite abstract approximation, let us add a further qualification, namely the dependency of all individuals on the totality which they form. In such a totality, everyone is also dependent on everyone else. The whole survives only through the unity of the functions which its members fulfill. Each individual without exception must take some function on himself in order to prolong his existence; indeed, while his function lasts, he is taught to express his gratitude for it.

It is on account of this functional structure that the notion of society can not be grasped in any immediate fashion, nor is it susceptible of drastic verification, as are the laws of the natural sciences. Positivistic currents in sociology tend therefore to dismiss it as a mere philosophical survival. Yet such realism is itself unrealistic. For while the notion of society may not be deduced from any individual facts, nor on the other hand be apprehended as an individual fact itself, there is nonetheless no social fact which is not determined by society as a whole. Society appears as a whole behind each concrete social situation. Conflicts such as the characteristic ones between manager and employees are not some ultimate reality that is wholly comprehensible without reference to anything outside itself. They are rather the symptoms of deeper antagonisms. Yet one cannot subsume individual conflicts under those larger phenomena as the specific to the general. First and foremost, such antagonisms serve as the laws according to which such conflicts are located in time and space. Thus for example the so-called wage-satisfaction which is so popular in current management-sociology is only apparently related to the conditions in a given factory and in a given branch of production. In reality it depends on the whole price system as it is related to the specific branches; on the parallel forces which result in the price system in the first place and which far exceed the struggles between the various groups of entrepreneurs and workers, inasmuch as the latter have already been built into the system, and represent a voter potential that does not always correspond to their organizational affiliation. What is decisive, in the case of wage satisfaction as well as in all others, is the power structure, whether direct or indirect, the control by the entrepreneurs over the machinery of production. Without a concrete awareness of this fact, it is impossible adequately to understand any given individual situation without assigning to the part what really belongs to the whole. Just as social mediation cannot exist without that which is mediated, without its elements: individual human beings, institutions, situations; in the same way the latter cannot exist without the former's mediation. When details come to seem the strongest reality of all, on account of their tangible immediacy, they blind the eye to genuine perception.

Because society can neither be defined as a concept in the current logical sense, nor empirically demonstrated, while in the meantime social phenomena continue to call out for some kind of conceptualization, the proper organ of the latter is speculative *theory*. Only a thoroughgoing theory of society can tell us what society really is. Recently it has been objected that it is unscientific to insist on concepts such as that of society, inasmuch as truth and falsehood are characteristics of sentences alone, and not of ideas as a whole. Such an objection confuses a self-validation concept such as that of society with a traditional kind of definition. The former must develop as it is being understood, and cannot be fixed in arbitrary terminology to the benefit of some supposed mental tidiness.

The requirement that society must be defined through theory—a requirement, which is itself a theory of society—must further address itself to the suspicion that such theory lags far behind the model of the natural sciences, still tacitly assumed to be binding on it. In the natural sciences theory represents a clear point of contact between well-defined concepts and repeatable experiments. A self-developing theory of society, however, need not concern itself with this intimidating model, given its enigmatic claim to mediation. For the objection measures the concept of society against the criterion of immediacy and presence, and if society is mediation, then these criteria have no validity for it. The next step is the ideal of knowledge of things from the inside: it is claimed that the theory of society entrenches itself behind such subjectivity. This would only serve to hinder progress in the sciences, so this argument runs, and in the most flourishing ones has been long since eliminated. Yet we must point out that society is both known and not known from the inside. Inasmuch as society remains a product of human activity, its living subjects are still able to recognize themselves in it, as from across a great distance, in a manner radically different than is the case for the objects of chemistry and physics. It is a fact that in middle-class society, rational action is objectively just as "comprehensible" as it is motivated. This was the great lesson of the generation of Max Weber and Dilthey. Yet their ideal of comprehension remained onesided, insofar as it precluded everything in society that resisted identification by the observer. This was the sense of Durkheim's rule that one should treat social facts like objects, should first and foremost renounce any effort to "understand" them. He was firmly persuaded that society meets each individual primarily as that which is alien and threatening, as constraint. Insofar as that is true, genuine reflection on the nature of society would begin precisely where "comprehension" ceased. The scientific method which Durkheim stands for thus registers that Hegelian "second nature" which society comes to form, against its living members. This antithesis to Max Weber remains just as partial as the latter's thesis, in that it cannot transcend the idea of society's basic incomprehensibility any more than Weber can transcend that of society's basic comprehensibility. Yet this resistance of society to rational comprehension should be understood first and foremost as the sign of relationships between men which have grown increasingly independent of them, opaque, now standing off against human beings like some different substance. It ought to be the task of sociology today to comprehend the incomprehensible, the advance of human beings into the inhuman.

Besides which, the anti-theoretical concepts of that older sociology which had emerged from philosophy are themselves fragments of forgotten or repressed theory. The early twentieth-century German notion of comprehension is a mere secularization of the Hegelian absolute spirit, of the notion of a totality to be grasped; only it limits itself to particular acts, to characteristic images, without any consideration of that totality of society from which the phenomenon to be understood alone derives its meaning. Enthusiasm for the incomprehensible, on the other hand, transforms chronic social antagonisms into *quaestiones facti*. The situation itself, unreconciled, is contemplated without theory, in a kind of mental asceticism, and what is accepted thus ultimately comes to be glorified: society as a mechanism of collective constraint.

In the same way, with equally significant consequences, the dominant categories of contemporary sociology are also fragments of theoretical relationships which it refuses to recognize as such on account of its positivistic leanings. The notion of a "role" has for instance frequently been offered in recent years as one of the keys to sociology and to the understanding of human action in general. This notion is derived from the pure being-for-others of individual men, from that which binds them together with one another in social constraint, unreconciled, each unidentical with himself. Human beings find their "roles" in that structural mechanism of society which trains them to pure self-conservation at the same time that it denies them conservation of their Selves. The all-powerful principle of identity itself, the abstract interchangeability of social tasks, works towards the extinction of their personal identities. It is no accident that the notion of "role" (a notion which claims to be value-free) is derived from the theater, where actors are not in fact the identities they play at being. This divergence is merely an expression of underlying social antagonisms. A genuine theory of society ought to be able to move from such immediate observation of phenomena towards an understanding of their deeper social causes: why human beings today are still sworn to the playing of roles. The Marxist notion of character-masks, which not only anticipates the later category but deduces and founds it socially, was able to account for this implicitly. But if the science of society continues to operate with such concepts, at the same time drawing back in terror from that theory which puts them in perspective and gives them their ultimate meaning, then it merely ends up in the service of ideology. The concept of role, lifted without analysis from the social facade, helps perpetuate the monstrosity of role-playing itself.

A notion of society which was not satisfied to remain at that level would be a *critical* one. It would go far beyond the trivial idea that everything is interrelated. The emptiness and abstractness of this idea is not so much the sign of feeble thinking as it is that of a shabby permanency in the constitution of society itself: that of the market system in modern-day society. The first, objective abstraction takes place, not so much in scientific thought, as in the universal development of the exchange system itself; which happens independently of the qualitative attitudes of producer and consumer, of the mode of production, even of need, which the social mechanism tends to satisfy as a kind of secondary by-product. Profit comes first. A humanity fashioned into a vast network of consumers, the human beings who actually have the needs, have been socially pre-formed beyond anything which one might naively imagine, and this not only by the level of industrial development but also by the economic relationships themselves into which they enter, even though this is far more difficult to observe empirically. Above and beyond all specific forms of social differentiation, the abstraction implicit in the market system represents the domination of the general over the particular, of society over its captive membership. It is not at all a socially neutral phenomenon, as the logistics of reduction, of uniformity of work time, might suggest. Behind the reduction of men to agents and bearers of exchange value lies the domination of men over men. This remains the basic fact, in spite of the difficulties with which from time to time many of the categories of political science are confronted. The form of the total system requires everyone to respect the law of exchange if he does not wish to be destroyed, irrespective of whether profit is his subjective motivation or not.

This universal law of the market system is not in the least invalidated by the survival of retrograde areas and archaic social forms in various parts of the world. The older theory of imperialism already pointed out the functional relationship between the economies of the advanced capitalistic countries and those of the non-capitalistic areas, as they were then called. The two were not merely juxtaposed, each maintained the other in existence. When old-fashioned colonialism was eliminated, all that was transformed into *political* interests and relationships. In this context, rational economic and developmental aid is scarcely a luxury. Within the exchange society, the pre-capitalistic remnants and enclaves are by no means something alien, mere relics of the past: they are vital necessities for the market system. Irrational institutions are useful to the stubborn irrationality of a society which is rational in its means but not in its ends. An institution such as the family, which finds its origins in nature and whose binary structure escapes regulation by the equivalency of exchange, owes its relative power of resistance to the fact that without its help, as an irrational component, certain specific modes of existence such as the small peasantry would hardly be able to survive, being themselves impossible to rationalize without the collapse of the entire middle-class edifice.

The process of increasing social rationalization, of universal extension of the market system, is not something that takes place beyond the specific social conflicts and antagonisms, or in spite of them. It works through those antagonisms themselves, the latter, at the same time tearing society apart in the process. For in the institution of exchange there is created and reproduced that antagonism which could at any time bring organized society to ultimate catastrophe and destroy it. The whole business keeps creaking and groaning on, at unspeakable human cost, only on account of the profit motive and the interiorization by individuals of the breach torn in society as a whole. Society remains class struggle, today just as in the period when that concept originated; the repression current in the eastern countries shows that things are no different there either. Although the prediction of increasing pauperization of the proletariat has not proved true over a long period of time, the disappearance of classes as such is mere illusion, epiphenomenon. It is quite possible that subjective class consciousness has weakened in the advanced countries; in America it was never very strong in the first place. But social theory is not supposed to be predicated on subjective awareness. And as society increasingly controls the very forms of consciousness itself, this is more and more the case. Even the oft-touted equilibrium between habits of consumption and possibilities for education is a subjective phenomenon, part of the consciousness of the individual member of society, rather than an objective social fact. And even from a subjective viewpoint the class relationship is not quite so easy to dismiss as the ruling ideology would have us believe. The most recent empirical sociological investigation has been able to distinguish essential differences in attitude between those assigned in a general statistical way to the upper and the lower classes. The lower classes have fewer illusions, are less "idealistic." The *happy few* hold such "materialism" against them. As in the past, workers today still see society as something split into an upper and a lower. It is well known that the formal possibility of equal education does not correspond in the least to the actual proportion of working class children in the schools and universities.

Screened from subjectivity, the difference between the classes grows objectively with the increasing concentration of capital. This plays a decisive part in the existence of individuals; if it were not so, the notion of class would merely be fetishization. Even though consumers' needs are growing more standardized—for the middle class, in contrast to the older feodality, has always been willing to moderate expenditures over intake, except in the first period of capitalist accumulation—the separation of social power from social helplessness has never been greater than it is now. Almost everyone knows from his own personal experience that his social existence can scarcely be said to have resulted from his own personal initiative; rather he has had to search for gaps, "openings," jobs from which to make a living, irrespective of what seem to him his own human possibilities or talents, should he indeed still have any kind of vague inkling of the latter. The profoundly social-darwinistic notion of adaptation, borrowed from biology and applied to the so-called sciences of man in a normative manner, expresses this and is indeed its ideology. Not to speak of the degree to which the class situation has been transposed onto the relationship between nations, between the technically developed and underdeveloped countries.

That even so society goes on as successfully as it does is to be attributed to its control over the relationship of basic social forces, which has long since been extended to all the countries of the globe. This control necessarily reinforces the totalitarian tendencies of the social order, and is a political equivalent for and adaptation to the total penetration by the market economy. With this control, however, the very danger increases which such controls are designed to prevent, at least on this side of the Soviet and Chinese empires. It is not the fault of technical development or industrialization as such. The latter is only the image of human productivity itself, cybernetics and computers merely being an extension of the human senses: technical advancement is therefore only a moment in the dialectic between the forces of production and the relationships of production, and not some third thing, demonically self-sufficient. In the established order, industrialization functions in a centralistic way; on its own, it could function differently. Where people think they are closest to things, as with television, delivered into their very living room, nearness is itself mediated through social distance, through great concentration of power. Nothing offers a more striking symbol for the fact that people's lives, what they hold for the closest to them and the greatest reality, personal, maintained in being by them, actually receive their concrete content in large measure from above. Private life is, more than we can even imagine, mere re-privatization; the realities to which men hold have become unreal. "Life itself is a lifeless thing."

A rational and genuinely free society could do without administration as little as it could do without the division of labor itself. But all over the globe, administrations have tended under constraint towards a greater self-sufficiency and independence from their administered subjects, reducing the latter to objects of abstractly normed behavior. As Max Weber saw, such a tendency points back to the ultimate means-ends rationality of the economy itself. Because the latter is indifferent to its end, namely that of a rational society, and as long as it remains indifferent to such an end, for so long will it be irrational for its own subjects. The Expert is the rational form that such irrationality takes. His rationality is founded on specialization in technical and other processes, but has its ideological side as well. The ever smaller units into which the work process is divided begin to resemble each other again, once more losing their need for specialized qualifications.

Inasmuch as these massive social forces and institutions were once human ones, are essentially the reified work of living human beings, this appearance of self-sufficiency and independence in them would seem to be something ideological, a socially necessary mirage which one ought to be able to break through, to change. Yet such pure appearance is the *ens realissimum* in the immediate life of men. The force of gravity of social relationships serves only to strengthen that appearance more and more. In sharp contrast to the period around 1848, when the class struggle revealed itself as a conflict between a group immanent to society, the middle class, and one which was half outside it, the proletariat, Spencer's notion of integration, the very ground law of increasing social rationalization itself, has begun to seize on the very minds of those who are to be integrated into society. Both automatically and deliberately, subjects are hindered from coming to consciousness of themselves as subjects. The supply of goods that floods across them has that result, as does the industry of culture and countless other direct and indirect mechanisms of intellectual control. The culture industry sprang from the profit-making tendency of capital. It developed under the law of the market, the obligation to adapt your consumers to your goods, and then, by a dialectical reversal, ended up having the result of solidifying the existing forms of consciousness and the intellectual status quo. Society needs this tireless intellectual reduplication of everything that is, because without this praise of the monotonously alike and with waning efforts to justify that which exists on the grounds of its mere existence, men would ultimately do away with this state of things in impatience.

Integration goes even further than this. That adaptation of men to social relationships and processes which constitutes history and without which it would have been difficult for the human race to survive has left its mark on them such that the very possibility of breaking free without terrible instinctual conflicts—even breaking free mentally—has come to seem a feeble and a distant one. Men have come to be—triumph of integration!—identified in their innermost behavior patterns with their fate in modern society. In a mockery of all the hopes of philosophy, subject and object have attained ultimate reconciliation. The process is fed by the fact that men owe their life to what is being done to them. The affective rearrangement of industry, the mass appeal of sports, the fetishization of consumers' goods, are all symptoms of this trend. The cement which once ideologies supplied is now furnished by these phenomena, which hold the massive social institutions together on the one hand, the psychological constitution of human beings on the other. If we were looking for an ideological justification of a situation in which men are little better than cogs to their own machines, we might claim without much exaggeration that present-day human beings serve as such an ideology in their own existence, for they seek of their own free will to perpetuate what is obviously a perversion of real life. So we come full circle. Men must act in order to change the present petrified conditions of existence, but the latter have left their mark so deeply on people, have deprived them of so much of their life and individuation, that they scarcely seem capable of the spontaneity necessary to do so. From this, apologists for the existing order draw new power for their argument that humanity is not yet ripe. Even to point the vicious circle out breaks a taboo of the integral society. Just as it hardly tolerates anything radically different, so also it keeps an eye out to make sure that anything which is thought or said serves some specific change or has, as they put it, something positive to offer. Thought is subjected to the subtlest censorship of the *terminus ad quem:* whenever it appears critically, it has to indicate the positive steps desired. If such positive goals turn out to be inaccessible to present thinking, why then thought itself ought to come across resigned and tired, as though such obstruction were its own fault and not the signature of the thing itself. That is the point at which society can be recognized as a universal block, both within men and outside them at the same time. Concrete and positive suggestions for change merely strengthen this hindrance, either as ways of administrating the unadministrable, or by calling down repression from the monstrous totality itself. The concept and the theory of society are legitimate only when they do not allow themselves to be attracted by either of these solutions, when they merely hold in negative fashion to the basic possibility inherent in them: that of expressing the fact that such possibility is threatened with suffocation. Such awareness, without any preconceptions as to where it might lead, would be the first condition for an ultimate break in society's omnipotence.

Translated by Fredric R. Jameson

When the Government Is Lying . . .

BY HENRY PACHTER

Even a hideous parricide has an attorney to safeguard his rights in court: however reluctantly, some appointed lawyer will plead, for instance, insanity. A similar defense, however, cannot be entered on behalf of a government that has been caught lying. Nobody misleads people in a fit of absent-mindedness; on the contrary: the only argument that has at least a ring of plausibility is that the government was acting for the best reasons, after due deliberation, and in the interest of precisely those people it was obliged to lie to. That is to say, the crime was committed from an excess of lucidity!

But here the trouble for the defense has only begun. Suppose the claim can be proved: the government acted, not in vicious pursuit of unavowable aims but—perhaps mistakenly but in perfectly good faith—for an excellent cause. Then it has not answered the real charge at all—which is not that it did the wrong thing but that it did the right thing in the wrong way: without getting the people's consent. (In the recent case of alleged CIA surveillance activities, many people who had not been bothered by FBI raids on Black Panthers, e.g., were appalled when they learned that the CIA had been used clandestinely for similar purposes.)

It is true that the substantive and the formal charges are often confused. One who disagrees with a policy is apt to find that he has not been adequately advised of it. President Wilson knew very well, for instance, that the United States would be drawn into World War I, yet he not only campaigned on a peace platform but he forbade his Naval Secretary, then the young F.D.R., to take any precautionary measures against that eventuality because, he said, when it happens "the record must show that we were unprepared." He was safeguarding the good name of the United States; neither his good faith nor the appropriateness of his action is in question (or else, those who disagree with his policy must attack it on its demerits). But for us, the problem is not whether Wilson's enemies have additional ammunition for electoral mud-slinging but whether his friends can defend a conduct so patently at variance with the image of innocence it was meant to project.

If this were Europe, the case would hardly need to be argued. People there have been brought up in the tradition of the God-ordained State which cannot, by definition, commit crimes (*princeps legibus solutus*), or have accepted the Machiavellian doctrine that *raison d'etat* rather than the Gospel governs the behavior of rulers. Although no one will deny that some kind of moral code must secure the intercourse of governments, it is generally agreed that such a code is different from the ethics of private citizens.

Not so in the United States. Here most people agree that in practical affairs a citizen may not always remember the precepts of his nursery school teacher; but everybody expects the government to behave as though these were indeed its guiding principles. A leading politician must be an exemplary father of his family and his finances must be clean as a hound's tooth. And the boy who could not tell a lie grew up to be the country's first president.

There must be a lesson in this difference between the European and the American approach. The story about George Washington and the apple tree may not be true—historians are doubtful and laymen no longer like to be seen as believers in patriotic cliches. But the historical truth is immaterial vis-a-vis the enormous significance of a legend that shows what Americans like to believe about their country. The criterium of TRUTHFULNESS has been impressed on generations of American children as the characteristic of valor that makes a man worthy of gaining the country's highest honors.

One hardly needs to be a Freudian to understand that authority in the state and authority in the family flow from the same source, or that the structure of the one reflects the structure of the other. In Europe, the patriarchal family has for hundreds of years reinforced the paternalistic state: both the father and the king must be trusted implicitly; their arbitrary decisions need not be understood and approved any more than those of a similarly whimsical God. In the United States obedience must be secured by consent, in the family as well as in the state, and authority is based on merit; respect must be earned. The super-ego can function only if and as long as it is reasonable and not too different from the ego.

To represent and reinforce truthfulness, the super-ego must itself be truthful. An authority that flaunts its own laws is hardly worthy of its name. Indeed, we observe that law and order break down when the citizens no longer trust their government's honesty. Moreover, those who traditionally provide the cultural glue of society—clergy, teachers, artists—either have no ground to stand on or will refuse to fulfill that function whenever authority itself loses its relationship with Truth.

Needless to say, what is true of a conservative government applies with even greater force to a revolutionary party. Its claim is always to tear the mask from government prevarication, and it is under constant constraint to expose its points to the test of proof. One of the most telling charges Trotsky hurled at Stalin was: "His concern is to save his face by cynical distortion of the facts; there can be no greater proof of the intellectual downfall of a revolutionary politician than deception of the masses." Yet it was this same Trotsky who spoke contemptuously of "their (bourgeois, formalist) morality and ours," vindicating deception in the interest of the cause.

Likewise, of course, we all know that lies in our enemies' mouths always seem big and in our friends', small; they also are interpreted as signs of corruption in the former and as concessions to dire necessity in the latter case. Moreover, we not only know that our government is lying: we expect it to, and on occasion will even praise it for that. We assume that our diplomats are cunning and our spies effective. We elect representatives and governments so that they can uphold our party's interests and keep our skeletons in appropriate closets. We expect them to maintain and enforce the whole web of conventional functions on which our society rests, and in so doing to proclaim the highest principles in which we know they don't believe. We expect them to enounce those principles at election time and then to make those wise, practical compromises we call statesmanship. We know that a candidate for office will not be able to fulfill his promises, but we insist that he make them. It is not he who wants to mislead us but we who want to be misled.

But I am not concerned with such comparatively simple instances of misrepresentation. The very structure of our institutions requires a kind of insincerity which is much more serious. We may elect a man to fill an office because we like him and trust him as a human being; but then we ask him to divest himself of these human characteristics and to become an impartial judge who can be moved only by facts. He must impersonate a character he is not; he must play the role of an official, a judge, an arbiter. He must be capable of making decisions which he knows may hurt some people and be unpopular with others. He must wear a mask—and we remember that "persona" was originally a mask—which conceals his private fears and likes; his social nature must be totally alienated from his natural person. We demand this hypocrisy from him as the greatest sacrifice in his service to the community precisely because we do wish to be ruled by laws, not by men with their weaknesses, their prejudices, their jealousies and their vengefulness; not even their pity should be allowed to bend Justice.

It is clear that for the past ten years young people have demonstrated against precisely this denial of nature in our society. They have demanded a public show of that "authenticity" which is possible only to the private individual, and they were disappointed when they found that Power knows neither honesty nor conviction. But it would be superficial to hold the lack of personal morality responsible for a condition that seems to be inherent in the exercise of power. Some public officials have always known this. The late Secretary-General of the United Nations, Dag Hammarskjold, noted in his Diary: "The most dangerous of all moral dilemmas: when we are obliged to conceal the truth in order to help the victory of truth," and he added with sorrow: "Should this at any time become our duty in the office which fate assigns to us—how straight must be our path at all times if we are not to perish."

He did not really finish the thought, for he may have experienced this "most dangerous dilemma" many a time; he was sparing in his communications to the press and always admonished the reporters to have faith in "quiet diplomacy." What he did not confide even to his Diary was his conviction that, since his own path was "straight," he owed no account to others. He was one of the last few men in the modern world who followed their "calling." Others were Churchill and de Gaulle, F.D.R. and Lenin (to name persons from a variety of political camps); all were prepared to go rather crooked ways in pursuit of their respective "straight paths," and they used the shocking truth and the soothing lie as the need of the moment required it to serve their ultimate ends, deeply persuaded that posterity would pronounce their purposes moral.

Perhaps these examples are unfairly selected. Some of our readers may agree that F.D.R. acted out of high responsibility; others may deny this, and they may not be satisfied unless I can show that a Gandhi or a Castro also lied. I shall do more, I shall prove that their followers wanted them to lie.

When Castro needed Russian help very urgently, he proclaimed on a solemn occasion: "I have always been a Leninist"—a gratuitous assertion which certainly did not fool Khrushchev or any reader of Castro's early speeches. (In fact, until three months before the March on Havana the Communists still held him to be a romantic adventurer.) But what did the Cubans feel? Here their leader was telling them cynically that he had deliberately misled them when he pretended to fight Batista only to restore Cuba's democratic Constitution; that secretly he had been planning all along to install a Communist dictatorship—yet the people followed him jubilantly into his new "Leninist" phase.

If anything, the case of Gandhi is even more startling. He had taught his people that non-violence was a sacred weapon—as long as the enemy had superior arms. After Independence he rejected non-violence and not only managed to remain a saint, but his followers now went around preaching on that non-violent man's authority that it was necessary to use violence.

So far our melancholy conclusion has been that the morality of lying resides entirely in the person who, or the side which, is doing the lying. If a leader has been recognized as carrying a mission, then he may discard all scruples; for he is serving a transcendent authority—God, an idea, a class or nation—and that will absolve him not just on pragmatic grounds but on the claim of a "higher ethics." We are told that, to attain the "substance" of the highest good, one must not submit to "formalistic" hesitations, sicklied over with the pale cast of bourgeois philosophy. As soon as I am satisfied that the purpose is right (and it must also be a sufficiently "ultimate" purpose) and the leader's character is pure, he may break the rules of formal ethics; and paradoxically: the less I doubt his inner sincerity, the less I ask him to give concrete proof of it. Only a truthful man may lie; a liar must be truthful. "Fidel does not lie," said the people who had accepted his lies.

Crazy though this sounds, it is what most people think and what the philosophers have taught since ancient times. Plato has admirably and honestly and in great detail shown that only a man widely known for his probity should rule a city. But then he turns around and tells us that this is so because only such a man will be believed implicitly when he has to tell lies. And there are many lies: small ones in the daily course of business, and big ones, myths in fact, which hold the city together and insure the working of the laws. Benevolent lies will convince the citizens that they must obey the gods. Of course, in Plato's Utopia liars are severely punished if they are private citizens. But the ruler is by definition truthful and whatever myth or lie he may have to use is by that very act the truth.

Had Stalin or Mao ever read Plato, they would have liked him, I am sure. But their followers are inconsistent. They would hold their enemies, the "bourgeois," to that formalistic ethics which they do not propose to follow themselves. They condemn "formalism" but they forget that as long as they are private citizens they are not in a position to say what is truth and morality; the rulers alone are in that position. Nor are they aware that this ability is also a burden and a predicament. New truths cannot be created except under dire necessity and with heavy responsibilities. Great men are praised in history books not for good behavior but for decisive policies: Mere whims or arbitrary, selfish decisions cannot be proclaimed as new truths but will soon be revealed to be lies, and therewith the great man loses his charisma, the reputation of probity.

We see that to tell a lie is not as easy as a small man, for instance Richard Nixon, thought it to be. Hegel has said that the Emperor of China was the least free of all men. We therefore find an additional criterium of the permissible lie: not only must its purpose be high-minded and the person of the liar be truthful, not only must the lie be used by the highest magistrate and for the benefit of the city; its historical significance also must be Greatness. It will not do for a court historian to reinterpret a retreat as victory, or a defeat as a strategic retreat. To do that, one must have history on his side. Gregory VII was a truly great pope: to assert the superiority of the Church over the Emperor he perpetrated one of the greatest hoaxes ever thought up by a public-relations man. As you may remember from your high school class in world history, Emperor Henry IV besieged the Pope in his Canossa castle, forced him to lift the ban, to give him absolution and to dissolve the dangerous coalition of princes he had assembled. But the clever chancellery of the Vatican gave out that Henry IV had been standing in the snow outside the castle for several days, had humbled himself and begged the Pope to forgive him—which the Pope eventually and graciously granted. To this day, "Canossa" means the humbling of the state by the Church.

Another example of manipulative interpretation occurred after the Cuban missile crisis. The conflict was settled by the withdrawal of the Soviet ICBMs; but Khrushchev was not forced to admit that he had ever installed missiles on Cuba. Moreover, Kennedy promised to remove from Turkey some obsolete Jupiter rockets which were due for withdrawal anyway. So Kennedy could claim, vis-a-vis the hawks in Congress, that he had made no real concession in return for withdrawal of the Soviet missiles (and the understanding was never published). Khrushchev, on his part, could claim, vis-a-vis the hawks in his military establishment and the Chinese, that he had not withdrawn anything and that in return for it he had obtained the withdrawal of American missiles from Turkey. Thus not only was peace preserved in 1962 but both contestants could claim victory.

Contrast with this wisdom now the more recent mishandling of the

U.S.-Soviet detente. The Russians were very anxious to receive most-favored nation status, substantial credit concessions, and access to U.S. technology. I think the United States should in return have received similar substantial concessions either in the economic field or in the theater of world politics. Instead, under the impact of a reckless lobby powered by an ambitious senator, we insisted that the Soviets guarantee a certain number of exit visas for Jews—a demand that is non-germane and very unusual because it infringes upon the sovereignty of the other nation. Foreign Minister Gromyko obtained the Politburo's consent to this foolish deal—which was indeed very cheap for the Soviet Union—provided, however, that the Soviet Union did not have to admit it. In fact, Gromyko gave Kissinger a letter disowning the whole deal, and threatened to publish it if the United States should ever claim any "right" to interfere with the Soviet Union's treatment of minorities.

All would have been well if the agreement had been kept a secret. The Soviet Union would have received credits at the rate that it gave Jews permission to leave. But certain Jewish organizations and the aforementioned Senator, a presidential candidate who certainly will not get my vote, insisted that the Secretary of State spell out the agreement so that they would get the credit for their dubious achievement. As everybody now knows, the Russians had no choice but to denounce the deal, and U.S. detente policies were greatly embarrassed. The pressures for disclosure had also been strengthened by certain "cold war" forces hostile to the detente idea, and "truthfulness" here was used as a weapon to sabotage the diplomacy of peace, whereas the ambiguity of Mr. Kissinger's and Mr. Gromyko's understanding might have decreased the tensions not only between the two superpowers but also in the Middle East. It amazes me that that senator still passes for a friend of Israel.

Another instance where ambiguity might have served peace better than the truth occurred during a recent war in Southeast Asia. The rationale of that war is not under discussion here; I am using the example only to point up a lesson. In that war, troops of country N were using the territory of a certain Prince to launch attacks on a certain country S. The Prince was embarrassed; but he also was loath to see his country drawn into the war entirely. Therefore, he gave permission, reluctantly I am sure, that bombers from country S should harass the encampments of country N's forces inside his own country—provided that his face was saved and country S denied what its airplanes were doing in his country. Thus, although of course all participants knew what was going on, and while pacifists in the United States were denouncing the bomb attacks, the government stubbornly denied any wrong-doing—thereby preserving peace for 99 per cent of the Prince's country. It was not until the truth was forced out that open war came to the whole of that unfortunate country.

These are examples from foreign policy, the field where obviously Machiavelli is still the greatest teacher. But we already have seen that matters which seemingly belong to international affairs have a domestic side; in fact, the issue of prevarication or misrepresentation usually comes up because some opposition party or ambitious pretender decides to assume a "hawkish" posture in foreign affairs.* But I shall cite at least one example on strictly domestic affairs and, more specifically, on local issues, where it seems clear that the government must try to withhold information and, if cornered, must misinform the public.

Supposing a city is planning a housing development. It has quietly bought up some land. Should a reporter be alerted to the project, land prices would rise abruptly, making the project that much more expensive or possibly endangering its completion altogether. Asked point-blank in a news conference, the Mayor has the duty to deny that anything is afoot, or he may have to develop a "cover story." Should he succeed, the citizens will later forgive him; but should anything go wrong, he may lose all credibility. There is no administrator in the world, whether in business or in national or in local government, who will not occasionally take a short cut toward some desirable goal, hoping that he might earn praise for "decisive action" if he succeeds.

The unsavory revelations about the Nixon administration—where selfishness and pettiness were married to evasiveness—have thrown opprobrium on all behavior normally condoned in the political community. We are notably forgiving in cases where a chief stands by his subordinates or where peers show solidarity and team spirit. This is true not only of governments; every football club will expect its members to stick together in adversity, to protect each other and, if necessary, to tell lies to the public. It is sheer hypocrisy to pretend that "our" party is always cleaner than "theirs," or that ordinary people are less hypocritical than politicians.

It is true, of course, that politicians have more occasion to lie, or at least to withhold the full truth. There seems to be a well-articulated ladder from outright, conscious and intentional deceit to the "white lie," the evasive answer and the fib, the blunder and the failure to disclose the full truth. Finally, there is the need to protect one's sources (claimed by both the police and the news reporters) and the highly controversial

*In order to obtain ratification of a treaty, therefore, the government has to "lie," i.e. to exaggerate what we get out of it and minimize the benefits to the other party.

question of confidential advice. It is generally agreed that a doctor and a lawyer, as well as a priest, may not reveal, even in the most worthy interest of the public, what they have been told in strictest confidence. Governments have often claimed the same relationship between the politician, who is responsible to his voters, and his advisers, who must present to him all the options and will do that only under the protection of confidentiality. This is essential for the smooth functioning of any executive office, whether in business, government, church, university, club or association.

Those who plead for participatory democracy, total publicity and instant disclosure of all government deliberations, fail to understand the principle of representative government. We elect or hire people to conduct business for us, and judge them periodically by their success. When the time comes to reelect or reject them, we compare their performance with our own preferences and desiderata. But we cannot judge their performance if we peek over their shoulder and prevent them from making decisions. The so-called participatory or "instant" democracy gives influence to pressure groups and may in fact hand control of the government over to the least responsible agents who have never faced the electorate, above all the press.

The need to avoid such influences then leads to new stratagems of concealment, which plague democracies most severely. It is a peculiar paradox that authoritarian governments, which cannot be asked questions, do not have to lie; democratic governments must answer parliamentary inquiries and therefore resort to manoeuvering in order to avoid telling either the truth or lies. An example well known to historians occurred before World War I. When England and France concluded the Entente Cordiale, the British Prime Minister was afraid that he might be asked in Parliament whether England had made any military commitments. He therefore avoided any reference of that sort when he met his French counterpart, but he saw to it that the two chiefs-of-staff met. The two officers made very detailed plans, and when Germany declared war on France in 1914, an astonished Foreign Secretary Grey was told that France's northern flank would be unprotected unless England fulfilled her obligation.

The question is whether lying by government is in a different category than lying by business corporations or private persons or social clubs; whether lying on behalf of an institution or an idea is less reprehensible or perhaps even more necessary than lying for selfish purposes.

We may easily distinguish various attitudes toward this problem. Conservatives take their cue from Plato or Hobbes: governments may not derive from God, but they follow an ethics of their own. Even though few admit that lying belongs to good rulers' tools, they will deny that it is the citizens' business to check on governments—and that amounts to the same thing. Liberals tend to be pragmatic and would probably admit that governments must use any means to serve a good purpose; but since they are also committed to the idea that governments must be controlled by public opinion, they cannot at the same time grant their government immunity for concealment, misinformation or outright lying. They will therefore vary their attitude from time to time: when in power, they will invoke "executive privilege," as did President Truman when he was beset by investigative Republicans in Congress and Senator Joseph McCarthy's terrorist quest for "disclosure." When the shoe was on the other foot, a Democratic Congress happily overrode President Nixon's claims of the same privilege.

Radicals are even more cynical. They will frankly proclaim that fighters for a good cause may indict their enemies for lying but may themselves use every subterfuge to advance their cause. They will call the tolerance they are enjoying "repressive"; the repression of truth, when they deem it necessary, will be dubbed "liberative." Thus, Sartre broke with Camus because he felt that Camus's attack on Stalin's concentration camps was inopportune; in leftist circles it is still considered bad manners to wonder whether President Allende of Chile may have made some fatal mistakes that cost him his office and his life. One must not admit mistakes committed by one's friends, and that is the political philosophy of conservatives, liberals and radicals alike.

The intention here need not be dishonorable. Just as Gabriel Borkman in Ibsen's play, the councilmen in the Stavisky affair thought that everybody would get his money back if only the embezzlement could be kept secret for another month. Obviously, if I am struggling to keep bankruptcy away, I must try to conceal this information from those who might start a run on my bank and thereby make the failure a certainty. Or to take another case, from a different field: recently, a grand jury proceeding was revealed, with the obvious intention, on the part of interests, to forestall the appointment of a public official; neither the person whose reputation was damaged nor the government whose purposes were frustrated had any recourse against the defamation, and the papers that had lent their columns to the propagation of the rumor claimed that it was their duty to report what they knew—these were the same papers, incidentally, which had condemned the same practice at the time of Senator Joseph McCarthy.

I think that in democracies this war between the forces that want full disclosure and the forces that try to protect state secrets will go on indefinitely. No government is entirely trustworthy; officials therefore must be controlled even at the risk of paralyzing their effectiveness, of making their operations indecisive, of defeating the purpose of their policies, or of endangering the world's peace. But these risks show that the function of controlling the government can be abused, whether by the government's enemies or simply by a sensationalist press that feels no responsibility to the common good; a responsible government must strive to free itself from these fetters. Suppose a city is threatened by an epidemic and its mayor is preparing evacuation of the children; but before he can arrange for reception centers elsewhere, provide checks against further spread of the disease by the evacuees, and take all necessary measures, some reporter gets hold of the news prematurely, broadcasts it over the radio and produces a panic with broken-down cars blocking the exit roads and carriers of the disease spreading it to the evacuation centers. The principle of the First Amendment can be murderous if it is applied dogmatically and thoughtlessly.

There must be a minimum of trust in the authorities if a country is to survive. A government should not be obliged to exaggerate the benefits of a treaty it has concluded in order to obtain its ratification; it should not have to conceal its motives in order to obtain cooperation on measures it deems beneficial. Such confidence, however, exists only where the body politic feels identity of purpose with its representatives and government. We trust and obey orders of the fire department, of a health officer, and of similar functionaries whose jobs are close to our own interests. If we do not have similar confidence in other authorities, something fundamental has gone wrong. We must not inquire, in such cases, whether and why someone is lying but why there is a "credibility gap" at all. Distrust of the government is a symptom of deeper problems in society. Lying in government is not a disease that can be cured in isolation from the rest of the social fabric.

Although I know that many Americans right now are more indignant about the previous administration's untruthfulness than about its policies, it is my contention that the issue would hardly have grown so bitter if the people had felt comfortable with this government and its policies. They objected to the substance and therefore criticized the form. For the past two years now we have been on a truthfulness binge and have hounded the government with disclosures and revelations, thereby undermining its usefulness. We have behaved like Gregers Werle in Ibsen's *Wild Duck*, who ruins his friend's family by fanatically insisting on telling the truth to everybody.

We attach to truthfulness a higher value than to many other principles that might rule our behavior. Truth seems to have something philosophical about it—for is not the philosopher first of all dedicated to truth? Indeed, so he is; but lest we overestimate this principle, let us listen to the foremost philosopher of antiquity, Aristotle. I have previously quoted Plato to the effect that only a truthful man may lie. Perhaps with a glance at his teacher, Aristotle issued this warning to posterity: Don't trust philosophers, and above all don't entrust to them the burden of government. They are too much dedicated to principles that are good to contemplate but not so good in practical affairs. Philosophers are too much involved with their personal salvation, and that is not good for transaction in the public interest. The great lies are usually told in the name of some great principle. Rather trust ordinary people, who may not know the highest truths but do know what to expect from their fellow citizens. In sharp contrast to Plato, Aristotle said that sinful men may make good citizens. All democracy is "transactional."

The larger the state, the lesser is the chance to build it on virtue. Even as small a commonwealth as Geneva was too large to form that kind of community where the public and the private affairs are merged so completely that each is governed only by himself and if he were to lie he would be lying only to himself. I have deliberately used here the very words of Jean-Jacques Rousseau: he knew quite well that his ideal community could be realized only in the narrow valleys of the remotest cantons of Switzerland, and that the price for such participatory democracy was general dullness.

He was only dimly aware of another possibility to constitute a community without lying. But unfortunately in the age of technological communication and manipulation, after the experience of totalitarian governments and the negative utopias of Huxley and Orwell, this has come closer to realization: the deliberate creation by the government of uncontrovertible truth. Hobbes foresaw that if ever powers-that-be should find the theorem, "In the triangle the sum of the angles is 180°" contrary to their interests, they would not hesitate to burn the geometry books. Totalitarian governments have structured and built for their subjects a sham reality. In this case the government does not tell lies but the entire system in which it operates is a lie, and nobody, not even the government itself, may be aware of it. As one of my Russian friends at the United Nations once said at the climax of a heated debate: "Why should I want to criticize a Communist government since it is right anyway?"

The Western counterpart to this weirdness is a technique that is only seemingly the opposite of sham. Photographers know how the camera can lie by appearing to depict nothing but stark reality. By presenting the appropriate angle or cut or enlargement, the camera can transform the greatest beauty into a repulsive agglomeration of sores. Any truth isolated from its context can become a lie; the more little truisms one tells about the great reality, the less does he reveal about the big truth. During the great Constitutional crisis of 1974, when most Americans were passionately and fanatically pursuing the truth about Watergate, I felt that some scheming manipulator could have designed the scandal to divert our attention from the much bigger corruption in Congress and in the economy. While America was busily discovering the truth that its President had involved himself in a shabby little cover-up, the corporations were stealing billions off our backs, despoiling the exchange value of the dollar vis-a-vis other currencies, eroding its internal value, and setting the stage for a depression. Nobody cared to hear these big truths.

Such attempts to create artificial universes are not without danger. If the Arab governments build their existence on the bugaboo of a threatening Israel, they may eventually have to fight a war for which they are not prepared. When Harry Truman justified the Marshall Plan by the exaggerated picture of a communist scheme to take over the world, he created a paranoic state of mind in America that made the McCarthy terror possible. In other words, even the most highly developed technique of manipulation has its limits: it always reaches a point where its further application will backfire.

In conclusion, therefore, I see government lying hemmed in on many sides: by the liberals' hesitations, by the radicals' demands for truth, by the inherent difficulties of justifying prolonged deception, by the inability of even the cleverest manipulator to control the consequences of his efforts, by the need of even the conservative paternalist to earn the confidence of those whom he must persuade that he has the calling and the office from God—Who, of course, would not trust a liar.

Not only is lying restricted; it must be avoided for another reason. A government that must often resort to deception thereby indicates to itself that it is weak, and its efforts to cover up previous lies will weaken it further. Finally, if deceptions are discovered or even if only a serious doubt has arisen about the government's trustworthiness, that in itself is a sign that the entire structure of the state lacks integration and is weak. The credibility gap did not arise from lying, but the lying became necessary because the government lacked credibility. The forces that contend for power in society must at all times find an equilibrium or an overarching ideology—perhaps a myth—that holds the structure together. But if they cannot agree what is truth and what is lie, what is convention and what is hypocrisy, what is legitimate prerogative of the government and what is illegitimate concealment, then exposure of the lie is no longer the corrective of isolated cases of mismanagement but the denunciation of the social contract.

On the surface, therefore, we see a struggle between, on the one hand, a government (or for that matter a corporation, a church, a newspaper, a research institution, a hospital, etc.) trying to protect its secrets and its retainers, and on the other hand the opposition, legitimate or self-appointed watchdogs of the public, concerned and other interested parties which are all trying to place these agents in goldfish bowls or playing politics with the popularity of such demands. In a wider context, however, these forces give expression to a deeper, more philosophical and more principled contest between two basic attitudes: one, which we have called conservative, is resigned to the insight that all human institutions are imperfect; the other, which we have called liberal, builds on the conviction that institutions can be made more perfect under the management of good men. From these attitudes radicals or pseudoradicals have drawn different conclusions: the conservative one leads to the idea that with good institutions one need not worry about good men; the liberal one leads to the rejection of all institutions. These attitudes are represented by world historical movements whose basic features have kept repeating themselves throughout the ages. Some will always claim the ethics of responsibility as their guide, others the ethics of conscience. Some will always demand that public morality be governed by the same code as private conduct; others will always invoke overriding principles of morality in the service of higher values. Some will justify the means by the end, others will judge the end by its means. Between the two, they are making history.

Bleaching the Black Lie: The Case of Theresienstadt

BY LUCY S. DAWIDOWICZ

"In Germany," Friedrich Reck-Malleczewen noted in his diary in February 1942, "the lies have a blond character." German nationalism colored, indeed double-dyed, all life, painting the dirty deeds of National Socialism in blond hues. Heinrich Himmler, himself no mean liar, informed his SS officers in 1943 that truthfulness had become a rare virtue in Germany. Lying prevailed in Germany no doubt because Adolf Hitler, High Master of the Big Lie, had demonstrated time and again that lying in the service of the National Socialist state and the German *Volk* was not only ideologically commendable, but was also politically rewarding. Furthermore, in Hitler's Germany lying was regarded not as a policy to be exercised exclusively by elite rulers in behalf of the state, as prescribed in Plato's *Republic*, but as a necessary technique to be used at all levels of state and party hierarchies in implementing National Socialist policy.

Not all German lies were blond. When the Ninth Commandment was violated to conceal the transgression of the Fifth, German lies were black as hell, black as murder. The blackest of German lies were concocted to carry out the "Final Solution of the Jewish Question."

The "Final Solution of the Jewish Question" was the German code name for the planned, systematic murder of the European Jews. Under cover of this code, the Germans annihilated six million Jewish men, women, and children and destroyed the thousand-year-old civilization of East European Jewry. Assigned top priority by Hitler, the Final Solution was carried out with determination and the requisite efficiency, even at considerable cost to the conduct of the war against Russia and the Western Allies.[1] To facilitate this vast undertaking of mass murder, the Germans spun intricate webs of lies, most designed to disarm and

1. Cf. my book, *The War Against the Jews 1933-1945* (New York, 1975), especially pp. 140-147.

deceive their victims, being "aggressive lies" (Ira S. Wile's classification), lies to advance German goals and thwart resistance to them. The Germans also erected facades of lies to deceive the bystanders, the world's putative watchful eyes and wakeful consciences—the Red Cross, the churches and their clergy, resistance movements, Allied political leaders. These were the "defensive lies," fabricated to avoid detection of and punishment for crimes far more heinous than lying. All over Europe the Germans told the Jews that they were being sent away elsewhere for labor service. "Resettlement for work in the East" became the master cover lie, concealing mass murder carried out through mass shootings by specially trained units in the open air on territory seized from Russia or through mass gassings in the specially constructed death camps on Polish territory.

In Kiev in September 1941, for instance, German occupation authorities posted notices ordering the Jews to assemble for "resettlement" and marched them off to the outskirts of Kiev at the desolate ravine of Babi Yar. There the SS murder squads, designated as *Einsatzgruppen* ("special-duty" groups) shot over 33,000 Jews in two days. In Lublin, the SS officers in charge of the "evacuation" of the Jews which began in March 1942 told the officials of the Jewish Council, half of whom were to be "evacuated," that they would reassume their administrative functions in their new residence.[2] But they, along with some 30,000 Jews from Lublin, were sent straight to the death camp at Belzec and into the gas chambers. In the Warsaw ghetto, the official German orders to the Jewish Council on July 22, 1942, stated that "all Jewish persons, regardless of age and sex," would "be resettled in the East," and that "each Jew to be resettled" would be allowed to take fifteen kilograms of luggage with him and provisions for three days.

Often the Germans elaborated on the official lies to adapt to particular situations. In small towns and villages, for instance, many Jews, having learned that "resettlement" meant death, fled to adjacent forests or found other nearby hiding places when they learned that the Germans were organizing round-ups of Jews. The Germans then improvised new lies and ruses. Allowing an interval of several days to elapse, they dispersed their forces and planted reports designed to reach the Jews in hiding that the coast was clear, that the Jews could return home safely. Seduced by the lie, the Jews returned and were trapped. In some places, the idea of "resettlement" was embellished by German

2. The texts of these and other documents in my forthcoming book *A Holocaust Reader*, to be published by Behrman House late in 1975.

sadism. Loading unwitting Jews on trains destined for death camps, the SS told them that they were being transported to Palestine.

At Treblinka, a death camp where 800,000 Jews were murdered, Commandant Franz Stangl had a sham railway station built, with a clock, ticket windows, timetables, and signs indicating train connections to Warsaw and Bialystok, contrived to create in the minds of the arriving Jews the false notion that Treblinka was a place from which departure was just as possible as arrival.

The lies continued into the inmost chamber of murder. Following the style set in the euphemistically titled "euthanasia" stations, where thousands of mentally ill and incurably sick Germans were murdered, the gas chambers in the death camps were identified as "shower baths." The Jews were told that they and their clothes had to be disinfected before they could be assigned to their new places of work. Crowding the Jews into the gas chambers, even then, the Germans continued to lie, instructing them to breathe deeply and thus cleanse their lungs.

While planning the final details involved in executing the Final Solution, Reingard Heydrich, head of the most dreaded police institution of all Europe, the *Reichssicherheitshauptamt*—RSHA (Reich security main office), who had been entrusted with the task of coordinating all aspects of the Final Solution, evolved another stratagem in the web of lies. (He called it a "tactical measure.") He would establish a camp for Jews that, while fulfilling routine functions in connection with the Final Solution, would also be—to be accurate, would appear to be—a model institution whose existence could refute charges that the Germans mistreated or even killed Jews. Such a model camp would be the blond lie to disguise the black lie, an ambitious and intricate falsehood designed to "document" the "truth" of a still greater falsehood. As a locus for this model camp, Heydrich chose the town of Theresienstadt in Bohemia, about thirty miles north of Prague.

*

Built in 1780 by Joseph II to commemorate his mother, Empress Maria Theresa, Theresienstadt was a walled fortress town at the confluence of two rivers, with some 200 two-story buildings and fourteen huge stone barracks. Abandoned as a garrison by the 1880s, Theresienstadt languished as a civilian town with a stagnant economy. Its population was some 7,000, when the Germans early in 1939 annexed the Czech provinces of Bohemia and Moravia (Slovakia became a separate puppet state), designating them as a German protectorate.

On September 24, 1941, Hitler appointed Heydrich as Protector of Bohemia and Moravia, in the expectation that this ruthless man, whom he later eulogized as "the man with the iron heart," would exercise the requisite terror to subdue the widespread unrest which the Czech population was then manifesting. Heydrich's new assignment was not intended to—and definitely did not—divert him from his responsibilities with regard to the Final Solution nor did it diminish his consuming interest in the Final Solution; it merely enlarged his area of operations, putting at his disposal the resources of Bohemia and Moravia.

On October 10, 1941, less than two weeks after assuming his new office, Heydrich was already familiar with Theresienstadt and had decided that it was admirably suited as an assemble place where the Czech Jews could be concentrated prior to being deported to death in accordance with plans and schedules still to be worked out.[3] Across the river from Theresienstadt stood a small fortress, called just that—*die kleine Festung*, which was designated as Gestapo headquarters for Theresienstadt operations, and which would also house a prison, convenient to the camp, yet discreetly out of sight. In a few weeks, Jewish forced-labor brigades, recruited from Prague and Brno for heavy construction work at Theresienstadt, began to transform the fortress town and its barracks into a detention camp. The Czech Jews began to arrive at the end of 1941 and the local civilian population was shortly thereafter evacuated. (In keeping with the habitual sequence of events in National Socialist Germany, the official decree establishing Theresienstadt as a "Jewish settlement" and ordering the evacuation of the local Czechs, was issued, after the fact, on February 16, 1942.)

Already in October 1941 Heydrich had darkly adumbrated his cunning plan to make Theresienstadt more than a transit camp for the Czech Jews on their way to annihilation. He elaborated more concretely on the idea to set it up as a "privileged camp" at the Wannsee Conference on January 20, 1942.[4]

The Wannsee Conference—its name taken from the meeting's site at the pleasant suburban Berlin lake—was an interministerial conference called by Heydrich to coordinate administrative matters relating to the Final Solution as they impinged on the various jurisdictions of the

3. For my narrative about Theresienstadt I have relied primarily on the two authoritative books by H.G. Adler: *Theresienstadt 1941-1945: Das Antlitz einer Zwangsgemeinschaft* (Tubingen, 1955) and *Die verheimlichte Wahrheit: Theresienstadter Dokumente* (Tubingen, 1950).

4. The minutes of the Wannsee Conference appear in full in *A Holocaust Reader*, cited above.

German state and Nazi party bureaucracies. There, in an expansive presentation outlining the development of the Final Solution, Heydrich described also his plan to assign to an old-age ghetto Jews from the Greater Reich (Germany, Austria, and the Protectorate) who were over 65 years old. Theresienstadt, he said, was under consideration for this purpose. Also Jews with World War I war decorations (Iron Cross, First Class), and with serious wartime disabilities would be assigned to old-age ghettos. "With this efficient solution," Heydrich summed up triumphantly, "the many interventions"—presumably by Germans in high office who still had connections with Jews or part-Jews—"will be eliminated at one stroke."

The idea of exemptions for Jewish veterans from the German dictatorship's anti-Jewish measures had originated with Marshal Paul von Hindenburg back in April 1933, when he had appealed to Hitler against the summary dismissals from the civil service of war-wounded judges, lawyers, and civil servants in the judiciary: "If they were worthy to fight and bleed for Germany, then they should also be considered worthy to continue serving the Fatherland in their professions." Hitler promised, somewhat gracelessly, to take the Marshal's "Noble Motives" into consideration in the legislation then being drafted to legitimate the removal of the Jews from the civil service. Subsequent anti-Jewish legislation did indeed exempt various categories of Jewish World War I veterans and permitted them to retain their jobs, but by 1938 even those exemptions were revoked. Still, personal interventions continued to be made from time to time for prominent persons and Heydrich, aware of the possibility that a general might apply on behalf of a much decorated "non-Aryan" war hero or that a top government bureaucrat might intervene for a part-Jewish partner in a mixed marriage, envisaged Theresienstadt as a wholesale solution to such requests for exemption. In Theresienstadt these individuals would be separated from the "Aryan" population, interned, yet would remain on tap if need be, in response to inquiry or investigation.

While elaborating this aspect of Theresienstadt's simulating function, an even craftier idea occurred to Heydrich and Himmler: the operation of Theresienstadt as an old-age ghetto would in itself supply the cover for the more monstrous lie of the Final Solution, "resettlement for work in the East." The existence of a model old-age ghetto, consisting of elderly Jews exempted from labor service in the East because it would be too severe a hardship for them to sustain, would give credence to German claims that the Jews had indeed been deported to labor and not to death.

During the early months of 1942 Heydrich perfected his design for the "propaganda camp," as Theresienstadt was thenceforth to be called by insiders in the SS bureaucracy. Most Czech Jews who first populated the camp, except for selected ones over 65, were dispatched on their ultimate journey eastwards—to ghettos and death camps—in the spring to make room for the "privileged" Jews. When Heydrich was assassinated in May 1942 by members of the Czech underground, the whole scheme to operate Theresienstadt as a cover for the Final Solution had already been worked out. Administrative responsibility for Theresienstadt was thereafter lodged with the RSHA office IV B 4, "Jewish Affairs and Evacuation Affairs," headed by Adolf Eichmann, who had worked under Heydrich. Theresienstadt's three successive commandants were all recruited from Eichmann's staff.

In June 1942 thousands of elderly Jews and war-wounded and war-decorated Jewish veterans began to arrive at Theresienstadt, to become unwitting actors in the sinister charade. They were duped even before they were sent away, the RSHA having evolved a minor-scale deception that would bring the German dictatorship material gain as well as propaganda benefit. German and Austrian Jews who still had some personal property and private means were induced to sign "home-purchase contracts," under which they assigned their remaining assets in exchange for a "lifelong guarantee of residential accommodations and board," including also medical care.[5] But when the Jews came to Theresienstadt, with their possessions, clothing, and books, they were assigned not to the modest private quarters they had been hoaxed into buying, but to tiered bunks in cheerless barracks. Remonstrating, they exhibited their contracts, their title to decent accommodations and board, but it did not take them long to realize they had been defrauded and deceived.

Actually Theresienstadt was operated like the ghettos in Eastern Europe. Its Jewish population was forcibly enclosed within a circumscribed area from which unauthorized departure was punishable by death. The old Habsburg barracks and the dilapidated two-story buildings, including the unused store fronts, were turned into communal quarters where at times as many as 50,000 Jews were crowded in misery and distress. Bunks were constructed in four and five decks, so close one upon the other that no one could sit upright at the edge of a bunk. Often people did not have even enough room to stretch out.[6]

5. The official instructions regarding such home-purchase contracts are published with commentary in Adler, *Die verheimlichte Wahrheit*, pp. 48-52, 55-57.

6. Leo Baeck, "A People Stands Before Its God," in Eric H. Boehm, ed., *We Survived* (Santa Barbara, Cal., 1966), pp 290-291.

Hunger, cold, and disease stalked the ghetto, ravaging the aged men and women already afflicted by the emotional shock of displacement and rejection. The ghetto hearse, an ornate four-posted wagon, a macabre relic of the past, now drawn not by horses but by Jews, transported the dead to the cemetery and delivered bread to the public kitchens, sometimes simultaneously.[7]

The SS ruled the ghetto with terror. Ghetto Jews were punished for writing unauthorized letters, for covering up escapes, for drawing and painting scenes of the authentic misery of Theresienstadt. The RSHA wielded the only power in the ghetto, but to reinforce Theresienstadt's fraudulent facade, they assigned the management of the ghetto's internal administration to a Jewish council, whose three top officers represented the uprooted Jewish communities of Berlin, Vienna, and Prague. Thus the imposture of "Jewish autonomy" was established, but in fact the only truly autonomous activity of the Jewish captives in Theresienstadt was the expression of their stubborn will to live and to survive the Third Reich.

*

In February 1943, Ernst Kaltenbrunner, Heydrich's successor, believing there were too many Jews in Theresienstadt—the count then stood at 46,735, nearly half over sixty years old—and using as justification the possible spread of a typhus epidemic, proposed to Himmler that five thousand of those over sixty be removed and sent to Auschwitz. Aware of Theresienstadt's role as a "propaganda camp," Kaltenbrunner assured Himmler that, as had been done with previous deportations from Theresienstadt to Auschwitz, the Jews to be taken would be exclusively those "who have no special connections or contacts to draw on and who hold no high war decorations of any kind." But Himmler, who precisely at that time was ordering the total destruction of the Warsaw ghetto, sent a message through his personal secretary rejecting Kaltenbrunner's proposal:

> The Reichsfuhrer SS does not desire the deportation of Jews from Theresienstadt because thereby the intention that the Jews in the old-age ghetto of Theresienstadt live and die in peace would be obstructed.[8]

The facade of Theresienstadt as a propaganda camp was, then, to be preserved, even though for the time being it was not exhibited. The stage

7. The artists of Theresienstadt left a poignant record. See Gerald Green, *The Artists of Terezin* (New York, 1969) and *The Book of Alfred Kantor* (New York, 1971).

8. The documents are reproduced in Adler, *Die verheimlichte Wahrheit*, pp. 296-299.

and cast were being held in readiness for the occasion when the show would be put on. The first tryout came in June 1943, when Theresienstadt was opened to two representatives of the German Red Cross. Their guide was one Eberhard von Thadden, Eichmann's opposite number in the Foreign Office, who dutifully followed Eichmann's instructions as to what to show. From the RSHA's standpoint, that visit was not successful. The German Red Cross representatives were reportedly "very upset and unfavorably impressed by their visit," having found the ghetto "frightfully overcrowded," the Jews "seriously undernourished," and medical care entirely insufficient.[9] After that visit, occasional parcels from the International Red Cross, mostly drugs and medical supplies, were permitted to be shipped to Theresienstadt.[10] Perhaps the German Red Cross made its point, but more likely the RSHA eased up so that the arrival and receipt, however infrequent, of such parcels, would give credence to the claims of the propaganda camp.

To ease the overcrowded conditions, Eichmann did in September 1943 what Kaltenbrunner had unsuccessfully proposed to Himmler the previous February. He shipped over five thousand Jews from Theresienstadt to Auschwitz, but the deportation this time had a new twist, intended to preserve the fiction of Theresienstadt. Instead of deporting just old people or those unfit to work, Eichmann selected families and allowed them to take their possessions. They were kept in isolation on the vast grounds of Auschwitz for six months, during which period they were forced to send postcards to friends and relatives in Theresienstadt praising their new accommodations. Thus the RSHA expected to dispel suspicion and disquieting rumors about where those five thousand Jews had been sent. (Only thirty-seven of them survived.)[11]

During the next few months von Thadden several times conducted visiting dignitaries around Theresienstadt, but no special efforts appear to have been made to enhance the camp's conditions, presumably because those guests were well disposed toward the German dictatorship and cared little about the Jews.

Theresienstadt, meanwhile, was fulfilling its function as propaganda camp in bolstering the German effort to deport the Jews from Denmark.

9. Roswell D. McClelland to John W. Pehle, Executive Director of the War Refugee Board, confidential letter, October 26, 1944. A copy of this letter is in my possession. See also Adler, *Die verheimlichte Wahrheit*, pp. 304-307.

10. Leni Yahil, *The Rescue of Danish Jewry* (Philadelphia, 1969), p. 292.

11. Gerald Reitlinger, *The Final Solution: The Attempt to Exterminate the Jews of Europe 1939-1945*, 2nd rev. and aug. ed. (South Brunswick, N.J., 1968), p 182.

In no European country had the Germans encountered as much resistance as in Denmark in September 1943, when the planned deportation measures aroused the opposition of Danish leadership and the entire Danish population. To reassure top Danish officials that no harm would befall their Jewish nationals, Werner Best, German Plenipotentiary in Denmark, told them on the eve of the attempted roundup, that the aged and unemployable would be sent to Theresienstadt, "where the Jews enjoyed self-government and lived in decent conditions."[12] But few Danes believed him. A few days before the roundup scheduled for the night of October 1, the Danes managed to warn, conceal, and then transport most of the 7,000 Danish Jews to safety in Sweden. Somewhat fewer than 500 Danish Jews fell into German hands. They were all sent to Theresienstadt rather than Auschwitz, as had been the case with the Norwegian Jews, no doubt because the RSHA now realized with what persistence the Danes would pursue the fate of their nationals. Indeed, immediately after the roundup, Danish authorities began to demand from Best and other German authorities the release and return of the deported Jews. Danish welfare authorities right away applied for permission to send letters and parcels to Theresienstadt. (The Germans never approved the shipment of parcels, but nonetheless the Danes sent about seven hundred parcels monthly containing food, medicine, and vitamin pills, some of which were let through.) The Danish Red Cross petitioned to visit Theresienstadt to see the Jews and their conditions.

Pressured by the Danes on all sides, Best appealed to Eichmann, who was in Copenhagen on November 2, opportunistically urging Eichmann to accede to Danish demands. Two days later, Eichmann, back in Berlin, having cleared with headquarters, wired Best that the RSHA agreed in principle that the Danish Red Cross could visit Theresienstadt, but not before the spring of 1944. The Danes insisted on an earlier date, but were rebuffed by Eichmann himself on December 14, 1943, and again in February 1944, when he said that a visit before May "would be undesirable." On May 16 Himmler himself gave permission for the visit and finally, on June 13, 1944, eight months after the deportation of the Danish Jews, the RSHA informed the Red Cross that the date for the visit to Theresienstadt had been fixed for June 23, 1944.[13]

The long postponement of the Danish request is surely to be attributed to the RSHA's determination to proceed with caution,

12. Raul Hilberg, *The Destruction of European Jewry* (Chicago, 1967), p. 362.
13. Yahil, *op. cit.*, pp. 291-305.

avoiding the blunders of overconfidence which had bungled the visit of the German Red Cross in June 1943. The RSHA realized that the forthcoming Danish Red Cross visit, if properly prepared, organized, and managed, could provide a neat opportunity to demonstrate to the world at large Germany's solicitude for elderly Jews and dispel reports about slave labor and death camps. This supersanguine expectation stimulated the SS to a grandiose scheme. They would transform Theresienstadt's exterior into a dazzling fantasy, while the misery would persist unchanged behind the false front.

At the end of 1943 the bitter comedy of Theresienstadt's potemkinization[14] began under the guise of a major "beautification" program. A new camp commandant, SS Obersturmfuhrer Karl Rahm, was brought in to set the pace in overhauling Theresienstadt. Neither money nor effort was spared. Even nature was enlisted: Eichmann was said to have postponed the Danish visit to the spring because the trees in bloom would enhance the landscape.

Under Rahm's brisk supervision, the streets began to be repaired, smoothed, and cleaned. Some abandoned buildings in poor condition were torn down. Others were repaired, cleaned, and painted on the outside. Block by block, the beautification program proceeded. The stores which had been converted into living quarters were now transformed into elegant shops, painted, refurbished, with charming outdoor signs designating them: "grocery," "bakery," "pharmacy," "lingerie," "perfumery." (These false fronts appear frequently in the work of the Theresienstadt artists as grotesqueries.) The SS even brought in appropriate merchandise as stock to authenticate the fraud.

The town square, which had been closed off, was now opened and its grounds cultivated. A splendid lawn was laid with little bypaths for strollers. A total of 1,200 rose bushes were planted. A music pavilion, complete with band stand and park benches, was erected. A cafe with sidewalk tables added to the illusion of a delightful spa. A children's playground, with up-to-date installations, furniture, and adornments, was constructed. The hospital, various children's quarters, public kitchens, as well as other institutions to be on the tour of inspection, were renovated, refurnished; necessary equipment was brought in. Every place was cleaned and scrubbed.

With accelerating frequency inspection teams and supervisory committees checked on the progress of the beautification program.

14. Modern history destroys our childhood myths. The scholars now say that Grigori Aleksandrovich Potemkin was an efficient and responsible administrator who most likely did not loot the treasury of Catherine II and did not erect sham villages to deceive her.

Each review generated new orders for further improvements. By May most of the exterior transformation had been accomplished. A Theresienstadt prisoner remarked that "even the great Potemkin would have been green with envy at the sight of so much ingenuity."

The next stage was to provide the sort of living accommodations for the so-called "prominent" Jews and many of the Danish Jews that would attest to the lie of Theresienstadt. To make space and at the same time to fortify Theresienstadt's reputation as an old-age ghetto, the RSHA in May 1944 deported about 7,500 Jews to Auschwitz, most of them young and able-bodied. The space that became available was used to set up new residential quarters, all on the ground floor of the small buildings. Since the RSHA did not plan to take its visitors upstairs, Jews vacated from the lower floor were crammed into the communal quarters upstairs, where the only beautification was the placement of flowerpots on the outside windowsills.

The living quarters of the prominent Jews were refurnished, cleaned and painted. Paintings which had been robbed from the abandoned homes of Czech Jews sent to Auschwitz were hung on the walls. The places which had been prepared for some of the Danish Jews were not assigned, however, before June 20. The next day they were allowed to inspect their new quarters and only on June 22, just the day before the Red Cross visit, were they permitted to move in with their few belongings. A Danish couple with a five-year-old son rejoiced in the ultimate luxury, the privacy of a room of their own. The amenities delighted them:

> . . . a real lamp shade, curtains for the windows, and a flowerpot; besides the three beds, a wardrobe, a real table, and a proper chair (what a thrill!), and a night table. There was no more space for any more furniture. A trim nameplate on the door and a blue quilt on the bed.[15]

About seventy Danish Jews, for whom such accommodations were not available or not considered worth providing, were invited to attend a nonexistent concert in a barracks and were kept there in isolation for the duration of the Red Cross visit.

In the last days of preparation, the SS authorities, using terror as their educational tool, began to coach the Jews as to their behavior while the foreign visitors would be on the grounds of Theresienstadt. The Jews were instructed and rehearsed as to how they were to dress, where they were to be stationed, and what they were to say. Children too were

15. Account by Corrie and Sven Meyer in Adler, *Die verheimlichte Wahrheit*, pp. 309-310.

coached and bribed with food about what to say and how to behave. The adults were warned against trying to pass unauthorized information about Theresienstadt and its real conditions. The Danish Jews especially were reminded that their continued exemption from being deported was contingent on their obedience to SS orders. Those whose families had been sent to slave-labor camps and about whom some inquiry might be raised were interned during the Red Cross visit under Gestapo surveillance in barracks out of bounds of the guided tour. Ailing, emaciated, ragged, and crippled Jews were warned to remain in their upper-floor barracks and keep off the streets. Just before the visitors were due, white gloves were distributed to the Jewish workers who delivered the bread to wear while on exhibit. At the last minute the pavements were washed with soap and polished as if they were parquet floors.

As the deadline for the Red Cross visit neared, tension in the Theresienstadt ghetto increased. The Jewish Council was particularly apprehensive, since the Germans had threatened to hold them responsible for any untoward conduct on the part of the Theresienstadt Jews. But with that traditional Jewish optimism which history has so frequently belied, many Jews hoped that some good, some change for the better, might ensue from the visit.

*

At last June 23, 1944 came, a pleasant summer day on which the visiting commission arrived. It consisted of two Danes and a Swiss medical man, Dr. M. Rossel, representing the International Committee of the Red Cross (ICRC). The Danes, who had never met Dr. Rossel before, were Dr. Frants Hvass, head of the Political Section of the Danish Foreign Ministry, and Dr. E. Juel-Henningsen, vice-chairman of the health administration in the Danish Ministry of Interior, the latter representing the Danish Red Cross.

The welcoming committee consisted of a half dozen SS officers, but only Rahm wore his SS uniform; the rest—even the head of the Security Police and Security Service in the Protectorate, even the top SS officials from Berlin—were dressed in the false colors of mufti. Von Thadden and a delegate of the German Red Cross were also present. When the Danes and the Swiss entered the gates of the Theresienstadt ghetto, they were received by Dr. Paul Eppstein, the "Eldest," of the Jewish "self-government." In the ghetto's town hall to which the delegation first went, Eppstein delivered a short lecture on how the ghetto was organized and administered, in accordance with the briefing he had been given by the RSHA. Like all the Jews of Theresienstadt, Eppstein had been instructed by terror, the German threats of reprisals having ensured his compliance. In fact, the day the visitors arrived, Eppstein still had a black-and-blue mark under his eye, the lingering evidence of a blow Rahm had given him a few days before.

The visitors were then conducted on the tour which had been so long and diligently in preparation. They stayed in Theresienstadt for about eight hours and were shown everything that had been constructed, cleaned, painted, and adorned especially for the occasion. The visitors talked to ghetto Jews whom they encountered on their tour—those encounters too were planned—or whom the Danes particularly inquired about, but except for one fleeting moment no conversation was conducted out of the earshot of the SS. Once Dr. Rossel had the opportunity for a private word with Dr. Eppstein, asking him what he thought would be the ultimate fate of the ghetto population. Dr. Eppstein said that he knew no answer to this question and added that he personally "saw no way out."[16] That was Eppstein's desperate attempt at esoteric communication, but it fell on deaf ears. Dr. Rossel proved to be the ideal dupe, more gullible and credulous than any old, frightened Berlin Jew hoaxed into buying an apartment at Theresienstadt. The Danish officials, for their part, persisted in their inquiries about their nationals in the ghetto, but showed little interest in the others.

For the Reich Jews in Theresienstadt that day was one of anguished disappointment. Their expectation that the Red Cross Commission might see behind the facade and penetrate the truth of Theresienstadt was crushed. Leo Baeck himself commented:

> They appeared to be completely taken in by the false front put up for their benefit . . . . Perhaps they knew the real conditions—but it looked as if they did not want to know the truth. The effect on our morale was devastating. We felt forgotten and forsaken.[17]

*

On July 19, 1944, Dr. Hvass and Dr. Juel-Henningsen reported at the Danish legation in Stockholm on their visit to Theresienstadt to a small group of interested Jews, two of whom represented the Committee to Aid Persons Deported from Denmark. Their summary of Hvass's remarks intimates that the Danes had opted for prudence rather than faultfinding, as a more judicious means of serving the interests of the

16. McClelland to Pehle (Footnote 9).

17. Baeck, *loc. cit.*, p. 294.

incarcerated Danish Jews. Though Hvass appeared for the record to be moderately satisfied with conditions as he saw them, at least with regard to Danish nationals, the report reflects a state of credence suspended, judgment suspended, censure suspended. Dr. Hvass pointed out that at Theresienstadt conversations had been "discreetly" observed.[18] The Danes had apparently decided that by appearing to have been hoodwinked, by making the Germans think they had been taken in by the grand pretense, they could continue, perhaps even intensify, their aid to the Danish prisoners. Indeed, their vigilance in the end saved the Danish Jews from the fate which was the common lot of the German, Austrian, Czech, and Dutch Jews in Theresienstadt—deportation to the gas chambers of Auschwitz. Those other Jews were truly forgotten and forsaken.

As for Dr. Rossel, the Swiss ICRC representative, his acceptance of everything he had seen (his own eyes!) and everything he had been told (his own ears!) was total and complacent. The report which he prepared for his superiors in the Red Cross was exactly what the Germans had hoped for as the outcome of their grand beautification program—a totally uncritical, even approving affirmation of their propaganda.[19] Rossel's report does not sufficiently illuminate his personality or motives. Was he merely deficient in intelligence or common sense? That would be a sad reflection on his genetic heritage. Was he simply a pompous vain man swayed by flattery and the VIP treatment which the Germans gave him? A sad reflection on his character. Or was he nurturing certain political sympathies for the Third Reich? A most sad and unfortunate reflection on the institution which employed him. The report itself can serve various classroom exercises, not the least, as a model for the unreliability of eye-witness reports in establishing historical truth.

"Immediately on entering the ghetto," Rossel wrote, "we were convinced that its population did not suffer from undernourishment." He was even persuaded by German assurances that the Jews in Theresienstadt ate not just as well but even better than non-Jews elsewhere in the Protectorate. In fact, he remarked, "certain articles even reach the ghetto, which are almost impossible to find in Prague." The Jews of Theresienstadt were well dressed too, he noted:

18. "Conditions in Theresienstadt, according to Danish Report," October 13, 1944, prepared by Otto Leyvsohn and Kai Smonsen, on a meeting at the Danish Legation in Stockholm on July 19, 1944. An English translation is in my possession.

19. "The Theresienstadt Ghetto," report of visit of June 23, 1944, by Dr. M. Rossel, delegate of the International Committee of the Red Cross. An English translation from the French original is in my possession. The McClelland letter, cited in Footnote 9, contains a penetrating commentary of Rossel's report.

> The smarter women were all wearing silk stockings, hats, foulards and carried modern handbags. The young men seemed also well turned out, some of them even were flashily dressed.

Furthermore, Dr. Rossel commented, "certainly there are few populations whose health is as carefully looked after as in Theresienstadt."

In his summation, Rossel was all naivete:

> We must say that we were astonished to find out that the ghetto was a community leading an almost normal existence, as we were prepared for the worst. We told the SS officers who escorted us that what astonished us most was that it should have been so difficult for us to obtain permission to visit Theresienstadt.

That "almost normal existence" was what Rossel had characterized variously as a "collectivist" or "communistic" society, as if in some way insinuating something about Jewish political preferences. The aftertaste of those remarks is definitely unpleasant.

Most perilously poised between obtuse neutrality and Nazi sympathy was Rossel's concluding paragraph. In its entirety it read:

> Our report will change nobody's opinion. Each one remains free to condemn the Reich's attitude towards the solution of the Jewish problem. If, however, this report should contribute in some small measure to dispelling the mystery surrounding the Theresienstadt ghetto, we shall be satisfied.

In Rossel's mind, impartiality was the fair approach toward the "Reich's attitude towards the solution of the Jewish problem." While he granted everyone the freedom to condemn the Reich in this regard, his report clearly indicated that he himself did not do so and that he considered Theresienstadt a wholly appropriate and unobjectionable solution to the Jewish question.

Rossel believed the false German assurances that Theresienstadt was an *Endlager*, a camp of final destination, from which no one was deported elsewhere. But in the months following the Red Cross visit, some 25,000 of the Theresienstadt Jews were sent to the gas ovens in Auschwitz. Only 10,000 remained by the end of 1944. But the comedy continued to run for selected audiences. On April 6, 1945, when the battle of Germany was raging, with Russian and American forces converging from east and west, two Swiss Red Cross delegates visited Theresienstadt, seeing only what the Germans wanted them to see. "The total picture of the town," they reported with acumen equal to Rossel's, "makes a very favorable impression."[20]

20. Extracts of this report in Adler, *Die verheimlichte Wahrheit*, pp. 355-357.

Two weeks later, when Berlin was already surrounded, Himmler was ready to betray his lifelong Fuhrer and save his skin through phoney negotiations on behalf of Jews who were already nearly all murdered. Theresienstadt was one of his bargaining points:

> Theresienstadt is not a camp in the ordinary sense of the word, but a town inhabited by Jews and governed by them, in which every manner of work is to be done. This type of camp was designed by me and my friend Heydrich, and so we intended all camps to be.[21]

Thus the man who had complained that truthfulness had become a rare virtue in Germany, at the very end exploiting the lie of Theresienstadt as his passport to legitimacy. But it was then too late for fraud and deception. The charnel smell of Europe under Hitler's Germany gave away the whole dark truth.

21. Quoted in Reitlinger, *op. cit.*, p. 179.

Lying on the Couch

BY LESLIE H. FARBER

It is virtually impossible to find references in the psychoanalytic literature to liars or lying, even in the form of studies of the impostor or the confidence man. If we are surprised by the psychoanalytic neglect of such a commonplace activity in our ordinary lives as lying, we should remind ourselves that psychoanalysis has, like other professions, had its share of practitioners of the lie. In fact, one of the early stalwarts of psychoanalysis, Wilhelm Stekel, at the time an editor of the *Psychoanalytische Zentralblatt*, was expelled by Freud from the inner circle for precisely this reason. I quote briefly from a letter of Freud's to Dr. Stekel, dated January 13, 1924:

Dear Dr. Stekel:

I acknowledge receipt of your letter of December 31, 1923, and thank you for your good wishes regarding the improvement of my health. But I cannot refrain from contradicting you on a few important points.

You are mistaken if you think that I hate or have hated you. The facts are that after an initial sympathy . . I had reason for many years to be annoyed with you while at the same time having to defend you against the aversion of everyone around me, and that I broke with you after *you had deceived me on a certain occasion in the most heinous manner*. . I lost confidence in you at that time and since then you have not provided me with any experience that would help me to regain it.

I also contradict your often repeated assertion that you were rejected by me on account of scientific differences. This sounds quite good in public, but it doesn't correspond to the truth. It was exclusively your personal qualities — usually described as character and behavior — which made collaboration with you impossible for my friends and myself. Since you most certainly will not change — you don't need to, for nature has endowed you with an unusual degree of self-complacency — our relationship stands no chance of becoming any different from what it has been during the past 12 years. With good wishes, yours faithfully, Freud.

Without knowing the content of Stekel's alleged deceit, I am rather heartened by Freud's response. He does not turn to psychoanalytic theory to accuse Stekel of trying to murder the father of the movement — as he had with other apostates. Instead he says, in effect, "Wilhelm, you have a rotten character, which, given your self-complacency, is not going to change. So let's call it quits."

We would be mistaken to assume from Freud's outrage that he regarded the human being as essentially truthful. Stekel's deliberate deception caught him off-guard, I imagine, but I am sure that his customary pessimism about the human condition remained unshaken. It was only a few years before that he had written the Reverend Oskar Pfister, "I don't cudgel my brains much about good and evil, but I have not found much 'good' in the average human being. Most of them are in my experience riff-raff, whether they proclaim this or that ethical doctrine or none at all."*

While psychoanalysis paid little or no attention to the conventional notion of the deliberate lie, it compounded man's capacity for deceit by adding to his concept of himself what we might call the unconscious lie — i.e. the lie that is hidden from our conscious awareness. The early literature on hysteria and repression suggested that the neurotic disorder itself was the result of a disagreeable bit of personal history that had been unconsciously disowned. Treatment required that the truth behind this neurotic deceit be retrieved and exposed to consciousness and responsibility. Since the beginnings of psychoanalysis, there have been several techniques for penetrating the unconscious and retrieving the truth behind the neurotic deceit. At first hypnosis was the method of choice. But then it became apparent that not everyone was subject to hypnosis. Worse yet, whatever the hypnotic state might be — to whatever degree it seemed to resemble the unconscious itself, it soon became clear the state was not lie-proof: in fact, hypnosis seemed to offer an histrionic setting for lying which enhanced the capacity for deception. Drugs still find favor as lie-detectors. Ancient sexual encounters, acts of cowardice or brutality on the battlefield have been vividly re-enacted with the stimulation of various drugs, but again, as

* See Leslie H. Farber, "Psychoanalysis and Morality", *Commentary*, November, 1965.

with hypnosis, dramatic verisimilitude proved to be no guarantee of truth. After hypnosis, the technique of preference in psychoanalysis became free association — and, of course, the interpretation of dreams through free association.

I should now like to offer an example of the hazards of free association from my early days in psychoanalysis when I was first a candidate in training with a psychoanalytic institute. I am compelled to warn you that my initial conception of free association was rather cinematic in character. As nearly as I can recall, I believed this esoteric art was primarily visual — a sort of movie which would be projected on the screen of my inner eyelids after I had closed my eyes. Naturally I considered myself honorbound to describe to my analyst, without deletion or censorship, the course of this movie, that description being what I considered free association.

On the day I have in mind I had lain down on the couch, closed my eyes, and was now waiting for the movie to begin. I saw no more than an image or two when I heard what could only have been a fairly young child practicing the violin in a room nearby. I could close my eyes but not my ears, and my movie stopped altogether as I listened to the kind of screeching that can be obtained only from an out-of-tune violin played forcefully by a novice with no ear at all. It struck me as a hopeless situation: the two of us could not pursue our artforms at the same time. Summoning up my courage (after all, I was paying for my time) I asked my analyst if it would be possible for the young man (her son, perhaps?) to do his practicing at a time that didn't coincide with my analytic hour, because I found it impossible to free associate (I did not reveal the idiosyncratic nature of my free association, which I felt was my own business) so long as the young man fiddled. Out of politeness I spared her any critique of his music-making, implying that even Heifetz would have got in my way. "Of course," she said, and moved quickly to that portion of the house to silence the young violinist. When she had returned to her easy chair behind the couch, she said, "I didn't realize you were interested in music." Caught completely off guard by such a remark, I blurted out, "Well, of course, but I wouldn't tell *you* about that!" For a moment I was somewhat amused by my snotty remark, which suggested that while I was willing to recount all manner of sexual indiscretion or infantilism, there remained a few other matters that were too private for psychoanalytic dalliance. However, my amusement was short-lived; in no time I became ashamed of my pretentious nonsense. And as I awaited my movie, violinist now silenced, my eyes shut, not surprisingly my mind turned to early musical experiences of my own, in particular a painful time when I engaged in a state violin contest, all of us young fiddlers being assigned Sibelius's *Valse Triste*, a lugubrious little tune consisting of long sustained mournful tones. Stage fright overcame me, a tremor overtook my bow arm, Valse Triste became Valse Stacatto. My opponent, known throughout the community as my inferior — I was, in fact, considered a shoo-in for first place — my opponent was an easy winner, if for no other reason than his steady bow arm. When I returned home that night my father asked me how the contest had gone. "I lost," I said mournfully. The movie began to go very slowly in this portion of my associations. Looking at my father's face I saw no trace of commiseration on his features. To the contrary he looked furious, as though my defeat was a cruel reward for all those months of listening to me rehearse my dreadful piece. As I tried, in my analytic hour, to describe the effect of his anger piled cruelly on top of my humiliation over my musical collapse, my eyes filled with tears, my voice choked and, to my astonishment, I found myself weeping noisily. Ordinarily I do not weep, so my tears seemed fraught with significance. It was as though without warning I had been plunged into a sizeable pocket of grief that I never knew existed. I seemed to have stumbled on a momentous event explaining a parting of the ways between my father and me. As if that were not meaning enough, I thought I now understood, or so I explained to my analyst, why I had chosen not to pursue a musical career. That renunciation, to judge from my tears, represented a far greater loss than I had ever been willing to acknowledge. Afterwards, as I mulled over this tumultuous hour, I thought to myself: What a marvelous thing is this psychoanalysis, that it should provide me with such revelations. I felt illuminated — though saddened — by my insights and also, I confess, quite exhilarated to be a part of this remarkable profession, whose extraordinary theories I had just verified in my own analytic experience.

My revelatory binge proved to have little staying power, however, giving way shortly to a sobriety in which I was compelled to make certain important revisions:

1. There never was a dramatic parting of the ways between my father and me. Our life together was hectic, full of struggle and reconciliation, both rewarding and disagreeable, depending on forces I shall describe in my next novel.

2. My musical talent was modest and I knew it. There was never a serious inclination, leaving my fantasies aside, to make music my profession. When the time came to pack up my violin and get on with my medical studies, I did so with relief, not grief.

If we recall Freud's pessimism about human character in general we may be able better to understand the curious circuitry that connects psychoanalysis to truth and truth-telling to psychoanalysis. The aim of the enterprise is, of course, truth, and an essential rule of the contract is truth-telling. On the other hand, the party who will be doing most of the telling is also deemed inadequate to the task on prima facie grounds: most people lie and deceive themselves a lot anyhow, and even an unusual truth-telling person wouldn't be able to speak *the real* truth about himself, since it, by definition, is hidden from his conscious mind, and may be discerned only by: first, outwitting consciousness, using the various devices I have mentioned (hypnosis, drugs, free-association and so on), and second, subjecting the material thus produced to the analyst for decoding.

While the analyst remains the principal decoder (being the one trained in the basic Freudian lexicon of human nature and therefore the one who owns the decoding manual), the patient is usually encouraged to participate as fully as possible on these archeological expeditions; true, he is only an amateur, on the other hand it is *his* dream, *his* free association that is the shard of pot, the splinter of bone. And not only *his* dream, *his* free association, but also *his* therapeutic moment, *his* scene, *his* production at-and-of-the moment — and momentousness — of discovery. The revelation of his revelation.

At this point the paradoxical relations between psychoanalysis and truth become even more complex.

It is given to human experience not only to contemplate its own nature and existence, but to historicize itself. Of epochs and eras and periods we hear much from chroniclers of public life. But rare is the individual who does not seek, in one way and another, to trace his own trajectory in time and context, to question his own life for shape and direction. Here I am today, 62 years beyond my beginning, the embodiment — and refugee — and survivor — and witness — of the forces that have moved across and within my life. As I survey this pastness that belongs to me alone: this unique tangle of public-private, shared-solitary, accidental-intentional, known-unknown that is my life-so-far, and is in some way accountable for my arrival in this present, and for whatever present-ness is yet to come, for me, — what I long to find is some particularity, some singularity that makes it not only in fact, but in truth, mine.

I search for some continuity that is more than mechanical, for something thematic in the moving parts; I search, above all, for a *point*, a meaning; and the truth is that if there is a meaning *I am* the meaning.

(Some lives could, I suppose, be considered useful for making general points, cautionary or exemplary, but not yours or mine, I trust.) I say "if there is a meaning" not because some lives have meaning and some don't, but because some lives *find* meaning, and some don't. And where is it found? It is found in the search for truth — about what one has been and done, about what one is and is doing. So, it turns out, Freud and I have no disagreement here. The point is to look for truth, and truth is the point. But, what sort of truth now becomes crucial. And what sort will of course determine to some extent the means to be employed in finding it — if indeed the means have not already determined what sort.

The truth I have in mind to look for is not the sort that once you find it you can have it wrapped to go. And once you get it home it fits right in and never wears out. My view of the truth is that there is such a thing, and that I can only approach it if I keep in mind the impossibility of my ultimately grasping it. Martin Buber, (who, you will notice, was comfortable with terms that do not come easily to us in our calling) put it this way: "The truth belongs to God alone. But there is a human truth, namely to be devoted to the truth."

The truth that interests me is problematical, partial, modest — and still breathing. It is not normally dramatic or revelatory, and its attainment depends far more on thinking hard than feeling freely. To put it another way: I think that speaking truthfully is a more fitting ambition than speaking the truth.

It is a different kind of truth that is sought and produced by the devices of psychoanalysis. It is revelatory; it is usually attended by — indeed identified by — considerable emotion, which is often understood to have been repressed or denied and is only now breaking through to the surface — a formulation I find somewhat dubious, quite incompatible with much of anything else we know about emotion, which is hard to conceive of — in actuality — as something not-present. In any case, the truths yielded up by these means are remarkable for their clarity, their completeness, their shapeliness, so to speak. Revelation tends to have a certain loveliness of form that is quite unrelated to — in fact may be quite in defiance of — what is revealed. "I see it now: I am a monster of self-absorption," may not seem especially self-congratulatory, but it is the sort of pronouncement that yields genuine satisfactions to the pronouncer — and these satisfactions are essentially esthetic in character.

There is, in my view, Keats to the contrary notwithstanding, no natural or inevitable affinity between truth and beauty; or, to put it another way, one would do well to cultivate an alert suspicion of any claimed connections. I do not mean to say, of course, that this probable incompatibility of art and life pertains to art — only to life. In one's pursuit of meaning in one's own life one is inevitably tempted to estheticize not only one's experiences but one's conclusions as well, in both cases not so much — or so specifically — beautifying what was ugly (in fact just as often uglifying what was difficult or confused or uncertain) as giving more deliberate and dramatic form to occasions and relations than they merited, or could, without falsification, accept. Everyone has, I imagine, experienced this temptation — and the difficulties it produces — in trying to present himself (to *tell it all*) to a highly prized new friend. He swoops and sweeps across the past — and into the present — shaping, structuring, summarizing, condensing — lying, lying. That is not how it was; that is not who he is; not at all.

I had once in supervision a young psychoanalytic candidate who was enthralled — as I had been, briefly, those many years ago — by the possibilities of psychoanalytic revelation. His specialty was dream analysis, and he was marvelous — inventive, enthusiastic, colorful — his interpretations were radiant with ingenious plausibility. The only problem was — and this dismayed him — his patient refused to get better. "I'm giving him all this great stuff, every time, and it never makes any difference at all," he complained again and again. Possibly, of course, the patient was merely a pathologically stubborn fellow, or — possibly he just wasn't as subject to revelatory rapture as his therapist. The Aha phenomenon is more compelling for some than for others. And of course for an analysis — or a friendship — or a marriage — to proceed compatibly according to the principles of revelation it does require *two* Aha hounds for its participants.

Revelation is addicting because the pursuit of the esthetic — at the expense of the accurate — is essentially coarsening. Ordinary, fragmentary truth, on a more modest scale, appears by contrast trivial and inadequate — it appears, in short, untrue, since it so conspicuously lacks the splendor and intensity of feeling by which one has come to recognize the validity of revelation. In this way one's assumptions about truth fasten on the revelatory, and this habit of discovery quickly becomes addictive.

It is clear by now, I expect, that I have come to consider the revelatory mode to be a form of lying. It yields something that calls itself the truth but is untrue, is an essential falsification of its subject.

But can it be called lying? I think of myself on the couch that day I have described. I had accepted whole heartedly the ideology that taught me such things were possible. My tears, being so unaccustomed, seemed then, as I said, fraught with significance. (It seems to me now that since my tears were so unaccustomed they should have seemed fraught with false significance.) However, everything about my experience on the couch, and the conclusions I drew from my emotions, seemed utterly genuine, without guile, in good faith. Does the fact that some short while later I decided the evidence all pointed a different way mean anything more than that I had originally been mistaken? It could be quibbled over, but I would rather not. The same evidence that persuaded me of the genuineness of my revelation at the time — that is, my tears, my thrilling, painful emotions, the general commotion — I later saw to be the very clue that might have restored my sanity during the occasion itself had I grasped it. That performance was not merely uncharacteristic of me — it was alien and unnatural, it was inherently false — and I should have known it. Enthralled already by the ideology that permitted — indeed provoked — these novelties of self-expression, and too naive — or too cowardly — to heed my tiny intimations of doubt about the authenticity of my behavior, I played out the drama of my willed self-deception to the hilt. Self-deception, but deliberate. Also known as lying.

It is interesting to note that just as psychoanalysis, in its origins, was rigidly mechanistic and utterly committed to revelation, so too the pop therapeutic spin-offs that surround us today — group encounter in various forms, self-actualization, primal scream, and so on — all share this dependence on the revelatory mode. That is, the paths to salvation take different turns, but salvation itself is a real — and realistic — goal. It is represented in psychoanalytic doctrine, of course, as the state of being "completely analyzed". It is some time since I myself gave up my allegiance to that possibility. Now I am truly gratified if a patient gets somewhat better.

In these remarks about revelation let me stress that I do not wish to challenge the possibility of genuine revelation. What I do mean to convey is my distrust of any psychological — or, for that matter, religious or artistic — doctrine in which revelation is obligatory and ideological. What such a doctrine requires is the repeated fancying up of some item of experience — memory, dream, feeling, what have you — to give it an epistemological razzle dazzle it couldn't manage on its own — and in the process essentially falsifying it. I spoke earlier of the "paradoxical relations between psychoanalysis and truth". The paradox is this: the entire enterprise of psychoanalysis is predicated on a person's capacity for truth-telling. And yet the very devices and strategies traditionally employed for facilitating his search for truth (devised, as I mentioned, to outwit his *in*capacity for truth-telling) — not to mention the tools for deciphering and celebrating the truth, once it is found — all seem to encourage the patient's capacity to embellish, to dramatize — in short, to lie.

When an anthropology or psychology gives insufficient weight to the possibility and reality of lying, the chances are increased of the double lie — namely that one not only lies, but lies about lying, claiming to be speaking the truth, particularly if truth-finding has become an important part of the ideology. The more a given psychology (or any creed) approaches a form of gnosticism, the more vulnerable it is — indeed the more imperiously it requires — the lie that passes as truth. In gnosticism, quoting from Hans Jonas' book *The Gnostic Religion*, "knowledge as a mental act is vastly different from the rational cognition of philosophy. On the one hand it is closely bound up with revelatory experience, so the *reception* of the truth either through sacred and secret lore or through inner illumination replaces rational argument and theory (though this extra-rational basis may then provide scope for independent speculation); on the other hand, being concerned with the secrets of salvation, 'knowledge' is not just theoretical information about certain things, but is itself, as a modification of the human condition, charged with performing a function in the bringing about of salvation." That day on my analyst's couch when I had those (false, as it turned out) revelations about music and my father, it was psychoanalytic doctrine, psychoanalytic training and psychoanalytic technique that led me to a gnostic certainty about my discoveries — a certainty depending far more on faith than fact or reason. Gnostic certainty is, not surprisingly, characterized by contempt for the world, which is regarded as irretrievably evil. It is not difficult to see how agreeably Freud's grim view of man fits into this picture, and how inevitably psychoanalysis took on from the beginning a gnostic cast. One of the curiosities of gnostic certainty is that it renders the believer so gullible. There are psychoanalysts who will believe absolutely anything a patient tells them about himself provided it is sufficient testimony to his morbid — or pathological — condition. Having said that, let me also point out that there are all sorts of psychoanalysts who go about their business in our profession without falling into the gnostic temptations that our traditional doctrine provides.

Let me leave the field of dubious revelation and move now to a more ingratiating form of lying, an instance of which occurred during the supervisory part of my psychoanalytic training. After finishing my psychiatric residency at St. Elizabeths Hospital in Washington, D.C., I found a position on the staff of Chestnut Lodge Sanatarium in Rockville, Maryland. Under the influence of Frieda Fromm-Reichmann and Harry Stack Sullivan the young therapists were caught up in the intoxicating possibility of treating schizophrenia with a form of psychoanalytic psychotherapy. I was assigned to treat a 13 year old schizophrenic boy who had already been mute for several years. Frieda Fromm-Reichmann was to give me an hour of supervision once a week. Under ordinary circumstances I would have felt myself enormously privileged to undergo this apprenticeship with such an estimable psychoanalyst. By ordinary circumstances I mean having a patient who would afford me something to talk about with my supervisor. Five days a week for an hour each of those days I sat with the boy. Sometimes I was as mute as he, seeming to emulate the silent psychoanalyst of tradition. Other times I tried to make conversation in one way or another, always unsuccessfully. Whether I, myself, free associated, or read aloud to him, or sulked, our impasse remained absolutely intact. Meanwhile I would meet once a week with Frieda, talking mostly of the ways in which I tried to get something going. Frieda's suggestions were not uninteresting. She came up with ways different from my own, correctly charged me with impatience with the boy's silence, and urged me to try to examine my inflated therapeutic ambitions in my own analysis, and to try to be more imaginative about the inner life of this young adolescent. All this seemed fair enough. None of her interpretations of my therapeutic endeavors would qualify as a cheap shot. Still, week after week, regardless of what she suggested and I did or didn't do, the boy's silence remained unbroken. I began to dread each hour with my patient, and dreaded even more each supervisory hour when Frieda and I would try once again to make something out of nothing. After a few weeks I was ready to throw in the towel, suggesting my patient and I were mismatched, that surely he would do better with another therapist. Frieda seemed to regard my wish to be relieved of my assignment as *quitting*, and she turned what I can only call stubborn. I should emphasize that the mythology at this sanatarium included the vainglorious conceit that there was no one so disordered that he could not be effectively reached with psychoanalytic psychotherapy. Stories circulated around the staff dining hall about patients who awakened suddenly from years of catatonic stupor to pass the time of day with the therapist who had devotedly, or perhaps doggedly, appeared each day for the obligatory hour. This was a different sort of gnosticism, more like the martyrs of the East who sought God from the isolation of their cave in the desert year after year.

In the aforegoing passage I have sought to give something of the background of the particular supervisory hour when Frieda asked me once again to describe what had happened in the previous week, and I said, "To tell you the truth, Frieda, nothing comes to mind. My mind is a blank." My lie was beginning: I was resorting to a stale psychologism, in order to avoid saying once again, "Nothing happened. Five more empty hours." Looking at her expectant face and knowing my own emptiness, I don't know whether I felt sorrier for her or for myself. Both of us were famished in our craving for some kind of therapeutic meaning. "It's peculiar you don't remember anything," she said. "Perhaps your amnesia has something to do with our relation." "Perhaps," I said hopefully. I knew where we were headed: a familiar psychoanalytic shore lay ahead that at the moment struck me as better than anything I had to offer. I heard her continue, "After all, I am an older woman, no doubt about the same age as your mother." Two more dissimilar human beings I could not imagine. Any comparison would be truly absurd. And yet, I found myself thinking, Why not? If it pleases her I can learn to like it, too. "You may have something there, Frieda," I answered. "I do remember times when I had nothing to say to my mother, when I resisted all her entreaties." She nodded thoughtfully and suppressed a sigh of gratitude. I hastened on. "Perhaps it is possible I've fallen into an old pattern . . ." and so on. We spent a fairly pleasant hour in this manner, handling each other helpfully and courteously across this stretch of time we had to spend together, that but for this invention loomed vast and meaningless.

As for whether it was lying, I cannot convict Frieda. She was a true believer. But as for me, I didn't even have revelation for an excuse. Certainly there were times during the hour when I entertained — or tried to entertain — the possibility that all this might contain some sort of truth. But on the whole I have to say that mine was an expedient and deliberate deceit, undertaken to relieve us both and indulged in with the certainty that it would be received not only graciously but uncritically. In other words, I was bound to get away with it.

Although I am the villain in this story, I have to say I don't think there is anything about my experience in this instance that is unique — either in psychoanalytic training or practice. Psychoanalysis is backbreaking work constantly threatened by loss of meaning. Since almost any content, no matter how debased or even untrue, is more bearable than meaninglessness itself, it is both our fortune and our misfortune to have a doctrine that makes itself available to our hunger for content at any cost.

It is not merely of course in therapy that meaning fails. Friend and friend, lover and beloved, parent and child, husband and wife, teacher and student — all important relations in this life are subject to meaninglessness from time to time, and vulnerable to invasion by one deceit or another to revive meaning that has been lost.

The construction of fictions — of various degrees of falsity — to ease our path occasionally, to repair a faltering relation — this is one of the functions of imagination, and we would do well to be in no hurry to despise imagination, upon which we are also dependent, after all, for the construction of non-fictions, which we can hardly do without. That is: imagination is the ally of both lying and truth-telling. It is double edged; it has its uses and abuses, its privileges and penalties. On the one hand it is one of our most powerful tools for knowing reality, and on the other it reverts to its original idolatrous form of image-making, which is inevitably destructive of truth.

Let me suggest here that lying may be divided crudely but serviceably into two categories. One category contains those gestures of kindness, convenience, cowardice, courtesy and so on that are less than candid — sometimes a great deal less — and sometimes appropriate and even admirable, and sometimes inappropriate and deplorable, but which, as a category, share one thing: they leave somehow open-ended their relation to utter truth; that is, they do not identify themselves as deceit, but neither do they pose as truth. In this essay I have concerned myself with lying of the second category.

There is a proverb that goes "Man is a creature who was given a tongue to speak and words to conceal his thoughts." When I was reminded of that saying but couldn't recollect it properly, I reconstructed it as: "Man is a creature who was given words with which to think and a tongue to conceal his thoughts." Neither formulation really quite gets to the heart of the matter, which is that man is a creature who can speak truthfully, and who lies. That's not very catchy, but it's closer. We all lie — to ourselves, to others, to the world itself. It is in our nature to lie, but I think I must add that it is also in our nature *not* to lie.

Lying, however natural to us, is also in another sense a treachery against ourselves. A lie is a desecration of the given. And the given is exactly that — that which is given to us to receive by calling it by name. When I suffered my revelation about my father I lost him. He literally disappeared from my imagination and was replaced by a sort of cartoon figure I could barely recognize. I had lost him and I had to work to get him back. I remember that occasion, too. When, after considerable struggle, I changed my mind about my revelations, when I repudiated the simplicity of my therapeutic inspirations in favor of the much more complex and difficult realities of my relation with my father, I experienced this change of mind — and heart — with a sense of deep relief: I suppose it could be called joy. I would not have so named it at the time; it didn't seize my consciousness with cries of "I am Joy! An important emotion! Observe how I fill you with feeling!" On the contrary, what I felt then was a profound rightness about my decision, I felt that something significant and truthful had been restored to me; I had retrieved one of my givens.

I seem to have had many harsh things to say in this essay about feeling, and I would like to clarify my position somewhat. There has been a rumor around for a couple of hundred years, probably more, that you only know it's a feeling if it bites you on the nose. Or, to put it differently, there is a decibel scale of emotion (often curiously congruent with the more familiar decibel scale of sound), on which intensity, significance and validity are all directly proportional, and increase as they climb the scale. Of course I have emotions of this nature, as we all do, but it is usually my inclination to endure rather than to cherish them. There is another sort of feeling that I do cherish — but only in retrospect, or in theory — for it does not single itself out as feeling during the experience to which it belongs. It stays bound to its subject, its content, as it did in my reconciliation — in my own mind — with the reality of my father. I suppose this might be called the feeling of truth telling.

Mental Illness *Is* Illness

BY PETER SEDGWICK

I am going to develop some thoughts which have arisen out of a study I am at present conducting into the work of the distinguished anti-psychiatrist (or ex-anti-psychiatrist), R. D. Laing. I do not propose to take up the specific questions raised by the work of Laing and the school of thought around him (which is in any case very desultory and unsystematic). Instead I am going to face squarely the central issue raised by all the sociological or quasi-sociological "revisionists" of the idea of mental illness. It appears to me that none of them have begun by asking the question: What is *illness?* Only in the light of an answer to *this* question could we determine our answer to the question: Is mental illness really illness in the 'medical' sense?

Let me begin by identifying who I am talking about. Not all of the "revisers" of mental health are sociologists; and not all sociologists working in mental-health problems are revisers. The influential work of Thomas Szasz, the Professor of Psychiatry at the State University of New York, rarely contains any material from the deviancy experts of the sociological profession (though it is braced by many striking allusions drawn from political science, law, economics, fiction and medical and psychoanalytic literature).[1] Michel Foucault, whose book *Madness and Civilisation*[2] has become deservedly famous in studies of the cultural relativism of psychiatric concepts, is a historical analyst of ideas in

NB: Notes are given in abbreviated fashion; the title of a work will be presented only once, and in subsequent references mentioned by an initial form (e.g., MMI for *The Myth of Mental Illness*), followed by the number of the footnote in which the full title is given.

1. *The Myth of Mental Illness* (New York, 1961) deals mostly with hysteria and malingering. *Law, Liberty and Psychiatry* (New York, 1963) is Szasz's fullest treatment but draws most of its examples from the forensic field. Szasz nowhere presents a comprehensive theory of mental illness which closely examines the different typologies of psychiatric diagnosis. *Ideology and Insanity* (New York 1970) is a collection of essays repeating old themes and suggested reforms of psychiatric practice. *The Manufacture of Madness* (New York, 1970) largely consists of an extended analogy between psychiatry and medieval witch-spotting.
2. New York, 1965.

the social and natural sciences who appears to have worked in complete independence from the academic specialism of sociology, in either its American or its European branches. On the other hand, the bulk of 'medical-sociological' writing in the subject-matter of psychiatry merely represents a parallel with the developed science of 'epidemiology' in the prevalence and incidence of physical diseases by different social classes, age-ranges, cultures and other social variables: these researches take it for granted that 'mental illnesses' exist as facts of life (to be correlated with other social facts) and do not discuss the logical status or the social nature of either diagnosis or therapy in the psychopathological field. Even the more advanced and closely focussed studies of 'family process' or 'psychiatrically-induced mental disorder' which are characteristic of the best work in British and American social psychiatry begin their analysis at a very late stage of the *total possible analysis* of mental illness. Chronic mental patients deteriorate, we are told, through spending long years in overcrowded locked wards: but what, pray, is a 'mental patient'? How does such a person come to exist, in terms of his own definition "I am a mental patient", the definitions of others, to the same effect, and the relations between these ascribed and self-ascribed identities? Family pressures, according to the American schizophrenia-researchers, impel susceptible people into severe breakdowns which necessitate their treatment in a suitably equipped clinical institution: the problem is to discover how the illness began, so that once again our very notion of a mental illness is never posed as constituting any kind of problem. That trend in the sociology of psychiatric classification and treatment which, on the contrary, takes 'mental illness' and its 'treatment' as being problematic, to be analysed as value-laden *social constructions,* is an unpopular trend in psychological medicine—though it dominates the teaching of deviancy-sociology in many American colleges. We have a contrast, in brief, between what might be called an *exterior* sociology of mental illness and an *immanent* (or in-dwelling) sociology of 'mental-illness-as-a-social-construct.' The same contrast, as a matter of fact, is visible in the sociological treatment of several social-problem areas outside the aetiology of madness: prostitution, homosexuality, drug addiction and criminal delinquency are all topics which can be discussed in the literature either via an external sociology analysing pathological 'givens' or from an immanent, critical perspective which sees the official counts and categories of deviancy as mere projections of society's formal or informal control-process, and performs an imaginative entry into the deviant's own actions, viewing these as an attempt to manufacture significance for his life within and against a rejecting, 'labelling' world.[3]

3. See Earl Rubington and Martin Weinberg, *The Study of Social Problems: Five Perspectives* (New York, 1971), especially Chapters 6 and 7, for a good presentation of the differing vantage-points on deviancy problems.

Immanent theorists of mental illness, whether in sociology or outside it, have usually had to begin by denying the validity of a natural-science perspective on psychological abnormalities. Thus we have Szasz, Leifer and Goffman drawing a sharp distinction between the natural-scientific, value-free language of physical medicine and the socially and politically loaded language of psychiatry. Szasz believes that, in physical illnesses, "the notion of a bodily symptom is tied to an *anatomical* and *genetic* context" as distinct from the social or ethical context which informs psychiatric judgments: our description of the norm of physical health (a deviation from which constitutes a physical illness or disease) is just a description, which "can be stated in anatomical and physiological terms".[4] Leifer, while thoroughly aware of the social grounding of medicine as a profession, insists that in physical diagnosis and treatment "the term 'disease' refers to phenomena that are not regulated by social custom, morality and law, namely bodily structure and function"; psychiatric concepts of disease refer, on the contrary, to "behaviour, which is subject to the regulation of custom, morality and law".[5]

Erving Goffman, the most influential sociological theorist in the 'anti-psychiatry' tradition, offers in different works a number of quite distinct approaches in the demarcation of physical from psychiatric disorders. One of his most readable books, *Stigma,* applies a careful phenomenological and interpersonal analysis to the victims of physical handicap and disfigurement, with a method very similar to that adopted in his celebrated study of "The Moral Career of the Mental Patient".[6]

Thus far, Goffman would appear to be using a unitary schema in which the division of the patients' case-files into 'psychiatric' versus 'physical' categories would contribute nothing to our further understanding of the difficulties experienced by the subject in his various social settings and encounters. Elsewhere, a more definite distinction between physical and psychiatric symptom construction is propounded. At one point, the 'political' vested interests surrounding the procedures of mental medicine are contrasted with the presumably apolitical practices of ordinary doctoring: thus, decisions concerning behavioural (psychiatric) pathology "tend to be political, in the sense of expressing the interest of some particular faction or person rather than interests that can be said to be above the concerns of any particular grouping as in the case of pathology". There is an assumption here that the language of body-pathology works within a unanimously common culture, rising above the historically-evolved social formations whose notorious diver-

4. Thomas S. Szasz, "The Myth of Mental Illness", *The American Psychologist,* February 1960.
5. Ronald Leifer, *In the Name of Mental Health* (New York, 1969), p. 35. Leifer is a disciple and systematic expounder of Szaszian doctrine with a much more sophisticated use of sociological theory than Szasz has.
6. *Stigma* (New York, 1961); *Asylums* (New York, 1961), pp. 125–70.

sity has been an important traditional beginning-point of sociological investigation; we shall have occasion later to question this assumption and to provide a few examples of wide cultural variation within man's conceptions of physical illness. Even in the strange sense of 'political' whereby politics means only open dissent among factions (so that, e.g., there could be no such thing as the 'politics' of a successfully manipulated consensus), it is extremely sweeping of Goffman to announce that decisions about physical pathology never involve conflicting interests between different parties to the situation. It is perhaps not surprising that, in his most recent exposition of the difference between 'mental' and 'medical' symptom-patterns,[7] Goffman falls back on an unsophisticated Szasz-type contrast between the purely biological, value-free substrate of medical classifications and the socially-determined character of judgments about mental symptoms.

"Signs and symptoms of a *medical* disorder presumably refer to underlying pathologies in the individual organism, and these constitute deviations from biological norms maintained by the homeostatic functioning of the human machine. The system of reference here is plainly *(sic)* the individual organism, and the term 'norm', ideally at least, has no moral or social connotation . . . biological and social norms are quite different things. . . ."[8]

The position of the Laing School is different again. Unlike Szasz and Leifer, Laing does not give a general endorsement to face-to-face psychoanalysis as the method *par excellence* for dealing with disturbed patients in an ethically acceptable (because non-medical) framework, but instead devotes much effort to the critique of psychoanalytic and psychological explanations of human pathology, on the grounds that they do not, with the exception of his own perspective, do justice to the actual experience of persons.[9] The argument is extended by David Cooper in a distinction between "two types of rationality" within the range of scientific knowledge. The study of humankind is to be conducted through a *dialectical rationality* which uses a historical-biographical method modelled on Sartre's interpretation of Jean Genet's life. *Analytic rationality* is the method of the natural sciences, which works for 'inert' data in physics, biology, etc., but is inapplicable to the study of people.[10] It is not clear where this leaves the role of medical science. Cooper concurs with Szasz and Goffman in assigning

7. In the Appendix, "The Insanity of Place", to *Relations in Public* (London, 1971), pp. 335–90.
8. RP (No. 7), pp. 345, 346.
9. See, eg *The Politics of Experience* (London, 1967), pp. 17–18, 41–44; *The Divided Self* (London, 1960), pp. 19–25; *Interpersonal Perception* (London, 1966), pp. 6–7, 40–41.
10. *Psychiatry and Anti-Psychiatry* (New York, 1971 edition), pp. 7–14.

physiological descriptions of human bodily states to a sphere that lies outside the proper understanding of people. Physiological explanation amounts to a 'reductive analysis', the misuse of analytic rationality in an area (the science of persons) for which it is inappropriate. But learning-theory and psychoanalysis, at any rate in the Freudian form, are equally 'reductive analyses', and just as bad as physiology. However, the Laingian classification of the sciences still has room for the medical role in the treatment of patients. Laing refers to himself as a physician and a psychiatrist,[11] and Cooper offers similar identifiers, complaining only that other doctors should deal with the physical ailments of schizophrenics and that non-medical administrators should attend to the procedural paraphernalia that are at present left to hospital psychiatrists.[12]

To sum up these rather complex alignments of position: it looks as though Laingians deny the applicability of a natural-science method of human investigations but claim that psychiatry (or else anti-psychiatry—which must be 'anti' only in the sense that the Anti-Popes were rivalling the Popes) can still be scientifically based within a suitable Sartrean methodology. There is no special division between the study of bodily states and the study of people: wrong forms of people-study are on one side of the divide, along with the psychiatric misuse of physiology and body-science generally, while the other brighter shore is occupied by a Laingian 'science of persons' which is admittedly still being developed. Szaszians, in contrast, allocate the natural sciences to an area dealing with medically reputable complaints (those referring to diseased organs of the body) and then set up another, non-medical autonomous zone for what is at present called psychiatry; concepts and methods are admitted rather eclectically to this liberated territory, on the sole proviso that psychiatric practitioners must see themselves as consultants responsible to their clients rather than as social agents programming the mentally ill. The 'scientific' status of Free Psychiatry is left indeterminate: Szasz writes at one point as if it had a descriptive, empirical foundation in the cataloguing of developmental levels during social maturation, but more recently has celebrated the 'moral science' of a liberated psychiatry which refuses any classification of persons—including (one may take it) a classification in terms of their level of social development.[13]

The position of the cultural historian Michel Foucault is hard to compare with any of the above theoreticians of present-day psychiatry. Foucault is not concerned to destroy the concepts of psychiatric diagnosis and treatment, but wishes only to point out that each age of

11. See, for example, his *Intervention in Social Situations* (London, 1969), p. 17.
12. David Cooper, "The Anti-Hospital: An Experiment in Social Psychiatry", *New Society*, March 11, 1965.
13. MMI (No. 1), pp. 143–5, II (No. 1), pp. 234, 210–11.

civilisation, from the medieval period to modern times, has had its own view of madness which closely reflects the general social and logical preoccupations of the time. Psychopathology is not independent of social history, for each age has drawn the split between madness and reason at a different point and in a fundamentally different fashion. Still it is permissible to seek a psychodynamic or a genetic or an existential account of an individual patient's behaviour, so long as we do not "make these aspects of the illness into ontological forms", real essences which then require "a mythological explanation like the evolution of psychic structure, or the theory of instincts, or an existential anthropology" to support them.[14]

Psychological descriptions of insanity "are not to be suppressed by some explanatory or reductive principle which is exterior to them", but simply situated within the forgotten social-historical framework which has given them birth. It is possible, for example, to speak of the psychological state of 'regression' (i.e., of a resumption of infantile patterns) only in a society which has separated infancy as a pre-adult refuge: "neuroses of regression do not display the neurotic character of childhood, but incriminate the archaic nature of the institutions which are concerned with children". Thus, unlike the sociological and other redefiners of mental illness, Foucault does not *eliminate* the psychological and the medical enterprises: instead he brackets them, and shows the text of other human meanings which lies just outside the thin bounds of the parenthesis. And, while for other critics the present world may have room for a liberated region of psychiatry—Szasz's "moral science" for neurotic life-problems or Laing's existential therapy for schizophrenia—which will be immune from the deceits and compulsions of the orthodox medical tradition, there is no such sanctuary in Foucault's psychiatric universe. The moral tyranny and the cultural bondage of the Reasonable Man's superior confrontation with Unreason are just as manifest in the psychoanalyst's consulting-room as in the locked wards of the asylum: they are no less implicit in our social attitudes towards neurosis than in our dismissal of the madman's rantings. The images of psychoanalysis, with their percipient charting of defense-shields, traumas, anxieties and other embodiments of conflict, do not (as the analysts imagine) reveal the true workings of an inner psychic machinery, but rather reflect "how mankind has made mankind into a contradiction-laden experience", hag-ridden by the theme of "competition, exploitation, group-rivalry and class struggle". Normal social structure is always the hidden truth of the psychology of the abnormal: so that if we may believe that one day, perhaps a genuine communion between Reason and Unreason can be restored, it will be within a new

14. *Maladie Mentale et Psychologie* (Paris, 1966), p. 101.

form of society which will see, as one of its natural consequences, the liberation of human thought from psychology.[15] In the here and now, we are left with no hopes for a reformed or even radicalised psychology of madness, and no choice, in working with patients, except to use the psychologised descriptions which have been bequeathed to us as the deposit and the disguise of social classifications made by previous centuries.

The various 'immanent' theorists of mental illness thus diverge, radically in theory and drastically for practice, in the same breath that they converge, as criticism and as negation, upon the established doctrines of psychiatric medicine. Immanentist theory does not present itself as a solid, cumulative mass of concepts which can be wielded as a single heavy weapon against the institutions of psychiatry. The prickled barbs of its various critiques project and tend in so many opposed directions that any attempt to grasp them for use as a unitary whole will wound the critic to the bone of his own logic. It is quite erroneous to speak, as one journalistic enthusiast has already done (in a manner which would be applauded by many other devotees), of a "school of thought" including Szasz, Goffman, Bateson, Cooper and Laing, "which offers this radical reformulation in our ideas about the true nature of mental illness, with its corresponding subversive critique of the established society and culture".[16] Not all of these theorists have expressed beliefs about "the true nature of mental illness": the views of Laing and Cooper (and Bateson) are confined to schizophrenia alone, and Goffman's theory of mental illness comes from quite a different "school of thought" from that of Szasz. Neither Goffman nor Szasz offers any "subversive critique" of larger social institutions, and indeed it appears that these two authors offer an explicitly conservative vision of societal process, founded in Goffman's case on a total immobilism of micro-structures and a total indifference to macro-structures, and in Szasz on the glorification of private medical practice at the expense of social welfare and on an anticollective individualism which savors far more of America's 'radical-libertarian' Right Wing than of any revolutionary social philosophy. Foucault, as we have seen, is some kind of Marxist, sceptical of the neo-Freudian and existentialist perspectives on humankind that are favoured by the Laing school. Other immanentist writers like Scheff and Lemert are quite silent on the general nature of American (or of capitalist) society, being content to apply, within the special field of mental illness, the concepts of a 'labelling theory' that have been developed by their school of sociology for many types and settings of social deviancy. We have not got here a colony of 'subversives', or

15. Ibid, pp. 102–3, 96, 97–8, 89.
16. From the Editorial Text to the "Sanity-Insanity: Madness: Violence" issue of *Peace News*, May 19, 1967.

even the theoretical base for an 'anti-psychiatry' which would be able to agree on some working alternatives—conceptual or tactical—to the current dominant framework of psychiatric treatment.

What we do have is a consistent and convergent *tendency of opposition* directed against *positivist method* in the study of abnormal human behaviour. 'Positivism', for the present discussion, may be taken to refer to an approach towards the investigation of human pathology which, modelling itself upon antecedents which it believes to be characteristic of the natural sciences, *(a)* postulates a radical separation between 'facts' and 'values' (declaring only the former to be the subject-matter of the professional investigator) and *(b)* suppresses the interactive relationship between the investigator and the 'facts' on which he works.[17] The psychiatric labels which are catalogues in textbooks of medicine and clinical psychology are, on a positivist account, terms which represent, or at least approximate towards, existent processes inhabiting an objective structure within the individual: the structure may be his psyche, his autonomic nervous system, perhaps even in the last resort his brain, but it stands towards the investigator as the ultimate object of reference towards which his hypotheses, his empirical techniques and his standards of validation all tend. To be sure, we may remain suitably guarded in the finality or the completeness of the claims we may make for our disease-categories. The judgments of psychiatrists on individual patients are notoriously prone to discordance: a fact which, in one variant of the positivist school, has stimulated the search for more accurate 'measurements' of the deeper dimensions on which personality-characteristics may be said to lie. Or it may be pointed out that we are working, at best, with hypothetical constructs of our own devising: a confession which offers little in the way of modest disavowal, since on the positivist account all scientific concepts whatsoever, from atomic particles to the Germ Theory of Disease, from chemical valencies to the mechanics of blood coagulation, are equally the inventive constructions of the mind, provisional models which may be more firmly based in empirical evidence and theoretical elegance than, say, the Hippocratic humours or the nineteenth century Ether, but are still artifacts of human production. The stance of the scientific investigator before the categories of psychopathology differs, on the positivist case, in no essential way from his relationship to the categories of

17. There are several very different descriptions of what 'positivism' is, referring to quite separate philosophical tendencies. My short definition above is somewhat indebted to Leszek Kolakowski's *The Alienation of Reason* (New York, 1969), but has been invented purely to contrast 'immanent' sociological descriptions of mental illness with the alternative methodological frameworks in medicine and psychology: it is not meant to provide any clues to what 'positivism' might be in other controversies or other fields.

biological disease, to the molecular arrangements of the elements, or to the orderings of animal species suggested by evolutionary theory. Our conceptual units for the subdivision and understanding of the natural world are, if you like, solid; or, if you like, tenuous; but in any case of a muchness. The chair in which the psychiatrist sits and the motions he engages in to sign a certificate exist and function at different levels of the organisation of matter; their existence and functioning may be understood in different departments of the organisation of theory. And the categories of human disorder which he employs in making his professional decisions about patients come from yet another area of the natural sciences, clouded (it is true) by greater complexities of error and uncertainty; they refer to yet another, higher level of the organisation of reality, to the precise inspection of which our instruments have not yet advanced.

Even the most advanced areas of clinical psychiatry bear, in their most basic terminology, the impress of this positivist tradition. We have the thriving discipline of 'the epidemiology of mental disorders', which has repeatedly displayed the considerable social variation, across classes and communities, in the incidence of the major psychological illnesses; yet it achieves this social insight by regarding the contours of the boxes into which its numerations fall as uncontroversial, objective boundaries, analogous to the physical disease-categories which are studied in other branches of the same discipline. ('Epidemiology' means originally, after all, the study of epidemics, that is to say of infectiously transmitted diseases like cholera and tuberculosis, and if the concept of an epidemic is nowadays commonly extended to the germless plagues of heart-disease, heroin-addiction or schizophrenia, it is still supposed to mark the occurrence of morbid conditions as distinct and unambiguous as those produced by actual bacilli.) Similarly, in the application of statistical techniques for the fresh classification of mental disorders (in an attempt to reach groupings of symptoms which will be more systematic than those drawn from clinical experience), we find a reliance on the methods of a 'numerical taxonomy' which was originally devised for the sorting of microbes according to the clustering of their objective characteristics.[18] The judgmental, valuational element in psychiatric assessments, in other words their *social* and cultural quality, is simply ignored in these taxonomic investigations. And the same can be said of the manifold drug-trials, behaviour-therapy studies, reports on hospital-ward reform, symptom-questionnaires and the like, which comprises

18. e.g., C. J. Klett and D. M. McNair, *Syndromes of Psychosis*, (New York, 1963); R. R. Sokal and P.A. Sneath, *Principles of Numerical Taxonomy* (London, 1963).

the bulk of the serious journals of present-day clinical psychology and psychiatry.[19]

It is to the permanent credit of the immanentist critics of psychiatry that they have exposed the inadequacy of this positivist framework for the understanding of mental illness. Whatever exaggerations the more radical anti-psychiatrists and labelling-theory sociologists have engaged in, they have shown convincingly that both diagnoses and treatment-measures in psychiatry are founded on ethical judgments and social demands whose content is sometimes reactionary, often controversial and nearly always left unstated. Mental illness is a social construction: psychiatry is a social institution, incorporating the values and demands of its surrounding society. These conclusions, and their supporting arguments, deserve to be placed in the forefront of all teaching material aimed towards those who seek guidance on the problems of mental illness. Foucault and Laing, Goffman and Szasz, Scheff and Lemert, should be made part of the curriculum for all aspirant therapists, nurses and social workers in this field. Never again should it be possible for a lecturer to instruct his students, or the public, that 'mental illnesses may be caused by heredity, the environment, or a combination of both' or that 'outcome in psychopathology depends on a combination of exterior stress and the inner predisposition of the patient'. For such dicta, however seemingly authoritative and 'scientifically grounded', simply obscure a number of central features of mental illness and its associated agencies of treatment and care. For to say that somebody is mentally ill, or to announce oneself as mentally ill, is to attach complex social meanings to acts and behaviours that in other societies, or in different contingencies within our own society, would be interpreted in the light of quite different concepts. The accidents of heredity and the blows of environment do not add up or multiply into the social position and personal identity of being 'mentally ill', any more than in bygone years they combined sufficiently to form the status of being 'a witch', or of being 'possessed by spirits', or of being 'under the infiuence of black bile' (to name a few of the alternative significations that have been attached to the behaviours nowadays classified in the light of 'mental illness' concepts). 'Stress' and 'predisposition' are valuable categories for the understanding of organisms and their malfunctioning; but we are concerned, in the understanding of human beings, with the impact of stressful meanings as these affect the predisposition of individuals to screen and consolidate these meanings into their established images of self and

19. This observation is not intended as a dismissal of these studies, whose method is often compatible with the valuational outlook on mental illness that will be developed later in this paper.

society. Trauma and resistance to trauma can, in the human case, be understood not on the analogy of a physical force striking a more or less brittle object, nor on the lines of the invasion of an organism by hostile bacteria, but only through the transformation of elements in a person's identity and his capacity to relate to other persons and social collectives. And what positivist accounts of mental illness most flagrantly omit is the serious 'stress' (of socially-charged meanings, and not of physical or biological influences) imposed on the subject-patient by the acts of diagnosis, classification, hospitalization and (even, in many cases) 'treatment'. As Marx criticised the Utopian Socialists for arriving at a position which involved dividing society into two parts of which one (themselves) was seen as 'superior to society', so must the clinical positivism of 'psychopathology' stand condemned for its stance of cultural smugness, its erection of a local, twentieth-century style of assessment into a timeless biological universal, its failure to take stock of its own social role. The Utopians, Marx observed, were so busy trying to educate society into Socialism that they forgot that "the educator must himself be educated"; the clinical positivists are so involved in uncovering the factual, objective basis of psychopathology that they have forgotten the subjective valuations which impregnate their whole enterprise. Sooner or later, for good or ill, the valuators must themselves be valued, and their judgments judged.

But the immanentist critique of clinical positivism (and of the latter's ally, the purely exterior 'medical sociology') has begun the task of this evaluation at a somewhat odd starting-point. In seizing on the value-laden, subjective, 'political' elements of psychiatric diagnosis and treatment, they have implicitly—and sometimes, indeed, explicitly—conceded the value-free, apolitical and 'objective' character of medicine-in-general: their dismissal of positivism in psychiatry is founded on a contract with non-psychiatric medicine which actually depends on the acceptance of positivism as a possible method in vital areas of human decision-making. The split between fact and value is reinstated at a superordinate, strategic level precisely in order to attack it in the tactical onslaught against the particular medical specialism of psychiatry. Physical medicine belongs to the world of Fact, of the natural sciences, of anatomy and physiology, of objectively ascertainable disturbed conditions of the body or its 'functioning', and psychiatry belongs to the world of Value, of ethical judgments on behaviour, of factional coalitions against the unhappy victim, or covert and malignant social and political control. The immanentists *have accomplished the feat of criticising the concept of mental illness without ever examining the (surely more inclusive, and logically prior) concept of illness*. They have focussed a merciless lens on psychiatric treatment, detailing its foibles, its fallacies, and its destructiveness towards human self-respect, while at the same time maintaining a posture of reverent myopia towards the chemical, surgical and other therapeutic procedures that are directed by doctors against the many targets of the human organism that lie outside the gray and white matter of the cerebrum. For one who (like myself) has searched the sociological and critical-philosophical literature dealing in the various fields of medicine, the evidence of selective myopia is simply overwhelming. There is no sociological examination of illness, or of medical theory and practice, which corresponds to Scheff's *Becoming Mentally Ill,* or to Goffman's "Mental Symptoms and Public Order", within the psychiatric specialty. There is no popular critical review of practices and concepts in general physical medicine which in any way parallels the thoughtful anti-psychiatric writings of Thomas Szasz and Ronald Leifer: Shaw's play *The Doctor's Dilemma* (along with the searching Preface to its printed edition) remains as a classic locus in this practically nonexistent genre. *The Journal of Health and Social Behaviour,* established by the American Sociological Association as an organ for theoretical and empirical contributions in the sociology of health and disease, concentrates (at least in its more conceptually oriented articles) on the social character of psychiatric practices and institutions, to the virtual neglect of all other branches of therapy. In the anthropological study of medical practice across different cultures, the literature of the folk-medicine of physical ailments is small besides the immense bulk of reports on 'ethno-psychiatry' in the more primitive societies of the world: I know of no journal, for instance, which performs for physical medicine the service provided by the excellent journal *Transcultural Psychiatric Research,* published from McGill University, Montreal. Among critical philosophers, no book or article on physical maladies parallels, for example, Foucault's *Madness and Civilisation,* or the many reappraisals of Freudian psychopathology. The philosophers of 'ordinary language' in the post-Wittgenstein tradition have singularly refrained from any logical analysis of what it means to be ill or to seek treatment: the classic phenomenological and linguistic-philosophical discussions of the notions of pain, or of the body, always take place in a curiously non-medical context, in the logician's proverbial armchair rather than on the hard seat of the waiting-room or the Casualty Department's stretcher. Doubtless there exist substantial reasons for this chronically repetitive suspension of the critical faculty in the face of general medicine. Physical medicine and surgery have achieved, after all, extraordinary advances, to the blessing of countless millions: who wants to pick a quarrel with success, particularly with the success of a miraculous technology projected in the service of universally acclaimed ideals? Yet the problem remains: We cannot review the social institutions of mental illness independently of, or prior to, the institutions and constructions that men have elaborated for the case of plain illness.[20]

What, then, is 'illness'? It will be recalled that critical theory in psychiatry has tended to postulate a fundamental separation between mental illnesses and the general run of human ailments: the former are the expression of social norms, the latter proceed from ascertainable bodily states which have an 'objective' existence within the individual. One critic of psychopathological concepts, Barbara Wooton, has suggested that the expurgation of normative references from psychiatry is at least a theoretical ideal, though one immensely difficult of achievement: ". . . anti-social behaviour is the precipitating factor that leads to mental treatment. But at the same time the fact of the illness is itself inferred from the behaviour. . . . But any disease, the morbidity of which is established only by the social failure that it involves, must rank as fundamentally different from those of which the symptoms are independent of the social norms . . . long indeed is the road to be travelled before we can hope to reach a definition of mental-cum-physical health which is objective, scientific, and wholly free of social value judgments and before we shall be able, consistently and without qualification, to treat mental and physical disorders on exactly the same footing."[21] Wooton's view has stimulated at least one attempt to begin the task of purging all cultural norms—with their inconvenient variability from one society to another—from the diagnosis of mental illness: Dr. Joseph Zubin has reported some work on 'culture-free' assessments of schizophrenia which involve the analysis of reaction-times, responses to electrical stimulation, and the like, among schizophrenic patients.[22] It would be fair to say that research in the refinement of psychiatric categories has been mounted with a similar perspective in mind, straining towards the physical-medicine ideal of a set of symptom-descriptions "independent of the social norms." Value-judgments and cultural stereotypes are

20. Talcott Parsons did develop an analysis of "the sick role", in Chapter 10 of *The Social System* (Glencoe, 1951), but this refers more to the status of *being a patient,* within a system of medical facilities, than to the concept of *being ill.* He has a more extensive discussion of health and illness in Chapter 10 of his *Social Structure and Personality* (New York, 1964), but for reasons too detailed to relate here, I cannot accept his terms. David Mechanic's *Medical Sociology* (New York, 1968) begins with a specification of disease which I find somewhat too general: "some deviation from normal functioning which has undesirable consequences, because it produces personal discomfort or adversely affects the individual's future health status" (p. 15). It would not be possible to distinguish illness from fatigue or bereavement on this definition, since these deviations from "normal functioning" are undoubtedly uncomfortable.

21. *Social Science and Social Pathology* (London, 1959), p. 225.

22. J. Zubin, "A Cross-Cultural Approach to Psychopathology and its Implications for Diagnostic Classifications", pp. 43–82 in L. D. Eron (ed.), *The Classification of Behavior Disorders* (Chicago, 1966).

seen as one form of 'error' coming between the investigator and his desired data, and the ultimate standard sought in the description of illness is to be taken to be a sociologically inert, culturally sterile specification of facts and processes which are grounded in bacteriology, biochemistry, physiology or perhaps some variety of cybernetic systems-theory.

But this enterprise, tending constantly towards the microscopic and molecular analysis of the 'objective' substrate of behaviour, forms only one of the ways in which we might begin to place mental and physical illnesses "on exactly the same footing". If we examine the logical structure of our judgments of illness (whether 'physical' or 'mental') it may prove possible to reduce the distance between psychiatry and other streams of medicine by working in the reverse direction to Wooton: not by annexing psychopathology to the technical instrumentation of the natural sciences but by revealing the character of illness and disease, health and treatment, as social constructions. For social constructions they most certainly are. All departments of nature below the level of mankind are exempt both from disease and from treatment—until man intervenes with his own human classifications of disease and treatment. The blight that strikes at corn or at potatoes is a *human invention*, for if man wished to cultivate parasites (rather than potatoes or corn) there would be no 'blight', but simply the necessary foddering of the parasite-crop. Animals do not have diseases either, prior to the presence of man in a meaningful relation with them. A tiger may experience pain or feebleness from a variety of causes (we do not intend to build our case on the supposition that animals, especially higher animals, cannot have experiences or feelings). It may be infected by a germ, trodden by an elephant, scratched by another tiger, or subjected to the ageing processes of its own cells. It does not present itself as being *ill* (though it may present itself as being highly distressed or uncomfortable) except in the eyes of a human observer who can discriminate illness from other sources of pain or enfeeblement. Outside the significances that man voluntarily attaches to certain conditions, *there are no illnesses or diseases in nature*. We are nowadays so heavily indoctrinated with deriving from the technical medical discoveries of the last century-and-a-half that we are tempted to think that nature does contain diseases. Just as the sophisticated New Yorker classes the excrement of dogs and cats as one more form of 'pollution' ruining the pre-established harmony of pavements and gardens, so does modern technologised man perceive nature to be mined and infested with all kinds of specifically morbid entities and agencies. What, he will protest, are there no diseases in nature? Are there not infectious and contagious bacilli? Are there not definite and objective lesions in the cellular structures of the human body? Are there not fractures of bones, the fatal ruptures of tissues, the malignant multiplications of tumorous growths? Are not these, surely, events of nature? Yet these, as natural events, do not—prior to the human social meanings we attach to them—constitute illnesses, sicknesses or diseases. The fracture of a septuagenarian's femur has, within the world of nature, no more significance than the snapping of an autumn leaf from its twig: and the invasion of a human organism by cholera-germs carries with it no more the stamp of 'illness' than does the souring of milk by other forms of bacteria.[23] Human beings, like all other naturally occurring structures, are characterised by a variety of inbuilt limitations or liabilities, any of which may (given the presence of further stressful circumstances) lead to the weakening or the collapse of the organism. Mountains as well as moles, stars as well as shrubs, protozoa no less than persons have their dates of expiry set in advance, over a time-span which varies greatly over different classes of structure but which is usually at least roughly predictable. Out of his anthropocentric self-interest, man has chosen to consider as 'illnesses' or 'diseases' those natural circumstances which precipitate the death (or the failure to function according to certain values) of a limited number of biological species: man himself, his pets and other cherished livestock, and the plant-varieties he cultivates for gain or pleasure. Around these select areas of structural failure man creates, in proportion to the progress of his technology, specialized combat-institutions for the control and cure of 'disease': the different branches of the medical and nursing profession, veterinary doctors, and the botanical specialists in plant-disease. Despite their common concern with disease, and their common use of experimental natural science, these institutions operate according to very different criteria and codes; the use of euthanasia by vets, and of ruthless eugenic policies by plant-pathologists, departs from most current medical practice with human patients. All the same, the fact that these specialisms share the categories of disease and illness indicates the selective quality of our perceptions in this field. Children and cattle may fall ill, have diseases, and seem as sick; but who has ever imagined that spiders or lizards can be sick or diseased? Plant-diseases may strike at tulips, turnips or such prized features of the natural landscape as elm trees: but if some plant-species in which man had no interest (a desert grass, let us say) were to be attacked by a fungus or parasite, we should speak not of a disease, but merely of the competition between two species. The medical enterprise is from its inception value-loaded; it is not simply an applied biology, but a biology applied in accordance with the dictates of social interest.

It could be argued that the discussion of animal and plant pathology deals in cases that are too marginal to our central concepts of health and illness to form a satisfactory basis for analysis. Such marginal instances

23. The above discussion is heavily indebted to Rene Dubos' masterly *The Mirage of Health* (New York, 1971), especially pp. 30–128.

are of course frequently used by logicians in the analysis of concepts since their peripheral character often usefully tests the limits within which our ideas can be seen to be applicable or inapplicable. However, a careful examination of the concept of illness in man himself will reveal the same value-impregnation, the same dependency of apparently descriptive, natural-scientific notions upon our norms of what is desirable. To complain of illness, or to ascribe illness to another person, is not to make a descriptive statement about physiology or anatomy. Concepts of illness were in use among men for centuries before the advent of any reliable knowledge of the human body, and are still employed today within societies which favour a non-physiological (magical or religious) account of the nature of human maladies. Our own classification and explanation of specific illnesses or diseases is of course tremendously different from the categories that are current in earlier ages or in contemporary tribal societies, but it is implausible to suppose that the state of illness itself has no common logical features over different types of society. Homer's sick warriors were tended by magical incantations as well as by herbs and other primitive technical remedies,[24] but the avowal and ascription of illness in Homer does not set up a distance between his characters and ourselves but rather (like his descriptions of bereavement or of sexual attraction) a powerful resonance across the ages. Similarly, the meaning of illness among primitive peoples is usually sufficiently close to our own to enable them to take advantage of modern medical facilities when these are made accessible within their territories: tribesmen and peasants do not have to be indoctrinated into Western physiological concepts before they can accept help from physicians and nurses trained in advanced societies. Sickness and disease may be conceptualised, in different cultures, as originating within bodily states, or within perturbations of the spirit, or as a mixture of both. Yet there appear to be common features in the declaration or attribution of the sick state, regardless of the causal explanation that is invoked.

All sickness is essentially deviancy. That is to say, no attribution of sickness to any being can be made without the expectation of some alternative state of affairs which is considered more desirable. In the absence of this normative alternative, the presence of a particular bodily or subjective state will not in itself lead to an attribution of illness, Thus, where an entire community is by Western standards 'ill', because it has been infected for generations by parasites which diminish energy, illness will not be recognized in any individual except by outsiders.[25]

24. See the excellent account of Homeric medicine in P. Lain Entralgo, *The Therapy of the Word in Classical Antiquity* (New Haven, 1970).
25. I have taken this observation from Dr. L Robbins' discussion in Eron, CBD (No. 22).

The Rockefeller Sanitary Commission on Hookworm found in 1911 that this disease was regarded as part of normal health in some areas of North Africa.[26] And in one South American Indian tribe the disease of dyschromic spirochetosis, which is marked by the appearance of coloured spots on the skin, was so 'normal' that those who did not have them were regarded as pathological and excluded from marriage.[27] Even within modern urbanised nations we cannot assume that aches, pains and other discomforts are uniformly categorised as signs of illness among all sections of the community. Although little work has been done on social-class variations in the construction of what constitutes 'health' and 'sickness',[28] the example of tooth-decay is suggestive: among millions of British working-class families, it is taken for granted that children will lose their teeth and require artificial dentures. The process of tooth-loss is not seen as a disease but as something like an act of fate. Among dentists, on the other hand, and in those more-educated sections of the community who are socialised into dental ideology, the loss of teeth arises through a definite disease-process known as caries, whose aetiology is established.[29] Social and cultural norms also plainly govern the varying perception, either as essentially 'normal', or as essentially 'pathological', of such characterics as baldness, obesity, infestation by lice, venereal infection, and the presence of tonsils and foreskins among children.

Once again it can be argued that these cultural variations apply only to marginal cases of sickness and health, that there are some physical or psychological conditions which are *ipso facto* symptomatic of illness, whether among Bushmen or Brobdignagians, duchesses or dockworkers. But there is no reason to believe that the 'standardised' varieties of human pathology operate according to a different logic from the 'culturally dependent' varieties. The existence of common or even universal illnesses testifies, not to the absence of a normative framework for judging pathology, but to the presence of very widespread norms. To be ill, after all, is not the same thing as to feel pain, or to experience weakness, or to fail to manifest this or that kind of behaviour. Rather it is to experience discomfort (or to manifest behavioural failure) in a

26. Cited by A. L. Knudsen, *The Individual, Society and Health Behavior* (New York, 1965), p. 49.
27. Cited by Mechanic, MS (No. 20), p. 16.
28. Knudsen, ISHB (No. 26), p. 48, quotes one New York study showing lower-class indifference to the need for medical attention for such conditions as ankle-swelling and backache. But these should still have been regarded as illness by the respondents, who could have had their own reasons (such as lack of cash) for refusing to consider medical treatment.
29. There is now some doubt among dental experts as to whether 'caries' is a genuine disease-entity or an artifact of diagnostic labelling.

context of a particular kind. Consider the following imaginary conversations between physician and client:

(a) *Client* Doctor, I want you to examine me, I keep feeling terrible pains in my right shoulder.
Doctor Really? What are they like?
Client Stabbing and intense.
Doctor How often do they happen?
Client Every evening after I get home from work.
Doctor Always in the same spot?
Client Yes, just in the place where my wife hits me with the rolling-pin.

(b) *Client* (Telephoning Doctor) Doctor, I haven't consulted you before but things are getting desperate. I'm feeling so weak, I can't lift anything heavy.
Doctor Goodness, when does this come on you?
Client Every time I try to lift something or make an effort. I have to walk quite slowly up the stairs and last night when I was packing the big suitcase I found I couldn't lift it off the bed.
Doctor Well, let's have some details about you before you come in. Name?
Client John Smith.
Doctor Age?
Client Ninety-two last February.

In the first example, the 'patient's' pain is not an illness because we expect pain as a normal response to being hit in tender places; indeed, if he did *not* feel pain when he was hit or prodded he would be taken to be suffering from some disease involving nerve-degeneration. In the second example, the patient's infirmity would usually be ascribed not to the category of "illness' but to that of 'ageing'. (If he had given his age as 'twenty-two' the case would be different.) In our culture we expect old people to find difficulty in lifting heavy weights, although it is easy to conceive of a culture in which mass rejuvenation among the aged had been perfected (perhaps by the injection of hormones, vitamins or other pep-pills into the water-supply) and where, in consequence, a dialogue of the type recounted would lead to a perfectly ordinary referral for medical treatment. The attribution of illness always proceeds from the computation of a gap between presented behaviour (or feeling) and some social norm. In practice of course we take the norm for granted, so that the broken arm or the elevated temperature is seen alone as the illness. But the broken arm would be no more of an illness than a broken fingernail unless it stopped us from achieving certain socially constructed goals; just as, if we could all function according to approved social requirements within any range of body-temperature, thermometers would disappear from the household medical kit.

This is not to say that illness amounts to any deviancy whatsoever from social expectations about how men should function. Some deviancies are regarded as instances not of sickness but of criminality, wickedness, poor upbringing or bad manners (though not all cultures do in fact draw a firm line between illness and these other deviations, e.g., primitive societies for whom illness is also a moral flaw and modern liberal circles for whom drug-addiction is categorised in medical as well as moral terms). Looking over the very wide range of folk-concepts and technical ideas about illness which exist in the history of human societies, one finds it difficult to discern a common structural element which distinguishes the notion of illness from other attributions of social failure. Provisionally, it is possible to suggest that illness is set apart from other deviancies insofar as the description (or, at a deeper level, the explanation) of the sick state is located within a relatively restricted set of causal factors operating within the boundaries of the individual human being. One may become ill as the result of being infected by germs, or through being entered by evil demons, or visited by a curse from the Almighty. Each culturally specific account of illness must involve a theory of the person, of the boundaries between the person and the world 'outside' him, and of the ways in which adverse influences can trespass over these limits and besiege or grip him. If the current theory of the person is positivistic and physical, the agencies of illness will be seen as arising from factors within (or at the boundaries of) his body; in cultures with an animistic tradition, the invasion will be one of the spirit or soul. But, however variously the nature of illness is specified from culture to culture, the attribution of illness appears to include a *quest for explanation,* or at least the descriptive delimiting of certain types of causal factor, as well as the normative component outlined above. It is indeed likely that the concept of illness has arisen in close parallel with the social practice of therapy, i.e., with the development of techniques to control those human afflictions which can be controlled at the boundaries of the individual person. It is hard to see how the category of illness, as a distinct construction separate from other kinds of misfortune, could have arisen without the discovery that some varieties of pain and affliction could be succoured through individual specialised attention to the afflicted person. In traditional societies, of course, the institution of medicine is not crystallised out as an applied branch of natural science: 'Therapy' for the Greeks was simply the word used for looking after or tending somebody, and, in Greece as well as elsewhere, a great deal of therapy goes on either in the patient's household or in conjunction with religious and magical specialisms. A specifically 'medical' framework of treatment is not necessary to provide the link between illness and practical action.

Practice and concept continue their mutual modification over the ages. In a society where the treatment of the sick is still conducted through religious ritual, the notion of illness will not be entirely distinct from the notion of sinfulness or pollution. Correspondingly, with the growth of progressively more technical and more autonomous specialisms of therapy, the concepts of disease and illness themselves become more technical, and thereby more alienated from their implicit normative background. Thus we reach the position of the present day where any characterisation of an 'illness' which is not amenable to a diagnosis drawn from physiology or to a therapy based on chemical, electrical or surgical technique becomes suspect as not constituting, perhaps, an illness at all. Such has been the fate of mental illness in our own epoch. It has been much easier for societies with an animistic theory of the person (and of his boundaries and susceptibilities to influence) to view mental disturbances on a par with bodily ailments. Ceremonies of ritual purgation and demon-expulsion, along with primitive 'medical' methods of a herbal or surgical type, are used indifferently by traditional healers on patients with a mental or with a bodily dysfunction. Fever and madness, the broken limb or the broken spirit are situated within the same normative frame, within the same explanatory and therapeutic system. Even the development of a technical-physiological specialism of medicine, such as emerged with the Hippocratic tradition which runs in fits and starts from antiquity to modern times, does not impair the possibility of a unitary perspective on physical and mental illness, *so long as a common structure of valuation and explanation applies over the whole range of disorders of the person.* The medicine of the seventeenth and eighteenth centuries in Western Europe, for instance, was able to interpret our present-day 'mental' disorders as a group of illnesses inhabiting the embodied person on much the same plane as other sorts of malady: the insane or the emotionally disturbed patient was suffering from a fault of 'the vapours', 'the nerves', 'the fluids', 'the animal spirits', 'the spleen', 'the humours', 'the head', or the forces and qualities of the body.[30] This unitary integration of human illnesses was of course only achieved at the cost of a stupendously inaccurate and speculative physiology. But an integrated theory of illness, whether achieved within a unitary-animistic or a unitary-physicalistic doctrine of the person, has one singular advantage over a more fragmentary perspective: it is not beset by the kind of crisis we now have in psychopathology and psychiatry, whose conceptual and moral founda-

30. See Foucault, MC (No. 2), pp. 119, 121, 123, 129 and 151 ff. Entralgo, in TWCA (No. 24) has similar explanations collected from ancient Hippocratic medicine.

tion has been exploded now that 'illness' has acquired a technical-physical definition excluding disorders of the whole person from its purview. Animistic and unitary-physicalistic accounts of illness both dealt in the whole embodied individual, but the medical technology of the nineteenth century and onwards has succeeded in classifying illnesses as particular states of the body only. Psychiatry is left with two seeming alternatives: either to say that personal, psychological and emotional disorders are really states of the body, objective features of the brain-tissue, the organism-under stress, the genes or what have you; or else to deny that such disorders are illnesses at all. If the latter, then the way is open to treat mental illnesses as the expression of social value-judgments about the patient, and psychiatry's role will not belong to the disciplines of objective, body-state medicine. Instead, it will be analogous to the value-laden and non-medical disciplines of moral education, police interrogation, criminal punishment or religion (depending on how low or how lofty a view one takes of the values inherent in psychiatric practice).

This dilemma will perhaps seem somewhat to dissolve if we recapitulate what was previously said about the nature of illness as a social construction. *All* illness, whether conceived in localised bodily terms or within a larger view of human functioning, expresses both a social value-judgment (contrasting a person's condition with certain understood and accepted norms) and an attempt at explanation (with a view to controlling the disvalued condition). The physicalistic psychiatrists are wrong in their belief that they can find objective disease-entities representing the psychopathological analogues to diabetes, tuberculosis and post-syphilitic paresis. Quite correctly, the anti-psychiatrists have pointed out that psychopathological categories refer to value-judgments and that mental illness is deviancy. On the other hand, the anti-psychiatric critics themselves are wrong when they imagine physical medicine to be essentially different in its logic from psychiatry. A diagnosis of diabetes, or paresis, includes the recognition of norms or values. Anti-psychiatry can only operate by positing a mechanical and inaccurate model of physical illness and its medical diagnosis.

In my own judgement, then, mental illnesses can be conceptualised just as easily within the disease framework as physical maladies such as lumbago or TB.

There are several misunderstandings that might arise, or indeed have arisen, from my declaration of this position: let me try to remove these misapprehensions at once. In the first place, it does not follow from my statement that the existing 'official' diagnostic categories of mental illness are the most useful or truthful ones that we can reach. I believe, for example, that 'psychopathy' represents no more than an attempt at social labelling, for control purposes, by psychiatrists working in tandem with the judicial authorities. It is likely, also, that 'schizophrenia' is a pretty useless dustbin category for a variety of psychic ills which have little logically or biologically in common with one another. Equally, though, I have no doubt that many current diagnostic categories in physical medicine will disappear in the next century or so, and be replaced by others apparently (and provisionally) more adequate. I can see that, for example, by the year 2072 nobody will be classed as having diabetes or asthma, though they will undergo feelings of discomfort similar to those experienced by present-day diabetics and asthmatics. In the future development of our species, we can anticipate *either* that some conditions now classified as illnesses will be re-allocated to a different framework of deviancy (or, more drastically, become regarded as essentially normal and non-deviant); *or* that, on the contrary, conditions which are nowadays viewed in a non-illness category of deviancy (as sins, perhaps, or as consequences of ageing or excessive effort) will be re-grouped into the range of the illnesses or diseases. The latter prospect—the progressive annexation of not-illness into illness—seems at the moment much more likely to happen than the former, especially since the stupendous achievements of medical technology make it more and more difficult for doctors to sign death certificates under the rubric 'died of natural causes'. The natural causes of death are becoming, more and more, causes that we can control: so that the terminally ill, and their relatives, will be putting strong pressures on the medical profession to redefine the natural (and inevitable) causes of fatality, rendering them into medical (and hence controllable) pathologies which require the services of a doctor rather than of a mortician. *The future belongs to illness:* we just are going to get more and more diseases, since our expectations of health are going to become more expansive and sophisticated. Maybe one day there will be a backlash, perhaps at the point when everybody has become so luxuriantly ill, physically or mentally, that there will be poster-parades of protest outside medical conventions with slogans like ILLNESS IS NOT SO BAD, YOU KNOW? or DISEASE IS THE HIGHEST FORM OF HEALTH. But for the moment, it seems that illness is going to be 'in': a rising tide of really chronic sickness. Even despite the Canutes of deviancy-sociology.

Secondly and much more importantly, nothing in my argument confirms the technologising of illness; the specialised medical model of illness is not the only possible one, as I have already indicated. As Dubos points out in his fundamental work *The Mirage of Health* (to which this paper is merely more or less a vulgarised addendum), the greatest advances in the control of disease have often come about through non-medical measures, and in particular through social and political change. The insertion of windows into working-class houses (with the consequent beneficial influx of sunlight), or the provision of a pure water-supply and an efficient sewage-disposal, did more to clear up the plagues of modern epidemic infection than did the identification of particular microbes or the synthesis of 'medical discoveries' like the various antibiotics and antitoxins. There are some authorities, notably Osmond and his collaborators,[31] who argue that, since the category of illness is infinitely preferable, from the standpoint of the mentally deranged, to any other variety of deviancy, we have to concentrate entirely on a narrow medical model for explaining diseases and curing them; in their view, social explanations for the onset of illnesses like schizophrenia and drug-addiction are incompatible with any illness-model, and so should be ruthlessly jettisoned. But we do not need to technologise illness beyond the point at which we decide that it is helpful to do so; even with physical illness, the concept of a 'social disease' is indispensable in the understanding and treatment of, for example, tuberculosis. Preventive medicine and public medicine are bound to invoke social explanations and social measures, to occupy a space which occurs, in short, at the intersection of medicine and politics. My case points, not to the technologising of illness, to the medicalisation of moral values (so obvious in the practice of psychiatry that it needs no fresh rehearsal here): but, on the contrary, to the politicisation of medical goals. I am arguing that, without the concept of illness—including that of mental illness since to exclude it would constitute the crudest dualism—we shall be unable to *make demands* on the health-service facilities of the society that we live in.

Those labelling theorists who like to yearn for the Lost Territories of deviancy now occupied by the invading armies of medical diagnosis, are committing a *sociological irredentism* quite as offensive as the better-known bogey of Psychiatric Imperialism. Assemblies of deviancy-experts remind me of nothing so much as the sad, moral-boosting reunions of Sudeten Germans in the Federal Republic: they appear dangerous to the Czechs, but basically such gatherings are those of the devotees of a lost cause, joining in old songs and refurbished regional accents in order to maintain a losing identity against the harsh world which offers many rival opportunities for re-socialisation. The 'demands' of the Sudeten Germans are, in 1972, a ritual, even if they were not so in 1938. The demands of the sociological revisionists of mental illness are not very obvious even as ritual: they appear to want more money for their own research, and one or two of their allies want to be left undisturbed to carry on rewarding private psychoanalytic prac-

31. Miriam Siegler and Humphry Osmond, "Models of Madness", *British Journal of Psychiatry*, 1966 Vol. 112, pp. 1193–1203; Miriam Siegler and Humphry Osmond, "Models of Drug Addiction", *International Journal of the Addictions*, 1968, Vol. 3, No. 1, pp. 3–24.

tices.[32] But theirs is a passive irredentism; after all, the sociologists never actually lived in the territories that the psychiatric colonizers have now taken over, so there cannot be very much energy in their grumbles. This very passivity is, however, highly dangerous in the present historical period when the amount of public money available for investment in the health services is so grossly inadequate. The voice of labelling sociology, including a good many of the 'immanentist' theoreticians, chimes in with the cautious, restrictive tones of the cheese-paring politician who is out to deny the priority of resource-allocation for the public psychiatric services (at the same time as he budgets lavishly for the military). Public psychiatry, as the result of the onslaughts of Szasz, Goffman and Laing and—to a smaller extent—of the other academic 'anti-psychiatrists', has become thoroughly unpopular with the general reading public. And since this middle-class public forms the great reservoir of candidates from which the officer-class of possible pressure-groups gets selected, the unpopularity of public-health psychiatry is an important factor which prevents the crystallisation of a vocal and determined lobby for the provision of intensive psychiatric facilities on a mass scale. Mental illness, like mental health, is a fundamentally *critical* concept: or can be made into one provided that those who use it are prepared to place demands and pressures on the existing organisation of society. In trying to remove and reduce the concept of mental illness, the revisionist theorists have made it that bit

32. The whole literary oeuvre of Szasz and Leifer is an attempt to justify one important way in which they earn their living: they are both psychoanalysts in private practice, accepting fees, sufficient to compensate them for the loss of time they might be spending in other work, from people who are in agony. Like any other intellectual, each of them has to justify what he is doing. They have to say: 'Well, at least it's better than what other people (e.g., psychiatrists in the community health services) are doing.' They also have to say: 'There is something rather important and special about this private fee-paying relationship: for example, it guarantees confidentiality and the responsibility of the therapist to the client alone, in a way which the psychiatrists in a publicly financed and organised health service, with their necessarily divided loyalties, cannot manage.' Hence their imperative need to destroy, intellectually (they cannot of course do it in practice, and would probably feel guilty if they could) the public mental-health service through attacking its main ideology, the category of 'mental illness'. There are of course serious problems, of the kind they adeptly stigmatise, in the bureaucratised psychiatric professions; divided loyalties are a fairly common fact of everyday life, but not everybody with a division of loyalties is a traitor. A psychiatrist or counsellor in a publicly financed institution is expected to be something of a double agent who can of course lay himself open to accusations of betrayal from either cause that he serves, i.e., from the institution or from the client. But being a double agent can be a perfectly honourable profession, at least before the court of honour which is the agent's own conscience. Whether other people believe that a person with divided loyalties is honourable or treacherous is, of course, a matter of *their* judgment alone.

much harder for a powerful campaign of reform in the mental-health services to get off the ground. The revisionists have thought themselves, and their public, into a state of complete inertia: they can expose the hypocrisies and annotate the tragedies of official psychiatry, but the concepts which they have developed enable them to engage in no public action which is grander than that of wringing their hands. Of course they do it beautifully. But the tragic stance of labelling theory and anti-psychiatric sociology cannot be taken seriously as a posture which is 'above the battle' for the priorities of spending within our bureaucratised and militarised capitalism. It is *in* the battle, on the wrong side: the side of those who want to close down intensive psychiatric units and throw the victims of mental illness on to the streets, with the occasional shot of tranquilliser injected in them to assure the public that something medical is still happening.

It may surprise some readers to hear that I, as a revolutionary socialist and Marxist, am so desirous of stimulating effective reforms in the mental-health field. But for a modern, engaged Marxism, the evolution of *transitional demands* on the existing social and political structure is essential. Just as the revolutionary exposes and pressurises Parliamentary 'democracy' by demanding *consistent democracy;* just as he exposes and fights the courts of bourgeois 'justice' by demanding *consistent justice:* so he must expose and combat the evils of our anti-therapeutic institutions of 'psychiatry' by demanding *consistent psychiatry*. A transitional demand in Trotsky's classic conception, is one which is placed on the system in the full knowledge that the system cannot grant it: the failure of the system to deliver its declared pledges will then expose its reactionary character before the masses. In the present era, which is characterised by mass demands for adequate medical treatment, *all* demands for public-health provision (including the demand for mass psychiatric services) are transitional in quality. The revolutionary can enter a united front with reformists (as he does all the time, for instance, in trade-union work), to place new pressures on the social order: if the system really can grant all that it claims to be able to do, the Marxist will have no quarrel with it, or with the reformists and liberals who expect it to carry out its promises. If (as the Marxist expects) the system cannot deliver the goods, then his liberal or reformist allies will become radicalised, and may even join the ranks of his Marxist comrades. So a united front is always possible, and indeed must always be sought, between revolutionaries and reformers. But no united front and no dialogue is possible between revolutionaries and cynics. Cynics are, quite simply, people who have no hope, and therefore have no capacity to express any demands for the future. The sociological critics of the 'mental illness' concept are, as ideologues, deeply cynical: if they do have hope, or any possibility of formulating demands in the mental-health field, such hope is not made manifest through the ideas contained in their books and articles. And the cynic cannot really be a critic; the radical who is only a radical nihilist, or a radical tragedian, is for practical purposes the most adamant of conservatives.

I have caught, in some discussions of a draft of this paper, a certain pervasive anxiety among my audience, an anxiety which is afraid lest psychiatry may, in the service of our abominable social and economic order, succeed in 'adjusting' the mentally ill to its goals. It is as though people believe that there is only a finite pool of grievances and maladjustments available in this society for radicals to work with: the fear is that psychiatry, with its tranquillisers, hospitals and whatnot, may succeed in mopping up this limited supply of miseries, discharging its patients into the hell of the factory and the purgatory of the home as permanently 'cured' and adjusted robots. Once again: if capitalism could really 'adjust' people, through psychiatry or any other technology, who would want to quarrel with it? I myself am perfectly happy to see as many mentally-ill persons as possible treated, fully and effectively, in this society; for no matter how many maladjustments may become adjusted through expert techniques, the workings of capitalism will ever create newer and larger discontents, infinitely more dangerous to the system than any number of individual neuroses or manias. Some people in this audience have seemed to me to be wanting to hoard the existing supply of neuroses and insanities, by leaving them untreated as long as possible, in the conviction that these are the best grievances we have got, and once they have gone, where will we get any more? I can suggest plenty more alternative sources of maladjustment, within our present-day society. But I forebear from doing so; for there is no arguing with people who will not read the newspapers.

Lewis Mumford and the Myth of the Machine

BY CHRISTOPHER LASCH

The hope of cultural renewal, briefly shared by so many intellectuals at the time of World War I, derived much of its energy from a widespread revolt against positivism. Both in Europe and in the United States, the scientific pretensions of positive philosophy came under attack by those who suspected that its "objectivity," its separation of fact and value, its divorce of theory from practice, concealed a defense of the social and economic status quo. Dissident intellectuals, self-consciously identifying themselves as a younger generation in revolt against their elders, condemned positivism as the characteristic cultural expression of a social order founded on the subordination of impulse to routine, the rational calculation of profit and loss, the impoverishment of the imagination. They condemned it, in other words, as a mirror image of industrial capitalism. The capitalist division of labor, as George Lukács wrote in *History and Class Consciousness*, reproduces itself in thought as " 'isolated' facts, 'isolated' complexes of facts, separate, specialist disciplines . . . whose very appearance seems to have done much to pave the way for such scientific methods."[1]

1 Not wishing to litter the text of this essay with reference notes, I propose to omit page references and other scholarly paraphernalia — a practice followed by Mumford himself. Almost all of Mumford's books are still in print, hence readily available. His correspondence with Van Wyck Brooks, edited by Robert E. Spiller, was published by Dutton in 1970. Michael R. Hughes has edited *The Letters of Lewis Mumford and Frederic J. Osborn* (New York: Praeger, 1972). Mumford's *Findings and Keepings: Analects for an Autobiography* (New York: Harcourt Brace Jovanovich, 1975), contains journal extracts, essays, correspondence, and the autobiographical novel, "The Little Testament of Bernard Martin," originally published in *The Second American Caravan* (New York, 1928). Another such collection, *My Works and Days: A Personal Chronicle*, has been published by Harcourt Brace Jovanovich in 1979. See also Mumford's *Interpretations and Forecasts, 1922-1972* (New York: Harcourt Brace Jovanovich, 1972), a collection of essays and excerpts from his books, and the collection edited by Harry T. Moore

The rebellion against positivism took many forms: vitalism, pragmatism, neo-Marxism, psychoanalysis, the sociology of knowledge. Some thinkers, like Max Weber, John Dewey, and Karl Mannheim, directed their attention to the study of consciousness, ignored or misunderstood by the positivists, but retained a positivistic faith in "scientific method." Others celebrated impulse, will, the power of "social myths." These two reactions had more in common than first met the eye. As Lewis Mumford wrote many years later, "The irrational avant-garde of the arts and the meticulously 'rational' avant-garde of computerdom are heading toward the same goal." A more important challenge to positivism came from those who revived dialectical modes of thought – as in psychoanalysis and neo-Marxism – in order to criticize both the illusion of scientific objectivity and the illusion of free will – both technological determinism and the irrationalist cults ostensibly opposed to it. A number of European Marxists, recognizing that Marxism itself had been "contaminated" by "positivistic and naturalistic encrustations," in Antonio Gramsci's words, turned to the idealist tradition in philosophy, and to its contemporary restatements by Dilthy and Croce, in search of theories with which to counter the mechanistic, fatalistic Marxism that too often served, in their eyes, as "a popular substitute of the cry 'God wills it.'" Rejecting the notion that material "base" determines cultural "superstructure," they came to the conclusion that a "renewal of culture," an "intellectual rebirth," a rehabilitation of the "devastated realm of the spirit," had to inform and perhaps even to precede a political revolution.

In the United States, the movement for cultural renewal remained mostly uninformed by Marxism. Given the intellectual poverty of American Marxism, it was not surprising that men like Mumford early decided that the "old-fashioned revolutionists are just as bitterly the enemies of our kind of game as the financiers and rulers are." In America, those who brushed aside the socialist version of positivism brushed aside almost all of Marxism as well, even though they shared many of the same concerns as their European counterparts: Lukács, Gramsci, Karl Korsch, and the Frankfurt

and Karl W. Deutsch, *The Human Prospect* (Carbondale, Illinois: Southern Illinois University Press, 1955). The utopian essay by Mumford, referred to near the end of this account, appeared in *Forum*, v. 88 (December, 1932), pp. 338-42, and his critique of Huizinga, "The Shadow of Yesterday," in *New Republic*, v. 88 (30 September 1936), pp. 230-1.

school.[2] The cultural movement in America, vaguely socialist in its original orientation, came to identify itself with the belief that a revolution in thought not only had to precede political change but would make a political revolution unnecessary. By 1930, Mumford had decided that "the situation demanded, not specific attacks on specific evils and specific points of danger, but a wholesale rethinking of the basis of modern life and thought . . . a new orientation . . . a new philosophical idea." Marxism and capitalism served the same "underlying ideals," in his view, the same "mechanistic plan of life." Nothing less than a "complete philosophical and social reorientation" would "guarantee a more satisfactory social order."

Like many others of his generation, Mumford had "grown up on Shaw and Wells." Before he was twenty, these writers, together with William James, had turned him "in one year . . . from a weak-kneed conservative . . . to a rather wild young man with a brick in my right hand and a red flag in my buttonhole." By 1914, he was already denouncing Shaw as a conservative. But for some time he continued to accept without question the scientific world-view of Fabian socialism and the "naive hope," as he later called it, that scientific and technical progress would usher in a new age of peace and plenty. At one point he planned to become an electrical engineer — the most "progressive" kind of engineer, in his view — and he mastered enough of the trade to serve during World War I as a radio operator in the Navy. Later he came to believe that his "early acceptance of — indeed, high excitement over — the doctrine of progress has given me a vivid understanding of my 'progressive,' power-infatuated contemporaries."

2 On the "affinity" between European neo-Marxism and the work of Randolph Bourne and other American thinkers, see Olaf Hansen's introduction to his collection of writings by Bourne, *The Radical Will* (New York: Urizen Books, 1977). Historians of American social thought, always faced among other things with the central fact of the absence of a Marxian intellectual tradition in America, and with the far-reaching implications of this fact, would do well to follow Hansen's advice to spend less time tracing "the meandering path of antidialectical thinking within the American radical tradition from decade to decade" — following the "pitfalls of various attempts to pragmatize Marx, seeing him as a 'scientist' of future revolutions, or simply 'americanizing' him" — and to concentrate instead "on those intellectual efforts which come nearest to fulfilling their promise as an equivalent to the explanatory scope and coherence of Marxist thought." Among those efforts, the work of Lewis Mumford offers one of the clearest examples of the way in which the "persistent rejection of Marxism" in America, as Hansen puts it, has created "new affinities to it."

Having come to socialism through the Fabians, he left it — or at least deepened his understanding of the problems Fabian socialism failed to address — with the help of another English tradition, the criticism of culture formulated by Ruskin and Morris and revived in America by Van Wyck Brooks.[3] By 1918, in an essay on museums — which seemed to him in retrospect to have "struck the essential chord of the rest of my intellectual life" — Mumford drew on Ruskin, Morris, and Patrick Geddes to support his argument for the integration of art and practical life, and for social reforms that would give back "to the artist the opportunity for public service which disappeared with the decline of the Middle Ages."

Mumford had more than a purely intellectual stake in the integration of art and the practical world of affairs. For several years, he wavered between a literary career and work in sociology and town planning as a disciple of Geddes, whom he regarded for some time as the "most prodigious thinker in the modern world." His decision to become a writer, in the face of Geddes' contempt for journalism, coincided with a decision to marry and to strike roots in America instead of continuing his sociological studies in England. In order to justify these choices to his master, he argued that his journalism represented "notes" for more extended works of scholarship. He added a more revealing argument, designed not so much to justify the choice of a literary career as to explain the difficulty of choosing a career in the first place. His generation, Mumford told Geddes, had grown up in the shadow of war and found it hard to believe in the future. An older man like Geddes, product of an age of hope, could not understand the "paralyzing effect of that pessimism . . . upon those whose personal careers had not yet acquired any momentum" before 1917. The collapse of a sense of historical continuity, he wrote elsewhere, called the very idea of a calling into question, undermining "all work that depends for its sustenance upon a heritage from the past, and is lured forward . . . by the gleam of the future."

In later years, Mumford attributed his choice of a career to the influence and example of Van Wyck Brooks. In 1932, he wrote to

3 In 1932, Mumford described himself, in a letter to Brooks, as a "post-Marxian." Statements scattered through his early writings, to the effect that socialists wished merely to stage an "uprising," or that they mistakenly "took machines to be prime-movers," suggest that Mumford rejected socialism as merely another mechanistic philosophy of life, another form of the "pragmatic acquiescence" bereft of any cultural vision to set against the corrupt values of a machine civilization. Here again, anti-Marxist thought in the United States led to conclusions similar to those reached by European Marxists, who criticized positivistic Marxism in much the same terms.

Brooks that it "was one of your *Freeman* notebooks, that I read on a journey to York in 1920, that sent me back to America, instead of continuing as a sociologist in England — and I have never regretted my choice!" In a fictionalized autobiography published in 1928, he says that he urged Geddes to read Brooks's *Ordeal of Mark Twain* if he wanted to understand why American "pioneers must settle down." Yet neither his initial commitment to a Brooksian style of social and cultural criticism nor the composition of his first two books, *The Story of Utopias* (1922) and *Sticks and Stones* (1924), resolved Mumford's doubts about his calling, which seem to have been intensified by the first years of his marriage to a high-spirited woman whom he found it hard to "master." Those doubts receded only in 1925-26, when he realized that a rediscovery of the American past entailed a reexamination of European history as well, and that a "synthesis" of past experience, moreover, might enable his contemporaries to arrive at a "vision to live by again." It was at this point that he set himself a task that both exhilirated and "frightened" him by its magnitude: "to describe what has happened to the western European mind since the breakdown of the medieval synthesis, and to trace out the effects of this in America."

Mumford's decision to return to the United States and to devote himself to a wide-ranging study of cultural history ran counter, as he well knew, to the self-imposed exile of other intellectuals and to their belief that modern men had to learn to live in a world utterly without order. His initial explorations of the American past convinced him that "there's promise in all this." By 1931, he had completed studies of the antebellum awakening in New England, of Herman Melville, and of the "buried renaissance" of 1865-1895; this work, together with that of Brooks, Waldo Frank, and Constance Rourke, seemed to him to establish an "active connecting link" with traditions that challenged the spirit of pioneering and furnished the "ingredients for a completely human society." A growing awareness of the neglected "ideal and esthetic aspect" of American life, Mumford thought, gave him and his contemporaries "new strength for our own task." In 1973, he wrote that the rediscovery of America in the twenties had constituted that decade's "most important contribution" to American culture.

This seems a curious judgment on the work of a period distinguished precisely by its penetrating criticism of American life — in the novels of Sinclair Lewis and Fitzgerald, the sociological satire of *Middletown*, the historical satire of Thomas Beer's *Mauve Decade*, and the writings of Brooks, Frank, and Mumford themselves. The postwar critique of American culture reached one of its highest points in Mumford's own essay, *The Golden Day* (1926), which struck Brooks as "the last word on all we have been thinking and writing about America during these last ten years." More appreciative in its treatment of Transcendentalism than Brooks had been in *America's Coming-of-Age*, this book nevertheless carried further the themes of Brooks's early work, showing how the promise of a "golden day" had evaporated in the post-Civil War era; how the best writers of the late nineteenth and early twentieth centuries had either acquiesced in the cult of material progress, as in the case of Mark Twain, or fled to Europe, which they treated, as in the case of Henry James, as a museum, finding in the "pillage of the past" a kind of "sublimation of the dominant impulses" of the time. The dominant philosophy, pragmatism, raised the cult of practical results to an indigenous ideology. Even the socialists, according to Mumford, conceived of revolution simply as a "change in power and control" and "could envisage only a bourgeois order of society, in which every one would have the comforts and conveniences of the middle classes."[4] In *America's Coming-of-Age,* Brooks had described nineteenth-century America as polarized between "transcendent theory" and the sordid pursuit of gain. Mumford deepened the indictment by showing that even thinkers who sought to come to grips with practical life ended by "idealizing the real," sinking into a "sluggish acceptance of the blind drift of things."[5]

4 "Thus Friedrich Engels [in *The Housing Question*] not merely opposed all 'palliative' measures to provide better housing for the working classes: he seems to have held the innocent notion that the problem would be solved eventually for the proletariat by a revolutionary seizure of the commodious quarters occupied by the bourgeoisie." Engels' idea, Mumford wrote in *The Culture of Cities*, was "fatuously optimistic" from a quantitative point of view, while "socially speaking, it merely urged as a revolutionary measure a process that had gone on in the older towns as the richer classes moved out of their original quarters and divided them up for working class occupation. But above all the suggestion was extremely naive because it did not perceive that the standards embodied in the more pretentious residences were *below* those which were desirable for human life."

5 Mumford claimed "no originality" in formulating his criticism of the "pragmatic acquiescence." "Bourne reached it before me: so did Van Wyck Brooks in *Letters and Leadership*: so did Waldo Frank in *Our America*. We were, perhaps, the ungrateful heirs of William James's great liberation; but it was part of our sad experience to find that the philosophy which had rescued the academic world from an arid theological provincialism was in itself also a provincialism." Like their European counterparts, who sought in the idealist tradition of philosophy (Vico, Hegel, Dilthey, Croce) an antidote to positivistic Marxism, American intellectuals looking for a corrective to pragmatism turned, as Mumford put it, to "Spinoza, Santayana, Croce, or in my particular case, Plato and Patrick Geddes" for a "hold on wider realms of thought and life than the pragmatists have been interested in." (*New Republic*, 19 January 1927, pp. 250-1)

If the twenties seem important today because they laid the basis for a more thoroughgoing criticism of pragmatism and the whole progressive tradition from which it came, this is not the way the period appeared, even at the time, to Brooks or Mumford. These critics saw their work as a contribution not to an emerging tradition of critical thought but to the affirmation of positive "values." When Brooks praised *The Golden Day*, he told Mumford that the book's "glowing appreciation of the *golden* age" had "done the *positive* thing which the rest of us had mostly left out." Brooks himself had already moved away from "*analytical work*," which he had prematurely decided was "done," to "synthesis." His earlier work had explored the "*dark* side of the moon," and he now set out, with considerable relief, to "re-assert the idealistic point of view," urging Mumford to do the same.

In 1922, Brooks still saw his own work as a kind of "sociology." He described the "contemporary literary mind" as "sociological" in its outlook, and he deplored the inability of the "severely classical mind" (exemplified by Albert Jay Nock, editor of *The Freeman*) to grasp the new style of discourse. By 1931, however, he was imploring Mumford to write "the History of American Culture, in six volumes, on the scale of Gibbon's *Rome*," and to write in "the grand style and from a point of view that is absolutely and everlastingly *central*." Fortunately Mumford took Plato, he said — not Gibbon — as his guide, and began his *Renewal of Life* series not in Brooks's mood of fond retrospection but in a more combative spirit, conceiving the first volume as "a book to out-Bentham the Benthamites, to out-Marx the Marxians, and in general, to put almost anybody and everybody who has written about the machine or modern industrialism or the promise of the future into his or her place."[6]

6 The record of the literary friendship between Brooks and Mumford, especially in its later stages, makes depressing reading. Although Brooks continued to acclaim Mumford as a "giver of laws," a "genuine prophet," a "world mind," a "true man of letters," and "the number 1 humanist of our day," he also complained that Mumford's writing was too "exclusively scientific" and urged him instead of writing about technology to immerse himself in study of "literary moralists." Mumford replied with equally conventional and unconvincing praise of Brooks's "deeply healthy" literary chronicles. Instead of confronting the growing divergence of their ideas, he vented his impatience with Brooks on a trivial offense: the decision of the National Institute of Arts and Letters, of which Brooks was a prominent officer, to honor Charles A. Beard with its medal of honor in 1947. Overdramatizing his own standing as a "pariah" and Melvillean outcast, Mumford contended that Beard's "success in gaining the ear of this generation" represented the measure of his own "failure." He castigated Brooks not merely for honoring a thinker who had "served the purposes of traitors and fascists" but for turning

Books written to settle accounts with earlier interpreters, even with the avowed intention of putting them in the shade, usually turn out to be more interesting to read than books aspiring to the "monumental, the classic thing," as Brooks put it in another of his exhortations. Whereas Mumford undertook the *Renewal of Life* as a "piece of unmitigated and unpardonable impudence," Brooks spoke of what a "wonderful thing" it was "to have a life occupied for years with an immense work" devoted to the rescue of "'neglected' figures" and the restoration of "heroic and classic models." The work of synthesis that Brooks urged on Mumford materialized in the form of his own *Makers and Finders* series, that tiresome tribute to the American literary past. Mumford, on the other hand, produced a series of books that demolish the myth of technological determinism (anticipating in this regard the findings of later scholars) and brilliantly explain how social patterns reproduce themselves at every level of life. The first two volumes of the *Renewal of Life* series are surpassed only by his own reexamination of these subjects in *The Myth of the Machine*. The history of technology and its relation to the growth of cities provided Mumford with an ideal focus. The subject brought together his varied interests — literature, architecture, science, and technology — and by forcing him to deal with the whole sweep of modern history, delivered him from the temptation to spend the rest of his life "rediscovering" America. The formidable task of historical analysis that Mumford imposed on himself also helped to check his tendency — freely indulged in too many of his other works and even to some degree in these — to spin out utopian visions of the future, to preach about "humane values and ethical principles," and to affirm the "organic," life-giving "philosophy of the whole." If *Technics and Civilization* and *The Culture of Cities* far surpass the concluding volumes of the series, *The Condition of Man* and *The Conduct of Life*, it is precisely because they deal not with the "human condition" but with the concrete historical problems associated with the rise of

his back on contemporary events, immersing himself in the past, and ignoring the "tragic choices" faced by intellectuals of his own time. In going along with the decision to honor Beard's work as a historian without taking his isolationism into account, Brooks had aligned himself, in Mumford's view, with the same kind of "gentlemenly men" who had once rejected Thoreau, Melville, and Whitman as "barbarous, hysterical or mad, because they made inconvenient issues over matters that gentlemenly men were careful never to take a position on."

Brooks argued in his own defense: "The idea that by voting for Beard I was voting against you was something that could never have entered my head."

capitalism, the spread of the scientific world view, the growth of the state, the industrial revolution, and the eventual emergence of a bureaucratic, managerial type of capitalism that organizes even leisure and consumption along industrial lines.

Mumford's central thesis, that modern technology has developed in the historical setting of capitalist accumulation and has been shaped at every point by the requirements of capitalist production, undercuts both the naive determinism that sees technology as the driving force in history and more sophisticated theories of the "autonomy of technique," as Jacques Ellul calls it. Whatever its liberating possibilities, Mumford insists, modern technology has created new forms of enslavement because it has grown up as the servant of national self-aggrandizement, war, and the insatiable appetite for profits. Acquisitive individualism, the glorification of privacy, the spirit of free scientific inquiry, the development of accurate methods of measuring time and movement, and the conquest of nature all belong to the same historical development, which culminates in the industrial or "post-industrial" order of our own time and its metropolitan round of life. The bureaucratization of work and play in the modern city, that "human filing case," completes the individual's reduction to a vicarious consumer of experience, dependent on the market for the satisfaction of his needs, on advertising and mass culture for instruction in the art of living, and on manufactured images for the illusion of reality. Urban density carried too far obstructs association and atomizes social life, just as the machine, absorbed into a general system of consumption, erodes older skills. The atrophy of competence, the invasion of everyday life by expertise, and the growth of a universal market that assimilates everything — even art and love — into the apparatus of commodity production appear from Mumford's perspective as the erosion of local and regional cultures by the advancing metropolis, which parasitically depends on the cultural organisms it devours and on a proliferating array of services that drive it toward bankruptcy.

Mumford's indictment of the modern city reaches its climax, not in the "neotechnic" visions of the future against which he plays it off, but in a critique of the "metropolitan mind" with its educated contempt for roots. In the course of his studies, supplemented by a fruitful correspondence with the English town planner Frederic J. Osborn, Mumford seems to have come to a deeper understanding of the progressive tradition from which he had already begun to free himself. He now saw that ostensibly revolutionary movements often reinforced the central tendency of bourgeois society in their misguided attempt to emancipate the individual from his past, from family ties, from the sense of place, and from nature itself. When Osborn read *The Culture of Cities*, he found in this and other books by Mumford a "god-sent reinforcement to my own sometimes desperate struggle for family living-space standards." For years, Osborn had fought against a "highbrow pseudo-modern aesthetic school of planners" who took for granted the obsolescence of the family and proposed to replace it with technology and with communal arrangements – "gadgets inside the house, nursery schools, school meals, crêches, and communal meals outside" – which in Osborn's view merely reinforced the "megalopolitan trend." Whereas "ninety-nine per cent of our people really want the house-and-garden type of dwelling," an enlightened elite of social critics, esthetes, and social reformers had already consigned it to the scrap heap of history. The Labor party, which might have been expected to register popular demands, had fallen under the control of a combination of old-guard trade unionists and a "rather urbanised, feminist, 'neo-technic', middle-class type who prefer nursery schools to babies." As for the Communists, they doted, Osborn wrote, on "steel-and-glass and Metro and communal cocktail bars in blocks of flats." Having himself been "brought up on Wells and Shaw and the world-minded who sneer at this country," Osborn had only recently begun, he confessed, to appreciate the "unique sanity, balance, and capacity of my own people" and to trust the preferences of "ordinary house-centered urban workers" over the "fashionable literary attitudes" that condemned the "out-of-date and despised cult of the family."

Osborn's insistence on the "connection between housing-planning and family idealism," together with his diatribes against the "Le Corbusier outlook," the "fashionable literary attitudes" underlying denigration of the family, the "provincials of Piccadilly" and the "metropolitan coteries" that made a cult of the "communal life," must have had a considerable impact on Mumford, especially when these ideas coexisted in Osborn's letters with sincere praise of *The Culture of Cities* and the books that soon followed. Osborn's criticism of highbrow cultural *chic* overlapped with Mumford's criticism of highbrow pacifism, which emerged as an increasingly important theme in his writings at a time when the fascist powers were beginning to expand their domination over the European continent. "I myself reacted definitely," Osborn wrote, "with outward violence but inner mildness from the Victorian bourgeois atmosphere when I was 17, and for five or six years I was thoroughly taken in by Bloomsbury and its absorption in ephemeral movements and its scorn of stability." Mumford had passed through a similar development, and in the late thirties he began to see his own experience as part of the prolonged crisis of liberalism that had led to the rise of fascism and the outbreak of World War II. The pacifism of the American left made him more and more contemptuous of the "moral paralysis" encouraged by the whole progressive tradition — the "specious social interpretations" by means of which progressives blamed "conditions," not men, for the rise of fascism and excused Hitler's aggression on the grounds that he sought merely to right wrongs inflicted on Germany by the Allies at Versailles. When Osborn denounced the "depravity and pessimism of the twenties" in his own country, he struck a responsive chord in Mumford. "Our weakness goes much deeper," Mumford replied. "Our young intellectuals — and I was one of them! — were more disillusioned by the First World War than the weakest spirits in Europe: and the drivel of our radio programmes, the whine of self-pity in our popular music, are symptoms of a formidable kind of escapism which gives me great concern." Again and again, Mumford ridiculed the "maudlin errors and myths that have been built up around Germany's guiltlessness and the sins of Versailles" — myths to which he too, he said, had once subscribed. In *Men Must Act* (1939), *Faith for Living* (1940), *The Condition of Man* (1944), and *Values for Survival* (1946), he deplored the "corruption of liberalism" and called not merely for a renewal of "purpose" and "values" but for recognition of the need for the "discipline of daily life."[7]

7 Liberals replied to this indictment in language that confirmed its accuracy. The editors of the *New Republic*, attempting to refute not only Mumford's argument for intervention but his charge that liberalism had lost all moral rigor, claimed that liberalism had outgrown a naive and optimistic faith in reason and human goodness, without, however, embracing updated ideologies of original sin. Modern psychology offered scientific insight into the "emotional depths in the personality" but simultaneously established the futility of "moral condemnation of the mentally immature" — the kind of moralizing Mumford fell into, according to the editors, when he denounced anti-interventionists as morally irresponsible. "No doctor would maintain that straitjackets and iron shackles have any therapeutic value. . . . The only possible means of salvation for the emotionally sick is . . . an objective and sympathetic understanding." This reasoning went far to bear out the contention that liberals had exchanged moral realism for a therapeutic ethic of moral nonaccountability.

As for the issue of intervention, the editors advised Mumford to "remember the deep shock to the sense of human dignity which was suffered by the incurring of [horrible] losses twenty-five years ago for causes which turned out to be deception and illusion." (*New Republic,* v. 102 [29 April 1940], p. 563)

These books indulged far too freely Mumford's penchant for exhortation and his fondness for the slogans of progressive humanist regionalism: "creation and preservation of values"; "growth, reproduction, development, creation"; "re-birth of the positive values of life"; "conscious recovery of regional roots"; "central core of purpose."[8] The vehemence of his hatred of fascism made him call for a "totalitarian" liberalism with which to counter it. When he deplored the "crazy ethical absolutism" that prompted the American Civil Liberties Union to defend American Nazis' right to free speech, he undermined his own criticism of moral relativity. The books that Mumford churned out in rapid order in the 1940s, for all their weaknesses, nevertheless contain a more heightened understanding of the "culture of liberalism" than he had previously achieved. This understanding rested on the simple proposition — taken for granted by the democratic theorists of the early nineteenth century but forgotten by twentieth-century progressives — that "a self-governing, self-acting, and self-respecting person is the very foundation of a democracy." In advanced industrial society, Mumford argued, the dominance of experts, the "ruthless destruction of the household arts and crafts, on the assumption that the equivalent can be purchased at a shop," and the concentration of technical knowledge at the top of the social hierarchy undermine everyday self-reliance. These developments make it possible for the ordinary man to live a "carefree" existence, in the sense that society relieves him of the need to provide for his own needs and of the moral responsibility for his actions. Mumford argued in effect that progressive ideology legitimizes this state of affairs and thus participates in the attack on the individual's moral autonomy.

The "sleek progressive mind," according to Mumford, holds that human nature is deflected from its natural goodness only by external conditions beyond the individual's control. Having no sense of sin, the progressive discounts inherent obstacles to moral development and therefore cannot grasp the need for a "form-giving discipline of the personality." The progressive mind scorns the past — the only

8 At its worst, Mumford's work in this period invited, and even to some extent deserved, the savage criticism it received from Meyer Schapiro, Richard Chase, and other writers associated with *Partisan Review* (see Schapiro's "Looking Forward to Looking Backward," v. 5 [July 1938], pp. 12-24, and Chase's "The Armed Obscurantist," v. 11 [summer 1944], pp. 346-8). Chase, reviewing *The Condition of Man*, observed that "the first three words of the introduction — "What is man?" — do not impress the reader with Mumford's ability to ask fruitful questions."

body of experience on which to base such a discipline. It scorns religion, even though modern socialist utopias, Mumford began to suspect, themselves live off the "unearned increment of religion." Progressivism scorns the discipline gained through manual labor, the endurance of discomfort, and the nurture of the young. It seeks to free mankind from all manner of hardship and adversity, from the boredom of domestic drudgery, and from natural processes in general. A society based on progressive principles, according to Mumford, renounces every transcendent goal in favor of the "private enjoyment of life." Thus American society has created a race of men and women who "deny because of their lack of experience that life has any other meanings or values or possibilities." Such people "eat, drink, marry, bear children and go to their grave in a state that is at best hilarious anesthesia, and at its worst is anxiety, fear, and envy, for lack of the necessary means to achieve the fashionable minimum of sensation."

Pragmatic liberalism, as Mumford called it, had lost the "tragic sense of life." It refused to confront the reality of death, hoping that "science's steady advances in hygiene and medicine might postpone further and further that unpleasant occasion." In 1940, he reported a conversation with a liberal who told him that he could not support a political decision that might lead to war and thereby bring about the death of other human beings. "When I objected that the failure to make such a decision in the existing international situation would certainly lead to the less fruitful death of these same human beings six months or six years hence, he confessed that for him any extra time spared for the private enjoyment of life seemed that much gained." This man had "ceased to live in a meaningful world," Mumford concluded. "For a meaningful world is one that holds a future that extends beyond the incomplete personal life of the individual; so that a life sacrificed at the right moment is a life well spent, while a life too carefully hoarded, too ignominiously preserved, is a life utterly wasted."

By 1940, Mumford no longer found himself altogether alone in his attack on the moral paralysis of American liberalism. Other interventionists, notably Reinhold Niebuhr, had come to similar conclusions. After Pearl Harbor, some of these attitudes became more common among liberals, even fashionable. Arthur Schlesinger said in 1949 that Niebuhr's writings had opened up to his generation a "new dimension of experience – the dimension of anxiety, guilt and corruption." Unfortunately, the tough-minded liberalism of

Schlesinger and Niebuhr soon showed itself to be another form of the "pragmatic acquiescence." Schlesinger and other liberal critics of liberalism sounded like Mumford when they denounced the "modern tendency to seek in optimistic sentimentalism an escape from the severe demands of moral decision." After the war, however, the new "realism" dissolved into uncritical support of the cold war policies of the United States government. Even Niebuhr defined the cold war as a conflict between Marxist "despotism" and the "open society" of the West, thus ignoring the possibility that the Western democracies had already taken on many of the features of the totalitarian regimes they sought to defeat or contain. Mumford, on the other hand, understood as early as 1945 that the "practice of obliteration bombing," culminating in Hiroshima and Nagasaki, had "made us the same kind of moral nihilists as our enemies." He did not hesitate to admit that the "confidence I had in 1940 about our ability to fight fascism without being infected with it has proved unsound."

Mumford saw more deeply into the corruption of liberal thought and practice than those who chose "pragmatic" over "utopian" liberalism and promptly defined the cold war as one more choice between freedom and "appeasement." He understood that pragmatic liberalism, superficially tough-minded, mounted no challenge to the modern cult of technology, which emerged in his writings of the 1940s and 1950s as the central element in the crisis of twentieth-century culture. Nor did pragmatic liberals, on the other hand, seriously challenge the irrationalist ideologies that put themselves forward as the negation of technological domination. Itself the "main ingredient of the Western mind," pragmatism, in Mumford's view, embodied a more benign version of the fascist impulse, which combines total regimentation with a celebration of irrational impulse. In his postwar diatribes against what he saw as the suicidal folly of nuclear armaments, Mumford returned to the criticism of pragmatism first set forth in *The Golden Day*, and now elaborated in *The Conduct of Life* (1951) and *In the Name of Sanity* (1954). He argued that pragmatism, and the progressive tradition in general, served as the ideology of modern science — the philosophy of power. The progressive's attempt to overcome "personal bias" and to disengage himself from imagination and emotion provided one more rationale for the scientific "abdication of responsibility" and the scientific "detachment from all other needs and values than those of knowledge and power." The triumph of the scientific world view went hand in hand, Mumford thought, with the "uprising of Caliban," the modern celebration of violence and instinctual release. "We have lived to witness the joining, in intimate partnership, of the automaton and the id, the id rising from the lower depths of the unconscious, and the automaton, the machine-like thinker and the man-like machine, wholly detached from other life-maintaining functions and human reactions, descending from the heights of conscious thought."

The pragmatic liberals who banded together in organizations like Americans for Democratic Action and the Congress for Cultural Freedom pictured themselves as unpopular teachers of hard truths. "Nothing exists in history," wrote Schlesinger, "to assure us that the great moral dilemmas can be resolved without pain." Schlesinger's attack on "historical sentimentalism," Lionel Trilling's plea for moral realism in *The Liberal Imagination*, and innumerable outpourings on the theme of *la trahison des clercs* expressed a general revulsion against the left-wing pieties of the thirties. Cold war liberals, however, disengaged themselves from the platitudes of the Popular Front only to embrace the crackpot realism (as C. Wright Mills called it) of nuclear deterrence and American globalism. Far from working against the grain, they took positions that found widespread support in official circles. Eventually many of them became advisers to the Kennedy administration, which at once gave official sanction to cold war liberalism and made the commitments to the defense of "freedom" in Vietnam that proved to be its undoing.

Mumford steered a more consistent course. Perhaps because he had never flirted with Stalinism in the thirties, he felt no compulsion to embrace the patriotic ideology of anti-communism in the fifties. He too attacked the moral sentimentalism that blames society for the wrongs perpetrated by individuals, but it never occurred to him to locate the corrective in a militant Americanism based on nuclear supremacy. The underlying weakness of liberalism all along, he came to believe, lay precisely in its idolatry of technological power. The moral passivity liberals had once shown in dealing with Hitler and Stalin originated in a deeper acquiescence to the machine. The "real *trahison des clercs*," according to Mumford, lay in the undeviating support they gave to the modern scientific enterprise of emancipating mankind from the controlling forces of nature — a project that "met so fully the id's infantile wish for unrestrained power." The modern intellectual, having grasped the principle that knowledge confers power on those who master the secrets of nature, had made power the "main object of knowledge." By turning his back on "emotion, imagination, and dreams," the man of knowledge had "deliberately fabricated for himself a defective personality."

In the forties and fifties, Mumford's criticism of science, technology, and the intellectual's infatuation with power fell for the most part on deaf ears. Beginning with *The Condition of Man*, his books met with a "blank wall" of public indifference. He found himself increasingly "unable to speak to my own countrymen." Not only did the public ignore his warnings about the danger of nuclear power but architects and city planners for the most part paid no attention to his critical analysis of the modern metropolis. The "tide has been entirely against us," he wrote to Osborn in 1966, adding that he felt like a "forgotten man in my own country." Osborn admitted a similar sense of futility. "What a holy failure our sixty-year effort has been to connect up planning and town development logically with the human passion for the single-family house and yard!" The garden city had ironically materialized, in the postwar period, in the form of suburbia — a parody of the garden city ideal.

The letters Mumford exchanged with Osborn, during this period of frustration and neglect, show how Mumford's long-standing quarrel with pragmatism gradually broadened into a more comprehensive indictment of progressive political culture.[9] Both men had been raised in the progressive tradition, as they continued to remind each other. "I was a 'state socialist,'" Osborn recalled, "under the inspiration, first, of Bellamy, then of H. G. Wells and very soon after of the Fabian Society, which I joined about 1906, and which was dead against Owenite 'communitarianism.' I at once accepted Webb's *Socialism: True and False* (1894) as the milk of the gospel." Only when he became manager of the model town of Letchworth, and later of Welwyn Garden City — in other words, when he began to deal with practical problems of town planning — did Osborn, according to his own account, begin to see the limitations of "scientific" socialism. Ebenezer Howard himself, he later discovered — the founder of the garden city movement — had experienced a some-

9 In the course of a philippic (1943) against the *Architectural Review* — a journal devoted, Osborn believed, to "the idea that we are passing into an age when buildings express the communal life which is to replace, rather than supplement, the family life" — Osborn wrote to Mumford: "I think their annoyance with you is that up to a point they had misread you as a modernist *tout simple*, and nothing could annoy them more than to find you in essential alliance with my school of thought *and* a defender of the out-of-date and despised cult of the family."

what similar deconversion from socialism, in this case the socialism of Edward Bellamy. "What Howard got from Bellamy was, he told me, the enthusiasm for a socialist community, and it was as a socialist community that he first thought of the ideal town. . . . Then he saw the great difficulty of municipal agriculture, so he thought, 'Why not let agriculture be carried on by private enterprise, the land being owned by the public and the increments of urban value thus being secured. . . . The fact that Howard first reacted from the simple communism with which Bellamy had overwhelmed him by reflecting on the difficulty of agriculture . . . is really significant."[10]

In England, public debates about the rebuilding of postwar London widened the breach between advocates of the garden city and advocates of "Marxism, Megalopolitanism and uncritical Modernism," as Osborn called them. Opposition to "greenbelt" cities, he thought, rested on the prejudice that the "family home is a dying institution, and that we are on the threshold of a new world in which, somehow, man will be born again as a social animal. . . . When I was a young member of the Fabian Society I was surrounded by people who felt like that." Mumford believed the "reaction" against garden cities expressed a "combination of communist snobbery and old-fashioned upper class snobbery, which has affixed the label of 'middle-class' to the Garden City idea." Like Osborn, Mumford objected to the "highbrow planning circle" not because he believed in the blessings of free enterprise but because too many planners, dismissing popular attachment to the family and the single-family house as evidence of a reactionary state of mind, arrogantly invoked the gods of historical inevitability and

10 The vast human devastation that has attended the forcible collectivization of agriculture in the Soviet Union and other socialist states shows that these premonitions about the "difficulty of agriculture" under state socialism were well founded. Precisely because Howard and his followers rejected collectivism, however, it is important to note that they did not equate "private enterprise" with unrestricted private ownership of land. Both Mumford and Osborn believed that public ownership was the only way to guarantee stable occupancy and to prevent the patterns of land speculation and rapid turnover that underlie the contemporary urban crisis. "Capitalist society has confused ownership with security of tenure and continuity of effort," Mumford wrote in *Technics and Civilization*, "and in the very effort to foster ownership while maintaining the speculative market it has destroyed security of tenure. It is the latter condition that is necessary for conservative farming; and not until the community holds the land will the position of the farmer be a desirable one. . . . Such ownership and planning by the community do not necessarily mean large-scale farming . . . [or] the extinction of the small family farming group, with the skill and initiative and general intelligence that distinguishes the farmer favorably from the over-specialized factory worker of the old style."

technological progress in their campaign to impose their own enlightened prejudices on the masses. Mumford insisted that on many issues, he himself was "not merely ready to go as far as a socialist or a communist, but possibly a little further." At the same time, he shared Osborn's impatience with "mechanically socialist" panaceas.

Osborn noted in 1952 that "highbrow types" had captured the "BBC Third Programme and television" and were "always seeking new opportunities of showing common people how they should live." "Home-centred culture," he wrote on another occasion, conflicted with the "'Bloomsbury' type of culture" many planners saw as the essence of city living — "theatres, ballet, lectures, eating, Johnsonian coffee-house celebration, etc." In opposition to the ideal of "urbanity" prevailing among most planners, Osborn argued again and again that most Englishmen preferred a life centered on family and neighborhood "if they can't have both." When Mumford criticized plans for urban renewal that would have had the effect of pushing family life out of the cities, Osborn agreed, adding: "I attach very little importance indeed to a consensus of opinion among [architects and other] technicians on a matter of this kind. I have so much direct evidence that they do not know what people like — or even what they *are* like. This is partly a class matter. One could develop a Marxist theory of the thing."

Neither Mumford nor Osborn went on to work out a class theory of the ascendancy of experts in modern society or the role of avant garde fashions in the development of the "myth of the machine." Instead Mumford turned in the mid-fifties to the task of rewriting *The Culture of Cities* — a more modest task in the pursuit of which, however, he inquired more deeply than before into the relations between technology and culture, revised many of his earlier ideas, weeded out the remnants of utopianism in his own thinking, and finally produced three books of major importance: *The City in History* (1961), *Technics and Human Development* (1967), and *The Pentagon of Power* (1970). In 1960, he called Osborn's attention to the contrast between the "very sombre final chapter" of *The City in History* and its counterpart in his earlier *Culture of Cities*, which confidently predicted the coming of a "new urban order." In 1937, Mumford still believed that technology, liberated from "capitalist canons of reputability and expense," would prove to be an agency of human liberation. In *The City in History*, on the other hand, he did not flinch from the "terminal possibilities" of the contemporary city. His worst forebodings, he wrote, had now come true. Passages in *The Culture of Cities* in which he had deliberately imagined the worst — passages criticized at the time as "unduly pessimistic, indeed perversely exaggerated and morbidly unrealistic" — had been overtaken by the march of events, which carried technological development to the point of making a "universal extermination camp the ideal terminus of this whole civilization."

Mumford's early work on the relation of technology to social change rested on the conventional assumption that capitalism and modern technology are at war with each other, and that technology needs only to be freed from capitalist constraints in order to serve human needs. In *Technics and Civilization*, he not only accepted Veblen's analysis of the "dissociation between capitalism and technics" but praised Frederick W. Taylor and Elton Mayo as pioneers of a "humanly controlled and effectively directed industrial production," which "awaited" merely the "formulation of non-capitalist modes of enterprise." He shared the common socialist illusion — one held also by Lenin — that Taylorism could be divorced from capitalist production and adapted to socialist regimes without recreating the hierarchical division of labor that concentrates planning and control in a managerial elite. Nor did he see that Elton Mayo's studies of the "human factor" of production attempted merely to palliate the worker's boredom and discontent while preserving the division of labor in which it originated. Mayo's work, Mumford thought in the early thirties, "pointed to a factor of efficiency in socialized industry, in which the worker himself is fully respected." In fact, Mayo proposed to destroy the workers' own traditions of solidarity and collective action, which had survived even the introduction of Taylorism, and to replace those traditions with the managerially imposed collectivism of "human relations." The work of Taylor and Mayo, instead of demonstrating the liberating potential of technological expertise, suggests that capitalism has created a technology that serves at the same time as a system of social control, while the history of industrial relations in the Soviet Union and other communist states shows that this system cannot be transferred to a socialist form of production without reinforcing capitalist patterns of domination and subordination under the fiction of a workers' state.

"None of us who pleaded for public housing in the 20s," Mumford wrote to Osborn in 1960, "can feel happy over what has been offered to us under that banner during the last twenty years." An awareness of "those consequences," he said, underlay the "sombre" conclusions of *The City in History*. Dissatisfaction with the results of progressive reform prompted Mumford to rethink the whole problem of technology and to lay new stress on the way in which "every technical advance" has always been "intermeshed with necessary psycho-social transformations both before and after." In *Technics and Human Development* and *The Pentagon of Power*, he gave up the naive distinction between technology and "pecuniary" interests. He now proposed a more fruitful distinction between labor-saving machinery and a form of social organization, first introduced by the divine kings of Egypt and Mesopotamia, in which society itself is collectivized as a vast "labor machine." Labor-saving machinery, often associated with small-scale enterprise and the progress of handicrafts, eliminates drudgery and frees human energies for more rewarding types of work. The "megamachine," on the other hand, creates new forms of drudgery, enlisting human energy in collective enterprises on a gigantic scale – epitomized in the pyramids or the modern assembly line – that gratify the power-hunger of the mighty but do little to improve the material conditions of everyday life. Originally modeled on the army, the megamachine – the "supreme feat of early civilization" – in turn "served as a model for all later forms of mechanical organization." Characterized by the interchangeability of parts, external direction of work, centralization of scientific and technical knowledge, and regimentation of the work force, the labor machine of ancient times already anticipated the central features of modern production, long before the so-called industrial revolution. Its initial introduction in the great hydraulic civilizations of antiquity, however, did not obliterate the "more modest and diversified modes of technology," which continued for centuries to "perform the larger part of the daily work." Only in the last two and a half centuries, according to Mumford, had the principles of the megamachine, formerly "confined to great mass enterprises," invaded the workshop itself – the real meaning of the industrial revolution. This development coincided, on Mumford's analysis, with a revival of the "old dream of unlimited power," the reintroduction of forced labor and genocide, the rise of states claiming and exercising absolute dominion, and finally, the emergence of a "new psychological type," the organization man or "bureaucratic personality" who lives in a condition of "submissive conformity" and "total dependence."

Though Mumford's description of modern society as the ultimate form of the "megamachine" makes too many facile analogies with ancient Egyptian and Sumerian civilizations, exaggerates its homogeneity, and minimizes the social tensions which modern capitalist production has not only not eradicated but in many ways intensified, it represents a considerable advance over his earlier work — and over conventional interpretations of the history of technology. Mumford's theory has the great merit of treating technology as a system of social relations and of recognizing the mutual dependence of technological change and social change. The essence of industrialization, according to Mumford, lies not in the introduction of machinery on a large scale but in the separation of planning from production, the monopolization of technical knowledge by a new priesthood of scientists and engineers, and the regimentation of the work force. These social changes represent the precondition, not the consequence, of large-scale mechanization — the extension to manufacture of the military-like discipline formerly confined to great enterprises of state. Modern industry has moved to a central position form of social organization and labor discipline that formerly once existed on the periphery of daily life. Hence the declining importance of the family, once the basic unit of production but now merely an obstacle to the complete regimentation of everyday activity. The logic of industrialization, according to Mumford's analysis, requires for its completion the extension into daily life of disciplines first perfected in the army and the monastery — institutions based on the renunciation of familial ties. "Ideally, the megamachine's personnel should consist of celibates, detached from family responsibilities, communal institutions, and ordinary human affections: such day-to-day celibacy as we actually find in armies, monasteries, and prisons." The celebration of sexuality in contemporary capitalist society does not contradict this line of analysis, since sexual "liberation" in the twentieth century goes hand in hand with the separation of sex from reproduction, from the ideal of romantic love, and finally from all its broader associations whatsoever. Far from affirming the biological basis of life, the biological differences between men and women, or the connections between human sexuality and the biological cycle of generation, decay, and renewal, the modern cult of sex holds up a purely mechanical standard of sexual satisfaction and equates sexual liberation with emancipation from nature. Thus it reaffirms the central aspiration of industrial society. The "liberation" of the sexual impulse, associated with the rejection of family ties and with an androgynous conception of personality, leads logically to the reduction of sexual pleasure to a momentary spasm — a momentary diversion from the routine of work, devoid of emotional content and serving, in Mumford's view, merely to pacify a population of drones. In Aldous Huxley's *Brave New World* — the prototype of advanced industrial civilization, in Mumford's view — a single drug, "soma," serves the entire sexual needs of the community.

By 1970, Mumford had come to the conclusion that Huxley's anti-utopia "spoke the final word" on everything "touched on in the concepts of a 'New World,' of Progress, of Utopia, and of Science Fiction." His own disenchantment with the utopian tradition — a long, gradual process — was now complete. From the very beginning of his career, Mumford had tried to fathom the meaning of utopian thought. His first book, *The Story of Utopias*, which foreshadows many of the themes of his later work, surveyed the literature of utopian speculation from Plato to H. G. Wells, treating it for the most part with sympathy and respect. Mumford saw utopianism, with its emphasis on "fundamentals," as a corrective to the "tepid and half-hearted discussions" engaged in by modern reformers and socialists, too preoccupied with "partial solutions" to concern themselves with the "life of the spirit." Utopianism, because it addressed itself to the design of the community as a whole, spoke to many of the same issues confronted by city planners. The tradition of Owenite socialism appealed to Mumford as an alternative to the "parliamentary chatter" and class "partisanship" of Marxian socialism. Although he could not suppress his distaste for the regimentation and elitism that ran through utopian thinking, he made no sustained argument against the essential emptiness of the utopian dream of a society without conflict, run by a revolutionary elite trained along monastic or military lines and freed from the discipline of daily life. In discussing Plato, Mumford took it as axiomatic that the "little utopia of the family is the enemy . . . of the beloved community." He endorsed Campanella's "remarkably keen" insight into the family's tendency to nurture the "self-love" that had to give way to love for the state. Unable in his own mind to resolve the question of how to keep the "common Utopia" from "being neglected through each one's concern for his little private utopia," he preferred to "leave this question in the air."

By 1930, Mumford had decided, as he put it in a private letter, that "life is better than utopia." The utopian tradition, he now thought, rested on the "fallacy that perfection is a legitimate goal of human existence." When he reprinted this letter in *Findings and Keepings* (1975), he added that "this conviction" was "already latent" in *The*

Story of Utopias and that after 1930 it ran through "all my writings." These remarks do not do justice to the continuing influence of utopianism on his writings of the 1930s. Both his major books of this period, *Technics and Civilization* and *The Culture of Cities*, end with the vision of a "neotechnic" utopia of steel and glass.[11] A chapter in *Faith for Living* (1940), "Life is Better than Utopia," confined itself to the commonplace argument that the "effort to achieve a permanent state of bliss would be self-negating." In 1932, Mumford published an unabashedly utopian essay in *Forum*, "The World Fifty Years from Now," which contains a compendium of clichés drawn from the tradition of both utopian and "scientific" socialism.[12] "By 1982," Mumford wrote, "the institution of private ownership . . . will have been completely deflated." Machine technology would create a new antiseptic environment and a new functionalism in art and industrial design. "Compared with the gross constructions of the coal and iron period, even the most gigantic structures of the new period will have a certain light elegance: the positive quality of the new Hudson River bridge, greatly magnified." Uneasily aware that his society of the future resembled a "well-drilled beehive," Mumford tried to counter the impression of uniformity by referring vaguely to new ways of "love-making, selective mating, the nurture of children." But the suggestion that human "breeding" would become the central science of the future hardly qualified the impression of regimentation Mumford sought to allay. His speculations about the organization of sexual life drew on the same left-wing clichés that underlay his vision of the "more refined, more efficient, more delicate" technology of the neotechnic regime. "Counter-balancing forces" that would neutralize the trend toward uniformity would "work themselves out," Mumford hoped, "on the level of communal and personal discipline, erotic and marital experiment, a whole series of new initiatives in the culture of personality."

Only in the 1960s did Mumford reject utopian thinking once and for all, together with the "dogmatic faith in technological progress"

11 The photographic sections of Mumford's book on technology and the city regularly end with glimpses of "modern machine art," the "new environment," the "new vernacular," "civic resurgence," etc. Even *The City in History* ends, pictorially, with examples of urban architecture uncomfortably reminiscent of the mood associated with the futuristic "international" style, elsewhere criticized so effectively by Mumford.

12 Notwithstanding the scorn Engels heaped on utopian socialism, "scientific" socialism differs from the utopian variety, in its vision of the good life, not because it rejects the sterile ideal of universal harmony but merely because it claims — often with little reason — to rest on a scientific study of society.

on which it rested. "I now regard utopias as instruction of What *Not* to Do," he wrote to Osborn in 1970, "or What to Avoid, since all the classic ones are static and authoritarian!" *The Pentagon of Power* contains a chapter, "Progress as Science Fiction," which brings to a close Mumford's fifty-year encounter with utopianism. Here he treats utopian fantasies not as blueprints for the good society but as unconscious "premonitions of disaster," "anticipatory subjective promptings" that demonstrate the malign possibilities of technology in advance yet break down resistance to technological "progress" by depicting it as inevitable. In *The Story of Utopias*, Mumford congratulated Edward Bellamy for his "fine motives" and criticized "only the outlets he imagined for them." He did not object to Bellamy's "conception of the good life," merely to the "structure he erected to shelter it." In *The Pentagon of Power*, on the other hand, Bellamy emerges as the spokesman for a "backward dream" – the "first authentic picture of National Socialism (German style), or State Capitalism (Russian style), in its most insidiously corrupting form, that of the providential Welfare State with all its disciplinary braces relaxed – though not removed" by the "massive bribe" of organized rewards equally distributed throughout the community.

Mumford's repudiation of utopian ideals marks the distance he travelled, during his long career as a social critic and cultural historian, from the culture of progressivism in which he and so many other intellectuals were brought up. In rejecting the progressive illusion of technological progress, however, Mumford did not join the ranks of the tired radicals who retire from social criticism or embrace conservative dogmas. His career cannot be described as a retreat to the right. On the contrary, his acknowledgment of the radical imperfectibility of human nature, his rejection of the dogma of progress, and his new respect for the character-forming discipline of daily life enabled him to become a more radical and persuasive critic of modern society. He threw off the optimistic faith that socialism (or some other program of state-sponsored social reform) will automatically liberate technology from its capitalist constraints, but he never embraced a politics of nostalgia or despair. Although he sometimes fell into the empty rhetoric of a humanism divested of social or critical content, he rejected the temptation to seek refuge in the type of humanism that condemns the present by holding it up against an idealized image of the past. A review of Huizinga's critique of modern society, *In the Shadow of Tomorrow*, published in the *New Republic* in 1936, shows that Mumford understood this temptation and firmly put it aside. Huizinga, like Mumford, deplored the contemporary drift toward barbarism, but he dismissed out of hand the entire tradition of modern thought, attributed the "lowering of the standards of critical judgment" to the influence of "Freudian psychiatry" and historical materialism, and thus deprived himself of any way of understanding the social origins of the "spiritual ailment" of modern times. In the end he left his readers only with the vague promise of a "purification of the spirit."

Mumford, on the other hand, remained true to the "sociological" mode of thought, eschewing the humanistic retreat exemplified by his friend Van Wyck Brooks and at a higher level by Huizinga. In seeking intellectual sustenance exclusively from the past, Mumford wrote, Huizinga tried "to draw warmth from the setting sun while every minute the air grows chillier." How could a modern man, "faced with many grave symptoms of collective madness, write about this dementia intelligently" if he turned his back on the work of Freud? How could a critic of modern culture, seeking to understand the connections between culture and social life, turn his back on Marx? Mumford himself condemned, no less harshly than Huizinga, the shallow modern cult of progress, its moral irresponsibility, and its "general attitude of permissiveness which has at its roots a general deflation of meaning and purpose"; but unlike Huizinga he never forgot that modern culture has itself given rise to the critical traditions that most adequately explain the contemporary crisis and point the way to its resolution. If the political implications of Mumford's work can be characterized neither as conservative nor "progressive," this is not because he pretended to stand above politics or, as superficial readers might be inclined to say, because he combined a conservative critique of modern culture with a progressive political program. Mumford's work defies political categorization because the conventional terms of political debate have lost their meaning. Work that transcends conventional categories, like Mumford's, will naturally be seen as a form of "cultural conservatism" by those who cling to the certainties of an outmoded progressive mystique. It is the champions of leftist orthodoxy, however, the "avant-garde minds cast in this old-fashioned 'progressive' mold," as Mumford once called them, who are now living in the past.

Christopher Lasch and *The Culture of Narcissism:* A Symposium

I. CRITICIZING CAPITALIST AMERICA*

BY MICHAEL FISCHER

* Review of Christopher Lasch, *The Culture of Narcissism: American Life in An Age of Diminishing Expectations* (New York: W. W. Norton, 1979).

Herbert Marcuse expressed the fears of many social critics when he lamented in *One-Dimensional Man* (1964) that "advanced industrial society is capable of containing qualitative change for the foreseeable future," not because the state represses protest or because the quality of life renders it unnecessary but because contemporary society seems able to accommodate those voices which oppose it. Eagerly embraced freedoms have only concealed "new, more effective, and more pleasant forms of social control and social cohesion." Faced with such a "greasily accommodating" status quo, to use Alfred Kazin's phrase, much radical thought (including Marcuse's) has undertaken an anxious search for grounds on which to stand, for a cultural and political base outside of capitalism from which to mount its attack. Christopher Lasch's writings, from *The New Radicalism in America* (1965) to *The Culture of Narcissism* (1979), have studied this search and sketched with singular precision the frustrations, contradictions and achievements which it has entailed. More than any other critic, he has combined sensitivity to the failings of radicalism with a defense of its underlying objectives.

The Culture of Narcissism, like *Haven in a Heartless World: The Family Besieged* (1977), advances beyond Lasch's earlier work by using psychology to complement social criticism. What Philip Rieff says of intellectuals in *The Triumph of the Therapeutic* (1966) and *Fellow Teachers* (1973) and Herbert Hendin observes of students in *The Age of Sensation* (1975) Lasch with some modifications extends to our culture as a whole, arguing that narcissism characterizes the dominant personality type of our time. He draws on the findings of clinicians to define its traits: "dependence on the vicarious warmth provided by others combined with a fear of dependence, a sense of inner emptiness, boundless repressed rage, and unsatisfied oral cravings" along with such secondary characteristics as "pseudo self-insight, calculating seductiveness, nervous, self-deprecatory humor." Unlike the nineteenth-century individualist, the "imperial self" or the "American Adam" analyzed by R. W. B. Lewis, Quentin Anderson, and others, the narcissist has no strong sense of self, so he relies on the admiration of others to give him self-esteem while at the same time resenting his dependency and their compliance. His self-absorption reflects not Emersonian egotism but its pathetic opposite, a desperate craving for attention in a world that does not seem to care or even exist.

Narcissism for Lasch registers "the psychological impact of recent social changes"; it is to our society what hysteria and obsessional neurosis were to Freud's. Our subjective response to social change obviously resists precise measurement, and not every reader will be as persuaded as I am by Lasch's evidence. He bases his attention to narcissism on the increasing rate of its occurrence in pathological form and on the presence of less severe narcissistic symptoms throughout our everyday life. These symptoms include our pervasive inability to mourn or accept old age and death; our loss of belief in the meaningfulness and even the reality of the external world, especially its persistence over time; our consequent living for the moment without regard to tradition or posterity; our anxious concern for appearances and our fascination with celebrities who have won the admiration that we covet; and, finally, our obsession with intimacy at a time when personal relations crumble under the demands for self-validation and immediate gratification that we bring to them. It is, of course, difficult to prove that these are in fact "our" attitudes but Lasch convincingly finds indications of them everywhere: in politics (where a preoccupation with spectacle has reduced political discussion to "meaningless babble" and protest to "self-promotion"); in literature (where the writer often "seeks not to provide an objective account or a representational piece of reality but to seduce others into giving him their attention, acclaim, or sympathy, and thus to shore up his faltering sense of self"); in humor (where self-deprecation has become a perfunctory "means of deflecting criticism and disclaiming responsibility"); in sexual relations (where concern for "performance" and "assertiveness" conceals a "deeper determination to manipulate the feelings of others to your own advantage"); and, finally, in the mass media (where the proliferation of images has shaken confidence in the objectivity of external reality, a commitment to novelty has weakened our sense of historical continuity, and the cult of the celebrity has exacerbated the feeling that "selfhood [is] dependent on the consumption of images of the self").

Lasch's most striking contention is that these narcissistic tendencies do not contradict American capitalism, as Daniel Bell and some conservatives would have it, but reflect what it has become. The bureaucratization of corporations has brought into the office the alienation experienced in the factory, preventing the individual from feeling responsibility for the products of his labor and from understanding its social repercussions. Service to self consequently displaces loyalty to impersonal, amorphous organizations and "success" gets defined as intra-bureaucratic advancement or survival. Because work is so abstract, moreover, the personality of the worker becomes as important as his productivity or skills in determining whether he will "get ahead." Such conditions, Lasch concludes, make narcissism not only tolerable but profitable:

> For all his inner suffering, the narcissist has many traits that make for success in bureaucratic institutions, which put a premium on the manipulation of interpersonal relations, discourage the formation of deep personal attachments, and at the same time provide the narcissist with the approval he needs in order to validate his self-esteem . . . . The management of personal impressions comes naturally to him, and his mastery of its intricacies serves him well in political and business organizations where performance now counts less than "visibility," "momentum," and a winning record. As the "organization man" gives way to the bureaucratic "gamesman"—the "loyalty era" of American business to the age of the "executive success game"—the narcissist comes into his own.

The redefinition of success at work makes leisure "an extension of commodity production" and not just in the often noted sense that the pleasures of consumption purportedly compensate for the drudgeries of one's job. Advertising intensifies the insecurity of the worker who has to sell himself to his superiors or colleagues and promises that the right commodities will give him a "winning image." Beneath the hedonistic surface of advertising lurks the message that we must survive the "war of all against all," or "the struggle for interpersonal advantage" which has invaded "even the ostensibly achievement-oriented realm of work."*

The erosion of the work ethic at the workplace and the collapse of its nineteenth-century moral and social justifications in part account for the ascendancy of narcissism. Lasch completes his etiology of narcissism by astutely noting the strains which the reorganization of work and leisure has put on education, family life, and sports, realms which put some distance between the individual and the economy. Formerly each provided relief from work and offered a critical perspective (often tacit) on its brutalizing competition. Today, however, each suffers from "the degradation of work" and becomes a new form of social control. In the family, for example, the absence of the father, the narcissism of the mother, the surrender of discipline to outside experts and ethics to the child's peer group all combine to "undermine the child's initiative and make it impossible for him to develop self-restraint or self-discipline." But, Lasch continues, "since American society no longer values these qualities anyway, the abdication of parental authority itself instills in the young the character traits demanded by a corrupt, permissive, hedonistic culture." Similarly, the weakening of liberal arts education and the inability to defend its rationale have reduced university instruction to "mindless eclecticism" and contributed to "the spread of intellectual torpor." But since the marketplace has little need for intellectual "enterprise and resourcefulness" and much less for critical thought, education equips students for work by giving them the requisite credentials without at the same time "overqualifying" them, that is, without teaching them how to think, read demanding texts, or take seriously the pre-modern past. Finally, while sports still offer rare opportunities for risk, concrete accomplishment, and physical exertion, they, too, have yielded to the prevailing distrust of group loyalties and achievement. Competition today often occurs not between the individual and standards of excellence or between teams that inspire fervid, long lasting partisanship. Contemporary athletes compete with each other, even with their own teammates, for publicity and celebrity status, making their performance on the field a relatively minor extension of what they do elsewhere (in interviews, movies,

* Lasch supports this point with reference to studies like Michael Maccoby's *The Gamesman: The New Corporate Leaders* (1976) and Stuart Ewen's *Captains of Consciousness: Advertising and the Social Roots of the Consumer Culture* (1976). Reviewing *The Culture of Narcissism* for the *Wall Street Journal*, Andrew Hacker objects that Lasch "peers at American society behind a barricade of books" and consequently succumbs to Maccoby's "all but total ignorance about how businessmen behave." But Hacker fails to specify where Lasch (and Maccoby) go wrong.

commercials, etc.). The "antagonistic cooperation" that characterizes teams comes to resemble the superficial togetherness of family life, the deceptive peace of a university campus, and the empty cohesiveness of bureaucratic institutions, all of which make for loneliness and anxious self-absorption.

If we accept this analysis, as I basically do, then we must conclude with R. P. Blackmur (whom Lasch quotes) that

> The crisis in our culture rises from the false belief that our society requires only enough mind to create and tend the machines together with enough of the new illiteracy for the other machines—those of our mass media—to exploit. This is perhaps the form of society most expensive and wasteful in human talent mankind has yet thrown off.

Lasch's disdain for inadequate solutions to this crisis seems as well-founded as his analysis of the crisis itself. The conservative argument, for example, superficially resembles his own: it also opposes, among other things, the trivialization of athletics, the disintegration of the family, and the dependence of individuals on the bureaucratized state and the "helping professions." But conservatives would remedy these ills without addressing their underlying causes, which for Lasch lie in the corruption of work under capitalism. The conservative is in the equivocal position of Michael Novak, for instance, who cries out for the insulation of sports from "business, entertainment, politics, and even gossip" without seeing that "the separation of work and leisure" that his argument presupposes "gives rise in the first place to this invasion of play by the standards of the workaday world." His escapist idea of leisure, in other words, takes for granted and indeed originates in the degradation of work; he tries to avoid the debasement of sport to entertainment which his own view of leisure makes inevitable. The conservative, in short, would reduce bureaucracy in government without contesting corporate control of production; he would restore discipline in the family without challenging the demands of a consumer economy for self-indulgence; and he would raise standards in the schools without confronting the mindlessness and shoddiness of most work elsewhere.

If conservatism is thus incomplete, what passes for radicalism in our society is self-deceived. Like Gerald Graff and others, Lasch argues that "cultural radicalism" assaults targets long since abandoned and ends up mirroring the status quo that it pretends to criticize. The "radical" critic of sports, for example, objects to their "seriousness" and "competitiveness," which presumably reinforce such "established" values as self-discipline, regimentation, and patriotism. But seriousness and competition, as Huizinga observed, are essential to athletics, and self-discipline and loyalty, Lasch adds, have little functional value in today's economy. What is wrong with sports is not their competitiveness but the specific form which competition has assumed, that is, its degeneration into struggles between individuals for attention, etc. In making sports less competitive, "radicals" collaborate with the widespread substitution of goals like self-fulfillment or peer approval for excellence and achievement; they conceal their collaboration under the guise of "liberation"; and they miss out on what remains genuinely radical about athletics, namely, the fact that they still reward effort, creativity, and cooperation in a society that has scant respect for such values. Lasch subjects the attack on "elitist" standards in education and "privatism" and "repression" in the nuclear family to much the same analysis. He rightly concludes that liberation from such constraints as the past, reason, and objective standards of truth and justice is today an empty *fait accompli*, a triumph of contemporary capitalism which "radicalism" unwittingly ratifies.

After he has distanced himself from these ostensibly radical and conservative positions, we of course wonder where Lasch himself stands. What would he have us do to rectify the conditions that he deplores? Many readers of Lasch's recent work think that he leaves this question dangling, either because he intends to pose, but not solve, the problems of our society or because he has no answer. He consequently seems to some "wholly pessimistic" and to others merely disgruntled, an ill-tempered malcontent expressing "a generalized hatred for modern life" that cannot issue in any program for change.*

These interpretations significantly do not mention that *The Culture of Narcissism*, like *Haven in a Heartless World*, resounds with solutions. Lasch calls repeatedly for a "struggle against capitalism" and the narcissistic culture that it has spawned, and for resistance to the new ruling class of "managers and professionals" who "promote and defend the system of corporate capitalism" and monopolize "the wealth that it

* In his review of *Haven in a Heartless World (New York Times Book Review*, January 15, 1978), Marshall Berman finds in Lasch this "generalized hatred" and adds that "it is perplexing and depressing to see Lasch, who was so perceptive in unmasking the radical simplifications of the 1960's seized by just the sort of nihilistic fury that marked the New Left at its worst." "Wholly pessimistic" are Frank Kermode's words, from his review of *The Culture of Narcissism* in the *New York Times Book Review*, January 14, 1979. He adds that Lasch has delivered "a civilized hellfire sermon, with little promise of salvation."

creates." "It does not seem unreasonable to believe," he writes, "even in the political passivity and quietism of the 1970's, that a thoroughgoing transformation of our social arrangements remains a possibility, and that a socialist revolution would abolish the new paternalism—the dependence of the ordinary citizen on experts, the degradation of both work and domestic life . . . ." To suggest that things can be better, that we made the present order and thus can remake it, Lasch appeals often to the pre-industrial past, not as a golden age which we should duplicate but as an alternative that calls into question the supposed necessity of our present arrangements and highlights the contradictions in our "progress." Lasch even points to "signs of new life" in the "revival and extension" of "earlier traditions of local action" and in the creation of independent "communities of competence." More bleakly, he draws on Freud in *Haven* to argue that no culture can completely socialize human nature and that outbreaks of defiance and aggression will survive the efforts of therapy and consumption to domesticate them. A reconstructed society would not eliminate pain and anxiety but neither would it have to intensify them to create a need for its commodities.

These suggestions are obviously incomplete; Lasch needs to say much more to show, for example, that a "socialist revolution" would reverse the degradation of work. It is less significant that some readers would want him to defend the adequacy of his solutions than that others, perhaps the majority, would react as if his solutions were indefensible, that is, as if their shortcomings were so obvious as to require no proof or even comment. Far from indicating toughmindedness, this jaded response may itself be the most destructive product of the crisis that Lasch would resolve. *The Culture of Narcissism* is important in part because it challenges the assumptions underlying the uncritical dismissal which it will doubtless receive from many readers. When Lasch uses the past as "a political and psychological treasury from which we draw the reserves (not necessarily in the form of 'lessons') that we need to cope with the future," he will seem to many readers to pass off as radical thinking what is actually reactionary nostalgia. But perhaps this judgment exposes not his backwardness but the imprisonment of much social criticism in a culture that despairs of the future because it is severing its links with the past. Similarly, when he appeals to "earlier traditions of local action," Lasch will appear to be pretending that a make-believe constituency is a potential political base. But maybe this criticism points not to his naivete but to the helplessness of those who make it, whose mutual distrust keeps such traditions from thriving. Finally, when he ties the need for a "socialist revolution" to such values as reason, compassion, and restraint, Lasch will seem to many critics to be anchoring his politics in airy nothing. But perhaps this retort, too, brings to light not his simplemindedness but the skepticism of a society which habitually assumes that "reason" is instrumental calculation, "authority" amoral power, and "freedom" the fleeting self-gratification that comes from outwitting or pleasing those who we keep in power.

The agony of the American left, to use the title of one of Lasch's best books, has always stemmed from its isolation from collective support and from a tradition of social criticism that would make opposition to capitalism not just a quixotic possibility but a cumulative program on which one could build. Understandably desiring influence, leftists have often modified the principles that isolate them, dignifying as "radicalism" what is actually the line of least resistance. *The Culture of Narcissism* makes no such concessions: Lasch unabashedly bases his comprehensive indictment of American culture in what will seem to many a non-existent alternative. What makes his book vulnerable to quick rejection is precisely what makes it so valuable. Lasch makes sense out of American society at a time when many of us routinely despair of mastering its "complexity" and so surrender the task of understanding it to "educators" and "experts," who splinter knowledge into expertise and thus perpetuate the very awareness of complexity that heightens dependency on their "services." He sees connections, especially between capitalism, work, and culture, where others see baffling "contradictions." He questions what conservatives unthinkingly assume is necessary and also what leftists just as dogmatically insist is radical. Challenging conventional ideas of liberation, he arrives at what may be the only way out of our present troubles.

II. THE SOLITUDE OF THE HEART: PERSONALITY AND DEMOCRATIC CULTURE

BY LARRY D. NACHMAN

"At a certain point in history," Lionel Trilling observed in his Norton Lectures, *Sincerity and Authenticity*, "men became individuals." They had arrived at a new conception of the human being and had come to view themselves in a new light. Apart from his works and deeds, apart from his social position, apart from his civic and legal standing, each person had an inner nature, a personality, which endowed his life with a special coloration and a unique significance. Like the idea of the soul of which it was a secularized version, it was universal, insofar as everyone had a personality, and it was unique, insofar as no two were identical. With the emergence of personality as the defining characteristic of the human being came the modern temptation to turn inward away from the world and worldly obligations in order to concentrate on the cultivation of the self and its inner life.

Tocqueville, who did not miss much, noted this important shift in his contemporaries' sense of their purposes and goals.

> 'Individualism' is a word recently coined to express a new idea. . . . Individualism is a calm and considered feeling which disposes each citizen to isolate himself from the mass of his fellows and withdraw into the circle of family and friends; within this little society formed to his taste, he gladly leaves the greater society to look after itself.

Tocqueville's analysis makes it clear that he was going beyond the traditional distinction between the private and the public life. He was attempting to describe a novel phenomenon which he thought to be a direct social consequence of the political revolutions of his time. He was charting the changes wrought by political democracy and its principle of human equality.

Aristocratic societies, Tocqueville held, generate stable and durable systems of relationships and institutions which situate each person in the social order and establish for him, as it did for his ancestors and will presumably continue to do for his descendants, a network of social obligations and responsibilities. Artistocratic societies, Tocqueville believed, maintain strong social bonds strengthened by family ties. These bonds were loosened by the new opportunities for social mobility which were created by the democratic upheavals of the recent past. Those newly arrived to eminence did not inherit their wealth but neither did they inherit social responsibilities. They entered a highly unstable social world in which people came and went and like all transients exhibited little care and concern for their temporary resting place. Now, each person feels he carries the burden of his life within himself. He has neither custom nor settled social conventions to help him set the course of his life. "Every man finds his beliefs within himself . . . [and] all his feelings are turned in on himself." These circumstances engender two unshakeable convictions. There is no interest other than self-interest. And one's "whole destiny" is completely within one's hands. Because it was a creation of democracy, Tocqueville believed that as democracy increased so would this new individualism.

> Thus, not only does democracy make men forget their ancestors, but [it] also clouds their view of their descendants and isolates them from their contemporaries. Each man is forever thrown back on himself alone, and there is a danger that he may be shut up in the solitude of his own heart.

It was in America that Tocqueville discerned this new man. Now, more than a century later, Christopher Lasch, in his *The Culture of Narcissism*, has written a harsh critique of contemporary America, a land whose people live, worldlessly and unaware of their worldloss, immersed in the solitude of their own hearts. It is an unlovely spectacle. In a society without binding loyalties, each person, as Tocqueville predicted, has become thrown back upon himself. The contemporary American is self-absorbed and paradoxically suffers from a diminution of self. Freudian analysis enables us to resolve this paradox. The ego, for Freud, develops at the point of contact between the human organism and the external world. The ego is a mediating agency between the instincts and reality. It is for the human being the source of rational understanding of the external world and of discovering what is possible and what is impossible. The human type which Lasch describes has not developed this faculty and remains permanently childlike, ineffective in dealing both with the world and with his own instincts.

Lasch's book depicts the deterioration of public life into a space suitable to a population of 'narcissists'. Events decay into mere experiences as attention shifts from acts which have real consequences to the inner responses of the spectators. Education is degraded, perhaps irreparably, as it abandons its responsibility to transmit knowledge about the social and natural worlds and degenerates into therapeutic exercises in self-expression. Art and literature no longer attempt to make intelligible an objective world that men share in common. On the contrary, by focusing on the purely subjective, contemporary art forms reinforce the sense people have that the world is chaotic and unknowable and that their shifting and contradictory subjective impressions are, in comparison to the external world, stable and reliable. Bureaucracies carve up the various components of human life into separate jurisdictions and enforce their claims that only specialists acting on behalf of the public interest are competent and entitled to manage matters which traditionally were regarded as private concerns. Individuals, having had important decisions taken out of their hands, become, in fact, incompetent to deal with reality. The one area left to people is the cultivation of their inner lives. The result of all this is an insatiable mass market for therapeutic cults and for new devices and strategies of self-improvement.

Lasch does well in his dissection of the social forms of privatism gone amuk. One would hope that those readers who have made *The Culture of Narcissism* a best seller would take his criticisms to heart. But it is hard to allay the suspicion that the book's success is itself a result of what Lasch attacks. The narcissist enjoys reading about himself and may well relegate the book to his growing shelf of self-awareness literature. If so, it would be a pity. The book deserves a better fate.

My quarrel with Lasch is not with his excellent portrayal of contemporary culture but with his theoretical and historical explanation of the emergence of a 'culture of narcissism'. For Lasch, the personality type and the culture associated with it are products of 'late industrial capitalism'. Lasch's attack is principally directed against not the owners of productive enterprises, who scarcely appear in his pages, but the new managerial, professional and governmental elites who have arrogated to themselves the power to direct the day-to-day behavior of masses of people.

In attacking progressive education, the bureaucracies of the social services, and the various institutions of psychobabble, Lasch is well aware that he is echoing parallel criticisms made by conservatives over the last generation. But inasmuch as his sources, descriptions, and analyses all have an exclusively American focus, it is unclear whether he is equally aware that this confluence of conservative and radical critiques is as old as industrial society. It was the conservative Carlyle who coined the term "cash nexus". Earlier, Coleridge and Southey had inveighed against the social destruction wrought by the selfishness of the new industrialists. And Burke himself protested against the coming age of "sophists, economists, and calculators". These earlier criticisms were directed, to be sure, against the individualism of 'economic man'. Now it is the individualism of 'psychological man' that has been called into account and yet again we see the convergence of conservative and radical positions.

This convergence of political polarities occurs because both conservatism and radicalism are engaged in a systematic opposition to the culture and politics of contemporary liberal democracy. They are drawn irresistably to a common set of targets and therefore often share a terminology and line of attack. It is important to recognize this triangular relationship of radicalism, conservatism and liberalism not only to sort out their differing social prescriptions but also to clarify the precise nature of their analyses of society.

One theme which is often employed both by conservatives and radicals is a vision of a better past set against which the present appears to be an age in decline. For the conservative, the decline is generally a matter of moral failing, the failure to retain the superior moral values of the past. For the radical, the past means the point before the current prevailing political and economic arrangements came into force. Conservatives and radicals often have a proclivity to make the past appear somewhat brighter than it actually was. Lasch's account of contemporary society is to a degree built up out of such an invidious comparison of the present with a better time in the past. He tells us that "the belief that in some ways the past was a happier time by no means rests on a sentimental illusion." But what was it in the past that prevented the emergence of narcissistic trends? To answer this question will help to test Lasch's thesis that the 'culture of narcissism' is a product of late industrial capitalism.

The world which preceded our own was based on authority. Because, as Hannah Arendt observed, "authority has vanished from the modern world", it is well to remember that authority once meant more than mere legitimacy and much more than simple respect. Authority meant the unconditional acceptance of an obligation to obey persons and institutions whose right to command was perceived as a datum of the world rather than as a result of rational persuasion or deliberate choice. Some historical examples may evoke this lost social bond. When Henry, Earl of Richmond and head of the house of Lancaster, defeated Richard III at Bosworth, he assumed the throne of England as Henry VII. Under Yorkist rule, he and other Lancastrian nobles had been under attaint. They were 'outlaws' and were deprived of all legal existence. Henry's first Parliament took up the question and one by one and in separate acts it removed the attaint from the Lancastrians. But when they came to the case of Henry, they did not act in a similar way to restore him to his rights. The learned members knew better. They merely observed for the record that he was "discharge dascun attainter eo facto que il prist sur luy le raigne & este Roy." ("discharged from any attaint by the fact that he had taken the realm upon himself and was King.") The king was king and could not have his status determined by those who gave justice under his authority. It is in the nature of authority to answer all challenges with the assertion, "I am that I am".

Much later, in the Seven Bishops' Case, a sedition trial arising in the turmoil of England in 1688, Judge Allybone presciently remarked,

> No man can take upon himself to write against the actual exercise of the government, unless he has leave of the government, for if

> once we come to impeach the government by way of argument, it is the argument that makes it the government or not the government.

Allybone believed that once government became a subject of discussion, of 'argument', government would no longer rest on its own authority but would be presumed to rest on the best or most persuasive argument, that is to say, on reason. In a world ruled by authority, institutions are not rationally defended because its defenders understand that reason is inherently subversive of authority.

One last, late echo of the dying world of authority is to be found in John Henry Newman's attack on liberalism.

> Now by Liberalism I mean false liberty of thought, or the exercise of thought upon matters, in which, from the constitution of the human mind, thought cannot be brought to any successful issue, and therefore is out of place. Among such matters are first principles of whatever kind. . . . Liberalism then is the mistake of subjecting to human judgement those revealed doctrines which are in their nature beyond and independent of it, and of claiming to determine on intrinsic grounds the truth and value of propositions which rest for their reception simply on the external authority of the Divine Word.

Newman, like Allybone, realized that the notion of reason, along with its counterpart, rational judgment, was incompatible with the principle of authority.

Before there were bureaucrats and experts, social service professionals and manuals of self-help, people did not act self-reliantly guided by their own intelligent judgments. They lived under the sway of authority and they knew what to do with their lives and with their children's because they received knowledge about these matters from authorities to whom all submitted.

Authority is associated with what Durkheim called the 'sacred' character of institutions as opposed to their 'profane' utilitarian functions. The emotional responses to authority partake of awe and dread. The binding force of morality was derived from the authority of the institutions which organized and gave coherence to each society. In the West, it was, above all, Christianity which affirmed the reality of the world as God's creation and, through the priesthood, gave direction to people's lives. Clearly, no matter how dismal the present, this is a past to which neither Lasch nor I would have us return. As Philip Rieff, the supreme diagnostician of psychological man, has put it,

> [Past communities] appear attractive only now, in distant retrospect, but the modern individual, faced with the necessity of merging his own life into communal effort, would have found them suffocating.

But if we can no longer live with authority, it is yet to be determined whether we can live without it.

Judge Allybone was indeed right. It was 'argument' that soon undermined the authority of institutions. The rationalism of the Enlightenment established two revolutionary principles: 1) that social and political institutions were not mysteries but were completely intelligible, and, 2) that institutions which could not give a rational account of their functions and benefits did not deserve to exist. This rationalization of society and politics had highly individualistic and democratic implications. It soon was widely held that any rational person could understand the principles of politics and that only ignorance, remedied by education, was a bar to universal participation in politics. Economic man was essentially a rational being capable of understanding his own interests and the best judge on how to achieve them.

Yet, this democratic and individualistic rationality did contain the starting-point for those bureaucratic and professional institutions which were later to claim that they alone were competent to make vital decisions about the lives of individuals. Lasch associates these institutions with late industrial capitalism and suggests that the scope and content of their activities are necessarily in conformity with the basic interests of the holders of economic power. But, as Lasch knows, social service bureaucracies have typically been reformist and strongly identified with their clients among the poor. Even today, corporate officials complain as bitterly of bureaucratic interference as Lasch does. Lasch, like many of those who speak of 'corporate liberalism', is too casual in his identification of contemporary liberals with defenders of economic elites. He blurs lines which are best kept distinct if liberalism is to be understood.

The impetus of contemporary liberalism is best suggested in the title of a work to which Lasch refers, *Euthenics: The Science of Controllable Environment*. Liberalism today is characterized by its almost unbounded faith in the possibility of controlling the environment. Liberalism asserts that all human problems are social, that they are solvable through the manipulation of social institutions, and that social institutions are completely amenable to the operations of human will and intelligence. The intellectual foundations of this strain in liberalism are to be found in the reigning behaviorism of American social science. Lasch is right to raise the question whether it would be preferable to take back from the social engineers some of the functions which they have assumed. But there is another question which ought to be asked first. Is what they say true? The claims of experts that they can produce desired results are rarely challenged. But before one gives them power to rear and educate children, rehabilitate criminals, transform cities, and establish new social relations, one ought at least to demand some evidence to back up the immodest claims that are routinely made.

Be that as it may, if I am right in this instance, that the roots of the bureaucratization of everyday life lie in principles which are also basic to the case for democracy and equality, a more general issue arises which touches the heart of Lasch's analysis. Lasch regards the narcissistic personality as a typical product of a stage of capitalism. Tocqueville's work, on the other hand, suggests another explanation. Tocqueville had insisted that the progress of democracy would inevitably lead to a retreat from social commitments towards exclusively privatistic concerns. Furthermore, Tocqueville believed that the triumph of the principle of equality was intimately linked with what we would today call 'modernization'. Lasch relates the evils he describes to one particular form of modern society. One may ask whether they are rather the necessary fruits of modernity itself.

The dissolution of tradition and authority, the rationalization of social life, and the termination of hereditary social status are essential to the process by which "men became individuals". The status of the human being was no longer settled by birth. Each person was presumed to have the opportunity to make a life for himself and therefore status came to be regarded as a personal and individual achievement. This change involved both a growth of personal freedom and an increased moral burden as matters which had traditionally been settled by society devolved upon the individual. Even religion became a matter of social choice. What had once been the guarantee of the reality of the created world and the basis of social cohesion had been reduced to another experience of the individual.

The principle of equality intensified this moral burden of the individual. I do not speak of juridical or political equality. It is rather that the notion of equality expanded beyond its political origins and came to be applied to the personality itself. Not only were all personalities equal but all inner feelings were equally valid. Authenticity replaced morality and sincerity replaced judgment. Each person had an equal claim to happiness, the only goal of life left to modern man, and each person had an unquestioned right to define for himself what happiness meant. Lasch omits an important characteristic of the self-absorbed personality, his naive ignorance of the tragic dimension. Like an infant crying in rage, he believes that it is possible for all desires to be satisfied. He cannot recognize those occasions when reality is truly intractible. Other people are regarded as instruments of satisfaction of desires. The furthest concession he will make to the independent existence of other human beings is to believe that they are like himself, that is to say, infantile. All human relationships are transformed into contracts for the mutual satisfaction of desires with the understanding that the contracts dissolve the moment they no longer produce pleasure. Each person exists as a world unto himself and is convinced that he has special talents which can be developed, special needs which must be met, and that all conflicts are actually resolvable problems of communication. Having made psychological demands upon society which cannot be met, modern man is no longer capable of demanding of society that which society alone can give, however imperfectly: justice. Happiness, as Freud remarked, may not be within "the plan of creation". But society can provide a measure of dignity, a limitation on deprivation and some moral foundation to life. What it cannot do is to give a guarantee of bliss and beatitude.

No society, however benign, can be adequate to the demands of the modern individual for psychic satisfaction. It is not puzzling why this most extreme positing of the claims of the self turns out to lead to such massive loss of self-confidence and sense of mastery of the world. The personality, doomed to disappointment by its own excessive expectations, must necessarily find itself thwarted and alternately blames the world and itself for not finding the end of its quest.

Lasch fails to confront the most dangerous vicissitude of the personality type he depicts. Such people, desperate for a place in a real human world, may be willing to sacrifice all personal freedom in return for admission into a human community. Rather than cling to their all too weak egos, they may turn to authoritarian communities where they will gain the presence of a strong super-ego, the leader who will care for and chastise them. This is not to say that a society bound by tradition and authority can actually be recreated in a modern world. It was the medieval Arabian philosopher, Al-Ghazali, who best explained why such a return is impossible.

> There is no hope in returning to a traditionalist faith after it has once been abandoned since the essential condition in the holder of a traditionalist faith is that he should not know he is a traditionalist.

The danger of all nostalgia, whether conservative or radical, for lost social worlds is that such nostalgia may issue in that which is well within the competence of modern man to choose and construct, totalitarian cults or societies. The communitarian solution to narcissism is not only not a solution but may represent a form of narcissism. Otto Fenichel has explored this phenomenon of secondary narcissism.

> Religious ecstasy, patriotism, and similar feelings are characterized by the ego's participation in something unattainably high. Many social phenomena are rooted in the "omnipotents'" promise to the powerless of the desired passive participation on condition of their fulfillment of certain rules.

Social controls are not necessarily imposed on people from above. Even severe controls may, on the contrary, be welcomed by large numbers of people not simply because of the practical benefits they receive but because they identify with the power represented by the controls.

Lasch believes that "the growth of management and the proliferation of the professions represent new forms of capitalist control". It is hard to understand what is gained by this explanation. Not all forms of control are capitalist and the term seems to lose its content when it is extended beyond its economic meaning of ownership of productive resources. The problem here, I believe, is primarily political. The technocratic impulse, which is so strong in contemporary liberalism, originated in the Enlightenment faith in man's ability to solve human problems rationally. Particularly in pre-Marxist socialism, this salutary creed expanded to a belief in the practical omnipotence of men to manipulate and control the human world at will. The belief that unlimited good may be accomplished leads easily to the demand for power to do that good. There has perhaps been no better motto for this technocracy than the one Engels provided. "The government of persons is replaced by the administration of things." It is just that the "things" administered have turned out to be human beings.

The narcissist and the technocrat share an incapacity to recognize those occasions when nothing can be done, when problems cannot be solved. They are caught up in what Freud called the 'omnipotence of thought', the infantile belief that wishes can spontaneously change the external world. A fragment from an ancient Egyptian medical text has been preserved which bears witness to the transition from magical to rational thinking. The text informs the apprentice physician that if a person has suffered an injury such that the crown of the head feels soft "like an infant's", the doctor should "walk away, for he can do nothing". The magician, of course, recognizing no limitation on his powers, would persist in his efforts to the very end. Opposed to the "omnipotence of thought" is the reality principle, the capacity to see the world as it is rather than as a projection of our wishes. The reality principle is nothing more than the idea of truth as it was developed in classical antiquity and handed down to us. This long tradition of truth-seeking and concern for knowledge of the world, the source of the only measure of mastery of the world available to us, is decaying before our eyes.

Lasch knows that the canons of intellectual inquiry are a corrective to the failings of modern man. He has aptly and intelligently defended these canons against those opponents who are, sad to say, to be found throughout the American educational system, both in higher and lower education. Perhaps the most melancholy product of the age of psychological man is the loss of the idea of truth as statements have come to be viewed solely as expressions of the self and are no longer regarded as having reference to the world shared in common. Lasch eloquently denounces the most recent "trahison des clercs" as educators no longer demand of themselves, their colleagues and their students the most elementary attention to evidence and proof or the rudiments of disciplined inquiry. This reluctance to recognize the possibility of truth is a prime instance of the modern rebellion against reality. But here too modern democracy has contributed to the processes undermining the reality principle.

It was Plato who first demonstrated that truth was a matter of knowledge as opposed to mere opinion. The modern political principle of democracy requires an equality of opinions in the political realm. Each person's judgment is to count equally. But this political requirement has overstepped its political boundaries and has been transformed into the general claim that all opinions, whatever their merit, are equally valid. All those who challenge this misapplication of democratic principles today are likely to be charged with being 'elitist'. (I am sure that Lasch, who perpetuates in his own work the rational and critical standards of truth-seeking, has had this epithet directed against him.) Still, those who would resist the final triumph of the course of contemporary culture would do well to cling to this slender and fragile reed of reason and rational discourse.

The contemporary situation is bleak. A retreat to a better past is impossible. What is all too possible is a plunge into a society whose deepest attraction would be its promise to curtail severely or annihilate all personal freedoms in order to provide men once again with the authority they crave. Given the present state of affairs, this is as likely to occur as is any intensification of the current trend towards a population of self-absorbed irresponsible individuals. The choices appear to be a population permanently stuck in adolescence or a population eagerly accepting the aegis of a severe, chastising parent.

Not only the contemporary personality but bureaucracy too is a product of modernity and of democracy. Bureaucracy replaced a system of privileged officeholders. Historically, bureaucracy was an instrument of kings who wished to become independent of the aristocracy which claimed to participate in government as a matter of hereditary right. This new form of administration was eminently adapted to the needs of democracy. The impersonality of bureaucracy is at least in part the consequence of the democratic demand for impartiality in the administration of government. What has become a cause of alarm in this century is the enlargement of the power of bureaucrats to make policy decisions and to exercise powers which were once regarded as properly legislative. But those who, like Lasch, deplore the absence of civic responsibility in the contemporary world might reflect that, though often submerged by cynicism, there is an exemplary tradition of democratic public service that is to be found among modern civil servants. One might consider that the modern culture-hero Faust, the prototypical self-seeker, found his contentment as a civil servant draining marshlands. That image meant much to the author of *Faust*, the Privy Councilor to the Duke of Saxe-Weimar.

If it is true that the current culture is a fixture of modernity, then its principal features will not be altered by social reform or radical reconstruction. The best strategy, perhaps, is to shore up those remaining elements of our culture which can serve as a counterpoise to its more destructive tendencies. Critical inquiry is one such. But there is another important element of our culture which preserves a conception of the individual that stands opposed to psychological man. I am speaking of the Anglo-American legal tradition in which the individual appears as a bearer of legal rights and responsibilities. Management by bureaucracies and a psychoanalytic account of the human being share in common a tendency to diffuse responsibility. Law, on the other hand, assigns responsibility solely to the individual and, by so doing, may be the last agency in our society to treat people as adults and moral agents. The individual as the law perceives him is a moral being who acts and whose acts have moral consequences. This is in marked contrast to the therapeutic conception of the individual whose acts are regarded as symptoms and emanations of the inner self. But even here, this strong and venerable tradition of law has been eroded as psychoanalytic and sociological concepts have penetrated into legal thought. To the extent that it is possible, we would do well to restore the older legal concepts and preserve the judicial system from being absorbed into the empire of psychological man.

Certainly, not all manifestations of modern individualism are to be condemned. Associated with the notion of legal responsibility is the conception of the individual as a bearer of rights—particularly rights against the government. Perhaps the greatest achievement of modern politics is the creation of a system of individual rights legally protected by the courts. In the century of totalitarianism the importance of libertarian ideas and institutions in resisting totalitarianism should be obvious. Moreover, although we may now be suffering from an excess of privatism, it should be remembered that it was not too long ago that large masses of people flocked to cities to escape the confined life of traditionalist communities. Lasch correctly senses that we have not yet learned to live well in the world that is ours. But he is overly optimistic in his expectation that a better society would resolve the dilemmas of modernity. At best, we can try to avert the worst of the vicissitudes of modern life. Beyond that, we can learn to have more modest and realistic expectations of what can be achieved in our personal and social life. Then and only then, we may discover how significant and important some small but real accretions in social and individual life can be. For the present, Philip Rieff has the best of advice.

> With no place to go for lessons in the conduct of contemporary life, every man must learn, as Freud teaches, to make himself at home in his own grim and gay little Vienna.

III. MOBILIZING THE RANKS OF REALITY

BY JANICE DOANE and DEVON LEIGH HODGES

Christopher Lasch is the most flamboyant of the contemporary writers who have declared war on "anti-realist" modes of representation. In a recent issue of *Salmagundi* (Summer-Fall, 1978) these writers—Gerald Graff, Lasch, and others—contributed to a forum on the "politics of anti-realism", a forum which took up arms against the chaos they claimed has been generated by modernist and post-modernist aesthetics. In his best-selling book, *The Culture of Narcissism*, Lasch continues to fight passionately for "reality itself," for the truth that lies outside the masks of words and images.[1] The war has escalated because American culture is permeated by unreality: literary texts no longer represent the real world, faith in history has collapsed, and most important, the very selfhood of man suffers from a "narcissistic impoverishment."[2]

As Lasch tells the story, this narcissistic impoverishment is emblematic of the final evolution of bourgeois individualism—our contemporary hedonistic, permissive, consumer society. The self-made Protestant who once stood solidly at the center of American society has been seduced away from his own truth by a professional elite that "has surrounded people with 'symbolically mediated information' and has substituted images of reality for reality itself" (CN, 221). This betrayal of an essential reality by what lies external to it both provokes and justifies his relentless attack on what he calls "prefabricated spectacles": modern literature, the theatre of the absurd, politics, sports, education, the awareness movement. Christopher Lasch, then, would seem to align himself with a familiar radical position which claims that decadence is the ultimate expression, the end point, of bourgeois individualism and its economic and political vehicle, capitalism.

Yet Lasch insists that he parts ways not only with political conservatives but also with cultural radicals. Both groups, Lasch contends, unconsciously support the society they would criticize. Cultural radicals attack "bastions long since surrendered: the patriarchal family, repressive sexual morality, the conventions of literary realism."[3] The corporation, the advertising industry, and the mass culture industry have long ago co-opted these demands by replacing patriarchy with "friendly" paternalism, and the work ethic with a consumer ethic which is not only tolerant of, but deeply dependent upon constant innovation and novelty, hedonistic morality and the rage for sexual and creative fulfillment. The conservatives, on the other hand, advocate the free expansion of the economy and so simply encourage more bureaucracy in both government and business. They, too, miss the right target—bureaucracy. The rise of bureaucracy has meant erosion of the standards with which Lasch is deeply sympathetic: self-sufficiency, discipline, order, sobriety, moderation, and thrifty industry.

1 Christopher Lasch, "Recovering Reality," *Salmagundi* No. 42 (Summer-Fall, 1978), p. 47.

2 Christopher Lasch, *The Culture of Narcissism: American Life In An Age of Diminishing Expectations* (New York: W.W. Norton & Co., 1978), p. xviii.

3 Lasch, "Recovering Reality," p. 44.

As the values he espouses indicate, Lasch is profoundly conservative, yet he recognizes—with deep regret—that there is no returning to the "patriarchal family", to the systems of authority which he sees as the only means of reinforcing those values. But though he unhappily admits his separation from a better past, Lasch will not allow himself the comfort of radical social theory with its optimistic teleology. He cannot attach himself to a political position, conservative or radical, because he sees political activity as trapped in the status quo of the present and unable to bring about real change. So he does not try to be political, if we understand by "political" a commitment to working towards change. Instead, he limits his intention to a "description" of what he calls in his subtitle "American Life in An Age of Diminishing Expectations." "Much could be written about the signs of new life in the United States. This book, however, describes a way of life that is dying..." (CN, xv).

As he ranges over every aspect of American society: our literature, forms of entertainment, education, businesses and political movements, Lasch narrates a history for each of these sectors of life which becomes a narration of degeneration and especially of *loss*. The "evidence" that supports this dark cultural history is, however, an illusion, a golden myth. Lasch believes in an ideal past, in the sobriety, enterprise and surprisingly "appropriate" acquisitiveness of the early capitalist. But if such a valorization of an earlier form of capitalism seems unlikely, and is hardly persuasive, he too is uneasy with it: "It is a tribute to the peculiar horror of contemporary life that it makes the worst features of earlier times—the stupefaction of the masses, the obsessed and driven lives of the bourgeois seem attractive by comparison . . . the prison life of the past looks in our own time like liberation itself" (CN, 99). Lasch attempts to make his idealization of "prison life" more palatable and more legitimate by claiming in his preface that "many radical movements of the past have drawn strength and sustenance from the myth or memory of a golden age in the still more distant past" (CN, xviii).

Myth or memory? Lasch's equivocation is revealing. Myth and memory are rhetorically opposed as alternative realms even as they collapse into the emergence of a nourishing illusion. The effect of his rhetorical gesture to keep these realms separate is that his own later narratives of the past—the sustaining illusion, if we keep in mind his preface—can then be offered as an objective account. It is no wonder, then, that Lasch speaks of the 19th century novel in glowing terms. For the central device of realism—offering an illusion as an objective truth—is his own device. Lasch conveniently neglects, or is ignorant of, the way in which 19th century novels were not only self-consciously aware of their status of duplicity but prompted that awareness on the part of their audiences.

Yet the 19th century novel did allow the pretense of faithful mimesis to be kept up and this illusion, according to Lasch, is good because it is sustaining, nourishing, and "healthy." Twentieth century art, on the other hand, is characterized as bordering upon the pathological because it puts into question the art work's previous status as a faithful copy of reality and focuses almost entirely upon its own conventions, forms and techniques. Twentieth century art can only be seen as degenerate if one can believe, as Lasch does, that the only form of illusion possible is traditional mimesis.

Mimesis is disrupted by the narcissist who is overly self-conscious and unable to suspend disbelief. And so it is not surprising that in the rise of the narcissist Lasch finds the most telling symptoms of the fatal malaise of contemporary society. Filled with nostalgia, yet incapable of learning from the past, the narcissist seeks only immediate gratification. Restless, empty, bored, the narcissist is hungry for self-knowledge yet capable of only pseudo self-insight. Deeply dependent, yet incapable of sustaining personal relationships, the narcissist has no access to a meaningful future. On the basis of a reported increase in the number of narcissistic patients in this country, Lasch generalizes his analysis of the narcissistic individual to collective behavior: "After the turmoil of the sixties, Americans have retreated to purely personal preoccupations" (CN, 4). From the self-made man of earlier times, the American has decayed to the self-depleted narcissist of the present.

Lasch's view of the narcissist is supposedly a psychoanalytic one, but Freud describes the narcissist as having not an "impoverished" self but an "intact" one. In his essay, "On Narcissism: An Introduction," Freud opposes the narcissist, who chooses himself as a love object, to the individual capable of loving objects that are truly other than himself. According to Freud, these two types of object-choice are related to the sex of the lover: real object-choice is characteristic of men, the narcissistic type is common in women. This sexual dichotomy leads to a certain "incongruity"—the narcissist is the object of apparently selfless desire:

> It seems very evident that one person's narcissism has a great attraction for others who have renounced part of their own narcissism and are seeking after object-love. . . . It is as if we envied them [women, children, animals] their power of retaining a blissful

> state of mind—an unassailable libido-position which we ourselves have since abandoned.[4]

In his longing for an "intact" self, Lasch reveals that he is captivated by the narcissism he seems to oppose.

René Girard has explored the "incongruity" of a selfless desire for an "intact" self. In "Narcissism: The Freudian Myth Demythified by Proust" he shows that the supposedly selfless desire for the narcissist is actually a desire for a mythic "self-sufficiency."

> Nothing is more logical, therefore, than the superficially paradoxical conjunction of self-centeredness and other-centeredness. Freud does not perceive that logic, or he refuses it because he insists on viewing what he calls 'object-desire' as a selfless gesture, a deliberate virtuous sacrifice of 'self-sufficiency,' rather than a fascination for an alien 'self-sufficiency,' forced upon us by a state of severe and involuntary deprivation in which human beings might generally find themselves in regard to that commodity.[5]

The proof that human beings are "deprived" of "self-sufficiency" is the fact of their desire: "Wherever there is self-sufficiency there is no desire; the notion of a narcissistic or self-sufficient desire is a contradiction in terms."[6]

In both Freud and Girard the notion of desire is crucial to understanding the concept of narcissism, and yet Lasch does not explicitly discuss desire. When Lasch uses the language of desire—words such as "restless", "hungry", "empty", "searching", all of which suggest the lack which generates desire—he uses it only in describing the narcissist. Thus it seems that only the narcissist desires and Lasch does not. He refuses to desire because it is not efficacious: the past is irretrievable, the future is empty, the present is occupied by narcissists. And the narcissists are notably deaf: "it does no good to confront the narcissist with a moral argument against this incapacity or to persuade or exhort him to change his ways" (CN,89). Suspicious both

4 Sigmund Freud, "On Narcissism: An Introduction," *General Psychological Theory*, ed. Philip Rieff (New York: Collier, 1976), p. 70.

5 René Girard, "Narcissism: The Freudian Myth Demythified by Proust," *Psychoanalysis, Creativity and Literature*, ed. Alan Roland (New York: Columbia University Press, 1978), p. 298.

6 *Ibid.*, p. 301.

of his own impulse to deliver sermons and of the capacity to change on the part of those who would most benefit from his address, Lasch is apparently condemned to an ineffectual discourse. This acknowledged ineffectuality, this knowledge of his own lack which both undercuts and yet informs his own intention, perhaps accounts for the obvious passion with which the book conducts its war. The contradiction between his claims and his aggressive rhetoric suggests that Lasch does not lack desire; he simply denies it.

As Girard points out, where there is desire there is no blissfully intact self. In so far as Lasch sees narcissists everywhere—those hungry, searching, depleted selves—he inadvertently admits the inescapable connection between desire and the loss of the self. However, by insisting that narcissism is only a contemporary condition, he protects himself from acknowledging his own desire, a desire that compels him to create a mythic past. How can we explain his investment in that golden past? An explanation would seem to require a revised notion of the self—one that would explain how desire, a lack within the subject, propels him toward the dream of an intact self. If we believe in the reality of this self, as Lasch does, we are condemned to feel guilty about our insufficiency and our desires. That is exactly what Lasch wants his readers to feel. But if we are more concerned with understanding our condition than condemning it, we must look beyond Lasch's puritan psychology.

A revised notion of the self is articulated in the writings of Jacques Lacan. In his well-known essay on the mirror stage, Lacan provides a radical psychoanalytic conception of the formation of the "I" that argues against Lasch's belief in the irreducible reality of the self. According to Lacan, the self is constituted when a child assumes the image of himself provided by a mirror. This narration of the self's formation links rather than separates self and image. "The mirror stage," says Lacan, "is a drama whose internal thrust is precipitated from insufficiency to anticipation—and which manufactures for the subject caught up in the lure of spatial identification, the succession of phantasies that extends from a fragmented body-image to a form of its totality that I shall call orthopaedic—and, lastly, to the assumption of the armour of an alienating identity, which will mark with its rigid structure the subject's entire mental development." In this history of the self, primary narcissism is a "jubilant" product of the mirror stage in which the child attaches himself to a specular image without recognizing that the "I" is objectified in something alien to itself. Lacan, then, is able to provide the self with a moment in which it obtains a satisfying unity with the image that constitutes it.

By contrast, in his history of the constitution of the psyche, Lasch bypasses the importance of the image by elevating the "real." The proper self of the past, he says, was able to internalize images of authority which guaranteed a sense of reality by inhibiting the archaic and aggressive phantasies of the id. The superego, thus formed and strengthened, became a guarantor of reality. When these authoritative images are not incorporated, as they are not in the present, the superego apparently becomes as phantastic as the id. Here we have a dichotomy between a self based in reality, the "proper" self, and one that is wholly fictional, the narcissist. This dichotomy, with its hierarchical valorization of the "real", is only possible because Lasch keeps under erasure the images which constitute the "proper" self in the first place. With similar acts of erasure Lasch privileges the categories of "reality" and the "past."

Lasch's aggressively antithetical system of representation relies not only upon keeping a whole series of realms opposed and separated: life and art, reality and image, work and play, male and female, self and other, but also on keeping the term on the left as a referent of the term on the right. And so does the narcissist become the whore, for narcissists—be they experimental novelists, advertising executives, corporation presidents, cultural radicals, black pride advocates or feminists—are notably unfaithful to the referent and responsible for its loss.

The self-controlled male of the nineteenth century, in other words, has given way to the self-indulgent woman of the present. "In our time," Lasch reports, "the happy hooker stands in place of Horatio Alger as the prototype of personal success. If Robinson Crusoe embodied the ideal type of economic man, the hero of bourgeois society in its ascendancy, the spirit of Moll Flanders presides over its dotage" (CN, 53).

The myth of the self-controlled male and the self-absorbed female is authorized by Freud's essay on narcissism. As we have seen, in this essay Freud creates the figures of the selfless man and the marvelous but self-centered woman he desires. In Freud's view this sexual incongruity produces a domestic tragedy: man loves a woman who cannot love him in return. But a man can assuage his disappointment with the knowledge that he has renounced narcissism and is therefore morally superior to the woman who scorns him. In Freud's scenario, then, woman occupies both the desired place of the intact self and the condemned position of the shallow narcissist. As Lasch points out, contemporary feminists have called into question this combined image of degradation and idealization; but their question is actually a profound threat. For when woman moves out of her "proper" position she breaks the mirror which establishes the "reality" of male identity and shatters the illusion of his superiority. When this happens, we move into the reign of woman.

According to Lasch, the reign of woman is equally destructive of men and women. Women are now deprived of the limited but secure social role that formerly protected them from male violence; men are increasingly impotent, having acquired a terrible fear of women: "the cruel, destructive, domineering woman, la belle dame sans merci, has moved from the periphery of literature and other arts to a position close to the center" (CN, 203). What is striking about this description is the horror with which it depicts the movement of the male into the position of the woman. The shifting location of men and women makes Lasch understandably hysterical—he loses part of himself. Lasch interprets this loss within the model of male domination: he suffers, and says that we all suffer, the condition of women dominated by men and dependent on them for survival. The "New Paternalism", the professional elite, gives us all the degraded status of women.

So emphatic is Lasch's need to enforce hierarchical structures that this abject conclusion is inevitable. He cannot imagine how the changing position of women and men could produce anything other than an even more oppressive society ruled by the father. But there is a gap in his logic. In collapsing oppositions so that art is no longer distinguishable from life, reality from image, work from play, male from female, the narcissist, the decentering woman, poses a powerful challenge to the patriarchal order. Lasch is more accurate than he knows when he writes in his preface: "Much more could be written about signs of new life in the United States. This book, however, describes a way of life that is dying. . . ." Or better, a privileged "reality" that is dying. The signs of new life cannot be spoken by Lasch because they subvert the antitheses — real and non-real, male and female — on which his text depends. It is in the play of figures which are not opposed to each other, and not the same, that a new symbolic order will be articulated.

The *New York Times Bestseller List* describes *The Culture of Narcissism* as a "hellfire sermon on the decay permeating American life." It is located on the list between two self-help books: a book which proposes another way to prevent decay—by extolling the joy of running, and a book which Lasch would undoubtedly deem worthy of a puritanical sermon—*How to Get Everything You Want Out of Life*. The placement of his text is easy to explain. Lasch's refusal of a modernist and post-modernist discourse, a refusal of the possibilities created by new modes of articulation, condemns him to repeat the discourse of the experts he berates. Those experts, like Lasch, insist that they can bring "reality" to a reader and help him discover his true self.

But perhaps Lasch's sense of an ending marks the close of the "faithful" language of mimesis he produces and castigates. This mode of representation gained its authority by asserting the unreality of the speech of others while denying its own artifice. By exposing this strategy, "anti-realists" have indeed subverted the power of traditional mimesis but they have not, as Lasch insists, repudiated politics. Without challenging the authoritarian ideologies which pretend to appropriate and master "reality" how can a writer hope to be political? Paradoxically it is Lasch, the "realist", who retreats from politics in the name of a ghostly reality of the past. And so he is melancholy. But the reader of *The Culture of Narcissism* may feel otherwise, for recorded in this book is the rise of a language located beyond the rhetoric of the "real"—a language which articulates new relations between men and women, masters and slaves.

IV. POLITICS AND SOCIAL THEORY: A REPLY TO THE CRITICS

BY CHRISTOPHER LASCH

Not only its detractors but even some of its admirers have misread *The Culture of Narcissism* as a "jeremiad," an "iconoclastic" exposure of our moral decay and self-seeking, a "sermon" on the evils of self-absorption and the baneful influence of special-interest groups. Although I have no intention of disavowing the ethical dimension of the book, I regard *The Culture of Narcissism* as a contribution to social theory and social criticism, not to the literature of moral indignation. Rooted in my earlier work, it attempts on the one hand to carry on and deepen the criticism of the American left begun in *The New Radicalism* and *The Agony of the American Left*, and on the other hand to show how changes in the American family, analyzed in *Haven in a Heartless World*, have produced a new type of personality structure, one that exhibits in varying degrees the characteristics of secondary or pathological narcissism.

In its concern with personality and the family, *The Culture of Narcissism* not only continues my own previous work but grows out of a long tradition of culture-and-personality studies, which have tried to establish links between the organization of culture and the psychological mechanisms through which culture is reproduced in individuals. The book derives also from a tradition of social criticism—the tradition of Herbert Marcuse, Max Horkheimer, the early Erich Fromm, and before them Marx and Freud—that has concerned itself with problems of authority, with the internalization of prevailing patterns of domination, and with the cultural and psychological devastation brought about by industrial capitalism.

My attack is directed not against selfishness or the pursuit of gain but against capitalism itself, which in its twentieth-century phase, often in spite of the best intentions of those who preside over its destiny, has steadily eroded the capacity for self-help and self-discipline, reduced large numbers of men and women to a condition of dependence, and has recently begun to encourage psychological traits associated with dependence and with unresolved conflicts dating from infancy. As more and more people find themselves disqualified, in effect, from the performance of adult responsibilities, the psychology of narcissistic dependence begins to pervade American culture, to replace the pursuit of gain with the more desperate goal of psychic survival, and to encourage a strategy of living for the moment, keeping your options open, and avoiding moral or emotional commitments.

In order precisely to forestall the temptation to misread my book as a moralistic indictment of self-seeking or as another protest against the "me decade," I have cited a large body of clinical evidence which suggests that grandiose illusions of omnipotence originate in early feelings of loss and deprivation, more precisely in defenses against a boundless rage, and that narcissism must therefore not be confused with normal rapacity and greed. Far from reflecting the "alarming growth of ego"—the "obvious" fact of our social life which several reviewers accuse me of belaboring at unnecessary length—narcissism signals a loss of ego, an invasion of the ego by social forces that have made it more and more difficult for people to grow up or even to contemplate the prospect of growing up without misgivings bordering on panic. To readers unable to master the distinction between individualistic egoism and narcissism, between self-seeking or self-absorption and the far more serious disorder in which the self loses its boundaries and merges with its surroundings, a psychological argument of this kind will appear to restate the "obvious" and to force commonplace observations, as a reviewer complains, into the "fashionable containers" of psychotherapeutic jargon. It is true that our therapeutic culture psychologizes everything and thereby trivializes everything, but this does not mean that we can dispense with the insights of psychoanalysis and fall back on common sense. Psychoanalytic theory not only provides indispensable insights into a therapeutic culture and the narcissistic personality who thrives in such a culture; it also serves, strangely enough, as the best innoculation against a psychologizing mode of thought. Those who have entered most fully into the study of psychoanalytic theory best understand its limits and have least inclination to generalize psychoanalysis into a cure-all or into a set of universal explanatory principles. Although psychoanalysis to be sure has been misused, distorted, and absorbed into a therapeutic culture that invokes medicine and psychiatry to justify a permanent suspension of the moral sense, Freud's theory still tells us more than any other about the inner workings of the mind, about the recreation of culture in unconscious mental life, and, indeed, about the crippling effects of a therapeutic culture on the individuals who have absorbed it.

The Culture of Narcissism, then, employs psychoanalytic ideas not to make a "sermon" more palatable to readers brought up on therapeutic jargon or to disguise "obvious" facts in obscure terminology, but to uncover patterns, both cultural and psychological, that remain far from obvious and largely inaccessible to common sense. Aware of the intricate, convoluted character of the links between culture and personality, painfully conscious of the pitfalls in studying them, and having no wish in any case to add to the outpouring of books claiming to offer highly personal and blindingly original statements about the sorry state of American society, I have relied heavily on the work of my predecessors in the sociology of culture. Risking the predictable rebuke that I look at American society "behind a barricade of books," I have tried to carry on a dialogue, both here and in *Haven*, with a long line of sociologists, anthropologists, psychoanalysts, and social critics. My efforts to revise the work of Riesman, Fromm, and the Frankfurt school—and elsewhere that of Talcott Parsons, Margaret Mead, Ruth Benedict, and Edward Sapir—should not obscure the extent of my indebtedness to those thinkers. I stress it here not merely to set the record straight (for the benefit of readers who can't spare the time to consult footnotes) but to dissociate my work, in the strongest possible way, from those "book-length diagnoses of our nation's maladies," those pseudo-critical confections, neither honest journalism nor honest sociology, which the publishing industry likes to pass off as profound social commentary. This work of dissociation becomes doubly important now that the publisher of the paperback edition has begun to advertise *The Culture of Narcissism* as a book that "ranks with four of the greatest books on society's changing values"—*Future Shock, The Greening of America, Passages*, and *My Mother Myself*. In view of this ill-conceived promotional campaign, I must repudiate more emphatically than ever the suggestion that my book represents the "latest addition to the 'what's wrong with us' bibliography," as one reviewer has characterized it. Pop sociology was exactly what I proposed to avoid by rooting criticism of American society in a well-established theoretical tradition, in doing which I deliberately rejected, moreover, the idiosyncratic, satirical, self-consciously provocative, iconoclastic style that has been the characteristic vice of American social criticism—even the best of it, as exemplified by the writings of Thorstein Veblen, Willard Waller, and C. Wright Mills.

A confrontation with established traditions of critical inquiry plays too little part in contemporary scholarship. Our would-be revisionists seldom grapple with the work they want so much to revise. Having no patience for a thorough study of the masters, they fall victim to fads, confusing boldness and originality with a slavish subservience to the latest Paris fashions. Thus Doane and Hodges, who don't even grasp the distinction between primary narcissism and secondary narcissism, predictably seize on the pretentious Lacanian system, with its chic new "revised notion of the self," as a corrective to Freud's "puritan psychology." As always, the search for "radical" alternatives to Freud springs from a need to put the best possible face on things, to get around the contradictions to which Freud called attention, and to restore a "satisfying unity" between the self and the object-world—in this case, the unity experienced by the infant who does not yet distinguish between himself and his surroundings, a unity recreated in adulthood by schizophrenia. It would be difficult to imagine a more pitiful proof of the exhaustion of Western culture than the delusion, shared by Laing, Cooper, Lacan, and their American admire hangers-on, that madness represents the only escape from alienation. Literary radicals understandably find in the idea of a new "symbolic order" an attractive alternative to political and social change, the prospect of which puts their nerves on edge. But their vision of a "new life," with its "subversion of antitheses" and effortless resolution of all contradictions, amounts in itself to a return to infancy, in which "the child attaches himself to a specular image without recognizing that the 'I' is objectified in something alien to itself."

Literary structuralism provides for timid but fashion-conscious intellectuals an easy escape not only from painful contradictions of all sorts but from politics itself. It gives them the comfortable illusion that exposure of "authoritarian ideologies" constitutes a political act, or that narcissism, by some strange twist of "dialectical" reasoning, somehow "poses a powerful challenge" to the dominant social order. Since patriarchal society has been dead for about two hundred years, at least in western Europe and the United States, it doesn't take much courage to attack its "authoritarian ideology." But then Doane and Hodges aren't interested in serious social and political analysis and don't know what to make of it when they come up against it. Like many critics of *The Culture of Narcissism*, they rely not on arguments but on accusations of "nostalgia," "belief in an ideal past," "profound conservatism," "deep regret," and "melancholy." I have answered such pseudo-criticisms before, but their persistence suggests a level of uneasiness impermeable to rational argument. Once and for all: I have no wish to return to the past, even if I thought a return to the past was possible. The solution to our social problems lies in a completion of the democratic movement inaugurated in the eighteenth century, not in a retreat to a pre-democratic way of life. Socialism, notwithstanding the horrors committed in its name, still represents the legitimate heir of liberal democracy. Marxism and psychoanalysis still offer the best guides to an understanding of modern society and to political action designed to make it more democratic.

I reject the humanist critique of modern culture (traces of which I detect in Nachman's essay) that blames Marx and Freud, along with Darwin, Einstein, and other pioneers of modern thought, for degrading the image of man and distracting attention from enduring moral truths. Far from rejecting a "modernist and post-modernist discourse," I hold that the modernist tradition has made history intelligible and retains the power to free mankind for the first time from subjection to blind historical necessity. Nor do I deny that a dying social order may contain seeds of a new and better system. I do insist, however, that signs of exhaustion, senility, and decay be recognized for what they are, not mistaken for "new life." The recognition of decline does not entail idealization of the past, merely a willingness to look facts in the face. Unlike Doane and Hodges, I don't believe that gratuitous attribution of unworthy motives to one's opponents can take the place of argument, but I begin to wonder if my critics' inability to distinguish an analysis of cultural decline from "nostalgia" doesn't betray a simple failure of nerve—an inability to admit that many things are in fact getting worse and may get a good deal worse than they are now. Doane and Hodges, like many other intellectuals, can't seem to see what is readily apparent to ordinary men and women, who have experienced an immediate and unmistakable deterioration not only in their standard of living but in the relations between parents and children and between men and women. Are intellectuals immune to the social pressures that beat against the family and every day threaten to dissolve the ego as well? Do they have no direct knowledge of the deterioration in the quality of life, which presents itself not only as a decline in purchasing power, a rise in crime and violence, and a rise in social tensions of all kinds but also as an intolerable series of psychic strains? Or is it that too many intellectuals think it would be unprogressive to acknowledge these facts, except as the birth-pangs of a new order? I am afraid that the Western intelligentsia as a class has invested too heavily in the political ideology of progressivism to admit that historical progress is by no means automatic. Intellectuals have what amounts to a class interest in misinterpreting the collapse of authority as personal liberation, the culture of pornography as sexual revolution, and the deterioration of political discourse as the "rise of a language located beyond the rhetoric of the 'real.'" Having written off demands for law and order as the expression of the proto-fascist mentality of the American working class, intellectuals wonder why working-class discontent often takes the form of anti-intellectualism, opposition to McGovernite "new politics," or as a "profound conservatism." When the alternatives held up to "middle America" are a totally permissive sexual paradise, a socialist utopia modeled on Cuba or the USSR, or a "language located beyond the rhetoric of the 'real,'" it is not surprising that ordinary working people in this country refuse to become revolutionary. Yet any movement for democratic change has to enlist the support of people who don't have much time to worry about the illusion of reality. Fashionable prattle about the "importance of the image" and the need to devalue reality becomes more than silly, it becomes morally repugnant when it comes from those who preen themselves on their "commitment to working toward change."

In any case, change is already upon us. The old order is dying—and this includes our new order as well, our advanced, ready-made ideas about socialism and feminism and sexual liberation and modernism and "post-modernism," themselves based on the despised bourgeois culture the collapse of which ironically brings with it the collapse of the adversary culture of the intellectuals. Old political pigeonholes no longer correspond to our rapidly changing cultural and political situation. Positions that once seemed radical have long since lost their power to shock or even to titillate. On the other hand, a "conservative" respect for order and authority has now become an essential ingredient of any radical movement that seeks to transcend the progressive and socialist pieties of an earlier time. In mindlessly embracing a politics of "cultural revolution," the American left has played into the hands of the corporations, which find it all too easy to exploit a radicalism that equates liberation with hedonistic self-indulgence and freedom from family ties. Meanwhile the left has turned its back on its proper constituency—the people who cling to family life, religion, the work ethic, and other ostensibly outmoded values and institutions as the only source of stability in an otherwise precarious existence. The left has chosen the wrong side in the cultural warfare between "middle America" and the educated or half-educated classes, which have absorbed avant garde ideas only to put them at the service of consumer capitalism. Lewis Mumford once regretted that "patriotism should be monopolized by reactionaries." The same thing applies to other "bourgeois" virtues. But the American left, in its unexamined commitment to positions it believes to be "anti-authoritarian," has repeatedly forced the legitimate need for authority, stability, and continuity to find reactionary political outlets. In default of the left, middle America turns to leaders like

Richard Nixon, the Reverend Moon, or the founder of that notable adventure in mass self-destruction, Jonesville.

In arguing that most of the allegedly radical alternatives advocated by aging revolutionaries reflect the culture of consumerism more than they challenge it, I do not wish to be misunderstood as saying that the culture of narcissism has eliminated the very possibility of opposition. On the contrary, its own demise can be predicted with assurance. As I have taken pains to point out more than once, it represents a way of life that is dying. Chronic shortages of energy, rising unemployment, runaway inflation, and the decline of western colonialism have undermined the economic foundations of hedonistic self-expression. They have destroyed the historic compromise of twentieth-century capitalism, in which people exchanged degrading conditions of work for the pleasures of consumption and commercialized leisure—the cultivation of the self, with its unappeasable appetite for new products, new sensations, new taste treats. It is now clear that the Western world can no longer afford a culture of narcissism, and I mean this statement not as a form of moral exhortation but as a description of fact. Our impending economic and ecological crisis—the crisis of uninhibited capitalist growth, now coming to an end—will demand not narcissistic self-exploration but collective discipline and sacrifice. There can no longer be any doubt about this; the only question is whether the necessary sacrifices will be democratically decided upon and distributed in a democratic manner or imposed by an authoritarian state. As Walter Dean Burnham and others have pointed out, the "massive public controls" needed to deal with the energy crisis "cannot be maintained without consent in a democracy." Burnham goes on to point out that "if democratic consent is to be won for the very hard public choices lying just over the horizon, a bona-fide, sustained, and more than rhetorical effort to approximate equality of sacrifice will have to be made by policy elites." Such an effort, he adds, presupposes a "revolutionary change in behavior norms among rank-and-file and elites alike."

To see the culture of immediate gratification as an unavoidable outgrowth of democracy and "modernization," as Nachman does, obscures both its historical origins and the political choices that will be forced on this country in the near future. Modernization theory, fixated on the dichotomy between "traditional" and "modern" societies and on the "transition," in Nachman's words, "from magical to rational thinking," overrides the concrete facts of historical development, assimilating all information to an overriding typological scheme that explains nothing. Even if we could accept Nachman's too simple opposition between "authority" and "democracy," as a highly abstract way of describing two broad social tendencies, it would still tell us nothing about the concrete forms authority has assumed in pre-modern society or about the long history of attempts, by no means negligible or hopelessly misguided, precisely to reconcile democracy and authority in the modern world. Modernization theory makes it impossible to distinguish between nineteenth-century individualism and twentieth-century narcissism, between "privatism" and the social invasion of the self, or even between communism and capitalism. When Nachman tries to recast my analysis of twentieth-century capitalism in the terms of modernization theory, he drains it of historical specificity and generalizes narcissism into yet another "product of modernity and of democracy." He then jumps to the conclusion that its "principal features will not be altered by social reform or radical reconstruction."

This interpretation is much too sweeping, and quite misleading in its political implications. The culture of narcissism has flourished in a specific social and economic environment, which first took shape in the twenties, matured (after the momentary check of the Depression) in the postwar period, and is now disintegrating at a rapid rate. In a climate of diminished economic growth, shortages of raw materials, and chronic inflation, struggles over the distribution of wealth, overlaid by cultural conflicts over patriotism, authority, and the status of women, will become increasingly desperate and bitter. Only a new movement for radical reform can provide a democratic focus for popular discontent. If on the other hand the demand for order and justice is diverted into a reactionary push for order at any price, the outcome will make narcissism look benign by comparison. Richard Sennett predicted a few years ago that sado-masochism would soon succeed narcissism as the new wave in pathology. Without conceding that narcissism is merely the "latest fashion in social disease," as a socialist paper sneeringly puts it, and without minimizing its staying power as an "alternate life style," I can foresee conditions in which a far more sinister form of paternalism would replace our managerial and bureaucratic state with an openly authoritarian system of controls, rooted in a psychology even more regressive and violent than narcissism.

All this takes us, of course, well beyond the "dilemmas of modernity." Such formulas, claiming to put the problem of narcissism into a broad historical context, merely serve as rationalizations of the "jaded response" to social criticism which, as Michael Fischer points out, contributes so heavily to the prevailing sense of resignation. Faced with Nachman's weariness on the one hand and with the phony structuralist radicalism of Doane and Hodges on the other, I am doubly grateful for Fischer's reminder that what makes genuine social criticism "vulnerable to quick rejection is precisely what makes it so valuable." I hope that other readers of *Salmagundi* will follow him in rejecting the clichés of pseudo-criticism, whether they hold out the false promise of a "new symbolic order" or wearily invoke the "dilemmas of modernity" as an all-purpose explanation of everything that ails us. Instead of rehearsing old positions and mouthing old catchwords, we need to open a new debate about our politics and culture. To begin such a debate, not to take sides in an old one, was all I hoped to accomplish in writing *The Culture of Narcissism*, and Fischer's response, along with a few others, gives me reason to hope that my labors were not altogether wasted.

The Divorce between the Sciences and the Humanities

BY SIR ISAIAH BERLIN

My topic is the relation of the natural sciences to the humanities, or, more specifically, the growing absence of relations between them, culminating in a divorce which, after many years of tension, finally, so it seems to me, took place in the early eighteenth century, even though it was not recognized for what it was until much later. It was not a divorce between "two cultures": I have never understood what was meant by describing two great fields of human endeavour—the natural sciences and the humanities—as cultures; but they do seem, once they became differentiated from each other, to have been concerned to answer somewhat different questions, different in principle, and for that reason to have pursued different aims and methods. This formulation (and perhaps the fact itself, if the formulation is valid) is likely to meet with some resistance from those who believe that this divorce, if ever it occurred, was a misfortune and, perhaps, could have been avoided; or else that it is an illusion and that the true practitioners in either field do, or at least should, pursue aims and use methods that are in principle identical or at any rate cognate to each other. Men who believe this, and they are not rare among academics and other intellectuals in modern society, stand in a noble tradition of those who believe that it is possible to make steady progress in the entire sphere of human knowledge; that methods and goals are, or should be, ultimately identical throughout this sphere; that the path to progress has been, as often as not—or perhaps a good deal more often—blocked by ignorance, fantasy, prejudice, superstition and other forms of unreason; that we have in our day reached a stage when the achievements of the natural sciences are such that it is possible to derive their structure from a single integrated set of clear principles or rules which, if correctly applied, make possible indefinite further progress in the unravelling of the mysteries of nature.

This approach is in line with a central tradition in Western thought which extends back at least as far as Plato. It appears to me to rest on at least three basic assumptions: (1) that every genuine question has one true answer and one only: all the others being false. Unless this is so, the question cannot be a real question—there is a confusion in it somewhere. This position, which has been made explicit by modern empiricist philosophers, is entailed no less firmly by the views of their theological and metaphysical predecessors against whom they have been engaged in long and uncompromising warfare. (2) The method which leads to correct solutions to all genuine problems is rational in character, and is in essence, if not in detailed application, identical in all fields. (3) These solutions, whether or not they are discovered, are true universally, eternally and immutably: true for all times, places and men: as in the old definition of Natural law, they are *quod semper, quod ubique, quod ab omnibus*.

Opinions within this tradition have, of course, differed about where the answers were to be sought: some thought they could only be discovered by specialists trained in, let us say, Plato's dialectical method, or Aristotle's more empirical type of investigations; or in the methods of various schools of Sophists, or of the thinkers who traced their descent from Socrates. Others maintained that such truths were more accessible to men of pure and innocent soul, not corrupted by philosophic subtleties or the sophistication of civilisation or destructive social institutions—as, for example, Rousseau and Tolstoy believed. There were those, especially in the seventeenth century, who believed that the only true path was that of systems based on rational insight (of which mathematical reasoning offered the perfect example), which yielded *a priori* truths; others put their faith in hypotheses confirmed or falsified by controlled observation and experiment; still others preferred to rely on what seemed to them plain common-sense—*le bon sens*—reinforced by careful observation, experiment, scientific method, but not replaceable by the sciences; and men have pointed to other roads to truth. What is common to all thinkers of this type is the belief that there is only one true method: and that what cannot be answered by it, cannot be answered at all. The implication of this position is that the world is a single system which can be described and explained by the use of rational methods; with the practical corollary that if man's life is to be organised at all, and not left to chaos and the play of uncontrolled nature and chance, then it can be organised only in the light of such principles and laws.

It is not surprising that this view was most strongly held and most influential in the hour of the greatest triumph of the natural sciences—surely a major, if not the major, achievement of the human mind: and especially, therefore, in the seventeenth century in Western Europe. From Descartes and Bacon and the followers of Galileo and Newton, from Voltaire and the Encyclopaedists to Saint-Simon, and Comte and

Buckle, and, in our own century, H. G. Wells and Bernal and Skinner and the Viennese Positivists, with their ideal of a unified system of all the sciences, natural and humane, this has been the programme of the modern Enlightenment; and it has played a decisive role in the social, legal and technological organisation of our world. This was perhaps bound to provoke reaction from those who felt that constructions of reason and science—of a single all-embracing system, whether it claimed to explain the nature of things, or to go further and dictate, in the light of this, what one should do and be and believe, were in some way constricting—an obstacle to their own vision of the world, chains on their imagination or feeling or will, a barrier to spiritual or political liberty. This is not the first occasion on which this phenomenon occurred: the domination of the philosophical Schools of Athens in the Hellenistic period was attended by a noticeable increase in mystery cults and other forms of occultism and emotionalism, in which non-rational elements in the human spirit sought an outlet. There was the great Christian revolt against the great organised legal systems, whether of the Jews or the Romans: there were medieval antinomian rebellions against the Scholastic establishment and the authority of the Church—movements of this kind from the Cathars to the Anabaptists are evidence enough of this; the Reformation was preceded and followed by the rise of powerful mystical and irrationalist currents. I will not dwell on more recent manifestations of this—in the German *Sturm und Drang,* in the Romanticism of the early nineteenth century, in Carlyle and Wagner and Nietszche and the vast spectrum of modern irrationalism both of the Right and of the Left. It is not, however, with this that I intend to deal, but with the critical attack upon the total claim of the new scientific method to dominate the entire field of human knowledge, whether in its metaphysical—*a priori,* or empirical—probabilistic, forms. This attack, whether or not its causes were psychological or social (and I am inclined to think that they were at least partly due to a reaction against the all-conquering advance of the physical sciences on the part of humanists, and especially the anti-materialistic Christians among them) was itself based on rational argument, and in due course led to the great divorce between the natural sciences and the humanities—*Naturwissenschaft* and *Geisteswissenschaft*—a divorce the validity of which has been challenged ever since and remains a central and highly controversial issue to this day.

As everyone knows, the great triumphs of natural science in the seventeenth century gave the proponents of the scientific method immense prestige. The great liberators of the age were Descartes and Bacon, who carried opposition to the authority of tradition, faith, dogma, prescription, into every realm of knowledge and opinion, armed with weapons used during the Renaissance and, indeed, earlier. Although there was much cautious avoidance of open defiance of Christian belief, the general thrust of the new movement was to bring everything before the bar of reason: the cruder forgeries and misinterpretations of texts, on which lawyers and clerics had rested their claims, had been exposed by humanists in Italy and Protestant reformers in France; appeals to the authority of the Bible, or Aristotle, or Roman law, had met with a good deal of acutely argued resistance based both on learning and on critical methods. Descartes made an epoch with his attempt to systematise these methods—notably in his *Discourse on Method* and its application in his *Meditations*—his two most popular and influential philosophical treatises. Spinoza's *Treatise On the Improvement of the Mind,* his quasi-geometrical method in the *Ethics* and the severely rationalist assumptions and rigorous logic in his political works and his criticisms of the Old Testament, had carried the war further into the enemy's camp. Bacon and Spinoza, in their different ways, sought to remove obstacles to clear, rational thinking. Bacon exposed what he considered the chief sources of delusion: "idols" of the tribe, of the den, market-place and theatre—effects, in his view, of the uncritical acceptance of the evidence of the senses or one's own predilections, of misunderstanding of words, and confusions bred by the speculative fantasies of philosophers and the like. Spinoza stressed the degree to which emotions clouded reason, and led to groundless fears and hatreds which led to destructive practice; from Valla to Locke and Berkeley there were frequent warnings and examples of fallacies and confusions due to the misuse of language. The general tendency of the new philosophy was to declare that if the human mind can be cleared of dogma, prejudice and cant, of the organised obscurities and Aristotelian patter of the Schoolmen, then Nature will at last be seen in the full symmetry and harmony of its elements, which can be described, analysed and represented by a logically appropriate language—the language of the mathematical and physical sciences. Leibniz believed not only in the possibility of constructing a logically perfect language, which would reflect the structure of reality, but in something not unlike a general science of discovery. His views spread far beyond philosophical or scientific circles—indeed, theoretical knowledge was still conceived as one undivided realm; the frontiers between philosophy, science, criticism, theology, were not sharply drawn. There were invasions and counter-invasions; grammar, rhetoric, jurisprudence, philosophy, made forays into the fields of historical learning and natural knowledge, and were attacked by them in turn. The new rationalism spread into the creative arts. Just as the Royal Society in England formally set itself against the use of metaphor and other forms of rhetorical speech, and demanded language that was plain and literal and precise, so there is in France at this time a corresponding avoidance of metaphor, embellishment and highly coloured expression in, for example, the plays of Racine or Moliere, in the verse of La Fontaine and Boileau, writers who dominated the European scene; and because such luxuriance was held to flourish in Italy, Italian literature was duly denounced in France for the impurity of its style. The new method sought to eliminate everything that could not be justified by the systematic use of rational methods, above all the fictions of the metaphysicians, the mystics, the poets; what were myth and legend but falsehoods with which primitive and barbarous societies were gulled during their early, helpless childhood? At best they were fancified and distorted accounts of real events and persons. Even the Catholic Church was influenced by the prevailing scientific temper, and the great archival labours of the Bellandists and Maurists were conducted in a semi-scientific spirit.[1]

It was natural enough that history was one of the earliest victims of what might be called the positivist character of the new scientific movement. Scepticism about historical veracity was no new thing: ignorance and fantasy, as well as malicious invention, had been attributed to Herodotus by Plutarch; and these charges against narrative history had been repeated at intervals by those who preferred certainty to conjecture. The sixteenth century in particular, perhaps as a result of the mobilisation of history in the religious wars by the various factions, saw a rise of scepticism and doubt: Cornelius Agrippa, in 1531, dwells on carelessness and the contradictions of historians, and their shameless inventions to cover up their ignorance or fill gaps in knowledge where there is no available evidence; on the absurdity of idealising the characters of the main actors in the story; he speaks of the distortion of the facts as being due to the historians' passions, wishes, hatreds and fears, desire to please a patron, patriotic motives, national pride, as when Plutarch glorifies the Greeks in comparison with the Romans; in his own day polemical writers extolled the virtues of Gauls over Franks and *vice versa*. How can truth emerge in these conditions? In the same vein Patrizzi, at the turn of the century, declares that all history ultimately rests on eye-witness evidence: and argues that those who are present are likely to be involved in the issues, and therefore liable to be partisan; while those who can afford to be objective because they are neutral and uninvolved are unlikely to see the evidence jealously preserved by the partisans, and have to depend upon the accounts of the interested parties. Such Pyrrhonism grows with the century: it is characteristic of Montaigne, Charron, LaMothe le Vayer, and of course, later in the century, in a more extreme form, of Pierre Bayle, to take but a few

1. Professor M. H. Fisch correctly points out that the dissolution of monasteries had released a mass of documentary evidence which had not hitherto been available, and this contributed to the fact that the Church, in repelling attacks on her historical claims, had recourse to historical weapons.

examples. So long as history is regarded as a school of virtue the purpose of which is to celebrate the good and expose the wicked, to show the unaltering character of human nature at all times, everywhere, to be simply moral and political philosophy teaching by examples, it may not matter greatly whether such history is accurate or not. But once a desire for truth for its own sake asserts itself, or—something more novel is born—the desire to create an advancing science: to accumulate knowledge, to know more than our predecessors and to be aware of this, this leads to the realisation that this can be achieved only if the reputable practitioners in the field recognise the validity of the same principles and methods and can test each other's conclusions, as was (and is) the case in physics or mathematics or astronomy and in all the new sciences. It is this new outlook that made the claims of history to be a province of knowledge seem so precarious.

Much of the most formidable attack came from Descartes. His views are well known: true science rests on axiomatic premises, from which, by the use of rational rules, irrefutable conclusions can be drawn: this is how we proceed in geometry, in algebra, in physics. Where are the axioms, the transformation rules, the inescapable conclusions, in historical writing? The progress of true knowledge is the discovery of eternal, unalterable, universal truths: every generation of seekers after truth stands on the shoulders of its predecessors and begins where these others left off, and adds to the growing sum of human knowledge. This is plainly not the case in historical writing, or indeed, the field of the humanities in general. Where, in this province, is the single, ever mounting edifice of science? A schoolboy today knows more geometry than Pythagoras. What do the greatest classical scholars of our time know about ancient Rome that was not known to Cicero's servant girl? What have they added to her store? What, then, is the use of all these learned labours? Descartes implies that he does not wish to prevent men from indulging in this pastime—they may find it agreeable enough to while away their leisure in these ways, it is no worse, he says, than learning some quaint dialect, say, Swiss or bas-Breton; but it is not an occupation for anyone seriously concerned with increasing knowledge. Malebranche dismisses history as gossip; this is echoed by other Cartesians; even Leibniz, who composed a huge historical work himself, gives a conventional defense of history as a means of satisfying curiosity about origins of families or states, and as a school of morals. Its inferiority to mathematics, and philosophy founded on the mathematical and natural sciences and the other discoveries of pure reason, must be obvious to all thinking men.

These attitudes did not, of course, kill historical studies. Methods of scholarship had advanced greatly since the middle of the fifteenth century, especially by the use made of antiquities. Monuments, legal documents, manuscripts, coins, medals, works of art, literature, buildings, inscriptions, popular ballads, legends, could be employed as aids to, and sometimes even substitutes for, unreliable narrative history. The great jurists of the sixteenth century, like Budé, Alciati, Cujas, Dumoulin, Hotman, Baudouin, and in the following century Coke and Matthew Hale in England, Vrank in the Low Countries, de Gregorio in Italy and Sparre in Sweden, performed major labours of reconstructing legal texts, both Roman and mediaeval. The school of universal historians in France—Pasquier, Le Roy, Le Caron, Vignier, La Popelinière, and indeed, the polymath Bodin, originated cultural history[2]; and were followed in the seventeenth century by writers like the Abbé de Saint Real, Dufresnoy, Charles Sorel, Père Gabriel Daniel, and, of course, Boulainvilliers and Fénelon. These beginnings of cultural history, and in particular the growing awareness of the differences rather than the similarities between different societies, ages, civilisations, was a novel development, which, in due course, revolutionised historical notions. Nevertheless, their proponents showed a greater propensity for denouncing useless erudition, and for making up programmes of what historians should do, than for indicating precise methods of performing these tasks or, indeed, performing them. Much of this was meta-history, or theories of history, rather than concrete historical writing. Moreover, the scientific model (or "paradigm") which dominated the century, with its strong implication that only that which was quantifiable, or at any rate measurable—that to which in principle mathematical methods were applicable—was real, strongly reinforced the old conviction that to every question there was only one true answer, universal, eternal, unchangeable; it was, or appeared to be, so in mathematics, physics, mechanics and astronomy and medicine, and soon would be in chemistry and botany and zoology and other natural sciences; with the corollary that the most reliable criterion of objective truth was logical demonstration, or measurement, or at least approximations to this. Spinoza's political theory is a good example of this approach: he supposes that the rational answer to the question of what is the best government for men is in principle discoverable by anyone, anywhere, in any circumstances. If men have not discovered these timeless solutions before, this must be due to weakness, or the clouding of reason by emotion, or perhaps bad luck: the truths of which he supposed himself to be giving a rational demonstration could have been discovered and

2. Phrases like *"les saisons et mutations de moeurs d'un peuple" or "la complexion et humour"* of a nation, or *"facons de vivre"*, or *"forme de vivre"*, *"la police"*, *"les motifs, les opinions et les pensées des hommes"*, *"le genie de siècle, des opinions, des moeurs, des idées dominantes"*, *"des passions qui conduisaient les hommes"* were very common throughout the sixteenth and seventeenth centuries.

applied by human reason at any time, so that mankind might have been spared many evils. Hobbes, an empiricist but equally dominated by a scientific model, presupposes this also. The notion of time, change, historical development, does not impinge upon these views at all. Furthermore, such truths, when discovered, must add to human welfare. Consequently the motive for the search is not curiosity, or desire to know the truth as such, so much as utilitarian—the promotion of a better life on earth by making men rational and therefore wise, just, virtuous and happy. The ends of man are given, given by God or nature. Reason, freed from its trammels, cannot help discovering what they are: all that is necessary is to find the right means for their attainment. This is the ideal from Francis Bacon to H. G. Wells and Julian Huxley and many of those who, in our day, believe in moral and political arrangements based on a scientific theory of sociology and psychology. The most famous figure in this entire movement, not in that of science itself, but of the applicaion of its discoveries to the lives of men—certainly its most gifted propagandist—was Voltaire. Its earliest and strongest opponent was the Neapolitan philosopher Giambattista Vico. The contrast between their views may serve to throw light upon the radical difference of attitudes which brought about a crucial parting of the ways.

II

Voltaire is the central figure of the Enlightenment, because he accepted its basic principles and used all his incomparable wit and energy and brilliant malice to propagate these principles and spread havoc in the enemy's camp. Ridicule kills more surely than savage indignation: and Voltaire did more for the triumph of civilised values than any writer who ever lived. What were these principles? Let me repeat the formula once more: there are eternal, timeless truths, identical in all the spheres of human activity—moral and political, social and economic, scientific and artistic; and there is only one way of recognising them: by means of reason, which Voltaire interpreted not as the deductive method of logic or mathematics, which was too abstract and unrelated to the facts and needs of daily life, but as *le bon sens,* the good sense which, while it may not lead to absolute certainty, attains to a degree of verisimilitude or probability quite sufficient for human affairs, for public and private life. Not many men are fully armed with this excellent faculty, for the majority appear to be incurably stupid; but those few who do possess it are responsible for the finest hours of mankind. All that is of interest in the past is these fine hours: from them alone we can learn how to make men good, that is, sane, rational, tolerant, or, at any rate, less brutish and stupid and cruel; how to enact laws and governments which will promote justice, beauty and happiness and diminish brutality, fanaticism, oppression, with which the greater part of human history is filled. The task of modern historians is therefore plain: to describe and celebrate these moments of high culture and contrast them with the surrounding darkness—the barbarous ages of faith, fanaticism, folly and abominable brutality. In order to do this historians must give more attention than the ancients to "customs, laws, manners, commerce, finance, agriculture, population": and also trade, industry, colonisation and the development of taste. This is far more important than accounts of wars, treaties, political institutions, conquerors, dynastic tables, public affairs, to which historians have attached far too much importance hitherto. Madame du Châtelet (Voltaire tells us) said to him "What is the point for a Frenchwoman like me of knowing that (in Sweden) Egli succeeded Haquin; or that Ottoman was the son of Ortugal?" She was perfectly right: the purpose of the work which he wrote, ostensibly for the illumination of this lady, (the famous *Essai sur les Moeurs)*, is therefore, "not to know in which year one Prince who doesn't deserve to be remembered succeeded another barbarian Prince of some uncouth nation". "I wish to show how human societies came into existence, how domestic life was lived, what arts were cultivated, rather than to tell again old stories of disasters and misfortunes . . . those familiar examples of human malice and depravity." He intends to "recount the achievement of the human spirit in the most enlightened of ages" (Introduction to the *Age of Louis XIV*), for "only that is worthy of mention which is worthy of posterity". Human history is an arid desert with few oases. There are only four great ages in the West in which human beings rose to their full stature and created civilisations of which they can be proud: the age of Alexander, in which he includes the classical age of Athens; the age of Augustus, in which he includes the Roman Republic and the Empire at their best; Florence during the Renaissance; and the age of Louis XIV in France. Voltaire assumes throughout that these are élitist civilisations, imposed by enlightened oligarchies on the masses, for the latter, with their lack of reason, want only to be amused and deceived, and so are naturally prey to religion—that is, for him, to abominable superstitions. "Only governments can . . . raise or lower the level of nations." The basic assumption is, of course, that the goals pursued in these four great civilisations are ultimately the same: truth, light, are the same everywhere, it is only error that has myriad forms. Moreover, it is absurd to confine enquiry to Europe and that portion of the Near East whence sprang little but the cruelties, fanaticism and nonsensical beliefs of the Jews and the Christians who, whatever Bossuet may seek to demonstrate, were and remain enemies of truth and progress and toleration. It is absurd to ignore the great and peaceful Kingdom of China, governed by enlightened Mandarins, or India, or Chaldaea and other parts of the world, which only the absurd vanity of Christian Europe excludes from the orbit of history. The purpose of history is to impart instructive truths, not to satisfy idle curiosity, and this can only be done by studying the peaks of human achievement, not the valleys. The historian should not peddle fables, like Herodotus, who is like an old woman telling stories to children, but teach us our duties without seeming to do so, by painting for posterity not the acts of a single man but the progress of the human spirit in the most enlightened ages. If you have no more to tell us than that one barbarian succeeded another barbarian on the banks of the Oxus or the Ixartes, what use are you to the public? Why should we be interested in the fact that Quancum succeeded Kincum, or Kincum succeeded Quancum? We do not wish to know about the life of Louis the Fat, or Louis the Obstinate, or even the barbarous Shakespeare and the tedious Milton: but about the achievements of Galileo, Newton, Tasso, Addison; who wants to know about Shalmaneser of Mardokempad? Historians must not clutter the minds of their readers with accounts of religious wars or other stupidities that degrade mankind unless it be to show them how low human beings can sink: accounts of Philip II of Spain, or Christian of Denmark, are cautionary tales to warn mankind of the dangers of tyranny; or if, like Voltaire himself, one does write a lively and entertaining biography of Charles XII of Sweden, it is for the sole end of pointing out to men the dangers of a life of reckless adventure. What *is* worth knowing is why the Emperor Charles V did not profit more by his capture of King Francis I of France; or what the value of sound finance was to Elizabeth of England, or Henry IV or Louis XIV in France, or the importance of the *dirigiste* policy of Colbert compared with that of his predecessor Sully. As for horrors, they too are to be detailed if we are to avoid another St. Bartholomew's Eve or another Cromwell. The task of the historian, he says again and again, is to recount the achievements of those regrettably rare periods when the arts and sciences flourished and nature was made to yield the necessities, comforts and pleasures of man. Meinecke rightly described Voltaire as the "banker of the Enlightenment", the keeper of its achievements, a kind of scorer in the contest of light against darkness, reason and civilisation against barbarism and religion, Athens and the Rome of the virtuous Caesars against Jerusalem and the Rome of the Popes, Julian the Apostate versus Gregory of Nazianzus. But how are we to tell what actually happened in the past? Has not Pierre Bayle thrown terrible doubts on the authenticity of particular reports of facts, and shown how unreliable and contradictory historical evidence can be? This may be so, but it is not particular facts that matter, according to Voltaire, so much as the general character of an age or a culture. The acts of single men are of small importance and individual character is too difficult to elucidate: when we can scarcely tell even what Mazarin was like, how can we possibly do this for the ancients? "Soul, character, dominant motives, all that sort of thing is an impenetrable chaos which can never be firmly grasped. Whoever, after centuries, would disentangle this chaos simply creates more." How, then, are we to recover the past? By the light of natural reason—*le bon sens*. "Anything not in keeping with natural science, with reason, with the nature *(trempe)* of the human heart is false"—why bother with the ravings of savages and the inventions of knaves?—We know that monuments are "historical lies" and "that there is not a single temple or college of priests, not a single Feast in the church, that does not originate in some stupidity". The human heart is the same everywhere; and good sense is enough to detect the truth. *Le bon sens* served him well: it enabled him to discredit much clerical propaganda, and a good many naive and pedantic absurdities. But it also told him that the empires of Babylon and Assyria could not possibly have co-existed next door to each other, in so confined a space; that accounts of temple prostitutes were obvious nonsense; that Cyrus and Croesus were fictional, that Themistocles could not have died of drinking ox blood; that Belus and Ninus could not have been Babylonian kings, for "us" is not a Babylonian ending, nor did Xerves flog the Hellespont. The Flood is an absurd fable: as for the shells found on tops of mountains, these may well have dropped from the hats of pilgrims. On the other hand, he found no difficulty at all in accepting the reality of satyrs, fauns, the Minotaur, Zeus, Theseus, Hercules, or the journey of Bacchus to India, and he happily accepted a forged Indian classic, the *Ezour-Veidan*. Yet Voltaire undoubtedly expanded the area of proper historical interest, beyond politics, wars, great men, by insisting on "the need to describe how men travelled, lived, slept, dressed, wrote, their social and economic and artistic activities". He complained that Puffendorf, who had had access to the state archives of Sweden, tells us nothing about its natural resources, the causes of its poverty, what part it played in the Gothic invasions; these are novel and important demands. He denounced Europocentrism; he sketched the need for social, economic, cultural history which, even though he did not himself fulfill his programme (his own histories are marvellously readable and entertaining but largely anecdotal in character—there is no real attempt at synthesis), stimulated the interest of successors in a wider field. At the same time he devalued the historical nature of history, for his interests are moral, aesthetic, social: as a *philosopher* he is part moralist, part tourist, and *feuille-toniste*, and wholly a journalist, albeit of incomparable genius. He does not recognise, even as a cultural historian—or cataloguer—the multiplicity and relativity of values at different times and places, or the genetic dimension in history: the notion of change and growth are alien to him. For him there are only bright ages and dark, and the dark are due to the crimes, follies and misfortunes of men. In this respect he is a good deal less historical than some of his predecessors in the Renaissance. He looks on history, in a loose fashion, as an accumulation of facts, casually connected, the purpose of which is to show men under what conditions those central purposes which nature has implanted in the heart of every man can best be realised: who are the enemies of progress, and how they are to be routed. Thereby Voltaire probably did more than anyone else to determine the entire direction of the Enlightenment: Hume and Gibbon are possessed by the same spirit. Not until the reaction against the classification of all human experience in terms of absolute and timeless values—a reaction which first began in Switzerland and England among critics and historians of Greek and Hebrew literature, and, penetrating to Germany, created the great intellectual revolution of which Herder was the most influential apostle—did history, as we understand it today, come into its own. Nevertheless, it is to Voltaire, Fontenelle and Montesquieu (who, contrary to the accepted view of him, was no less convinced of the absolute and timeless nature of ultimate human ends, however much means and methods might vary from clime to clime) that we owe the more scientific branches of later historical writing: economic history, the history of science and technology, historical sociology, demography, all the provinces of the knowledge of the past which owe their existence to statistical and other quantitative techniques. But the history of civilisation which Voltaire supposed himself to be initiating was in the end created by the Germans who looked on him as the arch-enemy of all that they held dear.

Yet even before the Counter-Enlightenment of the Swiss and the English and the Germans, a new conception of the study of history came into being. It was anti-Voltairean in character, and its author was an obscure Neapolitan of whom Voltaire had almost certainly never heard: and if he had, would have treated with disdain.

III

Giambattista Vico was born in Naples in 1668 and lived there or in its environs until his death in 1744. Throughout his long life he was little known, the very exemplar of a lonely thinker. He was educated by priests, worked for some years as a private tutor, and became a minor professor of rhetoric at the University of Naples, and after many years of composing inscriptions, Latin eulogies and laudatory biographies for the rich and the great to supplement his meagre income, was rewarded in the last years of his life by being appointed official historiographer to the Austrian Viceroy of Naples. He was steeped in the literature of humanism, in the classical authors and antiquities, and especially in Roman law. His mind was not analytical or scientific, but literary and intuitive. Naples under Spanish and Austrian rulers was not in the vanguard of the new scientific movement. Although experimental scientists were at work there, so were the Church and the Inquisition. If anything, the Kingdom of the Two Sicilies was something of a backwater, and Vico, by inclination a religious humanist with a rich historical imagination, was not in sympathy with the great scientific materialist movement that was determined to sweep away the last relics of the Scholastic metaphysics. Nevertheless, in his youth, he fell under the sway of the new current of thought: he read Lucretius, and the Epicurean conception of human development from primitive, semi-bestial beginnings, remained with him all his life. Influenced by the all-powerful Cartesian movement, he began by believing mathematics to be the queen of the sciences. But evidently something in him rebelled against this. In 1709, at the age of forty, in an inaugural lecture, with which professors in the University of Naples were obliged to start each academic year, he published a passionate defence of humanist education: men's minds *(ingenia)* were shaped by the language—the words and the images—which they inherited, as much as their minds, in their turn, shaped their moods of expression; the search after a neutral, plain style, like the attempt to train the young exclusively in the dry light of Cartesian analytic method, robbed them of imaginative power. Vico defended the rich, traditional Italian "rhetoric", inherited from the great humanists of the Renaissance, against the austere and deflationary style of the French science-influenced modernists. Evidently he continued to brood on the two contrasted methods, for in the following year he arrived at a truly startling conclusion: mathematics was indeed, as had always been claimed for it, a discipline which led to wholly clear, irrefutable propositions of universal validity. But this was so not because the language of mathematics was a reflection of the basic and unalterable structure of reality, as thinkers since the days of Plato or even Pythagoras had maintained: it was so because mathematics was not a reflection of anything. Mathematics was not a discovery but a human invention: starting from definitions and axioms of their own choosing, mathematicians could, by means of rules of which they or others were equally the authors, arrive at conclusions that did, indeed, follow, because the man-made rules, definitions and axioms saw to it that they did so. Mathematics was a kind of game (although Vico did not call it that), in which the counters and the rules were man-made; the moves and their implications were indeed certain, but at the cost of describing nothing—a play of abstractions controlled by their creators. Once this system was applied to the natural world—for instance, as in physics or mechanics—it yielded important truths, but inasmuch as nature had not been invented by men, and had its own characteristics and could not, like symbols, be freely manipulated, the conclusions became less clear, no longer wholly knowable. Mathematics was not a system of laws which governed reality, but a system of rules, in terms of which it was useful to generalise about, analyse and predict the behaviour of things in space. Here Vico made use of an ancient scholastic proposition at least as old as St. Augustine: that one could know fully only what one had oneself made. A man could understand fully his own intellectual or poetical construction, a work of art or a plan, because he had himself made it, and it was therefore transparent to him: everything in it had been created by his intellect and his imagination. Indeed, Hobbes had asserted as much in the case of political constitutions. The world—nature—had not been made by men: therefore only God, who had made it, could know it through and through. That is why mathematics seemed so marvellous an achievement, because it was the nearest to Divine creation that man could attain to. And there were those in the Renaissance who spoke of art, too, in this fashion, and said that the artist was a creator, *quasi deus,* of an imaginary world created alongside the real world, and the artist, the god who had created it, alone truly knew it. But there was something opaque about the world of external nature: men could describe it, and how it behaved in different situations and relationships, and offer hypotheses about the behaviour of physical bodies, but they could not tell why—for what reason—it was as it was, and behaved as it did: only he who made it, namely, God, knew that—men had only an outside view, as it were, of what went on on the stage of nature. Men could know "from the inside" only what they had made themselves and nothing else. The greater the man-made element in any object of knowledge, the more transparent to human vision it will be; the greater the ingredient of external nature, the more opaque and impenetrable to human understanding. There was an impassable gulf between the man-made and the natural: the constructed and the given. All provinces of knowledge could be classified along this scale of relative intelligibility.

Ten years later Vico took a radical step: there existed a field of knowledge besides those of the most obviously man-made constructions—works of art, or political schemes, or legal systems,—and indeed, all rule-determined disciplines—which men could know from within: human history, too, was made by men. Human history did not consist merely of things and events, their compresences and sequences (including those of human organisms viewed as natural objects), as the external world did; it was the story of human activities, of what men did, and thought, and suffered, of what they strove for, aimed at, imagined, of what their feelings were directed at. It was concerned, therefore, with motives, purposes, hopes, fears, loves and hatreds, jealousies, ambitions, outlooks and visions of reality; with the ways of seeing and ways of acting and creating, of individuals and groups. These activities we knew directly, because we were involved in them as actors, not spectators. There was a sense, therefore, in which we knew more about ourselves than we knew about the external world; when we studied, let us say, Roman law, we were not contemplating an object in nature of whose purposes, or whether it had any, we could know nothing. We had to ask ourselves what these Romans were at, what they strove to do, how they lived and thought, what kind of relationships with other men they were anxious to promote or frustrate. We could not ask this about natural objects: it was idle to ask what cows or trees or stones, or molecules or cells, were *at:* we had no reason to suppose that they pursued purposes; but if they did, we could not know what they were, for we had not made them and therefore had no God-like "inside" view of what ends, if any, they pursued or had been created to fulfill. There was, therefore, a clear sense in which we knew about intentional behaviour—that is, action—more than we did about the movement or position of bodies in space, the field of the magnificent triumphs of seventeenth century science. What was opaque to us when we contemplated the external world, was, if not wholly transparent, yet surely far more so, when we contemplated ourselves. It was therefore a perverse kind of self-denial to apply the rules and laws of physics or of the other natural sciences, to the world of mind and will and feeling; for by doing this we would be gratuitously debarring ourselves from much that we could know. If anthropomorphism was falsely to endow the inanimate world with human minds and wills, there was presumably a world which it was proper to endow with precisely these attributes, namely, the world of man. A natural science of men treated as purely natural entities, on a par with rivers and plants and stones, was an absurdity. With regard to ourselves we were privileged observers with an "inside" view: to ignore it in favour of the ideal of a unified science of all there is, a single method of investigation, was to insist on wilful ignorance (in the name of a materialist dogma) of what could be known. We know what is meant by action, purpose, effort, to achieve something or to understand something—we know these things through direct consciousness of them. We possess self awareness. Can we also tell what others are at? Vico never directly tells us how this is achieved, but takes it for granted that solipsism needs no refutation, and, moreover, that we communicate with others because we can and do grasp, in some direct way, less or more successfully, the purpose and meaning of their words, their gestures, their signs and symbols; for if there were no communication, there would be no language, no society, no humanity. But even if this applies to the present and the living, does it also apply to the past? Can we grasp the acts, the thoughts, the attitudes, the beliefs, explicit and implicit, the worlds of thought and feeling of societies dead and gone? And if so, how is this achieved? Vico's answer to this problem is perhaps the boldest and most original of his ideas.

He declared that there were three great doors that lead into the past:

language; myths; and rites; that is, institutional behaviour. We speak of metaphorical ways of expression. The aesthetic theorists of his day (Vico tells us) regard this simply as so much embellishment, a heightened form of speech used by poets as a deliberate device to give us pleasure or move us in particular ways, or ingenious ways of conveying important truths.[3] This rests on the assumption that what is expressed metaphorically could, at least in principle, be as well expressed in plain, literal prose, although this might be tedious and not give us the pleasure caused by poetic speech. But, Vico maintains, if you read primitive utterances (Latin and Greek antiquities, which he knew best, provide him with the majority of his examples) you will soon realise that what we call metaphorical speech is the natural mode of expression of these early men. When we say that our blood is boiling, this may for us be a conventional metaphor for anger, but for primitive man anger literally resembled the sensation of blood boiling within him; when we speak of the teeth of ploughs, or the mouths of rivers, or the lips of vases, these are dead metaphors or, at best, deliberate artifice intended to produce a certain effect upon the listener or reader. But to our remote ancestors ploughs actually appeared to have teeth; rivers, which for them were semi-animate, had mouths: land was endowed with necks and tongues, metals and minerals with veins, the earth had bowels, oaks had hearts, skies smiled and frowned, winds raged, the whole of nature was alive and active. Gradually, as human experience changed, this, once natural, speech, which Vico calls poetical, lingered on as turns of phrase in common speech whose origins had been forgotten or at least no longer felt, or as conventions used by sophisticated versifiers. Forms of speech express specific kinds of vision: there is no universal, "literal" speech which denotes a timeless reality. Before "poetical" language, men used hieroglyphs and ideograms which convey a vision of the world very different from our own—Vico declares that men sang before they

3. So Fontenelle, whose influence on his age was, perhaps, inferior only to Voltaire's identifies progress in the arts (as in everything else) with increase in order, clarity, precision, *nettete,* whose purest expression is geometry—the Cartesian method which cannot but improve whatever it touches, in every province of knowledge and creation. Mythology for him, as for Voltaire, is the product of savagery and ignorance. He is suspicious of all metaphors, but especially of *images fabuleuses* which spring from a "totally false and ridiculous" conception of things—their use can only help to disseminate error. Poets in primitive times employed mythological language ornamentally, but also as a strategem to represent themselves as directly inspired by the gods; modern writers should at least use *images spirituelles*—personified abstractions about, say, time, space, deity, which speak to reason, not to irrational feeling. The intellectual power, courage, humanity and unswerving pursuit of truth, with which the *lumieres* of the age fought against nonsense and obscurantism in theory and barbarous cruelties in practice, need not blind us to the vices of their virtues, which have exacted their own terrible price.

spoke, spoke in verse before they spoke in prose, as is made plain by the study of the kinds of signs and symbols that they used, and the types of use they made of them. The task before those who wish to grasp what kind of lives were led in societies different from one's own, is to understand their world: that is, to conceive what kind of vision of the world men who used a particular kind of language must have had for this type of language to be a natural expression of it. The difficulty of this task is brought home most forcibly by the mythological language which Vico cites. The Roman poet says *"Jovis omnia plena"*. What does this mean? Jove—Jupiter—is to us the father of the gods, a bearded thunderer, but the word also means sky or air. How can "everything" be "full" of a bearded thunderer, or the father of the gods? Yet this, evidently, is how men spoke. We must therefore ask ourselves what must the world have been like for those to whom such use of language, almost meaningless to us, made sense? What could be meant by speaking of Cybele as an enormous woman, and also, at the same time, as the whole of the earth, of Neptune as a bearded marine deity, wielding a trident, and also as all the seas and oceans of the world? Thus Herakles is a demi-god who slew the Hydra, but is, at the same time, an Athenian and a Spartan and an Argive and a Theban Herakles, who are many, and also one; Ceres is a female deity but also all the corn in the world. It is a very strange world that we must try, as it were, to transpose ourselves into, and Vico warns us that it is only with the most agonising and super-human effort that we can even attempt to enter the mentality of the primitive savages of whose vision of reality these myths and legends are records. Yet it can, to some degree, be achieved, for we possess a faculty that he calls *fantasia*—imagination—with which it is possible to enter minds very different from our own. How is this done? The nearest we can come to grasping Vico's thought is his parallel between the growth of a species and the growth of the individual: just as we are able to recollect the experiences of childhood (and in our day psycho-analysis has probed further than this), so it must be possible to recapture to some degree the early collective experience of our race, even though this may require terrible effort. This is based on the parallel of the macrocosm to the individual microcosm—phylogenesis as resembling ontogenesis, an idea which dates back at least to the Renaissance. There is an analogy between growth of an individual and that of a people. If I can recollect what it was to have been as a child, I have some inkling of what it was to have belonged to a primitive culture. Judging others by analogy with what I am now will not do: if animism is the false attribution of human characteristics to natural objects, a similar fallacy is involved in attributing to primitives our own sophisticated notions: memory, not analogy, seems closer to the required faculty of imaginative understanding—*fantasia*—whereby we reconstruct the past. (This is a contrast which Mr. Leon Pompa has stressed both in writing and in conversation. I am inclined to think that his interpretation is correct, and that I did not pay sufficient attention to this issue in my previous discussions of this subject.)

The categories of experience of different generations of men differ; but they proceed in a fixed order which Vico thinks he can reconstruct by asking the right questions of the evidence before us. If we ask what kind of experience is presupposed by, alone makes intelligible a particular use of symbols, that is, language, what particular vision is embodied in myths, religious rites, inscriptions, the monuments of the past, we shall be able to trace human growth and development, visualise, "enter" the minds of men creating their world by effort, by work, by struggle. Each phase of this process conveys, indeed, communicates its experience in its own characteristic forms—in hieroglyphs, in primitive song, in myths and legends, in dances and laws, in ceremonial and elaborate religious rites, which to Voltaire or Holbach or d'Alembert, were merely obsolete relics of a barbarous past or a mass of obscurantist hocus-pocus. The development of social consciousness and activity is, Vico maintains, traceable also in the evolution of etymology and syntax, which reflects successive phases of social life, and develop *pari passu* with them. Poetry is not conscious embellishment invented by sophisticated writers, nor is it secret wisdom in mnemonic form—it is a direct form of self-expression of our remote ancestors, collective and communal; Homer is the voice not of an individual poet but of the entire Greek people. This notion, in this specific formulation of it, was destined to have a rich flowering in the theories of Winckelmann and Herder who, when they first developed their ideas, had not, so far as one can tell, so much as heard of Vico. As for the unaltering character of basic human nature—the central concept of the Western tradition from the Greeks to Aquinas, from the Renaissance to Arotius, Spinoza, Locke, this could not be so, for man's creations—language, myth, ritual—tell a different story. The first men were savage brutes, cave dwellers who used "mute" signs—gestures and then hieroglyphs. The first peal of thunder filled them with terror. Awe—a sense of a power greater than themselves brooding over them—awakened in them. They gathered together for self-protection; there follows the "age of the gods" or *patres,* stern heads of primitive human tribes. Outside their fortifications there is no security: men attacked by other men stronger than themselves seek protection, and are given it by the "fathers" at the price of becoming slaves or clients. This marks the "heroic" age of oligarchies, of harsh and avaricious masters, who were of "poetic" speech, ruling over slaves and serfs. There comes a moment when these last revolt, extort concessions, particularly with regard to marriage and burial rites, which are the oldest forms of human institution. They cause their new rites to be recorded—this constitutes the earliest form of law. This, in turn, generates prose, which leads to argument and rhetoric, and so to questioning, philosophy, scepticism, egalitarian democracy, and, in the end, the subversion of the simple piety, solidarity and deference to authority of primitive societies, to their atomisation and disintegration, to destructive egoism and alienation,[4] and ultimate collapse, unless some Augustus restores authority and order, or an earlier, more primitive and vigorous tribe, with still unexhausted energies and firm discipline, conquers it; if this does not happen, there is a total breakdown. Then primitive life in caves begins again, and so the entire cycle repeats itself once more, *corsi e ricorsi,* from the barbarism of savage life to the second barbarism of decay.

There is no progress from the imperfect towards perfection, for the very notion of perfection entails an absolute criterion of value, there is only intelligible change. The stages are not mechanically caused each by its predecessor, but can be seen to flow from the new needs created by the satisfaction of the old ones in the unceasing self-creation and self-transformation of perpetually active men. In this process, war between the classes, in Vico's schema, plays a central role. Here again, Vico draws heavily on mythology. Voltaire tells us that myths are "the ravings of savages and the inventions of knaves", or at best, harmless fancies conjured up by poets to charm their readers. For Vico they are, as often as not, far-reaching images of past social conflicts out of which many diverse cultures grew. He is an ingenious and imaginative historical materialist: Cadmus, Ariadne, Pegasus, Apollo, Mars, Hercules, all symbolise various turning points in the history of social change.[5] What

4. The passage in Vico's *New Science* describing the end of a decadent civilisation is worth quoting: "Men, though physically thronging together, live like wild beasts in a solitude of spirit and will, scarcely any two being able to agree, since each follows his own pleasure and whim."
5. For instance, the story of Theseus and Ariadne is concerned with early sea-faring life: the Minotaur represents the pirates who abduct Athenians in ships, for the bull is a characteristic ancient emblem on a ship's prow, and piracy was held in high honour both by the Greeks, and the ancient Germans. Ariadne is the art of sea-faring, the thread is a symbol of navigation, and the Labyrinth is the Aegean Sea. Alternatively, the Minotaur is a half-caste child, a foreigner come to Crete—an early emblem of racial conflict. Cadmus is primitive man, and his slaying of the serpent is the clearing of the vast forest. He sows the serpent's teeth in the ground—the teeth of a plough, the stones he casts about him are the clods of earth which the oligarchy of Heroes retain against the land hungry serfs; the furrows are the orders of feudal society; the armed men who spring up from the teeth are Heroes, but they fight, not each other, as the myth relates (here Vico decides to "correct" the evidence), but the robbers and vagabonds, who threaten the lives of the settled farmers. The wounding of Mars by Minerva is the defeat of the plebeians by the patricians. In the case of Pegasus, wings represent the sky, the sky represents the birds, flight yields the all-important auspices. Wings plus a

to the rational thought of a later age seemed bizarre combinations of attributes—Cybele, who is both a woman and the earth, horses with wings, centaurs, dryads and the like—are in reality efforts by our ancestors to combine certain functions, or ideas, in a single concrete image. Vico calls such entities "impossible universals", images compounded of incompatible characteristics, for which their descendants, who think in concepts and not in sensuous terms, have substituted an abstract phraseology. The transformation of the denotations of particular words and their modifications can also, for Vico, open windows to the evolution of social structures. This is because "language tells us the history of the things signified by the words." Thus the career of the word "lex" tells us that life in "the great forests of the earth" was followed by life in huts, and after that villages, cities, academies.[6]

Vico's particular attributions are at times wholly implausible or wild. But this matters less than the fact that he conceived the idea of applying to the accumulated antiquities of the human race a species of Kant's transcendental method, that is, an attempt to conceive what the experience of a particular society must have been like for this or that myth, or method of worship, or language, or building, to be their characteristic expression. This opened new doors. It discredited the idea of some static kernel, a timeless and unchanging "human nature". It reinforced the old Epicurean-Lucretian notion of a process of slow growth from

horse is equivalent to horse-riding nobles with the right of taking auspices, and therefore authority over people. Myths represent powers, institutions embody radical changes in the social order; a mythological creature like Draco—a serpent found in China and Egypt too—or Hercules, or Aeneas (whose descent to Avernus is, of course, a symbol of sowing) were not historical persons, and, like Pythagoras and Solon for Vico, mere symbols of political structures, and cannot be fitted into a chronological framework at all.

6. Thus Vico groups together "lex" (acorn), "ilex", "aquilex", "legumen" and "legere", as typical "sylvan" words, plainly drawn from life in the forests, which then came to mean quite different activities and objects. At first, 'lex" "must have meant a collection of acorns". "Ilex" is "oak", for the oak produces the acorns by which the swine are drawn together (so, too, "aquilex" means "collector of waters"). "Lex" was next a collection of vegetables, from which the latter were called "legumina". Later on, at a time when "vulgar letters" had not yet been invented for writing down laws, "lex", by "a necessity of civil nature", must have meant a collection of citizens, or the public parliament; so that the presence of the people was the "lex" or "law" that solemnised the wills that were made *calatis comitiis*, in the presence of the assembled "comitia". Finally, collecting letters and making, as it were, a sheaf of them for each word, was called "legere", "reading" (N.S. 240). This is a piece of characteristically fanciful genetic sociological philology, a good illustration of Vico's doctrine of the relation of the evolution of symbols to the evolution of social life. In due course this approach led to rich and important branches of the humanities in the form of historical jurisprudence, social anthropology, comparative religion, and the like, particularly in their relations with the genetic and historical aspects of linguistic theory.

savage beginnings. There is no timeless, unalterable concept of justice or property or freedom or rights—these values alter as the social structure of which they are a part alters, and the objects created by mind and imagination in which these values are embodied alter from phase to phase. All talk of the matchless wisdom of the ancients is therefore a ludicrous fantasy: the ancients were frightening savages, *grossi bestioni,* roaming the great forests of the earth—creatures remote from us. There is no omnipresent natural law: the lists of absolute principles spelt out by the Stoics or Isidore of Seville or Thomas Aquinas or Grotius, were neither explicitly present in the minds, nor implicit in the acts, of the barbarous early Fathers, even of the Homeric heroes. The rational egoists of Hobbes, Locke or Spinoza are arbitrary and unhistorical; if men had been as they are depicted by these thinkers, their history becomes unintelligible.

Each stage of civilisation generates its own art, its own form of sensibility and imagination. Later forms are neither better nor worse than earlier, but simply different, to be judged, each as the expression of its own particular culture. How can early men, whose signs were "mute", who "spoke with their bodies", who sang before they spoke (as, Vico adds, stammerers still do), be judged by the criteria of our own sophisticated culture? At a time when the great French arbiters of taste believed in an absolute standard of artistic excellence, and knew that the verse of Racine, Corneille (or, indeed, Voltaire) was superior to anything by the shapeless Shakespeare or the unreadable Milton, or, before them, the bizarre Dante, and perhaps the works of the ancients too, Vico maintained that the Homeric poems were a sublime expression of a society dominated by the ambition, avarice and cruelty of its ruling class; for only a society of this kind could have produced this vision of life. Later ages may have perfected other aids to existence, but they cannot create the *Iliad,* which embodies the modes of thought and expression and emotion of one particular kind of way of life; these men literally saw what we do not see. The new history is to be the account of the succession and variety of men's experience and activity, of their continuous self transformation from one culture to another. This leans to a bold relativism, and kills, among other things, the notion of progress in the arts, whereby later cultures are necessarily improvements on, or retrogressions from, earlier ages, each measured by its distance from some fixed, immutable ideal, in terms of which all beauty, knowledge, virtue, must be judged. The famous quarrel between the ancients and the moderns can have no sense for Vico: every artistic tradition is intelligible only to those who grasp its own rules, the conventions that are internal to it, an "organic" part of its own, changing pattern of categories of thought and feeling. The notion of anachronism, even if others had some inkling of it, is rendered central by him. Polybius once said (and it might have been said in the eighteenth century) that it was a misfortune for mankind that it was priests and not philosophers who had presided over its birth; how much error and cruelty would have been spared it but for these mendacious charlatans, and Lucretius passionately reiterated this. To those who live after Vico, it is as if one were to suggest that Shakespeare could have written his plays at the court of Genghis Khan, or Mozart composed in ancient Sparta. Vico goes far beyond Bodin and Montaigne and Montesquieu:[7] they (and Voltaire) may have believed in different social *esprits,* but not in stages of historical evolution, each phase of which has its own modes of vision, forms of expression, whether one calls them art or science or religion. The idea of the cumulative growth of knowledge, a single corpus governed by single, universal criteria, so that what one generation of scientists has established, another generation need not repeat, does not fit this at all. This marks the great break between the notion of positive knowledge and that of understanding.

Vico does not deny the need for the latest scientific techniques in establishing facts. He claims no intuitive or metaphysical faculty which can dispense with empirical investigation. As tests for the authenticity of documents and other evidence, for dating, for chronological order, for establishing who did or suffered what and when and where, whether one is dealing with individuals or classes or societies, for establishing bare facts, the newly established scientific methods of investigation may well be indispensable. The same applies to the investigation of impersonal factors—geographical or environmental or social; the study of natural resources, fauna, flora, social structure, colonisation, com-

7. The difference of the earlier and later attitudes is brought out by the interest in myths and fables on the part of, say, Bodin and Bacon and even Montesquieu on the one hand, and Vico on the other. The two former thinkers do not think of myths and fables as inventions of lying priests or merely results of "human weakness" (to use Voltaire's phrase), but they look to antiquities of this kind for information about the *moeurs* and *facons de vivre* in early or remote societies for the express purpose of discovering whether there are historical lessons to be learned with relevance for their own times and circumstances. Even though temperamentally they may have been intensely curious about other societies, and collected these facts for their own sakes, the ostensible motive was certainly utilitarian—they wished to improve human life. Vico looks at myths as evidence of the different categories in which experience was organised—spectacles, unfamiliar to us, through which early man and remote peoples looked at the world in which they lived: the purpose is to understand whence we come, how we came to be where we are, how much or how little of the past we still carry with us. His approach is genetic, for it is only through its genesis, reconstructed by *fantasia* guided by rules which he thinks he has discovered, that anything can be truly understood: not by some intuition of timeless essences, or empirical description or analysis of any object's present state. This marks a genuine turning point in the conception of history and society.

merce, finance, must use the methods of science which establish the kind of probability of which Bodin and Voltaire spoke and every historian who uses sociological and statistical methods has done ever since. With all this Vico has no quarrel. What, then, is novel in his conception of history, over which he tells us he spent twenty years of continuous labour? It is, I think, this: that to understand history is to understand what men made of the world in which they found themselves, what they demanded of it, what their felt needs, aims, ideals were; he seeks to discover their vision of it, he asks what wants, what questions, what aspirations determined a society's view of reality; and he thinks that he has created a new method which will reveal to him the categories in terms of which men thought and acted and changed themselves and their worlds. This kind of knowledge is not knowledge of facts, or of logical truths provided by observation or the sciences or deductive reasoning; nor is it knowledge of how to do things, nor the knowledge provided by faith, based on divine revelation, in which Vico professed his belief. It is more like the knowledge we claim of a friend, of his character, of his ways of thought or action, the intuitive sense of the nuances of personality or feeling or ideas, which Montaigne describes so well, and which Montesquieu took into account. To do this, one must possess imaginative power of a high degree, such as artists, and in particular, novelists, require. And even this will not get us far in grasping ways of life too remote from us and unlike our own. Yet even then we need not totally despair, for what we are seeking to understand is men—human beings endowed as we are, with minds and purposes and inner lives; their works cannot be wholly unintelligible to us, unlike the impenetrable content of non-human nature. Without this power of "entering into" minds and situations, the past will remain a dead collection of objects in a museum for us. This sort of knowledge, not thought of in Descartes' philosophy, is based on the fact that we do know what men are, what action is, what it is to have intentions, motives, to seek to understand and interpret, in order to make oneself at home in the non-human world, what Hegel called *"bey sich selbst seyn"*. The most famous passage in *The New Science* expresses this central insight most vividly: "In the night of thick darkness which envelops the earliest antiquity, so remote from ourselves, there shines the eternal and never-failing light of a truth beyond all question: that the world of civil society has certainly been made by men, and that its principles are therefore to be found within the modifications of our own human mind. Whoever reflects on this cannot but marvel that the philosophers should have bent all their energies to the study of the world of nature, which, since God made it, He alone knows; and that they should have neglected the study of the world of nations or civil world, which, since men made it, men could come to know." Men have made their civil world—that is, their civilisation and institutions—but, as Marx was later to point out, not out of "whole cloth", not out of infinitely malleable material; the external world, men's own physical and psychical constitution, play their part. Of this Vico said nothing: he is interested only in the human contribution: and when he speaks of the unintended consequences of men's actions—that which they have not "made"—he attributes this to Providence, which guides men for their ultimate benefit in its own inscrutable way. That too, then, is outside man's conscious control. But what he means is that what one generation of men have experienced and done, and embodied in their works, another generation can grasp, though, it may be, with difficulty and imperfectly. For this one must possess a developed *fantasia*—Vico's term for imaginative insight, which he accuses the French theorists of undervaluing. This is the capacity: for conceiving more than one way of categorising reality, like the ability to understand what it is to be an artist, a revolutionary, a traitor, to know what it is to be poor, to wield authority, to be a child, a prisoner, a barbarian. Without some ability to get into the skin of others (what Keats called negative capability, which he attributed to Shakespeare), the human condition, history, what characterises one period or culture as against others—cannot be understood. The successive patterns of civilisation differ from other temporal processes—say, geological—by the fact that it is men—ourselves—who play a crucial part in creating them. This lies at the heart of the art or science of attribution: to tell what goes with one form of life and not with another, and then look for empirical evidence. Let me give you an example of Vico's method: he is arguing that the story that the Romans borrowed the Twelve Tables (the original Roman code of laws) from the Athens of Solon's day cannot be true; for it is not possible for such barbarians as the Romans must have been in Solon's time to have known where Athens was, or that it possessed a code that might be of value to them. Moreover, even on the improbable assumption that these early Romans knew that there was a more civilised or better organised society to the south-east of them (even though the barbarous tribes of early Rome could scarcely have entertained, however inchoately, such notions as civilisation or a city state), they could not have translated Attic words into idiomatic Latin without a trace of Greek influence on it, and in particular used such a word as *auctoritas,* for which no Greek equivalent existed. This kind of argument rests not on an accumulation of empirical evidence about human behaviour in many times and places, upon which sociological generalisations can be made to rest. Such notions as an advanced culture and what distinguishes it from barbarism, are for Vico not terms of value, but of the stages of the growth of self-awareness in individuals and societies; of the differences between the concepts and categories in use at one stage of growth from those that shape another, and of the genesis of one from another, which ultimately stems from knowing what childhood and maturity are. In the early fifteenth century, the Italian humanist Bruni had declared that whatever was said in Greek could equally well be said in Latin too. This is precisely what Vico denies, as the example of *auctoritas* shows; there is no immutable structure of experience, to reflect which a perfect language could be invented and into which imperfect approximations to such a language could be transposed. The language of so-called primitives is not an imperfect rendering of what later generations will express more accurately: it embodies its own unique vision of the world, which can be grasped, but not translated totally, into the language of another culture. One culture is not a less perfect vision of another: winter is not a rudimentary spring, summer is not an undeveloped autumn.

The worlds of Homer, or the Bible, or the Kalevala, cannot be understood at all if they are judged in terms of the absolute criteria of Voltaire or Helvétius or Buckle, and given marks according to their distance from the highest reaches of human civilisation, as exemplified in Voltaire's *Musée Imaginaire,* where the four great ages of man hang side by side, as aspects of the single, self-same peak of human attainment. To say this is a truism which I may be thought to have laboured far too long: it was not a truism in the early eighteenth century. The very notion that the task of historians was not merely to establish facts and give causal explanations for them, but to examine what a situation meant to those involved in it, what their outlook was, by what rules they were guided, what "absolute presuppositions" (as Collingwood called them) were entailed in what they (but not other societies, other cultures) said or did—all that is certainly novel and profoundly foreign to the thought of the *philosophes* and scientists of Paris. It coloured the thoughts of those who first reacted against the French Enlightenment, critics and historians of natural literatures in Switzerland, in England, in Germany—Bodmer and Breitinger and von Muralt, Lowth and Blackwell, Young and Adam Ferguson, Hamann and Möser and Herder. After them came the great generation of scholars, Wolf and Niebuhr, Savigny and Boeckh, who transformed the study of the ancient world, and whose work had a decisive influence on Burckhardt and Dilthey and their successors in the twentieth century. From these origins came comparative philology and comparative anthropology, comparative jurisprudence and religion and literature, comparative histories of art and civilisation and ideas—the fields in which not merely knowledge of facts and events, but understanding, what Herder was the first to call *Einfühlung*—empathy—is required. The use of informed imagination about and insight into systems of value, conceptions of life of entire societies, is not required in mathematics or physics or geology or zoology or even—though some would deny this—in economic history, or even sociology if it is conceived and practiced as a strictly natural science. This is an intentionally extreme statement, intended to emphasise the gap that opened between natural science and the humanities as the result of a new attitude to the human past. No doubt in practice there is a great overlap between impersonal history as it is conceived by, say, Condorcet or Buckle or Marx, who believed that human society could be studied by a human science in principle analogous to that which tells us about the behaviour of "bees or beavers" (to use Condorcet's analogy), contrasted with the history of what men believed in and lived by, the life of the spirit, blindness which Coleridge and Carlyle imputed to the Utilitarians, Acton to Buckle (in his famous attack upon him), Croce to the Positivists. Vico began the schism: after that there was a parting of the ways. The specific and unique versus the universal, the concrete versus the abstract, perpetual movement versus rest, the inner versus the outer, quality versus quantity, culture-bound versus timeless, principles, mental strife and self-transformation as a permanent condition of man versus the possibility (and desirability) of peace, order, final harmony and the satisfaction of all rational human wishes—these are some of the aspects of the contrast. Professor Erich Auerbach seems to me to have put this with eloquence and precision:[8] "When people realise that epochs and societies are not to be judged in terms of a pattern concept of what is desirable absolutely, but rather in every case in terms of their own premises, when people reckon among such premises not only natural factors like climate and soil, but also the intellectual and historical factors; when, in other words, they come to develop a sense of historical dynamics, of the incomparability of historical phenomena, so that each epoch appears as a whole whose character is reflected in each of its manifestations; when finally they accept the conviction that the meaning of events cannot be grasped in abstract and general forms of cognition, and that the material needed to understand it must not be sought in the upper strata of society and in major political events, but also in art, economy, material and intellectual culture, in the depths of the workaday world and its men and women, because it is only there that one can grasp what is unique, what is animated by inner forces, and what, in the more concrete and more profound sense, is universally valid . . ." I know of no better formulation of the difference between history as science and history as a form of self knowledge incapable of ever becoming fully organised, and to be achieved—as Vico warned us—only by "unbelievable effort".

This formulation, which is by now taken for granted by historians of literature, of ideas, of art, of law, and by historians of science too, and most of all by historians and sociologists of culture influenced by this

8. *Mimesis*, Princeton Paperback, 1963, p. 39.

tradition, is not, and does not need to be, assumed by natural scientists themselves. Yet, before the eighteenth century, there was, so far as I know, no sense of this contrast. Distinctions between the vast realm of philosophy—natural and metaphysical, theology, history, rhetoric, jurisprudence, were not too sharply drawn; there were disputes about method in the Renaissance, but the great cleavage between the provinces of natural science and the humanities was, for the first time, made, or at least revealed, for better or for worse, by Giambattista Vico. Thereby he started a great debate of which the end is not in sight.

Where did his most central insight originate? Did the idea of what culture is, and what it is to understand it in its unity and variety, and its likeness, but above all, unlikeness to other cultures, which undermines the doctrine of the identity of civilisation and scientific progress—spring fully armed like Pallas Athene out of his head? Who, before 1725, had had such thoughts? How did they percolate—if, indeed, they ever did—to Hamann and Herder in Germany, some of whose ideas are strikingly similar? These are problems on which, even now, not enough research has been done by historians of ideas. Yet fascinating as they are, their solution seems to me to be less important than the central discoveries themselves; most of all, the notion that the only way of achieving any degree of self-understanding is by re-tracing our steps, historically, psychologically and, above all, anthropologically, through the stages of social growth, governed by empirically discoverable laws, with whose workings we are acquainted in our own mental life but tending to no single, universal goal. Each of these forms of human experience has a structure and a style of its own, yet having enough in common with its successors, with which it forms a sufficiently continuous line of recognizable human activity, to be intelligible to them. Only in this fashion, if Vico is right, can we hope to understand the unity of human history:—the links that connect our own "magnificent age" to our beginnings in the great forests of the earth.

The Rebirth of God and the Death of Man

BY LESLIE FIEDLER

It has, I assume, become clear at this point to almost everyone that the successful Cultural Revolution we have been observing over the past fifteen or twenty years—here in the United States at least, and perhaps generally in the Western World—the emergence of what has been called variously the "Counter Culture," or "Consciousness III," or "The New Mutants," or the "Present Future," has been in large part, even essentially, a *Religious Revival:* the unforeseen, unsung and often quite misunderstood beginning of a New Age of Faith. The prophets of that Cultural Revolution, whether candid secularists like Wilhelm Reich and Herbert Marcuse or crypto-Thomists like Marshall MacLuhan, have, for reasons of their own, not emphasized this aspect of the movement they helped to create. And warm-hearted but superficial analysts and apologists after the fact like Charles Reich or Theodore Roszak have obscured the religious dimensions of the Counter Culture (along with much else) because of their commitment to chic journalistic vocabularies intended to sell rather than describe what must be made at all costs to sound Brand New.

To be sure, one French opposite number of such apologists, Edgar Morin, has recently declared his adherence to the New Movement, with the phrase: "I am joining the Childrens' Crusade!" But in context (M. Morin is a sociologist and ex-Communist, or rather, I suppose, meta-Communist) this sounded like a mere metaphor—demanding immediate translation into more secular terms. Looking backward from the end of 1972, however, it is possible to see (almost impossible to miss) what was, while it was happening, too obvious to be perceived: the fact that the recent Cultural Revolution has nurtured and, in a certain sense, *established* a dedicated minority, felt by the larger society to be somehow representative, exemplary—even "sacred." It is further evident that the values of that minority, as embodied in a life-style celebrated or deplored daily (it amounts to much the same thing) by the popular press, are much like those traditionally associated with earlier exemplary minorities: lay clergy and cloistered religious, isolated hermits and utopian religious communities, sponsored or somewhat reluctantly endorsed by the established Churches.

I do not intend to discuss here the life-style in which these values are embodied, though certain aspects of this, too, provide obvious analogies into religious practises of the past. The actual garb of the New Communicants, for instance, these robes and sandals so appropriate to the pilgrimages in which they habitually engage, seem to me to be superficial and symptomatic rather than essential, as does the show of poverty which characterizes their way of life. Their pilgrimages may be merely a new form of bourgeois tourism or even of American cultural imperialism while their much-vaunted poverty is, perhaps, more aptly described as conspicuous under-consumption. It is, therefore, at a deeper level that I propose to begin, by examining their value-system, at the center of which is the conviction that after all the contemplative life may be preferable to the active life. But, of course, to choose Rachel over Leah at this late date, the second wife of Jacob over his first, constitutes a radical rejection of the position defended against Catholic monasticism by an earlier Cultural Revolution launched by the Protestant churches: a position notoriously exploited by the secular heirs of Protestantism, the present Masters of our World, Capitalist and Communist alike.

From this major premise follow the corollaries that salvation rather than success is man's proper goal, and that, therefore, one must begin by rejecting goods in favor of the Good or even social welfare, and learn eventually to prefer being good to being well—a shocking anti-psychiatric position. Furthermore, once contemplation is valued more highly than action, Vision rather than understanding is proposed as the proper end of man's inner life, the life of the mind. Oddly enough, I first became aware of this revolutionary shift in values in the classroom, where I teach from time to time courses on Dante, having done so, in fact, over the past three decades. During the first two of these decades, I was vexed by the sense of having to explain a radically alien point of view to my students before they could have any notion of what the poetry of the *Divine Comedy* was really about. But since 1960, anyhow, there has been no need to spell out for students what "Vision" once meant to certain benighted believers since it is a category of experience to which they aspire even if they have not yet attained it. Still less is it necessary to expound for them the significance of the "Voyage", or, as it has become more fashionable to call it, the "Trip" through time to timelessness.

Never mind that the salvation sought by the New Religious is instant, here and now rather than at the end of days. Not they alone have become convinced that eternity does not lie beyond time, but intersects it. Still less must we be put off by the fact that the New Celebrants seek Vision by the use of once forbidden drugs, revelation not just through fasting and prayer and spiritual exercise, but by psycho-chemical means as well. All religions have employed intoxicants to initiate the entry into the Way—the grape, perfumes, music to aid in the trip toward ecstasy, where those means as well as everything else once prized and exploited will have become meaningless. After all, is not the ancient and holy practise of fasting itself a kind of negative psycho-chemistry?

We may *finally* be saved by that which comes out of the mouth rather than that which goes in, but all religions have initially concerned themselves with what is eaten as well as what is spoken: honoring not just the Word but Bread and Wine, as well as Dionysus and Ceres, the Gods poured out or consumed in honour of the other Gods. Besides, is there not implicit in the contemporary use of sacred drugs, of what is inadvertently sacred in the intendedly profane pursuits of Science, a commendable desire to democratize ecstasy, to make Mystical Vision no longer the privilege of a handful of adepts but of *everyone*. The New Religious are determined to be no inert congregation rehearsing the words of dead Visionaries and half-mythological Saints, but a living church of actual Visionaries and Saints. This constitutes, perhaps, a peculiarly American dream, in its most virulent form even madder than our dream of universal higher education, this dream of universal *Ekstasis;* but, by the same token, it is even more beautiful—not least because it may be finally impossible, a Way to Idolatry more often than a Door to Perception.

Less noticed, perhaps, than the redemption of the Contemplative Life but almost as critically important, has been the Revolt against Romantic Love everywhere present within the ranks of the Cultural Revolution: the quite conscious attempt to liquidate the anti-religion or quasi-religion or burlesque religion of Love, which has possessed the Arts of Western Christendom and haunted the imaginations of all who have read its texts, or looked at its ikons, or listened to its quasi-holy songs since Courtly Love and vernacular poetry were born together at the end of the 11th century in Provence. That essentially godless religion has come to seem to the New Communicants especially distasteful in its late Protestant-sentimental forms: that Angel-in-the-House tradition, in which the mock worship of women has been detached from adultery and linked to monogamous marriage and the bourgeois family.

Sometimes it is Sex—naked *libido,* unmythicized and polymorphous perverse—which the New Believers oppose to Courtly or Romantic or Sentimental Love. Sometimes it is *agape,* Holy Love, Sweet Charity, a universal bond which, by making all men and women Brothers and Sisters, challenges the authenticity of those exclusive bonds which define us as Sons and Daughters, Mothers and Fathers, husbands and wives, and especially faithful and jealous lovers of other single humans. Sometimes, under the New Dispensation, undifferentiated *libido* and universal *agape* blend into one ambiguous impulse, capable of motivating the sort of sub-orgasmic orgies often called these days "Sensitivity Sessions" or "Encounter Groups", or, more pretentiously and equivocally, "Tribal Experiences".

A wide variety of sexual behavior is tolerated under the New Dispensation, ranging from the total sublimation of passion, through multiple marriages to communities in which all are available in all possible ways to all; sex has become, like everything else, communal property. In no case, however, is exclusive heterosexual Love proposed as a means of Education and Civilization, a way of converting men and women, still moved by passion as dumbly and helplessly as beasts, into Ladies and Cavaliers, Courtiers distinguished by Gentle Hearts and the Intelligence of Love. And certainly the possibility has been preempted from the start of a compromise between *eros* and *agape,* the lust of the body and the longing of the soul, justified by the kind of Romantic Theology which begins with Dante's *Vita Nuova* and ends in the Anglican apologetics of Charles Williams, or the anti-Puritan Puritanism of D. H. Lawrence.

In addition to its attack on Work, Success and Romantic Love, the New Religion is marked by an onslaught against certain conceptions of the central importance of Literature in the humanizing of man, conceptions which had remained basically unshaken (despite the rivalry of Science) ever since the Renaissance recovered from the Classical Past the notion of Culture as Secular Salvation for an educated elite. It is not, as Marshall MacLuhan, for instance, has argued, that the New Communicants, being children of an age dominated by the post-Gutenberg media, have ceased to read. MacLuhan is simply wrong in this regard. I have never myself visited an Agricultural Commune which does not possess some books—a slim collection of highly prized and carefully read volumes. But these must not be thought of as constituting in any traditional sense a "Library". No, in their function and use, they are more like the household books of some pious Seventeenth Century New England Puritan than the contents of Nineteenth Century study shelves stacked with critically approved "Great Books," or an early Twentieth Century parlor table, loaded with the latest selections of the Book Clubs.

In place of the Puritan's Christian Bible, however, plus Milton and *Pilgrim's Progress,* one is likely to find a motley (but at last somehow standard) selection of some of the following: The *Tibetan Book of the Dead,* the *Whole Earth Catalogue,* and the *I Ching;* along with all three well-worn volumes of J. R. R. Tolkien's *Rings* trilogy, plus a Macrobiotic Cookbook, Kurt Vonnegut's *Cat's Cradle* or *Slaughterhouse*

Five, Castañeda's *The Teachings of Don Juan,* a couple of Hermann Hesse novels, and a complete file of the latest Stan Lee comic books. And, as I had almost forgotten, there would also be some pornography: a "Head Comic" by R. Crumm, or a more grossly sadomasochistic one by S. Clay Wilson, or perhaps, *The Kama Sutra.*

The point is not merely that the Scripture of various alien cultures have been given equal—or even superior—status with the Holy Book of Christianity, but that *any books which are read at all are read as Scripture,* which is to say, not for information or "cultural enrichment", much less to pass an idle hour, but as Guides to Salvation, and that even masturbatory fantasies are thus canonized. It does not matter, certainly, what the author of any particular text, chosen by some mysterious process associated with the market place and the mode, may have thought he was writing or why.

He may, like Robert Heinlein, for instance, when he corrected the last galleys of *A Stranger in a Strange Land,* have considered that he was producing just one more in a long line of Science Fiction novels, intended to provide entertainment and make a quick buck. After all, at that point Heinlein was already a long-established and well-rewarded hack. But he could not stay the process which kidnapped his work for "sacred" ends, extracting from it a new "holy" verb ("to grock") and supplying the initial inspiration, as well as a passage or two for Charlie Manson's syncretic Black Ritual. And it does no good to protest later, as Heinlein has, along with that master of Porno-S.F., Philip Jose Farmer, whose *The Lovers* apparently inspired him, that that is not what he meant at all. That *is* what they both meant *in context.*

Furthermore, it is neither accidental nor irrelevant that Heinlein's book comes from the area of Popular rather than High culture, the world of joyous junk rather than that of solemn art; for the new religion is essentially *Pop.* Pop Science is also raided in the endless search for a Pop Scriptures—as in the case of Ohsawa's various works on dietetics. Or perhaps one should rather describe the texts of the founder of Macrobiotics as Pop Science plus Pop Theology: a little vulgarized Zen Buddhism, mingled with some Pop Reflections on Yin and Yang, plus some practical admonitions at the level of the Home Medical Advisor on how to cure gonorrhea and avoid cancer by learning to eschew milk. It does not matter that none of this makes rational sense. What does matter is precisely that it does *not* make such sense, thus providing occasions for true acts of faith. "I believe because it is absurd," the naive believer has always cried, scandalizing the more sophisticated who had placed their faith in the rational.

Certainly, the skeptical have not given pause to any devotee, however anemic and wasted, nor disturbed his resolution to go ten days on "straight grains" in quest of health more spiritual than physical. Mere medical statistics seem as irrelevant to such a believer as they did earlier to the followers of Wilhelm Reich who crouched naked in their "Orgone Accumulators" in quest of an orgasm pure enough to inhibit cancer. Nor does the sober comment of academic psychiatrists turn anyone away from the palpable "hoax" of Scientology: creation of L. Ron Hubbard, who was himself a hack-writer of Science Fiction before he decided to peddle his fantasies as fact—thus becoming the Founder of a New Faith, in whose name he has grown as rich as any Robber Baron or Park Avenue "shrink." But, of course, being a *guru* rather than a business man or doctor or ordained clergyman, he finds it possible to remain immune to self-doubt or guilt. In an age of Underground Faith, the underground faithful rejoice especially in those leaders the established call "charlatans", in those who *are,* by established standards, charlatans in fact: from Hubbard and Leary and Manson to Wilhelm Reich.

But it is not charlatanism alone which moves the faithful. What are we to make, for instance, of the vogue of the Whole Earth Catalogue, the product not of showmen and hucksters, but of modest believers rather than arrogant Shamans, yet also a Pop, i.e., a commercial success? Is it not also a Bible for yet another Sect created in a time of Pop Science; and does it not reflect the teaching of yet another Science Fiction writer who has chosen life over art as his preferred medium: that odd blend of technocrat, *guru* and a nut inventor, R. Buckminster Fuller. To be sure, his doctrine has been oddly transformed by being translated from the Urban centers he loves to the New Mexico countryside by younger men, less sure than he that technology can solve the problems it has created by becoming super-technology. It is a kind of sub-technology, which the editors of The *Whole Earth Catalogue* prefer, a minimal technology, a technology of do-it-yourself. But they share his faith, his Religion of Gadgetry; and in 1972, their technocrat's Bible was given, scandalizing some and gratifying others, a National Book Award.

The judges who bestowed that award were merely attempting to certify as "literature" a somewhat pretentious collection of ads for goods still considered *"Kosher"* in a time of conspicuous under-consumption. But the early admirers of the *Whole Earth Catalogue* had already canonized it as "Scripture." So that even before the National Book Award, it had made its way on to the shelves of readers who would never use any of the products it advertised—having no desire to build super-geodesic domes or prefabricated Indian teepees, but merely to read or own a Holy Text.

How different has been the fate of the *Sears Roebuck Catalogue,* its predecessor and prototype, which only came to be esteemed and preserved when it had grown obsolete enough to the advanced to seem proper "camp". To be sure, the *Sears Roebuck Catalogue* evoked no holy names like that of Buckminster Fuller, no sacred theory like his. But this is not the real point; for in the declining Twentieth Century, what is most debased, most despised, most utterly vulgarized in the realm of para-literature, i.e., advertising, is all the more prized, so long as it can be used for presumed "sacred" ends: turning on, returning to nature, dropping out, avoiding pollution, ripping off the Establishment. It has, in fact, always been true in the case of Pop Religions, in America at least: in that of Christian Science, for example, and Mormonism, that the low literary value of New Scriptures has been taken as a warranty of their sincerity and truth.

And here, precisely, is where the habit of reading literature as Scripture so essential to the New Dispensation differs totally from the elitist "Culture Religion" whose great apostle was Matthew Arnold. For Arnold, what made literature, some literature, Scripture, or rather a replacement for Scripture in an age of declining faith and The Death of God, was its excellence as literature, and its consequent critical immortality. On the other hand, what makes literature, some literature, available as Scripture in an Age of the Revival of Faith and the rebirth of the Gods is its doctrinal content, in the light of which the very nature of literary excellence, in aesthetic or formalist terms, becomes not merely irrelevant, but offensive as well. Once more Faith drives out before it the criterion of Taste, which could only have flourished in its absence. It is not that literary excellence is felt as totally inimical to relevance or truth, for some of the canonical texts of the New Dispensation are worthy enough for formalist standards: Tolkien, for example, or Hesse, or Kurt Vonnegut. And yet even these contain a redeeming element of *schlock* or *schmaltz,* or at least *Kitsch*.

Beyond the rejection of the Puritan Ethos and Love and Literature, there resides at the heart of the current Religious revival a fourth rejection, not less noticed, perhaps, but certainly less clearly understood than any of the others; and yet without coming to terms with it, we cannot fully comprehend the meaning of the Cultural Revolution. This is the Rejection of the City, a flight from urban to rural, which seems at first glance merely a reaction (comprehensible enough, and even sympathetic) from the unseemly sprawl, the congestion and pollution, the anti-human pace and the aggravated offense against nature apparently inseparable from urban civilization. But the New Mutants in their agricultural communes cannot be understood merely as the last heirs of a tradition of revulsion which, over the past two or three centuries, has driven increasing numbers of sensitive souls to abandon the centers of large cities, and to create first the Romantic Suburb, then the Bourgeois Suburb, and finally, Exurbia: all bound still to the urban core by trains and buses and private cars, a network of two-way roads leading back and forth from markets and jobs and theatres at the center to gardens and bedrooms on the periphery. No, the agricultural commune is no ultimate exurb disguised as a rural slum, nor even a cross between Exurbia and Bohemia. It is an outward and visible manifestation of an inward and invisible rejection not just of the *metropolis* and the *megalopolis* but of the *polis* itself: not just of New York and Berlin and Tokyo and London, but of Rome and Athens, Florence and Urbino, Vicenza and Weimar, Green Belt and Bucks County.

There has been a deep ambivalence toward the city apparent at the heart of our culture ever since the city was re-invented sometime around the Twelfth Century. In Dante, for instance, innermost Hell, the heart of the Inferno, is thought of as a "sorrowful city," *la città dolente;* but in the ultimate Empyrean, he remembers the Holy City, stronghold of Empire and Papacy. And we are, therefore, not surprised when he draws on his tourist's memories of Rome for the setting of his final vision, portraying the Saints gathered together in an arena which is simultaneously a Rose and the Coliseum, the perfection of natural beauty and urban architecture. It is not the redeemed, the Heavenly City, which the New Religious dream but a world without cities—a world before or after cities, a world in which the Idea of the City has not yet been conceived or has been long forgotten. This is because Dante is already a Humanist, as the New Religious no longer are.

The idea of Man central to Humanism is inseparable from the Idea of the City: the notion of a complex community based on the division of labor, the centralization of specialized services, plus a concentration of talent, a maximization of cultural interchange, as well as the storage and distribution of the most varied kinds of goods. The actualization of this Idea made possible the creation of theatres and supermarkets, libraries and museums, hospitals and cathedrals, courts of law and parliaments, and supereminently, the University, the center and shrine, as it were, of dialectics and of the conversion of *mythos* to *logos,* the Shrine of Humanism. The End of the City, the death of the polis means, therefore, the End of Man as we have defined him over the past two and a half millennia. I scarcely need remind you of the Aristotelian text which is a chief source of that definition. *Man is a political animal; outside the polis, he is a beast or a god.*

Nor is it necessary to do more than mention the literary work which constitutes a kind of dramatic and still half-mythic prefiguration of that text, since it is a work which has pre-eminently possessed our imaginations over the past decade or so, becoming for us by all odds the favorite, the most living of all classic Greek dramas. I am referring, of course, to *The Bacchae* of Euripides, which renders with total clarity, though without simplification of the ambiguities involved, the crisis of the human which occurs when men grow weary of the institutions which have nurtured their humanity; or rather, perhaps, when those institutions rigidify to the point at which creative sublimation becomes deadly repression, and *logos* becomes madness both for those who remain behind in the dying city and those who abandon the *polis* in favor of the *thiasos,* the pack, the Dionysiac rout.

There is no other alternative; when we flee the City, we wake to find ourselves on Cithaeron, which is to say, in a world without order or tradition or law or distinction: the Dionysiac world, which it is possible to glorify by expurgation *à la* Nietzsche as a source of fertility and song (which it is), a place where madness has at least a sanctified function. But, as Euripides confessed long ago, it is also a world of ecstasy from which one awakens, inevitably, necessarily, to terror: the Mother discovering that the bloody head she holds in her hand is not that of some sacrificial beast, but of her Son who, refusing to sanctify madness in the name of the human, himself becomes simultaneously a beast and a God, though still somehow a mortal who must suffer and be destroyed.

But here precisely is the essence of the thiasic as opposed to political experience, of life in the pack as opposed to life in the city. For in the *thiasos,* all those distinctions are lost which made possible the play of dialectic and the reign of reason: between male and female, god and man, god and beast, drunkenness and sobriety, sanity and insanity, waking and sleeping, Yes and No. The realm of indistinction is, however, the realm of the metahuman: a realm we inhabit only in dreams, dreams in which, alas, we can no longer remain forever, like our prehuman ancestors, but from which we are doomed always to awake. This we tend to forget in the drunken roar of dionysiac release, at the Demonstration, the Orgy, the Rock Festival, the child's Saturday matinee at the movies, the adult's Sunday afternoon in the football stadium, when speech yields to noise (one name of the terrible God of the Pack is Bromios, the Roarer). It is, of course, in this world, the world of noise, of static and anti-messages, of overloaded circuits and amplifiers turned up to full that the New Religious live by choice, and the rest of us, willy-nilly, assaulted by record players or radios or the juke-box, bull-horns or the screaming of crowds.

Noise or silence—but not speech, dialogue, communication—are proper to the realm of the ineffable, the metapolitical, the divine. One pole of the possibilities inherent in the New Religions, the New Religiosity, is, then defined by the legend of Dionysus, as the adaptation of Euripides' play by Richard Schechner, *Dionysus in '69,* made clear—involving the audience itself, when it worked best, in the up-dated, naked Dionysiac rout it recreated in a theatre which ceased to be a theatre as the beholders became participants, followers of the Impostor God, the actor whose very act of imposture was proof of his Dionysiac claims. The God who was not a God but a neighborhood freak, in a theatre which was not a theatre but unstructured space, displaying his sex before spectators who, if moved, knew they were not spectators but celebrants and victims (they had paid to be so trifled with, so transformed): perhaps this was as close as we could come in our time to the true orgy, thiasic release. But maybe it was as close as anyone—after the building of cities, whether Thebes or New York—could *ever* come; emerging inevitably to other noises, other silences: the roar of the traffic which bears us home, the silence of our own house before we turn on the T.V. to watch the late, late show, or alternatively, the blaring insistence of the music our children are listening to when we enter. "Turn it down," we are likely to yell, glad to have a noise-level we can control—not off, but *down,* for we find total silence also an affront.

Not so those pledged to meditation, who pursue, through techniques adapted from Yoga—legs folded in the lotus position or pressed tight as they stand on their heads—what they learned to call (while Zen was fashionable) "the sound of one hand clapping." There is in our own Western tradition a myth of Silence equivalent to the Dionysiac Myth of Noise, which, I cannot help believing, is on the verge of moving once again to the center of our imagination. This is the Legend of the Holy Grail—that terrifying account of the destruction of a society based on chivalric valor and courtly love by the pursuit of what exists only outside of all communities, which is to say, Nowhere. The present age which has also turned its back on traditional notions of heroism and romance in its pursuit of vision should find this myth particularly sympathetic, yet there has been no contemporary adaptation of the Holy Grail story equivalent to Schechner's revision of *The Bacchae,* only children's stories and musical comedy versions of Arthurian story on the level of *Camelot,* or—more interestingly—infinitive variations in search of a new classic form in Science Fiction, short or long.

In fiction and verse, however, the major attempts to reveal the relevance of the Grail symbol to a time of reviving Faith have been made by writers whose religion is nostalgic rather than prophetic and whose aesthetic stance belongs to a moment when Modernism had not yet yielded to the post-Modern: John Cooper Powys in the *Glastonbury Romance,* Charles Williams in *War in Heaven,* and especially Eliot in his incoherent *The Wasteland,* framed on the one side by Jessie L. Weston's scholarly study, *From Ritual to Romance,* and on the other by Bernard Malamud's *The Natural.* Yet there is scarcely anyone among the New Mutants who is unfamiliar, through one child's adaptation or another, with Malory's *Morte d'Arthur,* that melancholy account of the end of the Round Table, the death of Arthur, and the destruction of Lancelot and Guinevere by the pure Knight who comes from silence and disappears into silence, creating nothing, only laying waste the world. If *The Bacchae,* especially as interpreted by Richard Schechner, was appropriate to the mounting ecstasy of the sixties, the Legend of the Grail seems an oracular prophecy, awaiting an interpreter, of the desolation which has succeeded it at a moment when the Rock Festivals have passed into the hands of the commercial exploiters, when the legendary fraternity of the Beatles falls apart in squabbles over money or prestige, when Lenny Bruce and Janice Joplin are dead—and the most devout among us withdraw into silent meditation.

In the world of silence, as in the world of noise, worship is possible as well as ecstasy, but not theology. The New Communicants begin where Thomas Aquinas ended, crying of his own *Summa Theologica,* "It is all rubbish." They know from the start that theology belongs to the realm of *Wissenschaft*—an alternative way toward vision, perhaps, quite like, though less sympathetic to them than the use of intoxicants and like the latter tending to become an occasion for Idolatry when considered an end rather than a means. And they sense somehow at this point that the Death-of-God Theology was the last theology of the West, since what it was talking about, what it foresaw was its own death; the death of a method rather than its subject.

We live at a moment when the God of the Science of God is dead, so that the Science of Religion, invented in the Eighteenth Century, has become as unviable as the Religion of Science invented at the same time. We must not be misled in this regard by the growing popularity of university courses in "Theology", courses crowded these days with precisely the New Communicants we have been discussing. Their uses of such courses are eccentric, illegitimate in fact from any "scholarly" point of view, since they enter them in quest of ecstasy and entertainment, more material to be stored in the do-it-yourself kits for salvation which they will take with them when they leave the University for the desert, the classroom for the Commune. Instinctively, they know that they must translate an ancient symbolic language into Pop Mythology, like that elaborated in the Stan Lee New Apocalypse series of comic books, in which Christian eschatology has replaced Captain Marvel and and the myth of the secular saviour bred in the modern city. To recover that ancient language they raid even classes in Theology, "spoiling the Egyptians," as the old phrase has it.

It must not be thought, however, that they share the rationalist or rationalizing motives of their teachers. Indeed, they stand on its head the humane and scholarly tradition which begins with the Socratic slogan, "The unexamined life is not worth living" and comes to a climax in the Freudian tag—inspired by Part II of *Goethe's Faust,* itself inspired by the secular triumphs of Deutschland reclamation: "Where *id* was *ego* shall be." The votaries of the noisiest of Gods and of the silence which follows his triumph have turned all that upside down—crying out in the rout (and minding not a bit if no one can really hear what they say):

"Only the unexamined life is worth living" and "Where *ego* is, *id* shall return!" No wonder, then, that the New Religious reject utterly not merely those churches of the West which have become hopelessly genteel but any which have compromised with Humanism. Christian Humanism, Judaeo-Humanism, any attempt to reconcile reason and faith, ecstasy and dialectic: this is the Enemy. "Dehumanize yourselves," cry the New anti-Humanists, "dare be more than human or less."

That is why, when they do not create for themselves home-made Churches out of Popular Science, they turn either to the religions of the original inhabitants of our own continent, or to those of those after whom they were named in error, the original Indians. The native American Church, that odd blend of protestant fundamentalism and the ritualized consumption of peyote buttons, has been especially appealing, since it involves the use of hallucinogens, and was blessed in the beginning by Timothy Leary. And what could be finally more sympathetic to the supermarket syncretism of our times than devotees who pray to Jesus, Mary and Peyote? But the East Indians have proved even more so, proving America once more, *still* the "Passage to India" which Whitman called it. Not only Whitman was moved in the 19th century to turn east in search of a new scriptures, but Emerson and Thoreau as well. Typically, however, the New Communicants resemble Whitman rather than Thoreau in that they tend to adapt rather than assimilate Indian religions, almost deliberately half-understanding them. In the end, therefore, whatever those religions may have meant to their original believers, to the New Religious in our midst they represent essentially what is least familiar in their world, most alien to their own believing ancestors: a polar opposition to Aquinas or Maimonides.

Typically, they respond to such religions in their shabbiest, their most vulgar forms: if Zen Buddhism, as in the late 50's, Zen as expounded by popularizers like Alan Watts. But it is more *lumpen* movements, like Krishna Consciousness, which they prefer, as anyone knows who has confronted on the street corners of the world in recent years those shaven headed youths clashing cymbals and crying for alms. So also they seek out the sect which developed around Meher Baba, that most Pop of avatars, who looked like the late great comedian, Jerry Colonna, loved movies and cricket and died ("dropped his body") without breaking his decades of silence as his followers had been long promised he would—a last vaudeville gag. If the mythology of Christianity has been accepted, begrudgingly and belatedly, by the New Religious, it is in its most Pop American revivalistic forms, the so-called "Jesus Freaks" being notoriously closer to Billy Graham or even Billy Sunday than to Ellery Channing or even Cotton Mather. Similarly, it is latter day Chasidism which appeals to converts out of all the possible varieties of

Judaism: to the followers of the Lubovitcher *Rebbe* recruiting with astonishing success among the long hairs, hippies and freaks by descending on American campuses chanting, P.O.T. means *p*ut *o*n *t*villim (phylacteries); L.S.D. means *l*et's *s*tart *d*avan-ing (praying).

But this is by no means the nadir or the acme of the New Crusade which has led also to a revival of Satanism and Witchcraft, limited most often to simple theatrics and the cry (without consequence): "Evil be thou my good!"; but occasionally eventuating in orgiastic Sabbaths and even (as the Manson affair made manifest) in ritual murder. Everywhere, however, the latest recrudescence of Black Magic has been essentially popular and democratic, sometimes downright shoddy and subliterate: a kind of Satanism for everyone—clearly distinguished from that elitist devil-worship which appealed to an aristocratic few at the end of the last century, and is memorialized in literary works intended for a highly educated audience, like Huysman's *Là Bas* or the poems of William Butler Yeats.

The New Diabolism reflects, in this sense, the redemption, so characteristic of the movement, of everything which Science and respectable Religion had agreed in labelling "mere superstition": alchemy, astrology, fortune-telling, all that had long been relegated to certain charlatans on shabby back streets or the filler columns in the popular press and the *Farmer's Almanac*. It is precisely the disreputable, anti-rational aura of these sub-sciences or anti-sciences which moves the young in an age which prefers astrology to astronomy, alchemy to chemistry, magic to technology: an age in which, among the New Mutants at least, the question "What are you?" is typically answered not with, "A student, a priest, a scientist," or even "A man;" but with "A Pisces" or "A Scorpio." And each eventless day is likely to begin with a casting of the *I Ching* or a shuffling through the Tarot Pack.

Moreover, this double revolt of visionary youth against rational religion and science is matched in some sense, perhaps essentially embodied in the re-appearance among them of certain "plagues" once nearly subdued by the combined efforts of laboratory researchers and medical technicians, plus a code of personal hygiene propagated first by primary school teachers, and then by the pseudo-Doctors in white coats on T.V. ads for toothpaste or sanitary napkins. There is something repulsive to anyone committed to living in his physical body and remaining faithful to his animal inheritance in the compulsive American drive (most recently and hysterically joined by upwardly mobile Blacks) to scrub, cleanse and deodorize oneself out of all semblance of physical humanity. Only when touring the remotest corners of the "backward" world, or lost in the midst of combat, or taken by chance or conscience into the houses of the hopeless poor, does the modern Western bourgeois catch a whiff of man's ancient smell, the true odor of mortality.

The invention of the flush toilet, perhaps, began it all—concealing from him his own wastes and precipitating an early ecological crisis, as the residue of what we had eaten and digested no longer fertilized what was to feed us next. This was succeeded by the cosmeticising and deodorizing of the dead, as a whole culture re-invented mummification in an effort to hide from sight the inevitability of death and decay. And what has finally followed everyone knows who watches daytime television, in which the truly sacred dramas (interspersed by secular ones, called significantly "Soap Operas" or just "Soaps") are Commercials dedicated to products guaranteed to remove mouth-odor, body-odor, kitchen-odors, toilet-odors, the natural smell of the genitals themselves: the basic scent of our dying bodies, without an awareness of which no religion seems necessary or possible.

No wonder the New Communicants have turned from this travesty-transformation of apocalyptic expectation into therapeutic hygiene, this attempt to create a redeemed and purified body Here and Now—along with the implicit Credo that cleanliness is not merely next to godliness but is all the godliness we need. No wonder they flee hot water and find pseudo-scientific reasons for eschewing soap, insisting that what in one sense cleans, in another, deeper sense pollutes. No wonder they leave behind "sanitary plumbing" and shit on the beaches and wooded hillsides of our own wilderness areas or whatever remote land they reach in their ceaseless pilgrimages, which seem not so much voyages to Holy Places, as flights from an unholy one: from the tiled bathroom with its locked door and stock of required reading.

More, however, is involved than the rejection of commercialized hygiene. The true, the ultimate enemy is modern medicine itself, most despised of the anti-magical sciences, most distrusted of the secular technologies. It is, in part, *institutionalized* medicine which the New Communicants fear, associating it, on the one hand, with that soulless totalitarian institution, The Hospital, especially its psychiatric wards, where ecstasy is labelled "madness," and "sanity" is enforced with shock treatments and lobotomies. On the other hand, they cannot separate it from the "Doctor," that $50,000 a year A.M.A. member, bad enough in reality and worse in their paranoic vision of him as a racist, sexist, exploiter of his patients—dedicated to supporting "unjust" wars while resisting "just" causes like socialized medicine, free access to drugs, euthanasia and legalized abortion.

For a while, the New Communicants opposed to that bogey man certain "good" doctors of their own, most notably, the famous "Dr. Hip-pocrates," whose columns of irreverent and fashionable hip advice appeared in the underground press. But Dr. Hip-pocrates has passed from favor for pointing out, in an access of responsibility, the danger to life itself of the famous ten-days "straight-grain" regime sponsored by the Macrobiotic Faith. It is quackery which they prefer, flagrant anti-science as preached by Ohsawa himself, or L. Ron Hubbard or Wilhelm Reich (anyone who seems more Medicine Man than professional practitioner). To be sure, some medical practices seem acceptable to the New Religious, especially if they are sponsored by regimes on the Left: Acupuncture, for instance, which has been officially blessed by Mao-Tse-Tung. But perhaps even its appeal is based not so much on its acceptance in Communist China as on its rejection by official circles in the United States, its aura of unredeemable disreputability. After all, it was first advertised on the American Scene not in some Mao-ist journal but in the pornographic pop novel, *Candy*.

Basically, however, there has been a movement away from all medical treatment, public as well as private, in favor of do-it-yourself techniques ranging from therapeutic diets to the use of hand-held vacuum devices for abortions. Birth-control has posed, in fact, a special problem, since contraceptive pills and the "loop" represent final achievements of the hated medical technology and its market-place *ethos*. Chastity and homosexuality seem more truly religious methods of population control, being more easily adapted to anti-technological myths; yet despite some talk of sexual abstinence and of *coitus riservatus* as practiced in certain Tantrist sects or among the Yogin, and the popularity in the Feminist movement of Lesbian unions, the major drift of the New Religious has been toward pan-sexuality and the Orgy—solutions which in a real sense pre-suppose modern contraception.

It is, in any case, infestation and disease which have tended to occupy the center of the rekindled religious imagination rather than purity or continence; so that even though no major sect has raised the cry, "Sickness is preferable to health" (except in the limited area of mental health), many new Communicants act *as if* this were an esssential article of their faith. And their rejection of established modes of prevention and treatment have eventuated in the return to the universities and the bourgeois suburbs of certain minor nuisances, once believed gone forever, like head lice and crab lice, as well as major diseases like gonorrhea and syphilis and infectious hepatitis. But hepatitis can be checked by careful sterilization of hypodermic needles (the chief source of its spread), and the common venereal diseases were on the point of disappearing in the decade after World War II, which had seen the development of ever more powerful antibiotics. Indeed, there is no "rational" explanation for their failure to become as obsolete as diphtheria and small-pox, no emergence of an especially virulent strain of *gonnochi* or *spirochetes* (as is sometimes believed) immune to these new "wonder drugs." No, what is involved is simply a refusal to be diagnosed or, once diagnosed, to follow prescribed treatments: a refusal based on a quite conscious contempt for science and a half-conscious longing for disease as some ultimate symbol of liberation.

It is no surprise that the highest incidence of venereal disease has occurred precisely in the holy places of the New Religious: the Haight-Ashbury, for example, and the Agricultural Communes, where a few instances of Plague have also been reported. The very universal love and emancipated sexuality which characterize the New Faiths at their best become a means of mutual infection and re-infection; while dirty needles used to inject ecstasy-producing drugs lead to stupor and coma and total collapse, as released bile invades the blood-streams of the devout.

It is possible, to be sure, to put all of this in historical context, reminding ourselves that all Crusades, i.e., resurgences of religious faith leading to the breaking of old cultural boundaries, have resulted in similar outbreaks of pestilence. We can think, for instance of how the late Medieval wars against Islam, presumably intended to repossess the Holy Land, brought back into Europe leprosy; or how the Discovery of America conducted by one who called himself the "Christ-bearing Dove" and sailed on a ship named after the Blessed Virgin, resulted in the first major outbreak of syphilis in the western world. To be sure, the Medieval Crusades were not fought solely, or perhaps even chiefly, to redeem Christian shrines; nor were the voyages of exploration primarily intended, as Roman Catholic apologists argued, to find a new source of souls as replacements for those lost to the Protestant Revolt. And one can read the body-wasting diseases that resulted as outward and visible signs of the impure motives, political and commercial, which underlay and undercut their avowed ends.

But perhaps it is better to understand such "plagues" as physical manifestations of profounder psychic events: the culture shocks resulting from an encounter with other societies based on differing concepts of the human and divine, as well as rival religions created to sanction such concepts. The current Cultural Revolution represents a movement in inner space rather than outer, a psychological rather than a geographical journey; but it, too, has resulted in an encounter with an alien type of man, the Barbarian inside of our old humanist selves. How appropriate, then, seems the re-invention of syphilis, a "disease" associated (quite like the natural hallucinogenic drugs) with the American Indian, in whom the New Mutants have found a model for their alternative life-style. No new Gods without new diseases seems to be the lesson of history; no resurgence of faith without new mortifications of the flesh at the unconscious or psychosomatic level, as well as on levels where reason and consciousness fully function. But this means, in the end, new definitions of "sickness" and "health."

We have known all along that when Dionysus comes he brings affliction to the spirit, "madness" in terms of the society he scourges. Why is it more difficult to accept the fact that he occasions afflictions of the flesh as well, "sickness" in the language of the world he teaches us to deny. And the same is surely true of the *deus absconditus* of the Grail Legend, that God who, unlike the Christian God, neither begets a Savior on the Jewish mother (the father of Galahad is Lancelot, which is to say, depraved and passionate man) nor reveals himself. In the end, the insufferably pure hero disappears from us, leaving the world a little worse than when he entered, since woman is bereft of her adulterous champion and the realm of its betrayed king. Even the symbols the Grail Knight *has* seen are symbols of infertility: Cup and Dish, Lance and Sword—the receptacles for Wine and Bread and the phallic weapons, one broken, one bleeding, eternally sundered from the female vessels. There is no Bible which follows such a revelation, only an unfinished, unfinishable popular poem by a hundred authors, and the pips on the Tarot deck, used first to tell fortunes and at last only to amuse the bored. How fitting that this myth survive among us chiefly in children's books and musical comedies, and finally in the literary texts (even Eliot's *Wasteland*) read only by scholars.

But he is a real God, though his name is never spoken, this God whose story begins in silence and failure only to end in silence and success. His unspoken name, I suppose, is death, *The Death of the King, Morte d'Arthur;* but he is nonetheless quite as genuine, as authentic as that other God whose names are many and cried aloud: Bacchus, Baccheus, Iacchos, Bassareus, Bromios, Evios, Sabazios, Zagreus, Thyoneus, Lenaios, Eleotheos, the Imposter, the Intoxicator, the Twice Born, the Phallus, the Ox, the Voice, the Pine Tree, Noise and Madness. When God is dead, a Christian theologian predicted not so long ago, the Gods will be reborn; or, to change the metaphor, once the Guardian at the Twin Gates of Dream, Ivory and Horn, has been removed, the undying Gods will re-appear. And why, then, would we hesitate to hail those who have opened the unguarded Gate, dancing at the head of a procession whose end no one can see, and shouting prophecies too loud to be heard? What if they scratch themselves, head and crotch, as they come; or even if the embrace they offer threatens infection and pain and death itself?

Not only have they performed the Hermetic function, turning themselves into *theopompoi,* heralds of the Gods. They have already begun to create a *cultus* appropriate to those Gods, as well as institutions to promulgate their faith and to preserve it in a hostile or indifferent world: The Demonstration, the Rock Festival, the Encounter Group. These variations on the Orgy (more like the American Revival Meeting, perhaps, than remoter Greek models), sublimated, half-sublimated, or totally de-sublimated, constitute their missionary institutions. And no vulgarization or commercialization can impugn them; for they are, by definition, vulgar and commercial, immune to "humanization" or polite piety. Nor does an eruption of violence, even murder, itself, such as "marred" the Rolling Stones' orgiastic moment at Altamont, undercut their effectiveness. Like the stoned-out kids or the exhibitionists publicly masturbating on flagpoles at Woodstock, Mick Jagger invoking death for unknown others is part of the meaning of it all: ugly, dark, dangerous, ambiguously suspended between *eros* and *thanatos* like the god himself.

Finally, however, it is their preservative institutions which seem the most vital and significant achievement of the New Age of Faiths: the asylums or refuges established for those already sanctified or in search of sanctity (or only tired and hungry and spaced out) in certain green interstices of our industrialized world: the Agricultural Communes. They have been sufficiently portrayed, in their bewildering variety and final unity, at all levels of scholarship and journalism; and the sense of their living reality has been rendered in fiction and verse as well as in film. There seems, therefore, little point in rehearsing either their virtues (the sense of community and peace, the possibility of nonmedical therapy) or their faults (the equivocal role of the *gurus* who lead them, their unstability, the hostility they engender in their neighbors). It is now clear that they are viable and that they will persist for better or worse, as we still say, in a world where few agree on the meaning of better or worse. But it is equally clear that they will persist in a larger world that will, by and large, not follow their example, but continue to emulate commercial, competitive and even violent social models.

Yet, like the monasteries of the Middle Ages, they have already altered the meaning of everything done around them, even in contempt of all they represent. Our Era can, in fact, be described as a Religious one not because all, or indeed most of us, live by a code which honors Contemplation and Vision, but because a few men and women, chiefly but not exclusively young, are laying up in isolation a kind of spiritual capital for us all, by living a life which many outside of their retreats are even now beginning to yearn for, or wish they yearned for, or wish they wished they yearned for. Certainly, most of us already envy them their presumed indolence, their boasted sexual freedom, their unashamed nakedness, and their apparent deliverance from urban *ennui*. There is, consequently, little doubt in my mind that in the near future our presiding form of hypocrisy will be the rhetorical tribute our vice pays to their virtue.

At that point, the analogy will be complete; and we will have as much right to call ourselves Dionysiacs or Anabaptists or orgiasts or ecstatic polytheists as the men of the Middle Ages had to call themselves Christians, despite their wars and un-charity and daily desecration of their official faith. For just as those would-be Christians endured or tolerated, sometimes even supported certain cloistered religious who *lived* the faith they could not really abide, so we are learning to endure or tolerate, even directly or by indirection support the hippies and freaks who are ushering in a New Dispensation we fear.

Yet how can we bring ourselves to applaud without reservation a group of believers who offer us a kind of salvation, to be sure, a way out of the secular trap in which we have been struggling, but who are themselves ridden by superstition, racked by diseases spread in the very act of love, dedicated to subverting sweet reason through the use of psychedelic drugs and the worship of madness, committed to orgiastic sex and doctrinaire sterility, pursuing ecstasy even when it debauches in murder, denying finally the very ideal of the human in whose name we have dubbed our species *homo sapiens?* If this is the price of religious renewal, who would not choose even the "quiet desperation" of Death-of-God Capitalism or Communism, both committed, in theory at least, to maximizing our earthly goods, minimizing suffering and pain, extending life and organizing the relations of the sexes in some rational and stable way.

Even if we stand in need of salvation rather than success or social welfare (as the equal though quite different anguish of rich and poor, male and female, Black and White, old and young among us suggests we do), surely we must look for that salvation to some other quarter. And yet I myself have been moved to the very verge of ecstasy, over the lintel of joy in precisely such religious communities as I have been describing; so that finally I can, *must* cast a balance in the most personal of terms.

Let me cite two instances. When my first grandson was born some four years ago, I found that I wanted him to be circumcized like all of his male ancestors for three thousand years; but not medically, therapeutically only and not certainly in the mumbled ritual of a tongue and faith no longer comprehensible to most of those who would be present. I decided, therefore, that I would myself adapt the ancient formulae to my own sense of the times, presiding, though leaving the actual cutting of the foreskin to a doctor from some church-sponsored hospital in New Mexico, Baptist or Methodist, I am no longer sure. The doctor, however, though a proper white-coated technologist, too emancipated certainly to suck a drop of blood from the child's penis like a traditional *moel,* was at least a Jew. Not so, the young congregation which assembled from a nearby commune called the Domes. They were, in overwhelming majority, *goyim,* though bearded and sandalled and robed quite like my own ultimate forebears: living great grandparents, as it were, a living past somehow grown younger than I. But is that not the way one remembers the grandparents of his grandparents, as he himself grows older in the trap of time which they have long since escaped?

There is one point in the ancient ceremony when the Celebrant says to the child, who actually bleeds in full view of all, his pain subdued by his first sip of wine, *"I say unto you, 'In your blood live!' Yea, I say unto you, 'In your blood live!'"* And the young man who stood behind me, blond-bearded and blue eyed, his gentile head half a foot above my own, responded, "Heavy trip, man!" and fainted. It was a response written in no prayerbook, but it was the right response. Because for once, for the first time in my fifty years of life, a *Brith,* a commemoration of our ancient Covenant with the God we thought dead was really *happening!* Before the ceremony was over, two other people had gone down, because (I was suddenly aware) they had learned again the meaning of Sacrifice and the required shedding of blood, beyond all rational talk of "symbolic wounds" or liberal horror at the persistence of cruel and archaic rites. Afterwards, we drank and danced, like my own Chasidic ancestors, for how many hours I cannot say, since we were out of time. And, at last, intoxicated and worn out, we slept, waking to joy with the next day. God knows (some reborn God) precisely what it was in me that danced and slept and waked and rejoiced: the undying child, perhaps, or the unredeemed savage, the unrecorded Polish rapist, or the half-remembered wonder-*rebbe* who healed the lame and raised the dead—maybe all of them, all of me except my customary professorial self, though, I suppose, that too. And why not?

So I danced again (I who cold-sober never dance, know when I am cold sober that, whatever I remember, I really never *have,* except maybe in my head), as I had actually danced at Purim services a year ago, my second son by my side. Purim is an odd holiday in the Jewish year to begin with, a mad occasion of masking and carnival release in honor of a woman: a Jewish girl, presumably, who began by dancing naked before a Pagan King, then married him, and ended saving her people from the destruction plotted by that King's evil prime minister. But Esther is finally no Jewish girl at all, her name a Hebrew variant of Ishtar-Ashtoreth-Astarte, just as the name of her presumed uncle, Mordecai, is another form of Marduk. She is, in short, the great Goddess herself smuggled into its imaginary history by the most patriarchal of faiths. But never mind, Jews have danced and sung in drunken joy life to her and death to her enemy, Haman (it is taught that on Purim a good Jew must get so drunk that he cannot tell Haman from Mordecai), for centuries now. And what better place to continue that tradition than in the converted clam bar which serves as a synagogue for that same Chasidic sect which cries on the campuses, "LSD means let's start *davan*ing." And *davan* we did, swaying and chanting in prayer, with a congregation consisting chiefly of half-converted long-hairs and freaks, though a few old men as well, and a handful of orthodox in their long black coats.

My son and I are joined in memory and love always, but seldom in pious practice. He is a food freak, a refugee from cities—who, while I am pounding my typewriter or opening my mail, will be crouched on the grass in lotus position or standing on his head bolt upright and stark naked in his lonely room. But for once we moved together in a common living present, joined by a magic to which, momentarily at least, we both subscribed. And our dead ancestors danced with us, at home with the bearded kids, high perhaps on grass, and the *chasidim,* a little drunk surely on rye whiskey. We had for that little while resurrected the dead, our own dead, given life to those who gave us the gift of life, and to the Father of us all, whose name we still did not say even when we knew he was dead. But his names are many, after all, since he is Many as well as One, is reborn as One when he dies as Many, twice reborn as Many when he dies as One: Jehovah and Elohim, Dionysus and Bacchus, or, alternatively, Astarte and Leukothea, Ishtar and Aphrodite and Cybele, it makes no difference. The women, young girls chiefly, were confined to the back of the synagogue, behind a screen, but somehow they knew. Together we had created the gods who created our humanity, male and female created we them. A minute later, of course, we were awake, sundered from each other, the past and those gods. But that, too, didn't, doesn't matter; couldn't, as the colloquial phrase has it, matter less.

And knowing this, I know what I must answer when the Priests and Professors, to whose world I return from the *Brith* and the ex-clam-bar, cry out (as my own ancestors first cried—for I am truly a Priest as well as a *chasid*—some two thousand years ago), "Can salvation come out of Galilee?" "Salvation always comes out of Galilee," I will answer out of the chasidic side of my mouth; which is to say, it comes out of the quarter from which we Priests and Professors had least expected it, the world we find it easiest to despise: not some Galilee of the past that we have sanctified and made safe for ritual and research, but a Galilee of the future which we still revile and fear.

But the dialogue, after all, is in each of our own heads, as well as in the community at large; and it cannot stop here. For even knowing and confessing that salvation comes out of Galilee, perhaps only knowing and confessing that piece of the truth, we are not delivered of our priestly and professorial obligations, not permitted to cry like some mindless gentile or wandering barbarian the matching slogan of contempt and terror, "Can wisdom come out of Athens or Jerusalem!!" Wisdom *always* comes out of Athens and Jerusalem, which is to say, out of worlds clean, healthy, reasonable and sane to the point of absurdity. Yet we dare not ignore the voice of wisdom when it insists, "The false prophet shall be put to death!" "The witch shall be put to death!" "The Messiah is yet to come!" "The Messiah is *always* yet to come!"

Only in the eternal tension of these two conflicting views, the irreconcilable dialogue of these two voices, Goyish and Jewish, prophetic and priestly, mad and sane, can the dearest of all possibilities be kept alive: the possibility (after the death and rebirth of the gods) of reinventing Man.

Leslie A. Fiedler
Buffalo, New York
Yom Kippur 1972

Oedipus in the Factory*

BY JEAN-MARIE DOMENACH

(translated by Anthony M. Nazzaro)

"Blow up Oedipus and Castration, intervene brutally each time that a subject intones the song of the myth or the verses of the tragedy, always bring him back to the factory."

(*Anti-Oedipus*, p. 374)

This complex was beginning to smell. One was awaiting a Molière in order to purge psychoanalysis. Deleuze and Guattari came along. They were not Molière, but rather Rabelais. Their verve slams the doors of the sacred closets where the "dirty little secret" is confessed. I recommend the reading of chapter 2, "Psychoanalysis and Familialism, the Sacred Family". It can only do good, as our priests used to say in the past. And besides, what verbal invention: *desiring machine, full body without organs, flux and schizes, sublime penis and transcending anus* . . . It's much more fun than Lacan.

Let's just enjoy this drollery for a moment. We don't have so many occasions to laugh. However, the spell of the language and the often pertinent vivacity of the polemic must not paralyse objections, for if this book has a happy side, it also has a sad one, and even a sinister one. "It transports everything,"[1] everything possible; it remains to be seen where. Its very mobility, so jolly and amusing, is for it a means of escaping definition and contradiction (a guerilla book, it has been rightly said). But I don't see what would oblige me to fall on my knees before a prose which doesn't respect anything (it is curious how one venerates, in Paris, everything which shatters what is venerated). There is bludgeoning in this book: at the essential points, no demonstration whatever, but linking phrases of the type: *it is evident that*, or identities: *this is that, this is the same thing as that*. Analyze its grammar a little bit, and you'll see.

* Review of G. Deleuze and F. Guattari, *Anti-Oedipus, Capitalism and Schizophrenia* (Edition de Minuit, 1972).

1. J. F. Lyotard, "Capitalism energumene" ("Fanatic Capitalism") (*Critique*, Nov. 1972).

I know: to criticize in the name of logic a book which presents itself as an apology for delirious discourse appears inadequate. But in the name of what would I be able to criticize, if not plain reason? Never will a delirium refute another delirium. Furthermore, I fear there is some hidden trick whose object is to void the question which bursts forth, categorical, from the very beginning, and which will not cease scratching and grumbling from one end to the other: the question of the subject. Just what are, according to our authors' own vision, these 460 pages in our hands? A product of *desiring production*? Or else a little "desired machine", but fabricated during numerous sleepless nights? It has indeed taken engineers to put together this piece of chatter. What is their position, what is their own action in the circuit? By itself, the process of fabricating the book belies the system exposed. And so on: as soon as one escapes from the cavalcade of funny abstractions, as soon as one stops at a concrete problem, the seduction evaporates. The polemic vigor of the book, its power of corrosion remain. But its historical, philosophical, political content seems to vanish when one questions it.

I would wish to contradict this book without depreciating it. I do not forget that it gives rise to these refutations. I also think that it will later appear to bear witness to an extremely advanced point, for it establishes itself beyond the circle foreseen by Nietzsche: when man's pretentious claim to knowledge about man becomes unbearable and manifests its vanity, it closes in upon itself, and a new form of knowledge becomes necessary: the "tragic knowledge"; the one which plunges into the new unknown. But "the preventive and curative virtue of art" is required. It is in this way that I take this book, in which laughter, jokes, petulance, roguish style are a form of art, a minor one certainly, but it frees us from horror and finally saves the book from its nihilistic destination.

Of Capitalism.

Compared to the gloomy structuralist system, the vision which dominates this book is indeed cheerful. One would believe he was visiting a factory gone mad. Gone are the constraining forms, the frozen geometry, the underground architecture where what the naive call human history is brought together . . . Here is a mechanism behaving like a firecracker, like trains at Christmas time in the store windows, sparking connections, overheated motors. One could ask: where does all this energy come from and where is it going? Which would pose both the problem of origin[2] and, above all, the problem of destination:all these

2. On this point, the thesis of *Anti-Oedipus* gives evidence of the same weakness as that of Marx: one can no more explain the origin of "social repression" than "primitive violence".

interconnected machines ought to tend toward the state of degenerating equilibrium which is called entropy. Besides, it is in this manner that Claude Lévi-Strauss envisages our fate in his terrible finale of *L'Homme nu.* But our authors are mute on this subject. Neither are they preoccupied with the fact that there exist some chains better constructed than others and which feed the latter,—engineers whose appearance and functioning cause a problem for a world-wide engineering. There are also sudden reappearances and shifts in direction, repetitions, recurrence of meanings which harmonize poorly with large-scale assembly and which require a minimum of historical perspective. But how could machines have a history? They wear out, that's all.

To consider the whole of human activity as desiring production renews and extends a vision which Marxism and Freudianism, more or less structuralized, had abusively formalized. To establish communication between political economy and libidinal economy, that old dream which today is exploding, is assuredly a fruitful undertaking, which unveils to us, in effect, the libidinal which Marx hid under politics and the political which Freud hid under the libidinal. It is indeed an *energetic*, as J. F. Lyotard writes, which is given to us there, as opposed to *meaning*. But this opposition is absurd, for one does not see what human energy could create—and where it could borrow—beyond meaning, myths, the old language which, unlike motor fuel which feeds machines, does not become exhausted in combustion. This book itself . . .

Nonetheless, however contestable it may be, this specular vision is salutary. *Anti-Oedipus* is related to the novels of Samuel Beckett: it displaces us right where we are, and we don't notice it—in the present case, machined and machining. If one has been able to interpret the structuralist vogue of the 1960's as an ideology of the rising technocracy, the vogue of *Anti-Oedipus* will be interpreted as an ideology of a prolific, exuberant, "fanatical" capitalism, as Lyotard says,—of a capitalism which refused to be taken in by crises and catastrophic predictions and, more than ever, sends its devices and its products to the four corners of the globe (including the socialist world) and now into space. Deleuze and Guattari take up again, sometimes in a sophisticated manner, the song of triumph intoned by Marx to the glory of expansive capitalism. In so doing, they can be credited for freeing the human sciences from the facile competitive use which is made of them and relating them to a world-wide situation dominated by capitalist activism.

We regret, however, that they use the word "capitalism" in such a vague and intemperate manner that we don't see its real nature and whether it is opposed to "socialism", or even if it has an opponent somewhere, an alternative of some kind. Must one consider that the U.S.S.R. depends on this "capitalism" and that the analysis is valid, at least partially, for her? And what about China? But as with M. Foucault when he links prisons with capitalism, one wonders to what extent capitalism, strictly speaking, is responsible, and how much is the result of the technical revolution and western productivism. As for *artificial and aberrant reterritorializations,* socialism, or at least what one knows under that name, seems to have operated on them to a greater extent, and more rigorously than capitalism, for it orchestrates production with a lyricism, a morality and a politics which have disappeared from contemporary capitalism, in which production is closer to desire than to the will.

Of Desire.

Some congratulate *Anti-Oedipus* for offering "a new theory of desire". I am struck, on the contrary, by the fact that desire, although it is abundantly utilized against all theories, depends on none of them. It is everywhere, but one will never know what it is,—desire of what? desire of whom? A vague concept, as "undecidable" as the Oedipus so much criticized. Thenceforth, there is nothing surprising in picking out here the fundamental contradiction: on the one hand, desire is everywhere, it invests the totality of the social field, it lives in the heart of even the most perverse productions, as fascism; on the other hand, "desire is revolutionary in itself, and as if involuntarily, wanting it wants."

Our authors are therefore forced into a corner and must decide. They get out of it by introducing, in quotes, the concept of "true" desire. But they immediately perceive its fragility, since repression can be desired just as much as satisfaction. So, how distinguish between true and false desire? Patience, they reply; "we claim the right to make a very slow analysis". The boring thing is that, three hundred pages further on, at the end of the book, we have gotten no further along.

There is a reason for this impasse: our authors can say nothing at all about desire, except to glorify it as productive energy in terms which, moreover, recall the invocations of the young Barrès, because they have deliberately avoided the terrain where desire could be situated, defined, hierarchized, this domain in which man produces man through meanings. From Plato to Hegel, by way of the Fathers of the Church, human desire has not ceased to be explored, and Freud has brought to it his tremendous contribution. But desire is the great absentee of this book, which speaks about it all the time, since it began by rejecting this human history which is woven between individuals, since it has reduced it to an abstract machinery whose motor fuel is undifferentiated desire, while at the same time (curious bilocation) being the negating and revolutionary agent. As R. Girard shows, in his masterly study of *Anti-Oedipus*,[3] between the *molecular* and the *molar*, between the *small parts* of the desiring machines and the large wholes, "the space in the heart of which we communicate" disappears. *Anti-Oedipus* bears witness indirectly that this space is shrinking and that communication is becoming mechanical. Must we not admit that it blurs it definitively, and that, while repudiating representations and myths, it finally has recourse to Christian mythology, one which transforms debasement into redemption, schizophrenia into revolution? But the song of raw desire is only a wild cry in the jungle which leaves us unarmed before our real problems, our real conflicts, or else it is already a work of art or of reason, a poem or a utopia,—Hölderlin or Fourier. Representation. Culture.

Of Culture.

German romanticism marked the cultural arrival of delirium. From Hölderlin to Céline, by way of Rimbaud, Nerval, Lautreamont and the surrealists, a black and white night surrounds the domain of reason. What, indeed, would our culture be without this background world? But both light and the monstrous issue from it, and it is not enough, to distinguish between them, to assign the fascist delirium to paranoia and the revolutionary desire to schizophrenia. The distinction, clinically and politically, is not so clear. (Was Sade, curiously absent from the book, paranoiac or schizophrenic? As for Marat, that paranoiac, he was a revolutionary. But should the Terror of 1793 be placed in the category of "true" or "false" desire?) Furthermore, all the mouths in the shadows do not speak in alexandrine verses. Our theaters, our screens are invaded by supposedly repressed and liberating discourse, but the discourse is immediately diluted in the parody of religion or of love—derisory deliriums,wretched machinery.

One will grant that the social turmoil brought about by profit and productivism leads toward the madness of repressed liberties, of frustrated or hallucinated desires. But can one conceive as easily as does *Anti-Oedipus* the overthrow and the cure? In the ideal world it suggests to us, "madness would no longer exist as madness, not because it had been transformed into 'mental illness' but, on the contrary, because it would receive contribution from all the other fluxes, including science

3. R. Girard, "Systeme du delire" ("System of Delirium") (*Critique*, Nov. 1972). Grasset has recently published R. Girard's *La Violence et le sacre (Violence and the Sacred)*.

and art" (383). Experience, on the contrary, allows us to affirm that the "insane" more easily find or recover a normal place in an organic society, or in a society temporarily drawn together (in time of war, for example), that is to say, by a "reterritorialization" whose social cost is high and whose nature is the inverse of the one Deleuze and Guattari are thinking about.

Moreover, doesn't it impoverish the meaning of delirium to link it to an economic-social structure whereas, long before capitalism, it said so many prophetic and oracular things about life and death, good and evil, the springs, the forests and the stars? The recourse to a nether world, if it is not already the organized world of that which does not speak, will bring only stuttering and ratiocination. The non-said does not save us every time from the corruption of language. In *Anti-Oedipus*, the Marxist dialectic sinks into an abstract negativism. Yes, Freudianism has become one of the parts of the capitalist system; yes, delirium had resisted Freudianism. It does not follow that schizophrenia is, with respect to capitalism, in the position where Marx had placed the proletariat. I understand that one is tired of the obscene apologies for work and culture which the bourgeois humanists and the Stalinists are pursuing. But I don't see what desire can produce without work, nor what delirium can produce without culture or without religion. Madness has, in fact, become a source of our common culture, and people as cultivated as the authors of *Anti-Oedipus* will not exclude it from it.[4] One must choose between the inside or the outside: "if delirium were really what one means it to be, why not enjoy it without worrying about founding it within a logical critique of all-delirious systems. (. . . .) The delirium which sweeps this work along is not and could not be the one which is claimed."[5]

Concerning the Institution.

Clearly, the target of the book is the nuclear institution: the family, whose psychoanalyst has become "the priest". But here the contradiction which we have just denounced reappears: how can desire be hierarchized, qualified, when one has made of it an all-inclusive energy. Thus, *Anti-Oedipus* criticizes the family which diverts desire and fixes it upon the State, then decrees that this desire which attaches

4. See on the subject what A. Beguin has written in *L'Ame romantique et le reve (The Romantic Soul and the Dream)* (Jose Corti), a work our authors don't seem to know, as well as his preface to the special issue of *Esprit*, Dec. 1952: "Misere de la psychiatrie" ("Poverty of Psychiatry"). For Beguin, the discourse of madness is not only an essential part of human exploration, but also a protest against "the norms of social utility". (One is mad in relation to a given society.) The difference with Deleuze and Guattari is that this discourse is in the order of the sacred and that this protest is one of liberty.

5. R. Girard, *op.cit.*

itself to the great "super-egotistic" entities is "shameful". In order to pronounce such judgments one must indeed set oneself up as an arbiter or as a new priest. In the name of what? Nietzsche had seen the difficulty and shown the way out: love your illusions to the point of making them exist differently, by yourself and for yourself. Transmutation, not destruction. One could say the same thing in a different way, using the Hegelian ruse. But the domain in which the individual runs up against the institution, the game they play together, all that is all shrivelled up, as we have said.

It is certainly a pleasure to hear psychoanalysis criticized as "the theater of the private man", "monstrous autism", and to see the authors link with economic and political life phenomena about which psychologists and psychoanalysts ordinarily give us an individualistic, inadequate interpretation. The dialectic of the "deterritorializations" (Barrés says uprooting; Berque says dispossession) provoked by capitalism, and artificial reterritorializations, seems right to me, even if it isn't new, but to what horizon does it lead? "When we consider what is deeply artificial in the perverse reterritorializations, but also in psychotic, hospital reterritorializations, or indeed in the neurotic family reterritorializations, we exclaim: Let there be still more perversion! Still more artifice! until the earth becomes so artificial that the movement of deterritorialization creates necessarily by itself a new earth." (*Anti-Oedipus*, 384). A policy of the worst sort, which it is difficult to take seriously. The problem of the institution and of public service remains unanswered. In a world of liberated desires, what will be the regulatory process? If one wishes to abolish the despotic State, one must also fear reviving it: universal anarchy leads to universal terror.

"There is neither good nor evil, there is only vegetation"; this sentence, which Hugo has a materialistic philosopher say, can be easily adapted to fit *Anti-Oedipus*: "there is neither good nor evil, there are only machines." And if the machine works "badly", this malfunction is, it seems, an element of the whole. Death itself "is a part of desiring machine" (397), a strange thing which would undoubtedly lead us, if we were to reflect upon it, toward the underlying plan and the true pathos of this book. But people still suffer, and they will not be relieved by being assured that their backfiring is useful to the great mechanism. You have to take care of them—not make them suffer more and along with them, step by step, the condemned society—but make them able to live this life, which we may judge mediocre, but which they prefer to death. Certainly, *Anti-Oedipus* nullifies mental illness and treats the psychiatric establishment harshly, not without good reasons. But it is useless for it to rehabilitate the schizophrenic.[6] The fact remains that the delirium of the latter is rarely bearable, for him and for his relatives, and that we find ourselves before a misfortune which we must indeed confront. One sometimes has the impression—this is unpleasant to say—that the schizo, this new substitute for the eternal privileged victim, is indeed very lucky—very lucky when we are the ones speaking about him. I reproach this book, because it has not confronted evil, for evading the question of suffering. One can say, using a pretty metaphor, "desiring machine"; it is more difficult to say "suffering machine".

The true boundary to be traced cuts across sickness and across nursing care: to struggle against social control, psychiatrization, Oedipianization, is not to deny infirmity, retardation and schizophrenia. There is a twilight zone where we can abandon neither those who suffer nor those who nurse.

Concerning the Subject.

At the end, the complaint of the sick person poses once again the initial question: *someone* suffers, just as we said at the beginning: *someone* wrote this book. The man-machine already amused the seventeenth and eighteenth centuries very much, and we can still draw much satisfaction from this: the humanity-factory of *Anti-Oedipus* gives us a fascinating view of it. (For me, this book is first and foremost what it repudiates most vehemently, a representation, a theater.) But how could a machine see the others and proclaim that they are machines? The same question arises at every level: "How could an unconscious which, we are told, is impersonal or transpersonal play a role analogous to that of the person, of the self, of the conscience in the systems of the past?"[7]—How can a being decide between the true and the false, good and evil without introspection? P. Weiss' Sade says it very well:

To distinguish what is false from what is right
One must know himself
Me
I don't know who I am.[8]

One is ashamed to recall what is obvious, but it is necessary, so obstinate is the contemporary furor against the subject, baptized "residual". "The real difference is not between the machine and the living person, between vitalism and mechanism, but between two states

6. They even dare to write "the schizo" when the specialists tell us: there are schizophrenics with multiple and sometimes very different symptoms . . .

7. R. Girard. *op.cit.*

8. Peter Weiss, *La Persecution et l'assasinat de J. P. Marat* (Seuil).

of the machine which are also two states of the living person" (*Anti-Oedipus*, 339). Up to a certain point, why not? Descartes had already advanced quite far in this direction. That there is mechanism in the living person, and something living in mechanism, we all agree. However, there is a small difference. I have heard a machine speak in a laboratory (not a tape recorder, but a machine which creates by itself the human voice); but when it said "I", it was not the I of the machine; one understood right away that it was a question of someone else, belonging to the human species. One sees men programming a machine, but one will never see a machine programming a man. Or else one must imagine a total programming of humanity—which leads us to another discussion, in the direction perhaps of Claude Lévi-Strauss.

This book, the most anti-metaphysical which has ever been written, leads us inevitably to the question of Being. From the moment when transcendence is rejected, evil no longer has a raison d'être, nor, as a consequence, does the subject, carrier of evil, who is unburdened only of his desire in order to fuel the motors of the whole factory. But what, then, is this desire, if one decrees that it doesn't come from any need? What is this negation, if we are assured that it isn't privation, insufficiency of being? In one way or another one must indeed think being or make there be some. It's difficult. But less so than to imagine a full void, like the one which *Anti-Oedipus* opens up on. I conclude with this sentence by R. Girard: "the true question is not: how to accede to universal delirium, but, how does it come about that there isn't just delirium and infinite violence, that is to say, nothing at all?"

Derrida, History, and Intellectuals*

BY FRANK LENTRICCHIA

For a while in the late 1960s and early 1970s, when in person and in print Jacques Derrida made his initial American public appearances, the ideas associated with his name appeared doomed to be of interest mainly to professors and students of critical theory at Yale, the Irvine campus of the University of California, and Johns Hopkins. Over the past seven or eight years, however, we have witnessed a remarkably steady flow of translations of Derrida's most important writings: *La Voix et le phénomène* in 1973, *De la grammatologie* in 1976, his translation and introduction to Husserl's *L'origine de la géométrie* in 1978, and now from the University of Chicago Press, in Alan Bass's elegant translation, *L'écriture et la difference*.[1] Chicago has recently added a translation of *Éperons* (1979) and promises translations in the not very distant future of *La dissémenation, Positions, Marges de la philosophie, La vérité en peinture* — and, perhaps, even *Glas*. I must rest my point about the Derrida vogue, in this essay, on the facts of academic publishing. For these facts not only implicitly address intellectual issues, but also economic realities. *Writing and Difference* is long, tough, and expensive, but already the paperback edition has appeared and a certain financial success seems assured.

I could add considerable evidence of a different sort to make the point that Derrida has fully arrived in the United States, that he is now dominating our critical landscape, and that some version of his thought (I do not say that it *is* his thought) may be on the verge of

* Review of Jacques Derrida, *Writing and Difference*, trans. Alan Bass (Univ. of Chicago Press, 1979).

1 *Writing and Difference* includes the following essays: "Force and Signification," "Cogito and the History of Madness," "Emond Jabès and the Question of the Book," "Violence and Metaphysics: An Essay on the Thought of Emmanuel Levinas," "'Genesis and Structure' and Phenomenology," "La Parole soufflée," "Freud and the Scene of Writing," "The Theater of Cruelty and the Closure of Representation," "From Restricted to General Economy: A Hegelianism Without Reserve," "Structure, Sign, and Play in the Discourse of the Human Sciences," and a concluding "Ellipsis."

being appropriated and normalized by an easily recognized conservative critical establishment whose goals, despite stark differences in rhetoric and philosophic authorities, may in the end succeed only in reenforcing the old new-critical business of "close" reading of the traditional canon of English and American literature. And I do mean *business:* one of the ends of the newest criticism is the production of articles and books on the canonical figures for the purpose of demonstrating, once again, that literary discourse is unto itself, self-mastering, free of all external determination. As recent jargon says, "self-deconstructing." According to the credo of a critic much shaped by Derrida, J. Hillis Miller: "I believe in the established canon of English and American literature and in the validity of the concept of privileged texts."[2] Deconstruction, Miller says, is common to all periods of history.[3] In other words, deconstruction is traditional – not a frightening deviation of contemporary theory. Miller should tell this to Gerald Graff, who sees in Derrida a barbaric relativism intent on destroying everything that is dear to traditionalist thought.[4]

It would be interesting to know how Derrida would respond to these two (increasingly typical) American readings of him. I will offer the opinion that neither Miller nor Graff has scored a bull's-eye, and the hope that *Writing and Difference* will show why. Their vigorous disagreement aside, Miller and Graff commonly affirm, in so many words, that the force of Derrida's work bears mainly on the internal interests of literary criticism. Without desiring to endorse the conventional separations of the disciplines, I am going to argue that Derrida can be received in another, perhaps more urgent way: as a writer whose strongest impact may be made on our historico-political consciousness.

1.

The advantage over his other major texts of *Writing and Difference*, for students of critical theory and the humanities at large, is that it puts forward in somewhat more accessible form issues that have

2 J. Hillis Miller, "The Function of Rhetorical Study at the Present Time," in *The State of the Discipline, 1970s–1980s* (a special issue of the *ADE Bulletin*, no. 62 [Sept.-Nov. 1979], 12).

3 *Ibid.*, 14.

4 Gerald Graff, *Literature Against Itself: Literary Ideas in Modern Society* (Chicago: The University of Chicago Press, 1979), p. 62.

always preoccupied Derrida and, for about a decade now, have pretty much captured theoretical dialogue in this country. The issues that have ruled Western thought since classical Greece — *representation, trace, structure,* the *subject,* the linguistic *sign* and the basis of its signifying capacities, the *book,* and perhaps the most significant and least understood of Derrida's interests, the issue of *history* — such terms and their contexts have fascinated Derrida from the beginning. The articulation of these terms in the network of their relationships to one another in *Writing and Difference* should make this text especially attractive to his American audience.

The deconstructive kind of reading that we associate with Derrida is on display in paradigmatic form in "'Genesis and Structure' and Phenomenology," an essay crucial to assessments of the history of contemporary critical theory and philosophy. Though conventionally seen as antagonists in binary opposition (in the 1950s and 1960s in France the struggle for hegemony in contemporary theory was fought out in just such melodramatic terms — genesis *or* structure, but not both), Derrida's effort is to disturb our perception of simple antagonism, to show in a shrewd reading of Husserl which complements the title essay of *Speech and Phenomena,* that the terms "genesis" and "structure" do not represent closed conceptual fortresses. In contemporary critical theory, genetic thinking, as a concern for the origin and the diachronic process implied by the origin, is radically opposed to structuralist thinking, a concern with totality, with a frozen (synchronized) temporality whose various elements are simultaneously present to consciousness. But for Husserl, Derrida concludes, there is no genesis-structure problem "but only a privilege of one or the other of these two operative concepts, according to the space of description. . ."[5] Husserl's ceaseless attempt, in fact, was one of reconciliation — to put together a "*structuralist* demand (which leads to the comprehensive description of a totality, of a form or a function organized according to an internal legality in which elements have meaning only in the solidarity of their correlation or their opposition) with the *genetic* demand (that is the search for origin and foundation of the structure)."[6] This conclusion, and the detailed argument leading to it, are not only of interest to historians of contemporary theory who have grown accustomed to thinking of "origin" and "structure" as mutually exclusive alternatives, and of the demand for "origin" as a

5 *Writing and Difference,* p. 156.

6 *Ibid.*, p. 157.

nostalgic urge laid to rest by the sophistications of structuralism (Emile Benveniste, among others, puts it in just about those terms). By reminding us that Husserl was not disallowing geneticism in general, but only the empirical or positivistic geneticisms of psychologism and historicism — Husserl favored a nonempirical intentionality, a transcendental origin of structure — Derrida begins to thicken and make more heterogeneous and difficult our sense of the history of modern philosophical and critical thought and their entangled lines of force. When he demonstrates that Husserl's investment in transcendental intentionality is at the same time an investment in structure — "an original structure, an archi-structure" — the strict binary of origin and structure is dissolved, and what is revealed is that a "certain structuralism has always been philosophy's most spontaneous gesture."[7]

Here, then, is one fundamental sense of deconstruction: a kind of analysis which dismantles not only the programmatic statement of philosophical intention (Cartesian, Kantian, phenomenological, *etc.*) but also the corresponding canonical reading which accepts at face value the claim of the programmatic statement (this is *my* turf — I discovered it, I own it). What Derrida's deconstruction tends to uncover, beneath the apparently unique philosophical program and its residence in the unique historical locale of its birth — locale and program exist in symbiotic relationship in traditional historicism — is a much longer and larger historical context, one governing all of these "unique" programs, through a set of rules for thinking that colors, compromises, qualifies, even subverts the philosopher's "unique" intention, and by so doing binds it over to the larger institutional enterprise of Western thought. That sort of dismantling is a primary task of deconstruction, and clearly it is a task for an historian, though not of the conventional kind.

That structuralist gesture which Derrida finds "spontaneous" — a natural, inevitable tendency of the philosophical mind? — he also finds "totalitarian"[8] because it desires to force a monolithic unity, a coherence of cultural productions and meanings, an exclusive and excluding historical totality that manifests a collective will to power, a relegation to nontruth and madness of all that is not consistent with the sense of rationality and sanity "inside" the totality. This sort of generalization of structuralism removes it from what we know as structuralism (an historically localized movement within the recent

7 *Ibid.*, p. 159.
8 *Ibid.*, p. 160.

French scene) and disperses its ruling desires to the point where "structuralism" becomes coincidental with the characteristic movement of Western philosophical intention. With its interests in determinate period unities, beginnings, endings, and the teleological processes which connect them, what we have known traditionally as historicism becomes a chief expression of this "spontaneous" structuralist gesture of Western philosophy. The root notion of "original structure" that Derrida finds animating Husserl's writings will, in its predication of *origin,* guarantee a certain determinate unfolding of temporal process, a fixed beginning moving toward a fixed end; while in its predication of *structure* it guarantees that the entire temporal process can be grasped synchronically, as if by a transcendental subject for whom the entire course of time can be mastered in a single glance. Time (in the inclusive Hegelian sense), or blocks of time, periods (as Lovejoy taught us to perceive them) become texts in this structuralizing of history (or its teleologizing — there is no difference), reduced to good behavior by an internal legality of rules. Heterogeneity — the undigestible — is excluded from homogeneous substance, or somehow reduced to compatibility with a presiding unity. One of Derrida's major criticisms of Husserl is that in the name of a structuralism which would avoid the positivistic (reductionist) historicisms of the nineteenth century, Husserl, in substituting a structuralism based on transcendental ground and attentive to the unity of cultural expressions, has reinstated the category of historicism in its most traditional philosophical form — as the methodology which creates and cherishes the "totalitarian structure."

"Totalitarian" is the word. In several of the essays in *Writing and Difference,* and in numerous places in his other writings, Derrida has recourse to political metaphor. So insistent is this metaphorics, in fact, so concentrated, and, very often, so crucially placed in the argument, that it is not possible to take this language casually. (Considering his extraordinary sense of figuration, I cannot believe that he would want us to take it casually.) His ostensible subject is the history of philosophy; his implied subject is the political and social quality of historical life; the nature of the relationship between philosophy and society is the great problem area in Derrida's work. It is in the essay on Michel Foucault's *Histoire de la folie* ("Cogito and the History of Madness") that the political and social implications are brought into decisive clarity of focus. Not that Derrida reaches a point of decisive, either-or choice: for him there is never a question of choice in that simple sense. It is that readers shaped (scarred) by contemporary theoretical debate are forced into making some decision about the main drift of Derrida's thought. Whether his contemporary readers, especially those who call themselves Derrideans, like it or not, Derrida's own discourse begs to be construed, and perhaps in a manner not unlike Derrida's own construction of the history of philosophy. With all allowances made for his intense consciousness of the duplicities of Western philosophical thought, and, at some level (he is the first to admit to this), for his own necessary complicity in that tradition — some judgment about where the main socio-political emphases of his work fall is necessary. The current Yale interpretation to the contrary notwithstanding, that judgment cannot fall into the category of the "undecidable," unless, that is, one's desire is to forego judgment.

The focus of Derrida's critique of Foucault is a brief passage of about three pages in which Foucault offers a reading of Descartes' first meditation. In this reading Foucault thinks he finds evidence of a historical rupture separating what he calls the "classical" period from what had come before it. The trademark of the classical, he thinks, is violent exclusion, the establishment of a contrary to reason (madness, folly, dementia, insanity, *etc.*). The Greek *logos,* which supposedly held sway until well into the seventeenth century, on the contrary *had no contrary* but rather a free interchange with *hybris.* I cannot go into the particulars of Derrida's and Foucault's readings of Descartes. (For my purposes those particulars are irrelevant.) I can only say here that Derrida's reading seems to me to be the more compelling one, and by far. In brief, what he does is to demonstrate, through an analysis of the play of textual voices projected by a series of minute but telling rhetorical gestures, that Descartes was not dismissing, excluding, or ostracizing madness from the philosopher's city, the "circle of philosophical dignity." "Descartes never interns madness," Derrida concludes, "neither at the stage of natural doubt nor at the stage of metaphysical doubt . . . Madness is . . . one *case* of thought (*within* thought)."[9] The conclusions that are drawn from this analysis are recognizably Derridean (but not in the Yale sense). 1) The central intellectual strategy which Foucault identifies with a discretely enclosed historical era has a much older, much longer lineage, one that escapes the block of time Foucault called the "classical age." The intellectual habit that Foucault wants to originate

9 *Ibid.*, pp. 55-56.

within Descartes has "always already" occurred. 2) This habit, this "structure of exclusion," not only does not originate in the later seventeenth century; it cannot be said to have originated at all (we cannot locate a "before"), and it is not what it seems to be. The "structure of exclusion"[10] represents the force of a desire (logocentric passion) that cannot be satisfied; nor can it be entirely lucid about its failure to generate perfect binary opposition (know itself in it logocentric passion, deconstruct itself). "Since" the Greek *logos* (I put "since" in quotation marks because such terms become problematic when simple origins are put out of the game), Reason in the guise of philosophy has desired to exclude both poetry (a term in Plato that refers to madness, irrationality, falsehood, writing, and women) and history in order to establish its protective barriers and to enclose its purity. But the very terms of such an effort work against clean ruptures which would guarantee segregated ontological identities for the discourses of philosophy, history, and poetry.

Let me offer an example of such philosophical desire, and its self-delusion, from a familiar place in a dominant Western text: the *Poetics* of Aristotle. I am referring to the section in which poetry and history are distinguished — apparently absolutely.[11] Poetry, the argument goes, imagines what may happen, according to laws of probability and necessity, while history reports on what has happened — the brute facts of things as they are. Quickly, however, a qualification enters. Poetry "tends" to express the universal, poetry speaks "more" of universals, poetry is "more concerned" with the universal, while history tends toward particularity. Which is to say that the stature granted to poetry by its supposed adherence to the laws of "probability" and "necessity" (veridically celebrated words which saturate the *Poetics*) is somewhat undercut: the difference between poetry and history is not a diametrical opposition, a difference in kind, but rather a difference in degree — poetry partakes (the logic of Aristotle's argument demands this conclusion) of *some* particularity, history of *some* universality.

But from what point of vantage are these judgments on poetry and history delivered? From the point of view of neither: from philosophy. Poetry is a "more philosophical and serious business than history," but by definition it cannot be *as* "serious," *as*

10 *Ibid.*, p. 40.

11 *Aristotle: "Poetics,"* trans., with an introduction and notes, Gerald F. Else (Ann Arbor: University of Michigan Press, 1967), pp. 32-34.

"philosophical" as philosophy itself, the discipline and discourse which speaks according to the truth of the probable and the necessary, a discourse governed totally by the universal to which it is (presumably) transparent. Also, by definition, history must be *somewhat* serious, *somewhat* philosophical: hence in some part governed by the laws of probability and necessity. Philosophy would exclude *both* poetry and history from pristine cognitive grasp of the realm of truth. In the act of defining its superior veridical status over poetry and history (in the act of defining itself), philosophy grants some measure of truth to both discourses. The differences between philosophy, poetry, and history are differences of degree. The relationship between poetry and history, or between philosophy on the one hand, and poetry and history on the other, is not definable as a structure of exclusion (however much Aristotle might desire that to be the case) but as a continuum which permits interchange and communication. The basis of communication among the three discourses is the universal. Aristotle's fear (hence his desire to enclose philosophy) is that all three may also be connected by a common partaking in mere particularity (falsehood, irrationality, madness). If philosophy, poetry, and history are situated on a "continuum" (the submerged metaphor of chapter 9 of the *Poetics*) and "particularity" is on the continuum, then philosophy cannot finally be free of contamination. To put it in another way, if we take the metaphor of the continuum seriously, then there cannot be a self-contained "inside" of truth and reason (philosophy) protected from an "outside" of falsehood and irrationality (poetry and history). (Our conventional academic habit of constituting the humanistic disciplines as autonomous islands of epistemic authority is thus subverted in one of the texts thought to lie at the very origin of the humanistic tradition; the hubris of the expert in philosophy — or in history or literary criticism — that his discipline has some unique claim to truth-telling is revealed for what it is.) This not quite successful exclusion of poetry and history by philosophy is one major meaning of logocentrism; the exposure of the failure to exclude another major sense of deconstruction. Some such form of failed exclusion constitutes the canonical tradition of Western philosophy; some such deconstructive reading marks Derrida's various dismantlings from Plato to Foucault.

It would follow from the deconstruction of the "structure of exclusion" that Foucault's intention to write a history of ostracized madness, condemned to silence, *from the point of view of silence itself,* is impossible. For what Derrida's deconstruction reveals is not a binary opposition which would present the historian with a simple either-or: either a history of madness itself, or a history of the language of psychiatry *on* madness, "on madness already crushed beneath psychiatry, dominated, beaten to the ground, interned."[12] What Derrida's deconstruction reveals is an imperfect binary (hence no binary at all), a difference *posing* as a binary, a mutually conditioning relationship of forces duplicitously masking itself as diametrical alternatives. Foucault's desire to reject on a global scale the order of reason and its discourses is a revolutionary desire to destroy that order, to step completely outside of it, and, by thus rupturing it utterly, free one's own discourse from its ensnaring and repressive consequences. Psychiatric reason, however, is but the "delegate" of societal and governmental reason, and the political order of reason is in turn but the delegate of the encompassing Western order of reason. "All of our European languages" are the "immense delegation" of the order of reason.[13] Derrida then anticipates the crucial point that he would make in a later essay, included in *Writing and Difference,* "Structure, Sign, and Play in the Discourse of the Human Sciences": "If the order of which we are speaking is so powerful, if its power is unique of its kind, this is so precisely by virtue of the universal, structural, and infinite complicity in which it compromises all those who understand it in its own language, even when this language provides them with the form of their own denunciation. Order is then denounced within order."[14] This order, which in the *Grammatology* he calls the *epistémè,* under the aegis of which all thought and all writing in the West is produced and determined, is the totality of all totalities — *"the greatest totality."*[15] His description of this epistemic totality is sobering, even depressing; it evokes a feeling of the dying fall: it is "unsurpassable, unique, and imperial"[16] in its grandeur. Not one determined historical structure among other possible structures, it is *the* structure. "There is no Trojan horse unconquerable by Reason,"[17] no revolution against reason except within reason, and even then to call the philosophical

12 *Writing and Difference,* p. 34.
13 *Ibid.*, p. 35.
14 *Ibid.*
15 *Of Grammatology,* trans. Gayatri Chakravorty Spivak (Baltimore: Johns Hopkins University Press, 1976), p. 46.
16 *Writing and Difference,* p. 36.
17 *Ibid.*

disturbance that one like Derrida is capable of creating a "revolution" would be rhetorical bombast of the first degree. As Derrida admits, the kind of disturbance he has in mind is to be understood "precisely in the language of a department of *internal* affairs."[18] He believes that the structure can be thoroughly shaken, but the wonder and awe that he expresses in the face of this immense structure of reason suggests that he believes it to be fundamentally invulnerable to change. The structure remains intact. There is no San Andreas fault of Reason.

And how shall we take the term "structure" in Derrida? It seems hopelessly late in the day to raise that question about a philosopher whose work constitutes one of the more forceful frontal attacks on structure and structuralism that one might imagine. More precisely, my question is, to what extent has Derrida himself been compromised by what he has so assiduously, even obsessively, deconstructed? In "Structure, Sign, and Play" he writes that there "is no sense in doing without the concepts of metaphysics in order to shake metaphysics. We have no language — no syntax and no lexicon — which is foreign to this history; we can pronounce not a single destructive proposition which has not already had to slip into the form, the logic, and the implicit postulation of precisely what it seeks to contest."[19] The example he gives is a telling one: in order to destroy the metaphysics of presence one would have to reject the concept and the word "sign," which, as "sign of," always promises the appropriation of presence. But this is precisely what cannot be done. Similarly, in order to destroy the metaphysics of presence one would have to reject the concept and the word "structure" — but neither can that be done. It will not do to charge Derrida with being a naive delegate of the order of reason, when in fact he has been exposing that order and its duplicities since the beginning of his career. In some sense, he would agree, he must be a delegate of that order, because it envelops and infects all those who write within it, whether they write for it or against it. Derrida has unveiled the assumptions and strategies of the classical concept of structure in "Structure, Sign, and Play." In one of the most penetrating essays on literary theory that I have read (the first essay in *Writing and Difference,* "Force and Signification"), he has also demonstrated that literary criticism is always and unremittingly structuralist, and that modern aesthetics, with its investments in spatial, geometric, and cinematic models — and, as we have seen already in the essay on Husserl, even with its

18 *Ibid.*
19 *Ibid.*, pp. 280-281.

investment in genesis and intention — is ruled by totalitarian structuralism which reduces time, passion, energy, force, and play, and which essentializes all heterogeneity. The intellectual agony of Jacques Derrida might be schematized in this way: on the one hand, he urges us not to abandon ourselves to structuralist formalism; on the other hand, emancipation from this massively enforced intellectual habit seems impossible. The injunction is to "resist"[20] (one cannot help but hear "the resistance" at this point), but in what terms, on what ground, with what chance of even modest success if we cannot help, even in our critical, deconstructive mood, repeating the repressive Western logic of logocentrism?

Let me defer, for a moment, the obvious question (how well does Derrida resist totalitarian structuralism?) and cite one of his most elegant statements on the tendency of structuralist thought to neutralize time and history: "the appearance of a new structure, of an original system, always comes about — and this is the very condition of its structural specificity — by a rupture with its past, its origin, and its cause. Therefore one can describe what is peculiar to the structural organization only by not taking into account, in the very moment of this description, its past conditions: by omitting to posit the problem of the transition from one structure to another, by putting history between brackets. In this 'structuralist' moment, the concepts of chance and discontinuity are indispensable."[21] It is clear that Derrida's deconstruction of the smaller, self-contained epistemological fields employed by Foucault in *Histoire de la folie,* and his replacement of such discontinuous totalities with "the greatest totality," the ever-persistent, pervasive, continuous and unavoidable *epistémè* he calls the order of reason side-steps the problems of discontinuity, of rupture with the past, of the embarrassment of an "historian" who must bracket history in order to deal with a structural totality in its "original" specificity. But does Derrida's "greatest totality" (the context of all contexts) avoid the totalitarian consequences of structural formalism? Is he himself a structuralist because, by his own argument, he can be, at bottom, nothing else?

If Foucault structuralizes historical discourse by blocking out discrete units (and unities) of epistemic substance, then it might be charged that Derrida structuralizes (synchronizes) the entire historical process with his order of reason and his tradition of logocentrism. "Structure. . . can be *methodically* threatened in order

20 *Ibid.*, p. 28.
21 *Ibid.*, p. 291.

to be comprehended more clearly and to reveal not only its supports but also that secret place in which it is neither construction nor ruin but lability. This operation is called (from the Latin) *soliciting*. In other words, *shaking* in a way related to the *whole* (from *sollus,* in archaic Latin 'the whole,' and from *citare,* 'to put in motion')."[22] To comprehend as *construction* would be to understand and endorse structure as totalitarian order; to wish to comprehend it as *ruin* (a futile wish) is to take the sentimental and deluded revolutionary position of Foucault when he claims to write the history of silence; to comprehend structure as Derrida does, from its "secret place," is to grant oneself privileged knowledge of the structure as *lability* — as the unstable contradiction that it is, as heterogeneous weaving without stabilizing origin or end.

In his early work on Husserl *(The Origin of Geometry)*, Derrida deconstructs the notion of tradition (in its most traditional sense) in order to show that "tradition," its concepts and its uses, is yet another strategem of the logocentric order of reason, another way of ensuring that heterogeneity will be understood as encrustation only, or a film of sediment, perhaps, that only momentarily obscures the essential process of tradition, the act of handing over, a process of preserving at all costs an ideal meaning, some impervious homogeneous stuff, some essential object whose ever-present presence guarantees the simple continuity of time as pure repetition (in other words, the death of time). To show, on the contrary, that so-called sedimentations are "essential" is to show, in so many words, that there is no "essence" in the metaphysical sense, no ideal object to be "obscured" or "sedimented."[23]

And yet, with all of these theoretical safeguards properly acknowledged and applauded, the nagging question remains: in Derrida's *practice,* in his actual deconstructions from Plato to Foucault, is "the structure" best characterized by stability or lability? Is "the tradition" of Western philosophical discourse unified or heterogeneous? If to uncover slippages in the would-be binaries governing the thought of Plato, or Kant, or Husserl, or Foucault is enough to demonstrate lability, then so be it. But to quiz that condition of lability from Plato onwards is to see, very quickly, that what is called instability is itself controlled totally by a set of rules for thought and writing which make the conclusions of Derrida's analyses

22 *Ibid.*, p. 6.

23 *Edmund Husserl's "Origin of Geometry": An Introduction,* trans., with a preface, John P. Leavey, Jr. (Stony Brook, N.Y.: Nicolas Hays, Ltd., 1978), pp. 29, 48-51.

predictable once we have grasped the method in any one of its demonstrations. The distinction between Plato and Husserl is finally (and here, I admit, I employ a distinction that Derrida does not accept) one of differences in respective cultural contents and cultural ambiences of their thought — not in the *form* of thought revealed. The effect of Derrida's various analyses of the philosophical tradition is not to affirm simple unity, but to demonstrate deep structural solidarity, unity of an extraordinarily complicated sort. It is this complex (and rather elusive) unity which makes (in Derrida's eyes) the order of reason an order too cunning and powerful to step outside of. The spatial sense of structure is constitutive even for this critic of structuralist geometrism. We exist "within" the order; our "disturbances" of "shaking" are of internal moment alone and are dealt with, tamed, even co-opted by some equivalent to a department of the interior.[24]

2.

In the more rigidified forms of Marxism, all superstructural phenomena are understood as simple determinates of an economic base: Derrida appears to accept an idealistic version of economism when he calls institutions "epiphenomena" and "delegates."[25] He does not tell us explicitly what they are epiphenomena *of*, but it seems undeniable that for him the cause (or base) of all things, the great motor principle, is philosophy itself. If philosophy is the "base" in the Marxist sense, and if structural totalitarianism is its "most spontaneous gesture," as Derrida puts it, then we need to take the notion of spontaneity very seriously. Philosophical totalitarianism appears inevitable, even instinctual. Like nature itself, philosophy in its repressive Western form is forever. Perhaps it is this deterministic notion of the base as repressive logocentric thinking which casts gloom on his prognosis for the future of reason and its many delegates. In the Marxist tradition change is not impossible, for history has shown us that the means of production have changed, and so have the relations which (as the ruling class) have controlled those means and hegemonized culture. There is no need in Marxist thought to project endless repetition of the status quo into the future. For Derrida, however, there seems to be no ground for hope. If Western philosophy is the cause of the forms of institutions, governments, languages, disciplines, *etc.*, and if that philosophical tradition has

24 *Writing and Difference,* p. 36.
25 *Ibid.*, p. 35, 40.

itself always been governed as to its form by certain spontaneous habits of thought, then it is understandable why Derrida (in all but words) would think those habits to be ineradicable.

If the free circulation of the mad, before their great confinement in the later seventeenth century, is but a "socioeconomic epiphenomenon on the surface of a reason divided against itself since the dawn of its Greek origin,"[26] then two things are clear. On behalf of Derrida it must be said that Foucault's isolation of a unique classical period was wrong; the repression is older and more insidiously pervasive than Foucault thought. On Foucault's behalf, however, we would have to conclude that Derrida appears to have instituted in his massive and continuous order of reason an epistemic force of monolithic determination, more efficient in its repressive work than anything dreamed of by Foucault when he instituted his series of discrete, smaller epistemes. Socioeconomic institutions are effects of a deep structure ("epiphenomena on the surface") which Derrida describes as a "oneness of Reason."[27] In his insistence that we take the spatial models of structuralism seriously, he writes that "metaphor is never innocent. It orients research and fixes results."[28] On the basis of this Nietzschean insight we would have to say that the metaphorics of "epiphenomenon," "spontaneity," and "department of internal affairs" are not innocent, that they are powerful structuralist metaphors, and that they have traditional implications. And I mean to recall Derrida's own attack on the essentializing and repressive implications of the notion of tradition, and his attack, in "Freud and the Scene of Writing," on the concept of the conscious author.

As the process of transmission of ideal objects, tradition requires a text produced in full lucidity of consciousness; a text fully present to itself. Such a text, in its serene immobile self-possession — like a statue, written stone, or archive whose signified content can be harmlessly, without loss, transported into a new milieu or a new language through a process of translation — would insure not only the security of translation (there *is* a self-present object to be translated), but also the "historicity" of the text (a negative term in Derrida which signifies the continuing hegemony of idealistic theories of history).[29] What is finally guaranteed by tradition (the basis of its

26 *Ibid.*, p. 40. I am grateful to James Holstun, a graduate student in my department, for pointing out to me the significance of this passage.

27 *Ibid.*, p. 36.

28 *Ibid.*, p. 17.

29 *Husserl's "Origin of Geometry,"* p. 51; *Writing and Difference*, p. 211.

appeal perhaps) is the ideality, the eternal value and truth of the discourse of the thinker who engages tradition, who enters into dialogue with it, who preserves an ideal meaning in his discourse in order to "hand it over" and "hand it down." I must say once again that Derrida knows all of this better than anyone else (he has taught us to know it), that it is his purpose to dismantle traditional notions of history, tradition, author, self-presence, representation, and translation. Still, with whom does Derrida speak? With the canonical figures of the tradition who hand down, from one to the other, and ultimately to Derrida himself, who at the moment is the end of the line, a weave of pure traces, reproductions unconsciously inscribed in texts which are *"always already"* transcriptions (appropriations of tradition) that will protend transcriptions to be.[30]

Vis-à-vis Western philosophy, Derrida is a critical intellectual who subjects the tradition to the most searching analysis of it we have yet seen. But his own discourse is necessarily a conservation, a handing down, a re-inscription of all that he is critical of; his own text keeps as well as breaks from the concepts of sign and structure, and hence in some part is "always already" a transcription of logocentric order. The notion of history that he implicitly promotes is a notion promoted by what Antonio Gramsci calls the traditional intellectual. Derrida is an unwilling and uncomfortable traditional thinker. No one who reads his deconstructions of various thinkers can fail to feel that he is witnessing subversion in process. Yet the structure itself is always left intact, however much it is shaken. Derrida will permit himself a "dream of emancipation"[31]; but with that sort of desire openly admitted one is tempted to read in another way the vigor of his attack on Foucault's revolutionary, utopian impulse. Real emancipation is impossible. Still, it is necessary to resist, he says. But given the alternatives (impossible utopianism vs. the monolithic Western order of reason) one is forced to ask: Why resist? How resist? To what end shall we resist?

We need, at this point, to approach the political status of deconstruction by considering Derrida's direct treatment of his method as a general strategy of reading. His political metaphors are pervasive and they speak for themselves: the heritage of Western philosophy and the various institutions it has spawned is the binary opposition which constitutes (all appearances to the contrary notwithstanding) not a "peaceful coexistence" (i.e., reason and

30 *Writing and Difference,* p. 211.
31 *Ibid.*, p. 28.

poetry, speech and writing, masculine and feminine) but a "violent hierarchy. One of the two terms controls the other (axiologically, logically, etc.), holds the superior position. To deconstruct the opposition is, first, at a given moment, to overthrow the hierarchy."[32] We must not delude ourselves, however, with a gesture of revolution, and attempt to leap beyond our heritage, Derrida warns, onto the terrain of a new, nonrepressive social order: to try to do so would be to give up all efforts of "intervening" in the order of reason which constitutes the state; simple rejection (as opposed to intervention) leaves the old order intact, its various mechanisms of repression undisturbed and ready to do their work again. Since the hierarchical set of oppositions which marks the "previous regime" will "always reconstitute itself," the analytic process of deconstruction must necessarily be interminable, constantly vigilant if the deconstructive reader is not to be content to reside within the system which he would dismantle. Deconstruction, then, must put forward a series of "undecidables" which cannot be appropriated by the oppositional structure of the "received order." Derrida's key terms *(supplément, hymen, différance,* etc.) somehow "escape from inclusion in the philosophic (binary) opposition" and yet *at the same time* "inhabit it, resist and disorganize it, but *without ever* constituting a third term. . . ."[33]

Now, if we ask what would appear to be an inevitable question — from where does Derrida derive the "secret" knowledge that enables deconstruction to shake up traditional structures? — he can only reply "from a certain external perspective which it [deconstruction] cannot name or describe."[34] As a mode of intervention, is deconstruction efficacious? Are violent hierarchies overthrown, or left intact? Overthrown for a while? And then reconstituted? All of the above? As a textual activity, deconstruction is politically marginal (in the usual and in the Derridean sense); "both faithful and violent," it moves "back and forth between the inside and the outside of philosophy." If this sort of action cannot have structural political impact, if from a practical standpoint it cannot be a "resistance," or an "intervention," it is, for those who can practice it, "a great

32 "Positions," *Diacritics,* 2 (Winter 1972), 36.

33 *Ibid.*

34 *Positions: Entretiens avec Henri Ronse, Julia Kristeva, Jean-Louis Houdebine, Guy Scarpetta* (Paris: Minuit, 1972), p. 15.

pleasure" *(un grand plaisir)*.[35] Deconstruction is a strategy whose larger theoretical consequences have not yet been spelled out.

I have the impression from reading Derrida that he believes that the inescapable fact of our historical situation, the fact that one is always and inevitably marked by the historical process, is necessarily a bar to progressive change, that "history" is synonymous with "repression" (a point hard to disagree with), and that historical repression can only reproduce itself endlessly into the future (a metaphysical point which turns history into nature). But why then resist? The image ofDerrida the writer that emerges from his texts is a reenactment of the myth of Sisyphus. Derrida fits well into Gramsci's characterization of the traditional intellectual futilely trying to free himself from old commitments: "Intellectuals develop slowly, far more slowly than any other social group, by their very nature and historical function. They represent the entire cultural tradition of a people, seeking to resume and synthesize all of its history. . . . To think it possible that such intellectuals, *en masse,* can break with the entire past and situate themselves totally upon a terrain of a new ideology, is absurd. It is absurd for the mass of intellectuals, and perhaps it is also absurd for many intellectuals taken individually as well — notwithstanding all the honorable efforts which they make and want to make."[36]

Derrida would, I think, reply to Gramsci that it is not possible for any sort of intellectual, whether traditional or on the left, to situate himself on the ground of a new ideology. Yet for all of his insistence on the massive constricting power of traditional Western ideology, Derrida's desire for the "new" surfaces when he points to the radically unstable nature of logocentrism (its "lability"). Again, from what privileged ground of "secret" knowledge is this judgment of instability delivered? What wish for the future does this judgment only barely mask, if not a wish for structural change? And yet what means (apart from the too problematic means of deconstruction) has Derrida explored for connecting theory and practice, and hence for making it possible for the intellectual to intervene? And how seriously can he be interested in intervention when largely he seems concerned with figuring out his relationship to Heidegger, Freud, Hegel, Kant, and so on back to the Greek fountains? In his extraordinary work *Keywords,* Raymond Williams pinpoints several senses of "tradition" which seem to me to threaten and perhaps even enervate Derrida's

35 *Ibid.*

36 Antonio Gramsci, *Selections from Political Writings: 1921-1926,* trans. and edited Quintin Hoare (New York: International Publishers, 1978), p. 462.

capacity to resist and disturb: delivery, handing down knowledge, passing on a doctrine, surrender or betrayal. I would add that tradition-making is an expression of the will to power; the idea of "handing down" is best understood as "forcing down." "But the word moves again and again," Williams concludes, "towards ceremony, duty and respect" — and especially toward the sort of duty and respect that sons are supposed to have for their fathers.[37]

If I appear to be using Gramsci's Marxism as a hammer with which to beat a thinker whose intellectual commitments deserve to be viewed in the light of a very different orientation, I can only say that Derrida makes me do it. Though I think he over-appreciates the role of philosophy in our socio-historical lives, his insistence that repression is as much culturally as it is economically executed is not far from the neo-Marxist emphasis represented by Gramsci himself. It would be hard to find a thinker who better fits Gramsci's definition of the critical consciousness: "Criticizing one's own conception of the world means . . . to make it coherent and unified and to raise it to the point reached by the most advanced modern thought. It also means criticizing all hitherto existing philosophy in so far as it has left layers incorporated into the popular philosophy. The beginning of the critical elaboration is the consciousness of what one really is, that is, a 'know thyself' as the product of the historical process which has left in you an infinity of traces gathered together without the advantage of an inventory. First of all it is necessary to compile such an inventory."[38] The anomaly of Derrida is that he has achieved such consciousness while viewing the order of reason within which he desires to intervene as a power of appropriation impossible to resist. Of course one cannot intervene in the order of reason if that order exists in splendid isolation from material reality. And there is no use in dealing with institutions in their material settings when these count only as "delegates" or "epiphenomena" of an ideal order of mind (a "oneness of Reason") itself beyond transformation. Philosophy is itself an institution (rather than a prime mover) existing in a network of institutions within which it does not play a privileged role. Philosophy is one of society's productions — not the producer of society and history.

37 Raymond Williams, *Keywords: A Vocabulary of Culture and Society* (New York: Oxford University Press, 1976), pp. 268-269.

38 Antonio Gramsci, *The Modern Prince and Other Writings*, trans. Louis Marks (New York: International Publishers, 1957), p. 59.

Psychoanalysis and Liberalism: The Case of Lionel Trilling

BY MARK SHECHNER

> In time, it may become apparent that Freud and his doctrine have undergone an inexorable disciplining by the culture, and that the exemplary cast of Freud's mind and character is more enduring than the particulars of his doctrine. In culture it is always the example that survives; the person is the immortal idea.
>
> —Philip Rieff

To consider the fate of those writers and intellectuals who started out in the thirties is to call to mind certain paradigms of experience and ideology that gave shape to their lives and were the hallmarks of their generational identity: the disillusionment with and retreat from progressive politics and the rightward drift of their sentiments and allegiances during the years roughly from 1937 to 1945. We think naturally of those repentant Communists and fellow-travellers like James Burnham, Sidney Hook, Irving Kristol, Whittaker Chambers, John Dos Passos, and Arthur Koestler (who, though not an American, became a leading spokesman for American Cold War attitudes in the late forties), whose headlong flights from one political extreme to the other were symptoms of the desperation and instability of those years. Of such moment was the experience that it could appear, in later years, to be the defining feature of the era's moral history: the very course of the *Zeitgeist*. By the early 1950s, these ex-leftists, acting out rituals of atonement for sins they had committed in the name of the future, as well as for many they had only imagined, could assume spokesmanship for the spirit of post-war accommodation that went by the name of realism, or pragmatism, or pluralism, or, as Daniel Bell phrased it, "the end of ideology." And as the charges that continue to be traded even now by such veterans of the old left as Lillian Hellman and Diana Trilling serve to remind us, there remain pockets of intellectual life in America in which one's moral credit is calculated from the year, even the month, in which one resigned or fell quietly away or confessed privately to the right people that one was troubled.

But in truth this paradigm of reaction is only a rare flower of the general experience, which seldom took so pure and symmetrical a shape. Not all post-war sentiment among retreating radicals Kristolized on the right, and not everyone who had once sworn solidarity with striking miners in Harlan County or subscribed to the policy of United Front From Below later signed up for duty with the Congress for Cultural Freedom or pled the case of the free world and its free market in the pages of the CIA-subsidized *Encounter*. A more comprehensive history of the great disillusionment turns up more complex and idiosyncratic careers, from those of staunch "revolutionists" like Dwight Macdonald and amazing holdouts for solidarity like Howard Fast, to those of the psychological converts, who forsook, or softened, or complicated their progressive views by taking up alienation or sensibility or psychoanalysis or whatever promising schemes for interior revitalization happened to be at hand.

In reading through the literary record of the 1940s, I have been drawn especially to these converts to the inner life, because the intellectual by-products of their apostasies, if that is the word for them, were particularly rich, and much of what was fresh in American writing after the war came down in the fertile precipitate of ideas and attitudes released into their thought by the chemistry of socialism on the wane. Elsewhere I've characterized the post-war "Jewish modernism" of Saul Bellow, Isaac Rosenfeld, and Delmore Schwartz as fiction in the wake of socialism, but in general the entire modernist milieu that cohered around *Partisan Review* in the forties and promoted not only the modernist line in fiction but brought together such critical voices as Edmund Wilson, W.H. Auden, Stephen Spender, Philip Rahv, Meyer Schapiro, George Orwell, Mary McCarthy, and Nicola Chiaromonte, took its departure from the fortuitous intersection of two historical movements: a fall and a rise. They were the decline of socialism and the triumph of big business.

For those intellectuals who had only a few years back been champions of the state's withering away, or at least of a redistribution of its goods and values, one consequence of America's economic boom and political hegemony after the war was a feeling of their own isolation and irrelevance, as the emergence of an unprecedented consumer economy at home and the rise of the Cold War abroad undercut their dreams of egalitarianism, socialism and international cooperation. The great depression came to an end, but the depression of the intellectuals lingered on, all the more poignant for being so wholly out of phase with the new American confidence. Into the emotional gap between the general elation and the intellectuals' sense of alienation flowed a volatile mix of ideas and energies that were expressive of such psychic dissociation. The literary phenomenon we've come to call the Jewish novel had its origins in the crisis of the intellectuals at a time when terms like alienation, victimization, and marginality were becoming popular definitions of Jewish sensibility and the Jew a stand-in for something known as "the universal homelessness of man." Among the post-war books to strike the note of isolation and drift were Saul Bellow's first novels, *Dangling Man* (1944) and *The Victim* (1947), Isaac Rosenfeld's novel, *Passage From Home* (1946), and his short stories, which were collected posthumously under the title *Alpha and Omega* (1966), Lionel Trilling's *The Middle of the Journey* (1947), Delmore Schwartz's stories in *The World is a Wedding* (1948), Arthur Miller's *Death of a Salesman* (1949), Paul Goodman's *The Breakup of Our Camp* (1949), Norman Mailer's *Barbary Shore* (1951) and *The Deer Park* (1955), Bernard Malamud's *The Natural* (1952) and *The Assistant* (1957), and Herbert Gold's *The Man Who Was Not With It* (1954).

Listening in upon this experience from the perspective of our own time, when this outburst of energy-in-anguish has largely exhausted itself, we may detect undertones of exuberance in the elegaic music, and, indeed, the real depression of these books shades off readily into the theatre of despair—as readily as *Dangling Man* shades off into *Herzog*. No one ever celebrated his own predicament more or held a more inspired view of his own tragic condition than did the forties' intellectuals at the very nadir of their defeat. If some, like Rosenfeld and Schwartz, eventually succumbed, unfulfilled, to the exhaustion of their powers, others found the atmosphere of disillusionment paradoxically bracing. In the 1940s, it seems, everyone wanted to be Franz Kafka.

It was in such a climate of aggressive malaise that psychoanalysis moved into the conceptual vacuum left by the retreat of socialism. For those who could make this shift of theoretical gears, the mental transformation from Marxist to Freudian was not so taxing as might be supposed. Marxism, in fact, served this generation as a school for abstract reasoning by preparing the mind for the rigors of grand theory. Psychoanalysis shares with Marxism the vanities of a comprehensive explanatory system, as ready to apply itself to a novel or a whole society as to a neurotic symptom or a dream. Like Marxism, its claims to deep explanation and radical insight promise to expose hidden and more authentic levels of cause and motivation beneath the deceptive appearances of social life, and, like Marxism, it is a code of values and an ostensible cure that offers the reassurance of scientific methods and the promise of practical results. But because it founds its moral calculus on the dynamics of the individual will, rather than the impersonal equations of economic evolution, it is a dialectics of choice, rather than of necessity; it places the instruments of redemption at the disposal of the individual rather than the group or class. For that reason it appealed strongly to the renegade Marxists, many, though not all, of whom were Trotskyists, who clustered about or at least paid attention to *Partisan Review* in the 1930s and 1940s. For them, Marxism had never been the unfolding of ineluctable historical laws, let alone the latest Comintern ukase, but a projection forward of dreams of economic liberation and social brotherhood—an ambience of hope based on nostalgia for an idealized *Gemeinschaft* and tied loosely to ideas about production and work. Marxists in name, they were largely utopian socialists in fact, and the libertarian bias of their brand of socialism responded naturally to views of the mind that put a premium upon individual will.

By the mid-forties, writers like Rosenfeld, Bellow, Trilling, and Goodman had embraced the assumptions of psychoanalysis as groundrules for their own habits of thought, as did Arthur Koestler, who found in psychoanalysis a potent tool for the debunking of socialist illusions. And a decade later, writers like Norman Mailer and Allen Ginsberg would also become converts to psychoanalysis, though in its Reichian modalities. If it can be charged against so many intellectuals that their psychoanalysis, like their modernism and their "sensibility," signalled an end to concern and a retreat from struggle, it can also be said that it expressed the deepening seriousness of their investigation into human predicaments and a less sentimental assessment of the real prospects for moral perfection and social reform. To be sure, in its militant, Reichian mode, psychoanalysis looked less like a retreat from history than a tactical regrouping for a new assault and a strategy to outflank the reactionary situation by internalizing the revolution. For those intellectuals who took him up in the forties, Reich was the Trotsky of the mind. But, in its more stoical, Freudian moods, psychoanalysis advanced the theme of *Civilization and Its Discontents* that the tension between human desires and social constraints is both inevitable and necessary, and that aggression and guilt are built-in features of human nature which are not subject to amelioration by social means. The later work of Freud, with its emphasis on aggression and its Manichaean biology of Eros and the "death instinct," was explicitly anti-utopian as well as anti-liberal, and therefore well-suited to the depressive aftermath of the war, especially for those intellectuals who had been stunned by their own helplessness in the face of the Nazi slaughter of the Jews and enraged by the general complicity of "civilization" in the crime. Freud was the ideal social philosopher for a generation whose initial post-war task was to come to terms with its own rage and guilt.

In addition to the mood of sober realism it appeared to endorse, psychoanalysis put forward a crisis model of the mind that suited well the emotional crisis of the intellectuals. It dispensed with the one-dimensional, utilitarian psychology shared in common by vulgar Marxism and American effort optimism in favor of a dialectical psychology in which doubt, ambivalence, inner struggle, and guilt were put forward as the very agencies of thought rather than signs of moral indulgence. Moreover, it cast doubt upon claims of moral certitude by declaring the inauthenticity, the essential defensiveness, of all organized self-assurances. Especially for the Jews, who were buffeted by so many historical and intellectual cross-currents, psychoanalysis was a way of justifying self-doubt and even raising it to the level of a moral standard. As so much post-war fiction gave testimony, uncertainty was not only a by-product of the modern crisis, but the very best way to meet it, so that John Laskell, the reformed progressive of Lionel Trilling's *The Middle of the Journey*, earns points toward maturity and moral realism by declining to take a stand on anything but his own negative capability. And Joseph, the paralyzed ex-socialist of Bellow's *Dangling Man*, negotiates his way through the thicket of modern ideas by refusing to be deterred by any of them. At an historical juncture when the disintegrated consciousness of modern life appeared to have achieved not only victory but stature among the intellectuals, psychoanalysis appealed to them as both ideology and cure, as justification and therapy.

But I don't wish to sound overly schematic in this view of the intellectual life of the forties. Psychoanalysis did not really make its debut among American writers on VJ Day, nor was its embrace invariably a sign that social concerns had been happily outgrown. The history of applied psychoanalysis in America is both long and, from the social point of view, honorable. We have the criticism of Kenneth Burke in the thirties, in which the dynamics of class and of the unconscious are brilliantly fused into a dazzling dialectical system, as evidence of an early and sophisticated application of psychoanalysis to literature and testimony too that syntheses could be devised that left the social conscience intact. More important and certainly more influential than the maverick voice of Burke, who was, in any case, a literary critic, not a social theorist, was the Left Hegelianism of the *Institut für Sozialforschung* or Frankfurt School, whose quarters in exile from 1933 to 1949 were on West 117th Street, adjacent to Columbia University. The varieties of critical theory that flourished at the *Institut*, especially in the work of Theodor Adorno, Max Horkheimer, and Herbert Marcuse, featured credible attempts to bring psychoanalysis and Marxism into common focus as elements of a broader dialectic of mind and society. And, of course, there was Wilhelm Reich, whose early books argued strongly for seeing social power as a reflection of sexual arrangements, and thus for regarding politics and culture as the natural objects of applied psychiatry, if not applied sexology. As we govern our emotions, or our families, or our genitals, goes the basic Reichian formula, so we run the state. In the forties and fifties, the literary Reichians like Goodman and Mailer showed no slackening of social passion, though their sexual critique of politics tended to call for remedies that were beyond the pale of social action.

* * * *

It was in the post-war climate of stalemate and reassessment that Lionel Trilling came to prominence as a spokesman for ambivalence, moral realism (that is, the acceptance of "good-and-evil"), ideas in modulation, and the tragic view of life. He emerged in the forties as a pivotal figure among the New York intellectuals, and though he quickly became among them a *primus inter pares*, a rough silhouette of his career would be a shadow of what they all had experienced. He was a Jew, and as a Jew had been schooled, briefly enough, in the left politics of the 1930s, whose programmatic views he was quick to forsake for the sense of intellectual "variousness and possibility" represented by Arnold, James, Forster, Mill, Freud, and Hegel. Like most New York intellectuals he styled himself a modernist, although he distrusted modernism and was more at ease with the 19th century, whose complex ideas and thick textures were more congenial to his own styles of moral concern. He shared with the others the view of literature as the expression of history, politics, class, *and* the *Zeitgeist* (though a Hegelian, he had sufficient appreciation of the material life to invoke class as an *idea* of great power), and made a practice of keeping watch over the trends and wrinkles of what his circle agreed to call the culture, which consisted largely of the opinions and social habits of the Eastern, liberal intelligentsia. And, after his fashion, he entered the mid-forties from the same position of alienation held in common by the intellectuals of his generation. He didn't call it that; he was, after all, a professor at

Columbia, not a graduate of the Federal Writers' Project, but the prevailing mood of his essays in the forties, as well as of his novel, *The Middle of the Journey*, was that of deracination and depression.

Though we don't usually think of Trilling as the historian of his own emotions, we can read the progression of moods he documented and the positions he defended as contributions to a Romantic autobiography: a case history of youthful precocity, mid-life emotional crisis, and eventual revival of the sort the nineteenth century held to be the very definition of the moral progress of the modern spirit. Mill's *Autobiography* comes to mind, as do such classic tales of crisis and conversion as Wordsworth's *The Prelude*, Byron's *Childe Harold's Pilgrimage*, Carlyle's *Sartor Resartus*, and Tennyson's *In Memoriam*. *The Middle of the Journey*, in its muted way, is such an account of spiritual death and rebirth, and the cycle of depression and revival in general is etched deeply into the larger movement of Trilling's work, as it was into the work of so many of his contemporaries. But what faith meant to Tennyson, the gospel of work to Carlyle, sentiment to Wordsworth, and Wordsworth himself to Mill, the entire emotional vista opened up by both psychoanalysis and modern literature was to Trilling. Trilling was aware of the precedents; psychoanalysis, as he understood it, was a codification of the great surge of self-discovery and self-healing that marked the literature of the nineteenth century. Mill in particular served him as a model of interior regeneration, and not only his *Autobiography* but the essays on Bentham and Coleridge stood behind the lessons on politics and the emotional life that Trilling himself delivered to his own generation in *The Liberal Imagination*.

In fact, what made Trilling's own version of the crisis of feeling so exemplary and influential a modern episode was his adherence to the example of Mill—the commitment to thinking the crisis through and drawing the connections between his own troubled emotions and the historical dilemma of his generation. Trilling had no difficulty considering himself a representative case, a "modern self" suffering from history. Thus he could turn the education of his own feelings through the exploration of inner conflict and the cultivation of sensibility into an ideological program: to reform the imagination of the prevailing liberal culture, or "To recall liberalism to its first essential imagination of variousness and possibility."

Trilling's case against the liberal imagination as he found it in the 1930s doesn't have to be reviewed here; his estimate of its intellectual shallowness is well known and generally accepted by now, even if the general recoil from ideology that liberalism's shortcomings appeared to justify is no longer celebrated as quite the wisdom it once seemed to be. I do want to talk about the part played by psychoanalysis in Trilling's efforts at intellectual revival and the flavor it added to his cultural politics as well as what it, in turn, derived from them. The dominant themes of Trilling's political and cultural thought in the forties grew in tandem with his interest in psychoanalysis; it is clear that his adoption of Freud was a special feature of those attitudes toward the progressive culture that were the polemical heart of *The Liberal Imagination*, though just how the politics of psychoanalysis shaped Trilling's use of it or affected those ideas that emerged under its sign is less clear.

The obvious starting point is to observe that psychoanalysis was to be administered to the intellectual culture at large, along with remedial doses of literature, as an elixir for weary emotions and an antidote to a progressivism that, in its instrumental view of reality and crude behaviorist orientation, "drifts toward a denial of the emotions and the imagination." Freudian man was a step upwards from liberal man in complication and mysteriousness, and was, in effect, his contradiction: he had an unconscious mind whose purposes were not always in accord with either his conscious will or his class interest; he was given to entertaining contrary ideas and emotions at the same time and to tormenting himself with his own ambiguities; he was prone to irrational fits of melancholy or guilt and to performing unexplained rites of apology and expiation for crimes he had not committed, and he had a fondness for self-defeat that made his failures seem more genuine expressions of will than his successes. How unlike the utilitarian man of liberalism, who maximizes pleasure at every meager opportunity, and how much closer to the neurotic hero of contemporary fiction, who confirms the modern character that Hegel called the "disintegrated consciousness!" For Trilling, the literary prototype of this version of psychological man was Rameau's nephew, Diderot's creature of lusts and deceits in whom he saw an epitome of the modern crisis and a preview of the psychoanalytic view of human nature: willful, insatiable, and contradictory. One thing psychoanalysis and contemporary fiction agree on is the alienation of modern consciousness from the wellsprings of will and desire, and for Trilling, the sufficient measure of liberalism's imaginative bankruptcy was its refusal to countenance the irrational component in human nature and, correspondingly, to gain expression in a major literature. It failed the tests of both psychoanalysis and fiction.

But that did not amount to a charge of political bankruptcy, for though Trilling despaired of liberalism's capacity to ameliorate the material conditions of life, nowhere did he venture an estimate of its political ideas or programs comparable in scope or trenchancy to his assessment of its imagination. Coming from a writer whose reputation owed so much to the climate of contemporary politics and who was so widely accepted as a political intellectual, Trilling's books yield surprisingly little concrete political thought. Trilling departed from the example of his English mentors: Coleridge, Arnold, and Mill, in profferring no social ideas of his own, only social sentiments and tastes which did not add up to an alternative liberalism or, for that matter, an alternative conservatism. His revitalized versions of the liberal imagination could never be put to any political tests but only aesthetic ones, for only in relation to literature and literary styles of representation could their validation be assured. By finessing all talk of policies, power, and institutions, except at levels of the highest abstraction, Trilling could chastise liberalism for its shallowness without having to confront on his own the world in which that shallowness had taken root. For what Trilling usually meant by politics was ideology, those large ideas of broad currency that frame reality, justify politics, and both constitute the rules of intellectual culture and regulate the very lives and emotions of the intellectuals. Only his view of ideology was not what a sociologist might see, a system of ideas serving to legitimate power or wealth or vested interest, but what a critic of literature might see, a *Weltanschauung* or aesthetics of vision, a principle of taste. In effect, Trilling left the dissection of liberal politics to others. The context of his ideas in the forties, after all, was the dismemberment of the left from all quarters, when everyone, the old Trotskyists in particular, wanted a piece of the corpse.

This deflection of attention from the world to the intellectuals and their perception of it was Trilling's way of detaching himself from the liberal mainstream to become its critic. And while such a politics of ideas could be vulgarized into a politics of opinions, which is what it commonly amounts to in the literary journalism of what used to be called the "little magazines," at its most acute it was a politics of vision and an epistemology. Trilling's finest essays were snapshots of the contemporary intellectuals in the act of observing and defining reality. His essays in *The Liberal Imagination* on Dreiser ("Reality in America") and the Kinsey Report are superb definitions of American and liberal styles of social knowledge, and if one learns little from them about the actualities of reality in America, one learns a great deal about the ideology of social perception in a society founded upon rationalized optimism. One also learns from Trilling something about the emotional impact of ideas and programs, what they feel like and what qualities of life they purvey. What he would recall most vividly of the thirties were its ideological failures and their devastating consequences for those who had committed their lives to its prevailing myths. In his introduction to

Tess Slesinger's *The Unpossessed* he recalled bitterly "the dryness and deadness that lay at the heart of [the intellectuals'] drama and that they had brought to the fore a peculiarly American dessication of temperament." Yet such sensitivity to ideology and its effects, based as it was upon a belief in the primacy of thought, was bought at a price; here, as elsewhere, Trilling suppressed those dimensions of social reality that progressive realism played up: the depression, the unemployment, the vicious labor battles, the advances of Fascism in Europe—in short, the general desperation. It was as though the world of dustbowls and breadlines were only a fantasy of liberal self-delusion, a pure artifact of proletarian art that could be seen through by a simple adjustment of vision. What comes into view when the camera dissolves from Harlan County to rural Connecticut is a movie of the 1930s featuring the self-deceived and self-destroying intellectuals themselves, and consequently dominated by its ideas of itself rather than the circumstances that had brought those ideas into prominence.

Both the strengths and limitations of Trilling's approach to the politics of culture are evident in *The Middle of the Journey*, his sole effort at yoking political thought to literary views in order to illuminate politics, rather than to venerate literature. That book was an attempt to bring to the politics of contemporary culture a sort of synthetic Victorian sensibility, an impasto of attitudes that Trilling had concocted for himself out of Mill, Arnold, Forster, Freud, and Keats, and to disclose the deadness at the core of liberalism by demonstrating how paradoxically stultifying was the embrace of its unremitting optimism upon the human heart. It was, as that may sound, a vote for the British nineteenth century over the American twentieth; Trilling's Anglophilia was always a moral preference first and foremost.

In later years Trilling himself observed that his intention had been to write a book about death, and about the refusal of intellectuals schooled in the liberal tradition to countenance it, because it lay outside the domain of their progressive fantasies. Or, as he would ask rhetorically in pointing up the way all things are politicized when dogma commands the imagination, "Was there not a sense in which death might be called reactionary?" John Laskell, Trilling's somewhat retiring spokesman in *The Middle of the Journey*, has recently lost the woman he loved to a sudden illness and has himself just recovered from a dangerous attack of scarlet fever. In his convalescence he visits the rustic Connecticut home of Arthur and Nancy Croom, vigorous, cheerful, and enlightened progressives who can scarcely pronounce the word death let alone draw tragic lessons from the presence of this walking *memento mori* in their midst. Arthur Croom is protected from depression by what Laskell calls "the armor of idealism." Laskell, however, needing to talk about his brush with death and to explore the meaning of that experience, finds that he is isolated from his friends and their sprightly intelligence, for he has looked into the abyss and seen there the end of ideology. He is joined at the Crooms' by another apostate from the Left, Gifford Maxim, a repentant Communist, indeed, secret agent turned staunch necessitarian or law-and-order man, whose political views have shifted radically to the right without surrendering an ounce of their millenarian zeal. Laskell thinks of him as "the man of the far future, the bloody, moral apocalyptic future that was sure to come." As we now know, Maxim is modelled upon Whittaker Chambers, whose transformation from espionage agent to prosecution witness won him a starring role in the soap opera of America's post-War revulsion against Communism. Though the plot of *The Middle of the Journey* is full of turns, including another sudden death, which supposedly puts to the test everyone's ideas about class, character, and "reality," the book is essentially a conversation piece; the moral element that Trilling was so intent upon pushing is contained in the by-play among these four, the Socratic dialectics of competing ideas whose overall purpose is to cast all ideas into doubt.

The Middle of the Journey just coruscates with intelligence and dialectical sparkle, and it remains the most illuminating document we have of the recoil of the political imagination from dogma under the pressure of the chastened realism of the late thirties and early forties—that fall into the quotidian that was the new era's particular form of disillusionment. Maxim, Laskell, and the Crooms are sharply drawn representative figures who stand for political positions and processes that engaged, and ruined, so many intellectuals in the thirties. But the book is first of all about *the imagination* under the sway of social ideas, or, as Trilling would entitle a monograph later in his career, about "mind in the modern world." It is a book about the mind and about those parts of it that take their cue from and find expression in political ideas. It is especially about that region of mind that is given neither to pure will nor pure idea, where the historical sense intersects the return of the repressed, and richly "overdetermined" motives take shape as political views. The politics of *The Middle of the Journey* is largely a politics of the mind and of character; the book's historical dimension is drastically foreshortened, and the context of actual events and circumstances so generalized as to be unimportant. The reader can scarcely fix the moment; only fleeting references to Spain and the Moscow Trials locate the novel in the late 1930s. Ideology, then, is not a theory of history but a matter of character, posture, and attitude. *The*

Middle of the Journey is very much a book about the morality of personal bearing and what Trilling liked to call "the self."

I don't want to oversell the book or claim for it more literary merit or thematic depth than I think it really has. To my mind it is more a document than a realized piece of fiction; its value lies in its grasp of an historical moment and of a generation's disillusionment and conversion, out of which came not only a revised and subdued politics but a reconstituted aesthetics as well. The crisis of the late thirties meant as much to art as it did to a politics, and *The Middle of the Journey* reflects not only the triumph of the will in repose over the will in action, of ideas in modulation over the logic of the next step, but of sensibility over agit-prop and modernism over realism.

I want to emphasize this last point. Though most readers of the book take John Laskell to be a stand-in for Trilling, as no doubt he largely is, they have also taken him and his spokesmanship for critical humanism for a moral standard by which Maxim and the Crooms may be judged, failing to observe, at the same time, what an odd and *modern* sort of character he really is. To be sure, we might say that Laskell has *no* character to speak of, only ideas, and it is true that he lacks either depth or definition, but there is a minimal character here, and certainly a strange one. The "disintegrated consciousness" that Trilling would later attribute to the modern character is apparent in Laskell, though in relatively benign form. Consider Laskell's situation: he is a dangling man, having neither parents nor anything that can be deemed a past; at thirty-three he has never been married and is not currently attached to a woman; he has no children and no apparent future, and is in recoil anyway from the very assumptions of futurity. His chief possessions are ideas, though he holds them with no great passion or conviction. As an intellectual, he is supposed to be a hero of maturity and moderation, but as a man, he is a bleak and unappealing figure whose chastity encompasses more than a resistance to dangerous ideologies. Though the political moment in *The Middle of the Journey* is the late thirties, the book is in other respects a typical product of the mid-forties. It is very much to the point that Laskell has been ill and is presently recuperating, for though we are told that he has been grappling with scarlet fever, *we know* that he has really been stricken with history and is recovering from the past. We know that the hot and molten Maxim and the cool Laskell, apparent antagonists, are really secret sharers, comparable American lives in search of second acts. Each is trying to recover in his own way from the same disease—*scarlet fever*, or an overdose of *red*—but where Maxim, afflicted by the more virulent strain, is riding the pendulum of atonement, Laskell just wants to take it easy. Maxim's politics are the politics of penance whose motive force is guilt, while Laskell's are the politics of convalescence: abstinence and moderation. The first law of recuperation is not to push yourself.

For all its apparent interiority and concern with the self, *The Middle of the Journey* can't be taken for a psychological novel. Except for Laskell's, and Trilling's, appreciation for ambivalence as a positive attitude, that is, as a precondition of moral realism, and the mystique of easeful death, for which Keats is as much responsible as Freud, there is scarcely a Freudian idea in the book, nor is there a fictional technique whose provenance might be traced to the climate of modern introspection. The *Middle of the Journey* is very much about the dilemmas of consciousness; the forces in contest are ideas, not instincts, and the inner dynamics of character are simple and shallow. It is also a conventional novel, indeed, almost deliberately unfashionable in its methods; its technical resources derive mainly from the line of philosophical humanism that runs from Austen and George Eliot to Forster and James. Against the claims of the more ideological brands of naturalism and realism that held sway in the thirties, it poses not the radical subjectivity of Joyce or Proust but the sensibility of the nineteenth century novel of thought.

The Middle of the Journey's link to psychoanalysis, then, lies neither in its ideas nor in its aesthetic strategies but in the deeper rhythm of experience that plots its moral curve; the rhythm of illness and recovery, or crisis and conversion that sets us to talking about ideological movements and revolutions in the language of disease and health. Laskell, Maxim, and the Crooms all suffer from ideas—they are literally sick with modern thought.

In the grim early forties, history could scarcely seem anything other than a disease, nor recovery anything less than the most pressing business at hand. The "Wasteland outlook," now so much bemoaned by Saul Bellow, seemed only common sense to an age that had seen the future collapse into barbarism. Trilling was not alone in pondering the ubiquity of neurosis and the cultural import of the Freudian dictum, "We are all ill." "Now," Trilling observed in his gloomy essay, "Art and Fortune," "the old margin [for doubt] no longer exists; the facade is down; society's resistance to the discovery of depravity has ceased; now everyone knows that Thackeray was wrong, Swift right." Note that it is not, say, Spengler or Hobbes who are called upon here in witness to the disintegration of culture but novelists, Thackeray and Swift. For the novel was, for Trilling, the definitive cultural document, the very measure of the *Zeitgeist,* and he was open to the thought that the contemporary decline of novelistic passion and the breakup of the synthesis of philosophy and precise social observation in modern fiction might well betoken nothing less than the much-advertised decline of the West.

> The novel is a kind of summary and paradigm of our cultural life, which is perhaps why we speak sooner of its death than of the death of any other form of thought. It has been of all literary forms the most devoted to the celebration and investigation of the human will; and the will of our society is dying of its own excess. The religious will, the political will, the sexual will, the artistic will—each is dying of its own excess.

Where Trilling stood apart from the general mood was not in his bleak diagnosis—even announcing *the* death of *the* sexual will was not so unique—but in the prescription for relief. He distinguished himself from both the Reichians (for whom *the* sexual will was also distressed) and the liberals and unreconstructed Marxists in his vote for psychoanalysis and the novel as correctives to the general malaise. Of course, it was not exactly relief that Trilling was after, not in the sense of either catharsis or adjustment to conditions, but a deeper level of rapprochement with the dilemma. Freudian that he was, he did not court a remission of symptoms so much as a reconstruction of his own character in ways that would allow him to face up to and survive the tragic situation on its terms. He was out to form, as he would put it, a "modern self," a resilient ego that would be equal to the demands of the age, and he attempted the transformation by immersing himself in literature and assimilating the exemplary monuments of unaging intellect. Though the formation of a reinvigorated but durable self was a personal quest, Trilling always treated it as the project of his generation through the neat rhetorical gambit of turning the experiencing "I" into a "we," thus both disguising the personal stakes involved and playing up the shared aspects of the crisis. The essays in *The Liberal Imagination* can be read both as chapters in a moral autobiography and showcases for the acculturated ego in the process of its self-reconstruction.

It seems an odd choice to seek emotional renewal for oneself, let alone for one's culture, through the agency of, of all things, *the* novel. Given the depths of the crisis, one would have thought such remedy beyond the powers of mere literature. But it was not so odd to Trilling, who had so high an estimation of the novel's capacity for social intelligence, and credited it, above all other expressions of human imagination, with representing the mind in its subtlest and most complex operations. For Trilling, after all, the modern crisis was not primarily a crisis of conditions, however awful they might be, but of emotions and imagination; it was to the impoverished inner life that the lessons in *The Liberal Imagination* were addressed. And it was in the novel, especially the great nineteenth century novels that are the richest examples of that genre, that Trilling saw the modern social imagination working at its highest pitch. Flaubert, Stendhal, Austen, James, Forster, and Tolstoy were for him not only exemplary artists but instances of civilized intelligence in full bloom; they were the flowering of a particular phase of Western social self-consciousness that had begun with the Enlightenment and reached its apogee in the middle of the nineteenth century.

But we should keep in mind that Trilling was almost always talking about himself, and that the essay in which his most exalted claims for the novel are made, "Art and Forture," is also a spiritual autobiography in miniature, done according to the Romantic paradigm. Ostensibly a meditation on the death of the novel, it is really about the death and rebirth of "the will," and there can hardly be any doubt about whose will is at issue. Moreover, in claiming for the novel the power to renovate the will, Trilling seems to have had in mind not only his own intimate relation to books but the example of Mill, whose youthful bout with depression was cured by the reading of Marmontel's *Mémoires* and whose convalescence and emotional re-education were abetted by therapeutic doses of Wordsworth. To reflect back upon *The Middle of the Journey* after reading *The Liberal Imagination* is to perceive the central weakness of Trilling's novel, which is his allowing John Laskell to speak for his convictions without giving Laskell the benefit of his vital experiences, that is to say, his reading. Laskell's recovery from liberal ideas, unmediated by anything but his post-operative meditation upon a bedside rose, rather than something more substantial, like *The Red and the Black*, is never credible. By contrast, Gifford Maxim's metamorphosis, motivated by a fierce and well-earned attack of remorse, is so much more real than Laskell's conversion to modulation and sensibility, which seems both unmotivated and intellectually flimsy. Laskell displays the sort of character that might be formed under the influence of the great moral themes of literature, for he is every inch the English teacher, but his convictions, lacking intellectual support, hardly rise above the level of genteel mannerisms.

Indeed, the problem of abstraction is general throughout the book, and is not just a flaw in the characterization of Laskell. By removing the action from some natural arena of conflict to a house in rural Connecticut—that is, to a world apart—Trilling was able to write a sort of moral pastoral whose characters are largely representative abstractions. Laskell in Connecticut is like Rasselas in Abyssinia, learning that you don't have to number the streaks of the tulip so long as you get the general drift. Gone are the factory and the meeting hall (and for the better, to be sure) but gone too are those settings, like the town or the family, in which issues can be worked out according to their own weight and complexity. Connecticut is not a metaphor for the world but for the seminar room, and the odd collection of friends and haphazard acquaintances who gather at the Crooms' has nothing to work out but ideas, for nothing dramatic is at stake. To throw the emphasis of dramatic action upon the collision of ideas in isolation, as Trilling does, is both to play up their historical importance *and* to exaggerate their political value.

* * * *

Seeing nothing less than the imaginative life of Western culture hanging in the balance, Trilling leapt readily to the defense of art when he saw it threatened, whether by the ideological demands of the political left or by the pedagogical reductions of the New Criticism or by psychoanalysis, in its claims that the pleasures of art were "substitute gratifications," and that poetry was a form of daydreaming, and art deeply connected to neurosis. Thus he was passionate in defending the essential health of art against Edmund Wilson's charge, in *The Wound and the Bow,* that it issues from neurosis and that, as in the legend of Philoctetes, the bow of artistic power is bound up with the "wound" of neurosis. For if literature were permitted to remain under the cloud of neurosis, as a mere symptom sublimated upward, then the whole moral point of appealing to the novel as a remedy for the social will "dying of its own excess" is lost, and so is the whole instructional premise of *The Liberal Imagination*—that politics has much to learn from literature. The cornerstone of Trilling's moral system was the *essential* balance and health of art, and Trilling took those writers whom he celebrated in his essays as object lessons in psychic composure. He endorsed Lamb's dictum that true genius is sane, that "the true poet dreams being awake. He is not possessed by his subject but has dominion over it." Laboring under the shadow of universal illness, that Freudian substitute for original sin, the artist is exemplary in his ability to exercise dominion over his conflicts and put them to use. "He is what he is by virtue of his successful objectification of his neurosis, by his shaping it and making it available to others in a way which has its effect upon their egos in struggle." Regardless of the conflicts and neuroses that may underlie his writing, what is healthy in the artist is his capacity for work, "that which gives him the power to conceive, to play, to work, and to bring his work to a conclusion."

But if literature was the cornerstone of a moral system, the morality of the mind was in turn the sought-after feature of literature. What Trilling always called attention to was the pedagogical example, and his most influential books, like *The Liberal Imagination* and *The Opposing Self*, are books of exemplary lives, exemplary minds, really, intellectual and therefore moral models whose ways of balancing pressures and reconciling tensions shine forth as salutary cases. James, Keats, Austen, Forster, Arnold, Mill, Orwell, and, especially, Freud, to rename the central figures in the pantheon, are heroes of thought, whose heroism consists of a judicious balancing of claims, a skeptical adherence to the cultural donnée, and a qualified acceptance of the conditioned nature of social existence. They are, in a phrase, mature adversaries of culture. Such virtues of mind sound oxymoronic, as they are supposed to, though Trilling thought of them as dialectical. He was a believer in chastened and wary rebellions that combined radical criticism of the existing order with tragic acceptance, and he admired, indeed, exalted the career of Sigmund Freud as the very paradigm of such a rebellion. Psychoanalysis, to the extent that it entered the moral system, did so as a principle of approbation rather than a tool of radical analysis—as an endorsement of certain civilized and modulated styles of managing pressure or doubt or despair. It was pressed into service as an ethical posture and a statement, in the idiom of a science, of the moral life of Sigmund Freud.

Which, in some measure, it is. As Phillip Rieff has shown in great detail, psychoanalysis is a moral psychology whose values are closely bound up with the character of Freud himself, with his skepticism, his intellectual restlessness, his militant rationalism, and his subjection of his own motives and dreams, as well as those of his patients, to rigorous scrutiny. Its very object is the moral character of the patient, the complex reticulation of habits and beliefs that constitutes his identity, and it was the most radical and enduring of Freud's discoveries that his neurotic patients were suffering from ideas rather than from neurological disorders, and that treatment had to start with an interpretation of the ideas themselves. Thus the interpretive tactics of psychoanalysis take their departure from values, and the very principle of treatment is to challenge the patient's moral system in an effort to peel away the film of bad faith and illusion that constitutes his illness. The aspects of mind that are now the hallmarks of the psychoanalytic view: repression, the dynamic unconscious, the belief that all manifestations of consciousness mask a latent and more significant level of meaning in which stunning, infantile motives are revealed, are moral concepts that portray ordinary consciousness as a form of deception, and show psychoanalysis to be a science of unmasking.

Trilling's admiration for the temper of mind expressed in such a science is a matter of record. As Steven Marcus has put it, "The figure of Freud was for him something very close to a moral ideal, or to an ideal of personal character and conduct. Freud's fierceness, boldness, honesty and independence, his sense of tragedy and stoical resistance all served or figured as models for him, models that he reaffirmed in his own person and tried to fulfill in his own existence." And yet, in view of Trilling's ardent declarations of admiration and intellectual indebtedness, perhaps nothing is so remarkable about him as the discrepancy between his zeal for Freud and his use of him. While many of Trilling's essays on literature and culture over the years may be read as applied Freud, they are largely applications of his character and his outlook rather than his ideas about the constitution of the mind. Indeed, the reader who has been struck by the discrepancy might feel justified in wondering whether such lionizing of Freud was not done at the expense of psychoanalysis as such, for it is plain that the figure of the man in Trilling's thought greatly overshadowed the method. I'm not thinking only of the shifts in emphasis from Trilling's early and detailed critiques of psychoanalysis in *The Liberal Imagination* ("Freud and Literature," "Art and Neurosis") to the later speculations on Freud's cultural thought, notably the essay, "Freud: Within and Beyond Culture" in *Beyond Culture*, but also of the general tenor of his criticism in which psychoanalytic gestures are often begun but never carried to completion. For Trilling's relation to psychoanalysis was characterized by his shyness about its explanatory conventions and his penchant for leavening his insights with large doses of rhetorical tact.

In part, this reflected Trilling's allegiance to intellectual modulation, the conviction that too strenuous a pursuit of radical ideas violated the delicate textures of complex thought and betrayed the ambiguities of social or literary situations. Trilling's exposure in the twenties and thirties to Marxist criticism, in which what passed for methodological precision was often just moral bullying and aesthetic obtuseness, turned him against systematic analysis and attempts to regiment the free play of thought. Though he, like other disenchanted left intellectuals in the 1940s, turned to Freud and cultivated innerness out of a disaffection from progressive ideology, his very style of embracing psychoanalysis reflected the scruples and habits of skepticism that constituted his new, circumspect style of liberalism. Nowhere in his long bibliography of literary studies do we find an instance of relentless psychoanalytic pursuit of latent meanings or a reaching after those distressing conclusions about infantile needs and irrational drives that are the special province of psychoanalysis as an interpretive system. He followed Freud himself in proclaiming the helplessness of the psychoanalyst before the mysteries of the creative gift and creative technique, and joined his mentor in disparaging the application of coarse clinical language to art. Nor did he believe that psychoanalysis could explain the artist's "unconscious intention as it exists apart from the work itself."

This reticence about, or, if you like, despair of, the analytic abilities of psychoanalysis in the face of literature may be one reason why Trilling gave short shrift to the early analytical books in Freud's oeuvre and concentrated his attention instead on the work of the later, speculative years when, starting with *Beyond the Pleasure Principle* in 1920, Freud turned his attention to cultural, social, and metaphysical questions and produced such adventures in analysis-at-a-distance as *Group Psychology and the Analysis of the Ego*, *The Future of an Illusion*, and *Civilization and Its Discontents*. This last was the indispensable book for Trilling, who considered it a milepost in the cultural history of the West for its conclusion that discontent was built into the condition of man in culture and therefore inevitable, and much of what passes for Freudian thought in Trilling's writing is really applied *Civilization and its Discontents*.

It is curious to contemplate this exaggerated emphasis on psychoanalysis at its most speculative and at its greatest remove from the clinic by such a rationalist whose initial defense of psychoanalysis, in the essay, "Freud and Literature," was to call attention to its elements of empiricism and reason. Yet a reading of Trilling's interpretations and uses of Freud turns up next to nothing of those great early books in which psychoanalysis tendered its strongest credentials to be taken as an empirical science. We hear almost nothing of *The Interpretation of Dreams, The Psychopathology of Everyday Life, Jokes and Their Relation to the Unconscious, Three Essays on the Theory of Sexuality,* and the major case histories in which Freud's clinical practices and interpretive strategies were most fully set forth. To be fair, I should add that many of Freud's early ideas are digested and assimilated in those essays that appear in *The Liberal Imagination,* but even with that in mind I find it difficult not to feel that much of psychoanalysis has been intentionally dismissed, if not evaded.

We may even come to view Trilling's psychoanalysis as largely a habit of dialectical thought that has been purged of its specific contents and elevated into a sort of Hegelianism in the head, a phenomenology of mind. Consider what is not to be found in it. Guilt is conspicuously absent, though Trilling never tired of adverting to the special insight into human depravity and the heart of darkness that psychoanalysis shares with modern fiction. The dynamic unconscious is missing entirely and with it the characteristic rhythm of repression and the return of the repressed that for Freud was the very mechanism of dreams, myths, and neuroses. Dreams themselves were apparently ruled out, as was the fantasy life of the artist, and with them went not only the distinction between manifest and latent levels of significance but the whole inventory of aesthetic transformations that Freud called dreamwork. We find only rare, and somewhat embarrassed, mention of infantile sexuality and its bodily stages and derivative passions and practices, though sex of any sort had little place in Trilling's conception of the moral imagination. As for what he might have gathered from the psychology of jokes or that of the errors and self-betrayals of daily life, Trilling makes no mention.

With so many vital ingredients of psychoanalysis discarded, we may reasonably ask whether Trilling was kidding himself about his Freudianism, and whether Marcus, who has stood up for these claims, has been pulling our leg. That is not necessarily the case; psychoanalysis is a rich and diverse body of clinical observations, modest inferences, and grand theories, and even with so much cast out there remains a residue of concepts possessing broad utility. What Trilling kept was largely the structural or dialectical model of the mind and the intrapsychic dynamism of ego, id, and superego that brings conflict, indecision, and self-torment to the forefront of our view of the emotions. He also adopted the cultural dialectic, the struggle of the ego to claim a niche for itself between instinct and culture, that is so central to *Civilization and its Discontents.* Trilling admired those cultural attitudes and personal gestures that bespoke Freud's concern for strengthening the distressed ego: his commitment to secular rationalism and his stands against the delusions of mythic and religious thinking, his wary and grudging approval of culture, his refusal to allow disappointment, resistance, and pain to weaken his convictions or interfere with his work, and his very definition of mental health as the capacity for love and work. But, above all else, Trilling embraced Freud's gloom, "the quality of grim poetry," as he called it, "[that] is characteristic of Freud's system and the ideas it generates for him." But such an endorsement identifies Trilling's Freud as the Freud of outlook, as opposed to the Freud of insight, and suggests that his admiration has been won at the cost of severing his "philosophy" from his depth psychology.

This weakness for the grim poetry of the Freudian outlook shows up in Trilling's thought as something quite distinct from psychoanalysis, and Trilling sometimes followed it to conclusions that look less like reasoned assessments of arguments and situations than assumptions of a grave and tragic posture. Certain of Freud's ideas, including the biological ubiquity of the death instinct, were valued for their reflection of his exemplary character and therefore as moral touchstones for modern man's self-evaluation, rather than for their philosophical cogency or correspondence to known evidence about the mind. Most readers of Trilling's work are familiar with his observation, in "The Fate of Pleasure" (in *Beyond Culture*), that Dostoevsky's underground man is no ordinary neurotic but modern man epitomized, who, disdaining the conditioned and predictable life of the middle-class, "has arranged his own misery—arranged it in the interests of his dignity, which is to say, of his freedom." Less well known, though, is the same formula brought to the defense of Freud's conception of the death instinct, which Freud proposed in *Beyond the Pleasure Principle* and which continued to occupy a place, though an uneasy one, in his writing thereafter. In a review of the third volume of Ernest Jones's biography of Freud, Trilling offered the surprising observation that the death instinct "may be understood as the intellectual expression of Freud's pride, of his passion for autonomy."

> The theory certainly would seem to be in the interests of human autonomy—if we accept it, we must see that it is no more absurd to say that a man wills to die than to say that he wills to eat or to copulate.

We may balk at this logic, since any idea we accept ceases instantly to be absurd, but what I want to emphasize here is not the logic but the detachment of a portion of Freud's psychology from the findings that support it and the consequences of its application, that is, from the science or craft of psychoanalysis, and its attachment to the character of the scientist. The validity and theoretical sufficiency of the death instinct is dispensed with in favor of its philosophical elegance and moral reference, what Freud called elsewhere "its grandeur, its ultimate tragic courage in acquiescence to fate." In other words, if the death instinct can't be entirely believed it may nonetheless, like the mind that conceived it, be admired.

Psychoanalysis itself, however, was not uniformly compelling for Trilling, and if he neglected to apply it with all the rigor and zeal that has been demonstrated by more recent practitioners, it is not because he misunderstood its interpretive strategies but because he lacked enthusiasm for the diagnostic reduction of complex feelings and perceptions. As a partisan of literature he was distressed by the psychoanalytic practice of analyzing downward in pursuit of reality among the infantile, the somatic, the irrational, and the unconscious levels of being. If the basic theorem of psychoanalysis is that the mind of every adult harbors a baby literally crying to be heard, Trilling's own preferences led him in just the opposite direction, to look in every great writer for the adult battling his or her way toward an adjustment of the pleasure and reality principles and toward his own psychological, and therefore moral, equilibrium. His inclination was to analyze upward toward the artist's moral posture, even toward the morality of art itself.

Thus, the fantasy life of the artist, to which psychoanalysis of more ordinary sorts pays attention, had no special purchase on Trilling's thought, which put a premium on the artist's compact with his energies and his commitment to reality. Trilling's praise for writers as different as Keats, Austen, Orwell, Flaubert, and Howells singled out the same quality of realization and acceptance; all acknowledged the conditioned nature of existence and yet embraced those conditions with a brand of attention and intellectual energy that had in it the quality of love.

There is admirable sanity in this, certainly if current forms of psychoanalytic criticism are the measure of the potential of psychoanalysis when brought to bear upon literature. Most of this criticism displays little evidence of love for literature and little sense of either the richness and depth of overdetermined meaning that psychoanalysis promises, or the dynamism of consciousness and culture that only a full view of the mind can provide. It does give us reason to feel that its collapsing of the rich possibilities of human desire and the nuances of literary expression into the lexicon of deep psychic wishes impoverishes the language of criticism. In this, psychoanalytic criticism is not so different from the brands of programmatic liberalism Trilling was familiar with in the 1930s and 1940s, or, of more recent vintage, the imported formalisms that have settled into such centers of academic power and influence as Yale and Johns Hopkins. Scarcely anyone who values literature can hope for these practices to spread. It is not difficult in such an academic environment as our own, with its bleak oversubscription to theories and methods and its mistaking of specialty for depth, to endorse Trilling's modulation of ideas, his transformation of psychoanalysis into a general dialectics that dispenses with its infantile programs, and his tendency to view life and art at the level of morality and "sensibility" rather than instinct.

But to commend Trilling's good sense by comparing him to the current ethos does not dispose of the question of whether his way of befriending art by denying the imagination's more turbulent recesses or by ignoring the patent fact that modern poets are often men, and women, in deep mental difficulty was not a weakening of the claims of art. Applying rhetorical etiquette is not the same thing as defending complex and subtle ideas against reductionism, and what passes in Trilling for balance or negative capability or a full and judicious view of situations is sometimes just a pulling of punches. Even a passing familiarity with psychoanalysis and its explanatory capabilities makes it relatively plain that Trilling was often guilty of turning away from his insights and finessing conclusions about the inner dimensions of fiction that the logic of inquiry entitled him to draw.

Only once did Trilling take the wraps off his psychoanalytic curiosity and allow himself the freedom of his insights. That was in the essay, "The Poet as Hero: Keats in his Letters" (in *The Opposing Self*), in which he brought to bear the authority of Freudian ideas to argue for Keats's geniality, his passion, and his courage. Not incidentally, the Keats essay is, in my judgment, Trilling's most splendid essay on a single author and his work. Certainly it is central to any appraisal of how Trilling felt about and handled psychoanalysis, not just because it contains the one straightforward demonstration of analytic reasoning in all his writing, but also because it advanced psychoanalytic interpretation in the spirit of Freudian moralism, placing its findings at the disposal of conceptions of maturity and responsibility that Freud recommended and Trilling labored to promote. As a critic armed with psychoanalysis was bound to see, Keats is the most voluptuous of the English poets, a man for whom "the sensory, the sensuous, and the sensual were all one" and the openness and vigor of appetite and taste tied overtly to an actively erotic imagination. "He is possibly unique among poets in the extensiveness of his reference to eating and drinking and to its pleasurable and distasteful sensations." But, having said that, Trilling felt obliged to enter the caveat that the characterization of Keats as an "oral" character, since that is what the diagnostic side of psychoanalysis recommends, would imply an unseemly passivity, an emphasis on appetites that ought to have been subordinated to more "manly" concerns, and a lingering emotional dependence upon a mother whose importance is everywhere implied, but, curiously, nowhere mentioned in any of her son's letters. (Indeed, Trilling admits to knowing almost nothing about her save a remark on her maternal solicitude by George Keats and an innuendo of questionable reliability upon her own generosity of appetite by Keats's guardian, Mr. Abbey.)

Yet, as everything in Keats's letters testifies, this writer who could celebrate the cool gush of a nectarine sliding down his throat and call out in his great "Ode to a Nightingale" for "a beaker of the warm South,/ . . . With beaded bubbles winking at the brim" was no aging infant or emotional invalid whose genius was founded upon psychic disproportion but an independent, sensible, spirited, intelligent, mature, self-accepting man, the sort of person both Freud and Trilling would agree to call an adult. Trilling's dilemma, then, was two-fold: to reconcile the indulgence of the poetry with the spirited intelligence of the letters, and to account for the ample eroticism and intimations of happy gluttony in the poetry of someone whose mother has seemingly been banished from his memory, though he can still speak habitually in such metaphors as, "The heart is the teat from which the mind or intelligence sucks identity."

There may have been some cause for confusion here for the moralist in Trilling but not for the dialectician; discrepancy was his very métier. Of the mother, to be sure, little could be said that did not lead to contradiction; her apparent absence from her son's thought, even in intimate letters to his brothers and sister, brought forth the estimation that "there was much, it would seem, to be forgotten." And yet, if the son's vigor and self-acceptance are to be understood and brother George's praise of her taken into account, "There would seem to be no reason to question, there is indeed, reason to suppose, her affectionate and indulgent nature—what we may call a biological generosity." Clearly, such a line of investigation—the reconstruction of the real Mrs. Keats—is a dead end. But not so the conjunction of sensory indulgence and mature good sense, of demanding childishness and heroic young manhood. This blending of opposites is built into the very developmental logic of the passions, and, in fact, by the age of five we already have evidence of the militant young Keats. "We read of the violent child of five who armed himself with a sword and brandished it on guard at the door and refused to let his mother leave the house; the story in this form is given by Haydon, who is not reliable, though usually apt, in the stories he tells; another version of the story is that Keats used the sword to keep anyone from entering his mother's room when she was ill." Such Oedipal sergeant-at-armsmanship is only the necessary prelude to the next stage of the emotions, indeed, to any sort of mature fortitude, or energy, or negative capability. "It is possible to say of Keats that the indulgence of his childhood goes far toward explaining the remarkable firmness of character, what I have spoken of as his heroic quality." The contradictions in Keats, then, come into view as mere phases of a natural growth in which the things of childhood were not put aside but assimilated and built upon, the whole man becoming the sum of all his biological potentials.

The figure thus drawn is the most familiar of all Trillingesque heroes, the opposing self or artist in contradiction, though in Keats's particular case the contradictions are happily resolved in the interests of energy, self-acceptance, and self-love. Still, despite the successfully resolved dialectic, the exercise is fraught with discomfort, and the ingenious developmental argument reads as though it was brought into play not just to save the critic from contradiction but to deliver the artist from the subversive charge of psychoanalysis itself. Trilling's strenuous defense of Keats's maturity and good sense is, of course, primarily an attempt to rescue him from the Romantic and popular view that he was a languid spokesman for sleep and poetry and a frail victim of the world's cruelties, who died, not of tuberculosis, but of reviews. But psychoanalysis endorses the Romantic impulse by looking upon the creative imagination as analogous to daydreaming and a continuation of child's play, and by showing a heightened regard for evidence of weakness, debility, yearning and dependence, in its relentless search for pathology.

Little wonder, then, that we find Trilling calling upon psychoanalysis here largely in an effort to get beyond it. For though "The Poet as Hero" is Trilling's one clearcut venture into Freudian interpretation (though the essay on Wordsworth's Immortality Ode in *The Liberal Imagination* contains some fragmentary psychoanalytic suggestions), psychoanalysis plays a small part in this essay which is devoted largely to a celebration of Keats's energy and moral realism. How far this is from the bias of psychoanalysis, which is to search for the wellsprings of imagination in regressed emotions, and to find meaning in the poet's *unconscious* symbolism. The Keats essay registers the strain between the subversiveness of psychoanalysis as a diagnostic art and the balance and tragic poise of the Freudian ethic, and thus explains Trilling's own choice of views. Henceforth, psychoanalysis would take a back seat to Freud, and the dynamics of creativity to the parameters of the "modern self" in the modern world.

This absorption in Keats's letters and character rather than his poetry was, like the elevation of Freud's *Weltanschauung* over his methods, a shying away from the asocial element in poetry itself. If psychoanalysis is laid to rest and Keats's "Ode to Indolence" judged less credible a guide to the cast of Keats's mind than his letters to his brother George, his spiritedness may be admired without extenuation. To rescue Keats from the distortions of the Romantic view is also to isolate him neatly from the driven and vulnerable parts of his own personality and thus from the very pressures and fears that energized his work and brought forth such a body of great poetry before his death at twenty-five. Lionel Trilling may have been a friend of literature but he was no fan of poetry, and his writing demonstrates amply that the novel, with its vistas and textures and examinations of character in society, suited his aesthetic and moral intuitions far better than did poetry, with its preference for the self in isolation and its traffic in those portions of the emotional life that lie below "character," that is, below scruples, judgment, values, reason, and the social instincts.

After the Keats essay, not only were there no more ventures into applied psychoanalysis—save, of course, the meditations on *Civilization and its Discontents*—but no more encounters with poetry. That side of the self that poetry and psychoanalysis hold in common was not the side that Trilling cared to pursue, at least not in public, and as James and Austen bulked larger in his thoughts, poetry diminished to the vanishing point. We hear nothing about the nineteenth century's poets, even such relatively social poets as Scott, Byron, Browning, or Tennyson, let alone bardic poets like Shelley and Swinburne. The century shapes up in Trilling's portrait as the exclusive domain of its great novelists.

Here, then, was a circumspect-partisanship of depths, a rhetoric of the depths, really, which extolled the inner life without giving it too much actual play. Trilling was captivated by the *idea* of the inner life, much as he was by the idea of politics or the idea of death; he Hegelianized psychoanalysis for the same reasons he Platonized politics: to refine out the cruder elements and isolate the essential ideas. Morris Dickstein has characterized Trilling as a Tory radical, which is a useful way to conceptualize his ambiguities, provided we keep in mind that the radical element was largely a genius for manipulating ideas and imagining ever more subtle essences, rather than a passion for uncovering irreducible motives or roots. If radical thought in its customary modern forms calls for the paring away of "superstructures" in order to lay bare the brute facts of biological need or infantile experience or class interest behind an idea or ideology, then Trilling's brand of radicalism was just the opposite: an upward distillation of the vapors of thought into their rarest and most abstract expressions.

Much can be said for such an unfashionable upward radicalism that reduces to paradigms rather than first conditions, for it is, like all radical styles, a way of precipitating essentials out of their solution of incidentals. And high-mindedness is not such a bad thing; we're just not used to seeing it applied so consistently from a position on the left (however minimally) side of the political fence. But Trilling's high-mindedness was influenced, and thus compromised, by his fastidiousness, which made his brand of negative capability sound on occasion like pure avoidance, and his dialectics like mere habits of fussiness. In reading Trilling, one often feels that he is holding too much at bay, as though his first consideration were to deny extremes. Certainly the habits of balance, skepticism, and irony that stood him in good stead during a decade of dogma and intellectual vulgarity also served to cut short lines of inquiry to which he was committed in principle but unwilling to put into practice. His first priority was to defend "mind" against whatever forces threatened to overwhelm it, even when those forces were not ideological or moral orthodoxy or unreason, but the mind's own natural propensity to explore. What passes, from one point of view, for negative capability or the ability to rest content with contradiction, may look like protective irony from another.

I certainly don't mean by this to derogate Trilling's work and make it sound any less vital than it was, but to point out that in his writing, as in the writing of anyone, even a literary critic, who manages to capture popular attention, obscure personal agendas are at work that manifest themselves as forms of intellectual insistence. To see one pressure behind Trilling's criticism as the attempt to fashion a moral self out of parts collected from books should not necessarily undercut his judgments but rather bring them into sharper relief. Once we grasp the idea, for example, that such self-construction was a work of deliberate and skillful artifice and that the adopted literary elements could become the very scaffolding of the ego, we can more plainly recognize the basic emotional premise of a book like *Sincerity and Authenticity*: that the culture of authenticity that took hold in the sixties posed a vital threat to those, like Trilling, who had assembled their social egos at other times according to different rules. We might say that the mask, once firmly in position, could not be put down, since it had become the face. How else to explain Trilling's misrepresentation of that culture by interpreting it through its parodists: R.D. Laing and David Cooper?

Trilling, we know, had little nostalgia for his Jewish origins and went so far as to observe, not incorrectly, that efforts made by Jewish-American writers of his generation to reclaim their roots were of no avail to their writing. Though he had begun publishing in 1925 in Elliot Cohen and Henry Hurwitz's *Menorah Journal*, the monthly publication of the Menorah Society, whose broad purpose was to form a non-sectarian, humanist, and progressive Jewish consciousness in America, he readily deserted that enterprise and its efforts at "cultivated" Jewishness in 1930 for the riptides of the intellectual mainstream, which meant largely *The Nation* and *The New Republic*, but included a brief and gingerly debut as a leftist in V.F. Calverton's *Modern Quarterly/Modern Monthly*. In 1944, reflecting on the depth and import of his Jewishness, he refused to waste any sentiment on his youthful torments over his Jewish identity, with which the better part of his *Menorah Journal* stories and essays were concerned, or to recognize any redeeming grace in the parochialism of organized Jewish life. "As the Jewish community now exists," he observed, "it can give no sustenance to the American artist or intellectual who is born a Jew. And so far as I am aware, it has not done so in the past. I know of writers who have used their Jewish experience as the subject of excellent work: I know of no writer in English who has added a micromillimetre to his stature by 'realizing his Jewishness', although I know of some who have curtailed their promise by trying to heighten their Jewish consciousness." Subsequently, he declined Elliot Cohen's invitation to join the editorial board of *Commentary* when it was being formed, and it is symptomatic of the chill that settled over his relations with that most forward looking of Jewish enterprises in the forties and fifties that *Commentary* neglected to review either *The Middle of the Journey* or *The Liberal Imagination* upon their publication. It is as difficult now for us to imagine Trilling a Jew as it was, apparently, for Trilling himself. The simulated English manner that was so integral a part of his bearing and voice was not just a literary taste or professional affectation; it was an identity.

Again, I don't intend here to call Trilling's integrity into question with an accusation of ethnic duplicity; I hold no particular brief for cultural uniformity or for the currently popular view of genealogy as a form of salvation. All the same, I think it worth noting that Trilling's break with the Jewish past, which apparently accompanied his break with *The Menorah Journal*, was more thoroughgoing and permanent than was the rule among second generation Jewish intellectuals. Trilling was no self-conscious rebel like Irving Howe, taking flight from his father's world in youth only to bow to its authority (which had now become its charm) in middle age. Nor was he an accomplished funambulist like Alfred Kazin, making an original synthesis for himself out of Winesburg and Williamsburg by wrapping his American dreams in folds of Russian melancholy. That, by the way, was the main line of imaginative assimilation, and the intellectuals who pursued it, including Kazin, Saul Bellow, Isaac Rosenfeld, Delmore Schwartz, and Philip Rahv, were adventurers in synthesis. Even Trilling's Freudian gloom and feel for the exigency of circumstances figure as a revamped racial melancholy. But Trilling *was* different in that new cultural blends and combinations did not appeal to him, and he shunned the exotic possibilities of the hyphenated identity. He was a refiner whose sensibility was established upon dissociation, upon cutting away parts of the self and suppressing the past. Jewishness was eclipsed, old associations kept at bay, the instincts soft-peddled, the unconscious squelched, "authenticity" taken to task, and a curriculum of reading taken on as a prosthetic identity. We shouldn't wonder that John Laskell has only a vestigial past, for memory is too great a risk. He is one of those born-again leftists whose new life is predicated upon amnesia. His watchword, if his existence could be reduced to a tag line, would be the credo of the self-estranged man: "Je est un autre.".

This sort of thing either matters or it doesn't, according to what we're looking for. If we want to find some consistency in Trilling's slant on psychoanalysis, that is, in the substitution of the Freudian character and *Weltanschauung* for the main points of doctrine, then the denial of Jewishness would appear to run true to form, corroborating our impression of Trilling's overall fastidiousness about the past. It also suggests something about how literature affected Trilling's moral equipoise, and why so much passion was invested in the literary imagination. For the moral drama of the novel, having been incorporated into the self, into the ego, may become indistinguishable from one's own, and the defense of the novel a surrogate defense of the self. And that drama, as Trilling would observe time and again, though most cogently in his essay, "Manners, Morals, and the Novel," is the drama of social mobility, of "the movement from one class to another." But it was characteristic of Trilling that while the advance from the ghetto to the middle-class was the great Jewish experience of his generation, he could approach the ubiquitous apprehensions about money, status, appearance, and manners that haunted the Jews in their campaign to become Americans only by way of the general idea, and that only through its literary sublimations, preferably in European literature. Thus, "Every situation in Dostoevski, no matter how spiritual, starts with a point of social pride and a certain number of rubles." The theme is one that would appeal naturally to a son of the ghetto, though the exact formulation comes from the Columbia professor. But, if you substitute Brooklyn for Dostoevski and dollars for rubles, you get something like the latent content of the formula. To look behind the figures of Julian Sorel, Tom Jones, Rastignac, Pip, Hyacinth Robinson, or any of the ambitious young provincials who bulk so large in Trilling's view of the novel is to discover the ungainly figure of David Levinsky, the rough beast from Zhitomir seeking his fortune in the garment district, his hour come round at last, slouching toward Gimbel's with his Fall line. It is appropriate that it should be a student of

Trilling's to finally remove the cloak of embarrassment from Jewish ambition and exhibit it as a point of pride, for it was Norman Podhoretz who brought social striving and its attendant concern with manners, masks, and money out from behind *the novel*, and issued a manifesto on the advantages of status, entitled, baldly, *Making It*. Podhoretz, it sometimes appears, is Trilling's latent content and what he might have sounded like had his career begun a generation later when his ponderous ironies and baroque indirections would be less in vogue. But then, it is the civilized sublimations for which we value Trilling; his circumlocutions were his power.

* * * *

But Trilling *is* elusive, especially in the face of efforts to pin down his ambiguities and link up his positions to his historical situation and to what he would call his "will." What is not ambiguous is his role in the post-War redefinition of liberalism, for he must be included among the intellectuals who transformed the prevailing rhetoric of liberalism from one of social progress and justice to one of sensibility and depth, all the while tidying up the depths by purging them of whatever was embarrassing, childish, or undignified. For the intellectuals, Trilling pointed the way from Henry Wallace to Adlai Stevenson, and from a politics of quantities that spoke of masses and dreamed of the greatest good for the greatest number, to one of qualities, that counselled personal self-development and individual self-restraint.

Trilling's brands of modulation and synthesis were a boon to his criticism; the range of voices and the purchase on ideas they brought him gave him a grasp and flexibility matched by few of his contemporaries. But such intellectual syntheses as he could effect, including the blending of psychoanalysis and liberalism, were often made at considerable cost, usually to the radical features of the original ideas. Thus psychoanalysis was asked to surrender its critical edge, while liberalism was called upon to forego its progressive fantasies. As a result, such upgrading, deepening, and enrichment as he brought to liberalism also robbed it of its historical mission: the amelioration of the conditions of life. And without a world to reform, liberalism found itself in the 1950s on the sidelines with nothing to do. Disenchanted with economics, disillusioned with "reality in America," ready at long last to embrace the basic structural supports of American society, and only casually interested in those elements of the self that can least tolerate the constraints of culture, liberalism set the conditions for its own demise in the 1960s, when its ideas in modulation would be asked, in their turn, how relevant they were to an unmodulated world.

Sincerity and Authenticity: A Symposium

PANELISTS: LIONEL TRILLING, IRVING HOWE, LESLIE H. FARBER, WILLIAM HAMILTON, ROBERT ORRILL, ROBERT BOYERS

Editor's Note:

This is an edited transcript of a symposium conducted at Skidmore College in March, 1974. The occasion was a two-day meeting convened to discuss Lionel Trilling's *Sincerity and Authenticity*. In the course of this meeting various panelists were able to engage Professor Trilling on a number of issues focussed in his book. One afternoon session—which had the participation of the novelist Curtis Harnack—dwelt especially on the nature of the modern self and the fate of autobiography in our time. Another session considered the relation between the Trilling book and Saul Bellow's novel *Mr. Sammler's Planet*, a novel Trilling was at first surprised to see linked with his book. He came after a while to agree that they belonged together, that both had much to say about the unfortunate drift of our present intellectual culture.

In all, we had almost ten hours of taped discussion to transcribe and edit. Much of that was given over to remarks by the panelists and members of the audience. In what we've thought to publish here, emphasis necessarily falls on what Trilling had to say. This is so, not alone because we have here an issue of SALMAGUNDI devoted to Lionel Trilling; it is so because those who gathered in Saratoga Springs in March, 1974 came primarily to listen to Trilling and to ask him to respond to their questions and observations. It is fair to say that no one among us was at all disappointed. I can only hope that, in the text that follows, we have managed to preserve some indication of the rare courtesy and spirited responsiveness that was Lionel Trilling's gift to those who knew him.

—Robert Boyers

ORRILL: Early in *Sincerity and Authenticity*, Professor Trilling concedes a certain ambivalence about his subject and about his approach to it. He sometimes feels when he reads Sophocles or Shakespeare or Homer, he tells us, "that human nature never varies, that the moral life is unitary and its terms perennial and that only a busy, intruding pedantry could ever have suggested otherwise." At other times he feels very differently, and considers that we cannot speak of morality in settled categorical terms. I would like to address my question to the entire panel. Does this ambivalence impair the book in any way? Does it make the book difficult?

TRILLING: I think that Mr. Orrill states my position quite accurately. And no, frankly, I don't think that this impairs the book. I don't think that the two modes of thought, the categorical mode and the dialectical mode, are necessarily contradictory of each other. I think one can say that both have validity even though they may suggest an apparent contradiction. As in science, the standpoint from which one looks at a phenomenon may change it. Sometimes one theory will serve best to explain a phenomenon, sometimes another and quite disparate theory will explain the same thing. And I think that scientists are willing to accept the disparateness of the two modes. Just so, though in judging others, in thinking about the conduct of others, the dialectical mode is likely to be the more appropriate, one does sometimes want to make categorical judgments. Clearly one serves the purposes of truth and of understanding best if one uses the dialectical mode in explaining how a person came to act in a particular way, and how changes came to take place in his behavior. This is especially true in discussing people in different cultures, figures in remote historical periods. I think that in judging one's own conduct one does best to stay with the categorical mode. One should assume, I think I do assume, that there is a fixed and permanent law; and I rightly judge myself by that. There is one point in my book where I come out for categorical judgment as against dialectical judgment. The passage comes at the end of chapter three where I'm talking about Jane Austen's *Mansfield Park*. And I say that "*Mansfield Park* ruthlessly rejects the dialectical mode and seeks to impose the categorical constraints the more firmly upon us. It does not confirm our characteristic modern intuition that the enlightened and generous mind can discern right and wrong and good and bad only under the aspect of process and development, of futurity and the interplay and resolution of contradictions. It does not invite us to any of the pleasures which are to be derived from the transcendence of immediate and pragmatic judgment, such as grave, large-minded detachment, or irony, or confidence in the unfolding future. It is antipathetic to the temporality of the dialectical mode; the only moment of judgment it acknowledges is *now*: it is in the exigent present that things are what they really are, not in the unfolding future. A work of art informed by so claustral a view might well distress our minds, might well give rise to anxiety [as indeed *Mansfield Park* does for many readers]. And not least because we understand it to be saying that even the reality of the reader himself is not, as he might wish to think, what it may become, but ineluctably what it is now. This is a dark thought, an archaic thought, one that detaches us from the predilections of our culture. But when its first unease has been accommodated, it can be seen to have in it a curious power of comfort." What that comfort is I don't say in the book and I'm not going to say now. But I . . .

ORRILL: But you can't stop there. Why aren't you willing to tell us?

TRILLING: Well then, the thought gives us a power of comfort which I'm calling curious because there is mixed in with it a certain amount of pain. I'm speaking of the sense that we may have, that we sometimes must force ourselves to have, that we are as we are and that we have a fate, a destiny, our own actuality. We are left with the person we really are and we are not to think of future developments. We are not to think of the exculpations of causalities. In this way we can perhaps accept ourselves as we are; and, as I say, there is a kind of wonderful actuality about that kind of realization of oneself.

ORRILL: Let me press this just a little bit further. Might it not be the case that the general historicism of your book serves to undermine that kind of certainty?

TRILLING: No, I don't think so. I think that, as I say, in different cases one uses a different kind of approach. I think historicism comes in on the side of generosity, understanding, and dealing with others. I think that what I've been calling the categorical mode of judgment—that this is the way we are, that we stand fixed and unchanging and not to be exculpated—applies very properly to oneself. This is a very old-fashioned view—I call it archaic in the passage I cited—but it's one I find I do respond to. I can also come along and say, well, the reason I am what I am is that I had this experience and this kind of parent, and they made this effect on me—I was brought up in this kind of culture, this kind of social class, and that explains it, but finally I don't think any of it explains it. In my sense of myself, if I were in analysis, yes, it would explain it. I would look to analysis to help me discover the causes and then seek to reverse their effect. But if I confront myself in my dark hours, or possibly my bright hours, I find that I am an essence, I am there, I am as it were a completed thing, for good or bad— not a completed thing really, but I am as I am. And I find that a comfort. By which I don't mean to say that I shrug my shoulders and say I can do no better. But to be able to receive oneself in that way seems a good thing; and to be able to think of other people in process—in quite another way—seems a good thing too.

HAMILTON: Let me object slightly to this line of questioning. I really don't see why ambivalence should be a pedagogical jeopardy in the seventies. We can confess ambivalence in a phony or an authentic way, and I'm assuming that Lionel confessed a genuine ambivalence at the beginning of his book. We confess it in a phony way when we want the students to identify with us and we want them to see that we too are seekers and we're like them. That of course is a contemptible ambivalent confession. But we confess ambivalence also when we're really uncertain about our intellectual and spiritual status. What do you think, Irving?

HOWE: I think that every serious person feels some nostalgia for the idea of a moral absolute, but he also manages to keep that nostalgia firmly in check. I think we all would like to believe that there are some commandments, but they're not the famous ten. We don't want to give up the idea of a commandment because the twentieth century suggests how dreadful life can be when everything is deemed to be possible; and yet, if we are asked to specify what the commandments are, then, like characters in Kafka, we are in a very serious predicament. We want to believe that there are moral limits, moral guidances, norms; and the difficulty we have is finding ways of making these precise. That's why I don't think there's any necessary trouble in Mr. Trilling's book between what you call the categorical and the dialectical, or the absolute and the historical because I think we have to try to find ways of working with both and of realizing in historical terms the still strong yearning for the absolute terms. We're all latecomers in history, it seems to me. There's never going to be an Aeneas or a Beowulf again. There will never be people of such absolute simplicity—heroic simplicity—directed and driven by God, by the idea of God's word. I don't think it is possible to will oneself back into the simplicity of a moral absolute. And yet to surrender that idea would seem to me dreadful; that is, to surrender the desire for that would seem to me dreadful. I'll stop by telling you a story about this which I think illustrates the point nicely. It's not my story, but a story in Solzhenitsyn's novel, *August 1914*. Though it is not, at least thus far, one of his best novels, an early section seems to me absolutely sensational. The book is an effort to write a Tolstoyan novel in the 20th century and much of what seems thus far wrong with the book is that it seems a pastiche, an excessive imitation of the Tolstoyan novel. But Solzhenitsyn, who is an extraordinarily intelligent, perceptive, and clever man; he knows what the difficulty of his project is, and he puts this difficulty, so to say, into the book. At the beginning of the book the hero, who's a young man obviously based on Solzhenitsyn in his youth, goes on a pilgrimage to see Count Tolstoy when he's a very old man. He's visiting, he feels, the most brilliant and distinguished mind of the 19th century. He wants to go back, he has that nostalgia which I've spoken of for the moral absolute which is embodied in Tolstoy. He wants to go back to Tolstoy. And he goes to Tolstoy's estate and he wanders around and he runs into the old man. The old man is by now irritable, he's sick and tired of young disciples or any other kind. He's had his say and he says in effect (I quote almost literally), What is it you want, boy? And the boy is struck dumb. He doesn't know what to ask but he knows if there's anyone of whom to ask a question it must be Tolstoy. So he says: What guidance do you have for us, and the old man grumbles and doesn't give really any answer. And the young man becomes desperately embarrassed and says: Do you still believe that the solution to human problems is the way of love? And Tolstoy says: Yes, I still believe that the solution to human problems is the way of love. And the young man that is Solzhenitsyn, in effect, is stricken dumb and leaves. And I think there's a wonderful moral, a wonderful idea in that, that though he does believe in Tolstoy's way and though the novel is to be organized around the Tolstoyan idea, he recognizes that the effort simply to turn back to the simple, coherent, unified, wholesome wisdom of Tolstoy is, for him, probably impossible.

BOYERS: If we all accept, as we seem to, that in the absence of moral norms considerations of sincerity and authenticity will have a great deal to do with our notion of the self, and that the self will be a problematic thing, perhaps we ought to consider how we come to identify the poor old ultimate actuality Lionel describes. What is the me that may be said to exist beneath the various roles to which each of us lends himself? Dr. Farber, in his book *The Ways of the Will*, suggests that there is a way, or a variety of ways of getting at this self, of distinguishing between this self and all of the possible projections of self which might be said to be falsely willed by a given individual. In your book, Les, you reduce the variety of functions, to an essential two: memory and imagination, two faculties which allow the individual to resist the unwarranted projections of self to which he is tempted.

FARBER: Well, yes, considerations of the actual me do occur, but usually after the fact, after some violation has occurred. Say I do something terribly crude, deliver an awful insult at a party. That night I'm struck with the enormity of my act and I ask myself, is this me? At this point I can confront what I've done, but if I'm not to go on to some pathological kind of brooding over weeks and weeks I'll have to be

Lionel Trilling

generous to myself; in other words I'll have to revert to what Professor Trilling has called a dialectical mode in looking at myself. Here's where my imagination begins to come in. I will have to both imagine the event as it occurred and the event as it might have occurred if I had been more sensible or more responsible; finally I'll have to imagine how much injury there was, and so on. I don't want to go on with this too long, but by my imagining of the event, its consequences, where it is in the future, where it is in the past, I can come to some notion, hopefully of me. It may take me half a lifetime but nevertheless, I'm rather optimistic about the possibility.

TRILLING: Leslie, how social is this analytical process? Is the true self in some sense a product of your imaginative reflection on the offense you've given or the forgiveness you've received, on the testimony you've received from comrades or loved ones?

FARBER: Yes, I believe the process is social and depends greatly on what goes on between me and those who suffered my insult, or who are close to me, just exactly as you say. But my imagination may not create an actual social exchange. I may not actually go on to ask for forgiveness of friends or family, I may keep it to myself, I may decide that forgiveness is not possible or I may decide that forgiveness is meaningless after all, that it is I who committed this act, and since it is not the greatest crime in the world I'll just have to live with it. I can become socially involved or not.

TRILLING: Your sense of yourself, though, could be social in the sense that you would read your friends as if they were mirrors of you. In your notion of yourself a large part surely is played by what you could ascribe to your friends in their opinion of you. They would say, well, Leslie is not the kind of man who generally goes in for that kind of irresponsible and insulting action which indeed was disgraceful; but this is most unlike him, they will say. And you will rather count on them to say that and you will say, after all, this was rather unlike me. Therefore in that sense you can triangulate yourself, can't you?

FARBER: No doubt there is that social dimension. I imagine how 'they' receive my action, how they forgive my action. If I'm feeling up, I imagine it one way; if I'm feeling down, I imagine it another way.

HOWE: It's interesting that exactly the same example occurred to me as occurred to Leslie; the sin we're considering is bad manners and it causes not much more than embarrassment. If I want to apologize for myself I ask myself which of my multiple selves committed the sin. If it was one of my social masks, so to say, I judge myself quite severely because I blame my snobbism as a professor or my ambition as an intellectual or my pretentions as a New Yorker. Whatever it may be, I find it something for which there is no excuse. And there I would say I behaved, to come back to our vocabulary, with shameful insincerity. But if I felt that I'd acted with what Professor Trilling calls my true self, that self which was formed by a certain conjunction of circumstances and cultural influences, I would have to say to myself, not with congratulations but rather ruefully, that alas, I'd performed in an authentic way.

FARBER: I want to add one word to what Irving has said. If this particular event wakes me up in the middle of the night, one of the discriminations I will have to make is whether my state is one of embarrassment, which I regard as a rather minor state, or whether I am shaken by having committed some real injury. And the answer to that question will seriously affect my experience of the event. I don't think it just follows from what I said that embarrassment is the only consequence of the offensive act.

ORRILL: Perhaps we can bring this around a little by having Lionel speak about our central terms, and asking everyone else to respond.

TRILLING: Well all right, why not. It seems to me sincerity has to do with one's relation to others; chiefly we know it in acts of communication. So that what one says is what one means, what one does is what one truly wants to do and has all the actuality it appears to have. In that sense sincerity is a public thing and—I'll go so far as to say for the purposes of simplicity—relates to one's public image, how other people think of you. And I try to make the point that the idea of sincerity comes into its full currency and full force at a time when we also have coming into its full being a public. That is, before the idea of sincerity was as forceful a concept as it later became, one had very small gatherings of people, one didn't see oneself in relation to very many people. So that's one's appearance, as it were, on the stage of society was infrequent if it occurred at all. It seems to me that sincerity is an act of self-presentation. One is telling the truth about oneself as best one can.

The notion of authenticity seems to me a more private thing, though obviously it has its public aspects too. It is one's self who judges whether or not one is authentic, that is to say that one is following one's true desires, following the laws of one's true being without any modifications, without responding to any of the sanctions or seductions of society. One is what one is. How one knows what one is one doesn't know but one doesn't go against one's own impulses. At a later time if we go on talking about authenticity and its meanings, I would like to recur to a short passage in which I speak of the etymology of the word as it comes from the Greek. I suggest there that there's a kind of violence in it. And I think that there is in the notion of authenticity, as against the notion of sincerity, a kind of assault being made, or a kind of defiance in which one says, 'Like it or not, this is the way I am and I will not put on a tie to come to dinner, or even a shirt, or anything else.' We won't go into the sincerity or authenticity of streaking, which is a very ambiguous thing. But there is—let me use this word—a defiance,—a defiant, self-assertion in the notion of authenticity so far as it may be said to exist in relation to society at all.

BOYERS: Would you accept that the violence which you identify as a component of authenticity is frequently directed not simply against the other but against the self? I am thinking of Carlyle's words (which you quote in the book): 'Close thy Byron, open thy Goethe'; according to these words, 'Know thyself' is to be abandoned as an altogether neurotic and unhealthy affliction of mind which ought to be replaced by 'Know what thou canst work at.' It would seem to me that the very notion of authenticity describes a kind of self-examination, which in itself is probably unhealthy and unfortunate for the self, whatever the positive values we have come to associate with it.

TRILLING: I would wholly agree with that statement. I tried to bring authenticity into as much disrepute as I could exactly on that ground. I, however, would go on to say that a concern with sincerity is equally inauthentic and insincere, that one simply cannot do it—one either is or is not a sincere person. One does try to tell the truth, one can make an effort in that direction, but as André Gide says, "You can't both be sincere and seem sincere at the same time'—I would say you can't be sincere if you try to be sincere. I think it's only on one's deathbed that one's friends and enemies and students and teachers can crowd around and say: you were sincere, you get an A for sincerity or a B+ for sincerity. These things follow from your actions, from the whole comportment of your life, and can be legitimately spoken only at the end.

HOWE: Well I think it may be useful to indicate that there are historical coordinates here, that we're not just taking two words and trying to define them and to cut very narrow refinements. I think by and large, as I understand it, the idea of sincerity would be roughly identified with the era of Romanticism, when people were struggling very much to create a self for themselves. And in that sense I think sincerity means a living up to some norm; it's a moral process, you struggle to become sincere and it occurs over, perhaps, an extended period of time; whereas authenticity seems to me to be identified largely with the phase of cultural modernism which begins roughly toward the last third of the 19th century. The man who says he wants to be authentic simply makes a rapid declaration, a leap so to say—it isn't the culmination of a process of training oneself or educating oneself, it's a rapid or perhaps instantaneous discovery—this is what I am, like it or not. A simple example, maybe overly simple, occurs to me: A student comes to see you and he or she says that he or she is very troubled and is trying to find out what his or her real place or purpose in the world is. The sincere way of coping with it is to discuss it and say look, you know, I haven't succeeded so well myself in finding out what my place in the world is, these things are very hard, etc.—perhaps the authentic way of saying it is, get out of here and stop bothering me because this is a hopeless discussion.

HAMILTON: Kierkegaard has crucial things to say on the subject of authenticity which we mustn't overlook. Historically it's a very specific idea. In the idea of authenticity there is a strong element of antagonism to philistine middle class culture. One of the secret meanings of authenticity is: I am a trouble maker and whenever possible I try to disturb bourgeois complacency. Now that's somewhat overstated, but there is that element in the 19th century genesis of the word.

ORRILL: I want to follow this up. At one point in his book, and correct me if I'm wrong, Professor Trilling argues that perhaps the violent assault on bourgeois society was necessary, but he seems to be saying now that in fact the tremendous emphasis we've come to place on authenticity is a very unfortunate thing. I find it very difficult to reconcile those two positions.

TRILLING: I can only respond by saying that we're in history and that there are no simplicities in history. Where I reject the idea of authenticity and seek to bring it into discredit is, how shall I put it, in its deteriorated form. I think I use the word in connection with developments in the late 19th century and the beginning of the 20th century. Then authenticity was a guiding principle, and artists would examine such a received traditional idea as representation and say look, I cannot possibly truly represent anything—I'm going now to create things, and this is going to be extremely troubling. In order to do my creating I may have to take things and tear them apart and put them together in a new way. There, the undertaking has a touch of heroism about it; there is a kind of historic necessity about it. The authentic is aggressive against something that really exists, against bourgeois respectability, and philistinism, but what happened, and I think this is true of sincerity too, is that they have become clichés. It is as simple as that. Authenticity and sincerity become confused with a kind of dress, with faded denims, perhaps, with a 'look' that's down to earth. As soon as you begin attaching moral meanings to a fashion, to a symbol of that kind and as soon as those meanings become accepted, become the mark of a certain kind of person who asks for a certain kind of respect, then I feel no, this is of no use. For the artist class in Paris in the 1840's to dress like workmen was understandable—to a point—because there had to be a movement against the respectability of the time; but when a revolt becomes an affectation, a cliché, I must withdraw from it. I think this is the ground on which my complication, my contradiction, exists.

ORRILL: It seems to me still that you're being somewhat elusive; you talk primarily about corrupt manifestations of authenticity—would you specify where historically you admire it and in what form and what context?

TRILLING: Well I think perhaps the word shifts its meaning and loses its force, as so many things do. Again I would come back to the notion of the public. One of the situations that modern man has to deal with is sheer numbers, that is, seeing himself and his conduct reproduced, mirrored in thousands and thousands of faces. And the impulse to try to separate oneself from those thousands of faces or certain segments of those thousands of faces by symbolic gestures which attest to one's right state of being, seems to me not a heinous way of behaving but rather small and of no particular account. When great claims are made for it, I feel I must reject it. There are moments when the word authenticity seems to me ridiculous—as when it's applied to a

certain Scotch whiskey, I don't remember which one, or to certain people. I find it difficult to talk about authentic people. All people are authentic because they're human beings, they look like people. I could attest to the authenticity of every person with a soul, presumably, and a mind, probably. That's a human being.
HOWE: I can give an example which may make this clearer. There was something heroic, say, in the career of a Flaubert, and something heroic in the career of a James Joyce, writers who were cut off from the mass audience, cut off from popular taste, even something heroic in the career of a Zola who took great risks for unpopular causes, and writers of this kind who conceived of themselves as part of an avant-garde which is rejecting bourgeois mediocrity and philistinism. Writers of this kind I think do have a heroic component in their lives, they make enormous commitments. But today, if a man is writing for *Playboy* and has a contract for his next book for three quarters of a million dollars, and is adored and idolized, a darling of the very bourgeoisie against whom Joyce and Flaubert were rebelling, it doesn't seem to be seemly that he should see himself in the line of Flaubert and Joyce.
FARBER: I like what I've been hearing, but I'm a little perplexed . . . I don't use the words 'sincerity' and 'authenticity' very often in my speech, yet I'm so taken by Professor Trilling's descriptions that I've wanted to make up words for them myself. For example, I thought about 'sincere' for a while and decided that a word I'm more apt to use is *serious*. I don't know just what to use for 'authenticity'.
HOWE: Genuine.
FARBER: Genuine, yeah. But I do want to preserve in this if we can the view that there is such a thing, suggested by sincerity, as telling the truth, honesty. Fair enough?
TRILLING: Oh, fair enough.
HOWE: I have a suspicion that some may wonder why all this matters; I think it matters enormously, and I want to try to say why: There was once a time when people weren't concerned about being either sincere or authentic or genuine. They were concerned with the truth and they believed that there was an objective truth, that the truth was there to be discovered; most people in western society believed that the truth was to be found in Christianity. It doesn't matter whether they were right or wrong but they believed that there was an objectively apprehensible truth. And at some point—I don't know exactly when, maybe in the 18th century, maybe a little earlier—there occurred an enormous change in the character of western culture. People no longer believed that they could discover the truth which existed as an element of external reality. People came to feel that their job was to be not so much true to the truth

but to themselves, that is true not to the 'facts' pronounced by various dogmas but to the fact of their own feelings. Now that is an enormous revolution in the history of humanity. All of us are trained, I believe, in our culture to believe in the primacy of our own feelings as against any notion of objective or measurable truth—and it wasn't always so. It comes, I think, to students and indeed other people, as a tremendous shock when they really apprehend that it wasn't always so. It's one thing to say it, but to really grasp that apprehension is enormously difficult.

ORRILL: I want to put your point in moral terms, Irving. I think what we're doing is important too—I think it's important because we want to be good and we want others to be good, but don't find any way of using that word any more. Our struggle with the categories of sincerity and authenticity is partly a struggle to avoid using the word good, which is empty and which doesn't serve the purposes to which we'd like to put it.

TRILLING: I also respond very positively to what you've said, Irving. I think that there's this to be added to it: That it's not only that the idea of truth was taken away but that the organization, that is to say the religion which proposed the truth and had been rejected, was now considered a fraud. And I think that what we should do in talking about authenticity or of sincerity is to observe how much we conceive society under the aspect of fraudulence. No idea, I'm sure, in our view of society is likely to win a quicker response than the idea that society itself has become fraudulent. This is an idea that we discover in the 18th century and the 19th century; we feel it all the more because in an odd way, an oddly specific way, our culture generates fraudulence. Consider for example the whole notion of advertising. We all mock advertising. The word Madison Avenue is a pejorative geographical term, isn't it? Why? Because we are a society which has created an art which undertakes to generate needs in us the satisfaction of which will make people rich. And we believe that the statements of advertising are in themselves fraudulent. We think of advertising as a contemptible seduction. And I think that can be taken as representative of what we feel about society in general. In a situation of that kind the notion of proving ourselves not merely good, but true, true to ourselves, true to our nature, true perhaps even to some notion that we have of what human beings ought to be, produces all the kinds of elementary and bizarre symbolic actions subsumed under the heading of the impulse to authenticity. And I think in that sense the subject is indeed of decisive importance.

BOYERS: Do you believe that there is an effectual way of organizing society to allow human beings to generate resistance to the seductive appeals you designate? Where is this resistance to come from?

TRILLING: Well, it comes from Ralph Nader apparently. I suppose

Nader is a kind of culture hero for us, for some people—he's rather boring to me—exactly because he says look, do not believe this kind of thing. He's very sincere. And *Consumer Reports* tells us this is the truth, this is the actuality about this or that product and do not be mislead. Imagine having a large literary industry called *Consumer Reports* which has to tell you whether the thing you're buying is authentic.

HOWE: I think I can make an example which is a little invidious. The example I offer would be the differing behaviors of two of our best writers: Saul Bellow and Norman Mailer. The point doesn't depend on which you prefer to the other, or whether one has genius and the other doesn't. In my judgment Bellow has behaved the way a serious writer should in resisting all the kinds of things you're talking about. Namely, he does his work, he doesn't appear on wretched talk shows, he doesn't lend himself to all the garbage of popular culture, of newspapers, T.V., of publicity and all the rest of it. And Mailer, though in some ways thinking of himself as more of a rebel against society, lends himself as a kind of clown to all the shoddy and spurious elements of the culture.

TRILLING: I'm trying to formulate a word in defense of Norman Mailer at this point. I think somehow, for me, that in becoming a clown he transcends this thing in ways that perhaps Hegel would understand. I think that his clowning somehow transcends what it is and becomes more significant. Maybe it's only because I do like him—very much as you do, Irving—and do admire him that I want to say this. I think that we must take into account the kind and amount of gratuitousness that has come into contemporary life for all sorts of reasons. That is, our choices are freer than they ought to be. The control of our lives by necessity is less than it formerly was. We are put under a diminishing pressure of what we can call duty, we are put under a diminishing pressure of what we call necessity. Not that these things have gone from us, but the confrontation of danger, the confrontation of death, the confrontation of suffering, this we do not have to make as frequently as people formerly did. We're pretty sure we're going to be fed, we're pretty sure that we will not die at one of those early ages that people used to die at. There are all sorts of things we can take for granted that people, even a hundred years ago, would have thought marks of an ultimate freedom, an ultimate luxury they would have wanted to possess. The number of bathrooms that exist now is one of the great cultural facts that nobody takes account of—the fact that you can have hot water if you want it and so on. I mention all these things to suggest how what we might call affluence, relative ease of material life leaves us confronting areas of choice which require us to look for a hardness somewhere, for a kernel of actuality and experience which perhaps we have to find for ourselves.

We may have more freedom than we are comfortable with. And, if one has confronted a period of danger in one's life—any kind of danger—one knows that some things are real and that one is real in confronting them. One does not begin to have phony thoughts when one is in danger of one's life, when on a raft trying to survive in mid-ocean, one is not fantasizing who one is—one simply is, and everything stops there.

FARBER: I would like to quibble just a little bit about that. It seems to me entirely within human possibility to confront danger and still succumb to sentimentalities about bravery and the ability to face death and so on. Don't you? I don't think that danger itself confers any kind of authenticity.

TRILLING: Well, it stops the process of self-examination, I think.

FARBER: Does it really?

TRILLING: Don't you think so?

FARBER: No. I've listened to plenty of people in great danger, for example in the second world war, and the process of self-examination went on. Of course my patients didn't generally use the terms authenticity and sincerity but they plagued themselves with whether they were really being brave or whether just—

TRILLING: Oh . . . yes, I think in war, perhaps, but I'm talking of a more ordinary kind of danger than that.

FARBER: Let's consider what's happened to death. Do you think that something has passed out of our culture in our way of confronting death?

TRILLING: Yes, I do.

FARBER: I assume you're talking about more than the mortician's industry.

TRILLING: Yes.

FARBER: OK, and I assume that what you are perhaps considering are the efforts of the medical profession to keep people living forever.

TRILLING: In part. But there are other things too I would speak of. For example, our feeling that we ought not mourn, which is a very common feeling among people today, that we ought to act as if nothing has happened to us when someone we love has died. This I think is an inauthenticity.

FARBER: Would you consider equally inauthentic the prescription somehow or other derived from psychoanalysis that we *should* mourn, that it's good for us?

TRILLING: Well you've got me there.

FARBER: Because I hear that all the time.

TRILLING: Well, then that's part of our inauthenticity. I certainly would never recommend to anybody that he mourn because it's good for

Lionel Trilling and Robert Boyers

him; he has to get over it, but I can see that there's something very wrong when it is felt to be culturally correct not to mourn, not to appear torn by grief. What I'm saying, then, is that as soon as you don't feel this pressure of what I'm calling necessity, as soon as life seems easy you may have questions of sincerity and authenticity which don't exist in certain kinds of cultures.

BOYERS: I'd like to see us address the question of sincerity in a defiantly blunt and simple way. Now there are contexts in which something like sincere behavior has to be assumed by all participants. For example, in a clinical or therapeutic encounter, the patient must assume that the therapist is sincere when he tells the patient what he thinks of his behavior. The therapist may not always want to speak openly, but insofar as he does, the patient must assume he is telling the truth. Now I wonder whether there aren't other contexts, even more familiar contexts, in which similar assumptions of sincerity are plausibly held. And I wonder also whether in fact it is possible to participate in the routines of daily life without those assumptions.

TRILLING: Well to that I think I can give you only the simplest of answers—which is, yes, that this is undoubtedly true. That is one reason that I take a peculiar pleasure in communal professional life. I like going to committee meetings at my university—I'm just one of those strange people who does—I like having conferences about problems because by and large the relationships exist on a level which is very reassuring to me. I think people say what they want and ask for what they want or need, and what they say is by and large to be trusted. These are not my intimate friends usually, but they are my colleagues, perhaps what you might call comrades, and I love them in a special way—I don't want to use that word *love* very lightly, but I have a special feeling for them because they're not my friends, they're my colleagues. And that is to say I think their relation to me and my relation to them can always be sincere. Yes, I quite agree with you there.

BOYERS: But there are, it seems to me, particular situations, perhaps most situations, in which this assumption of sincerity cannot be taken for granted. If I may, I'd like briefly to refer to an interesting story which Dr. Farber tells in *The Ways of the Will.* Perhaps it will enable us to address ourselves more specifically to this problem. He tells the story of the psychoanalyst Frieda Fromm-Reichmann, who as Dr. Farber represents her, was a rather well-bred, thoroughly refined, upper middle-class German lady. Dr. Farber speaks of a particular encounter:

> Dr. Fromm-Reichmann was seeing an extremely disabled young man who had been schizophrenic for years. He was habitually dirty and dishevelled; he rarely spoke and even more rarely achieved much coherence in what little speech he did produce. Without question, therapeutic work with this patient was a grim business, affording scant hope, little satisfaction, and few of even those fleeting rewards so precious to the therapist who specializes in the treatment of schizophrenia. One day, during a therapeutic hour, as this patient (mute, as usual) was sitting with Dr. Fromm-Reichmann in her office, she noticed that he was fingering his genitals with one hand that was crammed deep into the pocket of his trousers. It was also plain to her that he had an erection. She pondered the situation for a moment, then said to him, "If it will make you feel any better, please go ahead." Whereupon the young man unzipped his fly and proceeded to masturbate, while Dr. Fromm-Reichmann sat quietly across from him, her eyes down, her hands clasped in her lap. . . .
>
> Dr. Fromm-Reichmann was always a marvelous hostess, and something of her quality as hostess appears in the incident I have recounted about her and the mute young man who was encouraged to masturbate if it would help him to feel more comfortable. But I doubt as this man sat masturbating in her quiet office, full of tasteful mementos of her European past, she found much resemblance to her life as Groddeck's hostess. To some extent a hostess resembles an actress . . . she plays a role (in this case, one of amiability toward a group she may not know); she is not required to believe that her role is anything more than a role. As with an

> actress, believability is central to the effectiveness of the performance, but in order that it be achieved, actual personal sincerity—in regard to the scene itself—is unnecessary, if not irrelevant. In therapeutic encounters, on the other hand, the therapist's actual personal sincerity is considered absolutely essential to the occasion. I think that as Dr. Fromm-Reichmann described this incident with the mute and masturbating young man at a staff conference, she might well have blamed herself for some awkwardness in her invitation, and she would have been quick to acknowledge any erotic titillation she experienced. But she would have resisted the suggestion that there was anything unusual about her behavior, that while committed, in full sincerity, to her duties as psychotherapist she had suddenly found herself enacting the role of hostess. Her private conviction, I suspect, would have been, as in our previous example, that there was something real, something "down-to-earth" about this incident.

Now it seems to me that this is an incident which might be worth reflecting upon.

HOWE: Well it's an obviously brilliant passage and I think we're all grateful to you for having read it. It's the kind of thing that Leslie Farber gets off every once in a while. The thought that occurred to me is that it's very much like teaching. Any student who thinks that in my classroom I'm always being sincere is either utterly naive or out of his mind. My ultimate purpose I think is sincere: I want to teach, and I want to communicate, and I want to provoke, etc.; but at any given moment I have to play the role of a teacher, which can be provocative, nasty, amiable, cajoling, flirtatious, whatever—whatever works at the moment, and no one ever knows what is going to work at any given moment, how to hold attention or how to stir things up. So that it is a kind of performance with a great deal of preconceived deliberation and playfulness and artifice—that's the word I want. And in this sense it would be fun to read a passage from Professor Trilling's book in which he justifies Oscar Wilde's defence of the mask. Oscar Wilde speaks of people using masks as a way to perceive the truth about people which is better than when they unmask themselves.

TRILLING: You will think me insincere if I say that I was about to say exactly the same thing about teaching. It's full of subterfuges, full of guile. I lie constantly as a teacher, I'm hypocritical or whatever is the opposite of sincere. It seems to me that what we have to take into account here is one very important social institution—that of courtesy. The first stage of the simplistic impulse towards sincerity is certainly to attack courtesy. The forms of social intercourse as they are prescribed to allow for the expression of respect for our interlocutors or the people we are with in any relationship is a common thing. Alceste in Moliere's *Misanthrope* gets rid of all these courtesies. Though he's a gentleman and well-bred, as we say, he doesn't want to allow for those things to exist—not the polite lies, not any of the things that we say to which we attach no meaning but which if we don't say them makes us unsociable people.

HOWE: I want to come back to that fascinating passage Bob Boyers read from Leslie Farber. Am I right in thinking that if an ordinary guest had come into the home of Frieda Fromm-Reichmann and done in her living room as a guest what this patient did that she would have thrown him the hell out immediately? I know I'm right. I mean, it seems to me obvious, and I think that is a way to clarify the difference between her sense of what is appropriate in a direct personal relationship and what one may have to do in the performance of a professional obligation as an analyst.

FARBER: We have to raise one more point here. Would the young man be masturbating in her living room if he were not seriously disabled? The question is, was *he* being sincere?

HOWE: Was he being authentic—

FARBER: Authentic, indeed. This brings up what Professor Trilling has already mentioned about the violence that is attached to the word authentic. The young man was committing a kind of violence and Frieda was perhaps being unauthentic in not noting this.

HOWE: But was he trying to shock her? He knew that though she was a brilliant analyst she was a German lady, a very proper lady, and he was trying to see, as a patient often will with an analyst, what he could do to break that mask of composure, to make her cry out the way an ordinary human being yells out: 'For Christ's sake, cut it out!'

FARBER: Well, that's very much what I meant to say. Of course he was trying to shock her and she was unshockable given her premises about being able to blink almost anything.

HOWE: There's a great story about F. Scott Fitzgerald which I probably shouldn't go into . . .

TRILLING: You mustn't tease us, Irving.

HOWE: All right, I'll tell it to you very quickly. F. Scott Fitzgerald when a young man wrote his first book and dedicated it to Edith Wharton, who was then a very famous and great literary lady. He admired her intensely. He came to Paris, she was living in a suburb. The great lady said yes, you can come and visit me. He was terribly excited. As he went on the trip he stopped every few miles and had a drink. Each time he had another drink he got a little more angry at the idea that *he* was going to visit this great lady and pay her homage: who the hell was she anyway! By the time he got to see her he was thoroughly enraged and disoriented and he told her—you've got to have the image of Edith Wharton, a very unflappable lady indeed—that he and his wife Zelda were living in Paris in a bordello. She didn't even bat an eyelash and she said "Yes Mr. Fitzgerald, and what do they do in a bordello?" At that point he was absolutely undone and he ran home to Zelda and burst out in great grief and anger "She beat me, she beat me!" I thought of that story because in a sense Frieda Fromm-Reichmann did that very therapeutically.

TRILLING: What I'd like is to get at all this another way, by speaking of the relation of art to the notions of sincerity and authenticity we've been discussing. It seems to me that one of the things that we confront in looking for an actuality of self, as we do, is that we are a culture permeated by art. That is not my way of praising our culture, though it ought to be, and maybe twenty-five years ago it would have been, but I find myself often asking whether that wonderful Victorian confidence in the educative, moralizing power of art has been justified or if it can be accepted simply and without qualification. At several points in my book, as will be remembered by some of you who've read it, I raise the question, following my great master Rousseau, whether art is what people say it is—totally a benefit in our life. And if I may be the questioner here, I'd like to propose that as a question.

HOWE: In a way, Lionel, I think we may never have left the question of art. What we have before us is a kind of debasement of precious commodities. Paperback books may be a good example—I'm not sure. You know, when paperbacks first came out we were all terribly excited at the idea that we could go out and buy them and have them; we went out and bought far more books that we could read—we'd read them later, etc. . . . and now it seems to me in some way that the paperback thing has been a disaster for books—I won't try to say why, but there has been a cheapening process that's hard to describe. One doesn't want to have an aristocratic elitist view about art, about literature—and I don't—and yet, at the same time if one is honest, 'sincere', or 'authentic', one has to recognize that something has happened in modern culture which is terribly devastating and painful. I'm speaking of the mass vulgarization of the arts and of discourse about it. Now it may be that this is only a momentary phenomenon. It may be that with the continuing democratization of our culture we will discover new benefits; maybe there will be some value in everyone going to college, and buying cheap paperback books. At the moment it's a little hard to be optimistic about it.

TRILLING: Of course I agree with you but I'd like to catch you up on one word, Irving, and that word is vulgarization. That is an important phenomenon, no doubt, but it is not exactly what I think is the prime issue here. We are more properly concerned here with the capacity to make distinctions between the finest art and the less demanding kinds. We have to consider what has been made of art in the educated classes that are serious about it.

HOWE: I follow you, Lionel. I think you're speaking of the way art has been forced to take on certain roles, fulfill certain functions; and these functions are not appropriate to art. It takes on for many people a quasi-religious nature, it becomes a surrogate for moral life, for political life, and it shouldn't be that, it should just be art. And there is something about what you might call an art worship in our society which is a very painful and bad thing. It leads at worst to cultivation of beliefs, among many artists and writers, that are indefensible.

TRILLING: The other thing I had in mind was the actual direct influence art has on us, interposing between us and experience. We say it doesn't but I think it often does, I think it does in the way Rousseau thought it did; it keeps us from looking at the object directly, it keeps us from experiencing things directly.

HOWE: It's funny. I believe that in part, and yet anyone who teaches literature knows that half of his struggle with a class in America is to persuade them of the opposite; you struggle with freshmen and sophomores and even juniors and seniors, to persuade them that art is not a way of blinking or avoiding reality, but a way of apprehending reality, of enlarging your sense of reality. Here I think we come back to dialectics of a kind, that half of the art of teaching is to persuade the students of something and the other half is to dissuade them to the same thing.

ORRILL: Can anyone say who or what is responsible here? Is it the reader or the viewer who wants to be violated by art that's responsible?

TRILLING: No, I'm not blaming the audience. I'm going to take absolute perfect and wonderfully facile refuge in a superb word—what I'm blaming is the culture. I'm not blaming the audience, I'm blaming a set of circumstances. I'm not blaming any given audience at any time.

BOYERS: Perhaps we can fix responsibility on an important class in contemporary culture, on the academic intellectuals Lionel addresses in his book. In *Sincerity and Authenticity* he writes that "it is characteristic of the intellectual life of our culture that it fosters a form of assent which does not involve actual credence." That seems to me to describe better than anything I've read the besetting sin of the academic life. And I wonder if you could say something about the fundamental absence of what you call seriousness that so impoverishes discourse among intellectuals in our culture.

TRILLING: Well, I think one of the things that has happened in the academic profession is the suddenness of its growth. It seems to me that when you have a profession suddenly burgeoning, proliferating as ours has done, something happens to the sense of commitment. I think the academic profession, let's say fifty years ago, could probably show far fewer distinguished members—great scholars or great teachers of one kind or another. It was fashionable then to say that most academics were dull creatures. Nevertheless I think they were committed to the undertaking they had made in a very firm way. They may have been very dull but they were certainly serious—maybe seriousness and dullness have a natural affinity for each other—but they were serious. The academic life didn't seem to have much prestige attached to it, but suddenly things changed. The profession became attractive to lots of people; there was a loosening of the professional fibre, such as sometimes happens in other professions. The guild becomes a different kind of thing. When you speak of the academic profession, of course, you must speak of it as continuous with our intellectual life generally. And it's a strange thing about the intellectual class—it doesn't have a great sense of responsibility. It can take one position one moment and another at another moment and never say 'I'm sorry' about that first position, 'I apologise for having taken it, I did it because of this reason, now I'm right'; it just moves from one position to another with no sense that any change has taken place. I think one would have to go into the whole role as well as into the whole nature of the intellectual class to discover why this is, why it is one of their functions to make judgments on ideas and to relate themselves to ideas without considering the reality of their position. How often we make the disjunction between the intellectual functioning as intellectual and the intellectual functioning as a parent or husband or something of that kind, where his judgments are very different indeed.

BOYERS: Philip Rieff uses the word "weightless" to describe the transactions that occur in our time. He speaks also of "order-hopping" as the process wherein individuals allow themselves to be taken up by one ideological fad after another with no capacity to resist the seductions of ideas. I don't know if that seems clarifying . . .

TRILLING: Yes, in fact I respond to Rieff's terms very warmly indeed. There, I think, we're confronting a situation of the gravest import. The sense of commitment, the sense of actuality, the sense of weightiness-

(L. to R.) Irving Howe, Lionel Trilling, William Hamilton

gravity it used to be called—is going at the behest of a feeling for autonomy. That wonderful word which is so popular in our culture is a very dangerous word, indeed. We want to be autonomous in every possible way. At the same time we present in our colleges and universities something we call disciplines—the discipline of literature, the discipline of philosophy or of mathematics, which doesn't allow autonomy and which requires a service rendered to the object of study. I don't know what one can say further about this except to go on bemoaning it. I know of no way to be effectual in countering it.

HAMILTON: I guess I speak as a Protestant, and I'm more worried about the domination of the category of work, on both my mind and on my students' minds than you are. I would like to find responsible, and therefore serious, ways of beguiling my students away from the illusion that work is the only way of being related to the world, and therefore my function as a teacher surely, and art's function too in some way surely is to find the alternatives to work. Some of the great modern artists are in fact harlequins, clowns, and ought to be allowed to be so; we might do well to disassociate our students and ourselves from too earnest and too serious, too moralistic, too Protestant a relationship to the world.

TRILLING: Well, I think that what we're going to come out with is that there ought to be moderation in all things, even in moderation. Yes, of course work can be a falsity and there can be such a thing as too much commitment to work, but there can also be too much commitment to freedom and playfulness and the gratuitous and the fortuitous, as you would surely agree. I'm not sure that I would say that my students are

under the impression that work is their salvation; on the contrary I'm afraid . . .
HOWE: I think what you are speaking about is swinging or moral-sensationalism, or rootlessness or faddishness or something of that kind; and if that is what most of you are objecting to then maybe work is a good thing to recommend to young people. It's a great thing, after all; I remember William Faulkner once said that work is the only thing you can do all day long, and I think he was right. You don't have to be down on play to recommend work.
TRILLING: I think what Bob was objecting to originally is not only faddishness and triviality. Perhaps Saul Bellows' term of 'low seriousness' is very much to the point, it's a very useful phrase. Consider the typical feeling that one must have serious ideas about everything, one must have opinions, that one is not properly an intellectual person unless one can pronounce on almost everything, when by and large these things do not bear upon our lives and do not even bear upon our interest. The ability to test by one's own actual experience what one's opinions are seems to me a very hard thing to come by. Looking through my book I find I often make a disjunction between ourselves as readers and ourselves as persons in lives, as householders, heads of families, sons, whatever we are in our actual functions. And it seems to me that so long as we are not able to judge things not only as intellectuals but in our social roles, we are a failed class. I think this is the great sin of the intellectual: that he never tests his ideas by what it would mean to him if he were to undergo the experience that he is recommending.
BOYERS: Is Bellow's character Mr. Sammler responding to the issues in the spirit of your remarks? Is his mysticism somehow a response to the essential falseness of much intellectual discourse?
TRILLING: I would question whether Sammler is properly to be called a mystic. I think that the famous end of the book in which he utters the name of God in the vocative doesn't make him a mystic. Or if it does, we have to understand the term in a special way. A rather well-known and very scholarly rabbi who was once my teacher, Max Kirduschin, used the word. He talked, in speaking of the teachings of Rabbis, of normal mysticism. He said that they were controlled by normal mysticism. By which he meant that it was ingrained in their quotidian experience and was not moments and flashes of insight but was simply a kind of abiding faith that didn't need the moment of illumination. I suppose St. Teresa was a non-normal mystic. And if Sammler is to be called a mystic he is to be called a mystic only in the sense of one who responds to a normal mysticism. Which seems to me to have no ordinarily mystical content. He responds simply to the necessity

of making a certain kind of affirmation, of being categorical about certain things. When he says in that famous conclusion, which is deeply moving, that we know, we know, what is it we know? We know how to behave, we know what must be done. We pretend that we don't. We, as intellectuals, raise all kinds of questions. We ignore the fact that under certain kinds of situations there is only one way to act and there are no problems about it. I think this is all he is saying. He says somewhere earlier in the book that the intellectuals are the worse enemies of civilization. Sammler, I think, says that. And I think he would say they are the worst enemies of civilization because out of pride they insist on making problems. It's certainly a great achievement of intellectuals to propose problems. But as always there is a time and place for everything. I think that what Sammler is doing here, what Bellow is doing here, is saying these have become gratuitous, these problems. They are not real problems. And the questions that we'd like to raise about the moral life and our living of it are likely to be gratuitous. I think that's the sum of Sammler's mysticism.

Politics & History: Pathways in European Film

BY ROBERT BOYERS

European film-makers have demonstrated an interest in political subjects ever since the medium really took hold in the period after the First World War. Accordingly, a growing body of criticism has addressed issues associated with political reality and political commitment in a whole range of films, some of which seem not to have been made with deliberate political intentions of any kind. Indeed, it is fair to say that film theory itself, particularly in its formative stages, was often indistinguishable from political advocacy or, at least, political history. In the writings of Sergei Eisenstein, in Siegfried Kracauer's *From Caligari To Hitler*, we find attempts to understand the film medium and the historic occasion of its rise to prominence in what are essentially political terms. And though other critical works have lately achieved greater eminence — I am thinking especially of the works of André Bazin and of Christian Metz — the original impact of the early theories has not been seriously compromised. Because films have been taken to express 'reality' more immediately and recognizably than any other art, and because political events are thought to embody 'reality' more convincingly than other events, there still exists a lively interest in film as a means of political expression and as a gauge of historical truth.

Two of the more widely debated documents of recent commentary on film address particular movies as political phenomena which may best be understood by looking beyond the conscious intentions of film-makers. One document — by the French philosopher Michel Foucault* — takes its shape and direction within a still developing tradition of Marxist analysis; the other document — by the psychologist Bruno

* Michel Foucault, "Anti-Retro" in *L'Cahiers du Cinema*, July 1974; I wish to thank James O'Higgins and Mary Helen Wood for translating the text for me and for pointing out some of its merits and deficiencies.

Bettelheim* — is a relatively straightforward piece of humanistic argument, liberally peppered with bits of personal experience and moral misgiving. Though both documents 'correct' perspectives elaborated in contemporary European films, they fail in a variety of ways to look at these films as the films themselves ask us to examine them. Though Foucault and Bettelheim are gifted interpreters and — on other subjects — subtle theorists, neither seems to have much respect for the peculiar imaginative relation a good film establishes with its viewers. Both Foucault and Bettelheim think that even the best films have 'messages' and that, the better or more skillfully made the film, the more totally the 'messages' will be impressed. For Foucault it is a bourgeois delusion to believe that a good film invites a variety of responses which are suitably discriminating, dependent as they are on careful attention to details in the given film discourse. For Bettelheim, if there *are* a variety of responses to a film, they will fail in discrimination — the intellect will fall prey to confusion, emotion will swamp accurate evaluation, and a disastrous 'message' will take hold of us as surely as it would if the film were an undisguised piece of one-dimensional propaganda and we were its witting dupes.

Foucault's "Anti-Retro" is the edited text of an interview conducted by the film journal *L'Cahiers du Cinema.* The stated object of the interview is to look at a number of French films which have undertaken to 'recreate' history, more particularly the history of France and its people during the Nazi period; also, to discover why so many of these recent films should be devoted to what is, by now, an 'old' subject; and finally, to rescue from these films and from other political accounts of the past a ". . . .popular memory of all forms of struggle which has never really been able to speak" — in other words, also taken from the introductory remarks of the interviewers, "to uncover that which the official text suppresses, and lies forgotten in the accursed archives of the dominant class." One does not have to like the hysterical and imprecise rhetoric — "accursed archives of the dominant class" — to recognize in the stated intentions of the interview a number of important goals. There *have* been a great many recent films devoted to the Nazi period, not only in France, but in Italy and other countries as well. Though Foucault is primarily interested in Louis Malle's *Lacombe, Lucien* — certainly the most accomplished and memorable of these films — and in Cavani's *Nightporter*, he might as fruitfully have turned his attention to Vittorio De Sica's *Garden of the Finzi-Continis*, Michel Drach's *Les Violons du Bal*, and to other films distributed after the interview took

* Bruno Bettelheim, "Reflections: Survivors" in *The New Yorker*, August 2, 1976.

place. The most interesting of these later items is surely Lena Wertmuller's notorious *Seven Beauties*, the subject of Bettelheim's *New Yorker* essay. Why does Foucault largely limit his attention to French 'recreations'? By deliberately restricting his analytic focus in this way, Foucault believes he can elaborate a "context" for these films and explain how they are "inscribed in a history" which the film makers are not anxious to call by its rightful name. He can demonstrate how a number of films emerging from a particular political and cultural climate can implicitly elaborate a critique of previous historical myths and succumb at the same time to a variety of other myths no less dangerous. To accomplish this, Foucault must insist that French recreations of the Nazi period invariably reflect France's official explanatory myths, either by serving them up again with minimal adjustment or by positing counter-myths which are presumed to be more appropriate under present political circumstances. Whatever the inspiration of the individual film-maker, if he is French, he has to do the work of a Frenchman. He will do this work badly, however, unless he is equipped to perform a rigorous Marxist analysis of his materials and to move beyond inherited assumptions about the adequacy of his medium to express the historical truth. Though Louis Malle may have thought to show the French people "what they have been," he presents instead "what [he thinks] they should believe they have been."

It is not entirely clear, of course, that Malle's object — or Cavani's or DeSica's or Drach's — was to show anybody what actually happened during the Nazi period. Nor is it certain that anyone comes away from these films with a clear view of their national experience as ratified by particular moral or political imperatives. Foucault insists because he does not wish to look at the films themselves. He is interested in a phenomenon which began to take definitive shape with the appearance of Marcel Ophuls' long documentary film *The Sorrow And The Pity* (1972). Here was a film whose object was, quite clearly, to adjust the historical record, to set things straight. If it had a lesson to teach, a message to impart, it was not a personal 'reading' viewers felt they were getting but a portion of 'the truth.' A plural 'truth' it was, no doubt, but no less realistic or historically valid for being so. Foucault and his friends at *L'Cahiers* speak of the film as having opened up certain "flood gates," and it is indisputable that Ophuls persuasively accounted for the Nazi period in France in a way that no one had confidently embraced before. Grant that Malle and the others were stirred by *The Sorrow And The Pity*, that their films would not have been entirely possible without it; does this mean that their films attempt to do the same thing Ophuls did, to set the record straight and shape the historical memory of

Frenchmen? Foucault, apparently, cannot imagine an alternative possibility, namely, that Malle and the others wished to formulate a number of questions and to try out various responses without limiting themselves to documentary fact or tracing indelible patterns on the memory of Frenchmen.

The Foucault interview dwells, to the point of monotony, on what the philosopher takes to be a crucial deficiency in Malle's film and others like it: "The theme, roughly speaking, is that there have not been any popular struggles in the twentieth century. This affirmation has been formulated successively in two ways. The first time, soon after the war, by simply saying: 'The 20th century, what a century of heroes! There were Churchill, De Gaulle, there were the paratroopers and the squadrons, etc.' Which is another way of saying: 'There was no popular struggle, the real battle was that one.'....The other way, more recent, skeptical or cynical, if you like, consists of affirming purely and simply: 'Look at what in fact did happen. Where did you see struggles? Where do you see people rebelling, taking up arms?' " The consequence of which, according to Foucault and his friends, is that 'the people' are asked to believe that the French nation "collaborated with the Germans," that "they swallowed everything," and that there is no other way to 'remember' what happened. If Louis Malle made a film about collaboration, and it seems to confirm what Ophuls presented in a documentary format, Malle must have intended to show that no optimism is possible for those who think realistically about ordinary people and their relation to contemporary political systems. Though Malle may have thought to make an 'honest' film, to correct the Resistance-myths and inflated legends of popular struggle, he succeeded only in proving that neither he nor the rest of us can take seriously the idea of principled political resistance among ordinary men. "Is it actually possible to make a positive film about the struggles of the Resistance?" Foucault asks, and concludes that it is not. "One has the impression that that would make people laugh, or simply, that the film would not be seen."

Several questions present themselves at this point: 1-If people would laugh at any positive cinematic representation of popular resistance, would they do so because we have been ideologically conditioned to be skeptical of ordinary decency and simple courage? 2-Is it plausible that films have played a major role in this conditioning? 3-How likely is it that a complex and beautiful film like *Lacombe, Lucien* will convey and implant ideological messages? Would it not be more likely to open up possibilities than to close them off, to make viewers as potentially receptive to the idea of principled resistance as to the idea of perfect complicity in Nazi brutality? 4-Might we not be skeptical about popular struggle—especially in the context of the Nazi period—for good reason? Haven't we been given enough of the historical record to know what may no longer be supposed? Perhaps it is difficult to imagine an entire film about "the struggles of the Resistance" because such a film would probably suggest that we take positive hope on the basis of what had to be—in view of the historical record—a marginal response to Hitler?

Foucault believes that re-creations of the Nazi period in France falsify the fact of an objective possibility which the historical record cannot wholly compromise. It does not matter that most Frenchmen collaborated, or shut their eyes, or refused to lift a finger. What matters is that a significant number of Frenchmen did resist the Nazis, that many others would have resisted had they been able to imagine some means of effectually organizing themselves against the occupying forces. More, if Frenchmen are ever to imagine a means of popular resistance to whatever happens to be the dominant reality of the moment, they will have to be encouraged to think of themselves in a 'positive' way. This will not come to pass if the most accomplished artists tell people they are collaborators at heart, that they have nothing to remember but a tradition of dishonor, and that courage consists in the ability to face up to these sorry facts. What Malle and others take to be the facts of life are no more than reflections of a contemporary French political climate in which a deflationary ideological 'realism' has come to replace Gaullist 'grandeur' in the hearts of citizens. For Foucault, Malle is as much involved in the contemporary French situation as any French citizen. *Lacombe, Lucien* must be viewed as part of the political and cultural climate of its time—which is not 1944, when the action of the film is set, but 1973 when the film was shot.

Foucault's thesis rests upon an assumption that works of art are responsible to the constituencies they affect, that they may not 'innocently' address issues as if they were to be held accountable only in terms directly recommended by the works themselves. If Malle's film does not pass beyond the de-mythologizing functions assigned to it by Malle, if it is essentially nothing but a 'negative' representation, it needs to be 'corrected' in terms of what it might have been. This is not, in Foucault's understanding, a violation of the film but an attempt to place it, to retrieve for it a representative status which it seems not to have wanted. In proportion as Malle's film is directed to particular historical occasions and to the delineation of individual characters or agents, Foucault suspects that it may not be able to see what general understanding it will effect. By treating everything, including decisive local events and small heroic culminations, "*in passing*," as Foucault says, "*without capitalizing anything*" as especially important or broadly symptomatic, the film argues implicitly "that there is nothing worth remembering." If every detail has equal importance, if life is nothing but life, if to be ordinary is to be without significant redemptive prospect, then wisdom lies in cynical resignation. This Foucault cannot accept. Malle and the other film-makers, like the rest of us, must be instructed in what is really at stake in recent re-creations of the past.

The trouble with all of this is that *Lacombe, Lucien* does not affect us as Foucault thinks it would have to, given the political climate of France in recent years. For one thing, it is not a *French* film in the sense that Foucault suggests. It is so very close in spirit to other national re-creations that it must be said to express a European rather than a French sentiment. Nor is this sentiment what Foucault thinks it is. Its function is not, broadly speaking, demythologizing. No one watching the film in a properly responsive way will feel that Malle wishes to debunk particular inherited attitudes or to prove a point. What Foucault calls "popular struggles" are not at issue, one way or the other. To be attentive to the film is to understand throughout that there must have been struggles in Europe during the period of the Occupation; with so many people affected—for better or worse—some at least would have had to resist simply to protect their personal interests. Foucault cannot mean to suggest that he believes in popular struggles that have no relation to the concrete personal interests of individual citizens. There will always be a minority, of course, who act largely on the basis of political or moral conviction, but these are likely always to be the special cases, the heroes, if you will. If Malle refuses to underline their participation in the conflict, to celebrate their courage, we cannot fail all the same to think of them. Though they hover at the margins of our attention, never threaten really to displace the focus on Lucien Lacombe and his friends, they demand to be acknowledged, intermittently. Does Malle falsify anything when he has the district Resistance leader brought into Gestapo headquarters to be tortured, and refuses to let us dwell on the event, drawing us off with Lucien to other 'business'? We do not forget the image of the Resistance leader, his head fiercely dunked again and again in a tub of water, his captors standing by or participating dispassionately. Nor do we overlook the way Malle structures the event, framing it in a partially open doorway into which Lucien can peer, with the rest of us, only long enough to register what has happened before retreating downstairs to less immediately terrible pastimes.

Malle's film does not attempt to demythologize because there was nothing left to debunk by the time the film was made. Very few persons—French or otherwise—can have believed by 1974 that political resistance to the Nazi occupation took the form of a principled popular movement. Resentment may well have run high in occupied territories, but there is a considerable difference between resentment and resistance. A wide range of popular historical works and of speculative philosophical enquiries into the Nazi phenomenon had surely indicated—if nothing else—the failure of European populations to take effectual steps to protect the Jewish minority* and to deny the Nazis a foothold. Not even the French—and Foucault seems to think they are among those who cannot yet have heard the news—can have escaped the impact of such influential studies as Adorno's *The Authoritarian Personality*, Fromm's *Escape From Freedom*, Arendt's *Eichmann In Jerusalem*, or Sartre's *Anti-Semite And Jew*. Surely they cannot have missed the more serious novels and plays devoted to the combined issues of Nazism and Occupation, the international debates roused by European productions of Rolf Hochhuth's *The Deputy* ten years earlier, or by Peter Weiss's *The Investigation*. Foucault comes to Malle's film, and to the others, with a mistaken idea, and finds in the works he examines only what he expects to find.

Lacombe, Lucien is, in part, a film about collaboration, but it does not presume therefore to encompass the European experience of Fascism and Nazi occupation. There were, after all, many different kinds of collaboration, the most usual: collaboration from fear. This kind of collaboration we do not hear much about in Malle's film, which dwells instead on such factors as simple stupidity and power lust. No record is falsified because no one is given to understand that the entire historical record is at issue. Malle is proposing for himself, and for us, certain basic questions, to which he provides *possible* responses: Not, what were the kinds of collaboration by which the French people dishonored themselves, but what is the meaning of collaboration and how do we make sense of it? Not, collaboration represented the erosion of popular belief in particular democratic values or a collective failure of nerve in France, but collaboration cannot be understood apart from the experiences of individual human beings whose prospects for one sort of behavior or another are shaped by the concrete circumstances of their lives. In this sense the cool, relatively detached, seeming 'objectivity' of Malle's presentation consorts very well with his ultimate purposes. The film critic Pauline Kael observes, with characteristic shrewdness, that Malle's "...technique is to let the story seem to tell itself while he searches and observes. His gamble is that the camera will discover what the artist's imagination can't, and steadily, startlingly, the gamble pays

* The well-known Scandinavian exceptions only serve to underline the unpleasant facts of the matter.

off." There is no mystification of the medium and its magic power here, but an attempt to get at a phenomenon that resists easy attribution or summary. Malle's film leaves us with no message of any kind because he respects the intransigant particularity and terrible complexity of the materials he treats. To say that the camera discovers what we can't think hard enough or well enough to discover without it is to say that, in *Lacombe, Lucien*, we take something away that is not reducible to formulaic explanation. The European experience as such is at once larger and narrower than Malle's intention: larger, in the sense that it would have to involve a synthesis of diverse phenomena rather than unabashed conviction in the persuasive meaningfulness of a singular character or event; narrower, in the sense that it would involve only what we could give a name and relate to other comparably 'domesticated' historical experiences.

Ms. Kael also writes that "the movie is the boy's face. The magic is in the intense curiosity and intelligence behind the film—in Malle's perception that the answers to our questions about how people with no interest in politics become active participants in brutal torture are to be found in Lucien's plump-cheeked, narrow-eyed face." Foucault would no doubt respond that this is to capitulate with a vengeance to the ideology of film, according to which particular images are ever so 'convincing' by virtue of their pure visual intensity; an intensity, moreover, fully resistant to verbal translation and its consequent 'reduction.' I do not think Ms. Kael's evocation need yield to the charge. It is neither ideological nor evasive. She says, quite simply, what the film inevitably inpresses upon us: that it is possible to collaborate, to do terrible things, without knowing what one is doing or why one should cease. It is possible, that is, if one is Lucien, and if circumstances invite one to become comfortably involved without having to feel that anything to which one has genuinely belonged will be betrayed. I cannot agree with Ms. Kael that "the movie is the boy's face" because I do not think the questions are limited to collaboration and the participation in torture. But insofar as these are primary questions in the film, Ms. Kael is certainly instructive in telling us what kind of answers Malle is willing to provide.

Foucault does not think it is possible to make "a positive film about the struggles of the Resistance," and perhaps, in a special sense, he is right. If Lucien's face tells us as much as Ms. Kael thinks it does, one will have to wonder what sort of 'positive' organization may be expected to deal with it. How will such an organization lure him in? Will it promise him the sort of immediate gratification awarded by his participation in Gestapo activities? What will it substitute for the pleasure Lucien takes in expressing his rage towards the socially 'privileged' classes by sleeping with their daughters, sadistically forcing his way into their privacy, casually destroying their material supports—as Lucien breaks to pieces the model ship owned by the adolescent son of a Resistance doctor? Clearly, it would seem, if one is to make a 'positive' film such as Foucault recommends, and to be true to what most of us take our recent experience to be, one will have to select an alternative focus. Lucien will not do. This may mean, of course, that though one wishes to make a film about popular struggle, 'the people' will have to be rigorously excluded from one's persisting focus. Lucien's face, or faces like it, will create problems that no determinedly 'positive' film will be able to solve. The best one can do is to develop a range of Resistance figures who stand somewhere between 'the people' and the larger-than-life heroes who typically compromise any belief in popular struggle.* This Malle did not wish to do because, one supposes, he was interested in something else—not in a positive or negative film, but in a series of problems in the domain of imaginative re-creation which required the face of Lucien and of his principal antagonist, the Jewish tailor Albert Horn.

It is curious that Foucault should not have mentioned Horn at all. For though he does not occupy our attention as insistently as Lucien, Horn is an imposing presence throughout the film, as much for the boy as for us. There is much to be said for Lucien's face, for the open depths of its relative imperturbability. But there is more to be said, and fruitfully remembered, about the face of Albert Horn. His is the face of Western civilization itself, and of the ravages wrought by the modern barbarism. One doesn't want to make too much of this representative status, and it

* The best example of a moderately 'positive' film made along the lines I have indicated is Alain Resnais' *La Guerre Est Finie* (1966). Here the principal figure is an aging Spanish revolutionary named Diego who has been working for twenty-five years with a cadre of 'professionals' to overthrow the Franco regime. A text by Sartre used as an epigraph in the published film-script describes very well the arduous, frequently disheartening 'activist' Resistance enterprise: "As for the action itself, it must be called an undertaking, for it is a slow tenacious work of enlightenment which lasts indefinitely." This we feel, and admire, as we watch Resnais' film. Though we know, in studying it, that the anticipated popular struggle in Spain may be as far from coming to pass as it was twenty-five years earlier, the positive thrust of the action cannot be denied. Probably this is because its focus is mostly limited to Diego and his associates who, for all their misgivings and increasing weariness, continue to believe that they are doing what must be done. Though they do occasionally lose touch with the meaning of their actions, they demonstrate a considerable measure of what Diego calls "patience and irony." Most telling, I think, in the context of our larger argument, is that Resnais never gives us a glimpse of Lucien, which is to say, of his Spanish equivalent. Though there is much talk of popular resistance, of workers' movements and the like, the film never takes us inside Spain, to the workers themselves and their stubborn, casual limitations. Had it done so, it is unlikely that Resnais could have managed as much as he does in the way of hopeful anticipation.

is fair to say that Malle resists at every point the temptation to underline it. In fact, we understand Horn rather well in the first two or three minutes of our acquaintance with him—know him in his erect posture, his carriage, his poise, the restrained sorrow etched in the lines of the face, the worry and sleeplessness contained in and around the eyes. We recognize too the underlying softness in the slightly over-full pucker of the mouth, the promise of 'tasteful' compromise which is all he'll have to show for the impulse to resist what others wish to do with him. In every look and gesture, in the terrible restraint of his utterance and the easy elegance of his continuously muffled disapprovals, he is a stone in the path of any possible popular resistance struggle. It is not that he lacks courage or conviction, but that he is tired and does not understand what exactly he would have to fight against to put up an active resistance. He seems as genuinely incapable of hating Lucien as we, obviously, are meant to be. For it is Horn's fate to see what there is in Lucien that makes him attractive. Even as Lucien's victim he has to acknowledge the impressive 'reality' of unabashed animal vitality. There is even something fatherly in the way Horn observes the boy's adolescent preenings and absurd self-assertions—clearly disapproving, but fatherly all the same. The will to struggle, especially against those who feel no guilt and have no way of responding to a civil appeal, is all but extinct in Horn, and it will not do to complain that he is nothing but a bourgeois shop-keeper, not fit to embody the will-to-struggle Foucault thinks to find in the working classes. If he is no salvational figure—if he would seem to have no future at all—Horn is yet a moving representation of human qualities we shall need to draw upon if we are to construct a liveable future. I cannot imagine that Malle thought any less of Horn than that, or thought that we should somehow take him for less.

There are a variety of other figures in Malle's film, but its essential resonance is to be located in the steady opposition of Lucien Lacombe and Albert Horn. Malle's object was to bring one face right up close to the other, to see what effects might thereby be produced. In contriving to do this, Malle had to know that nothing 'positive' or fundamentally uplifting could possibly be made to emerge. He wanted to discover what it feels like to work upon a fragment of the recent past, what are and are not appropriate sensations in the face of horror and the small paradoxes of history. In the two central faces of his film he could watch the fine registration of states of feeling too fleeting and unsure to fix in words. It is a measure of his achievement that, though there are words in the film, though Malle will not foolishly give up the attempt to articulate some of the things his characters must feel, he lets the faces say most of what matters. This they can do not only because they belong to fine actors, but because Malle has played them against one another in a consistently interesting though unemphatic way. We take a great deal from our encounters with Albert Horn because we are permitted to see with him what must be dealt with in the person of Lucien; in the same way we can follow the notable increase in Lucien's avidity as a result of his regular intercourse with Horn—Lucien cannot say, really, what he wants, what moves or excites him, but we know, when we look with his eyes at the slightly rumpled and increasingly forlorn figure of his Jewish antagonist. It is not that he wishes literally to be like Horn, or to have what he has—Lucien can in any case take what he wants. What he envies is the demeanor of control, of grace under pressure, the air of one who has lived and cannot pretend in the interest of pride that he does not miss what he was. Lucien envies, perhaps most of all, the ability to assume the role of victim and suppliant without any corresponding inclination to grovel or to whine—as though it might be possible to have one's way after all, if only the right heartstring were plucked. There are limitations in this sort of 'strength,' and Horn deteriorates badly in the course of the film, letting himself and his appearance go to pieces more even than we'd quite been able to anticipate. But Lucien doesn't care for those limitations as we should. He can admire Horn, 'play' to him, just as much as he needs to while tormenting him. It is all very strange, and utterly believable.

To a point, Foucault admires what Malle has done, but he wishes that the French people might have been given a more accurate account of their experience. To accomplish this, he believes, Malle would have had to face up to the inscribing of his account in a history to which the film bears witness. This is the history of recent attempts to understand the phenomenon of collaboration and occupation. Had Malle faced up to the role of his film in 'writing' this history, he would have had to conceive and execute it along other lines. Though Foucault does not elaborate the prospect of an alternative development, it is clear from what he says that the character of Horn would have had to be drawn differently, and Lucien as well. As they stand, these characters demand a development which has little to do with politics. Politics has to do with power; with the desire for power and the consequences of its exercise. In *Lacombe, Lucien*, Foucault believes, the issue of power is displaced and evaded. The desire for power is converted to sexual desire, and the necessary resolution takes place at the level of erotic culmination rather than in the realization of political objectives.

Though Horn is not himself an erotic figure, he assists in the process of displacement whereby political conflict is turned to personal difference and the drama of character. But Foucault's indictment has more to do with Lucien. The boy had become involved in politics as a means of asserting a will-to-power which unmistakably answered to his needs. In the context of the film these needs are presumed to speak for the needs of other persons similarly unable to think through their desires and make sense of their meagre experience. Foucault and his associates resist the suggestion that popular needs are invariably reducible to erotic equivalents. Their conviction is that a genuine politics is possible even for people, like Lucien, who can be diverted all too easily from their attraction to popular movements. This can hardly be persuasive to anyone not already disposed to believe in the idea of popular struggle, but Foucault is nonetheless disarming in the concessions he makes to his antagonists. He sees as clearly as anyone might hope that Lucien is not a likely candidate for participation in resistance movements—though in the course of things, Malle suggests, he might accidentally have fallen in with resistance fighters as easily as he fell in with the Gestapo. For Foucault it is all a matter of potential: one must not close off a possibility by suggesting it could never have been realized, even when circumstances seemed to require that it come to pass. The artist's responsibility, at the very least, is not to confuse matters, not to pretend to be talking about politics while actually collapsing distinctions and displacing one progress for another. At issue are the artist's honesty and clarity of intention. These qualities it is possible to realize even when the complexity of the materials at hand is such as to daunt all confident projections.

"I wonder," Foucault says at one point, "if Marxist analyses are not to a certain extent victims of the abstract character of the notion of liberty. Under a regime like the Nazis', it is clear that one doesn't have liberty. But not to have liberty does not mean that one doesn't have power." What power does Lucien have? The power to exert some control over other lives, to be a factor where before he'd been a cipher. And the Nazis themselves? "We have to ask ourselves," Foucault suggests, "if that regime was nothing but a bloody dictatorship, how is it that on the third of May, 1945 there were still Germans ready to fight to the last drop of blood — if there was no mode of attachment of these people to power?" With liberty one thing and power, decidedly, another, Foucault is bound to be better in the course of these formulations at posing questions than at giving answers. This is all to the good, though the suggestion persists throughout the interview that Foucault is operating from a stable foundation on the basis of which Malle and the other directors come in for disapproval. It has to be taken as a little unreasonable that Foucault should expect a particular kind of clarity from Malle when he is himself so very free to poke and probe, to give out and take back in his own reflections on the subject. Why, after all, should Lucien be any less vulnerable to manipulation and to displacement of affect than he is? And where did Malle really go wrong in permitting Horn to 'personalize' the terms of the conflict for Lucien? Foucault's various concessions to the difficulty of it all indicate beyond a doubt that the idea of political liberty is likely to have but marginal importance for most people, and that any film-maker who thought it irresistable would fail to see its peculiarly inverse relation to the satisfactions of power. Malle, at the very least, must be given credit for seeing such things, and for demonstrating that it is possible to mount a political action without capitulating to the abstract dynamics of a purely political mechanism. Lucien and Albert Horn serve Malle so well because they require that he allow them to grow and to interact in accordance with the principles of their character. Had they been less coherently realized as characters, more susceptible to Malle's ulterior purposes in moving them about, the politics of the film would emerge as a mode of authorial calculation. Foucault doesn't address the problem from this point of view, but he should.

Bruno Bettelheim, in his long essay on *Seven Beauties*, has more in common with Foucault than either would be likely to admit. That their opinions clearly differ on important issues is less important for our purposes than the fact that they approach works of art with comparable expectations. The most interesting of these expectations is that works of art will answer to particular historical requirements even when the artists have indicated an intention to make use of history rather than to confirm or establish an historical record. Foucault wanted Louis Malle to resist the inscription of his film in a certain kind of 'revisionist' historical enterprise currently taking shape in France. Why? Not because he might thereby have made a better or more enduringly persuasive film, but because the cause of a parochial notion of popular struggle might thereby have been better served. Bettelheim wanted Lena Wertmuller to let us see the concentration camp experience as an experience different not only in degree but in kind from any other; also, to project the will-to-survive as consistent with the will to retain one's essential humanity — not with the will to get by at any price. Bettelheim's demands have more to do with the given world of *Seven Beauties* than Foucault's have with *Lacombe, Lucien,* but Bettelheim does not therefore serve our understanding any better. By coming to *Seven Beauties* with fixed expectations, by 'reading' the film with the eyes of one who feels he knows in advance all that may truly be said of the concentration camp experience, he denies the viewer's actual experience of surprise, provocation, and a special kind of disinterested contemplation.

Important distinctions must be made if Bettelheim's argument is to be properly answered. The contemporary historian John Lukacs has had enormously useful things to say about these distinctions. In an essay on E. L. Doctorow's novel *Ragtime*,* Lukacs contrasts a nineteenth century genre, "the historical novel," with a twentieth century form, uneasily labelled "novelized history." Lukacs does not think his categories as flexible as I do, and he would no doubt resist my suggestion that "cinematized history" would serve the basic point of his distinction as well as "novelized history." My reader will, however, follow my advice, for the moment at least, and substitute the one term for the other in pursuing Lukacs' argument: "The new genre is the converse of the historical novel. In *War And Peace* or in *Gone With The Wind* history is the background. In the [novelized history, like *Ragtime*, or Solzhenitsyn's *Nineteen-Fourteen*] history is the foreground. In the classic historical novel the great events of history are painted on a large canvas in order to lend depth to the story, to give an added dimension to the main characters. In the [novelized history] the reverse: the main characters serve for the purpose of illuminating the history of certain events, of a certain time. In this historical novel the author's principal interest is *the novel.* In [novelized history] the author's principal interest is *history* — perhaps a new kind of history, but history nonetheless." Though recent popular works of novelized history may distort the historical record, at their best they do represent, in Lukacs' view, an advance in historical consciousness. Bettelheim does not think that cinematized history (my term, not his) can represent a fruitful advance in any kind of consciousness unless it registers historical events with documentary accuracy and rests upon a sound humanistic foundation. Though he does not make use of Lukacs' distinction, does not argue the necessary relation between fact and fiction, individual and collective, in the conception of a film like *Seven Beauties*, his paper everywhere cries out for just that sort of theoretical underpinning.

But let us look at Lukacs' distinction more closely. The novelized history is said to use characters and portray particular encounters "for the purpose of illuminating the history of certain events, of a certain time." Illumination — the truth of the historical record — is the goal. Works of art typically propose to illuminate the truth, of course, but it is not always easy to say what kind of truth is available to a given novel or

* See "Doctorowurlitzer Or History In *Ragtime*" in SALMAGUNDI, #31-32, Fall 1975-Winter 1976.

film. When Lukacs writes that in the older genre—the historical novel—"the author's principal interest is *the novel*," he means to identify a certain kind of truth to which such works are principally suited. This is the truth of human feeling, a truth which is ratified by the accumulated experience of each reader or film-goer. Insofar as such works are persuasive, they appeal to our intuitive sense of things. If they present extraordinary persons involved in unusual exploits, they will develop their behavior and join events in such a way that our sense of the probable is tested no more than it may be without our turning from the spectacle in dismay. The truth to which we respond is, again, a truth of experience: we sense that, given a certain kind of extraordinary personage placed in very special circumstances, this is the way he would very likely behave; these are the likely consequences of initiating events; these are the sensations and thoughts an alert and intelligent observer ought to be permitted to have when confronted with such materials. This is the kind of truth we want and expect from most works of art.

Lukacs' notion of novelized history proposes to alter this expectation, to explain why it is we may be satisfied with another kind of truth when confronted with a book like *Ragtime*. It is the passion for historical truth which determines our response to these newer works, which have been created to answer to a demand earlier readers were not as likely to make as we: namely, the demand that no truth we are meant to accept be presented without the support of detailed context and place in time. Since all truth is presumed to be relative to particular circumstances and characterological disposition — itself a historical phenomenon which varies from one era to another — even a truth of feeling must be located in respect to time and general probability. Reader interest will tend to be less involved in the truth of human nature than in *a* truth of human nature in a given period. This is not to deny that general truths may emerge from the concentration on individual, specifically conditioned truths in their context, only that the terms of extrapolation will be differently weighted than they used to be. The issue is one of emphasis: as Lukacs writes, in the newer genre "the author's principal interest is *history*" — it is not the author's only interest, but his *principal* interest.

Bruno Bettelheim, in refusing to think through such distinctions, never really discovers what Wertmuller's *Seven Beauties* achieves. The issue here is not so much the success or failure of the film, but the expectations and responses it may be said to generate. Bettelheim assumes that Wertmuller's principal interest is history, that the film is an example of what we have called, following Lukacs, cinematized history. He assumes, moreover, that the film-goer cannot but be misled by the film, since what he is bound to find in it is a particular version of the historical truth which takes unforgiveable liberties with the actual historical record it presumes to enlarge upon. The actual record in this case is, of course, something with which Bruno Bettelheim is singularly familiar. As a concentration-camp survivor, as a scholarly authority in the field of holocaust studies, as author of several important works on terror and survivorship, he has at once a very large claim on our respect and attention. The problem is that his primary assumption is mistaken. No one believes while watching *Seven Beauties* that the historical record has been significantly clarified or enlarged. No one need feel that the actual experience of survivors has been betrayed, or demeaned. To argue the case as Bettelheim does is to mistake one kind of truth for another. There are more serious errors in Bettelheim's analysis ,but the first one is crucial in directing the course of the others.

Bettelheim remembers the opening of the film — like the other parts — very well indeed, and what he makes of it may be said to stand for his response to the entire film:

> Before the film's story begins, we are shown a series of newsreels of Fascism: demonstrations, marches, Mussolini exhorting the masses, Mussolini shaking Hitler's hand; war, the bombing and destruction of cities, the killing and maiming of people. Though all this is presented as horrible, we are entertained by an amusing, mocking cabaret song accompanying the newsreel scenes. And Mussolini and Hitler are also presented partly as comic figures — an approach that is supported by the song, in which all the contradictions of life are accepted at the same time. The song says "Oh yeah" equally to "the ones who have never had a fatal accident" and to "the ones who have had one." And though most of the lyrics and the singing bitingly reject the world of Fascism we see on the screen, they are also funny, and this quality simultaneously adds to the rejection and takes the sting of true seriousness out of it.
>
> . . .The newsreels and the song accompanying them in *Seven Beauties* take us back to the period when we thought that we did not need to take Hitler and Mussolini seriously. But the war scenes show us at the same time what happened because we didn't take these men seriously. This is a contradiction that runs all through the film.

So, a combination of newsreel footage and "mocking cabaret song" frames Wertmuller's film and instructs us in Wertmuller's approach to her materials. She works, according to Bettelheim, on a principle of contradiction and alternation: the ludicrous and the obscene mingle freely in her imagination with the terrible, the good with the bad, the playful with the serious. The result, in Bettelheim's view, is confusion and irrelevance. If viewers cannot confidently tell an appropriate response from an intolerable impropriety, if they are asked to laugh when they should cover their eyes in shame and horror, they may decide that one thing is much like another, that truth is in vividness of presentation and the power to evoke feeling — not in the substance of the vision. When audiences are so manipulated, Bettelheim argues, they will come to feel that they may not trust their responses at all — including decent and once reliable responses to cruelty and torture. They will find ways to deny that they have such responses at all, or that such responses are more legitimate, more worthy of their humanity, than others.

The opening of Wertmuller's film is no doubt full of incongruity and confusion, as Bettelheim rightly argues. What is its ostensible purpose and the effect it may be said to produce? As the frame for the film, rather than a part of the story, it may be said both to stand apart and to support or establish the central action. It stands apart in presenting what appears to be actual newsreel footage, while the central action is clearly fictional. No matter whether we take the story-line to reflect some accurate semblance of what actually took place in concentration camps. Insofar as the story is enacted; as it involves patently 'private' or 'exclusive' insights into very special characters; as it persistently juxtaposes the improbable and the probable with no trace of apology or regret — the audience knows that it watches the unfolding of a fiction. But what does it think as it labors to follow the opening sequence? Fact, or fiction? The distinction is not usually put so crudely when we speak of a film like *Seven Beauties,* but here there is no alternative. Bettelheim forces the issue in such a way that we cannot but go back to 'first' questions. If we take the newsreel footage to be authentic, which is to say, part of the documentary record — no matter how fragmentary —, must we therefore suppose that Wertmuller's intention was to prepare us for the unfolding of a cinematized history? The supposition might have been justified had the director not put in the accompanying cabaret song. As it is, the opening sequence undercuts any possible inference that Wertmuller is primarily interested in settling the historical record. If the song presents contradiction, if one interpretation of the holocaust experience vies with another — with no apparent means of reconciling them — the audience must see at once that it is not in for a definitive accounting. It is being asked to assimilate the frightening images on the screen to the shifting perspectives offered by the all-too-knowing lyrics mounted on the sound-track. Though the audience may try to manage this at first, it must recoil from the task with some unease after the opening minute or two of the film. Since there is no reliable way of adopting a single perspective on the imagery — not on the basis of the deliberately elusive cabaret lyrics, at any rate — the audience can do nothing but take in what is given, and wait for further 'instructions.' The unease we feel does not reflect the disappointed expectation that the definitive historical truth is about to be delivered. It reflects some feeling that we may have to work very hard to make sense of the film we are to see; also, that we shall be asked to focus not so much on what happened as on what the imagination is wont to make of the holocaust experience.

This is not an insignificant distinction, and the intelligence that registers the distinction in the opening minutes of the film will find its anticipations throughout unusually tense and uncertain. The film asks us to do several things at once: to compare and contrast what we know of the holocaust with the images projected on the screen—images which are patently fictional but which nonetheless refer unmistakably to real events we are not likely to forget; to think of the intrinsic dynamics of the imagination that contrives to move characters about and arrange events as peculiarly as it does in this film; to set up resistances to our own queasy impulses to reject what we are shown on the grounds that it violates a sombre decorum we take to be appropriate under the circumstances. In thinking about the way we perform these functions — here, as in our responses to many other works of art — we are required to differentiate between the way we ought to perform them, and the way we do perform them. Bettelheim thinks we ought to hold up the given images against the reality of the concentration camps and therefore to reject Wertmuller's images as specious and arbitrary — if *Seven Beauties* wanted to be taken as sheer fiction, it should not have suggested even for a moment that it was telling the historical truth. Also he thinks we ought not to be seriously interested in an imagination for which stacked corpses can as readily stimulate gallows-humor as evoke revulsion. Finally, Bettelheim feels that, far from resisting impulses to reject, we ought to dismiss *Seven Beauties* as a film which degrades and confuses — whatever the aesthetic discriminations we may feel tempted to introduce. Alas, we do not in general respond as we should. Wertmuller's images have a terrible authority which makes it difficult indeed to dismiss them as specious or arbitary. Even in the opening minutes of the film we are gripped by a central fact of human experience which is imposed upon us with ferocious authenticity: the fact that imagination can put to so many uses events which had seemed singular and astonishing almost to the point of numbing the senses which had long before engaged to deal with them. In witnessing *Seven Beauties*, though we may wish to turn away in horror or to cry out, we are persuaded by Wertmuller's invention to hang on, to watch for the trophies that persistent attention can win. Is it possible to laugh at stacked corpses and to do justice to the dead? The question here is almost beside the point. The film makes no pretense to do justice to the dead. Its business is another kind of remembering that has more to do with the dynamics of survival. Perhaps we ought always to think of the dead when we think of the Nazi period. Perhaps some of us are prone to think of little else, and may be blessed for so persisting. But it is a mistake to assume that everyone will be so disposed, or that *Seven Beauties* violates a mode of remembering to which it makes no claim, and to which it is obviously inadequate. If we resist impulses to reject what we are shown, we do so because those impulses are sometimes inflexible and unreliable, because they may inhibit the growth of our humanity as surely as Bettelheim thinks they will preserve and strengthen it.

But what exactly do we mean when we speak of this resistance? The film contains many sequences in which it is called into play. Not much resistance is required in the opening minutes because the presentation of materials there is so very tentative, the tension between image and cabaret song so deliberate that no 'statement' may be adduced, one way or another. If we are disposed to be sickened even by the newsreel footage and the 'improper' uses to which it is put we shall not be able to attend to the rest of the film in a satisfactory way, and there will be no more to consider. But resistance of the sort we have indicated *will* be required frequently afterwards. When the protagonist Pasqualino 'seduces' the monstrous female commandant in order to escape the fate to which others in the concentration camp are sentenced, we experience a revulsion so great that, for a moment, it threatens to swamp our more considered responses to the film. Pasqualino's behavior had been less than edifying in earlier sequences, but by this point, we feel, he has gone too far. The woman is as close to being a monster as we can imagine any human being to come. That Pasqualino should be willing to seduce her, to plead his love to one so fully terrible, in order to save his life, seems, at first, incredible. Why should she believe him? Why should he assume she'll find him appealing? How can a man who's been through so much seem to have learned so little, resorting to the tiresome deception by which men have so regularly sought to master women? Along with sheer physical revulsion at the prospect of a monstrous and unfeeling coupling, we experience a nausea that frequently accompanies an apprehension of the meaningless and incomprehensible. Though Wertmuller has had the effrontery to show us almost anything we can imagine — in *Seven Beauties* as in other films like *Swept Away* and *The Seduction Of Mimi* — we do not believe she will play out the seduction of the camp commandant. What point can possibly be made by pursuing an invention that so strains credulity and the limits of our tolerance?

Wertmuller allows us to resist impulses to reject the ghastly spectacle by detaching us from it and, strangely, by humanizing it. Resistance is an effect of discrimination, and discrimination is made possible by the complicating of an experience which had earlier seemed to offer nothing in the way of an enticing complexity. Revulsion is not so much overcome as, temporarily, held at bay, as the discriminative intelligence registers interesting distinctions between what we are given and what we'd expected. We resist the impulse to dismiss and to turn away because there is something for us in the spectacle, something we may not want to miss. This 'something' is signalled in the marks of Pasqualino's possession by his idea, his stratagem. He is so clearly given over to it, so fully convinced that he must act out his 'inspiration,' that we are almost persuaded he knows what he is doing. It is all thoroughly absurd, more than a little perverse, surely disgusting to think about too closely — but we are disposed progressively to feel that Pasqualino has to do what he has determined to do. We laugh at his overtures to the commandant, enjoy her amazement, anticipate that she may have him castrated and shot—didn't those big, 'sexless' German women go in for sexual butchery? we are apt to muse. Wertmuller detaches us from the spectacle by making us laugh at it and, simultaneously, by making us attend in a progressively disinterested way. We want to discover what it is about Pasqualino that drives him to the absurdity of his seduction-quest. We want to know why Wertmuller finds him so compelling, and how she manages almost to make him as interesting to us. But we know as well that, to the extent that we share this interest in Pasqualino, it is an interest not so much in his particular fate as in the peculiar, abstract depths of human invention. No one imagines that Pasqualino is Wertmuller's everyman, that anyone would be as likely as he to seduce the commandant. But no one will deny that he represents for us a certain kind of possibility to which present circumstances uniquely contribute. This is the possibility that human beings may well identify their humanity, their very sense of the self and of the values that sustain it, with the energy and cunning to remain alive and scamper, perpetually, beyond the outstretched hands of circumstance. If we are detached as we watch *Seven Beauties*, we experience nonetheless a very large interest in the issues raised, an interest we cannot satisfy by rooting for Pasqualino or against him; by passing secure judgments too quickly; or by giving in to the impulse to deny our laughter.

Bettelheim argues that detachment is fruitful only if we are detached from experiences that justify such a response. It is legitimate to conclude, early in the film, that Pasqualino is a relatively worthless person, and that we are therefore not required to feel concern for him. It is not legitimate to achieve detachment from the imagery of stacked corpses—whatever the way in which they are presented—, when to do so is inevitably to harden our responses to the murder of countless Jews. The operant principle here has to do with propriety, and it is not an idea anyone can take lightly. Over and over again, Bettelheim warns his reader that to confuse one mode of presentation with another is to forfeit the capacity to keep things in their rightful place. The comic and the horrible, persistently juxtaposed and intermixed, may make for a certain debased kind of aesthetic delight, but the "combination" will not yield to better purposes. Wertmuller's film, he argues, is a degrading experience because it induces us not to take anything seriously—not even something "that would ordinarily upset us greatly or move us deeply." Talk about detachment all you want, Bettelheim would seem to say. If the result is that the heart is hardened and the intelligence learns to yield too easily to the grotesque and fantastic, no good will come of what we call aesthetic discrimination and disinterestedness.

The problem is that, by failing to resist the impulse to condemn and recoil in sheer disgust, Bettelheim misses the film's invitation to participate in a crucial experience, wherein the dominant perspective is humanized with no corresponding refusal of judgment. This is an unfortunate feature of much self-consciously humanistic thinking. In insisting upon what it knows, it closes itself to all sorts of things it might otherwise have welcomed. To resist a "reflex" judgment is not, after all, to lose the capacity to judge, or to reflect, or to forfeit the right to judge at a later time. No doubt there is a sense in which we can take too much time making up our minds; a sense in which to wait, and split hairs, and search, perpetually, for nuance, is to lose any genuine prospect of moral intensity. But a film like *Seven Beauties*, after all, promises *something* in the way of a judgment. It is a work of art, of determinate length and scope and execution. The film, at least, may be judged, if nothing else, and there is bound to be some release of tension in this. We resist the impulse to judge and dismiss abruptly because we are secure in the knowledge that we shall have something on which to pass judgment later on. The film asks us to put up this necessary resistance by complicating our feelings and by humanizing our perceptions of what is going on. Bettelheim considers this sort of complication a disgrace. By making it difficult for us to know what we feel or, exactly, what we should be looking at, Wertmuller makes us doubt our right to judge. From such confusion, one thing looks much like another, a crime might just as well have been an act of charity, and we are left in a muddle from which nothing in the film will extricate us.

Bettelheim's moral knowledge is based upon a number of truths to which every decent person is supposed to be as devoted as he. Because the film seems to go against the grain of these simple truths. Bettelheim feels, it is clearly a violation of the given and a disservice to the survivors of the holocaust, who know what to make of their experience. Examples:

1—Pasqualino: ". . . charmingly portrayed by Giancarlo Giannini as the prototypical 'little man,' who will be a Fascist under Fascism, a Communist under Communism, and a democrat in a democracy. But this portrait of the little man, which the film makes us believe in, is a lie. The world's little men do not rape or kill—not under Fascism or Communism or in a democracy. These little men do not think of or manage an erection and intercourse with an absolutely abhorrent woman, even if their lives are at stake. The little man is banal, but he is not evil."

2—The Commandant: "The closer she gets to being a woman, the more grotesque this mass of flesh becomes, but also the more human, and the greater depth she reveals, not least because of the way she is acted by Shirley Stoler. She is not only shown imprisoned in her body but shown to feel it and to suffer from it. Her being disgusted by Pasqualino and his lie of loving her—which she, knowing how repulsive she is, does not believe for a moment—is but a small reflection of her disgust with herself . . . When she says that Pasqualino, because he managed an erection, will survive and win in the end, while she is doomed, her dreams unattainable, she implies that, unlike Pasqualino, she is unable to have sex without the appropriate feelings. . . .

. . . But this portrayal of a concentration-camp commander is no less a lie than the portrayal of Pasqualino as a sometimes charming but always utterly unimportant little man. If any one thing characterized the rulers of the concentration camps, it was their inability to reflect on themselves, to see themselves for what they were. Had they been able to recognize themselves as they really were—which the camp commander in this film is shown as being able to do—they could not have carried on for a moment. . . . Somebody with so much insight into herself could not behave toward the prisoners as we see her do."

In the first example, Bettelheim rejects the view of Pasqualino as capable of evil on the scale depicted in *Seven Beauties.* The little man as portrayed by Wertmuller "is a lie." How do we know? Bettelheim seems certain in his declarations on such matters, and assumes we will believe him. If Pasqualino were capable of evil on a grand scale, of indiscriminate killing and rape, he would not be a banal creature. This is the thrust of the argument. It is not, as such, a historical argument; nor is it an enlargement or application of a psychological thesis which has been experimentally validated. The argument is an argument from a body of shared knowledge which is often referred to as our fund of collective wisdom. "Little men do not rape or kill"—the conviction plainly expresses itself, with no hint of qualification or misgiving. Who, then, is responsible for the killing and raping? If not Pasqualino, presumably some other kind of social misfit will be held responsible. This misfit who commits evil deeds, according to Bettelheim, will not be banal. He will have some sense of what he is doing and what it means to do terrible things simply because one has been encouraged or empowered to do them. The evil man will not drift mindlessly into evil deeds, and will not think to defend himself by claiming he could not know how terrible his actions were. He will participate in brutality and terror because he stands to realize something from his participation, and he will know what he wants and how high the price may be. Pasqualino is incapacitated from this kind of participation by virtue of his mindless stumbling about from prospect to prospect with no resolute sense of what he really wants and may actually hope to achieve. He is banal because he is totally subject to the designs of others, and as such he is incapable of the resolve required to perform evil deeds which require a measure of fortitude, determination, even passion.

If I have properly represented Bettelheim's thought — and I do not see how I can have failed to represent it under the circumstances — I have also demonstrated that it is perfectly insupportable. It is a fact that many human beings in a number of European nations participated in brutal activities over a period of many years. That Hitler's programs were carried out by ordinary persons is not a fact anyone is in a position to dispute. It does not matter whether we call these ordinary persons banal or something else. We know what they did, and what they did was evil, if the word 'evil' has any ordinary meaning at all. To kill helpless people, to rape and pillage, is to do evil. Bettelheim argues that it is a slander upon ordinary men and women to show that they may be induced to support or to perform such evil actions. At one point he says he accepts Hannah Arendt's theory of Adolph Eichmann as the very embodiment of banality. But what can it mean to embrace the theory if one does not accept also what follows irrevocably from it? Namely, that banality is a condition to which human beings succumb; that certain cultures nurture in their citizens a complex of attitudes which incline them to deny responsibility for their deeds; and that such persons are to be judged by standards of civilized behavior whether or not they wish to assume responsibility for their actions. In this sense it is clear that banal persons are precisely those who, in our time, will perform evil deeds. Though they may pretend merely to be following orders, or to have acted out of confusion, they will be as capable of evil as though they had earnestly desired to murder Jews in order to steal their shoes or sleep with their daughters. For Bettelheim to deny the possibility of evil to banal little men is to deny that there have been responsible agents performing the many individual acts of brutality which together constitute the experience of the Nazi period.

Why does Bettelheim stake so much on this point? His concern is not really to assert that ordinary persons are fundamentally decent. He knows that any generalization of that kind is bound to seem dubious, at best. His more urgent contention is that Pasqualino, as the prototypical little man, can not have equated survival with the capacity to do terrible things. This is Bettelheim's central concern, to insist over and over again that survival in the Nazi period depended not upon the ability to kill or in other ways to dehumanize oneself, but to keep up one's sense of decency and honor. Though Terence Des Pres* and other scholars of the holocaust have lately argued that survival often meant learning how to "live beyond the compulsions of culture," Bettelheim argues that persons like Pasqualino can not be said to represent the meaning of survivorship. Though some, like Pasqualino, may have reverted to sheer animalism, and may somehow have survived, most who came through the concentration camp experience did so because they were lucky, and because they knew better than to succumb entirely to the examples of monstrous debasement continually held up to them. The portrait of Pasqualino is a lie because it shows him to have survived by virtue of his capacity to do terrible things — things, moreover, such a person cannot have done in light of the banal characteristics attributed to him.

The argument sends us back, as it must, to Wertmuller's film, or at least to what we can recall of it. At once we are compelled to remember that Pasqualino seemed always a peculiar fellow, slippery and outrageous, something of a buffoon, at times a caricature of what we take to be a familiar Italian figure. It is the figure of the Italian male as

*In *The Survivor* (1976).

the genial, simple-minded butt, hung up in the various ways played upon in a succession of popular films and novels. This is not *man*, but a certain kind of man, a certain kind of caricature of the Italian male animal. How do we know this? The opening sequences of the film had invited the viewer to wonder what might become the dominant perspective for an examination of the Nazi period. The peculiar tensions of the opening minutes — produced by a sound-track that seemed to know what it thought only to impress upon everyone the inherent uncertainty and contradiction of its knowledge — are extended to the entire film. The voice that glibly responds with an 'oh yeah' to everything it sees without being able to order its perceptions is the voice that controls the entire film. *Seven Beauties* is a vision of the past and of human possibility under the auspices of a cynicism whose manifest reason for being is the dominating presence of Pasqualino. Again, it is necessary to say, Pasqualino is not *man* — not for Wertmuller, not for the viewer of her film. He is a buffoon, a perennial victim who knows how to save his skin only by adopting the most transparent stratagems customarily available to the type. It never occurs to us to ask whether there is any actual human being who looks and behaves like the type because Pasqualino perfectly embodies what we have always taken the type to be.

Is it unreasonable that such a type should be said to have succeeded in saving his skin? Pasqualino may succeed, but nothing in the film suggests that anyone else would do as well in comparable circumstances. The strokes in Wertmuller's portrait are so broad, the caricature so playful and outrageously implausible, that no general conclusion may legitimately be drawn. We said earlier that the film asks us to focus "not so much on what happened as on what the imagination is wont to make of the holocaust experience." An imagination for which Pasqualino is a dominating presence is likely to be cynical in the extreme about the human truths revealed in the Nazi period. Who is to say, finally, what it takes to survive in a concentration camp? Surely Bettelheim understands that no program or strategy for survival was likely to be effective. Wertmuller's view is that while 'better men' perished, a man like Pasqualino might well have remained alive — not because he'd discovered a clever stratagem, but because he happened to be lucky. The film nowhere 'supports' Pasqualino or makes general claims for his shrewdness. On the contrary, he is ruthlessly exposed. We feel that he is detestable even as we want him to succeed in seducing the camp commander and saving his skin. When, finally, he shoots a fellow prisoner, he behaves only as we would expect him to under the circumstances. There is no use in denying that such a man might well do such a thing. Better men did worse things under pressure.

Bettelheim is surely mistaken in arguing that the film elaborates a morality of survivorship. There is nothing exemplary in Pasqualino's success, nothing anyone is encouraged to emulate. Wertmuller simply imposes upon us, with all the imaginative power at her command, an image we are not likely to forget. Though Pasqualino is not *man*, he is a figure of whom it is necessary to take stock when we think about our prospects and calculate the options. The imagination which cannot deal with Pasqualino, which cannot believe that he exists, does not know a very important part of the human condition. It may be that the type is overdrawn in Wertmuller's film; indeed, the elements of patent caricature and burlesque in the portrait encourage the view that Wertmuller deliberately exaggerated the features to provoke us and to indicate what were her major concerns. These have to do with the enlargement of imaginative potential, according to which it is possible to feel involved in Pasqualino's fate without capitulating to his view of the truth of things. Wertmuller's film succeeds precisely where Bettelheim thinks it fails: in its vivid distortions, in its strange conjunctions and grotesqueries, *Seven Beauties* compels a disinterested apprehension of issues. These are not primarily issues of historical fact but of imaginative resource: what, we consider, can the imagination do with the spectre of terror and banality acted out on a scale no one had previously imagined?

Bettelheim rejects not only the portrait of Pasqualino, but of the camp commander as well. The one is "no less a lie" than the other. Though the role is persuasively enacted by Shirley Stoler, though the viewer is led to "believe" in the character, she is a palpable untruth. This camp commander appears to know herself and to understand what makes other human beings behave as they do. In reality, camp commanders were nothing like this, Bettelheim argues. "Had they been able to recognize themselves as they really were . . . . they could not have carried on for a moment . . . . Somebody with so much insight into herself could not behave toward the prisoners as we see her do." This is one of those arguments it is difficult to win, whatever side you take. If you argue from experience, claiming that there are actual persons full of insight who nonetheless go right on doing terrible things, you will be told that such persons only *seem* to be in possession of the insights they display. Just so, in the film, it is Wertmuller's dexterous manipulation of images that makes the camp commander *seem* plausible. The director's 'success' is a form of trickery, and we are duped because we do not know how to resist this kind of deception.

But Bettelheim's side of the argument is no easier to defend. It may be logical to suppose that someone capable of speaking seriously to herself about dehumanization would consequently wish to avoid dehumanizing others and so degrading herself. It is not therefore unlikely that this person will do what she despises and deliberately enact what others already take her to be. The logic of Bettelheim's argument is limited. It has very little to do with the peculiar logic of imagination, according to which truth and contradiction are often indistinguishable. Wertmuller might justly be attacked had she simply yielded to this peculiar logic, but she doesn't. She works at it, strenuously, and finds over and over again that her general suspicion of easy humanistic truths will not be dislodged. She remains cynical and resolutely disabused, largely because she is stuck with the figure of Pasqualino. If he is decidedly a part of *the thing itself*, what can his final antagonist be but a defiantly improbable and all too believable character? The working logic of *Seven Beauties* insists that the improbable is as potentially true to our experience of life as the probable. This has only marginally to do with the familiar notion of the absurd as a determinative factor in our experience. Wertmuller doesn't incline to make broad metaphysical statements. She is intent on following out a number of broad imaginative paths laid out by her involvement with certain kinds of human beings. These figures are, in her films, as likely to work in a factory as to be swept away on a desert island or to find themselves in a concentration camp. To think the portrait of the camp commander a lie is to reject the kind of imagination for which particular kinds of conflict and paradox are both interesting and important. There is nothing in *Seven Beauties* to prompt so determined a rejection.

But let us return, for a moment, to the question of historical truth. Suppose it was true that camp commanders were not persons of considerable depth, and that it was possible to prove this to anyone's satisfaction. Would Wertmuller's portrait be therefore less 'true,' less believable than it is? The circumstance as described here is so hypothetical that we are hard put to answer, but we must try. If Wertmuller's character ran counter to everything we know of camp commanders, we should naturally have greater difficulty in believing what we are shown. We should not readily be made to believe in a camp commander who did his best to save the lives of Jews and worked to make other Nazi camp officers cooperate in the effort to prevent destruction. No more can we believe in a camp commander who is nothing but a blundering fool, an idiot who is regularly taken advantage of by inmates and other officers. When we think of qualities of personal depth and insight, however, we are on more treacherous ground. Even if someone had proven beyond the shadow of a doubt that no camp commander possessed such qualities, we might well be induced to entertain further doubts. So vivid a portrait as Wertmuller draws would surely have a chance of shaking our faith in the efficacy of instruments used to test for personal qualities. We would, at least, suspend our disbelief in the possibility of an insightful camp commander. And this suspension of disbelief might well continue for the duration of the film —for so long as we continued to feel that issues raised and conflicts played out had something useful and entertaining to recommend them. Which is to say, the historical truth of the matter is only important to us when the context is such that we have been made to expect that kind of truth. Otherwise we are likely to be tolerant of 'violations' and to look for other truths the film may better get at.

Bettelheim assumes that *Seven Beauties* is an example of what we have called, following John Lukacs, cinematized history. It is nothing of the sort. It is a political film; it adumbrates political issues and asks political questions it does not feel required to answer. Like other works of this kind, it refuses to be held responsible for espousing correct positions. Its responsibility is to make us alert to problems it takes to be important, and to trace out the implications of various positions in a reasonably consistent way. It has room for considerable improbability and contradiction, provided only that primary expectations are not wantonly or cruelly violated. History is more than a background used to give depth to character, but it is not an end in itself. At most, history is that circumstance within which political conflicts work themselves out, and in which characters achieve usable designations. Without such 'history' as is furnished us in a film like *Seven Beauties*, we can distinguish victims from oppressors only by observing what they do. We need to know as well what characters are supposed to be, what 'the record' has made of them. The early newsreel footage of the film indicates amply what we are to make of 'the record'; it can say ever so many different things depending on the predisposition we bring to it. Individual acts of brutality or cowardice are more difficult to get around. For Wertmuller, history is an uncertain domain within which we learn to fix particular acts and possibilities whose shape and meaning we both create and, in part, inherit. Politics, in a work for which history is more than background and less than determinate documentary fact, has to do with the problematic bringing to consciousness of social processes which for some persons always remain obscure and impenetrable. *Seven Beauties* is a political film in virtue of its persistent probing of the great social questions, in such a way that these questions come to seem unavoidable for each of us. Its use of history is instrumental to this end.

We have concluded that *Seven Beauties* is a political film. Is it possible to say what are its politics? Insofar as we can tell, it elaborates no consistent ideological position. It has its fixed interests, its dominant characters and conflicts, and it seems to make a number of points, to which Bettelheim, for one, attaches great importance. The most important of these points Bettelheim in fact takes to be the theme of the film:that there is no real difference between the world of the camps and the world beyond; that, since men behave badly, one way or another, they are never likely to resist the programs to which the Nazis and Fascists of this world will subject them; and that, finally, one contemporary political system is roughly equivalent to another. Whichever way you look, man being what he is, evil triumphs—the good being too weak to realize their decent ambitions. Is this what Wertmuller intended to convey? If she did not, and we do indeed take this to be the theme of her film, we are likely to agree with the film's critics who argue that it is at best confusing and irresponsible. For to suggest that those who 'liberated' the camps were no better than those who operated them is to fly in the face of everything we have ever thought to be true and certain. It is, moreover, to challenge the very possibility of a genuine politics, which depends, at least, on a capacity to make elementary distinctions.

What did Wertmuller wish to convey? It is true that the post-War Italian world, of which we are given a brief if fevered glimpse, is thoroughly unattractive; true, moreover, that the occupation troops (Americans!) have made it profitable even for otherwise 'good girls' to become whores. Bettelheim concludes that in these terms we may as well be back in the concentration camps—this, he argues, is the 'message' Wertmuller inevitably conveys. When the 'liberated' Pasqualino at film's end describes the future as a fight of all against all, he is articulating the film's final message, which is that there is nothing we can do with the evil all about us.

If Wertmuller had wished to convey this message, though, she would have had to do better than to express it in the words of Pasqualino. Everything we have witnessed in *Seven Beauties* inclines us to feel that Pasqualino is a degraded, albeit a pathetic and sometimes grotesquely funny, human being. His prediction of the war of all against all, which he has heard from someone else, is a pitiful reflection of his degraded conception of himself and of the utter impoverishment of his imagination. *Seven Beauties* stays with Pasqualino to the bitter end because it is he who stands in the way of any hopeful or purely humane exposition of our resources. If there is to be a politics worthy of our hope, Wertmuller suggests, it will have somehow to deal with this man, as Louis Malle knew we would have finally to come to terms with Lucien Lacombe. They are not really as different as they may seem, whatever the differences in their presentation.

For Wertmuller, again, we are to dwell not on what happened in the camps, but on what the political imagination is wont to make of our experience. In the figure of Pasqualino, we see what submission to brute fact amounts to. In his general yielding to the ongoing reality of his time, to what others reductively take to be the facts of life, Pasqualino indicates the failure of imagination to conceive possibility in human terms. The cynicism of Wertmuller's film is a reflection of its focus on this particular character and on the absence of hope to which he inevitably points. The politics of the film are no more than implicit, but not less actual for being so. In its elaborated critique of Pasqualino, in the sense it conveys of his debasement, and in the sense of relief we experience in the daylight world beyond the camp—whatever its modestly infernal dimension—,*Seven Beauties* gestures towards a politics that will reclaim the imagination of camp-survival for better purposes. Not survival merely, but a decent survival is what the film encourages us to think about and to want. By challenging us to reject Pasqualino, to discover a perspective from which it is possible to put him in his place, *Seven Beauties* asks us to conceive a politics that is more than a cynical resignation to a limited view of fact. In its energy and cunning, the film addresses the difficulty—but not the utter bleakness—of alternatives. Simply because it does not elaborate these alternatives is no reason to suppose it cannot put us in mind of our need to imagine them, and of the terms in which they will need to present themselves.

PART TWO

Literature and Literary Theory

Institutional Control of Interpretation

BY FRANK KERMODE

A very large number of people, of whom I am one, conceive of themselves as interpreters of texts. Whoever expounds a text (no matter at what level) and whoever castigates a text, is an interpreter. And no such person can go about the work of interpretation without some awareness of forces which limit, or try to limit, what he may say, and the ways in which he may say it. They may originate in the past, but will usually be felt as sanctions operated by one's contemporaries (this will be true whether or not one opposes and resents them). There is an organisation of opinion which may either facilitate or inhibit the individual's manner of doing interpretation, which will prescribe what may legitimately be subjected to intensive interpretative scrutiny, and determine whether a particular act of interpretation will be regarded as a success or a failure, be taken into account in licit future interpretation or not. The medium of these pressures and interventions is the institution.

In practice, the institution with which we have to deal is the professional community which interprets secular literature and teaches others to do so. There are better-defined and more despotic institutions, but their existence does not invalidate the present use of the expression. If we wanted to describe its actual social existence we should get involved in a complex account of its concrete manifestations in universities, colleges, associations of higher learning; and if we wanted to define its authority we should have to consider not only its statutory right to confer degrees and the like, but also the subtler forms of authority acquired and exercised by its senior and more gifted members. But we need not at present bother with these details. It can surely be agreed that we are talking about something quite easily identified: a professional community which has authority (not undisputed) to define (or indicate the limits of) a subject; to impose valuations and validate interpretations. Such are its characteristics. It has complex relations with other institutions. In so far as it has, undeniably, a political aspect, it trespasses on the world of power; but of itself, we will agree, it has little power, if by that one means power to bind and loose, to enforce compliance and anathematize deviation. Compared with other institutions, that is, the one we are talking about is a rather weak one. But it has none the less a family resemblance to the others.

Such a community may be described as a self-perpetuating, sempiternal corporation. It is, however unemphatically, however modestly, hierarchical in structure, because its continuance depends on the right of the old to instruct the young; the young submit because there is no other way to the succession. The old, or senior, apply at their discretion certain checks on the competence of those who seek to join, and eventually replace them. Their right to do this is accompanied by an assumption that they possess a degree of competence, partly tacit, partly a matter of techniques which may be examined and learnt; that one has acquired these latter is of course a claim that can be straightforwardly tested, but the possession of interpretative power, power of divination, is tested only by reference to the tacit knowledge of the seniors, who nevertheless claim, tacitly as a rule, that they can select candidates capable of acquiring these skills, and have the right to certify that they have achieved them. I am describing the world as it is or as we all know it, and am doing so only because its familiarity may have come to conceal from us its mode of operation.

The texts on which members of this institution practice their trade are not secret (though some of them are in practice inaccessible to the uninitiated) and the laity has, in principle, full access to them. But although the laity may, unaided or helped only by secondary or sub-institutional instruction (radio talks, Sunday newspapers, reading groups or literary clubs) acquire what in some circumstances might pass for competence, there is a necessary difference between them and persons whom we may think of as licensed practitioners. It is as if the latter were "in orders". Their right to practice is indicated by arbitrary signs, not only certificates, robes and titles, but also professional jargons. The activities of such persons, whether diagnostic or exegetical, are privileged, and they have access to senses that do not declare themselves to the laity. Moreover they are subject, in professional matters, to no censure but that of other licensed practitioners acting as a body; the opinion of the laity is of no consequence whatever, a state of affairs which did not exist before the institution now under consideration firmly established itself—as anyone may see by looking with a layman's eye on the prose its members habitually write, and comparing it with the prose of critics who still thought of themselves as writing for an educated general public, for *la cour et la ville*.

However, my concern here is to explore a little further the means by which the institution controls the exegetical activities of its members. Though it does so in part by fairly obvious means—for example, it controls the formation and the subsequent career of its members (who decides whether one is to have one's Ph.D?)—it has subtler resources, such as *canonical* and *hermeneutic* restrictions, and these are more interesting. By the first of these expressions I mean the determination of what may or ought to be interpreted, and by the second the decision as to whether a particular means of doing so is permissible. Of course canons change, especially in a "weak" institution; and so do styles of interpretation. How these changes occur is another part of my subject, and a subdivision of that part is the question of heresy.

I first considered these matters in a very brief essay written in 1974,[1] and I must ask leave to give a summary of what I said. The question was, how do we know an interpretation is wrong? We claim this knowledge, obviously; if a student in reading "my love is fair / As any she belied with false compare" construes "she" as a personal pronoun and not as a noun we have no compunction about saying he is wrong; though if William Empson said the "wrong" sense was present, as an instance of one or other (fourth to seventh) type of ambiguity (a "verbal nuance . . . which gives room for alternative reactions to the same piece of language") most of us would be less ready with our pencils. I.A. Richards, who did so much to encourage liberty of interpretation, has always been exercised as to the moment when this liberty becomes licence; he deplores people who have no sense "of what is and is not admissible in interpretation," and sees in some of Roman Jakobson's work means by which poetry may be defended against such "omnipossibilists". Yet it seems clear that the necessary decisions are rarely if ever arrived at methodically. What happens is rather that the institution requires interpretations to satisfy its tacit knowledge of the permitted range of sense; the requirement operates very simply when the disputed interpretation is the work of a novice, and may be harder or even, in the long run impossible, to apply if the author is known to be competent—one reason why the institutional consensus changes. But there clearly is a sense in which a professional body *knows*; how it does so was a preoccupation of Michael Polanyi's. There is an institutionalised competence, and what it finds unacceptable is incompetent. It does not, as a rule, have to think hard about individual cases—Polanyi gives amusing examples of the application of this tacit knowledge to scientific contributions which have every appearance of soundness but arrive at conclusions *known* to be impossible. Of course

1 *Art, Politics and Will: Essays in Honor of Lionel Trilling*, ed. Q. Anderson, S. Donadio and S. Marcus (New York, 1977), pp. 159-172.

there is no guarantee that this tacit knowledge is infallible; it is founded on the set of assumptions currently available—the paradigm, if you like, or, if you like, the *epistème*, and a revolution may change everything. Mendel is a famous instance; but such instances may be harder to come by outside the physical sciences. I cited Walter Whiter, and some lesser Shakespearian examples. But the immediate point is simply that it is upon the basis of a corpus of tacit knowledge, shared—with whatever qualifications—by the senior ranks of the hierarchy, that we allow or disallow an interpretation.

There is nothing astonishing about this conclusion, which might even be regarded as trite by members of other institutions no less quarrelsome though possibly more self-conscious than our own. In the psychoanalytic community, we are told, "the experience of insight results from the construction of a perspective most satisfying to the present communal initiative".[2] That is, what is found is the sort of thing it is agreed we ought to be looking for. True interpretation is, in fact, what Jürgen Habermas calls it: "a consensus among partners."[3] How else shall we judge its truth? Yet we should not altogether omit to mention that the institution also values originality; if there is agreement that some contribution has the force to modify or even transform what was formerly agreed, then that contribution is honored and may become the staple of a new pattern of consensus. Yet even such rare and revolutionary departures depend upon the consent of the hierarchy.

Of institutions having a primary duty to interpret texts, and to nominate a certain body of texts as deserving or requiring repeated exegesis (interminable exegesis, indeed) the Church is the most exemplary. Self-perpetuating, hierarchical, authoritative, much concerned with questions of canon, and wont, as we are, to distinguish sharply between initiate and uninitiate readings, it is a model we would do well to consider as we attempt to understand our own practice.

It is, of course, difficult to make such brief generalizations stick, and the Church has been prone to fission on precisely the issues I am discussing: authority, hierarchy, canon, initiation, and differential readings. But if it has something to teach us we must do what we can to overcome this difficulty. Let us first consider the canon. The word means "rod" or "rule" or "measure" and we all know, roughly, how it applies to the Old and New Testaments, or to Shakespeare: *Hamlet* belongs to the canon, *The Yorkshire Tragedy* to the Apocrypha, *Two Noble Kinsmen* is still among the latter, but many think it should belong to the former. Apocrypha meant "hidden ones", but came to mean

2 David Bleich, "The Logic of Interpretation," *Genre* 10 (Fall, 1977), p. 384.
3 *Knowledge and Human Interests.*

"spurious ones", and now just means "uncanonical ones". The canon possesses an authenticity which the Apocrypha lack. But to say in what that authenticity resided or resides is a very complicated matter.

The canon seems to have begun to crystallize in reaction against an heretical attempt to impose a rigorously restricted list of sacred books on the church of the mid-second century. Marcion rejected the whole of the Old Testament, accepted one gospel (Luke, much reduced) and added ten purged versions of Pauline letters to complete the canon. Marcion's canon may remind us at once of some rigoristic attempts (Leavis, Winters) to purge our own. He certainly knew what he wanted. In abolishing the Old Testament he was acting on a belief that its types and prophecies were false. This was a bold way of solving a difficulty of the early church. The establishment of a narrow canon eliminated, among other awkwardness, the problem of the status of the Old Testament. The first Christians had no scripture except the Old Testament, but as the Law ceased to be of prime importance to them their relation to it grew problematical; rejecting the agnostic rejection, they instituted a new way of reading it, as a repertory of types prefiguring Christianity. In so doing they virtually destroyed its value as history or as law; it became a set of scattered indications of events it did not itself report. But the correspondences between what was to be the New Testament and the Old were very important, since they were held to validate the Christian version. Marcion thought the Old Testament wrong and wicked, and he accepted the conclusion that Christianity up to his time had been erroneous, the true words of the founder adulterated.[4]

Marcion was certain that he knew what the original tradition was in its purity; he is the first in a long line of protestant reformers who enjoyed the same assurance. The magnitude of the crisis he brought upon the church is well described by Von Campenhausen. And he was for a time very successful. His was the first canon. The counter-offensive had to include the provision of a canon more acceptable to the consensus of the church. There is much dispute about the criteria employed. The Old Testament was defended, and out of a mass of gospels four were chosen as "authentic" (the rejected included of course Marcion's). All this took time; and the idea of closing the canon took more time, and was prompted by the threat of another heresy, namely Montanism, which used innumerable apocalyptic books. Thus was the canon achieved; and eventually the habit grew of thinking of it as two books, or two parts of one total, comprehensive book.

4 See Hans von Campenhausen, *The Formation of the Christian Bible*, trans. J.A. Baker (Philadelphia 1977 (1972)), pp. 147 ff.

Later came further benefits. For at various moments the institution, protecting its text, conferred upon it the virtues of apostolicity, infallibility, inexhaustibility and inspiration. Indeed, it took centuries of scholarly research and dispute to reach the point where the text was believed to possess all these qualities; the canon was not finally closed, even for Roman Catholics, till the Council of Trent, in 1546, when it was also pronounced equally authoritative in all its parts. The Lutheran tradition opposes this doctrine still. It is among Protestant theologians that one notes a tendency at present to re-open the canon - and perhaps admit the Gospel of St. Thomas, discovered at Nag Hammadi in 1945.[5]

This brief allusion to the history of the canon is meant simply to demonstrate the nature of the operations conducted by the institution which formulates and protects it, and the close relation between the character of an institution and the needs it satisfies by validating texts and interpretations of them. The desire to have a canon, more or less unchanging, and to protect it against charges of inauthenticity or low value (as the Church protected Hebrews, for example, against Luther) is an aspect of the necessary conservatism of a learned institution. An interesting example of this conservatism is the history of Erasmus' edition of the Greek New Testament, which was for three centuries the *textus receptus*. Erasmus hardly began the editorial job, even in terms of the manuscripts and editorial techniques then available; for some parts of the book he had no Greek text at all, and himself translated it from the Latin. His errors were obvious enough, but his successors dared not alter his text, reprinting the mistakes and putting the better readings in the notes. So it remained until Lachmann; and the vast editorial effort which he began still goes on. The institution had its own sources of truth, and purposes best served by claims of inerrancy, even in a text that could not (like vernacular translation) seduce the unlearned, or free interpretation from the control of Tradition held to be more authoritative even than the text itself.

It is obvious that control of interpretation is intimately connected with the valuations set upon texts. The decision as to canonicity depends upon a consensus that a book has the requisite qualities, the determination of which is, in part, a work of interpretation. And once a work becomes canonical the work of the interpreter begins again. For example, so long as the institution, assuming inerrancy, desires to minimize the contradictions and redundancies of the gospels, a main object of interpretation must be the achievement of harmony—"the

5 See David L. Dungan, "The New Testament Canon in Recent Study," *Interpretation*, 29 (1975), pp. 339-51; Albert C. Sundberg, "The Bible Canon and the Christian Doctrine of Inspiration," *Interpretation* 29 (1975), pp. 352-71.

concord of the canonical scriptures," as Augustine proclaims it in *The City of God*. There is a very long lapse of time between the first known "harmony" and the first known "synopsis," made in the nineteenth century under a new impulse to explain rather than explain away the discrepancies. They had been noted from the earliest times, and either elided (as in the *Diatessaron* of Tatian) or discounted (as by Origen and Augustine). Scrutiny of the gospels never ceased to be intense; but the attention they got was controlled by the desire of the institution to justify them as they were and find them harmonious; until, in the long course of time and under the pressure of changes in the general culture, a more secular form of attention prevailed.

The acceptance within the institution of the position that there is no separate discipline of sacred hermeneutics was very slow and is still incomplete. But one thing is true, whatever the measure of secularization achieved: at all stages the interpretation of the scriptures is primarily the task of professionals. The position that they are openly available to all men, yet in an important sense closed to everybody except approved institutional interpreters has been maintained from the beginning (in Mark, 4: 11) and is far from fully eroded. The work of the early interpreters was intended not only to establish harmonies between canonised texts, but also to elicit senses not available to persons of ordinary perceptions. Interpretation of the Old Testament was required to deal with its peculiar relation to the new established faith, to make it part, as Clement said, of the "symphony of senses".[6] Whatever seemed not to suit the institution's requirements had to be glossed into conformity. Gaps which opened between the apparent literal sense and the sense acceptable to doctrine or later-established custom had to be filled by interpretations, usually typological or allegorical. And always there were the secret senses, protected by the institution itself. At first these were oral, part of a tradition for which the institution was responsible; later there might be two texts, one generally available, the other reserved for initiates. And even of the public text there might be private interpretations. The Roman Catholic Church preserved at Trent (and I suppose in theory continues to preserve, though restrictions on Catholic exegetes have been much reduced) the position that it alone has the right, in the light of tradition, to determine interpretation. It was at Trent —in violent reaction against the enemy's bibliocentrism—that the inutility of scripture was seriously proposed; for since scripture was always subject to the superior traditional knowledge of the Church, it could be called redundant and, in the hands of ignorant outsiders, a source of error.

6 Quoted by Von Campenhausen, p.304.

Yet despite the success of protestants in contesting this institutional position, and despite the availability of the texts to a laity of much increased literacy, the interpretation of the works of the canon continued to be the duty of the clergy. Between the layman reading his bible and the modern exegete disintegrating the Pauline epistles or performing newly-validated hermeneutic operations—form-criticism, redaction-criticism, structuralist criticism—on the texts, there is as great a gulf as ever. The extent of it can be judged by anybody who looks at a modern gospel commentary written for professionals with one written for laymen—say, the Cambridge commentaries on the Greek New Testament, and the Cambridge commentaries on the New English Bible. The difference is astonishing, and cannot be explained in terms of the relative inaccessibility of the Greek text; the nature of the discussion is wholly altered.

It is clear, then, that there is, in the canonical texts, a reserve of privileged senses which are accessible only to people who in some measure have the kind of training, and are supported by the authority, of the learned institution to which they belong. And even in the most disinterested forms of interpretation—those which depend on historical enquiry or editorial techniques—there is, practically always, some effect from a prior doctrinal commitment. The practitioners believe, that is, in the religion whose doctors have instructed them in scholarship. This is not in the least surprising, but its obviousness ought not to prevent our taking it into account. It is a very important aspect of the sociology of interpretation. There are senses beyond the literal; but to divine them one needs to know where they are, how they relate to doctrine more broadly defined, and how it is permissible to attain them. Changes occur, certainly; a very radical change began in the late eighteenth century, and we have still not seen the last effects of it. For though they occur, they are slow and complicated; and they are attended by comparable changes in the institution itself, some of them signalled by public announcement and demonstration, as in Vatican II, some of them less obvious. A neat instance of the relation between the desires of the institution and the kinds of interpretation undertaken is this: after Leo XIII proposed the philosophy of St. Thomas Aquinas as a subject of neglected importance, there was a neo-scholastic revival. After Vatican II Catholic scholars acquired a new freedom in exegesis; disciplinary threats removed or diminished, they were able to do the kind of speculative research and commentary that had been largely forbidden them, so that modern biblical scholarship had been overwhelmingly non-Catholic. Of course we should remember that changes in different parts of the institution occur at very different speeds; the new liberty of Catholic scholarship is one thing; the fact that there are in the modern world many fundamentalisms, some merely popular but others belonging to highly organised institutions with control over interpretation, is another.

To labour the matter no further, let me turn to the literary institution and its canon. The points of comparison are that like its senior, though much less effectively, it controls the choice of canonical texts, limits their interpretation, and attends to the training of those who will inherit the presumption of institutional competence by which these sanctions are applied.

Can one really speak of a canon of literary-academic studies? It has perhaps grown a little more difficult to do so, but I think the answer is still yes. The only serious attempt at a description of its formation is, so far as I know, the sixteen-page essay by E.R. Curtius in his *European Literature in the Latin Middle Ages.*[7] Curtius shows that the ecclesiastical canon grew in importance, not only as a measure of the sacred writings, but also in the liturgical and juristic activities of the institution. So there was a canon of Fathers, a canon of Doctors; the notion that there was a set scheme for everything took hold. The medieval schools evolved a blend of pagan and Christian authors which also became canonical. It changed between the Middle Ages and the Renaissance, and it has changed again since then. The Renaissance also saw the first vernacular canon, which was Italian; other vernaculars followed suit, the French in the seventeenth, the English in the eighteenth centuries. I suppose we could say that the American canon is a formation of the present century. Curtius is somewhat impatient with these nationalistic canon-formations, and wants a canon of world literature which will put an end to such local conceptions.

The formation of a secular world canon is, however, outside the scope of existing institutions; the success of "comparative literature" in the academic world has been real but limited, partly because it does not work easily within the bureaucratic systems that give force to institutional decisions. The interest of Curtius' valuable and learned but inconclusive essay lies in his understanding of the fact that the relation between a canon and the historical situation of the institution which establishes it is close and complex; and he gives some support to the view that the formation and control of the secular canon we are now considering are historically related as well as analogous to those of the Church.

7 translated by Willard R. Trask, 1963 [1953], pp. 256 ff.

Of course we must not look, in an institution which lacks formal creeds and has no conceivable right to discipline a laity, for anything resembling that ecclesiastical rigor of which Trent is the image. The canon we are now discussing will necessarily be a more shadowy affair, even more subject to dispute than the ecclesiastic. The contenders for inclusion, and the apocrypha, will be more numerous, and it is impossible for us to settle the question by burning either the books or those who support their claim to inclusion.

Our institution is relatively new, and it is not so long since the question of the canon was simpler. It was defined, in a manner familiar to us from ecclesiastical history, by attacks upon it, which usually included moves to replace some member of the canon with another brought in from outside it. When did Donne become canonical? With Grierson's edition? Not quite; probably only with Eliot's essay of 1921, or even later, when that essay (itself a very late move in a campaign which had been going on intermittently for the best part of a century) gained academic support. Eliot was very much a canonist; the argument of "Tradition and the Individual Talent" presupposes a canon, though one to which works can be added in a timeless mix, the new affecting the sense of the old, much as the New Testament altered the sense of the Old.

As everybody knows, the accession of Donne was the cause of major alterations in the canon, or at any rate of attempts to change it radically. For example, the doctrinal changes which enabled that accession also implied a new valuation or even the extrusion of Milton, not to speak of the rewriting of the history of poetry in accordance with the law of the Dissociation of Sensibility. I myself was taught by enthusiasts who believed that Milton had been "dislodged," to use Dr. Leavis's celebrated word for it. The Chinese Wall had been outflanked. This movement began outside the academy, but was taken up within it. In the long run Milton stayed in; but great changes in the method of interpreting his texts became necessary, as anybody can see who compares the Miltonists of the early part of the century with those now dominant—say M.Y. Hughes with Stanley Fish, or Walter Raleigh with Christopher Ricks, whose book on Milton is indeed a splendid example of the ways in which a need to defend a canonical author may call forth new critical and exegetical resources. Meanwhile the motives of the anti-Miltonists were scrutinized with hostility.

Sociologists of religion tell us that institutions react, broadly, in two ways to threats from outside. Either they "legitimate" the new doctrine or text (the reception of Donne) or they "nihilate" it (the defeat of the attempt to dislodge Milton). In our institution the first of these is the more usual course, partly because of a relative lack of power, partly because of a looseness of organization, and partly because the tradition in which we work is predominantly Protestant. There is a measure of tolerance in all that we do. What we value most in work submitted to us by those who would like to join us is an originality that remains close to the consensual norms. Moreover we are, in general, inclined to pluralism and none too systematic, as scholars who take method seriously are often willing to tell us. And yet there is some rigor somewhere in the institution.

If you look at any M.L.A. December program you will see what looks like total license in regard to canon, or, to put that more liberally, an openness to innovation, a willingness to respond to legitimate pressures from the (political) world outside. There are sessions on Black literature, on neglected women writers, and the like; there are also discussions of relatively avant-garde critical and theoretical movements which have certainly not won their appeal to the senior consensus. On the other hand, the M.L.A. Bibliography shows a solid concentration of interpretative effort on the canonical figures. One concludes that here, as with the national and regional variations of canon that everybody is aware of, we have evidence of the ability of the institution to control marginal innovation and unrest. A few years ago the M.L.A. suffered something that looked for a moment like a revolution; but it was only a saturnalian interlude (appropriate to the season of their meeting), an episode of Misrule, tolerated because in the end reinforcing the stability of the institution. The boy bishops had their day, and the more usual, more authentically prelatical figures have resumed their places. We can tolerate even those who believe the institution should be destroyed. As Thoreau remarked, "They speak of moving society but have no resting place without it."

I have digressed from the question of our canon to speak of the forces within the institution which operate to change it, usually slowly. Over a period we can see marked differences. When I was a student nobody taught Dickens; we can trace his acceptance (in England, anyway) by the stages of Dr. Leavis's slow change of mind (he is the Marcion of the canon, unless that role is reserved for Yvor Winters). Few of my teachers even mentioned George Eliot. Blake hovered on the canonical margin, Joyce was still an outsider, though we read him. At Oxford all these problems were simplified somewhat by the decree that studiable, judgeable literature came to an end in 1830; nothing after that was licensed for exegesis.

How do changes in the canon occur? They usually depend on the penetration of the academy by enthusiastic movements from without. This is not always so; for example, there seems to be in progress at the moment an academic evaluation of early American literature; Cotton Mather is suddenly full of interest, Charles Brockden Brown is readable and capable of interpretation. But however the changes originate, there seems to be a law which says that the institution must validate texts before they are licensed for professional exegesis. After that there seems to be no limit, the exegetical progress is interminable. *Ulysses* is a good instance of this; a more remarkable one is Melville, ignored for sixty years or more and now fully canonical and endlessly explicated. George Eliot is another interesting case. The laity had probably gone on reading her, as it went on reading Dickens; but only lately, in my own time, has she become the subject of an apparently infinite series of interpretations, which are of quite a different kind from those which for years served as standard, say those of Leslie Stephen and Henry James.

Licensed for exegesis: such is the seal we place upon our canonical works. How do we license the exegesis itself? The intrusion of new work into the canon usually involves some change in the common wisdom of the institution as to permissible hermeneutic procedures. Thus the admission to American faculties of New Critics from outside the academy was a complex phenomenon, involving a quasi-political victory over the older philologists, a change in the canon (acceptance of Donne, Eliot, etc.) and a new hermeneutic, popularised by Brooks and Warren, and formalised by Wimsatt. The more evangelical success of Leavis resulted in the penetration of the English system of literary education by his followers; at the pastoral level they are still, probably, the most powerful teachers of reading in the country, and their moralistic contempt for non-believers—the unargued certitudes of the conventicle, the easy sneers of the epigoni—still makes its lamentable contribution to the tone of English literary debate. They hold to a rigorous canon (the line of wit, the great tradition, the wheelwright's shop) into which, from time to time, there are furtive insertions (Dickens, Tolstoi), uneasy candidatures (Emily Brontë), apocryphal appendices (L.H. Myers, Ronald Bottrall, Hawthorne).

From the institutional point of view the New Criticism and *Scrutiny* were (and still are) pretty successful heresies. They revised the canon and they changed the methods. The people initiated into reading by the institution began to read differently. Other attempts to alter canon and doctrine—those of Winters, Pound, James Reeves—had markedly less success. But we are now observing the progress of what may be more radical heresy. Unlike the theologians, we are not good at finding distinctive names for hermeneutic fashions; this is another New Criticism, or *nouvelle critique*, though it has moved a long way on from the French innovations of the sixties. The revival of Russian Formalism, the development of a new semiology, a new Marxism, a new psychoanalysis, a new post-Heideggerian anti-metaphysics, with new forms of cultural history—all the developments we associate with such names as Barthes, Lacan, Derrida, Foucault—have had some success within the institution, and may have more. A certain ideological fervour accompanies these manifestations, and they undoubtedly alter the shape of institutional interests in interpretation. Indeed they are avowedly subversive. They alter the limits of the subject, propose new views of history, institutions and meaning. This is not the place to enter into discussion of the validity of such new doctrine; I should, to keep within the boundaries of my topic, merely ask how we may expect the institution to contain or control it.

The fact that interpretation, under these new auspices, has a different sociology is not, in the end, subversive at all; it was probably necessary to move away from the aesthetic or iconic mode in which we spent a generation, and to view literary texts as texts among texts, all perhaps requiring "deconstructive" interpretation to give them another span of life. Certain kinds of literature, what the Germans call *kleinliteratur*, or "trivial literature," and also film, are accommodated in a sort of deuterocanonical sense. The institution, by hierarchical consensus, will try to protect itself against barbarism, but it will do so by control of appointments and promotions more than by working on the canon. For there is a risk that new hermeneutic procedures can be taken up by people interested only in new procedures, methodological mimics whose gestures seem empty, and who care nothing for any canon. They will have to be controlled in some other way. The new modes of interpretation, seriously practiced, are in themselves much less of a problem because of the underlying continuity between them and the traditional modes.

I hope that if I manage to explain what I mean by this I can justify the whole strategy of speaking about the institution of literary and critical scholarship as if it had some analogy with ecclesiastical and other institutions. First let us ask what kind of thing such institutions find on the whole to be acceptable as changes. The flatly unacceptable (a demonstration that the average gestation period of mammals is an integer multiple of the number II) is not even examined, and regarded as a joke. (But this example comes from the annals of an institution far more sure of itself than ours, or even the church, which, in its present uncertainties, lets all manner of things through the gate that would have been kept out even twenty years ago. In short, we must see that control over interpretation may vary with the social stability of the institution.)

On the other hand thousands of relatively unimportant findings, made within the confines of "normal" science, are tested and approved but not greatly applauded. In between are the works, very few of them, which, in Polanyi's words, "sharply modify accepted views" yet are themselves accepted; to them the authorities "pay their highest homage".[8] The authors of such contributions—Einstein, Dirac, Godel—have a security of fame within their institutions which is beyond the dreams of all others. In short, the institution does not resist, rather encourages change; but it monitors change with very sophisticated machinery.

Our practices, though less decisive, are analogous, and their traditional justification is much older. When we teach we do so (unless we are very dishonest) on the assumption that what we do is something that can be learned. This can be a worrying assumption; for example, it was by asking discriminating questions about it that Northrop Frye arrived at his negative theory of value, his view that what can be taught is literary taxonomy. But most of us suppose that we are doing more than that (if indeed we are doing that at all). And in practice we do more than that. We wean candidates from the habit of literal reading. Like the masters who reserved secret senses in the second century, we are in the business of conducting readers out of the sphere of the manifest. Our institutional readings are not those of the outsiders, so much is self-evident; though it is only when we see some intelligent non-professional confronted by a critical essay from our side of the fence that we see how esoteric we are. And in this respect we have to think of ourselves as exponents of various kinds of secondary interpretation—spiritual understandings, as it were, compared with carnal, and available only to those who, in second-century terms, have circumcized ears, that is, are trained by us.

And here we may reflect on the resemblance between ours and the psychoanalytical practice. Our concern, when we depart from the merely descriptive, is with latent sense. We learn, and teach others, to be alert to condensation and displacement in the text; we develop a strong taste for, and a power to divine, overdeterminations. That is why my reading of a Conrad novel, say, is different from an undergraduate's, though his will grow more like mine; and even more different from a layman's. The layman, we like to think, sees without perceiving, hears without understanding. He who has ears to hear, let him hear.

The continuity of the newest criticism with the early forms of interpretation licensed by the establishment is in the perpetuity of such assumptions. Poets may have a third eye, analysts a third ear, exegetes a

8 Michael Polanyi, *The Tacit Dimension*, 1967, p. 68. The paper on gestation periods is also from Polanyi, p. 64.

circumcized ear; these additional or purified organs are figures for the divinatory skills acquired within institutions. The deconstruction of a text is a bold figure for what exegetes *de métier* have always claimed the right to do. In the early enthusiastic stage the techniques employed may seem overbold, and attract the censure of the hierarchy—this is what happened to Empson, and to the anti-historical element of the New Criticism. But in the end the fate, so much dreaded by the newest critics, who are conscious enough of history and of the cultural forces of inertia, will overtake the enthusiasts; they will be "recuperated" or, if they are not, they will be nihilated. I do not offer an opinion as to whether this is right or just, but merely argue that when the charismatic becomes institutional some "routinization" is bound to occur; and if it does not become institutional it falls into neglect. As it has, in not too fanciful a sense, been institutional all along, and as nobody outside the institution has much chance of understanding it, I do not think there is much doubt about the outcome. How the experience will alter the future "tacit knowledge" of the institution it is impossible to guess.

I wonder whether some among my hearers, the younger perhaps, may not find what I have said a little cynical and gloomy. I believe that institutions confer value and privilege upon texts, and license modes of interpretation; and that qualification for senior membership of such institutions implies acceptance, not total of course, of this state of affairs. And I suppose one might well look upon this as an unhappy situation. Such institutions as ours do reflect the larger society which they somehow serve, and it may be an unjust society. But how else shall we protect the latent sense? The mysteries, said Clement, were not proclaimed openly, "in such a way that any listener could understand them"; they were spoken in parables, riddles, requiring exegesis.[9] And exegesis has its rules, on the foundation of which has been built the whole structure of modern hermeneutics. It is by recognizing the tacit authority of the institution that we achieve the measure of liberty we have in interpreting. It is a price to pay, but it purchases an incalculable boon; and for my own part I cannot bring myself to say that my conclusions concerning the power of the institution to validate texts and control interpretation are sad ones. They might even be a reason for moderate rejoicing.

9 Von Campenhausen, p. 303.

Literature and Culture: An Interview with Saul Bellow*

Q.: *Mr. Bellow, I'd like to begin by asking you whether you think the writer and/or the artist has a special task to perform at this point in time, whether you yourself feel that you have a special task to perform?*

BELLOW: If there's anything good that he can do the writer should certainly do it at once. In fact, the question is a little difficult to answer because writers don't think of themselves very often as people who are holding the line for civilization threatened by the old threat of barbarism and so on. Mostly they are people who are thinking very hard about the stories they might be writing or are writing. The cultural assignment is something else again, and that cultural assignment is perhaps more in the minds of university professors than it is in the minds of writers, who don't really see things in quite the same way. Sometime in the 19th century it became apparent that writers would have to do something to replace the churches which were dying out and vanishing in influence, and writers took this requirement quite seriously. I think some writers are aware that what they write belongs to the culture of their society; other writers don't care much one way or the other whether the culture is thriving or not—they think of it as an academic question. Sometimes I'm on one side of the matter and sometimes I'm on the other. Occasionally I worry about what's happening to culture in the United States, but on other days I think there is no culture in the United States, and there's no point in worrying about it. Have I answered your question?

Q.: *In part, yes, but perhaps I can press you a bit farther. You have approved, at least at one point in time, Collingwood's conception of the artist, to the effect that "he is one who tells the audience, at the risk of their displeasure, the secrets of their own hearts." Is that in some way picking up the last function of the clergy?*

* This is an edited transcript of a public interview conducted at Skidmore College on November 8, 1973. Interviewing Saul Bellow were Robert Boyers, Robert Orrill, Ralph Ciancio, and Edwin Moseley, all members of the Skidmore faculty.

BELLOW: Well, to be serious for a moment, I do not think that writers often feel that this is what they are doing, that is to say, when they themselves have reached some point of emotional and intellectual excitement in which they feel that they are telling the truth. Sometimes the writer experiences this when, at the moment in which he thinks about what he is saying, it so moves his own heart that he feels other people's hearts must be moved in the same way. And this has a value, which has something to do with the solidarity of the species as a whole. It's a generous impulse that artists sometimes have when they themselves are strongly moved, and they wish to make an offering to everybody else. I don't know how much fancy dress this feeling can stand. It's true that I quoted Collingwood once—I thought he had said a very good thing, and when I read that paragraph of his I agreed strongly with it. But I'm often worried about the responsibility which is thrust upon the writer, responsibilities which are didactic, moral, and so on. After all, we are, most of us, frail vessels: how much do we think we can do, what the devil do we think we are doing anyway? Do we really believe, in a country, a society, a civilization like this, that we can make that much difference? I don't like the feeling of super-erogation that goes with this. I don't even know how many times Shelley would have said poets are the unacknowledged legislators of mankind, if he had lived beyond the age of forty—perhaps it would have tired him out saying it over and over again. Possibly he would have changed his mind. What a writer does feel is the demand of the public upon him that he should be a legislator and that he should perform a moral function, and that he should provide emotional, spiritual stuff—those are rather old fashioned ideas, but I don't think that people have really given up old fashioned ideas—they just scoff at them, while in reality they continue to live by them. And I include writers in this.

Q.: *While reading your novels I often have the sense that various protagonist figures betray many of the essential qualities of the embattled writer in contemporary culture. I refer now not merely to such qualities as heightened sensitivity, but to a feeling he carries within him that no one cares or listens attentively. Do you tend to think of your protagonists as especially disturbed by such feelings?*

BELLOW: Well, hardly anybody is heard very much—everybody has his moment and people listen for a while, but they have a dial that they can turn, and they can always get another station or another network: if they don't like your show they can go on to the next. This is an amusement society for the most part, and I don't think that most writers that I know have too many illusions about how seriously they are being harkened unto.

Q.: *Is it conceivable, do you think, that in a culture such as ours what one might call supreme values could be generated anew? Malraux wrote, not long ago, that we recognize such values, supreme values, by the fact that men are ready to die for them. Are we ready to die for anything, do you think? Ought we to be ready?*

BELLOW: Well, I think lots of people are ready to die because they can't stand life anymore. And I don't think there's anything so extraordinary about that. Of course, Malraux is a romantic fellow, and he has these ideas of the romantic will. That's very nice and I'm all for that sort of thing. I don't think there's any particular reluctance to die. Of course the idea for which one dies may not be very clear in anybody's mind, that's true enough. But that just means that we're in some sort of ideological or moral interregnum, that we're between epochs, that we've used up all the old ideas and that people believe in very few of them. Of course, people are very odd; on the one hand they pay lip service to the accepted beliefs of their society, on the other hand they embrace the scepticism of their society. That's what I would call head culture: almost everybody believes the same thing in matters of head culture. On the other hand there are internal beliefs (I know this about myself): if you asked me any civilized question I would give you the civilized answer, because I know what the civilized answer is; if you asked me what I really feel in my heart, that's something else again. You can depend upon educated people to tell you that of course they are agnostic rationalists, but what they really are is their own very well kept secret. And the reason is that there's really no language for these secrets at the moment, and very few people whom you can take into your confidence. And there's very little independent self-confidence in most people, so that they subscribe, pretty much, to received opinions. If you ask people what they think they tell you what they learned in college. If you ask me what I really think, if I knew you very well, and trusted you, I might tell you. Of course there are two different speeches, and everybody knows that by now. There are the things you say, civilly, in polite society; and there are the things you say to yourself before you fall asleep. There are the people you bless and there are the prayers that you say to yourself which you wouldn't say to anyone else. Am I saying anything that's strange to you? I don't think so.

Q.: *Mr. Bellow, I'd like to ask you about the implication of a passage which appears in* Mr. Sammler's Planet. *At one point, talking, I believe, about formal experimentation in the arts, Mr. Sammler sides with the ancients. He maintains that imitation is necessary, that we must have models, that to think of greatness without models is an impossibility. In view of this passage (and whether Sammler is speaking for you or not) would you comment on your notion of originality, especially in the literary arts, on whether or not you believe that there have been any breakthroughs in the novel in recent years.*

BELLOW: No, I don't think there have been any true breakthroughs, I think there have been lots of people who have told the world that they were doing original things and deliberately breaking through, but I haven't seen anything very original in quite a long time. Of course, originality is welcome in any form, but as part of a cultural craze it becomes an obligatory thing: all writers and painters are to do something new, to belong to the modernist revolution. After all, there are not so many ideas that humankind has; whether it knows it or not, it continues to repeat the same themes. Sometimes I open up a strange set of books, *Hasting's Encyclopedia of Religion and Ethics*, when I want to understand what people are doing on the west coast. Invariably I can find it in *Hastings* because the human species rarely invents anything. But in the 19th and 20th centuries there's been this strange conviction that something new must be said with every breath. I suppose that Mr. Sammler is thinking of someone like Don Quixote, who said of course that you can't have anything worthwhile unless you imitate classical models—and that's a classical idea. Romanticism would have us believe that something startling, daring and new can be found as soon as you purge the film from the inner eye, or as soon as you break away from received ideas. This has been the standard of art for the last century and a half or so. The other standard, however, is that we simply do again what has already been done, marvelously. The fact is that most stories have been told, and told again, and again. Because, after all, human beings tend to make the same discoveries over and over again. The difference is not in the story but in the individual to whom the story occurs, or in the actors in the story. The individuals are different, the story tends to be the same. After all, how different can it be? We are all born, helpless, and we have to be nurtured, cared for, until we can stand on our own feet. Then we have children and they have to be educated and prepared for the experiences of life. Though we may think there is something smashingly new about the way we think in the 20th century, it is really not so new as all that. The difference is in the individuals, *they* are new; since individuals can't really invent themselves, I don't see why so much anxiety should be generated about this. I think the important thing they should discover is what they are, who they are; that is the novelty, that is what is new.

Q.: *When you say that the artist retells the same story, I'm reminded of*

Faulkner's introduction to The Sound and the Fury *in which he says a number of suggestive things about the creative process. He says that originally he meant to tell Quentin's story, or what had been Quentin's story, and that after he had told Quentin's story he didn't think he had done it right, so he went on and told the same story from Benjy's point of view, and still he believed he hadn't done it right, so he went on to tell the story from Jason's point of view. Would you say that some useful analogy can be drawn between what Faulkner describes in relation to* The Sound and the Fury *and your own work?*

BELLOW: Well, I think the best way to answer this is to tell one of my favorite jokes. I sometimes think the wisdom of life can be discovered in about 10 or 15 jokes. I'll tell you one which, I think, answers this question, if it is a question. An American tenor was performing, making his debut at La Scala. He sings his first aria early in the first act. The applause is tremendous and people shout "Ancora, vita, vita." So he sings the aria once more. The second time the applause is even more tremendous; the Scala roof seems to go off with everybody shrieking "Ancora, vita," so he sings the aria a third time. After he's sung it a third time, they call for it a fourth time. He holds up his hands and, with tears in his eyes, he makes a little speech. He says he never hoped for anything like this, that this is the greatest hour of his life, that his mother is a poor laundress in Kansas City and that his father decamped early and left them alone and after a cheap, rotten start he'd studied at the Juilliard, and he'd studied in Paris, and in Rome, and in Milan, and this was an unforgettable night for him, it justified a belief in himself, justified himself to his mother. But, the cast is waiting, the Maestro is waiting, the orchestra is waiting, we must go on with the performance. But the crowd shouts—"No, no!" and he says "how many times must I sing this aria?" Someone shouts, "you gonna sing until you get it right!" I know we all often feel like that.

Q.: *Just to follow up on this for a minute, Sammler seems to feel that it is not only artists and intellectuals who are determined to be original, but that all of us really are determined to be what he calls "interesting," and that we are, in fact, placed in peril by the frailty of our imaginations. Do you think you could comment on what Sammler means by that?*

BELLOW: Well, I think that it's a cancer of American life, that people believe that they must be interesting. I think that it comes out of a sense of dullness, boredom and inadequacy. They die to be interesting to each other; I think it's one reason why there's so little secrecy in Washington. I think that people run about as soon as they've learned something and tell it to each other. During the war, this was the despair of America's allies in Europe: no secret could be kept, everybody was talking. The German secret service could not believe that these stories weren't planted; what they didn't realize was that Americans were simply doing their damndest to be interesting to one another, and to everybody else that they met. As soon as they had discovered something, they burned with a fever to tell.

A woman once came to me and said that she was going to the country for a weekend of winter sports and skiing; she didn't ski but she was going to sit by the fire and make herself interesting. She was going to read a book all weekend and as she read a page she would crumple it up and throw it into the fire. Could I recommend a book that was suitable!

If I were terribly moralistic I would scold everyone about this, but as it is I will leave you with this: that people do feel that there's something wrong, unappetising, unappealing in the ordinary—that they have to do something super-erogatory, make themselves appeal; that the world is very boring, that they, themselves, are very boring and that they must discover some way not to be. So the task of entertaining one another is becoming a sort of social service. It accounts for the way people dress, for what people call a "life style" (deadly phrase), etc., etc. And in literature too, the question is: what is one to tell that will be truly interesting, and how can a writer compete with the great events of this century? What is he going to say after the revolution of 1905, World War I, the Russian revolution, the rise of Fascism, the great depression, World War II, the atomic bomb and all these other tremendous movements of destiny which have charmed mankind out of its shoes. I rather should say, charmed their survivors, not the people who experienced the events. Life, in this sense, has become very current-eventish. People think that they are political when they are immersed in these events—vicariously. They scold you as someone who thinks only of art for art's sake when you suggest to them that perhaps they are in a delirium and that they ought to be doing and thinking something else, that society is monopolizing their brains, and taking their souls away from them by this interest, by the news, by spurious politics. But I come back to this: what is one to offer that will be particularly interesting to mankind? We think now that we are mortal and that we have only one life; we've given up all belief in an afterlife, and our time has become more valuable because of this. People say, don't waste my time, don't tell me anything superfluous, give me something necessary, really necessary. I saw an ad in the New York subway a few years ago which went—If I have only one life to live, let me live it as a Clairol blond—made a great appeal to me. For just this reason, that writers feel that they are under the gun, that they dare not come to the public with superfluities, that they must be quintessential, that they must be as interesting as they can possibly be, that they will not waste this brief mortal time, that they're contemporary. I feel this very keenly, I wouldn't dream of publishing anything that would waste people's time. If I felt it was not worth reading, I would burn it—I often do.

Q.: *Have writers felt otherwise in your lifetime as a writer? Have there been changes in the attitude of most writers with respect to such matters?*

BELLOW: Well, I think most writers are like most surgeons: after they've completed a course on how to open up somebody's belly, they just go on doing it. They feel that they have a license to do it, and whether they do it well or badly doesn't matter so much. I also find that writers, after they have made some initial discovery about how to write a book, continue to write a book in that way, and just settle back into bourgeois comfort.

Q.: *I'm curious about the relationship between your work and the New York intellectual community, a community with which your work has always been very closely identified. It's clear that in recent years you've left the New York intellectual community, that your work no longer appears in* Partisan Review, *for example. Can you speak a little bit about the breakdown of that community?*

BELLOW: Oh, gladly. It's an infuriating subject and I'd be glad to speak about it. As a young provincial, of course, I had the obligation of going to the big town and taking it on. This has been the immemorial pattern of young hicks. I came from the sticks in order to take New York; I naturally had the fantasy of trouncing and stunning everybody. I did pretty well in that line, I think. I went to New York at a fortunate moment: just before World War II, and then again just after. There was a literary intellectual life in New York in the late 40's. There was the *Partisan Review*, there was Columbia University, there were many independent writers, painters, and critics. The big money had not yet hit, the media had not yet developed their full power, the universities had not yet entered the picture as patrons of the arts. Between the media and the universities, the literary life of this country was annihilated. People were drawn either to *Time* magazine or to the networks, or to the advertising agencies on the one side, or to the universities on the other. The universities were flushed, they began to buy up the literary magazines, they destroyed anything that you might describe as an independent literary culture in this country. They didn't attempt to do so, but that was the result. They bought up the avant guard magazines just as they bought up anything else. The universities sponsored anything—the more avant garde, the better. They had literary journals, they had the dance, they had the theatre, they had the music, and they had the painting; they had it all. And there was no extra-institutional and independent environment for writers. *Partisan Review*, itself, became very corrupt and doddery when acquired by Rutgers University. It was taken over by a new group of people and the old editors succumbed to age and the usual things. I began, in the late 50's, to think about leaving the eastern seaboard, because I didn't want to belong to any of the gangs, and I felt the madness of the 60's approaching. I think the 60's will be remembered as the decade of frenzy, and violent agitation, having very little to do with literature or art. I think the 60's was the decade of the politicization (a disagreeable word, even difficult to pronounce) of writers, painters and intellectuals in this country.

Q.: *Do you think that this development had something to do, as well, with the emergence of the counter culture, or the youth culture, if you will, in the period of the 60's? I speak of the degree to which the counter culture was taken up by the media, and became, in fact, very attractive to many professional intellectuals, including those prominently associated with the* Partisan Review*?*

BELLOW: Well, the *Partisan Review* had already entered the skeleton closet at that time; there was nothing much left. I'm not rejecting what people call the counter culture as counter culture. I just demand to see what it can do in the way of literature and art. It was great in the invention of what we call "life styles." It was wonderful as interior decoration or costume, but it was not exactly stupendous in drama or in literature. That, really, is the only basis on which I judge these matters.

Q.: *The counter culture has been a central concern, it appears to me, in the fiction of a number of writers: yourself in* Mr. Sammler's Planet, *Malamud, Updike and others. I always feel, in those books, a kind of ambivalence towards the counter culture, an obscure kind of fascination with forces actually subversive of civilization, an affirmation, in a sense, of the primitive.*

BELLOW: Well, there are two separate questions here: one of them is a question of affirmation. I've always thought that both pessimism and optimism were a racket as far as a writer is concerned. People want joy or gloom, so most writers stand on both sides of the joy or gloom abyss and provide joy or gloom, I think that's nonsensical, really, I think that people want writers' reasons to go on living and I don't think writers are capable of providing reasons to go on living. I don't believe that they are capable of originating a moral power by themselves—in conjunction with something else, yes, in conjunction, that is, with an ideology or a church, a belief or something of that sort; but writers who tell you life is beautiful or writers who tell you life is vile are, alike, imbeciles. Beautiful and vile have nothing to do with the matter; what does have something to do with the matter is something that is demonstrated in fact, an independent detail in the telling of the story. But as for matters on the ideological side, there is very little to be said for them. I think that most writers who ever lived were on the side of life in this: that they didn't think they should give up on the human species. Very few writers actually have given up on the human species and said that it didn't really deserve to exist. I think of someone like Jonathan Swift. I think of Tolstoy in certain moods, but I can think of very few other writers who really said that mankind does not deserve to continue. Nothing is legitimate in literature or any work of art which does not have the support of some kind of emotional conviction. The ideological conviction means almost nothing. The emotional conviction means everything.

Q.: *In his private moments, when Sammler wants to listen to someone, he turns to Meister Eckhart. Are there people who, if you would trust us, you would quietly recommend that we could listen to if we chose to do so? Or are there writers writing today that we might attend to?*

BELLOW: Well, I can tell you my own choice. I think Silone, the Italian novelist, is one writer doing something that one can listen to without fear of being deceived. There really aren't very many. But after all, this is a responsibility that, perhaps, literature can not support. It is, after all, by origin one of the "play" activities rather than one of the moral activities. I don't mean "play" in a frivolous sense—I mean "play" in a much deeper sense. But I think that the burden of moral authority for modern writers is a burden that none of them can sustain. I don't know of any who can. And yet the demand is there that they do something that mankind needs and craves and—where is it coming from?

Q.: *One has a sense that perhaps it is the nature of the city itself which has much to do with the condition you describe in your novels and in this dialogue. I wonder if you think that the city has a future, and whether, in fact, some of the young people in the counter culture aren't on to something in their flight from the city, the attempt to, even in some primitivistic sense, return to the earth. In any number of your novels you speak of the city itself as the source of much of what we understand to be contemporary chaos. You speak, for example, of our language as having degenerated specifically in connection with the life of the city. I wonder if you think there's any way that we might avoid the city, or that the city might be restructured for the better.*

BELLOW: Well, I think the evils can reach people everywhere very easily now. They aren't restricted to the city—people can have them out in the country. They can annihilate their minds and souls just as well out in the sticks as they can in New York. As a matter of fact, the characteristic life of the city today, as drawn by Joyce in *Ulysses* at the latest, is not really visible in America at this moment. People are not out in the streets as Leopold Bloom was in 1904, they're in the suburbs. The inner city is blighted, the scene of violence, crime and horror. People there are not reading books. All the same, I think these bucolic dreams are rather touching and I think that it's nice to go where the air is fresher. Destroying your brain with dope out in the quiet countryside is probably more agreeable than doing it in the city. Sometimes I think if I were a capitalist I would invest in old people's homes for the young—with the way some of these communes are going, they're going to be prematurely decrepid and there's going to be a big business in rehabilitation.

Q.: *I'd like to shift gears a little; would you be willing to speak about the place of comedy in your work—apart from its obvious entertainment value in your novels? What function does comedy play? Is comedy related to any of the subjects you've just addressed?*

BELLOW: Sometimes you think, what else can you do but laugh at these things. Perhaps that's the only thing—there's mercy and forgiveness in laughter. But let me try to put it this way: the Victorians told us how important high seriousness was, the 20th century has proved how deadly low seriousness is. What can one do with low seriousness? One watches what goes on and is convinced that despite the preaching of the doctrine of high seriousness, it's low seriousness that's won. I don't want to become political, but when you watch our poor President Nixon on television, what can you think but that he has cheapened scandal and brought it into disrepute—what really, can you say about that? I really don't know what else to do but laugh, and besides, it comes natural, and I shouldn't apologise for anything that comes natural, or even try to explain it, because what comes natural is most mysterious and we owe it our loyalty—unless of course it's crime that comes natural.

Q.: *Your mention of President Nixon inevitably calls me to more somber questions, to the notion of banality addressed by Hannah Arendt in her famous, some would say notorious, book on Adolf Eichmann. Sammler takes issue, in* Mr. Sammler's Planet, *with Arendt's notion of the banality of evil as a conceptual framework in which to deal with a figure like Eichmann. I'm not sure I understand exactly what Sammler suggests in his remarks. He seems to suggest that if Eichmann is to be taken as a banal figure, potentially merely one of us, that he really can not be evil, not inspire in us the proper revulsion. Is it necessary, do you think, to refrain from demystifying a figure like Eichmann if we would truly understand him?*

BELLOW: Well, I don't know that the banality of evil is an idea that demystifies—it just blames evil on modern mass civilization and on technological society and says that there is no *true* evil any more, that even this has become debased in a mass society. To me this is nonsense. I think that when human beings murder they know what they're doing. If they camouflage their murder, by one means or another, the magnitude of the evil doesn't change. Almost any human being knows what it means to take another man's life. What you gain by turning the thing around and blaming it on industrial mass society, saying that this man's mind is a mass of clichés, that he didn't know what he was doing—this is to remove the guilt from him and to place it upon society as a whole and upon the rest of us. Until we are convinced that each individual of us has committed murders we cannot be expected to share in that very guilt. I think also that the heroic, dramatic idea of evil, the idea that one must be a Richard the Third or an Iago in order to commit evil, gives evil a sort of literary character. We must simply examine the thing as it is and as it comes and as it happens. So I really do not believe in shifting the blame from the murderer to those of us who, perhaps in our minds, have done violent and terrible things, but who have, in fact, done nothing of the kind. In my own mind this is a distinction between the Jewish and Christian outlook: Jesus said that if you lusted after a woman in your heart then you might as well have committed the adultery. The Jewish outlook is that unless you have actually committed the crime you are not guilty of it, no matter what you have thought. The mental capacity to do this thing we mustn't forget, but neither must we think that the evil happens in a dream: it happens in fact, and those who commit the evil in fact are in fact evil. Those who only imagine it and suppress it cannot be called evil in the same sense. They have at least overcome the impulse or the temptation—there is a difference between the act and the imagination of the act, which we mustn't forget. If we forget it, we confuse the moral categories. This, I think, is a serious mistake. I think there is also such a thing as cunning in human beings which enables them to conceal their evil in banality: there's nothing useful in the view that Hitler's scheme of extermination showed a lack of imagination. The evil imagination was very great there, and anyone who describes it as a function of banality is himself, or herself, banal. Hitler's was a conspiracy so vast and so subtle that the very idea of blame disappeared from it. This was no small achievement—this was what Mr. Sammler meant when he said that, after all, the evil is too vast to be called banal.

Q.: *I'd like to ask you a related question: you've said that we must be loyal to what comes naturally. Some writers and thinkers, though, Melville and Freud for example, would tell us that murder and treachery are usually what comes naturally. You may disagree, of course, but given what we know of ourselves, isn't it a little hard to trust in what comes naturally?*

BELLOW: Well, there are many ways of explaining what comes naturally. There is the naturalistic mode of explaining what is natural, or a Freudian mode. I don't happen to agree with these. I do think that human nature is full of many kinds of wickedness which must be fought.

Q.: *Would it be useful to make a distinction between individual and social wickedness and the guilt that might be generated from these?*

BELLOW: Well, if I may say so, this conversation is turning me into a philosopher, which I am not. Writers are not cast in the role of philosophers. They have many ideas, but which ideas they believe is sometimes hard to find out, and is very difficult for them to know. Do we know what Skakespeare's ideas really were? He says "As flies to wanton boys are we to the gods, they kill us for their sport"; in the same play he says "The gods are just, and of our pleasant devices make instruments to plague us". These are contradictory statements. Which one did Shakespeare believe— One, or both, or neither? I don't know, but there was nobody to put him on the spot.

Q.: *Mr. Bellow, can we come back then to your art, to your use of language, and put to you a question that is prompted by a passage in* Herzog. *Near the end of that novel, referring to the composition of his own letters, Herzog might well be describing your own struggle towards suitable words as a novelist. "I go after reality with language", Herzog states; "Perhaps I'd like to change it all into language. I put my whole heart into these constructions, but they are constructions." Herzog seems to be saying, among other things, that language fulfills a therapeutic need, that it is a projection of the inner life and an instrument of knowledge. In light of this passage, would you comment on the degree to which language and reality are inextricably related for you.*

BELLOW: Well, I will say first of all that I knew a psychotherapist at the University of Chicago, himself a bit of a nut, who said that people who spoke very well were much less likely to go off their rockers. As for translating everything into language, I could get very profound about this, but you wouldn't remember what I said, and neither would I. So I'll say that the passage to which you refer was just one of the marvelous things that Herzog felt like saying. Will you please excuse me from further comment?

Q.: *Let me try another angle, which you can also put aside if you like. To what degree are your novels to be taken merely as verbal constructions, "merely" as fiction?*

BELLOW: Well, they should be taken as fiction, because even if I thought they were true, were literally real, they would still need to be taken as fiction, because I'm not sure that any account I gave of what I thought was really real would be anything except fiction. That's the way my mind informs or deforms. And to tell the literal truth, as everybody knows, is very hard. Think of all the great confessions in literature—are they really true? If I hold with Freud in anything I would hold with him in this one matter, that reality is a projection of something or other. Fictions are fascinating and relatively coherent projections. I don't often believe that the truth could be as easy as that. We love it, we seek it (I'm speaking of the truth, or of reality) but we must be happy when we can approximate it, somewhat. I know that I'm approximating it when I write something to which there is some sort of clear reaction from people. Beyond that, I don't really know very much about it.

Q.: *You mentioned Freud, and you seem, in much of your fiction, to carry on a kind of running battle with him. I think one of your characters says that psychoanalysis is one of the more interesting mistakes of the 20th century. In what way do you think Freud was mistaken?*

BELLOW: Well, if I was sitting on some grand metaphysical steam roller, I would be glad to run him over: beyond that, my feelings go something like this. First of all I think Freud was a great genius, but I worry about these great geniuses who create systems which then take the mind captive. It's very difficult to escape from any system of metaphors which successfully imposes itself upon you. You begin to think that way and pretty soon you can't think in any other way. You may begin to think of things as Marx thought of them, and then you're a gone goose for quite a while—you'll see everything in terms of the class struggle. Or you can begin to think of things as Freud thought of them and then you're equally sunk, because those powerful metaphors take control of your imagination and direct your thought. It's very hard to get out of this. I remember what my feelings were quite early in my life when I began to read Freud. It was hard not to see the world in terms of instinct and repression, not to see it in terms of concavity and convexity, not to see it in terms of the struggle of the child with his parents, and so on. All of these metaphors are very powerful and they're very compelling. Are they the last word? Is this it? No artist could actually tell himself that that vision was more true than another vision: the vision of Kant or the vision of Locke or the visions of Plato. How are all these things to live together? We must make our own minds up among these systems, empirically, using our own judgment, and also being faithful to our own imagination of reality and of the truth. Once you've given yourself over to one of these systems, you've lost your freedom in a very significant degree. Not so very long ago I was reading an essay of Freud's (I often read his papers at night to put myself to sleep), and I came across a very short statement which was fascinating to me. It went something like this (kept me awake for about half an hour): an American doctor had written a letter to Freud saying (after this American doctor had read Freud's little work *The Future of an Illusion*) 'I too at one time lost my faith and this was how it happened. I was a student in a dissecting room and a cadaver was brought in. It was the body of a very beautiful old woman. The sight of her face so touched my heart that I felt that life was wicked, and I could no longer believe in a god who delivered that body of such a beautiful person into the dissecting room. But after a time,' this doctor wrote to Freud, 'after bethinking myself, I changed my mind and I recovered my religious faith. I recommend that you, too, postpone a final decision on the existence of God for a time, until you have been able to think it over a little more completely.' Freud then writes, very condescendingly, that 'of course, what this man saw in the cadaver in the dissecting room was his mother.' At this moment I experienced a violent reaction against Freud. Was it not possible to experience beauty or pity without thinking of your mother, or without the Oedipus complex? The rigidity of this repels me. I felt that it was coarse and cruel. It's this sort of thing that I think of when I think of Freud. Then I try to think of it, with my smart brain, logically, and I say to myself: well, what is the unconscious after all? The unconscious is anything that human beings don't know. Is there any reason why we have to accept Freud's account of what it is that we don't know? Are there no other ways to explain what we don't know? Is it possible that what we don't know has a metaphysical character and not a Freudian, naturalistic character? I think that the unconscious is a concept that begs the question and simply returns us to our ignorance with an arrogant attitude of confidence, and this is why I'm against it. Does that answer your question?

Q.: *Very much so. But I'd like to go on to another: So many contemporary writers have exhibited a tendency towards self destruction. Is this a problem peculiar to our age, do you think?*

BELLOW: I suppose you are speaking of the fact that so many of our artists have committed suicide? If I told you that I could explain this I would be behaving like Freud, whom I just criticized. I don't know. This is a thing that baffles me, and I have seen many of my friends go that way—into death. The usual explanation is that America is a cruel and inhuman civilization which does not care for higher things and that people of particular sensitivity to such things can't enjoy this life, and wear themselves out in the effort. But I feel there is more to it than that. Some artists accept the challenge of philistinism in a peculiarly literal way in that they feel that it's incumbent upon the poet to be a sort of martyr, that he must be the wild, heedless and free person who throws his life away: by drink, by narcotics, by recklessness. It is something of a romantic image by now, I think. This doesn't mean that the agonies are not real, I think they are, I know they are, but once the mind is fixed in this particular mold of antagonism, there's hardly any way to get out of it. As for society, I mean now educated or so called cultivated society, it seems to take some satisfaction in the fact that poets don't make it but destroy themselves. It's as though there were some testimony in this to the awfulness of life, as if they were saying: I myself can take it, just barely, it's beating the hell out of me; but these others—the Berrymans or the Jarrells—they're far more sensitive organisms who simply cannot endure this. And there's a kind of self-congratulation in this, I think, on the part of many people. I was astounded, when I had written a short introduction to John Berryman's posthumous book, at the kind of reviews that I read, and at the mail that I received. People spoke of Berryman's suicide with some kind of gratification as though it were a marvelous thing to get up on the rail of a bridge and jump to your death, as though this was what poets probably ought to do with the conviction that this was their function, and perhaps even their duty: To die as they did in the gutter, to die as Hart Crane did, off the side of a ship. There is a kind of cannibalism revealed to one in the way that people relish this. I find that many of the reviewers of Berryman's books take a kind of relish in the fact that he lived and died as he did. In fact, I think Berryman had simply exhausted himself. He had used himself up, skin and bones, in the writing of those extraordinary poems. He had deteriorated very badly and he didn't want to continue to live. But one doesn't know why these things are done. I can only speculate about it all.

Q.: *How do you feel about recent developments in the art of fiction, developments we associate with writers like John Barth?*

BELLOW: I wish Barth, and the others, luck. I say alright, good. Does the man find a new story? The only book of Barth's I really know well is the one called *The Floating Opera*, which I liked very much. I haven't stories like "Leaving the Yellow House". Occasionally, when I write, I am beside myself with enthusiasm. When I wrote *Henderson*, I had no ideological feelings whatever. I live for those times and desire those states—always. That's what I feel that it's about. I can occasionally write very cleverly: I think of *Mr. Sammler's Planet* as a sort of polemical thing. I was moved to write it, but not in the same way. I didn't feel the terrible gratification of composition as I did when I was writing a book like *Henderson*, or, most of the time, *Herzog*. And that's what I go by. It's very hard for me to know what the result is of the feeling of pleasure and enthusiasm, or painful agitation, as it sometimes is. You know, it can be extremely painful, even when I'm laughing very hard as I do the thing. I like to think that those things which were written with feelings of the greatest pleasure and enthusiasm are the best, just as a woman might feel that the child she conceives by the man she likes most is the best child . . . but I don't know that those are the best children.

Q.: *You've had much to say about questions of sincerity and conviction—are sincere convictions necessary in the conception of a novel?*

BELLOW: Of course. I know of many books which novelists must have written out of the most powerful convictions; but it must be a powerful conviction in some very special sense, not simply an idea of what is good for mankind or good for society or morally desirable. If Tolstoy had not hated war with all his heart he would not have written *War and Peace* and we would have been poorer for it. But suppose he had only felt that it was his duty to hate war, if he really hadn't hated it, then he would have written a hell of a bad book. And this is what I frequently try to say, rather than what some have supposed, that these passionate convictions are in themselves to be criticized. On the contrary: it is where programmed beliefs substitute for the passions that you get into trouble. Sometimes I often wonder about the one-sidedness of the transaction between the writer and his culture. I often feel the demand upon the writer by society for constructive, didactic or moral attitudes. But I ask myself: what does society do for the writer that it should impose this demand upon him? I mean, it's Billy Graham, not me, who's welcome at the White House. Let him whoop it up for morality, why should I? And, besides, if I feel like whooping, if my conscience makes me do this, then it's another matter. But to whom do I owe this? And for what? Why is it that the majority of citizens in this country feel that they have the right to demand this from the few people who write books in this country? The demands on them are overwhelming and what are they based on? Is there any quid pro quo?

followed him in his more recent books, and don't know very much about him. On principle I don't think it's a very good idea for writers to try to work out the problem of the history of their art. That is to say: that's been done and that's been done, and that's been done, and now we must do something which has not been done. This historical approach, I think, is a very dangerous one because it hands us over to the demon of progress. I don't know that there is any progress in the arts and I don't know that the idea of progress is such a wonderful one, for art. Nor am I so sure that historical ideas about painting or literature are very good for literature or painting—respectively. I think of these mainly as cultural activities as I think of Picasso or Joyce as not only a painter and a writer but also as historians of culture. Are they very original historians of culture? I'm not as sure about that. What I do feel is that, in any work of art, imagination is always more powerful than any cognition, and that these historical ideas are, after all, cognitions. To try to find out by some kind of mental operation or study what the thing to write next is, what the thought properly should be, is a philosophical activity rather than an idea that properly belongs to art. Ever since Hegel, in the *Philosophy of History*, came out with this notion of the world historical character or the world historical personality, people have been convinced that there's only one note for any man of genius to sound in his own time, and that that one note is historically determined, and that one must find the crossroads of history. One must be contemporaneous, one must be modern, or one is obsolete. It seems to me, after a couple of centuries of this, that it's the ideas which have become obsolete and not the works of art. The works of art, when they are great, have a persuasive power of their own which is quite independent of the ideas. But if you try to make the correct historical reckoning, and if you use some sort of ideological astrolabe or sextant to take a reading of where you are, what you ought to write, that I think is false, and I think it's the origin of many of our difficulties at the present moment. Is the man with it, or is he square? We think of these as new terms, or relatively new terms, but actually they are about as new as 1820.

Q.: *Is there any one book of yours you prefer to all the others?*

BELLOW: Well, I think I had more pleasure in the writing of some than in the writing of others, but then I have a great deal of pleasure with women too, and I'm supposed to be very rough on them, or so some people were telling me at a reception earlier today. Seriously, though, I think back with great pleasure to the time when I wrote *Henderson the Rain King*. I greatly enjoyed the writing of that. I also liked writing something like "The Old System", a story of mine, and a few other

Q.: *How much can we believe Mr. Sammler when at the end of 'his' novel he speaks of what each man knows in his heart? Are we to be persuaded that he speaks here out of a conviction that you share?*

BELLOW: You're to believe in it as much as you can believe the New Testament, though I don't agree that absolutely all know in their hearts what's right and what's wrong. Look—you meet someone on the street and he says, give all you have and follow me—on what does he base this injunction? He bases it on the assumption that the truth is known. If that was good enough for the foundation of a religion, it's good enough for the conclusion of a book!

By Way of Mr. Sammler

BY JOHN BAYLEY

Mr. Sammler and, still more, his cousin, Elya Gruner, are honest men in the fine old bourgeois meaning of the word: they are deliberately created to be such; not heroes of our time, but heroes reconstituted to see if they can acclimatise to our time, take root in the mulch of its fiction, and inhabit the consciousness of that fiction without drawing too much attention to themselves. For such an experiment the American-Jewish novel offers the best available—indeed the only possible—conditions for success. It has the obvious but enormous advantage of continuity not only with the almost pre-fictional tradition of the *honnête homme*, but with the great humanistic liberal and Victorian novel world of Dickens, Thackeray and George Eliot, carried from the Anglo-Saxon heartland to every European country, naturalised especially in Russia, and grafted—though not altogether securely—to the developing American culture. A certain kind of Jewish image in fiction today is the product not of the Torah and the Hasidim but of *Little Dorrit* and John Stuart Mill.

What keeps this inheritance alive and vigorous is that it is not only an intellectual affair, a tradition of culture handed on to the most intelligent and receptive heirs available: it also appeals to a tribal and communal life-style. It is just conceivable that some pillar of the country-club could be celebrated by the spokesman of a wasp novelist as Bellow through Mr. Sammler celebrates Elya Gruner.

> Sammler in a mental whisper said, "Well, Elya. Well, well, Elya". And then in the same way he said, "Remember, God, the soul of Elya Gruner, who, as willingly as possible and as well as he was able, and even to an intolerable point, and even in suffocation and as death was coming was eager, even childishly perhaps (may I be forgiven for this), even with a certain servility, to do what was required of him. At his best this man was much kinder than at my very best I have ever been or could ever be. He was aware that he

must meet, and he did meet—through all the confusion and the degraded clowning of this life through which we are speeding—he did meet the terms of his contract. The terms which, in his inmost heart, each man knows. As I know mine. As all know. For that is the truth of it—that we all know, God, that we know, that we know, we know, we know".

He might do, but what should we have to think if he did? Our alert fragmented sensibilities, all programmed to "the modern", would have to look in every direction except that in which the words pointed. If intelligence were there irony would also have to be present, the ritual a parody of some well-meaning, but also well-heeled, Episcopalian parson; but that, and every other obvious lead would merely bring us back to the really terrible irony of contemporary form: there would be no way in which the words could not be referred to some intention or aspect of technique brooded in the book's—that is the writer's—consciousness. The unspeakable thing about the modern consciousness in fiction is the fact that it cannot refer to anything outside itself. Like Lawrence's "him with his tail in his mouth" it lets us into its continuum of every kind of possibility, every talking point for the seminar, except the presumption of a firm contract elsewhere.

Indeed it is obvious that the modern consciousness is not capable of taking the last paragraph of *Mr. Sammler's Planet* seriously. How could it? Why should it? Founded on what Lionel Trilling has defined as the concept of "authenticity", it cannot afford to look outside its own instincts without becoming inauthentic: it can only be instructed and diverted by new somersaults of stance, new departures in form. These can be presented in terms of a critical vocabulary of exchangable counters, the counters of pseudo-order and pseudo-morality—the discerning, the passionate, the compassionate, the committed, the horrifyingly funny, the deeply concerned. Those are some of the squarer ones. But since the authentic is by definition incapable of insincerity, and since these terms all carry some semantic assumptions about the sincere, they cannot be taken very seriously. Authenticity should be purely egocentric, its logical emotional expression sadism and masochism of various kinds, the destruction or mutilation of the self, or of others as a respite from the self. An element of indulgence has always secretly accompanied the composition of fiction, but it has now become the principle of the form: for the novelist a duty and an imperative. His indulgence authenticates the reader's.

The born writer of today—a Mailer or Burroughs, Hubert Selby, or Joyce Carol Oates—methodically explores this indulgence. It is also logical that his expression of the authentic consciousness should resemble—coincide rather—as far as possible with itself. If bored, it should be boring: language must mirror its obsessions, its paranoia: the opposite process from say, Jane Austen, where boredom and constriction are converted by an equally conscientious principle of art into entertainment and liberation. The coincidence was observed by Simone Weil, who remarked that the modern consciousness naturally took the form of fiction, and *vice-versa*. The world which consciousness turns into itself naturally has no idea of an absolute contract external to that world. Elya Gruner on his death-bed is not merely not a character seen in fiction (Tolstoy's Ivan Ilyich is also not such a one) but he is a character who does not—cannot—see his own consciousness in fictional terms.

Why not? The short answer is to be found in the ancestry of this novel. The progenitors of Bellow-Sammler did not have to answer the question why Little Dorrit is so staunch in looking after her father, or why the selfishness of young Pendennis is a disagreeable quality. They knew it "as all know"—even the reader. Bellow parodies this knowledge in the remarkable scene in which the huge negro pickpocket silently exhibits his penis to Mr. Sammler in the hall of the latter's apartment. "We hold some things to be self-evident, man". This is a scene straight out of the consciousness, the fictional consciousness, in which Lionel Feffer—existing as he does on another planet than Mr. Sammler's—lives and has his being. He is, of course, fascinated by the scene as fiction, and wants Mr. Sammler to tell him all about it. "How marvellous! what a . . . a sudden glory. It could be straight out of *Finnegan's Wake*. 'Everyone must bare his crotch'". Feffer's reaction is exactly typical of the consciousness as fiction, or the fiction as consciousness. The scene he reacts to is self-evidently authentic, and it also neatly illustrates the difference between the authentic as fiction and the thing we are all supposed to "know", the thing that fiction once could only dramatise and repeat to us because it assumed we did know.

Mr. Sammler is himself aware of the validity, as fiction, of his experience with the big negro. "Objectively I have little use for such experiences, but there is such an absurd craving for actions that connect with other actions, for coherency, for form, for mysteries or fables . . And I don't like it. I don't like any of it". How right he is. The experience in modern fiction always connects, not so much in accord with the famous precept of E. M. Forster as because it cannot help it. The critic today can always see unity in any novel he thinks good: he is not defining its quality but identifying its nature. This is particularly true of the American novel, which has always been dominated, even in the rambling composite world of Moby Dick, by the solitary Hegelian *geist*, whether that spirit manifests itself like Melville's in metaphysical terms, or — as in the case of Hemingway — through the absolute fiat of a new style. To occlude the spirit would also be to disperse its identifying unity, and in terms of the American tradition this is an exceedingly difficult thing to do. The admirable thing about *Mr. Sammler* is its successful evasion of this spiritual unity, which it parodies and makes use of for fictional purposes, its own point being way outside the united states of fiction.

Bellow courts with equanimity the fate of ostracisation as a modern novelist; and my own experience is that intellectuals whose inclination or duty compel them to welcome novelty in any form are indeed apt to look sideways at Mr. Sammler. So at least it is in England, and there is plenty of indication that this is also the standard reaction in America. I have already referred to Lionel Trilling's study in the ideology of the self, *Sincerity and Authenticity*, which makes brief mention of Bellow in dubious not to say doleful terms. There is not just the implication that Bellow has given up the struggle, turned his head aside from modernity, but that in attempting to reconstitute in fiction the idea of the good and sincere man—instead of exploring the possibilities of his modern authentic counterpart—Bellow is perpetrating something aesthetically ludicrous, vulgarly inapposite. So brilliant and persuasive is Trilling's general argument, and so unanswerable is his quiet rejection of any attempts to be "humane" or "compassionate" within the framework of the modern sensibility, that it is difficult not to agree. But the point does remain: Bellow's heroes are not competing in the same league with anything going on today: Sammler's disenchantment with the modern fictional image (confirmed by the brutal fiasco of his academic lecture) is as total as Elya Gruner's ignorance of it. The great thing about Bellow and his heroes is that they do not try to have it both ways, to be with it and "humane" at the same time.

It is of course true that Bellow has been a modern novelist, and that aspects of Mr. Sammler—his liking for Orwell and English mustard, his love of Bloomsbury and H. G. Wells—are excellent ways of shrugging off the burden of a "message" by making it appear more than a trifle absurd, even if endearingly so. They are perennial ways. Old-fashioned morality in Mr. Sammler is concealed behind the slightly prissy meticulous quality sometimes associated with it. Bellow's beautifully fastidious and discriminatory use of language is rightly abandoned in the emotion felt by Mr. Sammler in the last paragraph of his book, which I quoted. The contract cannot be made more acceptable by style. But in general Bellow's style is nowhere more emphatic than in this book, sardonically underlining the complex working out of moral intelligence required to nourish a society in which "all know". Delicacy and discrimination are not the same thing as knowing how to meet the terms of one's contract, but they have a sort of Jamesian association with it, which it pleases Bellow to define. He shows that style and language can exhibit all the stigmata of tradition and at the same time appear both tough and timeless; it is the language which really endorses and gives weight to the meaning, shows that the apparently reactionary is still very much alive.

Trilling's argument, based as it is on the survival or non-survival of *ideas*, overrides this obvious point: of course it is no good sounding humane and compassionate oneself—that is indeed to get left behind in a world that no longer exists—but while language can be reciprocally used and appreciated as it is in *Mr. Sammler* it makes no sense to talk of our cultural state as one in which only the authentic consciousness can prevail. George Steiner and others, more despairing than Trilling even, have foretold that the consciousness of today will dissolve and corrupt even the arts and discriminations of the written word. It may happen, but it is also the case that the patient is alive and well and probably living in New York.

Angus Wilson's recent novel, *As if by Magic*, seems apposite here. It is, as one might expect, a work of great brilliance, and the stratum of meaning that underlies it abuts also on Sammler territory. Both novels are aware that the modern consciousness is and requires to be its own state of fiction: both record the fact with a degree of sarcasm and satire: Bellow through his radical discrimination of different worlds and life-styles, Wilson—more obviously and more dangerously—by equating the idea of magic with the fictional "solution": his young persons think that seminars on Lawrence and George Eliot will teach them magically how to live; his middle-aged agronomist hopes that his new strain of "magic" rice will cure the world of poverty. Bellow's young man extolling the bizarre threats of pickpockets as "a sudden glory"; or Wilson's young woman bedding down in the parental couch with two male fellow-students—both regard themselves as liberated and egged on by the images of consciousness that fiction brings; in the latter case, indeed, the girl sees herself as completing on her own initiative and in the conceit of her own apotheosised *savoir-vivre*, a model of living and loving not fully in the tableau of *Women in Love*.

The drawback to Wilson's method, however, is the absence of any detachment or radical distinction within the world of the novel itself. Whether by intention or by instinct its style and manner collude too deeply with the kinds of magic that its sights are supposedly set on; for it it written badly, as if the author were aware (which he no doubt is) that in a TV world words don't get paid much individual attention to—the programme merely rushes on, getting in as much frenetic entertainment and viewing time as possible. Wilson's object is compromised by his desire to produce a wholly contemporary work that is also there to take off the contemporary. He is clearly in mortal fear of being left out, of not being where the action is; and thus the texture of the work becomes as slovenly as everything in it. The irony is that he can make the kind of conscious use of Victorian fiction—its spaciousness, organisation and breadth of attack—that appears much more obliquely and interestingly in Bellow's Jewish background of serious culture and the moral contract: but his horror of seeming in any sense to recreate or make use of the Victorian fictional tradition leaves him in the end out on a limb. Clarity and focus disappear from the method, even as the message attempts in its own peculiar way to endorse them.

The interest of this is that it shows to what extent Wilson, like almost every other modern novelist, takes for granted the idea of unity, the "organic wholeness" of a work of art, a novel in particular. The oneness of his style with his characters' attitudes and responses is depressing, indeed claustrophobic, as it is in most other modern fiction. Bellow, by contrast, succeeds in *Mr. Sammler* in producing a masterpiece in which none of the pieces especially fit together, or have any need to do so. Dr. Lal and his moon theories, which appeal to Sammler's old fondness for H. G. Wells (himself of course an almost grotesque example of an impure and "non-unified" approach to fiction) are simply around in the slightly mad way in which so much else is today. Bellow would no doubt go along with the Hegelian view of modern art as presenting a bunch of alternatives and possible diversions too variegated to allow the use of any yardstick of quality and kind; significant, though, that Wells is not "placed" as a writer, but left hovering as an aspect of the culture that set out to make sense of things.

Since discrimination holds its pieces together like embroidery, it becomes almost willy-nilly a parody of works to which the symbolism of "wholeness" is avowedly essential. Difficult not to believe that Bellow, who in his time has tried out almost every style of fictional approach, did not here intend the signs and symbols of fictional earnestness to act as self-born mockers of fiction's enterprise. I have never "taught" Mr. Sammler, but I can imagine with what routine alertness the seminar would move off on the scent, turning from the moon symbolism with raised eyebrows to Angela and Shula (they would be prepared to accept that for Sammler himself the moon is not a sex symbol) and then in full cry after Eisen, the powerful mechanical young Israeli, with his ruined marriage and his horrible baize bag full of metal objects. The climax of meaning here would come when Feffer is struggling in the grip of the great negro, the exiled African prince, whom he has snapped with a minox camera in the act of pickpocketing. The fictional consciousness doing its thing on life. Up steps Eisen, and at a word misunderstood from his father-in-law Sammler, slams the negro's head with his bag of modern bronzes, modishly rough pseudo-art replicas of tanks and other artifacts of progress. Young crude Israeli smashes out at older but more dignified kinds of malignancy, whose normal thing is to be left to their bad selves. Meanwhile Wallace, turning father Gruner's place upside-down in his search for stashed Mafia currency, accidently severs a water-main. Gruner himself, in hospital, dies when the screw on his carotid artery fails to stop an aneurism flooding his brain with blood.

Already in such a paraphrase fiction has arrived: and with it all the usual kinds of falsity. But by letting such matters protrude, Bellow had disarmed them of any occult fictional power. If I am right that Mr. Sammler offers us a specific rejection of the modern fictional image, it certainly does not reject the devices of art, and particularly of the arts of formalism. Bellow makes symbolism work for him even as he depreciates it: its effect is to remind us that life is not like the images of it such devices draw: instead of involving us in a novel they coolly remind us it is not one. The simplicity and the candour of the book, and especially of its ending, do not depend alone on the ease with which Bellow and his cast skip into the Victorian moral framework but also on the skill with which the techniques of the novel form are used against it.

This skill is as old as *Tristram Shandy* or *Evgeny Onegin*, both of which share with *Mr Sammler* the disconcerting gift of imparting a very plain sense of life—its "contract" in fact—through a highly sophisticated and amused art contrivance. Not for nothing is this admonition—not stated openly, as Bellow in his last paragraph nerves himself to do—conveyed through an epigraph in Pushkin's verse novel: "Il n'y de bonheour que dans les voies communes". Nabokov's error, an astounding one, which only so solipsistically brilliant a leprechaun could be stupid enough to make, is not to see that such a plain revelation is the only point of formalism, that without that bread and butter to fall back on everything else at the tea-party turns sickly and boring.

It seems to me a fact of great importance that no single consciousness broods over *Mr. Sammler* and is co-extensive with the book. The distinction here would be between the novel in which everything—and not merely Madame Bovary herself—is *moi*; and the novel in which the author has as it were made the acquaintance of, and got on terms with, a person whom he can use as a narrator and explorer. Sammler is in no sense Bellow's *alter ego*, but a formal projection of aspects of Bellow's awareness of things, which enable him—and this is the secret of success probably—to diminish and refine judgment. Judgment is all the clearer because the judge is cranky, odd, distinctly out of things. Herzog and Bellow's other previous *consciences*, back to the Dangling Man, encroached too much upon author and novel alike—they became the fictional consciousness. Mr. Sammler does not do that; he is too evidently *a côte*, as, for example, Fanny Price is in *Mansfield Park*. Jane Austen does not so much say things through Fanny Price as see what the world looks like through her eyes. She is a more helpless as well as a more partial viewer than the author, and the world she sees is all the more clearly focused for that reason—judged too, with a judgment that does not pretend to be anything than partial and non-unified, appealing as it does to sources outside the novel's world.

Mr. Sammler succeeds by being partial and incomplete, by rejecting the modern novel's paradigm of totality in the act of consciousness. But it is not a symposium or *Bildungsroman*, full of wise saws and modern instances. They are there, each with an appropriate mouthpiece, but the novel's exquisite sense of place and person, its shapely but unemphatic perspective, provides without any need for an aggressive display of wholeness the magic circle within which, as James laid down, all relations happily appear to stop. Bellow also rejects the meaningful, putting as little weight behind his imputations as behind his symbols. Every implication is of course tendentious. As a Jewish partisan in the misery of wartime Poland Mr. Sammler was entitled, we gather, to the relief and rapture of violence which modern man claims as a right in itself, one neither earned by persecutions nor justified by contemporary conditions. These past/present contrasts do possess an external authenticity however: they do not depend on being part of a novel. Compare again with *As if By Magic*. Having trounced modern magic, in its various forms, Wilson ends by giving his heroine an enormous legacy, and this liberates her as no attempts at hippy culture or communal love-making had done. Money is the only true magic; but this banal conclusion, which cannot be avoided by the novel, cannot be openly endorsed by it either: it remains in the limbo between the novel's autonomous consciousness and the assertions that might be said to float free of it.

This is the dilemma of the unified novel consciousness. Hard and clear pieces of separable intelligence and insight get lost in it. But Bellow does not lose them. They remain detached from the narrative, constellated only with the twin planets of civilisation and style. This, admittedly, is only a fancy way of saying that one likes Bellow's personality, which is that of a man, not of a novel, and makes his work well suited to the *ad hominem* approach. And indeed, where the novel is concerned, is there—should there be—any other? What sort of a man is the novelist? Is he really worth getting to know?—it is these queries that get overlaid by our acceptance of the consciousness as fiction, as by any of the ensuing preoccupations of formalism.

In the words of Wallace (everyone in Mr. Sammler is rightly given a crisp, discriminatory turn of phrase; is endowed by the author not with dominant consciousness but with his separable skills) our recollecting and discussing with Mr. Sammler "helps to keep the wolf of insignificance from the door". There seems to me the possibility that it is by meeting his people in appraisal and speculation, outside fictional metaphysic, that we can apprehend their virtues; with certainty, and yet without their author seeming to be under strain to produce "a good man". The "goodness" of characters in art depend more than is usually recognised on our ability to converse with them. We talk with Pierce, Prince Andrew, Levin, Dostoevsky's Alyosha: his Myshkin, on the other hand, like his Svidrigailov and Stavrogin, we merely contemplate with fascination as we would an actor, in Mr. Sammler's words "a man with a bit to play, like so many modern individuals". Mr. Sammler is firmly in agreement with Simone Weil that the modern consciousness takes to the form of a fiction, doing its thing, "Acting Human", laughing and crying and getting others to laugh and cry.

"But supposing that one dislikes all this theatre of the soul?" Mr. Sammler's query is pertinent, for it might be thought: how in that case write novels, absorb us, and move us? Again the sap in the tradition behind Sammler and his author provide the answer. In steely fashion he seals off the modern, magic persons, those who are fuzzy with "Acting Human"—Shula, Angela, Wallace—from those who, like Margotte and Elya Gruner, know the human contract by not playing Human. Sammler knows the world, not by doing his thing in it but by being—as most by tradition are and must be—its victim: his war-time experiences are not only traditional and local—like the irruption of the Slav Question at the end of *Anna Karenina*—but endless and timeless. Bellow has succeeded in creating a hero who in terms of feeling, emotion and experience represents—if one may be forgiven the phrase—the silent majority, even while his capacity to reflect on and give words to these things is that of an intellectual. Sorel's famous dictum does not have the last word here: Mr. Sammler is a clerk, but a clerk who commits no treasons.

The Politics of Anti-Realism

BY GERALD GRAFF

With the waning of the political radicalism of the sixties, "cultural radicalism" has grown proportionately in influence. The radical legacy of the New Left and the counter culture seems increasingly to lie in the sphere of culture rather than of politics. "Cultural radicalism" and "cultural revolution" are vague terms, of course. They denote no particular school of thought but rather a certain style of thinking, a pattern of typical oppositions and identifications whose rationale is usually left unformulated. This style of thinking can be found today in structuralists and post-structuralists, phenomenologists, post-Freudians and Jungians, existential and Hegelian Marxists, and innumerable other manifestations of the vanguard spirit in art, criticism, and social thought. More broadly still, the patterns of radical cultural thought have become part of the folk mythology of intellectuals as a group — and of those whose outlook is shaped by intellectuals. The names and the movements may change, but the structures of thought persist. Anybody today who endeavors to think "advanced" thoughts about culture and society is likely to think them through at least some of the patterns I try to describe in this essay.

Central to the outlook of cultural radicalism is a romantic theory of history which sees the progressive evolution of objective rationality as a fall from the organic unity of prereflective stages of being. One style of romanticism sought to overcome this fall, or escape its consequences, by an imaginative return to the preindustrial past — to antiquity, the Middle Ages, primitive or folk culture. Another style of romanticism aimed not to reverse the course of progress but to carry forward and fulfill its promise of human liberation. This "romanticism of the left" sought to overcome the fall into reason by using the imagination not retrospectively but prophetically, to further the recovery of organic unity through a revolution exemplified by the sensibility of art. This radical romanticism at once overturned the utopian assumptions of the

Enlightenment and restated them in a new form, the avant-garde quest for a progressive expansion of the frontiers of consciousness.

Radical Parallelisms

The assumption cultural radicalism inherits from this left wing romanticism is that a parallelism exists between psychological, epistemological, esthetic, and political categories of experience. Repression in psychology, rationalism in epistemology, representationalism and the elitism of high culture in esthetics are parallel expressions of bourgeois social domination. A statement by Joyce Carol Oates, in an essay entitled "New Heaven and Earth," illustrates the neatness of alignment sometimes attained by this parallelism:

> We have come to the end of, we are satiated with, the "objective," valueless philosophies that have always worked to preserve a status quo, however archaic. We are tired of the old dichotomies: Sane/Insane, Normal/Sick, Black/White, Man/Nature, Victor/Vanquished, and — above all this Cartesian dualism I/It. . . . They are no longer useful or pragmatic. They are no longer *true.*[1]

Political domination (Victor/Vanquished) is the correlative both of the epistemological separation of the knower from his object (I/It) and the psychological or medical differentiation of sanity from insanity. The central assumption here is that objective thought is the psychological and epistemological counterpart of political tyranny. There are several senses in which this is held: objective thought requires us to repress our emotions, to take a "valueless" stance in the interests of operational efficiency. This "reification" destroys the unity between ourselves and what we perceive and turns the "other" into an alien thing, ripe for domination and manipulations. In a parallel fashion, Western civilization turns both nature and human beings into manipulable things through technological mastery on the one hand and colonialism and exploitation on the other. Finally, by taking for granted the existence of a stable world "out there," objective thought presupposes a reality that is essentially unchangeable. By adjusting to the "reality principle," we reconcile ourselves to the established consensus as if it were an eternal law of nature. Thus Roland Barthes can assert that "the

1 Joyce Carol Oates, "New Heaven and Earth," *Saturday Review of the Arts*, Vol. LV, 45 (November, 1972), p. 53.

disease of thinking in essences . . . is at the bottom of every bourgeois mythology of man."[2]

Far from representing the culmination of man's struggle against ignorance and superstition, then, objective thought emerges as at best a precondition of the expanded material basis on which a non-aggressive society must depend, as a stage in the evolution of consciousness toward a reunified sensibility. It follows that the cultural revolution must be conceived as a revolt against the reality principle in the name of the pleasure principle, as the overcoming of repressive reason by imagination — or by a new "reason" based on Eros, fantasy, non-aggressive desire. The struggle, as Herbert Marcuse defines it, is "between the logic of domination and the will to gratification," both asserting their claims "for defining the reality principle. The traditional ontology is contested: against the conception of being in terms of Logos rises the conception of being in a-logical terms: will and joy. This countertrend struggles to formulate its own Logos: the logic of gratification."[3] By undermining the epistemological and instinctual bases of domination, the cultural revolution prepares the way for the political transformation of society, though the precise nature of this transformation may as yet be only vaguely foreseeable. At present, it may only be possible to say, as Richard Poirier says, that any political solutions "will require a radical change in the historical, philosophical, and psychological assumptions that are the foundation of any political or economic system. Some kind of cultural revolution is therefore the necessary prelude even to our capacity to think intelligently about political revolution."[4]

Art plays a key role in the social vision of the cultural revolution, but not as propaganda art or as socialist realism. For though in *content* these methods may be radical, in their *forms*, and the modes of perception embodied in their forms, they are conventional and reactionary. Overthrowing the established form of society means overthrowing realism, or going "beyond realism." Art, defined as an autonomous expression of the imagination, not passively receiving its laws from nature but freely dictating them to nature, is seen as the epitome of liberated sensibility. The romantic opposition between discursive and creative meaning, between language used as a practical

2 Roland Barthes, *Mythologies*, trans. A. Lavers (New York: Hill and Wang, 1972), p. 75.

3 Herbert Marcuse, *Eros and Civilization: A Philosophical Inquiry into Freud* (New York: Vintage Books, 1962), p. 113.

4 Richard Poirier, *The Performing Self: Compositions and Decompositions in the Languages of Contemporary Life* (New York: Oxford University Press, 1970), p. 144.

sign and language used as a constitutive *symbol,* corresponds to the distinction between tyranny and liberation. The imagination's independence from reality exemplifies the human spirit's break with political oppression and psychic repression, with all preestablished ideas of reality. As Frank Kermode writes, echoing Barthes, "the whole movement towards 'secretarial' realism" represents "an anachronistic myth of common understanding and shared universes of meaning."[5] By refusing to hold a mirror up to nature and by exploding the very idea of a stable "nature," art undermines the psychological and epistemological bases of the ruling order. The revolt against realism and representation is closely tied to the revolt against a unitary psychology of the self. As Leo Bersani argues in *A Future for Astyanax,* "the literary myth of a rigidly ordered self," a myth perpetuated by realism, "contributes to a pervasive cultural ideology of the self which serves the established social order."[6]

Radical art ruptures not only the forced unification of the self but also the linguistic "contracts" which impose uniform assumptions, reassuring us that reality is known in advance. Alain Robbe-Grillet says that "academic criticism in the West, as in the Communist countries, employs the word 'realism' as if reality were already entirely constituted (whether for good and all, or not) when the writer comes on the scene. Thus it supposes that the latter's role is limited to 'explaining' and to 'expressing' the reality of his period."[7] In a similar vein, Roland Barthes disparages the conventions of narrative fiction as "formal pacts made between the writer and society for the justification of the former and the serenity of the latter."[8] "Classical language," says Barthes, "is a bringer of euphoria because it is immediately social,"[9] implying a world known and agreed upon in advance — packaged, as it were, for the convenience of the consumer. Narrative realism is "the currency in use in a society apprised by the very form of words of the meaning of what it consumes."[10] Preestablished codes imply a myth of preestablished reality and order, and "the content of the word 'Order' always indicates repression."[11]

5 Frank Kermode, "Novels: Recognition and Deception," *Critical Inquiry*, Vol. I, 1 (Sept., 1974), p. 112.

6 Leo Bersani, *A Future for Astyanax: Character and Desire in Literature* (New York: Little, Brown, 1976), p. 56.

7 Alain Robbe-Grillet, *For a New Novel* (New York: Grove Press, 1965), p. 160.

8 Barthes, *Writing Degree Zero*, trans. A. Lavers (New York: Hill and Wang, 1953), p. 32.

9 *Ibid.*, p. 49.

10 *Ibid.*, p. 32.

11 *Ibid.*, p. 26.

The move beyond the "correspondence" theory of language entails a rejection of the mimetic view of criticism along with the mimetic view of literature. Just as literature must explode the bourgeois myth of a real world independent of human perception and fantasy, so criticism must divest itself of the academic myths of "the work itself," the "intention" of the author, and the "text" as a reified object. The theory that literature radically "defamiliarizes" our perception of reality spawns the corollary that criticism ought to defamiliarize our perception of literature. Just as the literary work destroys our complacent agreement about the nature of reality, criticism "deconstructs" the static, canonical interpretations by which conventional scholarship entraps the work and domesticates its potentially explosive energies. These moves beyond realism and beyond objective interpretation are paralleled in turn by a third impulse, which seeks to go beyond elitist hierarchies of high and low culture. The old-fashioned writer's conformity to a preestablished reality or the old-fashioned critic's conformity to an objective text or to a body of critical principles and criteria are emblems of the mass man's conformity to the propaganda and manipulation of organized technological society. These equations may not coexist in all radical theories, but they form a logical unity. I propose to examine them in turn.

Beyond Realism

One of the most systematic attempts at an anti-realistic theory of radical esthetics has been made by Herbert Marcuse, whom I shall treat at some length here. Unlike Barthes, Marcuse resists the equation of "classical language" and classical form with bourgeois political domination; he attacks Herbert Read and other avant-garde irrationalists for assuming that "classicism is the intellectual counterpart of political tyranny." Bourgeois art, including bourgeois realism, according to Marcuse, "transcends all particular class content." Through its expression of specifically bourgeois concerns, this art achieves a "universal meaning" that may be liberating for all classes.[12] Agreeing with Trotsky's strictures against an exclusively proletarian culture, Marcuse holds that the cultural revolution should not repudiate bourgeois culture, but should try to "recapture and transform" its "critical, negating, transcending qualities."[13] Marcuse's own esthetic theory attempts to use the concepts of Kant, Schiller, and Freud while overcoming their bourgeois limitations. Marcuse's respect for classical

12 Marcuse, *Counterrevolution and Revolt* (Boston: Beacon Press, 1972), pp. 89-90.
13 *Ibid.*, p. 93.

art distinguishes his position from that of Barthes. But Marcuse defends classical art only by describing it in romantic terms. Hence, he, like Barthes, opposes art to classical rationality and anything resembling mimesis. As thoroughly as any romantic theorist, Marcuse identifies art with the pleasure principle and denies its dependence on the reality principle. Following Kant and Schiller, Marcuse defines art as a "non-conceptual truth of the senses."[14] Though art may *use* concepts as part of its raw material, it is not obliged to reflect conceptual or theoretical truth. Marcuse thus rejects Lukács' praise of bourgeois critical realism for depicting "the basic laws which represent capitalist society." This requirement, he says "offends the very nature of art. For the basic structure and dynamic of society can never find sensuous, esthetic expression: they are, in Marxian theory, the essence behind the appearance, which can only be attained through scientific analysis, and formulated only in terms of such an analysis. The open form cannot close the gap between the scientific truth and its esthetic appearance."[15]

Such a passage suggests how ambivalent Marcuse can be with respect to classical rationality, how he hovers on the edge of romantic irrationalism without ever quite taking the plunge. On the one hand, he calls for a new "conception of being in a-logical terms: will and joy," a "logic of gratification."[16] On the other hand, he does not reject Marxist "scientific analysis." We shall return to this problem later. For the moment, the important point is that though Marcuse does not wholly deny the possibility or desirability of an objectivist or realistic epistemology, he distinguishes this epistemology from that of art, contrasting art with science in the customary romantic fashion. For the creative imagination, he says, summarizing Kant, "the experience in which the object is thus 'given' is totally different from the every-day as well as scientific experience; all links between the object and the world of theoretical and practical reason are severed, or rather suspended."[17] Presumably, these oppositions between the esthetic and the theoretical and practical realms are "transcended" by the work of art itself, or by the revolutionary realization of artistic vision in the society of the future. But art remains for Marcuse a non-conceptual mode of experience. It does not reflect reality.

A similar, though more equivocal rejection of realism characterizes much of the current revival of Marxist criticism. Siding with Brecht over

14 Marcuse, *Eros and Civilization,* p. 169. "The norms which govern the aesthetic order are *not* 'intellectual concepts'" (*Counterrevolution and Revolt*, p. 95).

15 Marcuse, *Counterrevolution and Revolt*, p. 125.

16 Marcuse, *Eros and Civilization*, p. 113.

17 *Ibid.*, p. 162.

Lukács, the New Marxism often leans toward the kind of analogical reasoning — long common in bourgeois avant-garde circles — which regards "open" forms as progressive, "closed" ones as reactionary. Thus Terry Eagleton, in *Criticism and Ideology*, opposes "Lukács' nostalgic organicism, his traditionalist preference for closed, symmetrical totalities," to "open, multiple forms which bear in their torsions the very imprint of the contradictions they lay bare."[18] But how can open, multiple forms "lay bare" contradictions when they are, so often, themselves expressions of a viewpoint distorted by alienation? Where does literature get the perspective that permits it to present distortion *as* distortion, to make itself a criticism of contradictions rather than a symptom of them?

In another book, *Marxism and Literary Criticism*, Eagleton hedges on these questions. He says that art can "yield us a kind of truth," but this truth is "not, to be sure, a scientific or theoretical truth." Rather, it is "the truth of how men experience their conditions of life and how they protest against them." In other words, "though art is not in itself a scientific mode of truth, it can, nevertheless, communicate the *experience* of such a scientific (i.e., revolutionary) understanding of society. This is the experience which *revolutionary* art can yield us." This sounds like a left-wing version of Susanne Langer's theory that art yields a "virtual experience" of understanding without the content of understanding, or like T. S. Eliot's view that poetry does not solicit beliefs but shows us "what it feels like" to have beliefs. The separation between the conceptual and the experiential, so familiar in bourgeois esthetic theory, is not overcome. Or is it? Eagleton does suggest that art somehow gives a critical perspective toward ideology:

> Science gives us conceptual knowledge of a situation; art gives us the experience of that situation, which is equivalent to ideology. But by doing this, it allows us to "see" the nature of that ideology, and thus begins to move us towards that full understanding of ideology which is scientific knowledge.[19]

It is not clear how a work of art can let us "see" the nature of an ideology (and why the quotation marks?) without communicating a conceptual apprehension of the ideology. Either the audience perceives the ideology *as* an ideology, in which case it conceptualizes it, or it does not see the

18 Terry Eagleton, *Criticism and Ideology: a Study in Marxist Literary Theory* (London: NLB, 1977), p. 161.

19 Eagleton, *Marxism and Literary Criticism* (Berkeley: University of California Press, 1976), p. 74, p. 83, n. 16.

ideology at all. The same equivocations over realism can be found in other current Hegelian and existential Marxists, but I cannot dwell on these theories here. One can appreciate the determination of the neo-Marxists to avoid the crudities of vulgar Stalinist realism with its dismissal of modernist experimental forms. But in their sympathy with the anti-realistic premises of modernism, the neo-Marxists may have abandoned the critical standpoint which makes Marxism a corrective to conventional modernist literary positions. Marcuse avoids these contradictions by unequivocally denying the realistic and theoretical nature of art. But Marcuse, too, as we shall see, has problems when he attempts to account for the subversive power of art.

How *does* Marcuse account for this subversive power? Marcuse says this power resides not in the content of art but in its form. It is art's freedom from conceptual reality, in fact, its ability to create out of the autonomy of the imagination that "other nature" which, as Kant theorized, supplies a "completeness of which there is no example in nature," that makes art a criticism of the existing order. By freely dreaming new possibilities of desire that have never been embodied in the actual world, art gives us a measure of the unsatisfactory reality around us. In this sense, all art for Marcuse is formalistic art — even realism. For though the world of a work of art may, as he says, be "derived from the existing one," it transforms this raw material according to the esthetic laws of art and the psychological laws of the mind.[20] In other words, though art may employ realistic conventions, it cannot serve a realistic ontology. "The norms governing the order of art are not those governing reality but rather the norms of its negation,"[21] a negation implicit in the form and style of art as such. Marcuse connects Kant's idea of the imagination and Schiller's idea of art as "play" with the Freudian concepts of the pleasure principle, Eros, and "the return of the repressed."[22]

Art then, regardless of its specific content, evokes "the power of the negative." Its very structure is made up of "the words, the images, the music of another reality, of another order repelled by the existing one and yet alive in memory and anticipation. . . ."[23] This means that even the artist who sets out to justify the established political order actually ends up subverting it. Marcuse thus arrives at a different sort of justification for explicitly "reactionary" art than that of traditional

20 Marcuse, *Counterrevolution and Revolt*, p. 92.

21 *Ibid.*, p. 95.

22 Marcuse, *Eros and Civilization*, p. 130.

23 Marcuse, *Counterrevolution and Revolt*, p. 92.

Marxist criticism, which also seeks to locate a "progressive" content unintended by the creator of the work. Marx, Engels, and Lukács praised the novels of Balzac for giving a picture of social reality unwittingly at odds with the author's intended legitimist message. For Marcuse, such writings are revolutionary not because they imitate the real world but because they negate it. Form is not transparent representation but transformation of reality, and for this reason subversive.

On the other hand, Marcuse holds that the purely esthetic nature of artistic negation limits the political effectiveness of art: "the critical function of art is self-defeating. The very commitment of art to form vitiates the negation of unfreedom in art." The element of "semblance" in art "necessarily subjects the represented reality to esthetic standards and thus deprives it of its terror."[24] This fact explains for Marcuse why societies have often been able to domesticate radical art and render its rebellion harmless. Marcuse's esthetic writings are studded with warnings against overestimating the power of art by itself to precipitate a revolution. Nevertheless, despite these cautions, Marcuse does not cease affirming that art embodies the very spirit of human liberation. And in *Essay on Liberation*, a kind of manifesto of the late sixties, Marcuse judged that the "disorderly, uncivil, farcical, artistic desublimation of culture constitutes an essential element of radical politics: of the subverting forces in transition."[25]

In the esthetic of the cultural left, one of the chief means by which art presumably exercises a subversive political effect is by shattering familiar modes of perception. This esthetic of "defamiliarization," as it has been called,[26] has its roots in the romantic idea that art strips away the veil of customary perception and permits us to see the world in a new light. At first sight, this doctrine appears anti-formalistic, and indeed it became one of the guiding assumptions of literary realism in the nineteenth century, in those realists who saw themselves as unmasking the false appearances of society. But formalism may itself appear as an esthetic of defamiliarization, an esthetic that seeks to explode the familiarities of realism. Formalism defamiliarizes experience not in order to reveal some truth behind the veil, but rather in order to dislodge

24 Marcuse, *Eros and Civilization*, p. 131.

25 Marcuse, *Essay on Liberation* (Boston: Beacon Press, 1969), p. 48.

26 See Robert Scholes' discussion of this concept in Russian formalist criticism in *Structuralism and Literature: an Introduction* (New Haven: Yale University Press, 1974), pp. 83-85, pp. 173-76; also Jonathan Culler, *Structuralist Poetics: Structuralism, Linguistics, and the Study of Literature* (Ithaca: Cornell University Press, 1975), p. 134.

us from our expectation of ever encountering truth. It is this use that Marcuse makes of the concept of esthetic defamiliarization, enabling him to reconcile his Kantian formalism with a kind of surrealism.

Marcuse writes of "surrealistic forms of protest and refusal" as the needed solvent of "repressive reason" in one-dimensional society.[27] He celebrates the verbal disruptions of experimental literature, which break the oppressive rule of the established language and images over the mind of man. He stresses that art dissolves the film of familiarity and cliché which, in advanced society, intercedes between reality and our perceptions:

> Non-objective, abstract painting and sculpture, stream-of-consciousness and formalist literature, twelve-tone composition, blues and jazz: these are not merely new modes of perception reorienting and intensifying the old ones, they rather dissolve the very structure of perception in order to make room — for what? The new object of art is not yet "given," but the familiar object has become impossible, false. From illusion, imitation, harmony to reality — but the reality is not yet "given"; it is not the one which is the object of "realism." Reality has to be discovered and projected. The senses must learn not to see things anymore in the medium of that law and order which has formed them; the bad functionalism which organizes our sensibility must be smashed.[28]

Art in this way brings into being a "new sensorium." In the universe of art, Marcuse says, everything "is 'new,' different — breaking the familiar context of perception and understanding, of sense certainty and reason in which men and nature are enclosed."[29]

This concept of radical perceptual disruption informs the esthetics of "self-conscious" fiction, science fiction, and other departures from realism. David Ketterer, for example, writes of the "radical disorientation" produced in the reader by science fiction conventions, and Darko Suvin calls this effect one of "cognitive estrangement." According to Ketterer, the new epistemology of science fiction tends to "destroy old assumptions and suggest a new, and often more visionary reality."[30] A similar view is advanced by Robert Scholes. Science fiction,

27 Marcuse, *Essay on Liberation*, p. 30.

28 *Ibid.*, pp. 38-9.

29 Marcuse, *Counterrevolution and Revolt*, p. 98.

30 Quoted by James Stupple, "Fiction Against the Future," *The American Scholar*, Vol. 46, 2 (Spring, 1977), p. 219.

Scholes says, "can regenerate a criticism of present life . . . through the construction of models of the future." Science fiction can serve this "model-making" critical function, according to Scholes, precisely because it is not burdened by the reactionary constraints of realistic probability but is "freed," as Scholes says, "of the problem of correspondence or noncorrespondence with some present actuality or some previously experienced past."[31] Similarly, for critics writing in this vein, literary reflexivity is radical: by calling into question the referential adequacy of the categories of understanding, it shakes us loose from our susceptibility to ideology.

Structuralism has served the purposes of radical esthetic theory by demonstrating that language is an affair of conventions, cultural creations that do not necessarily rest on truths of nature. Structuralism shows that signification is not a closed system, regulated by eternal meanings, but a process infinitely open to interpretation. In Barthes' use of structuralism, the departures of modern poetry from the "naturalized" cultural norms of prose have an exemplary value, shattering the illusion of a natural link between conventions, and the ideologies underlying them, and nature. Barthes contrasts realistic prose, that presupposes a closed, completed universe, with "the terror of an expression without laws" evoked by modern poetry, where "the word is no longer guided *in advance* by the general intention of a socialized discourse."[32] "Each poetic word is thus an unexpected object, a Pandora's box from which fly out all the potentialities of language" — a discourse "terrible and inhuman."[33] The modern poet in this way exposes the worthlessness of bourgeois "currency," for underlying it is only the fiction of an eternal order of reality.

Both Barthes and Marcuse are aware of the paradoxical and equivocal nature of this mode of artistic negation. Marcuse cites Barthes' *Writing Degree Zero* in *One-Dimensional Man* as an example of the kind of vanguard theory which is forced, by "the total mobilization of all media for the defense of the established reality," to call for a "break with communication" itself.[34] Marcuse recognizes that such anti-art may be politically innocuous, along with the art that expresses "a fashionably desublimated, verbal release of sexuality."[35]

31 Robert Scholes, "The Fictional Criticism of the Future," *TriQuarterly*, No. 34 (Fall, 1975), p. 242.

32 Barthes, *Writing Degree Zero*, p. 48.

33 *Ibid.*, p. 26.

34 Marcuse, *One-Dimensional Man: Studies in the Ideology of Advanced Industrial Society* (Boston: Beacon Press, 1964), p. 68.

35 Marcuse, *Counterrevolution and Revolt*, p. 118, n.

He condemns the irrationalism and mysticism of Norman O. Brown, Charles Reich, and the counter culture. He argues that the "revolution in perception" is vitiated when, through drugs or other stimulants, "its narcotic character brings temporary release not only from the reason and rationality of the established system but also from that other rationality which is to change the established system."[36] In the early seventies in particular, Marcuse seemed to retract some of the sympathy he had previously expressed for the irrationalistic ruptures of vanguard art. In *Counterrevolution and Revolt* (1972), Marcuse attacks Artaudian Theater of Cruelty, Living Theater, and rock culture as symptoms rather than criticisms of a sick society: "to the degree to which it makes itself part of real life," he says, this art "loses the transcendence which opposes art to the established order. . . ."[37] The criticism is well taken. What is not clear, however, is why Marcuse's own endorsement of formalism and surrealism, indeed Marcuse's definition of all art, should be immune to it. The shattering of the reality principle Marcuse calls for, the overcoming of the subject-object distinction, the emergence of a "new sensorium" — these things would seem to entail the very merging of art and life which Marcuse here deplores.

Radical esthetics without realism has been expounded by several American critics in a form that at first appears to be anti-political. In *The Confusion of Realms*, Richard Gilman attacks all artistic theory and practice which takes literature to be "an employment of language for ends beyond itself."[38] Invoking recent self-reflexive experimental fiction (Barthelme, Gass, Updike) and the criticism of Susan Sontag, Gilman argues that literary works are self-sufficient, self-justifying universes within themselves, not second-order representations of some already existing reality. Literature is properly an "increment," not a "complement," Gilman says;[39] it need not communicate "experience of any kind except an esthetic one,"[40] and it has "no reason for being other than to test and exemplify new forms of consciousness, which, moreover, have had to be invented precisely because actuality is incapable of generating them."[41] Elsewhere, Gilman applauds "the secularization of art," which is to say, "its chastening and the removal from it of the 'values' that ought to be obtained elsewhere, i.e., the moral, social, and philosophical values which literature and art were

36 Marcuse, *Essay on Liberation*, p. 37.

37 Marcuse, *Counterrevolution and Revolt*, p. 101.

38 Richard Gilman, *The Confusion of Realms* (New York: Random House, 1969), p. 49.

39 *Ibid.*, p. 264.

40 *Ibid.*, p. 48.

41 *Ibid.*, p. 72.

once expected to communicate."[42] Richard Poirier, advancing an esthetic of "the performing self," agrees with these sentiments. He endorses Gilman's attack on those who "confuse realms" by subordinating art to political ends and holds that "literature has only one responsibility — to be compelled and compelling about its own inventions."[43] In *A World Elsewhere*, Poirier argues that American literature, in its classic embodiments, can be seen as a series of attempts to create fictive worlds of pure "style" against the alien laws of politics, morality, and social behavior. These works create "an imaginative environment that excludes the standards of that 'real' one to which most critics subscribe."[44] A similarly anti-political formalism appears in the theories of Susan Sontag, Leo Bersani, and many others. These critics suggest that the psychic experimentalism of modern art is incompatible with the collective goals of humanitarian social reform, whether liberal or socialist. For them the cultural revolution speaks for antinomian energies which cannot be domesticated within the organized forms of politics and cannot be tailored to fit the requirements of any imaginable society, however ideal.

In its very disengagement from society and politics, however, this formalism reveals its political animus. The ostensibly chastened renunciation of humanistic pretentions for literature serves the aggressive aim of subverting the bourgeois mentality. Gilman's assertion that literature ought not be "an employment of language for ends beyond itself" contradicts his assertion that literature's purpose is to "test and exemplify new forms of consciousness," for the new forms of consciousness are obviously designed to subvert the old ones. Like Marcuse, Gilman proposes formalism as a weapon — the epistemological solvent of the bourgeois reality/principle and the "old Mediterranean values" which "are making some of us sick with a sense of lacerating irony."[45] The glorification of literature as a "world elsewhere," in the very process of divorcing literature from politics, betrays political resentment. It bespeaks a perception that, as Poirier puts it, "there is nothing within the real world, or in the systems which dominate it, that can possibly satisfy" our aspirations.[46] The same

42 Gilman, "The Idea of the Avant-Garde," *Partisan Review*, Vol. XXXIX (Summer, 1972), p. 395.

43 Poirier, *The Performing Self*. p. 31.

44 Poirier, *A World Elsewhere: the Place of Style in American Literature* (New York: Oxford University Press, 1966), p. 7.

45 Gilman, *The Confusion of Realms*, p. 19.

46 Poirier, *A World Elsewhere*, p. 5. I discuss Gilman and Poirier at greater length in "Aestheticism and Cultural Politics," *Social Research*, Vol. XL (Summer, 1973), pp. 311-343.

impulse that turns formalism against society turns it against radical politics, seen as a mere extension of the over-organized, over-rationalized social order.

Beyond Objective Criticism

As I have noted in a previous essay,[47] some recent commentators have seen the strangulation of art by criticism as a kind of literary counterpart of imperialism or industrial pollution. Thus Susan Sontag: "Like the fumes of the automobile and of heavy industry which befoul the urban atmosphere, the effusion of interpretations of art today poisons our sensibilities." Interpretation, she adds, is "the revenge of the intellect upon art."[48] It follows that art must get its own back by defining itself as the revenge of sensibility against the intellect, which is to say, against a culture whose political repressiveness is presumably exemplified in its overintellectuality. In this spirit, Leslie Fiedler calls for a postmodern criticism that abandons hollow pretentions to correctness and asserts itself unabashedly as creative writing, a criticism "poetic in form as well as in substance."[49] As if in response to Fiedler's call, a number of theories have arisen, including Ihab Hassan's "paracriticism" (which makes "mixed use of disconfirmation and discontinuity, of space, silence, self-query, and surprise"), Roland Barthes' evocation of the text as "a body of bliss consisting solely of erotic relations," Stanley Fish's "affective stylistics," and Harold Bloom and J. Hillis Miller's arguments for the necessity of "misreading."[50] These theories argue not only that the reader must create the text — a proposition defensible enough if understood in the right way — but that he must (or should) create it without reference to any control outside the fictions imposed by his subjectivity or by the open-ended possibilities of language. That the reader is thereby "liberated" in some way is taken to be beyond argument, even though not all these theories conceive the liberation in political terms.

But in some instances, the attack on objective interpretation has been given a Marxian twist, with the suggestion that the very concept of

47 See "What Was New Criticism? Literary Interpretation and Scientific Objectivity," *Salmagundi*, No. 27 (Fall, 1974), pp. 72-93.

48 Susan Sontag, *Against Interpretation* (New York: Delta Books, 1967), p. 7.

49 Leslie Fiedler, "Cross the Border, Close the Gap," *Playboy*, Vol. 16 (December, 1969), p. 230.

50 Ihab Hassan, "Joyce, Beckett, and the Postmodern Imagination," *TriQuarterly*, No. 34 (Fall 1975), p. 181; Barthes, *The Pleasure of the Text*, trans. R. Miller (New York: Hill and Wang, 1975), p. 16; Stanley Fish, "Interpreting the *Variorum*," *Critical Inquiry*, Vol. II, 3 (Spring, 1976), pp. 465-85; Harold Bloom, *A Map of Misreading* (New York: Oxford University Press, 1975); J. Hillis Miller, "Deconstructing the Deconstructers," *Diacritics* (Summer, 1975), p. 30.

textual determinacy is an extension of the system of private property. Again, the reasoning is highly analogical. Objectivity is a kind of police force suppressing the creative flow of interpretation. Or objective interpretation treats the text as a kind of "currency," bound by linguistic "contracts" to the existing class system. By freeing the text from the author's intended meaning and treating it as "multivalent," "plural," and open to the uninhibited and loving "play" of interpretation, the critic, it is implied, transgresses the bourgeois system of ownership:

> A multivalent text [Barthes argues] can carry out its basic duplicity only if it subverts the opposition between the true and the false, if it fails to attribute quotations (even when seeking to discredit them) to explicit authorities, if it flouts all respect for origin, paternity, propriety, if it destroys the voice which could give the text its ("organic") unity, in short, if it coldly and fraudulently abolishes quotation marks which must, as we say, in all *honesty*, enclose a quotation and juridically distribute the ownership of the sentences to their respective proprietors, like subdivisions of a field. For multivalence (contradicted by irony) is a transgression of ownership.[51]

Barthes' disengagement in *S/Z* of Balzac's "Sarrasine," then, from its author's apparent intention is aimed at bourgeois "propriety" (paralleled by bourgeois "paternity"), not merely the external propriety of social and literary decorum but the structures of possession and control this decorum rationalizes. At the very least, this kind of reading presumably undermines the ideology of professional literary study.

Critics who wish to liberate the reader from the determinacy of the text often write as if the only alternative were a kind of critical Final Solution that shuts off all disagreement out of a neurotic fear of uncertainty. Thus Barthes dismisses the problem of interpretive truth with the assertion that "the language each critic chooses does not come down to him from Heaven."[52] He thereby implies that if you are looking for truth in your interpretations, you are probably longing for some kind of theocratic authority to relieve you of the anxiety of choice. Start believing in the existence of an objective world or text, and the next thing you know you will be calling out the ideological police — demanding censorship and suppressing disagreement. At the very least, you convict yourself of existential cowardice. This reduction of the issue

51 Barthes, *S/Z*, trans. R. Miller (New York: Hill and Wang, 1974), pp. 44-45.

52 Barthes, "What is Criticism?", *Critical Essays*, trans. R. Howard (Evanston: Northwestern University Press, 1972), p. 260.

to a simple polarity of tyranny vs. freedom, bad faith vs. authenticity, is seen in an often-quoted statement by Derrida:

> There are thus two interpretations of interpretation, of structure, of sign, of freeplay. The one seeks to decipher, dreams of deciphering, a truth or an origin which is free from freeplay or from the order of the sign, and lives like an exile the necessity of interpretation. The other, which is no longer turned toward the origin, affirms freeplay and tries to pass beyond man and humanism, the name of man being the name of that being who, throughout the history of metaphysics or of ontotheology—in other words, through the history of all of his history—has dreamed of full presence, the reassuring foundation, the origin and the end of the game.[53]

Quoting this passage, Frank Kermode characterizes the contrast between types of interpretation as a contrast between "the old, Puritan, strict, limited, theocratic, radiating certainty about emblems and types," and "the new, which depends on the activity of the individual creative mind, on the light of imagination."[54] The choice having been reduced to one between defensive Puritanism and open-minded creativity, not much remains to argue about.

Beyond High Culture

Like literary realism and objective criticism, the distinction between high and low culture is attacked as a symptom of elitist ideology. Not only is a preference for high over mass culture presumably "elitist," but this label is sometimes applied to virtually any critical reservations about mass culture. Leslie Fiedler, for example, equates high culture with the "finicky canons of the genteel tradition."[55] Against this genteel tradition Fiedler poses an insurgent, anti-hierarchical, irreverent popular culture, and a postmodern art and criticism impatient with the old boundaries and determined to "cross the border, close the gap." "The final intrusion of pop into the citadels of high art," Fiedler says, presents "the exhilarating new possibility of making judgments about the goodness and badness of art quite separated from distinctions between high and low, with their concealed class bias."[56]

53 Jacques Derrida, "Structure, Sign, and Play in the Discourse of the Human Sciences," *The Structuralist Controversy: The Languages of Criticism and the Sciences of Man*, ed. E. Donato and R. Macksey (Baltimore: Johns Hopkins University Press, 1972), p. 264.

54 Kermode, "Novels: Recognition and Deception," p. 119.

55 Fiedler, "Cross the Border, Close the Gap," p. 230.

56 *Ibid.*, p. 256.

Richard Wasson expresses a similar exhilaration. The merging of high and mass culture in the sixties, Wasson believes, signalled the end of the dichotomy of action and contemplation that has kept the intellectual in a position of sterile isolation. The sixties, he writes, "give us a series of metaphors of culture which we might categorize as incarnational: culture leaves its sacred cloister and goes into the world to participate in the joys and sorrows of the human community and to work for its redemption."[57] One of Wasson's examples of this "incarnational" overcoming of distinctions is Northrop Frye's system of archetypes, which permits us to "demystify the discipline of English studies" by showing that the same mythic and generic structures pervade high and low forms alike. "That is why the standard criticism of Frye — that one can find archetypes everywhere — is so absurd; it's precisely because they are omnipresent that the literary critic can speak to the problems of civilization, can use his special competence to participate in the efforts of mankind to shape the world."[58] And again: "for Frye the job of the man of culture is not to defend highbrow culture but to demystify forms of communication by revealing their connections."[59] In Marcuse and Frye, Wasson concludes, "imaginative culture" transcends traditional distinctions; it "furthers the cause of Eros, of freedom, of liberation; it is not a spiritual discipline, an inner check, a hostile force opposed to the mass and popular arts, but a vehicle of liberation."[60]

The logic of this argument leads Wasson to congratulate Frye for declining to "consider advertising as 'bad' or 'false' or a mass media to be opposed by highbrow taste." He refers specifically to a statement by Frye that "to protect ourselves in a world such as ours" we have to look at advertising ironically, so that instead of rejecting it we "choose what we want out of what's offered to us and let the rest go." Here, Wasson comments, "advertising is appropriated into the total form of literature, into the world of archetypes. We react to advertising in the context of our understanding of verbal statements, of the visions of the world that literature gives, and in that context we accept or reject the vision. Literature, literary criticism, and literary education play then a decisive role in shaping the civilization we have and the civilization we want."[61]

57 Richard Wasson, "From Priest to Prometheus: Culture and Criticism in the Post-Modern Period," *Journal of Modern Literature*, Vol. III, 5 (July, 1974), p. 1201.

58 *Ibid.*, p. 1195.

59 *Ibid.*, p. 1197.

60 *Ibid.*, p. 1201.

61 *Ibid.*, p. 1197.

This argument is elusive: if, as Frye suggests, advertising is something from which we need to protect ourselves by means of irony, then where does this irony come from if not from some external perspective superior to advertising? Is not irony a bit condescending, a bit "elitist"? Wasson evidently recognizes the need to maintain a critical view of mass culture, yet the need to avoid the elitism of "highbrow taste" encourages the elimination of critical distance. What do we do when mass culture fails to correspond, precisely, to "the civilization we want"? And how do we know "what we want" unless we examine our desires critically and objectively? Critical principles seem to be required somewhere here, yet such principles seem incompatible with culture defined as an expression of the joys of Eros and of "incarnational unity of being." If detachment and dualism are equated with elitism, then the very resistance of intellectuals to society comes to be suspect. In the name of radical egalitarianism, criticism has to be liquidated.

Radical Contradictions

Here we can begin to see how the typical equations and oppositions of radical esthetics open it to difficulties. By equating imagination, Eros, and the pleasure principle with liberation and conceptual rationality with repression and elitism, radical esthetics accedes to the kind of technological dissociation of sensibility that it aims to oppose. Though this esthetics protests against positivistic and philistine reductions of art to the status of mere fantasy and myth, it reinstates these reductions in its own definition of art as an explosion of the unrationalized aspects of the psyche. Radical esthetics may claim to "reconcile" art and reason, but the reconciliation is prevented by the repudiation of mimetic theories of art and by the antinomy of theoretical and imaginative truth. Presupposing the degraded view of reason that identifies it with functional rationality, radical esthetics embarks on a self-defeating effort to make creative imagination, Eros, the senses do the work that only the reasoning intellect can do. This effort implants a familiar contradiction into radical culture: in exposing objective reason as an ideology, radicalism leaves itself no means of legitimizing its own critique of injustice and exploitation. If objectivity is a myth, then the rationale of tyranny is undermined, but so is the rationale of principled resistance to tyranny. Radical esthetics equates liberation with the transcendence of the subject-object distinction, as embodied in art and in the new sensibility. But such transcendence blurs the distinction between reality and myth and undermines the possibility of criticism.

The chronic ambiguity of its epistemology makes formalism an equivocal basis for an esthetic of radical intransigence. Formalism vacillates between opposing itself to reality and to the languages of practical discourse and appropriating them. Though formalism likes to oppose art to life, it also frequently confuses art with life, turning "life" itself into a set of literary fictions. When formalists like Gilman and Poirier suggest that "reality" is a myth of the imagination they perpetrate the "confusion of realms" they attack. If one strategy of formalism is to turn its back on politics and history and withdraw into the "world elsewhere" of art, another is to take revenge on politics and history by annexing them into the structures of art, turning them into manifestations of the imagination and the ego.

Thus Poirier, for example, asserts that "all expressed forms of life, reality and history" are "fictions": "Where is the Civil War and how do we know it? Where is the President and how does anyone know him? Is he a history book, an epic poem, or a cartoon by David Levine?"[62] Art reacts against the general invasion of life by theatricality and unreality by universalizing it, abolishing reality itself. In the process, art loses its critical perspective.

Radical esthetics confuses the acceptance of a common reality with capitulation of political tyranny. It is this confusion that causes Barthes, for example, to denounce the esthetics of representation and realism, for such an esthetics, deriving from "classical" (or in Derrida's term, "logocentric") assumptions about language, presupposes a common reality as the ground of language. As Jonathan Culler summarizes Barthes' argument (with apparent agreement), representational writing "depends heavily on readers' ability to naturalize it and to recognize the common world which serves as point of reference; and consequently changes in the social situation, which make it clear that the world is not one, undermine this *écriture*."[63] It is a historical fact that the loss of a sense of a common world, shared by the various classes and nations, was a principal cause of the decline of mimesis as a literary mode. But it does not follow that we can accept the absence of a common world as a literal philosophical truth, nor certainly as a shibboleth of radicalism. To reject the existence of a common world as a bourgeois myth is simply to invalidate political discourse, which depends on the possibility of giving a uniform reference to terms such as "exploitation," "justice," "equality," "oppressor," and "oppressed."[64]

62 Poirier, *Performing Self*, p. 29.

63 Culler, *Structuralist Poetics*, p. 135.

64 Culler acknowledges the necessity of a "common world" when he says that "the possibility of critical argument depends on shared notions of the acceptable and the

These terms, of course, may be perverted in systematic ways by the conventional languages of a particular ruling class, but our ability to identify the perversion as a perversion depends on our ability to refer to a common world. By mistaking shared reality and shared language with a stifling conformity, Barthes ends up attacking no particular society but the process of socialization. He is led to promote an antinomian definition of freedom as the refusal of community — a bourgeois definition of freedom if there ever was one.[65]

A radical esthetic based on formalism and defamiliarization encounters other kinds of problems. By breaking with the common language, such an esthetic deepens the division between art and society and perpetuates the spiral of artistic alienation and impotence. The more violently the arts overturn objective consciousness, the representational view of art, and the common language, the more surely do they guarantee their marginality and harmlessness — a condition which in its turn inspires renewed artistic attempts to overturn objective consciousness, representation, and common language. Aiming at intransigence, art ends up collaborating with its enemies, science, utilitarianism, and commerce, to ensure its unimportance. Redefining its alienation from society as a model of liberation, art boasts of its "secularization" as if it were a consciously chosen position rather than a consequence of antagonistic conditions. The strategic refusal of obedience to social demands on art permits the artist to ignore the fact that society has stopped making them.

The formalist strategy (and I include here those aggressive formalisms that do not retreat from life but absorb it through the projection of myth) is really a renunciation and an adaptation. It exploits the incidental virtues of the homelessness, impotence, and marginality which capitalism thrusts on the artistic intellectual. The esthetic affirmation of the spirit of "play," of the uninhibited exploration of the frontiers of consciousness, ignores the severely restricted boundaries within which this play and this exploration must take place. The play and the exploration presuppose the artist's

unacceptable, a common ground which is nothing other than the procedures of reading" (*Ibid.*, 124). Culler notes that Barthes occasionally concedes this too (*Ibid.*, pp. 190-91).

65 See Culler's critique of the *Tel Quel* group (*Ibid.*, pp. 241-54). Eagleton writes well against those who see criticism as "the repressive father who cuts short the erotic sport of sense between text and reader, binding with the briars of its metasystem the joyfully pluralist intercourse of meanings between them. A libertarianism of text and reader, in short, typical of the *Tel Quel* group, which like all libertarianism fatally inverts itself into a mirror-image of bourgeois social relations" (*Criticism and Ideology: a Study in Marxist Literary Theory* [London: NLB, 1977], pp. 42-3).

dispossession from an interpretation that would permit him to master social experience. The formalist vocabulary assumes the alienation of the artist from society, but with the understanding that alienation and estrangement do not need to call themselves by these names. Separation from society and the loss of the perspective by which this separation might be understood cease to be merely the unfortunate condition of art under a certain form of society, and become part of the very definition of art.

But the self-induced separatism of art represents only one side of a contradictory state of affairs. As the arts have wilfully separated from society they have, in certain new and paradoxical ways, become reunited with it. The estrangement of art from society has coincided with the estrangement of society, or of great segments of society, from itself. As the middle class has become disillusioned with science, commerce, affluence, and consumption and sceptical toward traditional bourgeois certainties, the separatism of the arts has actually drawn art and society into closer relation. Advanced art is, after all, not socially marginal; or rather, its very marginality makes it central in a society where displacement from the center (or no relation to the center, the sense that there is no center) has become the common fate.[66] If art, like the family and the church, has become what Christopher Lasch calls a "haven in a heartless world,"[67] a refuge of "humanness" that serves as a sort of vacation from the menacing world of work and competition, this fact only establishes its common ground with the community. If formalist esthetics is a way of living with alienation, this fact is more and more a source of social reconciliation than of social separation. In its ability to redescribe displacement from centrality as a revolutionary form of freedom and potency, advanced culture furnishes a model by which

66 As early as 1878, in *Anti-Dühring*, Engels saw the evolution of corporate capitalism rendering the capitalist himself superfluous:

> If the crises revealed the incapacity of the bourgeoisie any longer to control the modern productive forces, the conversion of the great organizations for production and communication into joint-stock companies and state property shows that for this purpose the bourgeoisie can be dispensed with. All the social functions of the capitalists are now carried out by salaried employees. The capitalist has no longer any social activity save the pocketing of revenues, the clipping of coupons, and gambling on the Stock Exchange, where the different capitalists fleece each other of their capital. Just as at first the capitalist mode of production displaced the workers, so now it displaces the capitalists, relegating them, just as it did the workers, to the superfluous population, even if in the first instance not to the industrial reserve army. (Frederick Engels, *Anti-Dühring*, trans. E. Burns [New York: International Publishers, 1972], p. 304).

67 Christopher Lasch, "The Family as a Haven in a Heartless World," *Salmagundi*, 35 (Fall, 1976), pp. 42-55.

social powerlessness can be experienced as gratification. In this sense, those (largely on the left) who think that intellectuals like themselves have no power and those (largely on the right) who think such intellectuals have too much are both right. In the cultural world today, powerlessness (and the command of its intellectual paradigms) confers power.

The terms in which it defines revolution and liberation make radical esthetics congenial to many elements of consumer society, for liberation from traditional constraints is an essential condition of the expansion of consumption. Consumer society, in its destruction of continuity through the exploitation of fashion, ephemeral novelty, and planned obsolescence, effects a "systematic derangement of the senses" that makes the disruptions and defamiliarizations of vanguard culture look puny by comparison. The superannuation of the past, the fluidity of personal relations, the malleability of the physical environment before technology and the spiritual environment before the myth-making of advertising, journalism, entertainment, and political propaganda combine not only to erode our assurance of reality but our ability to recognize this erosion and see it as harmful. Alienation from work, from the possibility of community, from belief in the possible intelligibility of reality have increasingly become the shared ground of middle class life. As this has occurred, adversary epistemologies that challenge the "logocentric" correspondence of language and mind with things lose their oppositional force. In demanding that words be liberated from the significations, fixed in advance, of socialized discourse, Barthes and other radical critics forget the extent to which advertising and mass culture have already accomplished this end. Their exposure of the inherently ideological nature of thought finds an echo in the popular cynicism that says that all judgments are "matters of opinion," and "who is to say" what is real and what is not?

Not only does consumer society generate feelings of social uselessness, it also helps shape the diagnoses of these feelings and the proposed remedies. Hence the emergence of new industries for the profitable dissemination of advanced theories of alienation and liberation. The politics of the self, which reduces history to the psychodrama of the autonomous imagination contending against a repressive superego, spreads from the esoteric discussions of intellectuals into everyday social and even commercial life. But again, commerce, advertising, and popular entertainment surpass the power of the most visionary art in offering a prospective escape from the limitations of ordinary human existence by way of a life of infinitely multiplying personalities, "life styles," and "environments." Through commodities symbolic of the open and liberated life, personal autonomy is consumed as a compensation for the superfluousness of the consumer. Recapitulating the fate of romantic art, the individual achieves autonomy at the very moment his contribution ceases to matter. Just as the autonomous artistic imagination is placed beyond criticism, the modern self is consoled for its dispossession from history, community and reality by having its "needs" placed beyond criticism. The "triumph of the therapeutic" closes the gap between sophisticated and lay cultures: no great distance separates the literary critic who looks to art for "a body of bliss consisting solely of erotic relations" from the encounter-group participant seeking to "get in touch with his body."

The "adversary culture," with its stylish powerlessness redefined as a form of erotic potency, thus becomes indistinguishable from the "adversary." Though advanced art is not necessarily popular or commercially successful, neither unpopularity nor commercial failure can any longer be plausibly attributed to the public's intolerance of innovation. The antinomian disparagement of "bourgeois values" is celebrated by the agencies of publicity, exploited by the manipulators of cultural fashion, and emulated in personal conduct — an additional reason why the ante of provocation and radical experiment must continually be raised if the arts are to justify their vanguard credentials. Perhaps only by refusing to assume material existence at all can art succeed in disappointing — though even this proposition is rendered dubious by the recent enthusiasm extended to Conceptual Art. The point seem to have been reached at which artistic intransigence is indistinguishable from celebration of the dynamisms of mass society. It is impossibie to say whether the artistic "vanguard" is actually leading society or struggling to keep up with it.

In short, cultural radicalism ignores the disappearance of the paternalistic repressions it seeks to dissolve. Though "conservatives" may here and there protest the triumph of godlessness and immorality, no conservatism opposes the necessary expansion of consumer markets. Whereas power once required the appearance of sanction by the spiritual ideas of high culture, power today finds it possible to do without such sanctions, to exploit a culture of radical pluralism and ideological dissonance. Far from representing tradition and "elitism," the contemporary corporation is hostile to the fixity of traditional standards, which stand in the way of progress. Hence the tolerance shown by corporate society to the kind of culture that crosses all the borders and closes all the gaps. Attacks on the vestiges of high cultural standards and realistic sensibility only further the transformation of culture into an appendage of the fashion industries, the subjection of all art and ideas to the law of planned obsolescence. The blurring of cultural levels celebrated by Fiedler and Wasson as an overcoming of "concealed class bias" only bespeaks the irrelevance of traditional discriminations of taste to the goals of managers and publicists. Insofar as radicalism makes the extirpation of high cultural snobbery the central objective, it encourages the illusion that mass culture is the democratic expression of the people, as if mass culture were not owned and operated by private interests.

The situation in the university departments of literature and the humanities echoes that of the social macrocosm. Just as the esthetics of radical defamiliarization blends with the dynamics of consumer society, attacks on the traditional modes of criticism and interpretation coincide with the spirit of academic professionalism. The departments of the humanities some time ago became the principal patron and expounder of esthetic innovation. There is no visible reason why they should not encourage radical innovation in criticism. The antithesis of "academic" and "avant-garde" is as obsolete as the antithesis of "bourgeois" and "bohemian." Just as a post-scarcity economy may depend on the liquidation of traditional social restraints, academic professionalism may even *require* radical critical innovation as a continuation of its expansion. Where quantitative "production" of scholarship and criticism is a chief measure of professional achievement, narrow canons of proof, evidence, and logical consistency impose a drag on progress. The new wave of paracritical improvisation in criticism and the transformation of interpretation into prose poetry may be arriving just in time now that conventional modes of qualifying for professional advancement seem to be wearing thin.

Repressive Desublimation

But the cultural radicals have not ignored these social changes. For some of them, the new accommodation of established society to vanguard art and ideas is merely the conclusive evidence that the revolution has already arrived. For those less sanguine about the present situation, this accommodation threatens the success of the cultural revolution — but by no means discredits its essential outlook. For Marcuse, the new popularity of vanguard cultural attitudes is a manifestation of "repressive desublimation" — the dominant society's repression of culturally revolutionary ideas by assimilating them in harmless forms. Marcuse observes acutely that high bourgeois culture, with its idealism, its love of beauty, renunciation, and sublimation, "has ceased to be the dominant culture." Therefore, a new question arises:

> if today we are witnessing a disintegration of bourgeois culture which is the work of the internal dynamic of contemporary capitalism and the adjustment of culture to the requirements of contemporary capitalism, is not the cultural revolution, then, inasmuch as it aims at the destruction of bourgeois culture, falling in line with the capitalist adjustment and redefinition of culture? Is it not thus defeating its own purpose, namely, to prepare the soil for a qualitatively different, a radically anticapitalist culture? Is there not a dangerous divergence, if not contradiction, between the political goals of the rebellion and its cultural theory and praxis? And must not the rebellion change its cultural "strategy" in order to resolve this contradiction?[68]

In the fifty pages following this passage in *Counterrevolution and Revolt,* I find no statement which addresses these extremely pertinent questions. Marcuse concedes that the revolutionary program has been all too easy to vulgarize and divert into frivolity and self-deception, but this fact is not permitted to call into question the program itself. Marcuse is content to reaffirm his faith that "the cultural revolution remains a radically progressive force."[69]

In other words, Marcuse declines to draw the logical conclusion to which his own social theory leads him: that the new sensibility in art and culture does not so much negate "one-dimensional society" as mirror it. And does not Marcuse's formalist esthetic mirror the self-validating autonomy which Marcuse and other social critics have discovered in the technological, bureaucratic, and economic processes of advanced society? In *One-Dimensional Man,* Marcuse says the language of one-dimensional society "controls by reducing the linguistic forms and symbols of reflection, abstraction, development, contradiction; by substituting images for concepts. It denies or absorbs the transcendent vocabulary."[70] But the substituting of images for concepts is according to Marcuse's Kantian esthetic the essence of art, which aims at "the non-conceptual truth of the senses." Defined as sensuous "experience"

68 Marcuse, *Counterrevolution and Revolt*, p. 85. See also Barthes' remarks about the political innocuousness of avant-garde theatre: "Whose Theater? Whose *Avant-Garde*?", *Critical Essays*, pp. 67-70.

69 Marcuse, *Counterrevolution and Revolt*, p. 103.

70 Marcuse, *One-Dimensional Man*, p. 103.

severed from conceptual correspondence with reality, art has no more basis than the technocratic language of one-dimensional society for transcending existing reality. It becomes an aspect of what it rebels against.

Here is the main difficulty with the subversive claims made widely for the disorienting and "model-making" powers of art, whether these claims are advanced specifically for certain anti-realistic genres or for art in general. It does not follow that a work that serves to "destroy old assumptions and suggest a new, more visionary reality" necessarily induces its audience to see the world more critically. The radical disorientation of perception and the cognitive estrangement brought about by self-reflexive fiction may result in a dulling of the audience's sense of reality or in a shell-shocked relativism suspicious not only of ideology but of truth. The "models for the future" seen by critics in science fiction may stimulate escapist fantasies rather than critical thinking, all the more probably if these models are inserted into an already uncritical, fad-worshipping mass culture. In other words, there is no way of determining the critical character of a literary work unless we know its disposition toward reality. If esthetic disruption and projection are not regulated by a rational respect for reality—that is, by a controlling realism—their critical value cannot be taken for granted. Radical esthetics, determined to liberate fantasy from "the problem of correspondence or noncorrespondence with some present actuality or some previously experienced past," has no way of making good its claims for the critical power of fantasy. James Stupple points to this problem with science fiction itself: "rather than encouraging analysis," Stupple writes, the use of disorienting conventions in this genre "actually impedes it, putting an end to critical thought."[71] Whether fantasy makes us more critical or merely more solipsistic and self-indulgent depends finally on its accountability to what is outside itself. But it is just such accountability that radical esthetics confuses with acquiescence.

That a great deal of putatively radical art has become an aspect of the confusion it rebels against is, as we have already seen, the very criticism Marcuse himself levels at the irrationalistic impulse in contemporary art and in the counter culture. In merging art with life, Marcuse observes, the new sensibility often "loses the transcendence which opposes art to the established order."[72] But this same criticism logically applies to Marcuse's own conception of art. Since he puts art under no obligation

71 Stupple, "Fiction Against the Future," p. 219.

72 Marcuse, *Counterrevolution and Revolt*, p. 101.

to reflect conceptual reality, Marcuse has no way of explaining why art should "transcend" established reality in a critical rather than a solipsistic or escapist fashion. His theory deprives itself of the critical principle needed to distinguish between substantial and trivial forms of artistic imagination. Marcuse sees art as "another reality, another order repelled by the existing one." But how can a work of art be "repelled" by existing reality unless it has the power to understand what that reality is? Art must be granted the power to conceptualize the existing reality, to see it *as* distorted, before it can effectively negate it.

Marcuse and other cultural radicals do not follow the logic of their position to its natural conclusions. If they were to do so they would have to abandon their belief in the parallelism of cultural and political revolution. They would have to acknowledge that the esthetic of defamiliarization and projection, of formalist assault on the reality principle, falls in line with "the capitalist adjustment and redefinition of culture." This, in turn, would call into question the larger assumption that the liberation of Eros and the pleasure principle from repression is a necessary counterpart of the revolt against oppression. And then one might ask, must we have a new cultural sensibility, a "new sensorium," a reorientation of perception, an "a-logical" celebration of being, a release of "will and joy" and Eros, a flight beyond humanism and the logocentric idea of man, if we seek to bring about greater justice and truthfulness? Or has the goal of relieving boredom replaced justice and truth as the purpose of politics? But to think these thoughts is to question the very foundation of cultural leftism. That the cultural revolution is regrettably vulnerable to "cooptation"—this can be conceded. But that the cultural revolution itself is fundamentally misconceived—this is unthinkable.

Groping for Trouts: On Metaphor

BY WILLIAM H. GASS

> Yonder man is carried to prison.
> Well; what has he done?
> A woman.
> But what's his offense?
> Groping for trouts in a peculiar river.

I want to begin with a problem that's also a bit of history. It may at first appear as far from my topic—art and order—as the Andes are from their valleys, or as such remote and glacial mountain slopes must seem to some swimmer whose nose is full of salt. The problem concerns the measurement of nature, and I don't in the least mind saying that on any number of counts it's like groping for trouts in a peculiar river.

We have each seen the motion in bodies. We ourselves live. The newsboy delivers the daily paper. The dime which has slipped from our fist runs in a tightening spiral till, like a bug, we flat it with our foot. Spirits rise, rumors travel, hopes fade. The flesh crawls, felts and satins roughen, and when we lick our ice cream we can even taste the melt. Yes, Heraclitus calls the tune, and like the sound of an accordion is the noisy meeting and passing of trains.

The movements everywhere around us—in us—seem, well . . . too numerous, too vague, too fragile and transitory to number, and that's terribly unsettling, for we always feel threatened when confronted with something we can't count. Why should we be surprised, then, to find out that creating and defending a connection between what William James called the buzzing, blooming confusion of normal consciousness—of daily life with its unstimulating bumps, its teaseless, enervating grinds—and the clear and orderly silences of mathematics, a connection which will give us meaning, security, and management, in one lump sum, is what our science—is what our art, law, love and magic—is principally about?

That newspaper—we might mistake it for the white wings of a passing pigeon. Do we see the line it draws? Think how Galileo would have rendered it. He'd notice neither newspaper nor pigeon. He discovered that the distance which the paper might be tossed could be expressed—how wonderful his image—as the area of a rectangle. The match-up was astonishing: velocity could be laid out on one side, time on another, and since he knew so much more about rectangles than he did about motion, his little Euclidean model (for that's what he'd managed), to the degree it held firm, would immediately make a science of physical movement possible . . . in terms of dots and dashes, points and paths . . . and he went on to describe all evenly accelerating motion in the cool and classic language of the triangle. Had Dante been more daring? I think not.

Now imagine that Alice (the girl conceived by Carroll—minister, poet, and logician), having eaten what she's been told to and drunk according to instructions, is swelling as she tiptoes through her tunnel, and imagine in addition that there is a light like those which warn low planes of towers, chimneys, or intrusive steeples, attached to the top of her head. Can't we see her as an elongating wand whose end is then a point upon a curve? A most monstrous metaphor, yet inspired. Any curve, Descartes decided, could be considered to enclose a set of lines whose ends like trimmed logs lay against it. Only moments later, so it seemed, so swift is thought translated into history, Descartes had devised a language to describe these points and lines, these curves and squares, in numbers. Every place upon a line had its address, and with that went directions: you went along Rue X a while, and then up Y till you were there. As simple as children, but all quite absurd, for motion only alters the overlaps of colors—we know that; there is nothing rectangular about passage; and surely squares and curves are never numbers—abstract, inert, and purely relational; they stretch their legs like cats. Yet in a generation (we speak now like the critics), Galileo, Fermat, and Descartes had first created, then speeded up, mechanics. Beyond the Pythagoreans' wildest dreams, motion had become number.

Again: how was it managed? The paperboy's paper is dispensed with. It becomes a point, its flight, a line. That curve itself is seen to be a row of dots, or so we might conceive a string of pearls if we were mathematically inclined. Next, each dot is said to represent the top of a slat, a vertical fixed like a post in the plane of the paperboy's feet. A picket fence, in short, has unfolded from his throw. If you prefer: it's a Venetian blind on its side, on edge. But no, the tip of each post is the elbow of an angle, the corner of that old friend, area, again, and thus this simple little daily act is actually, in our new poetry and picture book, exactly like a perfect fan of cards. Plato's intuition has been confirmed: the world we know and swim in is everywhere it flows a qualitative expression of serene, unchanging quantitative laws. The ambiguity of "point" makes many of these verses possible. Who knows? it may be the peak of a witches' cap, the climax of the geometer's cone. *Point:* it is truly a word to wonder at, this minute mark like a prick, this place in space less large than a hair's end or the sound of a silent clock, this piercing part and particular of discourse, this dimensionless speck which has been spelled, alone in English, sixteen different ways already—should we not salute it?

So yonder man is carried to prison. Shakespeare measures matters in quite another way. This sort of sexuality is seen as poaching . . . poaching in a peculiar river. The term is technical, and requires that we feel for the fish with our hands beneath an overhanging bank. "Fish must be grop't for, and be tickled too," Bunyan writes. When Hamlet tells Horatio how

> Up from my cabin,
> My sea-grown scarf'd about me, in the dark
> Groped I to find out them . . .

he is using "groped" less precisely, more generally, than in this passage from *Measure for Measure*. Tickling is apparently essential to it, for Maria awaits Malvolio, whom she plans to dupe, with the words: ". . . here comes the trout that must be caught with tickling." And what was thought as *peculiar* then was, in particular, private property.

For instance.

We hate to think that through much of our life we window shop and rarely purchase. Therefore, I suppose, it does dismay us to discover that of all the time we spend on sex—in thought, dreams, deed, in word, desire, or feeling—there is so little spending done to show for it that nothing's bought. Yet notice how predictably I've put it. I should be ashamed. First I spoke of spending time, and then I spoke of sperm—our sacred future—in the same way. Well, time is money, don't we say? and maybe our seeds are simply many pennies. Both, at least, are quantities—methods of accounting, blueprints, masterplots—and perhaps Protagoras really meant to tell us that man is the *measurer* of all things, not merely the measure, for I honestly believe it is his principal concern.

Certainly man will seem, in impoverished circumstances, to be interested only in getting himself fed, and of course if he feeds he will belch and break wind, he will wipe his behind with leaves, he will stopper his heart, allow his belly to rust, his skin to scale, and eventually he will inflate his bladder to embarrassment; but we cannot accurately measure man's nature in terms of what he *must* do (he must breathe, for example—all of us manage—yet few of us take much pleasure or even an interest in it); no, we have to observe him in the latitudes; in just those moments when the world unpins his shoulders from the mat; moments in which, if we were speaking of clocks, we would sense a wobble in the works. And if we think it's satisfaction that man wants, a simple easing of his needs like the release of stool or the fall of pants, remark how he collects in order to arrange (shells, coins, stamps); overeats to set a standard (ice cream, clams, corn, pie, cake, melons); makes rules as rapidly as clubs; commits to memory even fractional statistics, decimal notations (how fast six furlongs has been run, what Willie Mays is batting, what the market's done); turns the simplest "good day" into a social rite as empty, bored, and automatic as prayer or genuflection; passes laws and calls them measures; lays out all the acres of his days in stingy tracts with the ruthless greed of a plot developer. He arranges everything he hears, feels, sees, in decorous ranks like pallbearers beside him, and says he's "informing" his visual field. He lives a lot like a pin in a map—he calls it "growing up"—and there he indicates the drains. No, he does not copulate, he counts; he does not simply laugh or sneer or shout, he patiently explains. Regardless of the man or woman whom he mounts, throughout his wildest daydreams and even in the most persistent myths of his pornography, he will imagine in amounts. As our poet warns us, in the following boast:

> Some glory in their birth, some in their skill,
> Some in their wealth, some in their body's force;
> Some in their garments, though new-fangled ill;
> Some in their hawks and hounds, some in their horse;
> And every humour hath his adjunct pleasure,
> wherein it finds a joy above the rest:
> But these particulars are not my measure . . .

Some writers are worthwhile, even if the other virtues they possess are invisible, because, like cooling soup, all the scum is on the surface.

What does De Sade do, for example? He measures his thing; he organizes orgies; he makes change; he not only contrives novel entanglements, he classifies them, tagging participants, numbering the blasphemies, designing relationships, keeping count of screams. In short, he commands; he orders—on paper nowhere better—for no one slips from *his* pyramid of bodies with an "oops!"—not in *his* books—no one misses the mark or fails to come up to it or interrupts the action, that is to say, the argument; because there was nothing De Sade disliked more than the sense that matters were getting out of hand (do not be surprised to find a revolutionary loving order, they can't wait to issue edicts and pass laws), and where were they more likely to but during fornication? It's an unprotected time. Both soul and body are in danger, and Plato was neither the first nor last philosopher to suggest that lust was another name for chaos. Take off your clothing—did not the Doukhobors?—and you attack the state.

> We have strict statutes and most biting laws,
> The needful bits and curbs, to headstrong weeds,
> Which for this fourteen years we have let slip;
> . . . .
> (Now) liberty plucks justice by the nose;
> The baby beats the nurse, and quite athwart
> Goes all decorum.

This is the judgment of the duke in *Measure for Measure,* and this judgment motivates the plot. Take off your clothes. Be gymnastic. Public. Be perverse. Attack the deepest laws. De Sade, however, was no Galileo, even though his record as a prisoner was longer. The scientist represented motion geometrically because he wished to understand it. He did not so dangerously confuse his model with the world. But De Sade saw persons as pieces of earth in order to treat human beings like dirt. Sodomy was still a revolutionary act, but lust was some exasperation of the nerves, nevertheless, like a humming in tightly strung wires.

That light travels in straight lines; that a body set in motion will continue unchanged unless something else hinders it; that all things seek equilibrium or act to maintain themselves in any given state; that men seek only their own pleasure or act always to preserve their own lives; that we perceive only sense data; that we are machines: all of these are opinions so plainly desirable for the translation of data into abstract systems, as are both atoms and the void, that it seems unlikely they are more than rules of representation like the principles of perspective in painting.

It was Hobbes who understood the consequences of Galileo's model as a universal measure clearly. The advantage of thinking of matter in atomic terms was ultimately the resemblance of atoms to points, and as points stood for intersections, the corners of shapes, so atoms could be augmented by others and shrewdly arranged until the assemblage appeared as a visible object. If there were laws for the behavior of these, then might not men, considered as a house built of atomic bricks, be treated as moving bodies too; and finally, could not groups of them be regarded just like even larger bodies also on the move? In this way impressive sovereignties, in the drama Hobbes composed for them, became solarized systems, like vast constellations crashing through space, and the erratic rattle of humans against one another and the side of the State was no more confused in fact than the dance of shot in a metal bowl. Chaos, like darkness, had been snuffed out.

Chaos, of course, is an enemy of art, an inversion of one of its essential qualities; but chaos, as George Santayana has pointed out, is simply any order incompatible with a chosen good, like a set of files that's indexed alphabetically by middle name; and a world in which events leaf out at random—the honest card or crap game, for example—is still one where the odds can be stated with precision. The disorders of the streets, the fickleness of crowds, gangs, or mobs, like the heavy rushes of a bull, are often more predictable than the moves of a chess master, and we usually feel that even the quirks of great winds would be perfectly understandable if we knew their backgrounds better—who their parents were and how they were raised. The straw which a mighty storm has driven through a post, the house which has been moved a mile and set down like a tray, seem whimsical acts because, like putting the shot, so much energy has been expressed in them they ought to have been meant, and we believe, in our less faithful moments, they were not.

No, we can put order anywhere we like; there's not a trout we can't tickle, a fish for which we can't contrive a net; we can find forms in ink blots, clouds, the tubercular painter's spit; and to the ants we can impute designs which Alexander would have thought himself vain glorious to dream of. But to think of order and chaos in this relative way is not to confuse them, or put conditions out of the reach of judgment. There are clashes between orders, confusions of realms. Not every arrangement is equally effective. And we must keep in mind the relation of any order to the chosen good.

Descartes said that Euclid was too abstract and too dependent on figures: "it can exercise the understanding only on condition of greatly fatiguing the imagination." I know many books of that kind. Algebra, on the other hand, was overly rule-bound: "there results an art," he said, "full of confusion and obscurity calculated to embarrass, instead of a science fitted to cultivate the mind." Orders vary in both their vices and their virtues, in kind as well as in degree. Some are futile, others cheap. Among the worst are the illusory: politics and witchcraft, astrology and diets. Among the noblest are a few measurements of measure like Valéry's *Eupalinos*. It does not matter whether we are endeavoring to find an order for a given set of facts, or whether we are "arranging" things to fall into an order, the ordering is an act of mind which brings together like two hands that buzzing blooming confusion of which James spoke, and some sublimely empty abstract system like that which Euclid once devised, or the inventors of the diatonic scale . . . brings them together till they clap. The result is a quantity qualified—that's Plato's recipe for the world—and in the past the most successful systems have had their source in music and in mathematics, while we have found our models, as often as not, to be examples of physics and astronomy, religious books, long poetical plays or lengthy epical poetry.

Let us count.

One. We find, perhaps, on a lottery ticket, the most primitive use of number, in as much as the number is not even a name there, not even an elementary designation like "Peewee," "Nitwit," or "Gramps." The paper provides a place for their printing; it carries the figures, and these, by themselves, are mere grunts. Why do we number them at all? Why not print "Dimple" on one, "Nymphet" and "Spider" . . . then "Zealously," "Viper," and "Young." We don't care for sequence here, only for difference. In manufacturing such tickets, however, we want signs which can be simply produced, and a scheme for their production which will ensure there is no duplication. The ordinary number system pays that bill promptly. It can generate new and unique names indefinitely (no other is so efficient). Not even a language like Latin or English, each capable of a multitude of novel arrangements, can match its easy-going power.

Two. There are dog tags, Social Security, insurance, draft, or other numbers which name documents or people, marking them uniquely. These numbers are true names. They are almost too pure, for they tell us nothing else, and the figures themselves simply come from a convenient pool of signs.

Three. The next level is the ordinal use. The sequence of the numbers has a little meaning now. The numbering of the pages of a book is not quite an example, because it will tell me that some leaves are missing, or that, in my copy of *Under the Volcano,* a whole gathering has been repeated. For the first time, nevertheless, it makes sense to speak of measure. Take the scratch test for hardness: suppose I have five rocks. I scratch them turn and turn about as Beckett's Molloy sucked stones, and then I arrange them serially in terms of who scratches whom and who is scratched by whom, assigning any figures I like so long as they reflect that scratching order: 1 through 5, perhaps, or 0 , 4, 25, 92.3, and 112. Either list will do. Of course I could have called one Ruth, another Lou, and so on, but the names wouldn't tell me whether Ruth scratched Lou or Lou, Ruth, and that won't do. Even so, the stone labeled 5 in its sequence is not thereby that many times harder than 2, although this is a mistake which is frequently made.

Four. Counting is the cardinal use. What is the number of shoes in the store? Order alone is not enough here, and I must always proceed in whole units—that is assumed. The consequence of my counting, of course, is a sum, but the figure any particular shoe happens to receive is without significance. In the case of labeling hardness, I might have gone 0, 10, 25, instead of the 0, 4, 25 I used, but I could never have run 4, 0, 10, or 9, 6, 21. This floating or fastening of names is important in some metaphors.

Five. If you are number six in a simple count, it does not mean that you are in some way twice the fellow who was three. Addition is an additional property which we reach with luck and often genius only at this stage. Time and space are additive, hardness and heat are not. It is clear, by this time, isn't it? that my knowledge of the relations between numbered *things* depends wholly upon my knowledge of the relations between numbers. The Pythagoreans said grandly of justice that it was "4". Presumably this told us something of justice (actually it told us everything about justice, for the number was not only the *logos* (word) for justice, it was also *logos* (theory) of justice), but not even the zealots imagined that justice informed us about the number. Mathematical models (and this is important) are designed to tell us things about the data they shape, but the data are not expected or even allowed to snitch in the least on the system.

Rules of representation, I repeat, establish a link between the thing to be ordered and the order to be imposed. Let the face of this paper be the face of the earth. That is a rule of representation. The face of this paper is not the face of the earth, but neither is distance rectangular. Nevertheless, assuming one may enable me to find my way, assuming another may enable me to measure it.

Not all measurement, we have to notice, is direct. The scratch test is, but temperature taken with a thermometer is not. We measure the dance of the mercury because it undulates with the heat. My uncle's sweat, collected in a cup, would serve as well if only he were as reliable in his response as the metal.

Suppose I were to say, of a married couple, that in their life together the wife played left tackle. I haven't made a good model. Where are the other twenty players? Who are the coaches, trainers, where are the stands? Tennis would serve a loving couple better. Then I might be able to observe how the wife stayed on the baseline, seldom coming to the net; how she characteristically lobbed her return to his drives; what sort of spin she put on her serves, and so forth—*if that's what she did*. Or if I were to compare a football match to a chess game, I might carelessly see the two quarterbacks as the opponents—a mistake. The opponents have to be the coaches, since in chess the players are never pieces. And unless my measurements are meant to be skimpy, I have to assume that the moves of the athletes are fixed; that they only act as ordered. Well, my measurements *are* skimpy, my suit a poor fit, for when is that ever true?

Facts are not so stubborn as we sometimes like to think. The world may be a plenum, but it's also hollow as bamboo, both stiff as straw and limply flexible as string. We can often talk things into being only what we want to say about them.

Perhaps you know the game in which two players suddenly and simultaneously show one another either an open hand, two fingers or a fist. The open hand is paper, and it is said to be superior to stone, which the first represents, because paper covers stone, although the stone can blunt the scissor-shaped fingers, and they, in turn, can cut the paper when they meet. This unusual arrangement comprises a viciously circular pecking order. Imagine that only untouchables gave orders to kings. The superiority of each symbol to the other is inferred from the presumed properties of its name. Scissors cut paper, paper covers stone, stone blunts scissors. Totem names are like our numbers: metaphors seriously meant and socially applied, as instanced in this passage from Levi-Strauss's essay on social poetry and measurement, *The Savage Mind:*

> The following clans stand in a joking relationship to each other among the Luapula: the Leopard and Goat clans because the leopards eat goats, the Mushroom and Anthill clans because mushrooms grow on anthills, the Mush and Goat clans because men like meat in their mush, the Elephant and Clay clans because women in the old days used to carve out elephant's footprints from the ground and use these natural shapes as receptacles instead of fashioning pots. The Anthill clan is linked with the Snake clan and also with the Grass clan because grass grows tall on anthills and snakes hide there. The Iron clan jokes with all clans with animal names because animals are killed by metal spears and bullets. Reason of this kind allows the definition of a hierarchy of clans: the Leopard clan is superior to the Goat clan, the Iron clan to the animal clans and the Rain clan to the Iron clan because rain rusts iron. Moreover the Rain clan is superior to all the other clans because animals would die without it, one cannot make mush (a clan name) without it, clay (a clan name) cannot be worked without it, and so on.

When we number objects, animals, places, schemes, the things numbered remain unaware of their names (the Skunk Cabbage does not know that it is one), but when we label ourselves, we try to live up or down to our titles: I know I rust iron, and you know it too. Eventually we prove the matter to ourselves, and I rain down on you.

I've been groping for trout in a peculiar river, and perhaps I deserve to go to prison for it. Certainly the mathematician may feel that I'm poaching; but in all of my remarks I have merely been developing a metaphor for measure which will fit fiction, though I should like, like a sock, to see it stretched.

I ask you finally, then, to think of every English word as Euclid for the poet, a wildly ordered set of meanings and relations maybe, but settled down there, right at home there, nevertheless; to see that each one is, like a piece in chess, the center of a network of astonishing relations. A poem or a work of fiction is a system of such systems, and perhaps the novel, in particular, is an indirect measure of life. To do this it need not resemble, nor does it need to make, for the sake of a certain precision, the sacrifice which Galileo had to when he took all the color from mass or all grace from precision. We are sometimes inclined to think that measuring must thin its object—a line, in fact, has but one dimension—for where are the white wings of the pigeon when the paperboy's paper is transcribing its stringy trajectory? and if De Sade thinks of sex like a cook who opens cans, if many of us live like pins in maps, our hearts a red head, what can recommend measuring? It's true we should watch out for images which are merely telephonic sums for explanations which aren't really meant but are, like plastic bosoms and paste gems, only designed to dazzle. We confine ourselves to too few models, and sometimes live in them as if they were, themselves, the world.

Remember that as we moved from lotteries to temperatures, and from temperatures to the interplay of gravities, our models were able to take on more and more of the properties of the numbers which were being used to construct them, and that as we went along our knowledge did not dwindle but it grew. However numbers are morally and metaphysically neutral. They are nothing but relations, and quite orderly relations, too, while words are deposits of meaning made almost glacially, over ages. If the systems, in mathematics, exist mainly, like glasses, to be filled, they are also clear as crystal, and are not expected to stain anyone's white radiance; while words, again, are already names for thoughts and things, acts and other energies which only passion has command of; they are not blank, Barkis-willing, jelly labels. Prufrock did not measure out his life, One/Two, One/Two, but carefully in coffee spoons, from which the sugar slid, no doubt, like snow, and the beverage circled to their stir as soundlessly as a rolled eye. Mornings, evenings, afternoons: there was the polite chink as they came to rest in their saucers—chink chink chink . . . A complete world unfolds from the phrase like an auto map reveals its roads. In metaphor, meanings model one another, wear their clothes. What the poet tries to measure is the whole.

"Tell me, Apollo," Troilus cries, "what Cressid is, what Pandar, and what we. Her bed is India; there she lies, a pearl." Don't we know, then, where *we* stand? It is a distant and exotic place, the object of voyages by many men, rich in silks and spices, more guessed at and conjectured of than known. Our proper attitude should be one of wonderment and longing, curiosity, more than a little desire, more than a little greed.

But we must not suppose that "India" is merely a lens through which we peer at Cressida's bed as through some shard of colored glass we've found randomly at hand, since the syntax of our sentence is also odd, and thus the angle at which the lens is held is strange. It would be normal to say: her bed is big, or, her bed is walnut, her bed is unmade. It would be normal to say: her native land is India, or, her name is Cressida. And if we said that her bed was a boat, our grammar, at least, would be unexceptional. There would be no syntactical collision. But her bed *is* India.

When we measure nature with a yardstick or another sort of rule, the qualitative world does not seem to shadow us so obviously as normal sentences surround abnormal ones, because we are satisfied to say that we are measuring the height of the tree, not the tree, the frequency of light, not light, the temperature of the air—in short, an abstract property—but Shakespeare is not measuring some abstract exotic quality of Cressida's bed. Her entire sexual life becomes a matter of geography, history, danger, travel.

Each metaphor establishes between its terms a quite specific *angle of interaction,* and the movement of the mind which reaches, exploits, and dwells on this, so swiftly as to seem quite effortless, is nevertheless a momentous factor. Because of the comparative emptiness of numbers (something which I have not insisted upon so often I am ashamed to mention it again), when we raise our hand to the teacher, requesting to be excused to do, or otherwise perform, No. 1, we don't feel that our expression is metaphorical. The number is merely an evasive name; whereas if we had, instead, to say that we wished to leave the room to wash our car ("Excuse me, teach, but I got to go to wash my car"), then think what light (to seize a passing word) would eventually be shed on the relief of the bladder . . . or, for that matter, on actually washing one's automobile. The mind is a persistent logician. If doing No. 1 is: wash the car, then what is No. 2?

Let's go back to "bed" for a moment. In this Brobdingnagian image, if Cressida's bed is India, what must her dressing table be? Think of the size of Cressida herself. Truly, she must be a divinity. Some of these consequences occur to Shakespeare:

> Tell me, Apollo, for thy Daphne's love,
> What Cressida is, what Pandar, and what we.
> Her bed is India; there she lies, a pearl;
> Between our Ilium and where she resides,
> Let it be call'd the wild and wandering flood,
> Ourself the merchant, and this sailing Pandar
> Our doubtful hope, our convoy and our bark.

If "Her bed is India" enlarges her, the image which closes on it like the other half of a walnut is Lilliputian in its effect, since Cressida's bed becomes that of the oyster, and what once floated on the surface of the ocean, so to speak, has suddenly sunk in restful sleep beneath it. The conclusion is a proportion: that Cressida is to her bed as a pearl to its oyster, but this is reached by means of an intermediate step which is best forgotten, because initially we'd have to assume that Cressida lies in her bed the way oysters lie together in theirs. In that case there would have to be as many Cressidas quietly snuggled up beneath the sheets as anchovies in tins. The entire expression endeavors to play Descartes to

Galileo: to translate one model immediately into another, just as the offense of "doing" a woman is re-seen as poaching—the theft of private property.

So what the poet tries to measure is the whole *with* the whole—the paper as bird, the bird perhaps as paper—but he does not always succeed.

The Duke is in a sweat of explanation:

> We have strict statutes and most biting laws,
> The needful bits and curbs to headstrong weeds,
> Which for this fourteen years we have let slip;
> Even like an o'ergrown lion in a cave,
> That goes not out to prey. Now, as fond fathers,
> Having bound up the threatening twigs of birch,
> Only to stick it in their children's sight
> For terror, not to use, in time the rod
> Becomes more mock'd than fear'd; so our decrees,
> Dead to infliction, to themselves are dead;
> And liberty plucks justice by the nose;
> The baby beats the nurse, and quite athwart
> Goes all decorum.

What he wants to describe is a condition which eventually occurs in any state which sets aside its laws like a dirty fork in a fine café. He does not pile one image on another as if he were translating each to a higher sphere; rather, he looks rapidly through many eyes as though he were an insect, instantly, antennaed every eighth of every quarter inch. First, the laws are like the bit and bridle of a horse which, once let slip, will cause the horse (and heroine) to bolt; they are like the tools of cultivation left in idleness to rust their garden into weed; they are like the spared rod which spoils the child; and the king, himself, who will not keep the birches at their stinging, as though the smart burned both skins like a slap, is finally a lion who will not even leave his fattened sleep to hunt.

Most of these images have an equal weight, and consequently his description draws upon what otherwise would be conflicting areas of meaning without the least hesitation: the phrase, "biting laws," suggests "bits and curbs," which suggests "headstrong," something which horses sometimes are. But what are we to do with the word, 'weeds,' which has suddenly sprung up in the cultivated midst of our account? the bits and curbs of headstrong weeds? The poet slips from one role to another like an improvisor, each easily to each, because the passage does not merely say that the king and his decrees, the people and their condition, are as a farmer to his crops and fields, father to his children; it maintains that farmer, rider, lion, father, king, are *one*. This is the multiple metaphor which moves these lines to their conclusion: that "liberty plucks justice by the nose, the baby beats the nurse, and quite athwart goes all decorum."

"The baby beats the nurse" is a phrase which has certainly been singled out for popular acclaim, yet the form of the flip-flop intended is not quite right, because otherwise we'd have to think that nurses beat babies as a normal and happily ordered part of their duties, a practice encouraged in well-run states. Headstrong youths may be birched, possibly, but not babes. In the proper turn about, the baby would give suck to its nurse; but Shakespeare didn't want us to imagine the world turned simply topsy-turvy. Laws up-side-down would still be up-side-down laws. The Duke fears an absence of orders, a lapsing of powers, the disappearance of value.

Shakespeare was greedy. He wanted everything. He wanted Cressida shining in her bed, but he also wanted Troilus's eye there, and his straining loins. He was greedy, but that is what this bloody breathtaking business is all about. Paper covers stone. There are too many books in which the baby beats the nurse, in which form has been forgotten for the sake of some momentary fun.

Yonder man is carried to prison. But what's his offense? Violation. "What," Mistress Overdone exclaims, "is there a maid with child by him?" "No," her servant Pompey says, "but there's a woman with maid by him." No money to marry. The poor are always with us. Groping for trouts in a peculiar river.

Yet what is measured with these terms? To what shall we assign the number "grope"? and where do these trouts lay concealed? what is the name of the river? Yonder man . . . perhaps it's I? Then what's my crime? Between what banks did I reach down to touch, in darkness, and to tickle . . . My crime: where are its straight lines and equilateral dimensions?

But perhaps it would be best not to think about it.

Beginnings

BY EDWARD W. SAID

Where, or when, or what is a beginning? If I have begun to write, for example, and a line has started its way across the page, is that all that has happened? Clearly not. For by asking a question about the meaning of a beginning, I seem to have deposited a ghostly load of significance where none had been suspected. Levi-Strauss chillingly suggests that the mind's logic is such that "the principle underlying a classification can never be postulated in advance. It can only be discovered *a posteriori*." To identify a point as a beginning is to classify it after the fact, and so a beginning is always being left behind: to speculate about beginnings therefore is to be like Moliere's M. Jourdain, acquiring retrospective admiration for what we had always done in the regular course of things: only now, the classification seems to matter. Somehow, we know, we have always begun, whether to speak, to feel, to think or to act in one way rather than another, and we will continue to do so. If that is beginning then that is what we do. When? Where? How? At the beginning.

The tautology that tells us to begin at the beginning depends on the ability of both mind and language to reverse themselves, and thus to move in a circle, an ability which makes thought both intelligible and verging on obscurity at the same time. We clearly know what it means to begin, but why must our certainty be toyed with when we are reminded that in matters of mind beginning is not really a beginner's game? We deride the wishful thinker who pretends that the order of things can be reversed; yet at other times we avail ourselves of reversibility, if our case needs its effects. Swift's projectors in Book III of *Gulliver's Travels* who build houses from the roof down, live a fantasy of reversibility, but who more than Swift the hard-nosed pamphleteer wanted readers of his political writings to see things clearly, from the beginning—which meant wanting to reverse the ruinous trend of a European war policy, or the cancerous growth in English of neologism and cant?

Thus, one beginning is permissible, another one like it, at a different time perhaps, is not permissible. What are the conditions that allow us to call something a beginning? First of all there must be the desire and the true freedom to reverse oneself; for whether one looks to see where and when he began, or whether he looks in order to begin now, he cannot continue as he is. It is, however, very difficult to begin with a wholly new start. Too many old habits, loyalties and pressures inhibit the substitution of a novel enterprise for an old, established one. When God chooses to begin the world again he does it with Noah; things have been going very badly, and since it is his prerogative, God wishes a new beginning. Yet it is interesting that God himself seems not to begin completely from scratch. Noah and the Ark are a piece of the old world initiating the new world. As if in an oblique comment on the special status of beginnings Descartes observes in *Regles pour la direction de l'esprit:* "The human mind possesses in effect a *je-ne-sais-quoi* of the divine, where the first seeds of useful thought have been thrown, so that even though they have been neglected and choked off by studies contrary to their well-being, they spontaneously produce fruit." Every human being is a version of the divine, Descartes seems to be saying, and what seems spontaneous in man is in fact due to the resumption of man's beginning connection with God. To begin is to reverse the course of human progress for the sake of divine fruits.

A beginning must *be thought* possible, it must be *taken to be* possible, before it can be one, especially at the formal or concessive opening of a literary work; the "trouble" with *Tale of a Tub* is that its alleged writer does not really believe that he can get started. The mind's work, in order to be done, occasionally requires the possibility of freedom, of a new cleanness, of prospective achievement, of special and novel appropriation. It must have these in the course of its continuing enterprises, historical, sociological, scientific, psychological, or poetic. In other words it must be possible that Paul's injunction to the Romans, "Be ye transformed by the renewing of your mind," *can be* obeyed.

Finally, and almost inevitably, the beginning will emerge reflectively and, perhaps, unhappily, already engaged in a sense of its difficulty. This is true whether one thinks of beginnings in the past, the present, or even in the future. Thus at a very practical level Erik Erikson wonders where to begin in writing the biography of a great man: "how does one take a great man 'for what he was?' The very adjective seems to imply that something about him is too big, too awe-ful, too shiny to be encompassed." Huizinga, in accepting that history in some way deals with "facts" still wants to know how to begin to distinguish a "fact":

> To what extent may one isolate from the eternal flux of disparate units, specific, consistent groups as entity, as phenomena, and subject them to the intellect? In other words, in the historical world, where the simplest

thing is always endlessly complex, what are the units, the self-contained wholes (to give the German *Ganzheiten* an English equivalent)?

When Erich Auerbach sadly acknowledges that even a "lifetime seems too short to create even the preliminaries" for what he calls a work of literary and historical synthesis, he sees no hope, however, that an absolutely single-minded narrowness can accomplish the task.

> The scholar who does not consistently limit himself to a narrow field of specialization and to a world of concepts held in common with a small circle of like-minded colleagues, lives in the midst of a tumult of impressions and claims on him: for the scholar to do justice to these is almost impossible. Still, it is becoming increasingly unsatisfactory to limit oneself to only one field of specializaton. To be a Provencal specialist in our day and age, for example, and to command only the immediately relevant linguistic, paleological, and historical facts is hardly enough to be a good specialist. On the other hand, there are fields of specialization that have become so widely various that their mastery has become the task of a lifetime.

It might have been to all of this that Nietzsche, with his superb desperation and infuriation, said: *"Ich habe meine Grunde vergessen"* (I have forgotten my beginning). The wish to have a good grasp of how it is that one's activity either has started or will start forces these considerations, and sometimes an impatient response like the one given by Nietzsche; nevertheless, such a grasp always compels us into a rational severity and asceticism, an understanding of which will be a major task in the course of this discussion. In this essay, therefore, I hope first of all to draw attention to, perhaps even to exacerbate, the problem we face when we begin an intellectual job of work. My view is that an intensified, and an irritated, awareness of what really goes on when we begin—that is, when we are conscious of beginning—virtually transforms, corrects, and validates whatever the project in a very complete way. And this transformation ascertains both the direction of our enterprise and, also, its true possibilities. Second, I should like to understand, however stutteringly, what sorts of beginnings really exist; the word beginning itself is, and will remain, a general term, but like a pronoun, it has a specific discursive role or roles to play, but these are as much in the control of reasonable convention and rule, as they are in the control of reasonable assertion. I should like to examine all this as it bears on the possible kinds of beginnings available to us. Lastly, I should like to record a part of the rational activity generated in us when we deal with a beginning; and rational activity, it will become clear, includes rational sentiment, passion and urgency.

The beginning as primordial asceticism has an obsessive persistence in the mind which seems very often engaged in a retrospective examination of itself. We all like to believe we can always begin again, that a clean start will always be possible. This is true despite the mind's luxuriance in a wealth of knowledge about ongoing actuality, about what Husserl calls *lebendige Gegenwart* (the living present). There is a significant attention paid by the mind to a terminal in the past from which the present might have evolved, as well as a nervous solemnity—*when the question is thought of*—in the choice of a point of departure for an actual project. Indeed, in the case of the great modern re-thinkers the beginning is a way of grasping the whole project; Marx, to consider only one example, attacks Proudhon not only because of Proudhon's uncritically good intentions, but because of his misplaced priorities. "For M. Proudhon," Marx writes in *The Poverty of Philosophy,* "the circulation of the blood must be a consequence of the theory of Harvey." As Lukacs surmised in 1923, it was the job of Marx to show first that beginnings hitherto accepted by the forms of bourgeois thought contributed to, rather than lessened, the separation between man and his proper nature. Then Marx went on to demonstrate that, as Vico had demonstrated before him, man was in fact the beginning of all study, but man for whom "the *social* reality of nature, and *human* natural science, or the *natural science about man,* are identical terms." Clearly there has been a *radical* displacement of traditional thought, for in order to see man as the true origin of social change a new fusion between man and his activity must become possible and thereby re-thought in man's mind. The very act of beginning must no longer set man apart from his end, but must immediately suggest connections with it. Marx has cemented his own interpretive activity with man's human activity at a common revolutionary point of departure.

Formally the mind wants to conceive a point in either time or space at which all, or perhaps only a limited set of, things start, but like Oedipus the mind discovers at that point where all things will end. The beginning implies, or rather implicates, the end. If the search is a more modest one, the mind will look for a *possibility* in the past and will therefore propose the present and the future to it for reflection: the result will be three varieties, or stages, of possibility, linked in continuous sequence. This sequence, however, seems to be *there* at a distance from me, whereas my own problematic situation is *here* and *now*. For one rarely searches for beginnings unless the present matters a great deal. It is my present urgency, here and now, that will enable the sequence of beginning-middle-end, and transform it from a distant object *there,* into the subject of my reasoning. So conceived and fashioned, time and space make a drama realized according to an immanent text of significance and not a scenario contemplated in a way that will keep actor and text intact and separate. Ever the dialectician, Lukacs writes that "as the consciousness is not consciousness bearing on an object there, but the object's consciousness of itself, the act of being conscious overturns the form of objectivity of its object."

The verbal problems are very acute. A beginning suggests a) a time, b) a place, c) an object—in short, detachment. *My* beginning specializes all these a little more, and when I say *the* beginning, they are theologized, as Kenneth Burke very cogently argues in *The Rhetoric of Religion.* Once made the focus of consciousness, the beginning occupies the foreground, is no longer a beginning but has the status of an actuality, and when it cedes its place to what it pretends to give rise to, it can exist in the mind as virtuality. In all this "beginnings" vacillate in the mind's discriminations between thought beginning and thought about beginning, that is between the status of subject and object. Paraphrasing Hegel, we can say that formally the problem of beginning is the beginning of the problem. A beginning is a moment when the mind can start to allude to itself as a formal doctrine.

In language we must resign our thoughts to what Nietzsche saw was "something (that) impels them in a definite order, one after the other—to wit, the innate systematic structure and relationship of their concepts." Also, "the unconscious domination and guidance by similar grammatical functions," of which a system of concepts or words is only a strong disguise, merely leases the mind the right to a notion of formal beginnings. Language, as we perceive it in its universal use, has no beginning, and its origins are as marvelous as they are imagined, but they can only be imagined. Profoundly temporal in its self-evidence language nevertheless provides a utopian space and time, the prochronistic and the postpositional functions, over which its systematic determination does not immediately seem to hold firm sway. Thus "the beginning," as often belonging to myth as to logic, a temporal place, and a root and also an objective, remains a kind of gift inside language. I shall be returning to this notion a little later. Heidegger and Merleau-Ponty have made effective claims for the identity of temporality with significance, yet philosophically and linguistically theirs is a view that requires, I think, our recognition of the mind's self-concerned glosses on itself in time, the mind as its own philosophical anthropology. What sort of action therefore transpires at the beginning? How, necessarily submitting to the incessant flux of experience, can we insert—as we do—our reflections on beginning(s) into that flux? Is the beginning simply an artifice, a disguise that defies the ever-closing trap of forced continuity, or is it a meaning and a possibility genuinely allowable?

* * * * *

Literature is full of the lore of beginnings despite the tyranny of *in medias res,* a convention that allows a beginning to pretend that it is not one. Two of the wide and obvious categories under which to list types of literary starting points are, on the one hand, the hysterically deliberate, and hence the funniest, and on the other hand, the solemn-dedicated, the impressive and noble. The former category includes *Tristram Shandy* and *A Tale of a Tub,* two works that despite their existence cannot seem to get started; this is beginning forestalled in the interest of a kind of encyclopedic, but meaningful, playfulness which, like Panurge taking stock of marriage before falling into the water, delays one sort of action with another. The latter category includes *Paradise Lost,* a prelude to post-lapsarian existence, and *The Prelude,* which was to ready its author "for entering upon the arduous labour which he had proposed to himself." In both works the beginning has become the work itself. When a literary work does not dwell very self-consciously on its beginnings—as the works I have just named do—its actual start, as an intelligible unit, is usually deliberately formal or concessive. (I must evade the question of whether it is really possible to begin unself-consciously, since I am convinced that it is not really possible. The issue is one of degrees of self-consciousness: *Tristram Shandy* is uniquely sensitive about getting under way.) Yet I would argue that points of departure grew increasingly problematic during the eighteenth century, a development eloquently testified to as much in the titles of Frank Manuel's "The Eighteenth Century Confronts the Gods" and W. J. Bate's "The English Poet and the Burden of the Past, 1660–1820" as in their matter.

The search for such points is not only reflected but carried out in and, it comes to be evident to eighteenth century thinkers like Vico, *because* of language. Polytechnical as no other human activity, language is discovered as an "intelligible abode" in which questions of origin can profitably be asked for purely linguistic as well as social, moral and political reasons: Vico, in the misery and obscurity of his position at Naples sees the whole world of nations developing out of poetry, and Rousseau, for whom experience is clarified by words to which he is entitled, simply because he is a man of sentiments and a member of the *tiers etat.* Kant's *Prolegomenon to Any Future Metaphysics,* to speak now of a beginning that really aims to strip away the accretions of academic philosophy, undertakes a description of radical conditions which must be understood before philosophy can be practiced; nevertheless the *Prolegomenon* fully anticipates *The Metaphysic of Ethics* and *The Critique of Practical Reason*—it is coterminous with them—and the critical method with which Kant refashioned European philosophy. And in the essay "On Method" (in *The Friend*) Coleridge takes up the theme as follows, echoing Descartes: method distinguishes a noteworthy mind in its work, its discipline, its sustained intellectual energy and vigilance. Method, however, requires an "initiative," the absence of which makes things appear "distant, disjointed and impertinent to each other and to any common purpose." Together initiative and the method that follows from it "will become natural to the mind which has been accustomed to contemplate not *things* only, or for their own sake alone, but likewise and chiefly the relations of things, either their relations to each other, or to the observer, or to the state, and apprehensions of the reader."

All such investigations have in common what Wordsworth called "a cheerful optimism in things to come." What is really anterior to a search for a method, to search for a temporal beginning, is not merely an initiative, but a necessary certainty, a genetic optimism, that continuity is possible. Stretching from start to finish is a fillable space, or time, pretty much there but, like a foundling, awaiting an author, a speaker, or a writer to father it. Consciousness of a starting point, from the viewpoint of the continuity that succeeds it, is consciousness of a direction in which it is humanly possible to move, as well as a trust in continuity. Valery's intellectual portrait of Leonardo divulges the secret that Leonardo, like Napoleon, was forced to find the law of continuity between things whose connection with each other escapes us. Any point of Leonardo's thought will lead to another for, Valery says in the same essay, thinking of an abyss Leonardo thought also of a bridge across it. Consciousness, whether as pure universality or insurmountable generality or eternal actuality, has the character of an imperial ego; in this view Descartes' *cogito* was for Valery "l'effet d'un appel sonne par Descartes a ses puissances egotistes." The starting point is the reflexive action of the mind attending to itself, allowing itself to act (or dream) a construction of a world whose seed totally implicates its offspring. It is Wagner hearing an E Flat chord out of which *The Ring*, and the Rhine, will rush, or Nietzsche giving birth to tragedy and morals by ascending a ladder of inner genealogy, or Husserl asserting the radical originality of consciousness which will support "the whole storied edifice of universal knowledge."

Husserl requires a unique attention because the almost excessive purity of his whole philosophic project makes him, I think, the epitome of modern mind in search of its beginnings. The course of Husserl's development is, in the main, too controversial, too technical a subject to warrant further analysis, at least not here. Yet the meaning of his philosophical work is that he accepted "the infinite goals of reason" while seeking, at the same time, to ground understanding of these goals in lived human experience. Interpretation, which is a major task in the Husserlian and Heideggerian enterprises both, is thus committed to a radical undermining of itself, and not only because its goals are pushed further and further forward. For also its point of departure, no longer accepted as "naive"—that is, merely given, or *there*—stands revealed in the scrutiny of consciousness; as a result, the point of departure assumes a unique place as philosophy itself, "essentially a science of true beginnings . . . *rizomata panton,*" as well as an example of the science in action. Put differently, Husserl tries to seize the beginning proposing itself to the beginning *as* a beginning *in* the beginning. What emerges precisely is the sentiment of beginning, purged of any doubt, fully convinced of itself, intransitive, and yet from the standpoint of lay knowledge—which Husserl acknowledged to be "an unbearable need"—thoroughly aloof and almost incomprehensible. This kind of purely conceptual beginning is curiously reminiscent of these lines from Stevens' "Of Mere Being":

> The palm at the end of the mind,
> Beyond the last thought, rises
> In the bronze distance,
>
> A gold-feathered bird
> Sings in the palm, without human meaning,
> Without human feeling, a foreign song.

It is to Husserl that Valery's phrase "A specialist of the universal" is best applied. But I shall return to this queer, intransitive, purely conceptual but important kind of beginning very soon.

What is important to modern ascetic radicalism is the insistence on a rationalized beginning even as beginnings are shown to be at best polemical assertions, and at worst scarcely thinkable fantasies. Valery's Leonardo is a construction after all, and Husserl's phenomenological reduction temporarily "brackets" brute reality. The beginning, or the ending for that matter, is what Hans Vaihinger calls a summational fiction—and it is a summational fiction whether it is a temporal or a conceptual beginning—but I want to insist against Frank Kermode by stressing the primordial need for certainty at the beginning over the mere sense of an ending. Without at least a sense of a beginning nothing can really be done. This is as true for the literary critic as it is for the philosopher, the scientist, or the novelist. And the more crowded and confused a field appears, the more a beginning, whether fictional or not, seems imperative. A beginning gives us the chance to do work that consoles us for the tumbling disorder of brute reality, the exquisite environment of fact, that will not settle down.

Auerbach's retrospective analysis of his own work as a critic seems to suggest what I have been saying. In his essay *"Philologie der Weltliteratur,"* he at first rejects the possibility of making a continuity out of all literary production merely by endless fact-gathering; the immediate disorder of literature is too great for that. Then he proceeds to the description of a synthesis performed by the critic, a synthesis that depends on the choice of an appropriate *Ansatzpunkt,* or point of departure. "Myth" or "the Baroque," Auerbach stipulates, cannot be suitable points of departure for they are concepts as slippery as they are foreign to true literary thought; rather, a phrase like *la cour et la ville,* for instance, fully embedded in the verbal reality of an historical period, will itself *become* present (since it is an actual phrase, not a constituted one) to the researcher's mind, and will thereby link itself to the regulating, inner movement of the scrutinized, reflected-upon period. What is essential to Auerbach's meditations is the critic's willingness to begin with the proper instrument of discovery, one forged by language in the act of being locally itself.

Auerbach felt the *Ansatzpunkt* to be a term in the mind's operation. It appears at first as a simple, single digit; he uses the word *figura,* for instance, because it is found to have a special place in many Latin texts. Subtracted from history because of an insistence that attracts the researcher's puzzled attention, key words like *figura* seem suited, when strung together in sequence, for a new addition to our knowledge. Yet a mechanical arithmetic is avoided when the *Ansatzpunkt* is revealed as a symbol in a formidable algebra. A point of departure is intelligible, as x is intelligible in an algebraic function, as *figura* is intelligible in Cicero's orations, yet its value is also unknown until it is seen in repeated encounters with other terms in the function and with other functions or texts. Thus the importance of a word like *figura* or of the phrase *la cour et la ville;* in the research, both emerge from a catalogue to enter history, which Auerbach construes as ready in his mind to incarnate them; ready, that is, to change them, and be changed by them. No longer mere words or unknown symbols, in Auerbach's writing they enact "the enchainment of past and future woven in the weakness of the changing body." A mute term, relatively anonymous, has given rise to a special condition of mind and has evoked the poignancy of time. The beginning is an effort made on behalf of continuity; thus a term is converted into history, a unit into a synthesis.

At first a recurrence amongst other sentences, Auerbach's *Ansatzpunkt* turns into a question that asks the reason for its persistence. *Nihil est sine ratione.* And persistence will give the critic the opportunity to view a literature, or a so-called period, as an interrogator acting for a mute client. Interrogation itself creates notable effects, of which one is the phrasing of answers that are given *in terms* of the question. Thus the disparities between a text by Racine, by Corneille, by Vaugelas or Moliere are reduced in the interests of an overriding code of significance—embodied in a repeated phrase like *la cour et la ville* to which these texts seem directed—that links them all. The evidence Auerbach marshalls, however, has a form and an economy that is as particular as the forms of events in a nineteenth century novel, say a novel by Zola. It is not a mere collection of example, but a synthesized shaped whole. Elsewhere, Auerbach commends Zola for his daring, not to say his hopeless task, in attempting to deal with the tremendous complexity of the modern world; and this same world offers a panorama of warring "facts" faced no less by a literary critic of Auerbach's learning, or by a philosopher of Husserl's energy. In the latter's *Cartesian Meditations* he charges that "instead of a unitary living philosphy, we have a philosophical literature growing beyond all bounds and almost without coherence. Instead of a serious discussion among conflicting theories that, in their very conflict, demonstrate the intimacy with which they belong together, the commonness of their underlying convictions, and an unswerving belief in a true philosophy, we have a pseudo-reporting and a pseudo-criticizing, a mere semblance of philosophizing seriously with and for one another." Yet only through the voluntary imagining and the radical asceticism of a *formal willingness* to undertake the bolus synoptically can the researcher, whether novelist, critic or philosopher, even begin his task.

Beginnings and continuities so conceived are an appetite and a courage capable of taking in much of what is ordinarily indigestible. Sheer mass, for example, is compelled into a sentence, or a series of sentences. Books, names, ideas, passages, quotations—like the ones I have used—follow the sequence postulated for them; this is why Swift's "A Modest Proposal" is so perfectly illustrative of itself as a cannibalist tract, as well as of the operations of criticism, understood as re-thinking. For the obduracy of Irish peasant bodies that are coerced into a marvelously fluent prose is no more than the obduracy of books and ideas co-existing in something we call either verbal reality or verbal history. A literary critic, for example, who is fastened on a text, is a critic who, in demonstrating his right to speak, makes the text something which is continuous with his own discourse, and he does this by first discovering, thereby rationalizing a beginning. Thus the critic's prose—like Swift's as it mimics the Cannibalism it propounds by showing how easily human bodies can be assimilated by an amiable prose appetite—the critic's prose swallows resisting works, passes them into passages that decorate its own course, because it has found a beginning that allows such an operation. The beginning therefore is like a magical point that links critic and work criticized. The point is the meeting of critic and work, and it coerces the work into the critic's prose. In finding a point of departure invariably in the meeting of his criticism with the text criticized, is the critic merely re-finding his vision, his biases, in another's work? Does this entail the hope that "prior" texts have prepared one's validity or right to exist with charitable foresight? That *Ansatzpunkt* exist with one's name on them? What, in fine, is the critic's freedom?

* * * * *

These are difficult questions Let us examine Auerbach a little more. His *Ansatzpunkt,* as I said above, is a sentence or phrase, once spoken or written in a distance we call the past, but now mute: *la cour et la ville,* for instance. Yet the recognition of its wanting-to-speak, its importance in the present, transforms the *Ansatzpunkt* from an uninteresting but recurring motto into an instrument for the critic's work; like Aeneas' moly, it guides the critic through previously unnegotiable obstacles. There must of course be an act of endowment or assertion on the critic's part before an innocuous verbal "point" can turn into the privileged beginning of a critic's journey. The critic's belief, as well as his reflective examination of the point, together germinate into a criticism that is aware of what it is doing. Since a beginning of this sort projects a future for itself in cooperation with the protocols of critical prose—nowadays we speak of texts, meanings, and authors as co-existing in "literature"—the critic would like to devise a means for working with this set of conventions. He would also like to preserve what is unique and possibly strange in his own work. At the sheer level of the writing itself, the critic accepts the determination of linguistic and critical convention while hoping to retain the freedom of possibility: the former is governed by historical and social pressures, the latter by a point of departure that remains exposed to its contingent, and yet rational, status, one that encourages interrogation and retrospection. In the critic's work therefore a vigilant method and a record of that method's accomplishments are being produced together.

The point of departure, to return to it now, thus has two aspects that interanimate each other. One leads to the project being realized; this is the transitive aspect of the beginning—that is, beginning with (or for) end, or at least continuity, envisaged. The other aspect retains for the beginning the identity as *radical* starting-point: the intransitive and conceptual aspect, that which has no object but its own constant clarification. It is this second side that so fascinated Husserl, (I spoke earlier of a beginning *at* the beginning, *for* the beginning) and has continued to engage Heidegger. These two sides of the starting-point entail two styles of thought, and of imagination, one projective and descriptive, the other tautological and endlessly self-mimetic. The transitive mode is always hungering, like Lovelace perpetually chasing Clarissa, for an object it can never fully catch up with in either space or time; the intransitive, like Clarissa herself, can never have enough of itself; in short, expansion and concentration, or words in language, and the Word. The relationship between these two aspects of the starting-point is given by Merleau-Ponty: "Whether it is mythical or utopian, there is a place where everything that is or will be is preparing, at the same time, to be spoken." ("Qu'il soit mythique cu intelligible, il y a un lieu ou tout ce qui ést ou qui sera, se prapara on meme temps a etra dit.")

Mythical or a utopia, this place of which Merleau-Ponty speaks is probably the realm of silence in which transitive and intransitive beginnings jostle each other. Silence is the way language might dream of a golden age, and words, Blackmur says, are sometimes "burdened with the very cry of silence," with their very opposite and negation. Yet we do speak and we do write. We continue to use language, its burdens and confusions notwithstanding. The capabilities of language are not beggarly. For articulated language is also a way of apprehending, of alluding to, and even of dealing with what is unknown, or irrational, or foreign to it, whether we call the unknown a myth, a dream, utopia, or absolute silence. We never know, Eliot says, in any assertion just what or how much we are asserting. The unknown can even be called a beginning insofar as the beginning is a concept that resists the stream of language. Since in its use language is preeminently an actuality, a presence, any reference to what precedes it and what is quite different from it is an unknown. If, as I speak, I refer to a beginning, I am referring to what is not immediately present, unless I am referring to the transitive, useful beginning, the beginning defined as present for the purpose of the discourse. The intransitive beginning is locked outside of language; it is unknown, and so labelled. And yet I can and often must refer to it as Husserl did, even though it seems perpetually to refuse me.

Let me try another way of explaining this. When I read a page I must keep in mind that the page was written, or somehow produced in an act of writing. Writing is the unknown, or the beginning from which reading imagines and from which it departs in what Sartre calls a method of guided invention. But that is the reader's transitive point of view which is forced to imagine a prior unknown that the reader calls writing. From the point of view of the writer, however, his writing—as he does it—is perpetually at the beginning. Like Rilke's Malte he is a beginner in his own circumstances. He writes for no real sake but for his writing; he writes in order to write. What he has already written will always have a power over him. But it too, while he writes, in the presence of his act of writing, is an unknown. It is felt but not present. The writer is the widow of an insight. Eliot says:

> It seems to me that beyond the namable, classifiable emotions and motives of our conscious life when directed towards action—the part of life which prose drama is wholly adequate to express—there is a fringe of indefinite extent, out of the corner of the eye we can never completely focus; feeling of which we are only aware in a kind of temporary detachment from action.

The unknown absence, felt by the mind, is represented by modern poets, critics, and novelists as an antecedent power that incriminates and is refracted in the present; its mode of being, whether as horizon or as force, is discontinuous with the present and partial in appearance. The great prior reality—whether we call it history, the unconscious, God, or writing—is the Other (Milton's "great taskmaster's eye") present before, and crucial to our Now. The unknown is a metaphor for felt precedence that appears in glances backward, as an intimation of surrounding discomfort, as a threat of impending invasion, always ready to wreck our tenuously performed activity. It is Eliot's backward look, "the partial horror and ecstasy," Conrad's darkness, seemingly at bay yet ever closer to springing forward and obliterating mind and light, Kafka's trial that never takes place, but is planned before K can do anything, an endlessly circumvented trial but oppressively present in its very impingements, Borges' ruins that gradually reveal themselves as part of a terrible plan whose entirety one can never fully perceive but can always be felt as immortal. Or, in radical criticism, it is the deep anterior claim of the writing, sometimes willfully forgotten, sometimes deliberately attenuated, but always haunting the critic whose reading abuts the mountains and the caverns of an author's mind-at-work; such critics write critical poems imitating the behavior of the mind. At its best, radical criticism is full of its own changing, and haunted by its opposite, by the discontinuities of the dialectic of writing, which it must re-enact and record. Thus, according to Blackmur, "criticism keeps the sound of . . . footsteps live in our reading, so that we understand both the fury in the words and the words themselves."

Here, it seems to me, Freud's little essay of 1910, "The Antithetical Meaning of Primal Words," is very relevant. In the work of the philologist Karl Abel, Freud found linguistic and historical confirmations for his views that signs or words in a dream can mean either their opposite or something radically different from their appearance. Words in ancient Egyptian, according to Abel, contained a simultaneous recollection of their opposite and even of their negation. "Man," he goes on, "was not in fact able to acquire his oldest and simplest concepts except as contraries to their contraries, and only learnt by degrees to separate the two sides of an antithesis and think of one without conscious comparison with the other." Abel, unlike Freud, was a meliorist: Freud believed that words continue, in fact, to carry a recollection of their opposite, the unknown carrying with it a considerable freight of the unknown. Reading thus sends us back in a regressive movement away from the text to what the words drag along with them whether that is the memory of the writing, or some other hidden and perhaps unknown opposite.

Because we must deal with the unknown, whose nature by definition is speculative and outside the flowing chain of language, whatever we make of it will be no more than probability and not less than error. The awareness of possible error in speculation, and a continued speculation regardless of error, is an event in the history of modern rationalism whose importance, I think, cannot be over-emphasized; it is to some extent the subject of Frank Kermode's *The Sense of an Ending,* a book whose very justifiable bias is the connection between literature and the modes of fictional thought in a general sense. Nevertheless, the subject of how and when we become certain that what we are doing is wrong *but at least original* has yet to be studied in its full historical and intellectual richness. Such a study would, for instance, show us when and how a poet felt what he was doing was *only* writing poetry, how and when a philosopher attributed to his philosophy the power to predict its own invalidation, and when a historian saw the past dreaming about itself in his work.

* * * * *

Let me capitulate some of the things I have been trying to describe. The choice of a beginning is important to any enterprise even if, as is so often the case, a beginning is accepted as a beginning after we are long past beginning and after our apprenticeship is over. One of the special characteristics of thought from the eighteenth century until today is an obsession with beginnings that seems to infect and render exceedingly problematic the location of a beginning. Two kinds of beginning emerge, and they are really two sides of the same coin. One, which I called "temporal" and transitive, foresees a continuity that derives out of it. This kind of beginning is suited for work, for polemic, for discovery. It is what Emile Benveniste describes as the "axial moment which provides the zero point of the computation" that allows us to initiate, to direct, to measure time. Auerbach calls his *Ansatzpunkt* a handle by which to grasp literary history. We find it *for* a purpose, and at a time that is crucial to us, but it can never presume too much interrogation, examination, reflection unless we are willing to forego discipline on the mind that wants to think every turn of its thoughts from the beginning. Thoughts then appear linked in a meaningful series of constantly experienced moments.

There is always the danger of too much reflection upon beginnings. In a sense, what I have been doing in this paper proves the hazards of such an undertaking. In attempting to push oneself further and further back to what is only a beginning, a point that is stripped of every use but its classified standing in the mind as beginning, one is caught in a tautological circuit of beginnings about to begin. This is the other kind of beginning, the one I called intransitive and conceptual. It is very much a creature of the mind, very much a bristling paradox, yet also very much a figure of thought that draws special attention to itself. Its existence cannot be doubted, yet its pertinence is wholly to itself. Because it cannot truly be known, because it belongs more to silence than it does to language, because it is what has always been left behind, and because it challenges continuities that go cheerfully forward with *their* beginnings obediently affixed—it is something of a necessary fiction. It is perhaps our permanent concession as finite minds to an ungraspable absolute. Its felt absence has, I think, seemed particularly necessary to the modern mind, mainly because the modern mind finds it exceedingly difficult, perhaps impossible, to grasp presence immediately. To paraphrase A. D. in Malraux's *La tentation de l'occidents,* we lose the present twice: once when we make it, and again when we try to regain it. Even in the midst of powerful impressions upon us we find ourselves resorting to intervening techniques that deliver reality to us in palpable form. We are peripatetic converts to every mediation we learn, and learning, the process Vico described as auto-didactic philology, then seems more and more to be a matter of submitting to various linguistic fatalisms. A critic, for instance, cannot take in literature directly; as Auerbach said, the field is too minutely specialized now, and too vastly spread beyond our immediate ken. So we create sequence, periods, forms, measurements that suit our perceptual needs. Once we have seen them, these orders are left alone; we assume that they go on ordering to time's end, and there is nothing we can do about it. These mediating orders are in their turn commanded and informed by one or another moderately intelligible force, whether we call it history, time, mind, or, as is the case today, language. In *Le visible et l'invisible* Merleau-Ponty writes:

> If we dream of regaining the natural world or Time by our coincidence, our absolute identity, with either or both, if we dream of being the identical zero-point we see there, or the pure memory which within us governs our remembering, then language is a power for error, since it cuts the fabric that connects us vitally and directly both with things and with the past; language installs itself like a screen between us and things. The philosopher speaks, but that is his weakness, and an impossible one at that; he ought not to speak, he ought to meet things in silence, and in Being to rejoin a philosophy that has already been articulated. Yet despite that the philosopher wishes to verbalize a specific silence within him to which he listens. That absurd effort is his entire *oeuvre.*

Everything that is left after these orders of mediated presence are accepted we call unknown. But, as I have tried to show, the unknown remains with us to haunt us from its horizon. When we hint at the unknown we are involuntarily borrowing the words of our experience and using them to gesture beyond our experience. The archetypal unknown is the beginning. Newman called such a beginning an economy of God, and Vaihinger called it a summational fiction. We might call it radical inauthenticity, or the tautology at the end of the mind, or with

Freud, the primal word, literally, with an antithetical meaning. Such a beginning is the unknown event that makes us, and with us, our world, possible as a vessel of significance.

The most peculiar thing about such an unknown beginning—aside, that is, from its enduring shadow in our minds—is that we accept it at the same time that we realize that we are wrong, that it is wrong. It is useless, except when it shows us how much language, with its perpetual memories of silence, can do to summon fiction and reality to an equal space in the mind. In this space certain fiction and certain reality come together as identity. Yet we can never be certain what part of identity is true, what part fictional. This is the way it must remain—as long as part of the beginning eludes us, so long as we have language to help us and hinder us in finding it, and so long as language provides us with a word whose meaning is as certain as it is obscure.

A Conversation with V.S. Naipaul*

Interviewers: BHARATI MUKHERJEE, ROBERT BOYERS

RB: Somehow it seems strange to meet you here in this setting, in the sedate environs of a Wesleyan sitting room.
VSN: I don't belong here, of course, although everyone has been very gracious. It's an intolerable place, really. Do you know that my students can't find a shop that sells the *New York Review of Books*? The college store apparently has never been asked by a member of the faculty to carry such a publication. I don't think you will find your own magazine here.
R.B. Still, the experience of teaching bright students must have its pleasures.
VSN: Are they bright students? I don't know. I think it's bad to be mixing all the time with inferior minds. It's very, very damaging. To be with the young folk, the unformed mind, I think is damaging to one.
R.B. Where do you look for better minds? Where is your peer group?
VSN: There are people. And you know, few things excite me more than meeting a man I admire.
R.B. Do you have a literary circle as such?
VSN: No, but most of the people I know tend to be people who would be interested in my work, and have been for a long time. They are people whose interest I think is worth while.
B.M. One of the things you said years ago, I think, to Israel Shenker of the *New York Times*, I found very touching. You said that you write in London and don't have an audience, that you're just hanging in the air, doing the work of an artist in a vacuum, which is in a way absurd. You seemed to regret that you had no feedback. Do you feel that now, that sense of loss, that sense of insufficient feedback?

*This is the edited transcript of an interview conducted in May, 1979.

VSN: It's diminishing. That is diminishing because I think I've got a kind of audience now. At least I'm read by other writers. But the problem is really very important, and very simple, isn't it? The writing of books, the publishing of books, may be taken for granted by people who belong to a society in which those activities are part of the social routine. Even people who don't read books here know that there are other people who do. They know that there are book shops. But I don't spring out of that kind of society, and that is why I have felt that I am floating in a vacuum. I am an oddity, and have always felt that I was an oddity, since I have always been writing . . . I am an exotic to people who read my work, and also to people who don't read it but know that is what I do. Asiatics do not read, of course; they are a non-reading people. If they read at all, they read for magic. They read holy books, they read sacred hymns, or they read books of wisdom, books that will do them good. They do not read for the sake of inquiry or curiosity because their religion has filled the world for them completely. In the west, when you write you feel that you write for a certain kind of individual. And you assume that readers can feel themselves to be individuals. This is not an eternal in the world, not a constant. To write a kind of literature that I can find interesting you need to acquire an anxiety about man as an individual, and even in Europe this is a relatively new thing. There are some "Asiatics" writing, it is true. But they are recording for this outside audience their little tribal rites and they're seen really not as new writers enlarging the sensibilities of readers accustomed to works of real literary value.

B.M.: I am an extravagant admirer of your work and . . .

VSN: What do you find in it to admire?

B.M.: Well, you have articulated for people like me, for the first time, a post-colonial consciousness without making it appear exotic. Your writing is about unhousing and remaining unhoused and at the same time free. I not only sympathize with that condition; I want to share that sense of being cut off from a supporting world. But I'm also a little concerned with, or perhaps I don't understand, your dismissal of the Asiatics and their way of reading. Were you always as sure about Asians as you seem now to be?

VSN: Well, in the first place I think that this word "Asian" is quite an absurd word. It began to be used by Mr. Nehru in 1946 or '47 because, he said, "Asiatic" was a weak word. The Japanese when they used it to launch their propaganda in the 30's didn't think it was weak. Don't you think that if the word earned a bit more respect it would be a lovely word? Particularly as attached to a word like "prime" or "refined." That would sound very nice. On the other hand, "prime Asiatic mind" doesn't say as much to me as "dumb Asiatic mind." In any case, there is a sort of connection between the two. I think, as you can see, that you must get rid of the word "Asian" if you are to make your questions acceptable.

B.M.: But why should I be concerned about their being acceptable? I only want you to tell us about your attitudes to third world readers. And it is a fact that not only "Asians"—or "Asiatics"—but Africans read you . . .

VSN: No, I don't count the African readership and I don't think one should. Africa is a land of bush, again, not a very literary land. I don't see why it should get mixed up with Asia.

B.M.: You are determined to be quarrelsome. Shall we just say, "non-white commonwealth" readership?

VSN: That again is a very recent kind of division which I don't accept. You see, from the very early days I've been very careful in my work not to use words that produce the wrong associations. I don't use the word "imperialist" or "colonialist," for example. You say my work has some kind of meaning but you use words I can't use. In the 1950's those words or others like them might have had acceptable associations, but no longer. Now they are words that are used only by those chaps in the universities who make a specialty of putting things in political grooves. These are men who think they have a calling. They make investments in a political-academic stock market. Some are at present trading in African futures, creating a little calling. . . .

B.M.: But the point I was trying to make, a point you intend obviously to obscure, is that you do have two groups of admirers. One group sees you not as part of any kind of ethnic or exotic literature but as voicing a kind of aloneness or lostness which is recognizably a part of a literary tradition. The other readers are trying to recognize, even identify with something that they think they've also experienced in their own lives.

VSN: Yes, it's nice to think that there are readers who feel they can see their experience in what I've written. But finally the writer who thinks it's his business to get across the specificity of his material is making a great mistake. And I feel totally excluded by the works of writers like, shall we say, John Cheever, who are so much of their tribe that I think, as I read them, this is not for me, I mustn't enter there. I'm talking about what is really tribal literature, and I include in this even the stories of Hemingway, which can be quite good.

R.B.: In this sense we can say that there has been a marked shift in your own work. The word *tribal* as you use it would seem much more applicable to a book like *A House For Mr. Biswas*, for example, than to any of the works of the last ten years. *Biswas* does have a certain particularizing inclination which is absent in the later novels. And it is plausible then to see the recent work as marking an advance, a maturity.

VSN: Well yes, it's a good observation. Of course, when you're starting, you really have got to try to establish a world and it's much easier if you can even pretend that the tribal culture *is* a world, that the life of the street puts you in touch with the wider world. The early comedies make this pretense, I think, and they include *Biswas*, a book I think I remember, though I haven't read the book since I wrote it, you know. But even there, in a book like that, you can only pretend that you are totally shut in, that the condition is thoroughly imposed. You see that your goal is to get outside somehow by means of a tremendous intellectual exercise. I remember the anguish of those years, feeling always depleted. How was I to take the nature of my own life, which I couldn't refer to anything in my literary experience, and look for ways of entering the other life, a life led by people who would be strangers to one, people, say, living in London, with a history. It took me some years, even after I finished *Biswas*, to feel that I could do the job. I was still very shaky when I wrote *Mr. Stone*, the little book I wrote about England. Only after that did I really get going.

R.B.: Did you know as you were writing *Mr. Biswas* that this was something that in a sense you had to see through but would leave behind as you moved on? Did you shape the future as you were moving through it?

VSN: No, no, when one is writing one is always hoping at any stage to do it all, because — who knows? — you might die. You don't know, you never think about what's going to come next. I don't know what I'm going to do next year in my fiction. Even 8 months after I finish I'm just hoping that what I've written will lead on to something else.

B.M.: In the early years, the anguish you describe must have had a lot to do with the absence of available literary models for works that like *Biswas* sought to render a world that had not really been done before.

VSN: And of course for me this was complicated by the fact that I didn't even really belong in the exotic world I was born into and felt I had to write about. That life I wrote about in *Biswas* couldn't be the true nature of *my* life because I hadn't grown up in it feeling that it was mine. And that world itself was in fact turning when I entered it. How could one avoid the feeling of floating around? There are great mysteries in all this. It's a mystery that we in this room should all be talking the same language. And if I want to write about that mystery one thing I have to do is to avoid doing it in — here I'll use the word — in the way of the imperialist period novel. You know what I mean, the novel written by Hemingway or someone like that who always has the right passport and continues to pretend that it doesn't matter. But it would be quite different for someone like myself. I couldn't manage that pretense quite so easily.

R.B.: There must be advantages in the condition you describe, though the disadvantages had to seem insurmountable at first.

VSN: I will tell you. The good person, if he is dedicated, always makes his limitations into virtues. People looking at the work say, "God, you know, if only, if only, if only. . . ." That's true of me, too, I tend to complain of limitations. But there are virtues. Do you follow?

R.B.: Yes, I think so.

VSN: And there are after all financial limitations that are very much a part of this condition. I was just thinking about this today because for the first time in my life I actually sent off a note asking a magazine to commission a project. I've never done that before. I've always talked to people by word of mouth about ventures. I felt that my letter was a great humiliation after I posted it. And my mind went back to the utter humiliation I felt when my agent, who should have known better, made me take the manuscript of *Mr. Biswas* years ago to a hotel in London, where Mrs. Knopf of course rejected it instantly. They rejected the book because it was not publishable, and they were quite right, of course. It's not publishable because you don't write about Asiatics for a western audience which is in essence the only audience you can have. Such a book makes no commercial sense.

B.M.: But how then have you seduced, persuaded the publishers? Including those who run the house of Knopf?

VSN: By being around for a long time. Just by being around. I think it's fair in some ways. If you've been around for 25 years as a writer it means that there probably is something there. It isn't someone simply going through a phase or responding to a passing provocation.

I've sat out the Forster thing about relationships and a great many other temptations. You know how easy it would have been for me to subscribe to the pretentious stuff. How many people would have liked me to take as my slogan "only connect," that sort of thing. What other sort of things have I sat out? When I was young there was Kafka. But those temptations are gone.

R.B.: It's very interesting to go back to the reviews, and when you do, you find it's not always easy to understand why you should have had trouble. In general the reviews were very favorable, and the books were respectfully treated even in the major reviews.

VSN: Which ones? The American or British?

R.B.: American and British reviews, in fact. There were favorable early notices in the *New York Times*, in *Encounter*, and so on. Yet, as you say, it has taken considerable time for the impact to be felt — in the U.S. especially. It's a very curious thing to me . . . I can't think of any other writer so favorably and fairly reviewed who had to wait so long for a readership.

VSN: My books here used to sell six or seven hundred copies, you know.

R.B.: Yes, it's incredible.

VSN: Maybe libraries bought them.

B.M.: Do you feel that you've educated your audience? Have you created the audience that now reads the unpublishable books like *Biswas*?

VSN: No, I think it's all due to a number of very good, kind and generous people who have liked my work over the years, ever since I have been writing. I think it's entirely due to them, not to me.

R.B.: May we speak some more about your "origins"? Some time ago, you wrote about Conrad, and I am quoting: "Conrad's value to me is that he is someone who, 60 to 70 years ago, meditated on my world, a world I recognize today. I feel this about no other writer of the century . . ." Would you talk a little about this?

VSN: Oh yes, I'll tell you what I mean. I had a lot of trouble with Conrad when I was young because I read his work as a sign of what a novel should really entail — the psychological truth, etc. Conrad had a way of playing the fool in many ways, with his specious dramatizations. His cinematic eye often got him in a lot of trouble. I really don't think he has all the fine gifts of a novelist — doesn't have the true fantasy of a novelist. But in a practical way I cannot imagine Virginia Woolf or Proust or any of the other writers we admire considering the world I come from as being of any value. It is remarkable that Conrad could look at that world with the utmost seriousness. What an achievement! Can you imagine the pressure not to see it? Asiatics are people that simply didn't exist as individuals. In the novel of the 19th century they are just background, never more. Well, what a wonderful thing to do, to study the difference between two different kinds of people. With Conrad you have a great effort of understanding, of sympathy — do you feel that?

R.B.: What you say is really intriguing, since I have had the impression you resisted Conrad.

VSN: When I was young I did actually say — I think it was in *The Times* of 1962 — that I couldn't get on with Conrad.

R.B.: You went so far as to say that what you found "peculiar but depressing" about Conrad is that he comes to the fiction with ready made conclusions, where Ibsen's writing seemed a lot more exciting.

VSN: Yes, I still think there is much that is depressing in Conrad's writing. He begins very late, remember, he marries a lady who turns very fashionable, and he has all sorts of pressures on his time. He finds it necessary to churn out tales, tales. And his talent really never should have gone to producing all those tales. I find that very, very depressing. It is the wisdom that is not depressing. I believe he began to publish at about 38, though he began to write years before. So he was really very, very wise by the time he came to do the things most of us know.

B.M.: Are there any living writers you find exciting or wise in the same way? Writers whose work reflects the anxiety about change and an absorption in essential questions that you find bracing?

VSN: I know that literary intellectuals have a capacity to become excited about what's coming up next. I don't, and so I have a harder time than you in admiring current writers. Most of them seem to me terribly conventional. This doesn't mean that good ones don't exist. But who are they? I think that many recent writers have shared this view of mine, that even the better writers are perhaps missing the essence. I don't actually know all that many new American writers. Do you think I'm wrong?

R.B.: It's hard to say. We'd have to define what we mean by "essence," and we'd have to identify the different kinds of novels produced in this country. And that won't be fruitful here. But what of the current English novel?

VSN: I can't be interested in the latest English extravaganza. I can't be interested in a novel about the men in London. I can't – it's too far from me.

R.B.: That's too bad in a way. Since quite obviously that is what many American and English readers have said of you. They can't be interested in a novel about the people in Africa or the Caribbean. They're "too far" from us.

VSN: Yes, well one has one's limitations, and there it is. But I continue to think there is a difference here. I feel that the most interesting books have a certain instability about them which I don't find in current English fiction.

R.B.: An instability? I'm not sure I know what you mean. I suppose you mean something about the content of the work. And in this sense maybe it is someone like Orwell you'd prefer to the current crop.

VSN: Yes, Orwell remains very interesting, doesn't he? To break away from the stable English phase he had to pretend that he was a pauper. He had to learn to strip himself of all his earliest assumptions. He is the most imaginative writer, most imaginative man in English history. He travelled in a new direction. Don't you agree?

R.B.: I must confess that to me Orwell is most appealing as an essayist, a journalist – much more so than as a novelist.

VSN: The novels also are interesting. But whichever of his works you prefer, he does not write like the English writers I know. What I miss in the novels of London life, as also in the novels of suburban misery, is the instability. In them you have the assumption of being, that what is, has already been, and will continue. The Soviets too write most often about what is constant. I much prefer writers who can carry in their writing some sense of what is, wasn't always, has been made, and is about to change again and become something else.

R.B.: Orwell, of course, spent a good deal of time writing journalism, and so have you. Would you tell us a little bit about how journalism feeds into your fiction?

VSN: I'm getting too old to do it well, you know, though journalism is something that engages me and in a sense keeps me going. Those articles – many of them – called up the most complex skills. They required that I hold myself open for encounters, for adventures, that I always be alert without knowing what next to look out for. They had me wondering always what questions to ask, how to get on with people, how to let people talk. I had to learn to understand what would prejudice my grasp of any given country or situation, and I worked to acquire a travel skill that would let me know when the time had come for me to go away, to know when things had begun to repeat themselves. After a while you've got the material, but the writing is always altering that material. You've got to be alert to the various pressures, all the temptations to draw social lessons. Everything you know is engaged. It's a total exercise. I think it's the most difficult, the most complex thing you can do.

R.B.: Do you feel that the vision of things you arrive at in that way is very different from the conclusions you reach in the fiction?

VSN: They come out of two entirely different segments of the brain. And they're actually written differently. I just mentioned this to someone else the other day. The fiction begins on the typewriter, which allows when necessary for a certain speed, if there is anything there. The other has to be done very carefully, so it's done by hand, because it's very planned, you know? Have you ever had the experience of sort of picking your way around? You land in the airport and you stand there and ask yourself: What shall I do? Anything that begins that way is going to take shape very differently from a work of fiction. But the reporting helped me to study the world, helped me a lot really, though it was a great strain, a great effort when I began doing it.

B.M.: It has been said about some of the non-fiction — I'm thinking especially of *The Middle Passage* — that . . .

VSN: That was the first one. *The Middle Passage* — yes, a very funny book. I continue to like it a great deal.

B.M.: But it was said, when it appeared, that you were approaching the country with preconceived conclusions — that you went to confirm expectations rather than to explore what was before you.

VSN: Yes, there were complaints. In the 1960's people were shouting for certain political movements in those places I visited, so when I stepped in to say that this is stupid, that this is just routine, nothing more than public affairs, those who were shouting did not approve. By now of course I think they've given up. The particular holy man they were pushing at the time in those places has been abandoned. And you know, I think that the books of real writers, even when they are reporter's books, must be judged on their ability to stand up. A writer's book has to stand even after the events have changed. My book was written in '61, published in '62. So 18 years later it has to stand up or not. You read it now and I think you see that it's fair — it's fair. Or is it not fair? But obviously it offended people who had their own prejudices, who thought that shouting racist slogans in 1960 was wonderful. I thought they were horrible.

B.M.: But it has been said of *The Middle Passage* that you . . .

VSN: If *The Middle Passage* is found untrue today, 18 years later, then I will debate what seems untrue. If it remains true, if you cannot bring yourself to say, 'You were wrong here, and here, or here,' then there is no sense asking how I came to arrive at these things. I arrived at them because I refused to go in with preconceived notions. You know, people are always convinced that their political passion is wonderful, and then surprised when they find they've learned nothing from their experiences. You must read the book, and tell me that the chapter on Jamaica is not marvelously prescient, pre-visionary of what has happened lately. If you can tell me that, *then* attack me. Don't tell me otherwise that I shouldn't have said what I say about the illiterate black man shouting for racial redemption and found to get nowhere. Will you say they have gotten somewhere? I'll say they've gotten nowhere. They've destroyed their little world. I say they've taken several large steps back to the bush. And it's surprised me. I never thought that after 300 years of the new world an African people could return to the bush. That is very sad.

B.M.: What is amazing to me is the confidence with which you can say that the objective truth is they have returned to the bush.

VSN: I'm being very provocative, but I'm also speaking with a lot of bitterness. And much unhappiness. Because it is not pleasant to see the place where you were born destroyed, and that is the bottom of it. There are no institutions, nothing to refer to any longer. You cannot refer to any idea of law, or honesty about public money or the rights of all men, because racialist politics in a way rejects all these values. And I wish that people would see that in fact one is really bitter because of the collapse of human values. *I'm* not fighting a racial war; the people who ban me over there are fighting a racial war. And that is a sign of the collapse of civilization, of the possibility of movement forward.

B.M.: This revelation of the bitterness behind the easy generalization that . . .

VSN: Easy generalization? It's taken a long time to think about the bush. It's a big thing, there is no easy generalization or easy conclusion. It's as difficult as the conclusion you come to after being in India. It takes a long time in India to come to the simple conclusion that, by God, these people are just extraordinarily stupid! There is no hidden virtue in a man like Desai. There is no secret intelligence in these people. The people running the country and playing politics are just very, very stupid. Now *that's* a breakthrough, since these simple things elude one; because one is so full of received ideas one just doesn't see the truth.

R.B.: But why haven't you applied this kind of soul-searching and possible breakthrough of insight to British society, too? You haven't really dealt with England except in the early novel, have you?

VSN: That's right.

B.M.: And if you were to turn your whole intellectual machinery on the English, would they also be likely to come up seeming incredibly stupid?

VSN: They are in trouble. And it's the trouble that comes to every country that has really been tremendously successful. There have been few countries as successful as England in the world — and not successful only in one way but in almost all ways, except perhaps painting and music. Think of English literature, science, the institutions of law and government, their establishing the rights of man, their prodigious history. Have you read Darwin? Isn't it marvelous? As a young man I read *The Voyage of the Beagle*, and I thought, how wonderful that a young man who was a scientist, not a writer by profession, could write so magnificently.

B.M.: I think of Darwin and Freud and a number of others as literature, not as theory or science.

VSN: I think the finest English minds can be found outside the purely literary enterprise. But you know, great vanity can set in when a people are so successful. They begin to believe in racial magic, and finally exalt the form rather than the substance. Darwin's great because Darwin is, well . . . Darwin, but eventually he just becomes part of English Literature. And the general achievement extends then to manner of speaking, manner of addressing, to the shadow, the shadow, and a great tradition goes quickly into its decline. You can see it here in America. I'm sure that the fathers of the current student generation here had some feeling that it was necessary for them to work and achieve something. Already, in one generation after the consolidation of America's undoubted dominance in the world, you have people who are unlettered, extraordinarily vain, lazy, corrupt but at places like Wesleyan at least they take great care to dress the correct "preppy" way. The thing that they are *not* interested in is work or achievement. A great success begins to breed a kind of corrupting vanity. I'm afraid it's quite common in human society.

B.M.: Of course you are chiefly interested in another kind of society, a world largely unfamiliar to British and American audiences. For me, *Mr. Biswas* was a really exciting breakthrough because it went from the closed communal satire of the communal world to the study of unhousing and housing. But there were problems you had to solve in all of the early works. How did you, in the early novels, get across to the foreign audience the necessary sense of a wife-beating hero coming from a wife-beating culture? Your audience really couldn't know how to respond to a hero who is also a wife-beater. In a Cheever novel, if a character beats his wife, we know he is a bad guy. For you the situation had to be very different.

VSN: Well, I think of the words I used to describe that wife-beating. I said that it made them very close, or something like that. I've forgotten the sentence, which was written some years ago—23, I think. I remember it stuck in my mind, and I thought it might remain with others too.

B.M.: Yes, it was a memorable sentence. But, you see, that particular paragraph is a little troubling, because there's an easy assumption there about the couple's having fallen into their roles. Everything was comfortable, you suggest, the wife had been beaten, and each of them had fulfilled his assigned roles. I think that *that* kind of easy assumption — you won't like that phrase "easy assumption" — is no longer possible in your fiction.

VSN: Not at all. Absolutely. You can no longer do that. Everybody, everything has to be explained very carefully. But when you do that sort of subject, well, you find it's an unavoidably funny subject, no matter how you try to explain it. You know the joke: Do you still beat your wife? But the treatment of the subject needn't be malicious. It's a serious thing. Wife-beating is very prevalent, as I found out when I went to the courts and followed all the cases. One afternoon in my hotel I met one of these men. And I said: Do you really beat your wife? — and he said, I don't, but my neighbor does. These things can be very funny, but you can't always be sure your reader will take them in as you'd like.

R.B.: Do you consider the audience when you work out a scene or a crucial detail in your novels? I'm speaking, for example, of the scene in *Guerrillas* in which the very unlovely young woman is brutally sodomized. In drafting such a scene, would it be necessary for you to imagine the response of the reader, and perhaps to modify the treatment of that episode accordingly?

VSN: Yes, of course. I had to be careful. The novel, you know, hangs between two sexual scenes. The first explains the second. I was very nervous before I wrote the first one. And I was appalled by the second. I hope I was careful enough to remove from the sex scenes any association of the standard erotic writing. But I was appalled. Yet I couldn't remove all of the more erotic or excitatory associations of words. I know it's offended a lot of people. It really has. But you see, the terror of that book is inevitable. It's a book about lies and self deception and people inhabiting different worlds or cultures. It is the only book I know which is really about an act of murder. That is why it's shocking — and the fact that it shocks you is part of its success. But it's the wrong kind of success if you just think, God she was such an unpleasant girl. If she was really all that unpleasant, if you hadn't been made to understand her, you wouldn't have found her death to be so appalling.

R.B.: Were you surprised at the very favorable reception of the book in the United States?

VSN: The book lost me about half my readership in England. They couldn't take it.

R.B.: It's very strong medicine. But I was surprised, again, that someone like Hilton Kramer thought so very highly of the book. I would've thought that . . . .

VSN: I think he responded to the pain in the book, and to the fact that it's a moralistic book. It has very hard things to say about people who play at serious things, who think they can always escape, run back to their safe world. The woman in the novel is a study in vanity, and perhaps people like Kramer have strong feelings about that kind of vanity.

R.B.: You describe *Guerrillas* as a moralistic book. Do you then see yourself as having moved resolutely from satire into moral fiction?

VSN: I want to go back to comedy now. Oh yes, I want to go back to comedy. Having gone through those dark things, and drawing upon all my knowledge, I want to be funny once again. Why not? Why shouldn't one be funny?

R.B.: Would you describe your latest novel, *A Bend in the River*, as a comedy?

VSN: Well, I think it's a little funnier than the other book.

B.M.: It can't be funnier than *Guerrillas*! Can it?

VSN: Do you know *Guerrillas* is full of jokes? If I had read *Guerrillas* aloud you would be roaring with laughter. Really.

R.B.: This is something I'll have to think about. To accept what you say here would commit me to a separation of form and content that I'm not comfortable about. Though this would place you, in a way, closer to some of the more reflexive or self-regarding writers of contemporary fiction, who are not primarily "writing about," but "writing." Do you have any kind of interest at all in the kind of fiction we associate with writers like Donald Barthelme or William Gass? There seem to be a great many more prominent novelists of that kind in the United States than elsewhere.

VSN: How would you define their work?

R.B.: I sense that you are asking because you don't ordinarily read books by such writers. And of course there are drastic differences between a Gass and a Barthelme. For one such writer what counts more than anything else is a love of language for its own sake. For another what counts is the calling into being of the play function of the mind. In any of these writers the element of signification is decidedly modest. They disdain, for themselves, the representational possibilities of fiction.

VSN: I think it's a legitimate thing to do.

B.M.: You think this is a legitimate option for an unhoused writer?

VSN: To play with language?

B.M.: Yes. To be a Nabokov . . .

VSN: Oh yes, for any writer, I think it's quite legitimate. Whether it's satisfactory in the long run is another matter, but it's quite legitimate. I wouldn't run it down. I recognize it as one of the twists of the world, you know.

R.B.: You don't have the sense that the novel today has a specific function, a job of work to do . . . nothing of that sort. That's to the good, so far as I am concerned. And really what you say confirms my sense of *In a Free State*, or at least the sense of it I got when I reread it a few weeks ago. I found there a wonderful subversive quality, if I may use that term, a quality found only in fictions that deal with plausibly human persons, but which undermine all ordinary expectations attaching to familiar representations. Here you have two people on their way to a particular place, in a car, and a windshield which can be scratched the way it might be scratched in a naturalistic fiction. But one accepts at once in reading the novel that that isn't at all the level at which one is interested. One isn't interested at all in the scratch on the windshield or in the destination to which the car is headed, one is interested really in the way in which our familiar relation to the world is threatened. Nothing more than that. I have the sense that in the book what is real is the sense of menace. None of the particulars attaching to that menace matter. Does that make sense?

VSN: That was a very, very hard book to write. There is dialogue all the way through, and for that to work you have to establish the lives and relationships of all the people precisely. But you also have to get what is happening outside. Even the history of the land plays an important part. You stress the dramatic arrangement, I think. But when you stress that you say in effect that you don't feel that it's real, that the land is real.

R.B.: I didn't feel that as in any way a lack, a failure. For me the book aims at, and achieves, a negation of concreteness, a negation of real options, of the ordinary, and in that sense for me it is the most potent of all your works, though not the most appealing.

VSN: Oh, but I had them rolling in the aisles last week when I read in New York from the restaurant sequence. Though later on they were a little shocked to discover they were laughing at something people shouldn't really be laughing at. It was too late for them to regret their laughter.

R.B.: But even the humor there seems to be of a very special sort. It's not satirical in the way one expects from earlier books.

VSN: I agree it is an odd book. But of course one can't analyze one's work.

B.M.: To me it was terrifying, not only because of the terror of the situation, but because of the vision which said all politics is silly, and the African people will necessarily revert to the bush.

VSN: You know, I began to write the book in '69, before anyone can have seen exactly how accurate my predictions would be. I got a fabulous roasting when the book came out in 1971. Our African "strong man" hadn't really shown his hand then. The book offended a lot of people who just couldn't visualize these developments in a land like Uganda, which I drew with touches of Kenya and one or two other countries. My critics didn't see what could happen with someone who's kicked out the Asiatics and put the Europeans under seige. I was thinking again the other day how I got very frightened being there in 1966. I used to think, "I'm alone here . . . terrible things are coming here." But I could not have worked out the means by which in that pacific, lovely place, where people are so gentle and nice, there would suddenly be guns and killing and the prisons would be full of blood.

R.B.: Does your political passion lead you to read the newspapers every day? You sound like a man who needs to stay on top of events.

VSN: That's the trouble. Though I used to have an appetite for the papers when I was younger, I came to feel that they're unhealthy. They're bad for you like eating ice cream for breakfast, lunch and dinner. And they tell you nothing new. I spend more time on the news magazines. There are a number of good ones in this country.

B.M.: Can you tell me more about the politics you are most interested in?

VSN: I'll tell you a little story, though I won't mention names. There's an elegant lady in England . . . getting on now. She wrote a novel about a lady with a lover; the lady had a moral crisis — "Should I condemn others when I'm immoral . .", you know that kind of thing, all very delicate and beautiful. And this novel came out a few days before the pound took its enormous dive — it seemed it was going to touch one dollar fifty. And I thought, the dive of the pound — that extended event — has destroyed the value of this novel, which implies that this world is of value, that values are steady and are going to go on. But when your pound crashes, you cannot make those assumptions any more.

B.M.: Your story in a way addresses our earlier question about writers like Barthelme.

VSN: Well yes, I suppose all that assumes great security, that the world is going on; and that I can't assume, you see.

R.B.: Perhaps you insist too much that all is hopeless, that nothing can come from India or from other places in the third world. And perhaps you are mistaken when you say that European methods of historical inquiry "cannot be applied to Indian Civilization."

VSN: Clearly you have read Indian history. And so you must know that there are all sorts of things no Western historian can know what to do with.

B.M.: You say this over and over again, but I don't see that you've really made a case.

VSN: You think it can be done?

B.M.: Yes. And I guess the other problem that I have with your kind of vision is dismissal of the passions of people in these far-off places. I know it's absurd to be born in Calcutta or in Port of Spain . . . but it hurts those of us who have had that misfortune to hear you talk of it as you do.

VSN: Do I dismiss that passion?

B.M.: Well, to say that these people are incapable of serious thought on their own condition, or that they don't deserve a sympathetic and serious voice is, I think, tantamount to dismissal.

VSN: They've had too much sympathy, don't you think? They've had too many lovers of India loving them for their wretchedness and their misery and their slavery and their wish to keep others trapped.

B.M.: But no one I know wants to encourage that kind of Indophile.

VSN: Who do you want? You see, I'm not sure you know. What I want is for India to regard itself as a big country. It should be doing something in the world. It should have high standards of achievement. A country with 600 to 700 million people which is now offering the world nothing but illegitimate holy men should be ashamed of itself. And if that's the stupidity you've arrived at then you really should pull yourself up and say, "What can we do about it?" For a time I hoped my little proddings might start something. But clearly they're not going to start anything at all. And I do want you to see that I don't dismiss them because they're too far away. I'm very sad they've made themselves so negligible in the world. I think they pay a bitter price for being negligible. And I wish they could see that for themselves.

B.M.: Your books, then, really grow out of pain and irritation . . .

VSN: And a concern . . .

B.M.: Rather than contempt.

VSN: Oh, concern, oh certainly. One can't write out of contempt. If you try to do that, the book won't survive and won't irritate. Contempt can be ignored. But let's go back to your point about European methods applied to something as bizarre as Hindu history. Consider that in a way Hindu civilization stopped growing a long time ago. Nothing has been happening except plunder, war, decimation.

R.B.: But truly the alternative would not be to write the history from within Hindu culture. That cannot be what you propose. Said of course argues that to write about the Orient, one must entirely abandon any presumption of objectivity. One must, to do the job, write from a position of advocacy, from within. Only in this way will one want to do justice to one's subject. I don't see how this can be your view.

VSN: I think that any Hindu of intelligence who saw his history would be so appalled he would decide to go do something about it. And since things just go on as always, the Hindus must not see.

R.B.: Again, that's why I was curious about your rejection of European methods of historical analysis.

VSN: I'm not trying to reject, but to inquire. Let's think: Can you write a satisfactory history of England from the pre-Roman time up through the Roman occupation, the Roman withdrawal, the time of the little savage kings, and their being wiped out by the Danes—the consequence of all this being that nothing happened? It wouldn't make sense to write weighty histories about that; whereas, if you make all this a chapter of something larger, the material conceivably can stand that kind of inquiry. Remember what I wrote years ago, that history was built around achievement and creation.

R.B.: And in this sense, one might say, no form of history will presumably do justice to the complexities. They will require some other form entirely...

VSN: Probably something else is needed. Probably. As long as the same little things keep happening over and over again, with the same pointless stops and starts.

R.B.: But more seems to be involved here than the repudiation of particular historical forms. In *The Mimic Men* the narrator fails to see what good can come of the effort to put oneself in the place of those who are distressed. The effort, he concludes, we can make only "when we seek to forget ourselves by taking on the burden of others."

VSN: Did I write that?

R.B.: I think I've got it right. At least that's what your narrator says.

VSN: I wrote those words?

R.B.: Yes, you did.

VSN: Sometimes I forget, you know. But read it again for me, will you?

R.B.: He "tried to put myself in the place of those I thought were distressed." In so doing, he concludes, "I failed to see much. I minimized the quality of personality. But so it is when we seek to forget ourselves by taking on the burden of others." To what degree can the narrator in that novel be said to speak for you?

VSN: No, no, no. That isn't *me*. In fact, I had the other view, that there is more to people than their distress. That they are real people. And unless you understand that everyone has cause for self-esteem, you make a terrible political error. The Marxists tend to reduce people to their distress, or to their economic position. It's the sort of thing Conrad observes a little bit in *The Secret Agent*. He has another way of saying everyone has a cause for self-esteem. Everyone has something outside himself which gives him some idea of his own status. But you can't assume that people who live in a bleak condition have nothing at all to esteem in themselves, and will therefore answer any revolutionary call at all.

R.B.: May I shift ground a bit? In a review of *An Area of Darkness*, a well-known British critic makes some rather critical observations about the book. But then he goes on to say that the book has a great many strengths, and that it is, finally, "wonderfully enjoyable." Do you think that a satisfactory conclusion for a critic, or a reader?

VSN: I think it's entirely satisfactory. I think books should be fun. I think what is wrong with a writer like Conrad, for all his brilliance, is that you don't rush home and say, "Now I'm going to settle down and read a wonderful book." This is what you do for Balzac and for Tolstoy. And if this is good for them, why shouldn't we demand it from the rest of us?

B.M.: And you feel the same way about non-fiction? That its primary responsibility is, as it were, to be enjoyable?

VSN: There might be instances in which this response would not be appropriate. But I'm willing to believe that the element of pleasure is almost invariably paramount.

Imitations: Translation as Personal Mode

BY BEN BELITT

IT WOULD APPEAR that the domain of Robert Lowell's *Imitations* is public rather than private in character: a "small anthology of European poetry" from Homer to Pasternak and Montale, drawing upon five languages, including the Russian; with the customary omission of the Spanish. To some extent the concessions to Homer and Sappho are perfunctory: lip-service to the museum of the Sixth Century B.C., except in some fragments from Sappho which engage Lowell's lifelong preoccupation with cosmic and personal deprival. As a "small anthology of European poetry," however, the collection is obviously sparse and crotchety: what is important is the poet's readiness to explore the European intonation, try the agonies and the vagaries of the European subject in a way that his American contemporaries have not, and prove them by translation on his pulses. The effect of his anthology in the long run is to draw the reader's attention constantly to the person of the translator, and away from the ambiance of "Europe." It would appear that Lowell, like Pound and Eliot, has employed a mode of translation to enact a repertory of "personae" native to his irascible and inquiring genius; that what we have is, in fact, not an anthology of European poetry, but a species of dramatism: an artist's mimicry of other artists.

It is Lowell's startling expectation that all—Homer and Sappho, Der Wilde Alexander and François Villon, Leopardi, Hebel, Heine, Hugo, Baudelaire, Rimbaud, Mallarmé, Valéry, Rilke, Saba, Ungaretti, Montale, Annensky and Pasternak—"will be read as a sequence, one voice running through many personalities, contrasts, and repetitions." To this end, the mimetic brio of his assault upon the initiating voices is nothing short of ruthless. Sappho has been supplanted by "poems (which) are really new poems based on hers"; Villon has been "stripped"; Hebel has been "taken out of dialect"; Victor Hugo's "Gautier" has been "cut in half"; Mallarmé, Ungaretti, and Rimbaud have been "unclotted" at the translator's pleasure; a third of *Bateau*

Ivre has been jettisoned; two stanzas have been added to Rilke's "Roman Sarcophagus": "And so forth! I have dropped lines, moved lines, moved stanzas, changed images, and altered meter and intent."

The scandalized purist need not search long for a vantage point from which to sink his knives where self-righteous pedantry has always found fair game: indeed, Mr. Lowell in his Introduction delivers himself up to would-be assassins with the resolute fatalism of Caesar in the Roman Senate. His admissions and omissions seem almost wilfully suicidal: in that European cemetary of noble utterances and awesome identities which he inhabits, his actions appear vandalous and his appetites necrophilous. The question of Conscience, so touchy to critical moralists, seems never to have occurred to him. What remains is only his need, which is apparently insatiable: to "find ways to make (my originals) ring right for me"; to make Montale "still stronger in free verse"; to "keep something equivalent to the fire and finish of my originals"; to be "reckless with literal meaning" and labor "hard to get the tone"; "to write alive English"; "to rashly try to improve on other translations"; and most significantly, to *keep writing* "from time to time when I was unable to do anything of my own."

Connoisseurs of the translated word have every reason to ask where such wilful gerrymandering may not lead the professed translator: or *why* it is that certain translators translate. Taking Lowell at his own word, one would have to say that the cause is everywhere personal and solipsistic, as well as feral. More than ennui, certainly, must be postulated in his candid admission that he turned to "imitation" when the real thing was for a time denied him and he faced the virility of the world's eloquence "unable to do anything of my own." In the hard school of "*Sauve Qui Peut*" the cannibalism of the large talent at bay must be applauded for finding other means of dining with Landor and with Donne; and I count translation among the most taxing counsels of expedience. It requires, in the first place, an expenditure of self equal to the banquet set forth on the rich man's table. It deploys every skill given the poet's hand in the service of identities and prodigies not his own. As such, it is a form of austerity which finds sufficient recompense in the hard morality of Blake: "All Act is Virtue." Incidentally, it also accomplishes a kind of homeopathic therapy for purging past excesses and preparing for exertions yet to come, as when Lowell informs us that his Baudelaire, for all its stunning accomplishment, was "begun as exercises in couplets and quatrains and to get away from the longer, less concentrated problems of translating Racine's *Phèdre.*" At its worst, for which Lowell is also accountable, it "imitates" the bittersweet and the mistletoe in its search for symbiotic equivalences, attaching itself to a forest of host-plants to gratify its voracious determination to survive.

This is as much as to say that translation may serve the translator as a form of surrogate identity, as well as a labor of love. In the "parisitology" of translation, it is true, there are certain crustaceans which castrate their hosts, others which attach themselves to large aquatic mammals for the ride and prestige, others which strangle and infect: but the vitalism of Robert Lowell is another thing. I dwell upon it here precisely because his talent is massive enough to invite and master each of the dangers mentioned, in the service of a commanding identity, and survive. Modesty will get us nowhere in the attempt to arrive at any criteria of translation which may be said to underlie Lowell's accomplishment as intermediary for the European mind. The "one voice" "running through many personalities, contrasts, and repetitions" is unmistakably the voice of Robert Lowell—the most eventful and passionate voice of our epoch, whose voracity matters because it helps to give character to our century. Its impersonations, collapses, reassertions are never parasitical in the morbid sense of enacting flights from the poet's responsibility, or providing lines of least resistance in a peripheral struggle for existence.

On the other hand, little is to be gained from rushing to the defense of the *Imitations* with toplofty disclaimers which pay the poet the dubious compliment of removing him from the imputation of translation entirely. When Professor Alvarez informs prospective readers that the *Imitations* of Robert Lowell is "*Not* a book of translation"; that what we have is a "magnificent collection of new poems by Robert Lowell, based on the work of 18 European poets . . . in that constantly expanding imaginative universe in which Lowell orbits," no one is likely to benefit, least of all the translator. Robert Lowell cannot be dismissed as the space-man of recent American translation, circling the European scene in a rubbish of old sandwiches, astronautical weightlessness, and "expanding imagination." Doubtless, he winced, somewhere in the lower gasses, to find his "small anthology of European poetry" written off as "the most varied and moving book that this leader of mid-century poetry has yet produced" and "oddly, one of the most original." Edmund Wilson's equivocation is not much better: that the *Imitations* is probably "the only book of its kind in literature," whatever that happens to be. Nor can I, despite my mistrust of literalists dedicated to the subversion of inquiry and realism in translation, call the "complaint that Lowell has not followed

Baudelaire literally" an "absurd" one, with Mr. Wilson. The gift of absurdity is precisely what the literalist has not got; and it is possible that absurdity may do more than sanctimony to justify the deeper claim on our imagination for the passionate integrity of utterance which characterizes the finest of Lowell's "imitations."

What must be asked in the long empirical run is another question: what are we to understand by "imitation"? Precisely what or who is being imitated in the *Imitations*—Robert Lowell? his great originals? or "due process of translation?" Is the essential premise of imitation: (1) "I will now proceed to English this poem *as though I were* translating it"; or (2) "I will now English this poem as though it were part of my own sensibility, moving from element to element inside my own identity rather than the translator's, assembling and disassembling all inside my own nervous system, committed at all points to my own language rather than the language of the original?" Does the "imitator" differ from the "translator" in that he performs as a kind of versifying dowser sensitive to the indicated pulls of a *terra incognita* and is capable of turning all into *faits accomplis* of prosody? Is he a virtuoso asked to re-invent at second or third or fourth-hand (at, times he has no direct access to the language of the original) the occasion that was uniquely the poet's and the habits of mind and language that originally invested it? Are we concerned with fabrication rather than *mimesis*?

Current practise has no easy answers to these questions, and none is forthcoming in the term given the reader by Lowell. The word itself—imitation—has a notorious history of private and public misdemeanors from its awesome beginnings in Aristotle, up to the present. Life has been "imitated," Nature has been "imitated," Action has been "imitated," with nobody much the wiser. Indeed, the provenance of the "mimetic" factor is almost a certain guarantee of the surrender of the issue to polemical metaphysics and has helped to expose the bias of whole centuries. Thus, one generation talks of copies, phantoms, deceptions, in the name of imitation; another "holds the Mirror up to Nature"; another divinizes its literary models: "To copy Nature is to copy them"; another chooses "the mind's self-experience in the act of thinking" and re-invents Fancy and Imagination. Our own century has benefitted by the combined assaults of I. A. Richards, the debunkers of I. A. Richards, Butcher's preface to the *Poetics*, Francis Fergusson's bid for the "histrionic sensibility," and the long vista of verbal and compositional "dramatism" central to the poetics of Kenneth Burke.

None will serve to crystallize for us the intent of Robert Lowell in this volume. Among more recent symposia on the subject—notably, the barrage of 18 voices out of Harvard *On Translation*[1]—Jackson Mathews' "Third Thoughts on Translating Poetry" comes closest to the issue at hand, in decidedly cautionary terms. "The temptation," he writes, "is much greater in poetry than in prose to fall under the spell of the model, to try to *imitate* its obvious features, even its syntax, or to *mimic* the voice of the other poet. The usual mistake is to believe that the form of the model must somehow be *copied*." The spectrum remains the same—*imitate, mimic, copy*—but the paradox accomplished here is to force Lowell's word to account for all that he has repudiated in the name of "imitation." For whatever its shortcomings, Lowell's *Imitations* is no mocking-bird in an aviary of European originals.

II

Where, then, are we to turn for clues to the criteria of license and translation in Robert Lowell's anthology? In the absence of a "philosophy of composition," I would like to propose a direct reading of the "imitations" into which all has been metamorphosed by the translator himself—a collation of *his* choices, without any hint of paradigms known or imaginable to me, to which they might conform. Among the eerie truths learned by practising translators is the fact that the One True Translation which all pedants seem to have to hand and consult at will, exists nowhere at all. The particulars of Lowell's originals and the particulars of his "imitations" do, however, and together they may help us to construe the personal venture he has undertaken in behalf of his great models. For this purpose I have chosen two poems of Eugenio Montale—"Dora Markus" and "*Piccolo Testamento*"—for reasons which seem serviceable enough to me, though I am aware that all acts of translation are unique to themselves, especially where the range of voices and epochs is as orchestral as in Lowell.

Lowell's special fascination in Montale is already apparent in his prefatory remarks on his distinguished contemporary. "I had long been amazed by Montale, but had no idea how he might be worked until I saw that unlike most good poets—Horace and Petrarch are extremes—he was strong in simple prose and could be made stronger in free verse." Here is both the admirer's profession of engrossment in an appealing and powerful talent, and the translator's discovery of

1. *On Translation*, ed. Reuben A. Brower (Cambridge, Mass.: Harvard University Press, 1959).

a stance from which he might attempt an Archimedean moving of two worlds. Apart from such assurances—which are never idle in Lowell—there are a number of other considerations which confirm the appropriateness of such a choice. Despite Lowell's preference for Baudelaire as a *semblable* in spleen, guilt, and "*l'Inconnu*," despite his taste for the nostalgias and demoniacal historicity of Rimbaud as an artist "*maudit*," despite the neoclassical atavisms of Rilke and the delphic contemporaneity of Pasternak which he openly courts, the intonations and textures of Montale perhaps come closest to the temper of Robert Lowell himself. Like Montale, Lowell's prevailing cachet, after *Lord Weary's Castle*, is hard-bitten, melancholy, psychologically dense, with a subject that keeps curiously fluid despite the relentless pressure of despairing intentionality. Poem after poem in *For the Union Dead*, for example, eludes one in the midst of its restless thrust and circuition, as is also the case in Montale's "*Mottetti*," "*La Casa dei Dognani*," "*Iride*," "*La Primavera Hitleriana*," and countless others. For all Montale's declared predilection for "occasions" (he is content to call a whole volume *Le Occasioni*) what puzzles the reader most in both Montale and Lowell is the nature of the poetic occasion itself: *where* the poem's center was supposed to fall in the midst of the seething interplay of scruples, particulars, recriminations, and insurmountable rejections.

The Italians, with their civilized tolerance of the ineffable, have an admiring word for this phenomenon which they apply like a watermark to Montale: *hermetic*. The American reader has only the giddy afterthought: but what was it all about? Similarly, both Montale and Lowell carry a dense burden of personal and historical wretchedness, failed loves, psychological landscapes, existential incongruities inseparable from persons and places and electric with the pulsation of the moment. We have the unplumbed exacerbations of Montale's Bellosguardo, Eastbourne, Finistère, Proda di Versilia, to place alongside Lowell's Dunbarton, Nantucket Graveyard, Nautilus Island, Rapallo, and Boston Commons as stations of a spiritual itinerary. Like Lowell, Montale has written a "Ballad in a Clinic," watched storms from "The Coastguard's House," untangled the oddities of a "gnomelike world" from a "Café at Rapallo," scouted the ironies of "A Metropolitan Christmas," turned mordantly upon his own failed purposes in city parks, orchards, on trains and on beaches, leaving an inconclusive savor that troubles the attention without wholly disclosing itself. As in Lowell's volume by that name, a whole genre of heraldic "life studies" is opened up in Montale's "Dora Markus,"

"To Liuba Leaving," "Arsenio," "Carnival for Gerti," and "Visit to Fadin"; and it is hardly necessary to point out the "confessional" bias of poems like "Little Testament," "Letter Not Written," "Two in Twilight," "To My Mother," and the whole sequence of "Motets." The uncanny impression remains, after many readings of Montale's "Eastbourne," that it is a poem which might well bear the signature of both poets.

As an instance of "life study" Montale's "Dora Markus" is especially noteworthy. Here we have not only "one of the most poignant love elegies of all time" (in the opinion of Glauco Cambon) but a counterplay of intimacy, psychological divination, and the displaced "oriental" mind moving between Porto Corsini and the Austrian Alps. As a study in exile it combines a rich texture of deprival and unrest (*"irrequietudine"*) in a shimmering context of suspended outcomes: the poet's implacable vision of a "voice, legend, destiny" already "exhausted" or manhandled; the *"antica vita"* of a Jewess miraculously surviving from one day to the next by talismanic powers whimsically attributed to an ivory mouse in her jumble of lipstick, powderpuff, nailfile; and an immediate scene—majolica interiors, seaside *pensiones*, complete to the bayleaf that "survives for the kitchen." The aim of the poet is, above all, to recover the peculiar *"ansietà d'Oriente"* (Oriental anxiety) at once so fascinating and appalling to the Italian's appetite for melodrama: the capacity of Dora Markus to drift without outcome in a Levantine haze, instead of opting for fatality like a heroine in an opera by Verdi or Puccini.

Formally, it is among the most expansive and readily accessible of Montale's great set-pieces: open, conversational cadences undisturbed by the intrusion of eruptive afterthoughts—the *"dolce stil"* rather than the *"rime aspre"* of Montale's many voices, riding on its phrases, pauses, assonantal depths and graces with an unflinching objectivity. As such, it would not appear to offer the thorny talent of Robert Lowell an ideal vehicle of "imitation"; and it is hard to see how he was persuaded that Montale was either "strong in (the) simple prose of Kay's *Penguin Book of Italian Verse*" or "could be made stronger in free verse." The verse form chosen by Lowell is indeed free to the point of crudity: a prosody without pulse or that factor of inner rhyme which so often limbers the tensions and deepens the resonance of both Montale and Lowell. In comparison with the supple elegance of Montale, it is peculiarly shrill, prosy, angular, without reverberations. Its effect is that of an intermediate, rather than a final, draft, as though Lowell were still mired in the prose of *The Penguin*

Book of Italian Verse or preliminary renderings of his own. The presence of Robert Lowell, sometimes playing at "imitation," sometimes pressing for the bare sound and the tough reduction of intricate matters which is his true signature, comes and goes; the equivalences of Montale do not.

Nevertheless, the fact remains that "Dora Markus," for all its ineptitude, is a *translated*, and not an "imitated" poem. Every sequence of Montale's thinking has been retained intact, every image has been confronted, for the most part, in its own context; every effort has been directed with scrupulous and laborious integrity on unfolding the progressions of the poem as they are given the reader by the poet himself—with one maddeningly tone-deaf exception. The last line of all, indispensable to both the pathos and symmetry of the poem—what Sergio Solmi calls "the special curvature of Montale"—weighted with the total charge of Montale's induction of a "voice, legend, destiny," is suppressed: "But it is late, it grows later and later." Characteristically, Lowell has preferred to bleed off into suspension points and ignore the Dantean return to inexorable judgment of the original.

The digressions of Lowell's Montale deserve close scrutiny because they encompass whatever remains of the purely "imitative." It would be pointless and tedious to attempt an exhaustive collation of the two texts, since this is not a study in detection but a glimpse at the propinquities and equivalences of translation. Turning to the most harmless deviations first—the permissible variants or extensions of meaning forced upon the poet by exigency or "inspiration"—one might note the following in the first section of "Dora Markus." A "wooden pier" (*ponte di legno*) becomes a "plank pier": all to the good. The "almost motionless" (*quasi immoti*) fishermen become "dull as blocks" —possibly as extensions of the same plank pier; a "sign of the hand" (*segno della mano*) becomes a Lowellesque "toss of your thumb"; a dockyard (*darsena*) becomes "outlying shipyards"—very Bostonian; what was "shiny" (*lucida*) in Montale becomes "silvered" in Lowell; an impassive spring (*primavera inerte*) is a "depressed spring," and a way of life called "dappled" (*si screzia*) by Montale is curiously "subtilized" in Lowell. In a key-phrase to the poem as a whole, the "soft Oriental anxiety" of Dora Markus is diagnosed by Lowell as "nervous, Levantine anxiety"—and surely "Levantine" is a triumph of the *mot juste*: one of those windfalls of which one says the translator has pinned down what the original could not. The "stormy evenings" (*sere tempestose*), on the other hand, are levelled into "ugly nights," the admittedly equivocal *"dolcezza"* (a word intransigently foreign to English) turns into "ennui" rather than "sweetness" or "blandness"; and the "lake of indifference" (*lago d'indifferenza*) invoked by Montale as the heart of Dora Markus, is modified somewhat myopically into a "puddle of diffidence," as though the word had been read wrongly by the translator.

In most cases, the changes noted are legitimate ventures in interpretation, in which, as Valéry has pointed out, the translator not only presses for language, but "reconstitutes as nearly as possible the *effect* of a certain *cause* (a text in Italian) by means of another *cause* (a text in English)." More arbitrary departures, however, follow fast. Lowell elects to turn the simple "lowlands" or "flatlands" (*bassura*) of Montale into a "patch of town-sick country"—his own invention—and renders "its calms are even rarer" (*i suoi riposi sono anche piú rari*) with the heavy-handed "the let-ups are nonexistent," preempting what the author has left suspended. Other modifications seem merely inept or gratuitous to the quizzical reader: why, for example, "full of amnesia" for *"senza memoria"* (without memory)? Why clutter the *"antica vita"* (old life) of Montale with the needlessly explanatory "old world's way of surviving"?

Similarly, there are some troublesome admixtures of interpretation and fabrication in Part II of "Dora Markus." It is of the essence of Lowell's temperament, and as such, allowable, that the "ragged peaks" or pinnacles (*gl'irti pinnacoli*) of a seascape should turn up as "frowsy shorefront" in Lowell, the geese's cry (*gemiti d'oche*) turn into "catcalls," the "throbbing of motors" (*palpito dei motori*) metamorphose into "the put-put-put of the outboards," American-style, and "the evening that stretches out / over the humid inlet" (*la sera che si protende / sull'umida conca*) contract into "night blanketing / the fogging lake coves." There are also less allowable thrusts, however, which represent not "due process" of interpretation, but random piracies on the part of an "imitator" writing as he pleases, precisely as Lowell declares he intended to. Carinthia "of flowering myrtles and ponds" (*tua Carinzia di mirti fioriti e di stagni*) takes a curiously baroque turn of fancy: *"Your corsage is the crescent of* hedges of flowering myrtle." Where Dora Markus merely "stoops on the brink" (*china sul bordo*) Lowell's text explodes roguishly into "sashay on the curb of a stagnant pond"—certainly a strange outburst for the "exhausted" and "indifferent" Dora of Montale's legend. Similarly, there is a revving-up of the "big gold portraits" (*grandi ritratti d'oro*) which preside over her legend, into "ten-inch gold frames / of the grand hotels," as well as their subjects, whose "looks of men / with high(set) weak whiskers" (*quegli sguardi / di uomini che hanno fedine / altere e deboli*) shape up luridly as "the moist lips of sugar daddies / with weak masculine sideburns."

The passages cited, I repeat, constitute passing deflections, digressions, personal readings and renderings of detail; or incidental collapses and fumbled opportunities. Their telltale abundance in the case of "Dora Markus" constitutes a record of imprecision which forces one in the end to dismiss it as inept or provisional; the matrix of Lowell's English text itself, however, remains a *translated* rather than an "imitated" one. As such, "Dora Markus" presents a hard assay that need scandalize no one, however much it may disappoint the admirer of Robert Lowell who *asks* (as would I) for the sound of his voice and delights in following it as an attending presence through the translation it has chosen to inhabit. The failures of touch, the incidental occlusions of intent and tone, the occasional over-acting, over-posturing, over-reaching, the rare pratfalls into prosy approximations, are those of all poet-translators busy at their trade in the ordinary way, probing through that double identity which is the *néant* from which all true translation begins.

III

Precisely the same must be said for the modality and effect of Lowell's "*Piccolo Testamento*" (Little Testament). Here the translator's total encompassment of his original—his over-all felicity of touch, texture, compositional detail—is as impressive as the botched approximations of "Dora Markus." Perhaps one ought look no further for causes to such propitious effects, but merely acknowledge their existence as *faits accomplis* and pronounce the union of minds and languages fortunate. The nature of the original, in this case, however, in itself promises more compatible outcomes. In comparison with the pure line of "Dora Markus," the "Little Testament" is a poem more deeply scored with all the idiosyncratic merits of Montale—denser, stranger, nervier in its turns of rhythm and fancy, less immediate in its disclosure of the complex matters touched upon, more obdurate in its hermetic self-scrutiny, more oblique in its confidences. As such, it offers continuous resistance to all that is merely manipulative or "imitative" on the part of the translator and insists on its retention *intact*. At the same time, it is full of glancing turns of direction, texture, metaphorical and stylistic alignment, forging through its transpositions with a driving pulse, without the forfeit of a single misgiving or anxiety.

Presumably, this brings us closer to the vein of Lowell's "Skunk

Hour," "Colloquy in Black Rock," "The Flaw," and "The Severed Head": there should be less need, under the circumstances, for the translator to punctuate, revise, delete, and transpose matters to his satisfaction. Deviations from Montale's original persist here as in "Dora Markus," and one might even wonder about the justice of passing incursions. When Lowell gives us a "pearl necklace's snail's trail" for Montale's "snail's trail of mother-of-pearl" (*traccia madreperlacea di lumaca*), the visceral exudation of the snail is falsely represented by a necklace which has nothing to do with the context and omits the special iridescence sought by the poet. Similarly, when Montale, in the "crepuscular" vein of Italian modernism, writes the powder and mirror (*la cipria nello specchietto*) of a lady's compact (probably) into his poem as another instance of talismanic delusion, the poignancy of the ordinary is lost in the "*spectrum* of a pocket-mirror." I see no good reason, moreover, for turning the "soft coal wings" (*l'ali di bitume*) of Montale's descending Lucifer into "hard coal wings," his shadowy Lucifer (*un umbroso Lucifero*) into a "torch-bearing Lucifer," his dance (the "*sardana*") into an "orchestra," even if one grants that the Greek *orxestra* was actually a dancing-place. Lines 5–7, that universal stumbling-stone of translators of the "Little Testament"—and there are many—will of course please no one familiar with the elliptical fascinations of the original, and resists the best efforts of Lowell to improvise on his own. The "light of church or workshop / that neither the black nor the red cleric (acolyte?) / may nurture" (*lume di chiesa o d'officina / che alimenti / chierico rosso, o nero*), breathes heavily in Lowell's version: "The lamp in any church or office / tended by some adolescent altar boy / Communist or Papist, / in black or red." The question of which is the red and which the black, remains, as well as the pious orthodoxies of the adolescent Communist.

With every allowance made for near misses and far reaches such as these, I should still insist that the "Little Testament" of Lowell's Montale follows through from beginning to end as a *translated* venture of considerable beauty, intact in its own rhythms, illuminations, skills, and integrity: a meeting of minds and imaginations where they intersect in two artifacts—or Valéry's Italian "cause" wedded to his English "effect" which provides the reader, in turn, with a cause in itself. If this metaphysic is too hard or casuistical for the hasty to construe—and I suppose it is—the fault is not wholly Valéry's or Lowell's; or mine. It is part and parcel of a modern semantic bias which expects the croupier's handy transformation of blue chips into cash at the prevailing international exchange at each turn of the translator's wheel. For positivists such as these, the dropsical linguistics of Nabokov's "poetics" is a fitting crucifixion.

Debate on such matters is likely to be bottomless, discussion bad-tempered, and scholarship usurious. I prefer, instead, to dwell on the appropriateness of Lowell's continuing pursuit of translation as personal mode, in the years which have followed his initial *persona* as the castle-bound Lord Weary. Unlike the guerilla nationalists, professional bridge-blowers, rooftop snipers, and nocturnal infiltrators and assassins of the translator's domain, he has steadily gone on learning his trade by open assault in a variety of skirmishes and full-dress battles, in full view of the enemy, cap-a-pie, in single combat. It is already a very far cry from the glowing fabrications "after Rimbaud," "after Valéry," "after Rilke," in *Lord Weary's Castle*, with their reticent preface: "When I use the word *after* below the title of a poem, what follows is not a translation but an imitation which should be read as though it were an original." The author of *Imitations* and the translator of *Phèdre* and the *Oresteia* need never apologize for poems which presumably "come after" his sumptuous models. His English now lives *simultaneously* with the tongues and talents to which he is beholden.

Similarly, it can be said of his "dramatism" that translation has made it increasingly possible for him to depersonalize his penchant for heroic and patrician *personae*: Jonathan Edwards of the spiders and the "surprising conversions," the memoirs of General Thiebault, the confessions after Sextus Propertius, Valéry, Rimbaud, Rilke, Cobbett—all out of Lord Weary's castle—and move on to the province of drama as such. Here, Lowell's activity has been dazzling in both the pomp and diversity of its passion for transformation. More and more his medium has become theatrical in the literal sense that Lowell has increasingly sought out the provenance of the *played play*, rather than the pirated or inhabited identity of European masters. He has taken a craftsman's pains to "translate" Melville's Benito Cereno into objective theatrical artifacts, instead of appropriating the identity of Melville himself. He has translated the *theater* of Racine, rather than turning Racine into an impersonation of himself. And lest *grandeur* remain "still unsatisfied" in Calvary's turbulence, he has most recently thrown his total force against the full weight of Aeschylus' *Oresteia* in a bid for total theater.

It is to be hoped that with the passing of time and the channelization of a sensibility which hindsight now shows to have been constantly "histrionic," Lowell will continue to leaven the integrity of his translation. Ultimately, there should be no need for him whatever to remove himself from the rank and file of translators as such, or work in a special aura of privilege, in the name of "imitation." I say this without much hope that translators are ever any the wiser for having translated for a decade or a lifetime, or that they can ever hope for Adam's dream, who "awoke and found it true." Indeed, Babel is always with us. The moralist will say, for example: Translation is a long discipline of self-denial, a matter of fidelity or betrayal: *traduttore, traditore.* The vitalist will say: Translation is a matter of life and death, merely: the life of the original or the death of it. The poet will say: Translation is either the composition of a new poem in the language of the translator, or the systematic liquidation of a masterpiece from the language of the original. The epistemologist will say: Translation is an illusion of the original forced upon the translator at every turn because he has begun by substituting his own language and occasion for that of the poet's and must fabricate his reality as he goes. The Sibyl sees all and says : Translation is the truth of the original in the only language capable of rendering it "in truth": the original language untouched by translation.

Lowell's Graveyard

BY ROBERT HASS

It's probably a hopeless matter, writing about favorite poems. I came across "The Lost Son," "The Quaker Graveyard in Nantucket" and "Howl" at about the same time. Some of the lines are still married in my head and they still have talismanic power: *snail, snail, glister me forward; Mohammedan angels staggering on tenement roofs illuminated; this is the end of running on the waves*. I see now that they are all three lost son poems, but at the time I didn't see much of anything. I heard, and it was the incantatory power of the poems that moved me. Enchantment, literally. I wandered around San Francisco demolishing the twentieth century by mumbling to myself, *blue-lunged combers lumbered to the kill* and managed to mix up Roethke's *ordnung! ordnung! papa's coming* with the Lord who survived the rainbow of his will.

*

You can analyze the music of poetry but it's difficult to conduct an argument about its value, especially when it's gotten into the blood. It becomes autobiography there. The other night in a pub in Cambridgeshire (named The Prince Regent and built just before the regency in the year when the first man who tried to organize a craft union among weavers was whipped, drawn, quartered and disembowelled in a public ceremony in London) the subject of favorite poems came up and a mild-looking man who taught high school geology treated us to this:

For it's Din! Din! Din!
You limpin' lump o' brick dust, Gunga Din!
Though I've belted you and flayed you,
By the livin' Gawd that made you,
You're a better man than I am, Gunga Din!

And he began to talk about his father's library in a summer cottage in Devon. I thought of how my older brother had loved that poem, how we had taken turns reading Vachel Lindsay and Kipling aloud on summer nights in California, in our upstairs room that looked out on a dusty fig orchard and grapevines spilling over the wooden fence.

Poems take place in your life, or some of them do, like the day your younger sister arrives and replaces you as the bon enfant in the bosom of the family; or the day the trucks came and the men began to tear up the wooden sidewalks and the cobblestone gutters outside your house and laid down new cement curbs and asphalt streets. We put the paper bags on our feet to walk back and forth across the road which glistened with hot oil. That was just after the war. The town was about to become a suburb in the postwar boom. The fig orchard went just after the old road. I must have been six. Robert Lowell had just published in the *Partisan Review* a first version of "The Quaker Graveyard in Nantucket."

*

Thinking about this a long time later made me realize that "Quaker Graveyard" is not a political poem. I had assumed that it was, that its rage against the war and puritan will and the Quakers of Nantucket who financed the butchery of whales was an attack on American capitalism. But a political criticism of any social order implies both that a saner one can be imagined and the hope or conviction that it can be achieved. I had by then begun to have a way of describing such an order, got out of a melange of Paul Goodman, Camus and *To the Finland Station*, but what lay behind it was an imagination of early childhood, dusty fig leaves and sun and fields of wild fennel. Nostalgia locates desire in the past where it suffers no active conflict and can be yearned toward pleasantly. History is the antidote to this. When I saw that my paradise was Lowell's hell, I was forced to see that it was not a place in time I was thinking of, but a place in imagination. The fury of conflict is in "The Quaker Graveyard" but I went back to the poem looking for the vision of an alternative world. There is none. There's grief and moral rage but the poem imagines the whole of human life as sterile violence:

All you recovered from Poseidon died
With you, my cousin, and the harrowed brine
Is fruitless on the blue beard of the god . . .

and it identifies finally with the inhuman justice of God:

You could cut the brakish waters with a knife
Here in Nantucket, and cast up the time
When the Lord God formed man from the sea's slime
And breathed into his face the breath of life,
And blue-lunged combers lumbered to the kill.
The Lord survives the rainbow of his will.

There are no choices in this history of the experiment of evolution and so there can be no politics. "The Lost Son," all inward animal alertness and numbed panic, contains the possibility of a social order by imagining return. And "Howl" wants to imagine a fifth international of angels.

It struck me then that the poem was closer in sensibility to someone like Robinson Jeffers than to most of the poets that I had come to associate with Lowell. Both poets are forced to step outside the human process and claim the vision of some imperturbable godhead in which the long violence of human history looks small. But in "Quaker Graveyard" it is important to say that is the position the poem *finally* arrives at because it is a poem of process, and of anguish. Warren Winslow drowns, the Quakers drown, the wounded whale churns in an imagination of suffering and violence which it is the imperative of the poem to find release from, and each successive section of the poem is an attempt to discover a way out. When I was beginning to read poetry to learn what it was and what it could be, this seemed the originality of the poem and its greatness.

*

And it's still hard for me to dissociate it from the excitement of that first reading. The poem leapt off the page. Its music, its fury and grief, haunted me:

where the bones
Cry out in the long night for the hurt beast
Bobbing by Ahab's whaleboats in the East

By that time Lowell was writing in the later, more influential style, then controversial, now egregious orthodoxy:

These are the tranquilized fifties
and I am forty . . .

But I didn't know that, and I still find myself blinking incredulously when I read — in almost anything written about the poetry — that those early poems "clearly reflect the dictates of the new criticism," while the later ones are "less consciously wrought and extremely intimate." This is the view in which it is 'more intimate' and 'less conscious' to say "my mind's not right" than to imagine the moment when

> The death-lance churns into the sanctuary, tears
> The gun-blue swingle, heaving like a flail,
> An hacks the coiling life out . . .

which is to get things appallingly wrong.

*

Years later I heard a part of this judgement echoed in a curious way. I was listening to Yvor Winters, just before his death, lecturing on George Herbert. He was talking about Herbert's enjambments and, in one of his rare excursions into the present, he said in a bass grumble, "Young Lowell has got a bad enjambment which he got from Allen Tate who probably got it from Herbert." I though of "The Quaker Graveyard":

> Light
> Flashed from his matted head and marble feet
> Seagulls blink their heavy lids
> Seaward

It lit up the poem all over again. Lowell had just published this in one of the fashionable journals:

> Only man thinning out his kind
> sounds through the Sabbath noon, the blind
> swipe of the pruner and his knife
> busy about the tree of life. . .

Non est species, but plenty of *decor*. I'm still not sure what I think about these lines. There is enormous, ironic skill in the octosyllabic couplets, and terrible self-laceration in their poise. It is probably great writing in the sense that the state of mind couldn't be rendered more exactly. But I wondered about the state of mind and said a small prayer to the small gods — hilarity and carnality — that I could escape it. The writer, among other things, is getting a certain magisterial pleasure from seeming to be outside the picture. The writer of these lines is in it:

And rips the sperm-whale's midriff into rags,
Gobbets of blubber spill to wind and weather,
Sailor, and gulls go round the stoven timbers
Where the morning stars sing out together . . .

*

It is possible, I suppose, to object to the brilliance of the writing. Charles Olson is said to have complained that Lowell lacquered each of his poems and hung it in a museum. But this judgement, like the 'confessional' revolution envisaged by the professoriat, seems to be based on the sociology of Kenyon College or the fact of meter or Lowell's early models, on everything but a reading of the poems. Finish in poetry is, as Olson insisted, a question of form following function. "The Quaker Graveyard" is brilliantly written, and in a decade of amazing poetry: the *Pisan Cantos,* the first books of *Paterson, Four Quartets,* HD's *War Trilogy*, Stevens' "Credences of Summer," Roethke's "The Lost Son." But its brilliance seems neither dictated nor wrought; it is headlong, furious, and casual. There are moments that hover near grandiloquence — "Ask for no Orphean lute . . ." but they didn't bother me then and don't much now.

Everything about the sound of the poem seemed gorgeous on first reading. "A brakish reach of shoal off. . . " sounded like an impossible Russian word, sluggish and turbulent; the Indian-Yankee "Madaket" bit it off with wonderful abruptness. I still like to say it:

A brakish reach of shoal off Madaket, —

In the second line, the oddness of the sound, which is a substitution in the third foot, has a slightly startling effect:

The sea was still breaking violently. . .

The rhythm breaks "breaking," makes a violence out of slackness in a way that I had never seen before and it was clearly intended because *still* is an extra syllable:

The sea was still breaking violently and night

From here to the end of the stanza, the energy of the poem allows no rest —

Had steamed into our North Atlantic fleet,
When the drowned sailor clutched the drag-net. Light
Flashed from his matted head and marble feet,
He grappled at the net
With the coiled hurdling muscles of his thighs:

I loved the nervous restlessness of the rhyming, the way you accept "net" as the rhyme for "fleet" and "Madaket", then get the off-rhyme "light," so that when you arrive at "feet" it is hardly an arrival and you are pushed toward "net" again. It's like a man shooting at a target with such random desperation that the hits count for no more than the misses. This effect, together with "young Lowell's bad enjambment," transmute an acquired skill into articulate rage. And the colon after "net" is not a rest; it insists on the forward hurtle of the lines:

The corpse was bloodless. . .

*

Warren Winslow or not, it has always seemed to me that Lowell himself was the drowned sailor, just as Roethke is the lost son. Otherwise the sudden moments of direct address make no sense:

Sailor, will your sword
Whistle and fall and sink into the fat?
In the great ash-pit of Jehoshaphat
The bones cry for the blood of the white whale,
The fat flukes arch and whack about its ears,
The death lance churns into the sanctuary. . .

It is having it both ways to be the young man drowned in the "slush," in the "bilge and backwash," "the greased wash," "the sea's slime" where "the whale's viscera go and the roll of its corruption overruns the world" and to be at the same time the young poet who identifies with the vengeance of the earth-shaker, "green, unwearied, chaste" whose power outlasts the merely phallic brutality of the guns of the steeled fleet, but the impacted writing permits this and it is psychologically true. Distrust of birth is the beginning of one kind of religious emotion.

In the speed of the writing, the syntax comes apart; it dissolves into emotion, into music and the subterranean connections among images. Throughout the poem it is characteristic that the important associations occur in subordinate clauses or compounds so breathless that you have to sort your way back quite consciously to the starting point. This resembles the syntactical strategies of the French surrealists, particularly Desnos and Peret. The main clause is a pushing off place and the poem makes its meaning out of its momentum. It's a way of coming to terms with experience under pressure and not some extrinsic decision about style. Even the lines about the shark —

Where the heelheaded dogfish barks its nose
On Ahab's void and forehead

are not Clevelandizing; they are not even — in the period phrase — a metaphysical image because their force is not intellectual. The lines depend on our willingness to let barking dogs marry scavenging sharks in the deep places where men void and are voided. To complain about this is not to launch an attack on 'consciously wrought' but the reverse.

The current taste is for the explicit, however weird. Surrealism comes to mean the manufacture of peculiar imagery and not something in the sinews of a poem. The fish in "For the Union Dead" are a midpoint in this levelling process. They are transformed into sharks and then into cars as "a savage servility slides by on grease," but the delivery is slower, the context narrative and topographical. It is pretty much the same image as in "The Quaker Graveyard," but it has been clarified like broth, a fish stock served up as clam chowder to the peremptory gentleman in the cartoon who likes to see what he's eating.

And this won't do for Lowell because the power of his imagery has always been subliminal; it exists as the nervous underside of the thing said. Look at this, for example, from "Fourth of July in Maine." The poet is addressing Harriet Winslow:

Dear Cousin, life is much the same,
though only fossils know your name
here since you left this solitude,
gone, as the Christians say, for good.
Your house, still outwardly in form
lasts, though no emissary comes
to watch the garden running down,
or photograph the propped-up barn.

If memory is genius, you
had Homer's, enough gossip to
repeople Trollope's Barchester,
nurses, Negro, diplomat, down-easter,

cousins kept up with, nipped, corrected,
kindly, majorfully directed,
though family furniture, decor,
and rooms redone meant almost more.

How often when the telephone
brought you to us from Washington,
we had to look around the room
to find the objects you would name —
lying there, ten years' paralyzed,
half-blind, no voice unrecognized,
not trusting in the afterlife,
teasing us for a carving knife.

High New England summer, warm
and fortified against the storm
by nightly nips you once adored,
though never going overboard,
Harriet, when you used to play
your chosen Nadia Boulanger
Monteverdi, Purcell, and Bach's
precursors on the Magnavox.

This is affectionate, even cozy. And beneath that first sensation is deep pathos; and beneath that is something like terror, so that the force of the phrase "life is much the same" keeps changing—for the worse—as you read. The imagery of a life with fossil memory, a run-down garden, a propped-up barn, a devastated Troy and cursed Mycenae, a Barchester that needs repeopling, people who need to be nipped and corrected, or redone, a half-blind paralyzed woman (the syntax has a way of paralyzing her objects as well), the need to be fortified against summer (with nips: the carving knife lying suddenly across both the cozy drinking and the corrected behavior) all issue in, among time's other wreckage, a Magnavox, the great voice which reproduces a great religious passion in the form of a performer's art. Everything dwindles, is rendered. Boulanger's Monteverdi. Lowell's Harriet. It's easy to explicate poems and hard to get their tone. The tone here has one moment of extraordinary pathos which is deeper than the cat-like movement through entropy and corrosion:

half-blind, no voice unrecognized,
not trusting in the after-life,
teasing us for a carving knife.

High New England summer . . .

But in the end the tone has to do with rendering; the whole passage is majorfully directed. It is not the experience but a way of handling the experience. The imagery accumulates its desolating evidence, but in such a way that the terror in the poetry is perceived while the novelistic pathos is felt. The subterranean images, whether "consciously wrought" or not, are intellectual. In this way, it is exactly a metaphysical poem as nothing in *Lord Weary's Castle* is.

In the second section of "Quaker Graveyard" there's not much that could be called development. Four sentences, three of which use syntax only as a line of energy, do little more than elaborate an instance of what used to be called the pathetic fallacy, but they confront the experience of grief, of terror at the violence of things, directly:

> Whenever winds are moving and their breath
> Heaves at the roped-in bulwarks of this pier,
> The terns and seagulls tremble at your death
> In these home waters. Sailor, can you hear
> The Pequod's sea-wings, beating landward, fall
> Headlong and break on our Atlantic wall
> Off 'Sconset, where the yawing S-boats splash
> As the entangled screeching mainsheet clears
> The blocks: off Madaket, where lubbers lash
> The heavy surf and throw their long lead squids
> For blue-fish? Sea-gulls blink their heavy lids
> Seaward. The wind's wings beat upon the stones,
> Cousin, and scream for you and the claws rush
> At the sea's throat and wring it in the slush
> Of this old Quaker Graveyard where the bones
> Cry out in the long night for the hurt beast
> Bobbing by Ahab's whaleboats in the East.

The effect here is not simple, but for me it is the most beautiful moment in the poem. The whole of that first sentence relaxes. The lines break deliberately as if they were trying to hold the emotion in place. But the content is terrible and the perception is extraordinarily intense. The feathers of the gulls ruffling in the wind are made to hurt. And it's such an ordinary perception. "Whenever winds are moving," to my Pacific grounding, is almost always, so that the image registers the steady pain of merely seeing. For some reason this connected in my mind with a thing Levi-Strauss says near the end of *Tristes Tropiques:* "What I see is an affliction to me, what I cannot see a reproach." The power of this image connects all the description in the poem with the eyes of the dead sailor and the gulls' eyes and the profoundly becalmed eyes of the Virgin of Walsingham. It connects the wind's breath with the breath of the poet which accelerates into violence again in the next sentence. And that sentence is a good example of the expressive power of syntax in the poem. In its fierce accumulation of images, you lose any sense that it began, rather gently, as a rhetorical question. This is a way of being lost, of drowning in the dissolution of syntax. Surrealism, I'm tempted to say, is syntax: not weird images but the way the mind connects them. Here they swell and gather toward violence, toward a continuous breaking like the breaking of waves on the shore and the effort of control is conveyed by the way "the entangled screeching mainsheet clears the blocks."

So the poem must slow down again: "Seagulls blink their heavy lids/Seaward." This fixity, the imperturbable consciousness of the gull whose feathers a moment before were trembling in "home waters," is an enormous relief. It is not the dead staring eyes of the drowned sailor and it is not yet the seeing of Our Lady of Walsingham. That heavy-lidded blinking of gulls seems to have a wonderful Buddha-like somnolent alertness when you look at it. It accepts things as they are. It's when gulls are perched on piers, heads tucked in a little, eyes blinking matter-of-factly, that I'm suddenly aware they have no arms, no hands. Even if they don't like what they see, they're not going to do anything about it. And this is the relief. But gulls are also scavengers. Their seeing doesn't hope for much, but it belongs to the world of appetite and their appetites are not very ambitious. That is why the sailors, grasping at straws in section IV, are only three-quarters fools. They want something, have heard news "of IS, the whited monster." So the lines accelerate again. The sea, godly in the first section, is consumed in the general violence in this one and the section ends in a long wail for Moby Dick, the object of desire, monster and victim.

Almost all of "The Quaker Graveyard" works in this way. It's hard to get at without a lot of tedious explication, but look at the third section of the poem. If you ask yourself how the language or the thought proceeds, it's not easy to say. First sentence: All you recovered died with you. Second sentence: Guns blast the eelgrass. Third sentence: They died. .; only bones abide. Characteristically, the Quaker sailors appear at the extremity of a dependent clause; then their fate is seized on, midway through the section, as a subject, and the stanza unravels again into violence as the sailors drown proclaiming their justification. And it does not seem arbitrary. It seems inevitable, because this hopelessly repeated unravelling into violence is both the poem's theme and the source of its momentum. Hell is repetition and the structure of anger is repetition. In this poem history is also repetition, as it is the structure of religious incantation. They are all married here, desperately, and the grace of the poem has to exist in modulation of tone. This modulation, like the different textures of an abstract expressionist painting or like the very different modulations, that create the texture of Whitman's poems — "Song of Myself" comes to mind — is the grandeur and originality of "The Quaker Graveyard." Not theme, not irony or intimacy or the consciously wrought, but absolute attention to feeling at that moment in the poem's process.

*

"They died / When time was open-eyed, / Wooden and childish." It takes a while — or took me a while — to see that this is the one moment in the poem that reaches back into childhood. The image has about it the helplessness of childhood. Time here must be the wooden, openeyed figureheads on old whaling ships, probably seen in books or a maritime museum. The look of the eyes on those old sculptures, their startled and hopeful innocence, dawns on you and it creates the state of mind of the child looking up at them. *Was* not *seemed.* The verb makes the child's seeing sovereign and irrecoverable. Lost innocence is not the subject of the poem. There is a kind of pleading between the poet and the innocence of his cousin, the ensign who went to the war and did his duty. "All you recovered . . . died with you". But the innocence of the child, of the ensign, of the figureheads is only one syntactical leap away from the stupidity and self-righteousness of the Quaker sailors — "If God himself had not been on our side" — who are swallowed up without understanding a thing. Their eyes are "cabin-windows on a stranded hulk / Heavy with sand."

*

Sections IV and V continue this riding out of violence but the conclusions of both take a turn that brings us to the religious issue in the poem. It didn't puzzle me much in that first excited reading because I ignored it. I was living down a Catholic childhood and religious reference in poetry seemed to me not so much reactionary as fossilised and uninteresting. But it was surely there in a lot of what I was reading. Robert Duncan's work was thick with religious imagery, & the "Footnote to Howl" exclaimed, "Holy! Holy! Holy!" I didn't know

Lowell was a convert to Catholicism or that this was a momentous rejection of his heritage. For that matter, I didn't know what a Lowell was. But I could see that the poem was not Catholic in any sense that I understood. It is true that the implicit answer to the question "Who will dance the mast-lashed master of Leviathans / Up. . ." is Christ. Orpheus, the way of art, is explicitly dismissed at the beginning of the poem. And the fifth section, the most terrible, the one in which the whale receives the sexual wound of all human violence, ends with a prayer: "Hide / Our steel, Jonas Messias, in thy side."

But the first of these passages is a question and the second is a supplication, not a statement of faith. Insofar as the poem is Christian, it seemed to me to be a very peculiar Christianity. I was prepared to grant that the killing of the Whale was also an image of the crucifixion of Christ, but in the poem this act is the source and culmination of evil. "When the whale's viscera go. . . .its corruption over-runs this world." There is no sense here of the crucifixion as a redemption. I can imagine that three or four pages of theological explication could put it there, but it isn't in the poem. Typologically the legal torture and murder of the man-god is not the fall; in the Christian myth it is not cruelty and violence but pride and disobedience through which men fell. One can make a series of arguments, threading back through the blasphemous pride of Ahab to the dominion given man by God in the epigraph to the poem, and emerge with a case for cruelty as a form of pride, but cruelty is not pride. They're different things, and it is cruelty and death, not pride and the fall, that preoccupy the poet, no matter how much of Melville or theology we haul in to square this vision with orthodoxy.

Reading Robert Duncan has given me a way to think about this issue in Lowell:

> There was no law of Jesus then.
>   There was
>   only a desire of savior. . .

Somewhere in his prose at about the same time Duncan had written that the mistake of Christianity was to think that the soul's salvation was the only human adventure. That was an enormously liberating perception. It put Christ on equal footing with the other gods. And the gods, Pound had said in a phrasing that seems now late Victorian, were "eternal moods," forms of consciousness which men through learning, art, and contemplation could inhabit. They were not efficacious. We were not Mycenean warlords, burning bulls and hoping the good scent of roast beef found its way to attentive nostrils; and the Mother of Perpetual Help did not, as my aunts seemed to believe, repair carburetors or turn up lost purses. But the gods were real, forms of imagination in which we could dwell and through which we could see. "The verb," Pound had said with the wreckage of his life around him, "is 'to see' not 'walk on'."

I got my Catholicism from my mother's side, Foleys from Cork by way of Vermont who drank and taught school and practiced law on the frontiers of respectability until they landed in San Francisco at the turn of the century. My father's side was Protestant and every once in a while, weary probably with the catechisms of his children, he would try to teach us one of his childhood prayers. But he could never get past the first line: "In my father's house there are many mansions. . ." He would frown, squint, shake his head, but that was as far as he ever got and we children who were willing to believe Protestants capable of any stupidity including the idea that you could fit a lot of mansions into a house, would return to memorizing the four marks of the true church. (It was one, holy, catholic, and apostolic.) But that phrase came back to me as a way through the door of polytheism and into myth. If Pound could resurrect the goddesses, there was place for a temple of Christ, god of sorrows, desire of savior, restingplace of violence. I could have the memory of incense and the flickering candles and the battered figure on the cross with the infinitely sad and gentle face and have Aphrodite as well, "the fauns chiding Proteus/in the smell of hay under olive trees" and the intoning of Latin with which we began the mass: "*Introibo ad altare Dei.*" On these terms, Lowell's prayer moved me: "Hide our steel, Jonas Messias, in thy side." And I could accept cruelty as the first fall; it was truer to my experience than pride or disobedience which the violence of the state has made to seem, on the whole, sane and virtuous. Not the old dogma, but a piece of the unborn myth which American poetry was making. And this is the sense of things in the poem. There is no redemption promised in the prayer at the end of section V. There is only the god of sorrows and the receiving of the wound.

*

Sexual wounding: it is certainly there in section V, both in the imagery and in the way the section functions, literally, as a climax to the poem. This is the fall, the moment when corruption overruns the world. And the rhetorical question, "Sailor, will your sword/Whistle and fall and sink into the fat?" wants to make us all complicit. The passage is Calvinist in feeling; every day is judgement day:

> In the great ashpit of Jehoshaphat
> The bones cry for the blood of the white whale

In sexual imagery, not only the penetration by the death lance but the singing of stars, the dismemberment of the masthead, we are all judged:

The fat flukes arch and whack about its ears,
The death-lance churns into the sanctuary, tears
The gun-blue swingle, heaving like a flail,
And hacks the coiling life out: it works and drags
And rips the sperm-whale's midriff into rags,
Gobbets of blubber spill to wind and weather,
Sailor, and gulls go round the stoven timbers
Where the morning stars sing out together
And thunder shakes the white surf and dismembers
The red flag hammered in the masthead. . .

This needs to be seen straight on, so that we look at the sickening cruelty it actually describes. It's a relief and much easier to talk about myth or symbolic sexuality. This is an image of killing written by a pacifist who was willing to go to prison. It makes death horrifying; it makes the war horrifying, and the commerce of the Nantucket Quakers whom Melville reminded his readers to think of when they lit their cozy whale-oil lamps. "Light is where the landed blood of Cain . . ."

But, just as there is disgust with the mothering sea in the bilge and backwash throughout the poem, there is a deep abhorrence of sexual violence, of sexuality as violence. I'm not sure how to talk about it. There is Freud's gruesome little phrase, as gruesome in German as in English but lacking the pun: the sadistic conception of coitus. But calling it that doesn't take us very far. The fact is that there is an element of cruelty in human sexuality, though that isn't the reason for the Puritan distrust of sex. The Puritans distrusted sexuality because the sexual act dissolved human will for a moment, because — for a moment — men fell into the roots of their mammal nature. You can't have an orgasm and be a soldier of Christ. Thus *Samson Agonistes.* And the Puritan solution, hidden but real in the history of imagination whether in Rome or the Enlightenment, was to turn sex into an instrument of will, of the conscious cruelty which flowered in the writings of Sade. It is there in our history and Lowell is right to connect it with the annihilative rage of capitalism. Flesh is languor ("All of life's grandeur / is something with a girl in summer. . .") but it is also rage. It marries us to the world and the world is full of violence and cruelty. This is part of the bind of the poem which is also the Calvinist bind of determinism and free will. The way out is not-world, an identification at the end of the poem with the "unmarried" Atlantic and the Lord who survives the rainbow-covenant of evolution.

All of which would be pretty grim if it were not for "Our Lady of Walsingham." It's a remarkable moment in the poem, the most surprising of its modulations, a little tranquil island in all the fury. I imagine that for a lot of younger writers it was the place where they learned how far you could go away from the poem and still be in it. Pound says somewhere, sounding like a surly Matthew Arnold, that a history of poetry that's worth anything ought to be able to point to specific poems and passages in poems and say here, here and here are inventions that made something new possible in poetry. This is one of those places.

Its occurrence makes emotional sense because it follows section V. It is the peace of the satisfaction of the body's rage, a landscape of streams and country lanes. The nineteenth century would have described the writing as chaste or exquisite and I'm not sure we have better words to praise it with. It's wonderfully plain and exact:

> Our Lady, too small for her canopy,
> Sits near the altar. There's no comeliness
> At all or charm in that expressionless
> Face with its heavy eyelids. As before,
> This face, for centuries a memory,
> *Non est species, neque decor*,
> Expressionless, expresses God: it goes
> Past castled Sion. She knows what God knows,
> Not Calvary's cross nor the crib at Bethlehem
> Now, and the world shall come to Walsingham.

This is another temple, not the god of sorrows but the goddess of an almost incomprehensible peace. It appears to be the emphatically Catholic moment in the poem (which adds a peculiar comedy to the idea that "Lycidas" was somehow its model; I've just visited the cathedral at Ely where Milton's friend Thomas Cromwell personally beheaded all the statues in the Lady Chapel. If the setpiece digressions of Alexandrian pastoral taken over by Milton to scourge a Popish clergy have really become a hymn to the Virgin Mary, it is the kind of irony— funny, too elaborately bookish — that would please the author of *History*.). But I don't think it is Catholic, or not especially Catholic, and that is its interest.

The crucial phrase is "past castled Sion." Lowell is not after sacramental mediation but a contemplative peace beyond any manifestation in the flesh, beyond thought or understanding, and — most especially — beyond desire. This isn't incompatible with Catholic theology, but it's not central to its spirit which is embodiment: the

Orphean lute and the crib at Bethlehem. This apprehension of God, of a pure, calm, and utterly clear consciousness, belongs equally to all mysticisms, Christian or otherwise, and it has always seemed to me that the figure of Our Lady here looks a lot like Guatama Buddha. It is the embodiment of what can't be embodied. This is a contradiction, but it is one that belongs to any intellectual pointing toward mystical apprehension. It is the contradiction that made the world-denial of Buddhists and Cathars at the same time utterly compassionate toward and alert to the world and the flesh and makes the Buddhist Gary Snyder our best poet of nature. This is not the rejection of the world which the last lines of the poem suggest; it's something else and for me it's something much more attractive as a possibility of imagination.

But how does it square with the last lines? I don't think it does. Nor does it contradict them. That's the aesthetic daring of this section. What the Lady of Walsingham represents is past contention. She's just there. The method of the poem simply includes her among its elements, past argument, as a possibility through which all the painful seeing in the poem can be transformed and granted peace. She floats; everything else in the poem rises and breaks, relentlessly, like waves.

*

I finally got to hear Robert Lowell read a couple of years ago in Charlottesville, Virginia — in Jefferson Country where the roadsigns read like a rollcall of plump Hanoverian dowagers and America comes as close as it ever will to a munching English lane. The setting made me feel truculent anyway and when he began by murmuring an apology for the earlier poems — 'rather apocalyptic,' 'one felt so intense' — I found myself on the poems' side. And the voice startled me, probably because I'd been hearing the work in my own for so long. I thought it sounded bizarrely like an imitation of Lionel Barrymore. It was not a voice that could say, "Face of snow,/You are the flowers that country girls have caught,/ A wild bee-pillaged honeysuckle brought/To the returning bridegroom — the design/Has not yet left it, and the petals shine," without sounding like a disenchanted English actor reading an Elizabethan sonnet on American television.

I had felt vaguely hostile toward Lowell's later work, though I admired it. I thought, for one thing, that the brilliant invention of "The Quaker Graveyard" had come about because he had nothing to go on but nerve and that, when the form cloyed in *The Mills of the Kavanaughs,* he had traded in those formal risks for the sculpted anecdote and the Puritan autobiography, a form about as original as John Bunyan's *Grace Abounding*. Out of that manner had come, not so much in Lowell himself as in the slough of poetry *Life Studies* engendered, a lot of narrative beginning "Father, you . ." or "The corn died in the field that summer, Mother/when . . ." It struck stances toward experience, as if Williams had said, "No attitudes but in things!" I wanted the clarity that "Our Lady of Walsingham" looked toward and in "Waking Early Sunday Morning" I thought he had come to something like that earlier insight and abandoned it too easily:

I watch a glass of water wet
with a fine fuzz of icy sweat,
silvery colours touched with sky,
serene in their neutrality —
yet if I shift, or change my mood,
I see some object made of wood,
background behind it of brown grain,
to darken it, but not to stain.

O that the spirit could remain
tinged but untarnished by its strain!
Better dressed and stacking birch. . .

As if you had to choose between them or tarnishing were the issue. That glass of water interested me a lot more than the ironies about electric bells ringing "Faith of our fathers."

Anyway, when he began to read, all this buzzing of the head stopped. There was the sense, for one thing, of a body of work faithful to itself through all its phases (early, middle, and ceaseless revision). And there was the reading of "Near the Ocean." Hearing it, I began to understand the risks attendant on backing away from the drama and self-drama of *Lord Weary's Castle.* Pain has its own grandeur. This disenchanted seeing was not serene neutrality — it was not serene at all; it had the clarity of a diminished sense of things not flinched at. I thought it was a brave piece of writing and it revisits the territory of "The Quaker Graveyard," so it seems like a place to end:

Sand built the lost Atlantis . . . sand,
Atlantic ocean, condoms, sand.

Sleep, sleep. The ocean, grinding stones,
can only speak the present tense;
nothing will age, nothing will last,
or take corruption from the past.
A hand, your hand then! I'm afraid
to touch the crisp hair on your head —

John Berryman: A Question of Imperial Sway

BY JOHN BAYLEY

BERRYMAN, LIKE LOWELL and perhaps more so, is the poet of the time whose size and whose new kind of stylistic being shrugs off any attempt at enclosure. But one thing about both is obviously true. *Life Studies, Notebook,* and *Dream Songs* show that verses, old-fashioned *numbers,* are still capable of being what Byron wanted—"a form that's large enough to swim in and talk on any subject that I please"—and not only the capable but the imperially inevitable form. Compare their talking verse—dense as lead one moment and light as feathers the next—with the brutal monotony of that dimension of talking prose which Hemingway evolved, and which Miller, Mailer, Burroughs and others have practised in their various ways. In the *Dream Songs* and *Love and Fame* Berryman makes that kind of prose appear beside his verse not only doltish and limited but incapable even of straight talking.

Formalistically speaking, curiosity has no place in our reception of the Berryman experience. The medium makes the message all too clear. In spite of all the loose ends of talk, the name-dropping and the facts given, we have no urge to find out with whom, when, why, and what; and this is not a bit like Byron. "I perfect my metres," writes Berryman, "until no mosquito can get through." Let's hope he's right. In every context today we sup full of intimacies. The group therapy of our age is its total explicitness; privacy and reticence have lost all artistic function and status: and so a lack of curiosity is not abnormal in the reader or even unusual. But Berryman seals off curiosity with a degree of artistic justification against which there is no *ad hominem* appeal.

The implications of these two phenomena—a new verse and a new self in it—seem to me what discussion of Berryman has to be about. There is no point in prosing along with detailed technical discussion of his verse, for its idioms and techniques are all completely self-justifying and self-illuminating.

"Poetry," said Thoreau, "is a piece of very private history, which unostentatiously lets us into the secret of a man's life." The matter would only have been put thus by a North American, at once orphan and contemporary of romanticism. The triumph of Berryman's poetry is that in becoming itself it has learnt how to undermine the apparent relevance to the poetic art of that niggling adverb: by flinging it suddenly on its back he has revealed that utter and shameless ostentation can become the same thing as total form, and virtually the same thing as the impersonality which our knowledge and love of the traditions of poetry condition us to expect. To let us in unostentatiously usually means today to be *confiding*. Elizabeth Bishop makes her Fish her poem, but is at the same time both confiding and self-justifying, as is such a typical poem of Wallace Stevens's final period as "The Plant on The Table." So at the other extreme of length and technique is *Paterson*. These confidences produce the impression that the poet is (to turn Stevens's own words against him) "an obstruction, a man /Too exactly himself." Such confidences cease to be important when they are made by a poet as far back as Wordsworth, but in our own time they are very important because they collapse style, the only thing that enables us to guess at the authority of a modern poet. At the moment they are not "soluble in art" (the phrase from the prologue to *Berryman's Sonnets*) though they may dissolve in time—or the whole poem may.

One thing which that in other respects overrated European author Beckett shares with Berryman and Lowell is the masterly inability to confide. None of them are deadpan: indeed all seem very forthcoming, but what Berryman calls "imperial sway" (Pound was "not fated like his protegé Tom or drunky Jim/or hard-headed Willie for imperial sway") manifests in them as a kind of regal blankness: it is not for them to know or care whether or not their subjects are listening.

Berryman cannot be "exactly himself," for he is so present to us that the thought of the real live Berryman is inconceivable, and scarcely endurable. His poetry creates the poet by a process opposite to that in which a novelist creates a character. We get to know Macbeth, say, or Leopold Bloom, to the point where we enter into him and he becomes a part of us; like Eurydice in Rilke's poem he is *geben aus wie hundertfacher vorrat*—bestowed upon the world as a multitudinous product. Berryman, by contrast, creates himself as an entity so single that we cannot share with or be a part of him. Such an autobiography as his does not make him real in the fictional sense. Everything is there, but so is the poetry, "language/ so twisted and posed in a form/that it not only expresses the matter in hand/ but adds to the stock of available reality."

That is Blackmur, one of Berryman's heroes: his wisdom put into a lapidary stanza and three quarters, ending with the poet's comment: "I was never altogether the same man after *that*." *That* is after all, though, a conventional formalistic and Mallarméan utterance, and the great apparent size of Berryman and Lowell is that they have achieved a peculiarly American breakthrough: the emancipation of poetry from its European bondage as *chose preservée* and its elevation into a form which can challenge and defeat the authority and easygoingness of prose at every point. As Valèry perceived when he coined the phrase, Europe can never get over its tradition that poetry occupies a special place, and that prose has grown all round it like some rank and indestructably vital weed, isolating it in an unmistakable enclave. Wallace Stevens concedes the same thing, in his practice, in his Jamesian persona ("John D. Rockefeller drenched in attar of roses" as Mary McCarthy put it) and in his comment that "French and English constitute a single language" (exclusive of American presumably). Looking back in England we see that Wordsworth, the great seeming liberator, was more subjected than he knew; as he grew older the "poetic" engulfed him; Coleridge's attempts to write a "poetry that affects not to be poetry" renounce all tension, and lack even the circumnambulatory virtues of *Biographia Literaria*. But whatever the difficulties of emancipation American writers had to overcome, this was not one of them. Whitman showed the way. Pound, as he says, "made a pact" with him, and the *Cantos,* no less than *Leaves of Grass,* never strike us as tacitly admitting that the same kind of thing could be or is being said in prose.

For one thing, the "I" is wholly different. Coleridge's and Wordsworth's "I" is usually themselves, the "man speaking to men," in either verse or prose. Even in such a masterpiece as "Resolution and Independence" "I" is not metamorphosed by the medium, by the poetry. Hence, even there, the poetry is not doing its poetic job to the hilt. A prose Wordsworth is, or would be, perfectly acceptable, but a prose Whitman "I", or a prose "Henry" Berryman would be intolerable. To make a poetic "I" as free and even more free, as naturalistic and even more so, than a prose ego, and yet quite quite different: that is the secret of the American new poetry which appears to reach its apogee in Lowell and Berryman. By this they show not only that verse can still do more than prose, but that the more closely it is involved in the contingent, the more it can manifest itself as the aesthetically and formalistically absolute.

I must return to this point in a moment, but let us first dispose of Berryman's own comments about the "I" of the *Dream Songs*.

> Many opinions and errors in the songs are to be referred not to the character Henry, still less to the author, but to the title of the work . . . The poem, then, whatever its wide cast of characters, is essentially about an imaginary character, (not the poet, not me) named Henry, a white American in early middleage in blackface, who has suffered irreversible loss and talks about

> himself sometimes in the first person, sometimes in the third, sometimes even in the second; he has a friend, never named, who addresses him as Mr. Bones and variants thereof.

This of course is rubbish in one sense, but in another it is a perfectly salutary and justified reminder by the author that when he puts himself into a poem he formalises himself. To labour the point again: Mailer is always Mailer, but Berryman in verse is Berryman in verse. That does not mean that he is exaggerated or altered or dramatised: on the contrary, if he were so the poem would be quite different and much more conventional. Berryman of course deeply admired and was much influenced by Yeats, who helped him to acquire the poet's imperial sway over himself and us, but he is not in the least concerned with Yeats's doctrine of the Masks, and with trying out contrasting dramatic representations of the self; such a cumbrous and courtly device of European poetry does not go with American directness and the new American expansiveness. Why bother to put on masks when you can make the total creature writing all the form that is needed?

Byron and Pushkin also emphasised the formal nature of their poetic device, often in facetious terms and in the poems themselves—making characters meet real friends and themselves, etc.—Berryman's gambit to emphasise a comparable formalism has a long history. None the less his comments are misleading in so far as they imply something like a dramatic relation between characters and ideas in the *Dream Songs*. The hero of Meredith's *Modern Love* would be as impossible in any other art context as Henry, but he is in a dramatic situation, and in that situation we can—indeed we are positively invited to—judge him, as we judge Evgeny Onegin. And to judge here is to become a part of. The heroes of such poems with dramatic insides to them are not taken as seriously as heroes in prose; they are unstable and frenetic, capable of all or nothing, because we do not get accustomed to them: they appear and vanish in each line and rhyme. None the less they are stable enough to be sat in judgment on, and Berryman's Henry is not. Ultimately, the formal triumph of Henry is that because he is not us and never could be, he has—like our own solitary egos—passed beyond judgment.

The paradox is complete, and completely satisfying. Clearly Berryman knew it. "These songs are not meant to be understood you understand/ They are only meant to terrify and comfort" (366). But though it is not dramatic the interior of the *Dream Songs* is grippingly exciting, deep, detailed and spacious. Moreover it is not in the least claustrophobic in the sense in which the world of Sylvia Plath involuntarily constricts and imprisons: on the contrary, like the world of early Auden it is boisterously exhilarating and liberating. It has no corpus of exposition, sententiousness, or pet theory, which is why it is far more like

Modern Love or *Evgeny Onegin* than the *Cantos* or, say, *The Testament of Beauty*. It never expounds. Another thing in common with the Meredith and Pushkin is the nature of the pattern. Each "Number" is finished, as is each of the intricate stanzas of their long poems, but in reading the whole we go with curiosity unslaked and growing, as if reading a serial. The separate numbers of the *Dream Songs* published in magazines could not of course indicate this serial significance, which is not sequent, but taken as a whole reveals unity.

The Russian formalists have a term *pruzhina,* referring to the "sprung" interior of a successful poetic narration, the bits under tension which keep the parts apart and the dimensions open and inviting. Thus, in *Evgeny Onegin,* Tatiana is a heroine, a story-book heroine, and a parody of such a heroine; while Evgeny is, conversely, a "romantic" hero for her, a parody of such a hero, and a hero. The spring keeps each separable in the formal art of the poem, and the pair of them in isolation from each other. I am inclined to think that Berryman's quite consciously contrived *pruzhina* in the *Dream Songs* is a very simple and very radical one: to hold in opposed tension and full view the poet at his desk at the moment he was putting down the words, and the words themselves in their arrangement on the page as poetry. When one comes to think of it, it is surprising that no one has thought of exploiting this basic and intimate confrontation before. (The weary old stream of consciousness is something quite other, being composed like any other literature in the author's head, irrespective of where he was and what he was being at the time.) The extreme analogy of such a confrontation would be Shakespeare weaving into the words of "To be or not to be," or "Tomorrow and tomorrow and tomorrow" such instant reactions and reflections as "Shall I go for a piss now or hold it till I've done a few more lines"—or—"I wonder what size her clitoris is"—or—"We must be out of olive oil." Of course there is no effect of interpretation in Berryman; but the spring does hold apart, and constantly, a terrifying and comforting image of the poet as *there*—wrestling in his flesh and in his huddle of needs—while at the same time poetry is engraving itself permanently on the page. It is this that keeps our awed and round-eyed attention more than anything else: our simultaneous sense of the pain of being such a poet, and of the pleasure of being able to read his poetry.

It is also instrumental in our not judging. The poet is not asking us to pity his racked state, or to understand and sympathize with the wild bad obsessed exhibitionist behaviour it goes with. These things are simply there, as formal achievement, and Henry James, that great Whitman fan, would oddly enough, I am sure, have understood and been gratified by it. He suggests it in the advice he gave to the sculptor Andersen about how to convey the tension and the isolation in an embracing sculptured couple.

> Make the creatures palpitate, and their flesh tingle and flush, and their internal economy proceed and their bellies ache and their bladders fill—all in the mystery of your art.

"Hard-headed Willie" in his magisterial way, and with his "blood, imagination, intellect running together," might also have given a clue; but when he says "I walk through a long school-room questioning" or—

> I count those feathered balls of soot
> The moorhen guides upon the stream
> To silence the envy in my thought.

it is well understood that he is doing no such thing. This is the rhetoric of the moment, not its apparent actuality; the thought he is silencing and the questions he asks have all been cooked up in the study afterwards. His air of immediate imperiousness, with himself and us, is a bit of a fraud, and this seasons our admiration with an affectionate touch of decision. Yeats is the boss whose little tricks we can see through and like him the more for: all the same, we do judge.

And with Berryman we don't; the spring device forbids it. How judge someone who while talking and tormenting himself is also writing a poem about the talk and torment? Except that we know, deeper down, that this effect *is* a formalistic device and that Berryman's control of it is total. And this knowledge makes us watch the taut spring vibrating with even rapter attention. There is a parallel with the formalism so brilliantly pulled off by Lowell in *Life Studies,* where the poetry seemed itself the act of alienation and cancellation, as if poet and subject had died the instant the words hit the paper. The formal device or emblem above the door framing the two collections might be, in Lowell's case, a speech cut off by the moment of death: in Berryman's, a Word condemned to scratch itself eternally, in its chair and at its desk.

Lowell forsook that frame, and in *Notebook* approaches the idiom of the *Dream Songs* (I waive any enquiry, surely bound to be inconclusive, into questions of mutual sympathetic influencing). But in achieving the note of continuing casualness, in contriving to stay alive as it were, *Notebook* remains individual pieces, fascinating in themselves, but lacking the tension that makes *Dream Songs* a clear and quivering serial. The comparison may be unfair, because *Notebook* may not be intended to be a narrative poem, but it shows how much and how successfully *Dream Songs* is one, and *Love and Fame*.

If I am right in thinking that Berryman's aim is to hold in opposed tension and full view the poet and his words, I may also be right in supposing that *Homage To Mistress Bradstreet* was inspired, in the form it took, by the same preoccupation. What seems to have been the donnée for Berryman there was the contrast between the woman as she presumably was, and the poems that she wrote. Berryman's ways of suggesting this are on the whole crude—I do not see they could be anything else; but the idea obviously fascinates him. Why couldn't her poems be *her,* as he wills his to be him? The poem celebrates a gulf and a contrast.

> When by me in the dusk my child sits down
> I am myself. Simon, if it's that loose,
> Let me wiggle it out.
> You'll get a bigger one there, & bite.
> How they loft, how their sizes delight and grate.
> The proportioned, spiritless poems accumulate.
> And they publish them
> away in brutish London, for a hollow crown.

Homage to Mistress Bradstreet is far from being a masterpiece; it is a very provisional kind of poem. Its virtues grow on one, but so does a sense of the effort Berryman was making to push through a feat of recreation for which a clarified version of the style of Dylan Thomas was—hopefully—appropriate. Had Thomas, instead of lapsing into "Fern Hill," been able to write a long coherent poem on a real subject—the kind of subject touched on in "The Tombstone Told When She Died"—it might have been something like this. But Thomas never got so far. We know from *Love and Fame* that Berryman felt the impact of Thomas early—in Cambridge, England, before the war—found him better than anyone writing in America, and made great use of him, the kind of use a formidably developing poet can make of an arrested one. The superiority of *Mistress Bradstreet* over the poems that are unemancipated from Auden—"World-Telegram", "I September 1939", "Desire is a World by Night", etc.—strikingly show how Auden was far too intellectually in shape to be successfully digested by Berryman as Thomas had been.

The feeling imagination, the verbal love, in fact, of *Mistress Bradstreet,* is most moving; and the image of her reading Quarles and Sylvester ("her favourite poets; unfortunately") is, I am convinced, a counter-projection of the image later willed on us by the grand, fully "voiced" Berryman of his own self at his own desk. Finding his own voice is for Berryman a consummation in which his own self and his poetry become one. Nor would it be fanciful to see this as the climax of a historical as well as of a personal process. Poetry, in its old European sense, *was* very largely a matter of getting out of your own perishable tatty self into a timeless metaphysical world of order and beauty. We have only to think of Spenser scribbling in Kilcomman Castle, transforming the horrors of the Irish reality into the beauties of *The Faerie Queen;* while Donne—often taken as "modern"—is no less a transformer of the casual and the promiscuous into metaphysical fantasy and form.

From Bradstreet to "Henry," who is no mask but a nickname in the formal spousals of poet to reader, is therefore a journey of almost symbolic dimensions, and one which only Lowell and Berryman could have successfully accomplished. Whatever their technical interest and merits, all their early poems were strangely clangorous and muffled, as if a new god were trying to climb out from inside the machinery: they needed the machinery to establish but not to *be* themselves. *Berryman's Sonnets* are brilliantly donnish in the way they cavort around the traditions and idioms of the genre, and it is indeed part of that idiom that there is no inside to them, no personal, non-dramatic reality.

> Keep your eyes open when you kiss: do: when
> You kiss. All silly time else, close them to;

In combination with such admirable and witty pastiche the gins and limes and so on of the *Sonnets* strike one as mere modern properties, and quite singularly not about what Berryman is. His use of Donne here is more generous than Lowell's grabbings out of the past; yet if Lowell wears his versions more ruthlessly he does it also more comprehensively.

Their absolute need of at last finding, and then being, themselves, could be seen in the light of Auden's comment: "when I read a poem I look first at the contraption and then at the guy inside it." To both Auden and Yeats it would make no sense to be in search of their own voices. They remain what they were from the beginning. When Yeats says—"It is myself that I remake"—he is subsuming guy and contraption under a single flourish, but in fact the continuity between Yeats young and old is unbroken, and so with Auden. There is never any doubt what guy is in the contraption and that he is the same one. I would say, therefore, that there is a radical and important difference, *in this respect,* between the poetry of Auden and Yeats and that of Lowell and Berryman; and, interesting as it is, I would not agree with the conclusion that M. L. Rosenthal comes to in "The Poetry of Confession."* He feels that the Americans "are carrying on where Yeats left off" when he proposed that the time had come to make the literal Self poetry's central redeeming symbol:

> I must lie down where all the ladders start,
> In the foul rag-and-bone shop of the heart.

**The Modern Poets* (Oxford University Press). Reprinted in *Robert Lowell: A Portrait of the Artist in His Time,* edited by Michael London and Robert Boyers (David Lewis, New York, 1970).

But that is surely Yeats striking out a new line, apparently turning a somersault but really remaining the same old aesthete and tower-builder who chided the contingencies of this world for "wronging your image that blossoms a rose in the deeps of my heart." Yeats had always affirmed the self: he took it for granted, he did not have to find it: and in "Sailing to Byzantium" he exaggerates almost to the verge of parody the traditional view that seems to start Berryman off in *Mistress Bradstreet:* that "once out of nature" and in the world of art the perishable and tatty self enters a new dimension of being, becomes a poet. What is fascinating about Berryman's enterprise is that starting from "the proportioned spiritless poems" he tries to reconstitute, so to speak, the perishable being who so improbably produced them. That seems to me the significant American poetic journey—to discover the living ego as it has to be ("I renounce not even ragged glances, small teeth, nothing")—and it is the exact reverse of Yeats's pilgrimage. In finding themselves Lowell and Berryman must indeed renounce nothing, not a hair of their heads, "forever or/so long as I happen." Such an achievement is a triumph quite new to poetry and confers on it a new and unsuspected authority. Thomas Wolfe said something like: "I believe we are lost in America but I believe we shall be found." Lowell and Berryman could have nothing to do with the lush fervour of the sentiment. None the less, in terms of poetry they embody such a faith and justify it.

3

This is indeed glorious but not necessarily satisfactory. Let us try to see what has been lost as well as gained. My contention would be that the two poets reverse completely one canon of the European aesthetic tradition, as represented by Yeats, and those other European Magi Rilke and Valéry, but in another way they are willy-nilly bound to it.* Their spectacular breakthrough into contingency is only possible because of the other Magi article of belief that things have no existence except in the poet's mind. So that in the iron selfhood the two poets have created, the most apparently feeble, hasty, or obviously untrue comment, sloughed off from day to day, acquires an imperishable existence when it is unsubstantiated on the page. The poems in *Love and Fame,* where even the nick-name "Henry" has been dropped between

*Berryman's comment on Rilke in the *Dream Songs* is characteristically exhilarating.

Rilke was a *jerk.*
I admit his griefs and music
& title spelled all-disappointed ladies.
A threshold worse than the circles
where the vile settle and lurk,
Rilke's. As I said,—

us (as nick-names come to be dropped between old married couples) are apparently bar-room comments on Berryman's past, nothing more, and the people, events, feuds and boastings in them are as commonplace as the lunch-hour. The lines are like a late Picasso drawing, the realised personality of genius implicit in every flick of the pencil. (One wonders whether Edmund Wilson, who maintained in "Is Verse A Dying Technique?" that modern poetry is the prose of Flaubert, Joyce and Lawrence, had a chance to read them.)

And yet something is missing, the something that might join all these things to life itself. Such a poetry is not "earthed"—cannot be—for it has nothing of the *accidental* and inadvertent in it, no trace of genuine impurity. Art is all trickery, but it is a trickery which can join up with our own lives and dreams, events and responses, our own self-trickery maybe. And can it be that in so meticulously creating the contingent self Lowell and Berryman have had to cut it off from the outside world? That is what I meant by saying that the poet is created here by a process opposite to that in which the novelist creates his characters. The novelist arrives at the reality of the world because his art is not and cannot be fully under his control. He cannot make everything himself: his readers must supply it; and the people and things he writes of will become real not only because his readers are doing a lot of the work themselves but because what he invents will become true by repetition and by being taken for granted; the man he shapes for us on page 2 will have become his own man by page 200. And this is as true of Joyce as of Trollope; it is equally true of much poetry in which "things" and a "world" are created—*Evgeny Onegin* or "The Eve of St. Agnes." But it is not true of Lowell and Berryman, however much they may seem to be putting things and a world before us.

Some time ago, in a book called *The Romantic Survival,* I made a point about the world of Auden's poetry which I still think important, though the rest of the book no longer seems very relevant to me. It is that Auden, following Yeats, had carried the personal and legendary domain of that "Last Romantic" one stage further, creating his characteristically and ominously centripetal world of stylised meaningfulness—derelict factories, semi-detached houses, "the silent comb/ Where dogs have worried or a bird was shot." What gave this world its instant authority was its appearance of stern political and social finger-pointing with its actual invitation to conspiracy and relish in the landscape of the evil fairy, the Death Wish. "Auden has followed Yeats," I wrote, "in showing how the intense private world of symbolism can be brought right out into the open, eclectised, and pegged down to every point of interest in contemporary life." And yet Auden constantly reminded us—his wittiest spokesman was Caliban in "The Sea and The Mirror"—that the realities of such poetry are necessarily mirror realities.

> All the phenomena of an empirically ordered world are given. Extended objects appear to which events happen—old men catch dreadful coughs, little girls get their arms twisted . . . All the voluntary movements are possible—crawling through flues and old sewers, sauntering past shop-fronts, tip-toeing through quicksands and mined areas . . . all the modes of transport are available, but any sense of direction, any knowledge of where on earth one has come from or where on earth one is going to, is completely absent.

The *bien pensants* of contemporary culture have made so much of the desolating, but also heartening and "compassionate" sense of the pressures of life, of the sheer difficulty of being oneself, which Lowell and Berryman have conveyed in their poetry, that a qualification along these lines may be in order. Auden finds the trick to let out Yeats into a new world of legend: Lowell and Berryman—on a scale and with a virtuosity of which today only American poets are capable—let him out in his turn, into a place where "*all* the phenomena of an empirically ordered world are given," and "*all* the voluntary movements are possible." Its very completeness precludes any attachment to mundane eventfulness—"From a *poet?* Words/to menace action. O I don't think so." Berryman's remark echoes what Auden constantly reiterates. Theirs is a breath-taking achievement, with results not at all like Auden, but I doubt it could have been done without him. As Berryman so engagingly puts it in that superlative *Love and Fame* poem, "Two Organs":

> I didn't want my next poem to be *exactly* like Yeats
> or exactly like Auden
> since in that case where the hell was *I?*
> but what instead *did* I want it to sound like?

Temperamentally, one infers, Berryman could hardly be more different from either Yeats or Auden. He was "up against it" in a sense (I take it) unknown to their basically sane and self-centering personalities, but he adapts the mirror world of their invention to sound like what he wants to be. Success is shown by the failure of the alternatives taken by poets in a comparable situation (not of course of Berryman's stature, but that begs the question): the "confidences" of Anne Sexton and the "blown top" meaninglessness of Kenneth Fearing, for example. Berryman takes from Auden not only the mirror world but the wry unswerving knowledge of its use, which adds—as it does in Auden—a further dimension to the meaning of the poem. An instance would be 97 in the *Dream Poems,* which deliberately lapses delicately into gibberish and concludes:

> Front back and backside go bare!
> Cat's blackness, booze, blows, grunts, grand groans.

> Yo-bad yom i-oowaled bo v'ha'l lail awmer h're gawber!
> —Now, now, poor Bones.

This is not like Lear's fool, clowning to hide desolation and fear, though something like his voice can be heard at times in the *Dream Songs*. It is a humorous, rather than a witty, exploitation of the formal idiom; its camp "blackface" touch not unlike Auden's handling of Jewish Rosetta in *The Age of Anxiety*. Both poets know that they can only move us by means of a sort of carnival exploitation of the mirror world: Caliban, with his virtuoso eloquence, and Rosetta with her day dreams, would be equally at home among the exuberance and desperation of the *Dream Songs*. "A man speaking to men" does not say, as Henry does "He stared at ruin. Ruin stared straight back." The humour of Groucho Marx, even if corny, also belongs to the mirror world.

And so does the straight talk. We can have no objection to sentiments like

> Working & children & pals are the point of the thing for the grand sea
> awaits us which will then us toss & endlessly us undo.

or

> We will die, & the evidence
> is: nothing after that.
> Honey, we don't rejoin.
> The thing meanwhile, I suppose, is to be courageous and kind.

because they are less earnest than sparkles from the wheel, and have been so wholly cauterised by contrivance. We can have "a human relation," for what that's worth, with poets far less good than Berryman. We can enter into such and share their feelings in a way impossible with him, for all the openness and Olympianly inclusive naturalness of his method. It is strangely unsatisfactory that in his poetry the poet cannot put a foot wrong. He can go off the air (Auden can too) but that is a different thing. If any technological habit has unconsciously influenced this kind of poetry it may be the record player with its click on and off, its hairline acoustics and relentless sensitivity. Both Lowell's and Berryman's poems have the flat finality of something perfectly recorded, and just the right length for perfect transmission. I notice writing down quotations that they do not sound very good, even when I had admired them as part of the poem: for the proper rigorous effect every word of the poem must be there.

This again excludes the accidental. The tone does not change or modulate, does not sag accidentally or rise with deliberate effort; the "supernatural crafter" is too much in charge, as he gives us an inkling in "*The Heroes*."

I had, from my beginning, to adore heroes
& I elected that they witness to,
show forth, transfigure: life-suffering and pure heart
& hardly definable but central-weaknesses

for which they were to be enthroned and forgiven by me.
They had to come on like revolutionaries,
enemies throughout to accident and chance,
relentless travellers, long used to failure

in tasks that but for them would sit like hanging judges
on faithless and by no means up to it Man.
Humility and complex pride their badges,
every "third thought" their grave.

Compare and contrast with that the young Stephen Spender's hopefully confiding and altogether by no means up to it poem "I think continually of them that were truly great." Spender gives it away by the touching solemnity of knowing he is writing a poem, a poem about heroes, the truly great. An all too human poem, as human as the embarrassment with and for the author that flushes us as we read it, but at least we know from it what we do *not* feel about those who "left the vivid air signed with their honour," etc. By patronising it we engage with it: by disliking its sentiment we adjust our own. And we respond to it; it is not a null poem, even though it combines the inadvertent and the contrived in an unstable state.

Great as well as small poets are, or have been, rich with this inadvertence. Keats, writing in halcyon good faith,

Let the mad poets say whate'er they please
Of the sweets of peris, fairies, goddesses;
There is not such a treat among them all,
Haunters of cavern, lake, and waterfall,
As a real woman.

seems not to know how it was going to look, or what the reader was going to think, and certainly not how revealing of his genius the lines are. Byron always seems to know, with his posturing and easy anecdotage, and the wholly controlled and calculated swagger of the jotting on the back of *Don Juan*.

O would to God that I were so much clay
As I am blood, bone, marrow, passion, feeling,
Having got drunk exceedingly today
So that I seem to stand upon the ceiling. .

These lines mime a loss of control and a hungover truculence, and yet every so often he forgets himself genuinely in a way there is no mistaking, as in the lines written when he heard his wife was ill. The chagrined pity of its opening seems to try, and fail to be, all self-pity, until a kind of hangdog solicitude turns to and takes refuge in the relieved virulence of satiric declamation. There is even an unexpectedly startled and self-disconcerted note in the famous lines: "How little know we what we are, how less/What we may be." Hardy is in this kind of way the most vulnerable of all great poets, as witness the end of "After A Journey," where the poet revisits the sea-haunts where he had first fallen in love with a wife long estranged and now dead.

> Trust me, I mind not, though Life lours,
> The bringing me here; nay, bring me here again!
> I am just the same as when
> Our days were a joy and our paths through flowers.

"I am just the same as when . .": the reassurance he gives and needs to give has all the eager clumsiness of life: we can hear the relief of saying it, a relief all the greater because it can't be true.

I labour this incongruous mixed bag of examples because they all seem to me to contain something naive and direct that has vanished or is vanishing from the performance of good poetry. In them we seem to meet the poet when he doesn't expect it; like Sartre's voyeur he is looking at something else so intently that he is unaware of the reader behind him. And can it be that Berryman's preoccupation—for it appears to be that—with establishing the poet's existence in all its hopeless contingency ("I renounce not even ragged glances, small teeth, nothing,") is both an attempt at what earlier poets—and bad poets today—do without meaning to, and a recognition that only a formalisation of such directness is possible to him? We can see it in the cunning control of that same poem, *"The Heroes,"* which slides casually into the subject *a propos* of Pound, a "feline" figure ("zeroing in on feelings,/ hovering up to them, putting his tongue in their ear"); then goes on to distinguish this from the "imperial sway" exercised by Eliot, Joyce and Yeats; rises to the celebration of heroism already quoted; and in the last verse shows us where the first six came from.

> These gathering reflexions, against young women,
> against seven courses in my final term,
> I couldn't sculpt into my helpless verse yet.
> I wrote mostly about death.

The ideas are referred to a pre-poetic stage in the poet, when they were tumbling in the dark together with feelings about girls and resentment against classes. That self could not have written the poem, but it had the ideas, and is coincident with the self that is now sculpting the poetry effectively—perhaps more than coincident, because its topic was the inclusive and unsculpturable one of death. Imperial sway can only be exercised over the words that make up the self.

The last line does not nudge us; it simply looms up—a perspective on the dark contingency of the self that heroes don't have, for they can be sculptured into verse. The self that can't remains pervasively present, disembodied above the poem like a Cheshire Cat. There is no question of making or remaking that self in Yeatsian style, nor of making legendary figures out of the poet's *entourage,* as both Yeats and Lowell in their different ways have done. Professor Neff who gave Berryman a C out of malice at Columbia, in the next poem "Crisis" is paid the subtle compliment of a rapid, unimpartial write-off; there is no attempt to enshrine him in some immortal rogues' gallery, and Mark Van Doren in the poem is also and simply a real person, as in conversation. The poet's mother and father appear in an equally unspectacular way (contrast again with Lowell), figures briefly revealed by night, unless the night, or pre-dawn, time of most pieces, like the seeming traces of drink or drugs, is another convention for conveying the continuity and actuality of the self.

The self can appear in that dark past as in grand guignol, surrounded by ghosts indistinguishable from itself (129: "riots for Henry the unstructured dead") or it can be transposed into a hauntingly meticulous *doppelganger,* as in 242.

> About that "me." After a lecture once
> came up a lady asking to see me. "Of course.
> When would you like to?"
> Well, *now,* she said.

After a precise, casual, brittle account of the quotidian campus scene—the poet with lunch date, the lady looking distraught—comes the payoff.

> So I rose from the desk & closed it and turning back
> found her in tears—apologising—"No,
> go right ahead", I assur-
> ed her, "here's a handkerchief. Cry". She did. I did.
> When she got control, I said "What's the matter—if you want to talk?"
> "Nothing, Nothing's the matter." So.
> I am her.

Naturally: she could be nobody else. Only through Berryman can the poem move us, but it does move. The hopelessness, the stasis, is completely authentic. Not so, I think, those poems in *Love and Fame* about the others in the mental hospital, Jill and Eddie Jane and Tyson and Jo.

For all their "understanding" "The Hell Poem" and "*I* know" have something insecure about them, as if threatened by the presence of other people. The poet was not threatened of course—we feel his openness, his interest—but the poem is caught between its equation with contingency and the fact that, as form, its contingency can only be "me."

The Berryman *pruzhina,* or spring, snaps as the real presence of these others pulls it too far apart. For the young Berryman, as he tells us in "Two Organs," the longing was to write "big fat fresh original & characteristic poems."

> My longing, yes, was a woman's.
> She can't know can she *what kind* of a baby
> she's going with all the will in the world to produce?
> I suffered trouble over this.

"I couldn't sleep at night, I attribute my life-long insomnia/ to my uterine struggles." Nothing is more graphic in Berryman than the sickness and struggle of finding oneself about to become a poet, lumbered with an unknown foetus that when it arrives will be oneself. We may note that this is the exact opposite, in this mirror world, of true childbirth, which produces *another person.* Still, the pains are real enough, and so is the comedy. Indeed the black comedy of Beckett again comes to mind, a theatre of one. "By virtue of the aesthetic form," generalises Marcuse, the "play" creates its own atmosphere of "seriousness" which is *not* that of the given reality, but rather its "negation." That kind of portentousness is here in a way, and the theory of the "living theatre" has certain affinities with Berryman's drive—if I am right about it—to coincide poet as man with poem as thing.

Berryman's fascination with becoming himself as a poet has—given his genius—an almost equal fascination for us, but it has a drawback too. We can contemplate it but not share it—it is not really a part of the universally identifiable human experience, the experience in Byron or in Gray's *"elegy,"* to which, as Dru Johnson observed, every bosom returns an echo. What we have instead is extreme singularity, the Berrymanness of Berryman, which we and the poet stare at together: that he absorbs us as much as he absorbs himself is no mean feat. We want indeed to know "of what heroic stuff was warlock Henry made"—the American hero whose tale can be only of himself and who is (unlike Wordsworth) bored by it.

> Life, friends, is boring. We must not say so.
> After all, the sky flashes, the great sea yearns,
> we ourselves flash and yearn,
> and moreover my mother told me as a boy

> (repeatingly) "Ever to confess you're bored
> means you have no
>
> Inner Resources." I conclude now I have no
> inner resources, because I am heavy bored.
> Peoples bore me,
> literature bores me, especially great literature,
> Henry bores me. .

Delightful! Our bosoms return an echo to *that,* as to the celebration of the same mother in 100, and her "two and seventy years of chipped indignities," but what principally gets to us is the performance of birth, the pleasure of finding the foetus so triumphantly expelled.*"Le chair est triste, hélas, et J'ai lu tous les livres"*—that sensation, too, for Mallarmé, existed to end up in a book, and so it is with the perpetual endgame of Berryman—"after all has been said, and all *has* been said. ."

We do miss a *developing* world. Having found himself on the page the poet has found hell, or God—it is much the same, for in either case there is nothing further there. Compare with the world of Hardy, say, who was not bored but went on throughout a long calvary continuing to *notice* things outside himself, able to bring the outside world into his poetry while leaving it in its natural place (Marianne Moore and Elizabeth Bishop have done the same.) And among Hardy's preoccupations "the paralysed fear lest one's not one"—a poet that is—did not as far as we can see, figure. But it is the detriment and dynamic of Berryman's book. Hardy had things easier, for he did not in the least mind writing bad relaxed poems, and this itself helps to keep him in the outer world, the world of *true* contingency. His is the natural contrast to the place discovered and developed by our two in some ways equally Anglo-Saxon giants.

> I say the paralysed fear that one's not one
> is back with us forever. .

So it may be. The struggle to become a great poet, to exercise imperial sway, may indeed be increasingly and ruinously hard, obsessing the poet's whole outlook. But they have shown it can be done.

The novelists of our time have not succeeded in creating a new fictional form as they have created a new poetic one—and that seems to me to have real significance. The bonds that enclosed the novelist and compelled him into his form have up till lately been social as well as aesthetic ones. There was much that he could not say "in so many words," and which therefore had to be said by other means—a style had to be found for creating what society could not tolerate the open expression of: such a style as is created, for example, in the opening lines of

Tristram Shandy. But in a wholly permissive age the formal bonds of poetry remain drawn taut because they depend on sculpting a voice, graving a shape and pattern. The bonds of fiction slacken into unrecognisability because the pressures of society itself, not of mere craft, which used to enforce them, have withdrawn. The novel form today has no inevitable response to make to its unchartered freedom; it can only concoct unnecessary ones, resurrected devices like those of Barth, Burroughs, Vonnegut and others, which do not impress us with self-evident authority but act as an encumbrance, get in the way. Like the novelist the poet can say anything now, but he must exercise imperial sway as he does so. If he can, poetry has the edge again, and Lowell and Berryman have honed it to a razor sharpness. Despairing art critics, we learn, have been asking not what art is possible today but *is* art possible. As regards poetry, we have our answer. It is still adding to the stock of available reality while expressing the matter in hand.

"This Leaving-Out Business": The Poetry of John Ashbery

BY CHARLES MOLESWORTH

The first few books of John Ashbery contained a large proportion of a poetry of inconsequence. Borrowing freely from the traditions of French surrealism, and his friends Frank O'Hara and Kenneth Koch, Ashbery tried out a fairly narrow range of voice and subject matter. Subject matter, or rather the absence of it, helped form the core of his aesthetic, an aesthetic which refused to maintain a consistent attitude towards any fixed phenomena. The poems tumbled out of a whimsical, detached amusement that mixed with a quizzical melancholy. This aesthetic reached an extreme development with *The Tennis Court Oath* (1962), a book in which no poem makes even the slightest attempt to marshal a rational context or an identifiable argument. Line follows line without the sheerest hint of order or apparent plan; this studied inconsequence delighted some readers at the time. But this is not a book to re-read, and without seeing it in the context of rebellion against the too-conscious aesthetic then fostered by academic poetry, it is difficult to understand why the book was published. (Wesleyan seems an especially unlikely publisher, except their "program" was committed to innovation, and with this one title they seemed to fulfill that aim once and for all.) But with the exception of *The Tennis Court Oath*, Ashbery's first four commercially published books (the others are *Some Trees* (1956) *Rivers and Mountains* (1966), and *The Double Dream of Spring* (1970)) included some poems with interpretable meanings and recognizable structures. But reading the first four books together, one is struck by how precious are those poems which do make poetic sense, surrounded as they are by the incessant chatter of the poems of inconsequence. Slowly, however, it appears as if Ashbery has gained the confidence of his true project, and, as it unfolds, an indulgent reader can see how it needed those aggressively banal "experiments" in nonsense to protect its frailty. .Ashbery's later poetry often uses the traditions of prose discourse, but instead of a poetry of "statement" he has evolved a most tenuous, unassertive language. The first four books, one feels, would have turned out insufferably banal, or perhaps would have remained altogether unwritten, if Ashbery had faced his subject directly or made too various or rigorous demands on his limited language.

Some Trees was selected by W.H. Auden in the Yale Younger Poet competition, and one might guess Auden enjoyed the campy joke such a selection appeared to be. Rumor has it that Ashbery disliked Auden's introduction intensely, and when Corinth Books republished the volume in 1970, they excluded it. In the mid-'fifties there was little like Ashbery's poetry to be found, except of course for the poems of Frank O'Hara. But Ashbery's work at this time, despite its being the rival of O'Hara's for preciosity and surreal wit, had a more "literary" feel than that of his friend. This feel is hard to locate, but it grew with Ashbery's career, and in some way accounts for the partisanship some academic critics have recently shown for his work. In some of the poems in this book, we see a straightforward whimsy such as that often used by Kenneth Koch. The humor remains deadpan, the juxtapositions being between the high-minded expectations of "art" and the flat unheroic irony of the disaffected speaker. For example, "The Instruction Manual" and "The Painter" are like comically neuter protest poems, in which alienation is turned into a commonplace, and what might be the "howl" of the outsider sounds instead like the whimper of a repressed clerk. (The masterpiece of this sort of thing is Koch's "The Pleasures of Peace.") Also Ashbery includes a few examples of a favorite exercise of the so-called "New York School" of poets, the formula-poem which takes a simple grammatical structure and repeats it over and over with bizarre content. This method of generating whimsy may well owe its origin to the surreal concern with *objectif hasard*, where the consciously selected "format" is then juxtaposed to whatever chance associations the writer can release. Here is part of "He":

> He knows that his neck is frozen.
> He snorts in the vale of dim wolves.
> He writes to say, "If ever you visit this island,
> He'll grow you back to your childhood.
>
> "He is the liar behind the hedge
> He grew one morning out of candor.
> He is his own consolation prize.
> He has had his eye on you from the beginning."

He hears the weak cut down with a smile.
He waltzes tragically on the spitting housetops.
He is never near. What you need
He cancels with the air of one making a salad.

The poem unveils twelve such quatrains, and each line begins with "He" followed by a verb. "The vale of dim wolves" and the tragic waltz on "the spitting housetops" typify the imagery of Ashbery's early poetry: arbitrary, coy, disaffected, "smart." Moreover, the arbitrary continuation of the poem lies at the center of Ashbery's aesthetic, which seems a flirtation with nihilism, an autotelic art that apotheosizes symbolism's elevation of style over content. The stochastic movement of the poem reminds one of the music of John Cage; the levelling of values suggests the painting of Andy Warhol.

We can place along side the above passage from *Some Trees* the following excerpts from, respectively, *Rivers and Mountains* and *The Double Dream of Spring*:

The sedate one is this month's skittish one
Confirming the property that,
A timeless value, has changed hands.
And you could have a new automobile
Ping pong set and garage, but the thief
Stole everything like a miracle.

****

The mountain stopped shaking; its body
Arched into its own contradiction, its enjoyment
As far from us lights were put out, memories of boys and girls
Who walked here before the great change,

Before the air mirrored us,
Taking the opposite shape of our effort,
Its inseparable comment and corollary
But casting us further and further out.

These lines show how Ashbery's poetic sidles up to and slips away from meaning, as each line clearly links to the one before and after it, but the overall context remains vague and elliptical. Increasingly Ashbery resorts to the contextual devices of prose: pronominalization, appositive and subordinate clauses, logical co-ordination, and so forth.

But at the same time certain "poetic" devices come to the fore, for example, startling similes, metaphoric verbs, ambiguous suspension of predication, and highly figurative language—what Ashbery calls "the great 'as though'." Often the element of play in his poetic causes Ashbery to drift into a boring "castles in the air" approach, as if he were testing the limits of significance; likewise, he can become ponderous when his poetry takes on a pseudo-philosophical cast, where irony ought to be operating, but a sodden rumination drains off the flow of wit. Ashbery himself describes the perfect balance, when his language becomes most distinctive and most rewarding; this is from "Clepsydra," in *Rivers and Mountains*:

Each moment
Of utterance is the true one; likewise none are true,
Only is the bounding from air to air, a serpentine
Gesture which hides the truth behind a congruent
Message, the way air hides the sky. . .

Havelock Ellis once characterized decadence as a style that subordinates the whole to the part, and we can glimpse something analogous here with the sense that each moment of the poem is true (and the further implication that *only* in its moments is the poem true, as all larger significance is illusory). And the paradox that no moment is true (because its truth must immediately be displaced by the next moment) suggests a sort of polymorphous perversity of contextuality. Add to this Ashbery's equivocating suspension between a referential and an emotive sense of meaning (air doesn't really hide the sky, it *is* the sky, so meaning and utterance are perfectly equal; however, the utterance must be a serpentine gesture, something other than merely "factual") and you begin to understand why his poems seldom resort to traditional lyric modes of expression. Straight-forward narrative, direct spontaneous outcries or deeply urgent shows of authenticity: none of these will be readily available to Ashbery's readers. Each decadent style, as Ellis also suggests, must be seen against a classical style from which it has "fallen down," and throughout Ashbery's work we catch the dying echoes of English romanticism, especially those poets most haunted by the past, Wordsworth and Shelley. These echoes are driven by Ashbery's relation to language and meaning, a relation that is both tenuous and diffident, because his feelings are evanescent, and off-handed and condescending, because his utterance is derivative.

In many ways, *Rivers and Mountains* is Ashbery's most frustrating book, for it avoids the total meaninglessness of *The Tennis Court Oath,* and yet lacks the richness of *The Double Dream of Spring*. The book, full-sized as poetry books go, has only twelve poems in its sixty-three pages. But an average of five-page poems would be deceptive, for one poem takes up almost thirty pages; this poem, "The Skaters," is in many ways the quintessential Ashbery poem, the epitome of his career. Mixing bland, straightforwardly prosaic passages with the most inane, jumbled poetry of inconsequence, "The Skaters" is a nervous tour de force, a paean to solipsism and an anguished cry against its imprisonments. Few of the other poems in this book are especially distinctive, though "Into the Dusk Charged Air" offers a special instance of the tenacity of Ashbery's aesthetic paying unusual, inexplicable rewards:

Mountains hem in the Colorado
And the Oder is very deep, almost
As deep as the Congo is wide.
The plain banks of the Neva are
Gray.The dark Saone flows silently.
And the Volga is long and wide
As it flows across the brownish land. The Ebro
Is blue and slow. The Shannon flows
Swiftly between its banks.

And so it goes for over 150 lines, as if some catatonic were suddenly afflicted with logorrhea in the presence of an atlas. The last images of rivers are frozen, and the poem has a curious, baffled, anti-transcendent structure that seems somehow just right. The other feature of the book is a greater tendency to break up the flow of surreal images with occasional axioms, though these sometime take the form of bemused rhetorical questions or half-resuscitated cliches. This contributes to the "literary" feel of Ashbery's anti-literary attack on meaningful structure and universalizing particulars.

But obviously it is "The Skaters" that this volume features, and the poem itself introduces clearly one of Ashbery's most insistent self-questionings: what should he put in, and what leave out? "This poem... is in the form of falling snow," he ingenuously announces, and as the meanings float and melt, an overridingly reflective mood casts the poem into melancholy, which in turn throws up images of self-defense and self-abasement. Here is one entire stanza:

But this is an important aspect of the question
Which I am not ready to discuss, am not at all ready to,
This leaving-out business. On it hinges the very importance
of what's novel
Or autocratic, or dense or silly. It is as well to call
attention
To it by exaggeration, perhaps. But calling attention
Isn't the same thing as explaining, and as I said I am not
ready
To line phrases with the costly stuff of explanation, and
shall not,
Will not do so for the moment. Except to say that the
carnivorous
Way of these lines is to devour their own nature, leaving
Nothing but a bitter impression of absence, which as we
know involves presence, but still,
Nevertheless these are fundamental absences, struggling to
get up and be off themselves.

I think this passage says more about Ashbery's poetic than all that has been written about him, especially when some critics have forgotten that "calling attention / Isn't the same thing as explaining." But most evident here is Ashbery's fear of the banal, the "dense or silly," as well as his craving for the truly fresh, the "novel or autocratic," and more importantly his sense that it has become increasingly difficult to distinguish between them. The resort to surrealism can be seen as a response to this fear, for surrealism's levelling of values mixes the mysterious and the mundane, and so seeks to solve the problem by embracing it. At the same time, the impulse towards inconsequence can be seen as an elaborate flight, a defensive reaction against this fear of the meaningless, so the poet celebrates his own "carnivorous" quest for the meaning he knows will always elude him—unless he abandons his search and accepts reality as it is. The problem, however, remains one of locating the truly "fundamental" absences. For five or six pages later we find this entire stanza:

Uh. . .stupid song. . .that weather bonnet
Is all gone now. But the apothecary biscuits dwindled.
Where a little spectral
Cliffs, teeming over into irony's
Gotten silently inflicted on the passages
Morning undermines, the daughter is.

The worst part of it is that the absences here are apparently less than fundamental, and seeking connections in such a text is like playing cat's cradle with a rubber band. And in "The Skaters" we confront a stiffer problem yet, as the poetry of inconsequence mixes indiscriminately with some of the poet's more pellucid and lyric efforts, and this rather decreases the overall meaning that's available to most readers. (I suspect, however, for the "we" in the phrase "which as we know involves presence" this mixing is the stamp of excellence, the proof of Ashbery's suspension between the burden of traditional meaning and the bathos of playful absurdity.)

Other hallmarks of Ashbery's style show up in "The Skaters," and throughout *Rivers and Mountains*: most noticeably, a fear of social reality and a dire, overwrought emotionalism. These are central to the problem of putting in and leaving out, for apparently Ashbery is far from thoroughly comfortable in the role of aesthete or plangent late-Romantic. The very ambitiousness of a poem like "The Skaters" indicates he wants to address a wide spectrum of reality, even if large hunks of modern day reality are simply not assimilable to his style, and he must resort to rhetorical questioning, as in this passage:

> But another, more urgent question imposes itself—
> that of poverty.
> How to excuse it to oneself? The wetness and coldness?
> Dirt and grime?
> Uncomfortable, unsuitable lodgings, with a depressing view?
> The peeled geranium flowering in a rusted tomato can,
> Framed in a sickly ray of sunlight, a tragic chromo?

Only by aestheticizing the harsh reality, by turning the moment into a genre scene, can the poet imagine the other world and excuse it, notice, to himself. Later we are told (after a long section of aggressive solipsistic fantasy about being stranded on an island):

> In reality of course the middle-class apartment I live in is
> nothing like a desert island.
> Cozy and warm it is, with a good library and record collection.
> Yet I feel cut off from the life in the streets.

He describes himself at one point as a "professional exile," and like all such exiles must make a song of himself, a song that makes the universe and its secret meanings available to him, but only through the mediacy of strong feeling:

The west wind grazes my cheek, the droplets come pattering
down;
What matter now whether I wake or sleep?
The west wind grazes my cheek, the droplets come pattering
down;
A vast design shows in the meadow's parched and trampled
grasses.
Actually a game of "fox and cheese" has been played there,
but the real reality,
Beyond truer imaginings, is that it is a mystical design
full of a certain significance,
Burning, sealing its way into my consciousness.

Here the obvious echoes of poems by Shelley and Keats are undercut by the fey diction ("pattering down"), and the mystical meaning is simultaneously exposed as putative (and hence false) and esoteric (hence really real). But just as we can detect the essence of a wounded liberal conscience, however embarrassed, behind the passage on poverty, so we can hear real emotional loss, however ironically distilled, behind the wan textures of such passages.

And so, roughly half-way through his career to date, Ashbery's *Rivers and Mountains* demonstrated that he was in many ways still our most private and our most public poet, an egoist and an exile. But the style was coming clearer with each book, and the paradoxes, cultural and poetic, had intensified. Ashbery's poetry attained the acme of defensive irony, and yet might well offer a way beyond what had become such a limiting aesthetic. Even if Ashbery could not decide on what to put in and what to leave out, at least he had clearly identified this as the problem; however, as the later books were to show, stating the problem did not always reduce it, let alone dispense with it. "All right. The problem is that there is no new problem," as he says in the opening of the last section of *Three Poems* (1972). What saved Ashbery from the dessication of defensive irony was not just his hunger for innovation, nor his return to Romantic themes, but his willingness to come round (and round and round) onto the *sources* of his own feelings, as well as to speak openly about the non-appearance of feeling. We can even speculate that his sense of an audience grew more secure and slightly more public, and he slowly began to abandon his sense of being no more than a coterie poet. But we shouldn't make too much of this; the hermeticism is part of the project, and Ashbery will probably never achieve the free-wheeling humor of Kenneth Koch or the feckless self-definition of Frank O'Hara.

Much of the particular feel of Ashbery's poetry comes from the tension between its prose-like discursiveness and the random, sometimes elliptical tenuousness of its associative gatherings. The "self" in a typical Ashbery poem will almost stumble over a defensive displacement of what is really affecting him; at the same time, reticence never appears as a real possibility. This self wants your attention, but he is counting on your good taste not to inquire too rigorously or peremptorily. The author-reader contract emits a conspiratorial atmosphere for Ashbery, as he writes not simply for those "in the know," but for those whose dalliance is infinitely tolerant. Here is "The Chateau Hardware," the shortest poem in *The Double Dream of Spring*, but otherwise typical of Ashbery's rhetorical strategies:

It was always November there. The farms
Were a kind of precinct; a certain control
Had been exercised. The little birds
Used to collect along the fence.
It was the great "as though," the how the day went,
The excursions of the police
As I pursued my bodily functions, wanting
Neither fire nor water,
Vibrating to the distant pinch
And turning out the way I am, turning out to greet you.

Several phrases contribute to the elliptical structure of the poem; "a kind of," "a certain control," and "used to collect" all rely on an assumed body of shared knowledge or at least prior reference, and seem to take for granted an easy mix of comfortably common values and emotions. Note, too, how the fifth line suggests a predication that is never completed. The average reader might well look for a "that" clause, expecting to hear that it was the great "as though" *that*. . . But instead the last six lines of the poem are grammatically in apposition to the initial "It was" of line five. The poem, then, instead of gathering to some sort of dramatic resolution, trails off into a series of qualifying clauses governed by participles (wanting, vibrating, and turning). This structure strengthens the mundane "It was" that opens the poem; in a sense, the entire poem is simply an elaboration of that initial moment. (Note, too, that "moment" is both past and unchanging.) At the same time, as the elliptical details filter through the poem's meandering syntax they seem to deepen a mystery that is unresolvable. For example, the surreal juxtaposition of the police excursions and the speaker's bodily functions has an apparent logical context based on the adverbial relation ("as").

Yet this juxtaposition is no sooner set up than the bodily functions are further placed in another context, one of total sufficiency. What began as oppressive has suddenly become carefree. The "distant pinch" could metaphorically be something as threatening as death, like the "old catastrophe" of Stevens' "Sunday Morning," or something as reassuring as missing someone who nevertheless soon returns ("turning out to greet you.").

But this combination of the mundane and the mysterious gets reinforced by the imagery, combining "little birds" and "excursions of the police." Likewise, the poem yokes the plain declarative opening sentence with the last sentence in the poem, which combines the declarative with the bracketed "as though" that suggests the whole experience, or at least its experiential essence, takes place in a subjunctive, virtual framework. The farms appearing as a kind of "precinct," together with the exercise of a "certain control" and the mockly picturesque "little bird. . .along the fence" add up to something like an anti-pastoral. Clearly the speaker is too self-conscious, too urbane in his manipulation of pastoral markers to be celebrating the "green world" of literary tradition. Yet the surrounding police metaphors and activities help create the feeling that the poem is about an escape, a momentary temporal haven from the usual "wants," in which a sense of bodily wholeness and fellow feeling is restored. We never see the physical locale in any detail, nor do we clearly hear a celebratory tone. And the season being autumnal contributes to the elegaic mood, which in turn adds to the etiolated sense of diffidence at the core of the poem's affections. Forced to a summary statement of the poem's theme, we might say that it argues that the impulse towards pastoral can itself become imprisoning, yet such escapism allows the affections to reassert themselves with simplified dignity, with the feeling of fatedness. The poem obviously leaves out a great deal, and is rather fastidious, and at the same time off-handed, about what it puts in.

But something else that makes up the feel of Ashbery's poetry—it is both cause and effect of its distinctive quality—can best be described as its essentially prose-like movement. Ashbery eschews the ordinary lyricism of verse, seldom bothering with rhyme or alliteration or strict meter. At the same time the prosaic run of his sentences is neither Pateresque nor Euphuistic. This prose quality goes hand in hand with the flat, affectless tone as well as the diffident, self-questioning attitude. The run of his argument, the flow of the poem's display of itself suggests a ruminative impulse at work. Very seldom do the metaphors result from the pressure of emotion, and we miss the meter-making argument that

Emerson asked of poetry. Often the metaphors and similes seem illustrative rather than functional, supplied to the reader as a courtesy, lest the sinuosities of the ego's search for balance between a too-ready order and a hopeless chaos weary him beyond limits. This part of Ashbery's aesthetic is clearly pushed to extremes in his *Three Poems*, where the dense Jamesian prose is studded with cliches. Obviously Ashbery felt the ordinary reader's demands, for fresh images and authentic if not desperate emotions, had to be utterly denied. No reviewer of this work had the temerity to suggest it was a good-natured hoax, a jeux d'esprit in which the confessional impulses of contemporary poetry were so gluttonously satisfied that they were simultaneously being scorned. Ashbery stuffed his "poems" with so much mandarin prose, masking such banal content, or at least cultivating a stultifying surface banality, that the modesty of the book's title can be read as either a deadpan joke or a highhanded taunt. Modernism's insistence that no subject matter or language was intrinsically nonpoetic confronts a severe test in this instance.

But *Three Poems* isn't a hoax, despite the self-indulgence of its format and its seeming refusal to mediate its feelings into a language public enough to allow response. The work's main concern is the theme of individuation, the re-emergence of a new self out of the old. This theme, central to much contemporary American poetry, is of course an important modernist preoccupation as well. With Ashbery the temporal aspects of the theme emerge forcefully and the book becomes a severe meditation on time, the trappings of time as well as the trap of temporality. In fact, the two tutelary deities seem to be Walt Whitman and Marcel Proust. The poem seeks to embrace contradictions by recovering the past; but with Ashbery the recovery, or at least the attempt to recover, throws up such a welter of conflicting and unresolved emotions that the confusions of self, rather than its individuation, becomes the dominant focus. Here is a sample of how the pursuit of a subject becomes the subject:

> Are you sad about something today? On days like this the old flanking motion almost seems to be possible again. Certainly the whiff of nostalgia in the air is more than a hint, a glaring proof that the old irregular way of doing is not only some piece of furniture of the memory but is ours, if we had the initiative to use it. I have lost mine. It has been replaced by a strange kind of happiness within the limitations. The way is narrow but it is not hard, it seems almost to propel or push one along. One gets the narrowness into one's seeing, which also seems an inducement to moving forward into

> what one has already caught a glimpse of and which quickly becomes vision, in the visionary sense, except that in place of the panorama that used to be our customary setting and which we never made much use of, a limited but infinitely free space has established itself, useful as everyday life but transfigured so that its signs of wear no longer appear as a reproach but of indications of how beautiful a thing must have been to have been so much prized, and its noble aspect which must have been irksome before has now become interesting, you are fascinated and keep on studying it.

The push of mind here combines an anal retentiveness with an insistent shedding of disguises and contexts. "I thought that if I could put it all down, that would be one way. And next the thought came to me that to leave all out would be another, and truer, way," Ashbery says in the first sentence of the book. His self often takes a passive role ("the thought came to me"), but also draws on deep sources of meditative energy and is unwilling to surrender the slightest psychological clue, as he tracks down all traces of the self, its transformations and evasions. The mind, like time itself, knows no fixity, but neither can it escape the rigidities of the past and the irrevocable oncoming of the future.

As was often the case with the poems in *The Double Dream of Spring,* Ashbery's language and theme involve him in that mixing of the mysterious and the mundane, that transvaluation of value which is one of the major heritages of surrealism. The old humanistic assurances fail to satisfy the quester: "you will realize that just having a soul was not enough: you must yield it up, vanish into the oblivion prepared for you by your years of waiting that all your practice of stoicism was not enough to seal off." Nihilism's threat energizes the pursuit as thoroughly as any real hope, for Ashbery plainly agrees with Stevens that "Death is the mother of beauty." But death offers a mundane possibility too, almost a banal one, for everywhere he looks he sees exempla and simulacra of unexceptional dissolution.

> And you know at last the condition of weightlessness and everything it implies: for the future, the present and most of all for the past into which you now slip helplessly, no longer prevented by the grid of everyday language, remaining in suspension in that greenish aquarium light which is your new element, compelled to re-enact the same scene in the old park, with snow on the ground and the waiting look on the faces of the nearest buildings, some distance away. All this in the interests of getting at the truth.

Ashbery's speaker fitfully becomes aware of social reality, reacting with an almost paranoid suspicion of being watched, as in this passage where the buildings' faces hover expectantly over the scene. This social reality also mixes elements of the mysterious and the mundane, as we might expect in a poetry threatened and yet enticed by solipsism.

> And finally and above all the great urban centers with
> Their office buildings and populations, at the center
> of which
> We live our lives, made up of a great quantity of
> isolated instants
> So as to be lost at the heart of a multitude of things.

This is from a poem in *Double Dream*, but echoes can be found throughout Ashbery's work of this sort of dissociated fear and paralysis. A passage, too long to quote fully, from *Three Poems* begins:

> . . .but at this time of year the populations emerge again into the arena of life after the death of winter, and one is newly conscious of the multitudes that swarm past one in the street; there is something of death here too in the way they plunge past toward some unknown destination, leaving one a little shaken up on the edge of the sidewalk.

Like Eliot's "I had not thought death had undone so many," this passage shows mass urbanized man as threatening in his complexity, and indeed narcotizing in his lack of purpose. The "plunge" of the masses ironically resembles the quest of the enlarged individual ego for some psychological satiety (or even surcease). But Ashbery's rather flat tone here should not conceal his deep unease, for the mundane surfaces of life offer the most persistent challenge to his equanimity. At one point Ashbery describes mass man as an "imbroglio of defeated desires. . .a sort of Thirty Years' War of the human will." We have clearly come worlds away from Whitman's democratic idealism. Yet Ashbery often finds the mundane mysterious, just as he occasionally presents the mysterious in mundane colors—echoing Baudelaire's sigh of "I have read all the books."*

Despite its circuitous structure, *Three Poems* does have at least a partial climax and resolution, though its third and final part, "The

* Almost as if to show contempt for the theme of lost visionary power, Ashbery says in the *Double Dream*: "Finally he decided to take a turn past the old grade school he'd attended as a kid. . . . Time farted."

Recital," returns to a questioning and questing mood. It's in the middle section, "The System," that Ashbery adduces a tentative "lesson," for the book does have a moral hunger at its core, obscured though it often is by epistemological complexity and aesthetic play. The poem poses the problem of how to integrate a visionary happiness into the everyday; how, when the self is so kaleidoscopic in its fears and hopes, can a transcendent "light" be made to illumine everything we do.

The middle section, then, is Ashbery's grandest attempt to answer the unresolved problems, problems of mind and self and value, which are the legacy of English Romanticism. In many ways this is Ashbery's most serious writing, where his project is most insistently questioned, but at the same time it is where his defensiveness is most perplexing. We can understand his nervousness, his radical ambiguity, and his polymorphous syntax, only if we grant that it is a grand elliptical commentary on a problem that is never directly stated. As such, this section presents the reader with the central difficulty in reading Ashbery: one senses an enormous psychological uneasiness, but the high level of play, and the almost choking egocentricity of the language, call into question the author's ultimate seriousness. Should the reader be convinced of the validity, let alone the lucidity, of Ashbery's vision, he still must grapple with how this vision can be mediated into the world of his own everyday experience. The complexity, in other words, might not argue so much for a long tradition of meaning, or a shared cultural crisis, but rather a unique, idio-syncratic formulation that forbids any social application of whatever solace or transformation it might putatively promise. But Ashbery, ever the anticipator of problems, and problems within problems, sets out to answer just these questions.

And answering the question of what to do with this visionary light leads him to the choice, which turns out *not* to be a choice, of which sort of happiness he truly wants, one kind that "has already proved itself," and another "that could lead to greener pastures." But it isn't a choice because

> it is certain now that these two ways are the same, that we *have* them both, the risk and the security, merely through being human creatures subject to the vicissitudes of time, our earthly lot.

So we move from a Wordsworthian dilemma, torn between the sweet past forever lost, and the bittersweet compensation of an all-too-available present, to what seems an existential resolution, where we embrace our temporal sentences because they create the only precincts in which we can continue being human. Joined with this traditional

Romantic and late-Romantic nexus of paradox, we find offered Ashbery's praise of the ordinary.

> But that is the wonder of it: that you have returned not to the supernatural glow of heaven but to the ordinary daylight you knew so well before it passed from your view, and which continues to enrich you as it steeps you and your ageless chattels of mind, imagination, timid first love and quiet acceptance of experience in its revitalizing tide.

Our chattels can be enriched because they are of the mind, and the idealism of Ashbery continues to be his first burden and his final blessing. Consciousness can never dissolve the curse of consciousness, nor can time cure the blot of temporality. "We were surprised once, long ago; and now we can never be surprised again." The book is studded with willed and longed for consolations, but unremitting dolor is finally its major tone.

Ashbery's latest book, *Self-Portrait in a Convex Mirror* (1975), contains a mix of poems, and one masterpiece, the title poem. There are even a few lyrics that seem almost "regular," as if they could have been written by any number of other poets; they have more or less expectable metaphoric structures and thematic content, and their language is scarcely surreal. This group includes "Fear of Death," "Mixed Feelings," and "As One Put Drunk Into The Packet Boat," and these poems show how far behind are the puerilities of *The Tennis Court Oath*. There is another group of poems that reads like a series of glosses on the complex meditations of *Three Poems*: "Ode to Bill," "Voyage to the Blue," and "Grand Galop." The last of these presents the most succinct expression of Ashbery's concerns and strategies, though it is itself hardly a concise poem. It begins "All things seem mention of themselves / And the names which stem from them branch out to other referents" and it pursues that special kind of abstract thought that Ashbery excels in. Ashbery once said that his poems were

> about the experience of experience. . .and the particular experience is of lesser interest to me than the way it filters through to me. I believe this is the way it happens with most people, and I'm trying to record a kind of generalized transcript of what's really going on in our minds all day long.

"Grand Galop" exemplifies the approach that is adumbrated here, as it skillfully weaves a set of reflections together with musings on the very act of gathering and sorting and releasing such reflections. The poem clarifies much that was baffling and unproductive in the earlier books.

However, there are at least two poems of inconsequence in *Self-Portrait*, "Sand Pail" and "Foreboding", and the dogged nonsense of these two is at least fitfully present in some other poems as well, the "Farm" sequence, for example. So it is too early to announce that Ashbery has abandoned completely the practice of surrealism in its most inconsequential aspects. But Ashbery does seem more intent on circling reality than in arbitrarily dipping into its recesses and surfaces, as if he has realized (and commendably accepted his realization) that the search for patterns is, at the very least, more interesting than the willful neglect of all consequentiality.

And with his masterpiece, "Self-Portrait in a Convex Mirror," his circlings become majestic. As the title suggests, this poem is a meditation on solipsism, but it is also a cry against temporality as well as a celebration of the commonplace attempts we make to overcome its ravages. The poem is unusual in several respects, at least for Ashbery. For example, it is a rare instance of his announcing a fixed subject for a poem, in this case the Renaissance painter Parmigianino's masterpiece of "distorted" perspective. Also, Ashbery quotes not only Vasari on Parmigianino's work, but a modern art historian as well, gracefully blending in these "objective" reports with his own thoroughly subjective reading of the painting. The poem is over five hundred lines long, in a blank-verse of a relaxed sort, its diction and syntax being remarkably straightforward, again considering Ashbery's previous work. But what provides the masterly dimension of the work is its philosophical seriousness. Ashbery's connoisseur's eye, and his deep affection and puzzlement in the face of Parmigianino's art, have found ample expression by joining with a poetry that draws on both the "ordinary language" philosophy of the British tradition and the phenomenology of modern French and German thinkers. But the philosophical reflections, questions, and formulations are all lightly cast; the poem never resorts to a technical vocabulary. And the meditation on art serves admirably to focus the poem's energies as they arise out of a grappling with everyday experience and the "classic" problems of epistemology and time.

The poem begins with a meditative description of the portrait that introduces the problem of "putting in and taking out," but here presented as a problem of interpreting the gesture of the painting's subject and intention, what Ashbery calls the painting's desire "to protect / What it advertises":

> The time of the day or the density of the light
> Adhering to the face keeps it
> Lively and intact in a recurring wave

Of arrival. The soul established itself.
But how far can it swim out through the eyes
And still return safely to its nest?

What can the artist reveal, what can the ego, looking to sound its own depths, find as ground or containment that will insure its own continuity: this is the meditator's problem. Seen from a different angle, this problem threatens to be resolved by one's finding out that nothing can be put in to the soul, because everything has been left out:

The secret is too plain. The pity of it smarts,
Makes hot tears spurt: that the soul is not a soul,
Has no secret, is small, and it fits
Its hollow perfectly: its room, our moment of attention.
That is the tune but there are no words.

Clearly Ashbery is here confronting a fundamental absence, and we can see the threat as something like Berkleyean idealism, for only when we are attending moment by moment to our selves can we be said to have a principle of existence. Pursued logically this would mean there is no meaningful past; our self would be like the self in Hume's philosophy, without causality or connectivenes, remade at every moment, like "a ping pong ball/ Secure on its jet of water." Yet art is one way we do establish a usable past, for the fixity of art, whatever it may distort, assures us that we had ego functions—memory, desire, intention—at some other time.

But it is certain that
What is beautiful seems so only in relation to a specific
Life, experienced or not, channeled into some form
Steeped in the nostalgia of a collective past.

"Experienced or not" shows us that Ashbery believes in the empathetic powers of art, and art viewing, and the "collective past" indicates he might be willing to embrace some form of social reality, if only an elite and historically conscious one. But the solipsism isn't that easily cured, and the poem's many twistings and unfoldings indicate that grappling with such problems can't be "logically" concluded.

But what art offers, especially an art redeemed from temporal dissolution, is a radical form of "otherness," an evidence of another human will and consciousness, much like ourselves perhaps, but insistently other, hence again mundane and mysterious. And this otherness spreads out from the "enigmatic finish" of art to our common activities:

Is there anything
To be serious about beyond this otherness
That gets included in the most ordinary
Forms of daily activity, changing everything
Slightly and profoundly, and tearing the matter
Of creation, any creation, not just artistic creation
Out of our hands, to install it on some monstrous, near
Peak, too close to ignore, too far
For one to intervene? This otherness, this
"Not-being-us" is all there is to look at
In the mirror, though no one can say
How it came to be this way.

This is the poem's central insight, its highest truth, and its most reassuring consolation, suspended as it is between slight and profound change, near and remote distances. "The ordinary forms of daily activity" have attracted Ashbery all along, as if the aesthete in him needed just this ballast to steady him in the swells of self exploration. James Schuyler's "Hymn of Life" also makes this kind of affirmation, and it should be read along with "Self-Portrait" as the most brilliant extension of the poetic mode of "The New York School" since the death of Frank O'Hara.

"Self-Portrait" ends, as does *Three Poems*, with a coda that mutes any excessive feeling of "triumph," and the note of dolor, of autumnal falling sounds in the closing lines:

The hand holds no chalk
And each part of the whole falls off
And cannot know it knew, except
Here and there, in cold pockets
Of remembrance, whispers out of time.

The absence of sustaining warmth and integrating knowledge will always be Ashbery's true subject, his lasting concern; for him nothing is more fundamental. The surfaces of mundane reality *are* reality, and yet only our much more than superficial reflections can make that apply, and Ashbery's poetry will probably always be suspended between this admission of defeat and a calm claim of victory. He addresses Parmigianino, or rather his sustained surface in the self-portrait, with these words:

And just as there are no words for the surface, that is,
No words to say what it really is, that it is not
Superficial but a visible core, then there is
No way out of the problem of pathos vs. experience.
Your will stay on, restive, serene in
Your gesture which is neither embrace nor warning
But which holds something of both in pure
Affirmation that doesn't affirm anything.

Ashbery here clearly addresses himself, and his poetry, as well.

****

But this leaves us with the problem, if that is what it is, of Ashbery's recent fame, for how has this difficult, often abstruse poet found an audience? After Frank O'Hara's death in 1966, it appeared as if the "New York School" would slowly disintegrate. The coterie of poets around St. Mark's Church on the lower east side of New York had developed a second-generation, informally led by Ted Berrigan. Ashbery himself made few public appearances, though his work still attracted a group of fervent supporters. And of course the art scene, which had long served as the nexus of much of O'Hara and Ashbery's work, went through several transformations, from abstract expressionism to color-field painting to pop art, but picking up more public acceptance with each new phase. It was clearly becoming more difficult for the avant-garde to sustain anything like an adversary relation to the mainstream cultural forces. In fact, the original sense of the military term "avant-garde" was beginning to reassert itself, for the advance guard was meant to bring back news to the central command and thus support and facilitate its strategies. Ashbery has not commented publicly on his own development in the late sixties and early seventies, so we can't know if he tired of the poetry of inconsequence, or if he felt drawn to the traditional post-Romantic set of themes and problems after an intensive reading of, say, Wallace Stevens, or if he simply developed a calm philosophic mind to replace a wearied surreal eye. But we do know that *Self-Portrait in a Convex Mirror* was given the Pulitzer Prize, The National Book Award, and the National Book Critics Circle Award, an unprecedented sweep for a poet. And an inexpensive Penguin edition of this book went quickly into a second printing, aided no doubt by the prizes and their publicity, but also, I suspect, because not only was the poetry more "available" in its feelings and meanings, but because many academic critics were willing to push Ashbery as *the* major poet of the seventies. After the cultural confusion of the sixties, we probably shouldn't be surprised that a putatively major poet has produced six commercial books of poetry that include one volume that is totally meaningless and another written in prose! But clearly Ashbery's ascension, though partly the result of a unique talent, reflects larger cultural forces and energies, not least among which is the assimilation of the experimental impulses of modernism into the standard, though pluralistic, framework of contemporary poetry.

What stands behind Ashbery's rather sudden success d'estime is the triumph of a poetic mode. A mode demands less aesthetic energy than a truly individual style, but usually offers more gratification than an average school or "movement." Ashbery's mode has what most modes have, a distinctive blend of sensibility, verbal texture, and thematic concerns. In each of these categories, or elements, a mode must not become too rigid; its sensibility cannot turn into a set of static attitudes, its verbal texture cannot be reduceable to simple matters of vocabulary or verse forms, and its thematic concerns must allow for a range of subject matter. Successful modes, then, thrive on their distinctiveness, their ability to be set off against a larger, more public set of expectations. But the moment this distinctiveness becomes too rigid, the mode slips into self-parody, consciously or unconsciously. Just when and how a mode calcifies (or what is less likely, fails to achieve a distinctive feel), is hard for literary historians to measure precisely, especially in contemporary literature. But ample evidence for the existence of Ashbery's mode can be found in one of the first issues of *Partisan Review* for which he acted as poetry editor. Here are the openings of four poems from Volume XLIII, number 4:

First of all I'm naked
while I'm typing this,
only my rash is airbrushed,
the rest is visceral energy
for my poetry, in this case
depicted objects of tough minded
harsh light that emphasizes
the previous generation of
dismayed bridegrooms at the
altar of the cosmic alienation.

****

It's nice to sit down in the evening
With the rain out of doors
And the dog lapping water from the toilet bowl
To a dinner given in your honor

****

From my doorstep, at twenty,
Swinging in and out of the pastoral setting;
My father gone, my mother waiting idly
Beside the buzz of a hazy world—
Perceive it—at twenty—surrounded
By weak prospects and thin possibilities. . .

****

Of postures taken
Little indication was given
We were to spend hours watching slender
Black lines erratically divide fields
Of primary color. Clouds pursued me
With insinuations of previous neglect
Like a dried wash rag limply hanging
From a towel rack.

The sensibility here might roughly be described as that of mock confessional joined to the surrealistically coy; the verbal texture relies on a mix of the familiarly colloquial with the etiolated irony of self-conscious diction; and the themes all arise out of a search for priviliged moments of awareness, furtively snatched from a world where the madcap pluralism of values (and value-systems) is the almost-disconcerting norm.

These selections, written by four different poets, demonstrate a recognizable mode, whose chief immediate influence of course is the work of Frank O'Hara. But Ashbery's own contributions to the mode are significant, though one senses he has done more to keep the mode alive than to widen its possibilities. But this brings us back to the problem of the limits of a mode. Does Ashbery's sudden reputation reflect the adoption of his mode by other poets, or vice versa? Has the mode finally achieved respectability, or has its perfection, its final self-definition simply made it more immediately available to other poets? Certainly the panels who praise Ashbery's "originality," his "breathtaking freshness and adventures in which dazzling orchestrations of language open up whole areas of consciousness no other American poet has even begun to explore" (to quote a typical jacket blurb), must be made up of readers who simply don't follow contemporary poetry. Ashbery's relation to the mode in which he works seems little more adventurous than that of several other poets to their modes. Is it, then, the mode itself that impresses the judges as intrinsically more adventurous than the other modes currently being developed and practiced? This seems the most charitable explanation, though the obvious point must be made: the mode has been available since 1950 or so, jostling and sometimes obscurely mixing with other modes. Ashbery's domination of this mode is fully achieved, and in those terms his reputation is warranted. But his success may well have something to do with the cultural moment, and a weariness with moral and political fervor in poetry now that the 1960's are past. Ashbery's peculiar dissociation of feeling, his syntactical bracketing or suspension of affect, produces a poetry that simultaneously submerges itself in emotion and moves beyond it. "But the fantasy makes it ours, a kind of fence-sitting/ Raised to the level of an aesthetic ideal."

Observations on Psychoanalysis and Modern Literature

BY ERICH HELLER*

In the history of thought it occurs again and again that a privileged mind turns a long-nurtured suspicion into a system and puts it to the good or not so good uses of teachers and learners. When this happens, we say that it has been in the air for a long time. This is so in the case of psychoanalysis, and whatever its future fate, its historical importance is beyond doubt. For it is impossible not to come into contact with it or to avoid the collision, even if one merely wanted to say to it that it has no business being there. A theory owes this kind of inescapability to its long maturation in the womb of Time. It is born and casts its spell upon a world that seems to have been prepared for quite a while to receive it. Pallas Athene, it is said, emerged from her father's head in full armor. But surely, before this birth took place, Zeus must have spent many a day pondering Athenian thoughts and must have done so in the Athenian dialect; and our world had awaited Freud long before it heard his name.

This is why psychoanalysis appears to be more than merely one among many possible theories about the psyche; rather, it comes close to being the systematic consciousness that a certain epoch has of the nature and character of its soul. Therefore it would be an endless enterprise to speak of Freud's influence on modern literature; and literature, whatever else it may be, is also the esthetic form assumed by the self-awareness of an age. If a writer today speaks of fathers or sons, of mothers or dreams, of lovers or rivals, of accidents that determine destinies or destinies rooted in character, of the will to live or the longing for death — and what else is it that poets and writers talk about? — how

* This essay will also appear in *Psychiatry and the Humanities*, the forthcoming Festschrift for Edith Weigert, edited by Joseph H. Smith. It is printed here by arrangement with the Washington School of Psychiatry.

can he remain untouched by Freudian thoughts even if he has never read a line by Freud? And the more he were to try to extinguish or "repress" this "influence," the more he would become its victim. Could a post-Freudian poet say what Goethe's Egmont says: "As if whipped on by invisible demons, the sun-born horses of Time rush along with the fragile chariot of our destiny, and nothing is left to us but intrepidly to hold fast to the reins and keep the wheels from pushing against a wall of rock or driving into an abyss" (*Egmont*, II, 2) — could a contemporary writer put such words into the mouth of his hero without suspecting that he has learned it from Freud? That the invisible demons with their whip are really the Unconscious, the Id, and the rather helpless charioteer the Ego with its good intentions?

From Goethe, Novalis, the German arch-Romantic, and Kleist, the one and only naturally tragic poet of German literature (even if Goethe once cursed him as "*Unnatur*" — "*Diese verdammte Unnatur*," he said), and certainly from the literature we have uppermost in mind when speaking of the later nineteenth century, from Stendhal, Flaubert and Maupassant, from Tolstoy and Dostoyevsky, there is a much shorter way to Freud than the maps of literary history usually show; and the subsequent literature is altogether domiciled in a country the cartographer of which is Freud. It may not be the most pertinent of questions to ask whether Hofmannsthal, Schnitzler, Broch, Musil, Kafka, Rilke, Hermann Hesse or Thomas Mann have been "influenced" by Freud, or whether Joyce or Virginia Woolf, Hemingway or Faulkner have "learned" from him. For the question — to which the answer may be in some cases Yes and more frequently No — is almost as irrelevant as it would be to ask whether the first builders of aircraft were inspired by Newton. Airplanes fly in Newtonian space, trusting, as it were, in the validity of the law of gravity. What then are the qualities of the sphere of the psyche traversed by modern literature?

Out of its multitudinous characteristics I wish to select two from the writings of Thomas Mann. The first bears upon the problem of man's responsibility for his decisions and actions — that is, the problem of morality itself. A masterpiece among novellas, *Death in Venice*, supplies our first example. We remember the episode (in the third section of the story) that is decisive in the development of the plot, when Gustav von Aschenbach for the last time tries to take the moral initiative in the encounter with his destiny. He wants to escape from the sickly oppression: from the Venetian air, heavy and sultry with the sirocco, where the deadly epidemic would soon luxuriate, but also from his growing passion for the beautiful boy Tadzio. He determines to leave and orders his luggage to be taken to the railway station on the hotel's early morning motor boat, whereas he himself, believing that there is enough time for an unrushed breakfast and, without acknowledging this to himself, perhaps for a last silent encounter with Tadzio, chooses to take a later public steamship. But when he arrives at the station, his luggage has gone off on a wrong train. This accident makes his moral determination collapse. He decides to wait for his trunk in Venice, returns to his Lido hotel and to his erotic enchantment. He is ready now for the approaching disease and for death.

Fate and accident are ancient allies; yet only in the Freudian era could *this* accident have been woven in this manner into the texture of destiny. For as Thomas Mann tells the story, the accident is not, as any similar event in Greek tragedy would be, a weapon in the hands of a divine antagonist with whom the hero's will is interlocked in combat, and not a cunning maneuver of that friend or foe called Fate. It is rather the revelation of Aschenbach's true will that gives the lie to his declared intention to depart. If Aschenbach is clearly innocent of the mistake made in the dispatch of his luggage, he is innocent only after the canon of traditional moral judgments. According to the new dispensation he is responsible; and in his soul he knows this or comes to know it as he ecstatically welcomes that travel mishap as if it were the gift of Freedom itself. "Aschenbach," we read, "found it hard to let his face assume the expression that the news of the mishap required, for he was almost convulsed with reckless delight, an unbelievable joy."

The basic idea of Thomas Mann's novel *The Magic Mountain* can be stated almost in one sentence: Hans Castorp, a seemingly "well-adjusted" young shipbuilding engineer from Hamburg, has planned a visit of three weeks in a Swiss sanatorium for tubercular diseases where his cousin is a patient, but remains there for seven years. Certainly, he becomes ill himself, but his physical symptoms are by no means serious. What then is the *real* reason for his tarrying? It is his hidden wish, a secret perhaps to himself, to await the return of Clavdia Chauchat. He has fallen in love with the Russian woman and she, as she leaves, promises that she will return: and Hans Castorp waits seven years. His illness is the mere pretext for his waiting. Against all "humanistic" reasonableness and moral principles, his *true* will has asserted itself. And Thomas Mann began to read Freud only after he had written *The Magic Mountain.* Voila, the *Zeitgeist*!

Both *Death in Venice* and *The Magic Mountain* would be unthinkable were it not for the Romantic fascination with the alliance between love and sickness and death; and this is almost as much as to say: unthinkable without depth psychology. These works are situated in a territory of the psyche the ethics of which are radically different from those of the Enlightenment (to name only one of the preceding epochs). It is strange that the strongest hostile response evoked by Freud's teaching was, at least to begin with, moral indignation. Freud, it was held, undermined morality and catastrophically narrowed the domain in which ethical laws could be applied unquestioningly. A profounder criticism would have been to show that, on the contrary, he extended a person's responsibility so immeasurably that it became in practice all but unworkable. The rationalistic doctrine of morality, which until the Romantic period had dominated the moral philosophy of Western civilization, saw the moral person triumph or succumb in a *conscious* struggle with forces which, no matter whether they were called "nature" or "instinct" or "inclination," were the simple antagonists of the ethically wakeful human being. In Freud's doctrine, deeply indebted to the Romantic sensibility, the moral conflict becomes total warfare. It is waged even in places where once upon a time the warrior sought and found relaxation from the strains of morality: in sleep, in dreams, in fantasies, in innocently involuntary action. Let anyone say now: "I have only dreamt this," or "I did not intend to say this; it was a mere slip of the tongue," or "I was determined to do what I promised, but then I forgot": instantly he will be persuaded that he dreamt what he dreamt, said what he said, forgot what he forgot, because he was prompted by his deepest and truest will. While the moralist of the rational Enlightenment proved himself or failed in what he consciously *willed* or *did*, the Romantic and Freudian morality is once again concerned with the innermost character of a person, with his *being*. Once again: for there was a time, long ago, when a prophet struck fear and terror, albeit by speaking in a different idiom, into the minds of the Pharisees by putting the goodness of the hidden soul or the rebirth of the whole man ethically above the righteous observance of the law by the publicly displayed good will. This was the essence of the moral revolution of Christianity.

As psychoanalysis, with all its variations and eclectic modifications, is a dominant part of the epoch's consciousness, it has a share in its calamity. This manifests itself—speaking, as would seem appropriate, in medical terms — in the vast superiority of presumed diagnostic insights over therapeutic possibilities. Has there ever been a doctor who has diagnosed as many pathological irritations as Freud? The psyche is to him an inexhaustible reservoir of abnormalities, precariously dammed in by the most delicate concept of health. All pleasures and all oppressions of the soul, all sins and all virtues, the restlessness of the heart as well as the great constancy of love, the fear of evil as well as the faith in God — all these may in the twinkling of the diagnostic eye degenerate into signs of psychic imbalance. But what is the health of the soul? Compared to the resourcefulness and ingenuity of the diagnosis, the only answer that can be given within the limits of psychology is primitive, pedestrian and simple-minded: the ability to control the controllable conditions of existence and the adjustment to the unalterable. But who has drawn the frontier between the controllable and the unalterable? Where exactly does it run? Is it fixed by God, this fabrication of the father-bound neurotic psyche? Or by Nature who has created the boy after the image of Oedipus and then handed him over to the healing practices of psychological *ratio*? Or by society or the State? By *which* society and *which* State? By that Victorian society whose numerous pathological symptoms have called forth psychoanalysis? Or by the enlightened, generously liberal, thoroughly "demythologized" society that on both sides of the Atlantic sends swarms of patients into the consulting rooms of psychologists? Or by the tyrannical State that prohibits their activities?

The questions are endless and unanswerable. For it is true to say that if there were an answer, there would be no psychoanalysis. It would not have been invented, had it not been for the disappearance from our beliefs of any certainty concerning the nature of human being. Thus we have become the incurable patients of our all but nihilistic skepticism, indulging a conception of the soul that stipulates more, many more, psychic possibilities than can be contained in one existence. Whichever possibilities we choose, we miss out on the others—and distractedly feel our loss without being able ethically to justify it. Inevitably foregoing uncounted possibilities, we experience this as the betrayal of a vaguely conceived "fullness of life." For our beliefs do not acknowledge any reason to sacrifice possibilities in order to gain our reality — a reality that for us has assumed the character of the arbitrary and the indefinable. Thus we are haunted by as many dead possibilities as there is room for in the wide region of frustrations. It is the accomplished hypochondria of unbelief.

Paradoxically enough, Freud himself, over long stretches of his enterprise, was securely at home in that rationalistic Enlightenment faith whose increasing instability was the historical occasion of this doctrine, just as the doctrine in its turn added to the disturbance. But because he himself was hardly affected by it, he had no ear for the question his own theory raised, and certainly did not have the *philosophical* genius to meet it. With astonishing naivete he examined the "How" of psychic conditions, as if such labors could yield clear answers to the "What" of psychic phenomena, of their meaning and their possible relatedness to the possibly true nature of being. Thus he believed, for instance, that primeval murderers of their fathers created from the agony of their guilt a godfather to be worshipped — a theory which of course presupposes that those savage creatures in all their savagery possessed a conscience and the psychic disposition to believe in God. Yet Freud did not ask to what end human beings should have the ability to feel guilty or the capacity for religious beliefs, but took for granted that the conscience and the faith of his savages corresponded to nothing real in the world and fed on sheer illusions; and his readers, just as he himself did, looked upon certain *contents* of guilt and faith understandably as antiquated without paying attention to the *form* and quality of these psychic dispositions. But are those dispositions not exceedingly curious if they have no correlative whatever in the order of reality? Of course, Freud would rightly have said that this was not a psychological question, but a metaphysical or ontological one. True; but to doubt the very validity of such questions, quite apart from the inability to answer them, is the main psychological characteristic of the epoch that has produced psychoanalysis as its representative psychology.

One of its most important tenets is the theory of repression. From the beginning of his history man has suffered from the compulsion to "repress," and only because he "represses" has he a history, for historical epochs or cultures differ one from the other by the changing moulds in which they cast some human possibilities at the expense of others. This is why the ancient Greeks were despite Pythagoras and the Pythagoreans not rich in great natural scientists, but in artistic accomplishments unsurpassed by any other age; or why we have the most self-assured and effective technology, but arts that are exceedingly tentative, uncertain, restless and experimental; or why creations of nature have been, ever since the discovery of Nature, the great comfort and pleasure of the Romantic sensibility: because this tree or that range of mountains appears to be the sum total, without loss or sacrifice, of *all* its potentialities, and therefore never hurts our esthetic sense by insinuating to us that it might have done much better had it only chosen another career. For one of the things that set man apart from all other beings is that the sum of his potentialities by far exceeds the measure of their realizability in one human life or even in one historical epoch. Man has been given language (in the sense of all his means of expression) so that he can say what he has not chosen to be silent about. He is such an eloquent creature because he is unspeakably secretive. This is the natural-historical aspect of human transcendence, the psychological side of his "existential problem." Human existence is choice, resignation, sacrifice — and indeed neurotic repression if a man has to make his inescapable choices and sacrifices under the dim enforcement of social norms he no longer believes in, instead of basing his decisions upon the belief in the greater virtue of what he has chosen, no matter whether he does so consciously or unconsciously, from lucid insight or from faithful unreflective obedience. If he no longer feels that there is any compelling reason why he should forego this in order to achieve that; if his existence is not illuminated by any shimmer of its transcendence, then his rejected potentialities (or, for that matter, injuries sustained by the child in his religiously or ethically "agnostic" society) grow into neuroses in the darkness of the unconscious. And psychoanalysis shares with existential philosophy the tragic fate that, although it is, of course, founded upon the awareness of the universal human need to choose, to select and to sacrifice, it is at the same time, like most other creations of the age, deprived of the means to transcend this distressing human condition.

From this follows the "scientific" intention of psychoanalysis to disregard any hierarchy that religion or metaphysics or ethics or tradition has set up concerning the activities of consciousness. It may well be true to say that this has been the first such attempt in the history of man's efforts to know himself. There is for psychoanalysis no pre-established order of the psyche: it is impossible to discern, at least initially, what is important to it and what is unimportant. It is a theory that lets itself in with chaos. If there is to be any order, it has to be created — somewhat in keeping with the *apercu* of that arch-Romantic Novalis (in his celebrated fragment of 1799 "Christendom or Europe") that only anarchy will once again beget a true spiritual order: "Religion will rise from the chaos of destruction as the glorious founder of a new world." Psychoanalysis — like the sensibility of Romanticism (as opposed to that of Classicism) — is imbued with the suspicion that everything, every tatter of a dream, every scrap of memory, every seemingly arbitrary association our thinking makes between this and that, may be of hitherto unsuspected significance within the economy of the soul, just as Marcel (in the first volume of Proust's vast novel *À la recherche du temps perdu*) receives those sudden messages of a great and hidden truth, those unpredictable intimations of eternity, from a stone the surface of which reflected the sunlight, or from the clanging of a bell, or from the smell of fallen leaves — "a confused mass of different images, under which must have perished long ago the reality" — the absolute reality he was seeking. Nietzsche's great and truly dreadful experiment consisted in his assuming that the history of the Western mind was nothing but a conspiracy to conceal the truth; and where such concealment is looked upon as the rule, the suspicion is bound to arise that, vice versa, anything, literally anything, may unexpectedly "conduct" the mind toward a tremendous illumination. It is precisely this that distinguishes modern literature from, above all, the myth-bound poetry of ancient Greece. And what Hofmannsthal said in his poem "Lebenslied" of the "heir" of this long process of disinheritance, is as true of psychoanalysis as it is of the artist of the psychoanalytical age:

Ihm bietet jede Stelle
Geheimnisvoll die Schwelle —

meaning that he who is without a home in an ordered world will entrust himself to any current of chance to take him anywhere, for anywhere may be the threshold of the mystery.

Proust's great novelistic *oeuvre*, the attempt to catch hold of a withdrawing world by means of an exquisitely woven net of memories; James Joyce's *Ulysses*, this monster work of genius that turns the experience of one day into a kind of lyrical-epical encyclopedia; Hermann Broch's time-consuming record of Vergil's dying; not to mention the many minor 'stream of consciousness' novels—all this is the literary product of an epoch whose soul has been analyzed by Sigmund Freud. And whatever will remain of this literature will bear the imprint of a consciousness that Freud has helped to become conscious of itself— and thus, given the nature of consciousness, has helped to come into being. But can a consciousness that is so thoroughly conscious of itself ever achieve that "*geprägte Form*," as Goethe called it in "*Urworte-Orphisch*," the oneness of deliberate form and "naive" spontaneity that has always been the hallmark of great art?

Speaking of Freud and modern literature, we cannot help concerning ourselves with the unusual and in all probability critical situation of literature in an age that constantly is in search of an acceptable theory of its soul. For the relationship of art to that self-understanding of the soul which culminates in Freud is by no means free of conflicts, and these tensions have been in the making ever since the truth about man has been sought not in myth or religion but in psychology. Psychology — the psychology, for instance, that dominates the novel of the nineteenth century — is the science of disillusionment. Its climate is, as some of the Romantics believed, unfavorable to poetry; and in a serious sense it is true to say that the history of the psychological novel is the progressive dissolution of what traditionally has been regarded as poetic. Novalis, who wrote that psychology is one of the "ghosts" that have "usurped the place in the sanctuary where the monuments of gods should be," knew what he did when he countered the Romantic enthusiasm for Goethe's *Wilhelm Meister*, indeed his own fascination with that novel, by calling it a "Candide aimed at poetry," a satire of the poetic mode.

Goethe, in his turn, accused Kleist, this *Ur*-patient and *Ur*-practitioner of depth analysis, of aiming at the confusion of feelings. What he meant by this was very likely the war that Kleist's imagination, in love with the heroic and the mythic, fought with his analytical intelligence; and this intelligence was at the same time in unrelenting pursuit of the psychological truth. It is a feud that reverberates throughout Kleist's dramatic verse and prose. Indeed, the source of the particular fascination wielded by his dramas and stories is the clash, and at times the unquiet marriage, between poetry and neurosis. Goethe was bound to abhor this poet as intensely as Kafka admired him. For Goethe believed — at least at times — that poetry prospered only when it was left to grow and mature in the unconscious. He said so to Schiller and added that poetry presupposes in those who make it "a certain good-natured and even simple-minded love for the real which is the hiding-place of truth."

Unconscious, good-natured, simple-minded, trusting that the hidden truth may, after all, reveal itself to the naive mind in the phenomenal world — if one were to define Kleist's genius, indeed the spirit of modern literature by means of its perfect opposite, this would be its negative definition. Should it ever happen that a history of modern literature is written in honor of Sigmund Freud — by a literary historian who also possesses a thorough knowledge of psychoanalysis without having become intellectually enslaved to it — it might begin with Goethe's highly conscious praise of the unconscious, contemplate afterwards the Kleistean tension between mythology and psychology which is at the same time so characteristic of a whole literary epoch, and then arrive at the writings of Nietzsche, that astonishing prompter of psychoanalysis, "the first psychologist of Europe," as, not very modestly, he called himself (and Freud himself all but acknowledged his claim) — Nietzsche, who at the same time never tired of pointing to the perils of the mind's psychological pursuit of itself, and believed he knew that there was a kind of knowledge that may become "a handsome instrument for perdition." Such an essay in literary history might conclude with Kafka's dictum from "Reflections on Sin, Suffering, Hope, and the True Way": "Never again psychology!"

In honor of Sigmund Freud? Would it not rather be a polemical performance? No. For is the stance of the polemicist appropriate to the inevitable? Our imaginary historian of literature would show that there is a compelling logical development from German Romanticism, the fountain-head of so many currents in modern literature, to the works of Sigmund Freud. How is this? The medical sobriety of the founder of psychoanalysis brought into the vicinity of a literary-philosophical movement that is reputed to have fostered every conceivable extravagance of the fancy? Still, the connection exists; and it is a mistaken belief, hardly more than a facile superstition, that the early German Romantics were bent simply on discrediting realistic wakefulness in order to rescue the dreamily poetic, or on fortifying the domain of the imagination against the encroachments of the real. True, the poet in Novalis was sometimes outraged by the prosaic realism of Goethe's *Wilhelm Meister.* On these occasions he would say of it that it elevated "the economic nature of man" to the rank of his "only true nature" (and he might have said: the nature of man insofar as it is accessible to psychology); or that it was "a piece of poetic machinery to deal with recalcitrant material;" or that with this novel he made his final bid for quasi-bourgeois respectability: "The Pilgrim's Progress toward a knighthood." But in a different mood he called it a supreme masterpiece, "the novel *par excellence*," and its author "the true vicar of the poetic spirit on earth." It is clear that even Novalis, the true poet in the first group of German Romantics, played his part in the strategy of Romantic Irony, an attitude of mind which would surely be useless in any ferocious defense of the imagination against the attacks of rationality. No, Romantic Irony is a play played around a center of great seriousness. Its ambition is to save the authentic life of the imagination from the wreckage of illusions. Just as lifeboat instruction is given on luxurious ocean liners, so Romantic Irony aims at teaching the spirit of poetry how to keep afloat in the approaching floods of what Goethe named the Prosaic Age: the Age of Analysis.

Friedrich Schlegel, the Grand Intellectual Master of the early Romantics, demanded that poetry should be practiced like a science, while every science should become a new kind of poetry. This was Schlegel's *outré* manner of expressing what Schiller, in his celebrated essay "On Spontaneous and Reflective Poetry," hoped for: that at the highest point of consciousness man would acquire a new and higher "naiveté." Novalis said even more: "Those who uncritically believe in their health make the same mistake as those who uncritically regard themselves as sick: both are diseased" — because, one assumes, of their wanting in critical alertness; and still more: that certain kinds of physical sickness are best treated through treating the psyche because the soul has the same influence upon the body that the body has upon the soul. If these sayings were offered as utterances of Freud's, the attribution would not meet with much incredulity. And the following *is* all but by Freud although it too was said by Novalis: "All that is involuntary must come under the control of the conscious will." This means the same as "*Ego* shall be where *Id* was."

As one reads what Freud says of the relationship between "I" and "It," of the wounds which the struggles between the two inflict upon the soul, and how the soul may regain its lost integrity through the enhanced consciousness of itself, it is impossible not to relate this great psychological utopia to the vision of a future paradise with which Kleist ends his meditations "On the Marionette Theatre" — or rather, on the neurotic derangement, the false self-consciousness, of the inhibited psyche; and even though the Eden of the original innocence and unself-conscious grace is shut for ever, we must, Kleist writes, "embark on the journey around the world in order to find out whether we may not be received through a back door": In the future *perfection of consciousness* we may recover what we have lost in the Fall; we shall have to "eat of the Tree of Knowledge again to fall back into the state of innocence."

Schiller, in that essay on "Spontaneous and Reflective Poetry," means something similar, if not the same, when he speaks of our gaining a new and purified spontaneity through the infinite increase of our reflective power. And what else is it that the philosopher of Romantic pessimism, Schopenhauer, has in mind when he, intimately knowing the terror of the *Id*, the dark impulses of the Will, glorifies in his *magnum opus*, *The World as Will and Idea*, the freedom that the *Ego* may conquer through the understanding of that *Id* and itself? And finally Freud and Nietzsche: Even if the mountain tops of the prophet Zarathustra seem worlds apart from the consulting room of the analyst, they are nonetheless neighbors, and not only in the sequence of time. For one of Nietzsche's two divinities is Dionysus, the god of the intoxicated will to live, but the other is Apollo, the god who possesses the power of clear articulation and disciplined insight. Nietzsche too longed for the ultimate rule of Apollo — not *over* Dionysus but *together with him* in an utopian oneness of Mind and Will, intellect and impulse. Yet Nietzsche and Freud are neighbors above all by virtue — virtue? Well, sometimes it seems a necessity imposed by history — by virtue of the determination with which they pursued the truths of psychology, a psychological radicalism intolerant of any gods that were not more than the illusory comforters of sick souls. But if ever there comes the unimaginable day when men, beyond sickness and illusion, live in the integrity of being, then the spirits of Freud and Nietzsche may give their assent to Kafka's resolve, unrealizable in his time: "Never again psychology!"

Literature and Discontinuity[1]

BY ROLAND BARTHES

(Translated by Richard Howard)

Behind every collective rejection of a book by our stock criticism we must look for *what has been offended. Mobile* offended the very idea of the Book. A compilation—and even worse, for the compilation is a minor but received genre—a sequence of phrases, quotations, clippings, or paragraphs, words, block-letter capitals scattered over the (often nearly blank) surface of the page, all this concerning an object (America) whose very parts (the States of the Union) are presented in the most insipid of orders, which is the alphabetical order: here is a technique of exposition unworthy of the way our ancestors have taught us to make a book.

What aggravated *Mobile*'s case is that the liberty its author takes with regard to the Book is paradoxically associated with a genre, the *travel impression,* to which our society extends the greatest indulgence. A journey, we grant, may be freely described from day to day in frank subjectivity, in the manner of a private diary whose thread is continually broken by the pressure of days, sensations, ideas: a journey can be written elliptically *(Yesterday, ate an orange at Sibari),* the telegraphic style being sanctified by the genre's "naturalness." But society is reluctant to add to the liberty which it gives, a liberty which is taken. In a literature like ours where everything is in its place, and where only such an order generates security, morality, or more exactly, for it consists of a complex mixture of both, *hygiene,* it is poetry and poetry alone whose function is to collect all the phenomena subversive of the Book's material nature: since Mallarmé and Apollinaire no one can take exception to the typographical "eccentricity" or the rhetorical "disorder" of a poetic

1. Apropos to Michel Butor's *Mobile: Study for a Representation of the United States.* —The reference to a general disapproval by French critics was reflected by the characteristic American review—incredulous, derisive, outraged—the translation of the book received from Truman Capote.—Tr.

"composition". We recognize here a technique familiar to good society: to *freeze* such liberties as if they were an ulcer; consequently, aside from poetry no outrage upon the Book may be tolerated.

Butor's offence was all the graver in that his infraction was intentional. *Mobile* is not a "natural" or "familiar" book; no question here of "travel notes" or even of a "dossier" of various materials whose diversity might be accepted if one could call the thing, for instance, a *scrap book* (for naming exercises). For *Mobile* is a conscious composition: first of all, in its scope, which relates to those great poems, so foreign to us, which were the epic or the didactic poem; then, in its structure, which is neither a narrative nor an accumulation of notes, but a combination of selected units (to which we shall return); finally, in its very closure, since the object treated is defined by a number (the States of the Union) and since the book ends when this number is honored. If then *Mobile* violates the consecrated (*i.e.,* sacred) notion of the Book, this is not out of negligence but in the name of another idea of another Book. Which one? Before finding out, there are two lessons to be learned from *Mobile's* reception, lessons concerning the Book's nature.

The first is that any upset an author imposes on the typographic norms of a work constitutes an essential disturbance: to deploy isolated words on a page, to mix italic, roman, and capital letters with a purpose which is visibly not that of intellectual demonstration (for when we are concerned to teach *English* to our schoolchildren, we are quite indulgent of the splendid typographical eccentricity of our Carpentier-Fialip manuals), to break the material thread of the sentence by disparate paragraphs, to make a word equal in importance to a sentence—all these liberties contribute in short to the very destruction of the Book: *the Book-as-Object is materially identified with the Book-as-Idea,* the technique of printing with the literary institution, so that to attack the material regularity of the work is to attack the very idea of literature. In short, the typographical forms are a basic guarantee: normal printing attests to the normality of the discourse; to say of *Mobile* that *"it's not a book"* is obviously to enclose the being and the meaning of literature in a pure protocol, as if this same literature were a rite which would lose all effectiveness the day we formally violated any of its rules: the Book is a High Mass, and it matters little whether or not it is said with piety, provided its every element proceeds *in order*.

If everything which happens on the surface of the page wakens so intense a susceptibility, it is clear that this surface is the depository of an essential value, which is the *continuity* of literary discourse (and this will be the second lesson to be learned from *Mobile*'s reception). The (traditional) Book is an object which *connects, develops, runs* and *flows,* in short, has the profoundest *horror vacui.* Sympathetic metaphors of the Book are: fabric to be woven, water flowing, flour to be milled, paths to be followed, curtains parting, etc.; antipathetic metaphors are those of a fabricated object, *i.e.*, an object assembled out of discontinuous raw materials: on one side, the "flow" of living, organic substances, the charming unpredictability of spontaneous liaisons; on the other, the ungrateful sterility of mechanical contraption, of cold and creaking machinery (this is the theme of the *laborious*). For what is hidden behind this condemnation of discontinuity is obviously the myth of Life itself: the Book must *flow* because fundamentally, despite centuries of intellectualism, our criticism wants literature to be, always, a spontaneous, gracious activity conceded by a god, a muse, and if the god or muse happens to be a little reticent, one must at least "conceal one's labor": to write is to secrete words within that great category of the continuous which is narrative; all Literature, even if it is didactic or intellectual (after all, we must put up with some of the novel's poor relations), should be a narrative, a flow of words in the service of an event or an idea which "makes its way" toward its dénouement or its conclusion: not to "narrate" its object is, for the Book, to commit suicide.

This is why, in the eyes of our stock criticism, guardian of the sacred Book, any analytical explanation of the work is ultimately mistrusted. The continuous work requires a corresponding cosmetic criticism which covers the work without dividing it up; the two preferred operations are: to summarize and to judge; but it is not good to break down the Book into parts which are too small: that is Byzantine, that destroys the work's ineffable life (by which is meant: its *course*, its murmuring stream, guarantee of its life); all the suspicion attached to thematic or structural criticism comes from this: to divide is to dissect, to destroy, to profane the Book's "mystery", *i.e.*, its continuity. Granted, our criticism has gone to school, where it has been taught to discern "schemas" and to recognize those of others; but the divisions of the "schema" (three or four at most) are the main breaks of the journey, that is all; what underlies the "schema" is the *detail:* the *detail* is not a fundamental raw material, it is inessential small-change: major ideas are coined into "details" without for a moment entertaining the notion that major ideas can be generated from the mere arrangement and disposition of "details". Paraphrase is therefore the rational operation of a criticism which demands of the Book, above all, that it be continuous: we "caress" the Book, just as we ask the Book's continuous language to "caress" Life, the soul, evil, etc. Thus the discontinuous Book is tolerated only in very special circumstances: either as a compilation of fragments (Heraclitus, Pascal), the work's *unfinished* character (but are these works actually unfinished?) corroborating *a contrario* the excellence of continuity, outside of which there may be a sketch but never perfection; or as a compilation of aphorisms, for the aphorism is a tiny, dense piece of continuity, the theatrical affirmation that the void is horrible. In short, to be a Book, to satisfy its essence as Book, the work must either flow (like a narrative) or gleam (like a flash of light). Outside these two systems lies violation, outrage of the Book, a not very tempting sin against the hygiene of Letters.

Confronted with this problem of continuity, the author of *Mobile* has proceeded to a rigorous inversion of rhetorical values. What does traditional rhetoric say? That we must construct a work in large masses and let the details take care of themselves: salute to the "general schema", a scornful denial that the idea can be parcelled out beyond the paragraph; this is why our entire art of writing is based on the notion of *development:* an idea "develops" and this development constitutes part of the "schema"; thus the Book is always reassuringly composed of a *small number of well-developed ideas*. (We might of course ask what a "development" is, contest the very notion, acknowledge its mythic character and affirm on the contrary that there is a profound solitude, a *matte* nature of the authentic idea, in which case the essential Book—if there must be such a thing as an essence of the Book—would be precisely Pascal's *Pensées* which "develop" nothing at all.) Now it is precisely this rhetorical order which the author of *Mobile* has reversed: in *Mobile* the "general schema" is of no account and the detail is raised to the rank of structure; the ideas are not "developed" but distributed.

To present America without any "rational" schema, as moreover to accomplish for any object whatever a schema of no account, is a very difficult thing, for every order has a meaning, even that of the absence of order, which has a name, which is disorder. To express an object without order and without disorder is a feat. Is it therefore necessary? It can be, insofar as any classification, whatever it may be, is responsible for a meaning. We are beginning to know, in small measure since Durkheim, in large measure since Lévi-Strauss, that taxonomy can be an important part of the study of societies: *tell me how you classify and I'll tell you who you are*; on a certain scale, there are neither natural nor rational schemas, but only "cultural" schemas, in which is invested either a collective representation of the world or an individual imagination, which we might call a taxonomic imagination, which remains to be studied but of which a man like Fourier furnishes a great example.

Since, then, *any* classification is a commitment, since men inevitably give a meaning to forms (and is there a purer form than a classification?), the *neutrality* of an order becomes not only an adult problem but even an esthetic problem—one difficult to solve. It will appear absurd (and provocative) to suggest that alphabetical order (which the author has used in part to present the States of the Union and for which he has been censured) is an intelligent order, *i.e.*, an order concerned with an esthetic concept of the intelligible. Yet the alphabet—not to mention the profound circularity it can be given, as the mystic metaphor of "alpha and omega" testifies—the alphabet is a means of institutionalizing a zero degree of classification; it startles us because our society has always given an exorbitant privilege to charged signs and crudely identified a zero degree of things with their negation: for us, there is little place and little consideration for the *neutral*, which is always felt *morally* as an impotence to be or to destroy. Yet it has been possible to consider the notion of *mana* as a zero degree of signification, which is enough to indicate the importance of the neutral in a realm of human thought.

It hardly need be said that in *Mobile* the alphabetical presentation of the States of the Union also *signifies*, insofar as it rejects all other classifications (of a geographical or picturesque type); it reminds the reader of the federal, hence arbitrary, nature of the country described, affords throughout the entire course of the book that civic expression which results from the fact that the United States is a constructed nation, a list of units, none of which takes pre-eminence over the rest. Michelet too, undertaking in his time a "study for a representation" of France, organized our country as if it were a chemical body, the negative at the center, the active parts at the edge, balancing each other across this central, this *neutral* void (for Michelet did not fear the neutral), out of which had come our royalty; for the United States, nothing of the kind is possible: the United States is an accumulation of stars: here the alphabet consecrates a history, a mythological way of thought, a civic sentiment; it is at bottom the classification of appropriation, that of encyclopedias, *i.e.*, of any knowledge which seeks to dominate the plural of things without destroying their identity, and it is true that the United States was won like an encyclopedic substance, thing after thing, State after State.

Formally, alphabetical order has another virtue: by breaking, by rejecting the "natural" affinities of the States, it obliges the discovery of other relations, quite as intelligent as the first, since the meaning of this whole combination of territories has come *afterwards*, once they have been laid out on the splendid alphabetical list of the Constitution. In short, the order of the letters says that in the United States, there is no contiguity of spaces except in the abstract; look at the map of the States: what order are we to follow? No sooner does it set out than our forefinger loses track, the accounting evades us; there is no such thing as a "natural" contiguity; but precisely for this reason, the poetic contiguity is born, the powerful one which obliges an image to leap from Alabama to Alaska, from Clinton (Kentucky) to Clinton (Indiana), etc. under the pressure of this truth of forms, of literal parallels, whose heuristic power we have learned from all modern poetry: if Alabama and Alaska were not such close alphabetical relatives, how would they be merged in that night which is the same and different: simultaneous and yet divided by a whole day?

Alphabetical classification is sometimes completed by other associations of spaces, quite as formal. There is no lack in the United States of cities of the same name; in relation to the *truth of the human heart,* this circumstance is trivial enough; the author of *Mobile* has nonetheless paid it the closest attention; in a continent marked by a permanent identity crisis, the penury of proper names participates profoundly in the American phenomenon: a continent that is too big, a lexicon that is too small—a whole part of America is in this strange friction of words and things. By connecting homonymic cities, by referring spatial contiguity to a purely phonic identity, Butor reveals a certain secret of things; and it is in this that he is a writer: the writer is not defined by the use of specialized tools which parade literature (*discourse, poem, concept, rhythm, wit, metaphor,* according to the peremptory catalogue of one of our critics), unless we regard literature as an object of hygiene, but by the power of *surprising,* by some formal device, a particular collusion of man and nature, *i.e.,* a meaning: and in this "surprise", it is form which guides, form which keeps watch, which instructs, which knows, which thinks, which "commits"; this is why form has no other judge than what it reveals; and here, what it reveals is a certain *knowledge* concerning America. That this knowledge should not be enunciated in intellectual terms, but according to a particular table of signs, is precisely . . . literature: a code which we must agree to decipher. After all, is *Mobile* more difficult to understand, is its knowledge more difficult to reconstitute, than the rhetorical or *précieux* code of our seventeenth century? It is true that in that century the reader agreed to learn how to read: it did not seem exorbitant to know mythology or rhetoric in order to receive the meaning of a poem or of a discourse.

The fragmentary order of *Mobile* has another significance. By destroying within discourse the notion of "part", it refers us to an infinitely sensitive mobility of closed elements. What are these elements? They have no form in themselves; they are neither ideas nor images nor sensations nor even notations, for they do not emerge from a projected restoration of experience; they are, rather, an enumeration of signaletic objects, here a press clipping, here a paragraph from a book, here a quote from a prospectus, here finally, less than all that, the name of an ice-cream flavor, the color of a car or a shirt, or just a simple proper name. As if the writer resorts to "takes", various soundings, with no regard for their material origin. Yet these "takes" without stable form, anarchic as they seem on the level of the *detail* (since, without rhetorical transcendance, they are indeed nothing but details), paradoxically become object-units on the broadest level there is, the most intellectual level one might say, which is the level of history. The units are categorized with remarkable consistency, within three "bundles": the Indians, 1890, today. The "representation" which *Mobile* gives of America is thus anything but modernist; it is a representation, in depth, in which the perspective dimension is constituted by the past. This past is doubtless brief, its chief moments are contiguous, it is not far from peyote to Howard Johnson ice-cream flavors. As a matter of fact, moreover, the extent of the American diachrony has no importance; what is important is that by constantly mixing *ex abrupto* Indian narratives, an 1890 guidebook and today's automobiles, the author perceives, and allows us to perceive, America in an *oneiric* perspective, with this one stipulation—original when it concerns America—that the dream here is not exotic but historical: *Mobile* is a profound *anamnesis,* all the more singular in that it was written by a Frenchman, *i.e.,* by a writer from a nation which has ample sustenance for memory, and in that it should be applied to a nation mythologically "new"; *Mobile* thus destroys the traditional function of the European in America, which consists of being astonished, in the name of his own past, to discover a nation without roots, the better to describe the surprises of a civilization at once endowed with technology and deprived of culture.

Now *Mobile* gives America a culture. Of course this enumerative, broken, a-rhetorical discourse offers no dissertation on values: it is precisely because American culture is neither moralistic nor literary, but, paradoxically, despite the eminently technological condition of the country, "natural", *i.e.,* naturalistic: in no country of the world, perhaps, is nature, in the quasi-romantic sense of the term, so visible; Butor tells us that the first monument of American culture is precisely Audubon's work, *i.e.,*a flora and a fauna *represented* by an artist outside of any school or tendency. This fact is in a sense symbolic: culture does not necessarily consist of experiencing nature in metaphors or styles, but in subjecting what is *immediately* given to an intelligible order; it is of little importance whether this order is that of a scrupulous recension (Audubon), of a mythic narrative (that of the young Indian peyote-eater), of a newspaper chronicle (the *New York World* reporter), or of a canned-goods label: in all these cases, the American language constitutes a first transformation of nature into culture, *i.e.,* essentially an act of institution. All *Mobile* does, in short, is to recuperate this institution of America for the Americans and to *represent* it; the book's subtitle is "Study for a Representation of the United States", and it has indeed a plastic finality: it aims to provide an equivalent for a great historical (or more precisely, trans-historical) tableau in which the objects, in their very discontinuity, are at once shards of time and first thoughts.

For there are objects in *Mobile,* and these objects assure the work its degree of credibility—not realistic, but oneiric credibility. The objects are *starters:* they are mediators of culture infinitely faster than ideas, producers of hallucinations just as active as the "situations": they are most often at the very bottom of the situations and give them that *exciting, i.e.,* strictly mobilizing character which makes a literature truly alive. In the murder of Agamemnon, there is the obsessional veil which serves to blind him; in Nero's love, there are those torches glittering on Junia's tears; in the humiliation Boule de Suif, there is that basket of food, described to the last detail; in *Nadja* there is the Tour Saint-Jacques, the Hôtel des Grands-Hommes; in *Jealousy* there is an insect squashed on the wall; in *Mobile,* there is peyote, 28 flavors of ice-cream, 10 colors of cars (there are also the different colors of the blacks). This is what makes a work into a *memorable* event; like a childhood memory in which, beyond all hierarchies learned and meanings imposed (genre: "truth of the human heart"), shimmers the light of the essential accessory.

A single wide horizon, in the form of a mythic history, a profound flavor of the objects cited in this great catalogue of the United States, such is the perspective of *Mobile, i.e.,* what makes it, in short, a work of familiar culture. If this classicism of substance has been misunderstood, no doubt it is because Butor has given his discourse a discontinuous form (*crumbs of thought* was the scornful phrase). We have seen how subversive any attack on the myth of rhetorical "development" appears. But in *Mobile* there is worse still: discontinuity is here all the more scandalous in that the poem's "units" are not "varied" (in the sense this word can have in music) but merely *repeated:* unalterable cells are infinitely combined, without there ever having been any internal transformation of the elements. If indeed we grant that a work can be composed of several themes (though thematic criticism, if it parcels out the theme too much, is sharply contested): in spite of everything, the theme remains a literary object insofar as it submits itself to variation, *i.e.,* to development. Now in *Mobile,* there is no theme, from this point of view, and therefore no obsession: the repetition of elements clearly has no psychological value here, but only a structural one: it does not "betray" the author, but, entirely interior to the object described, visibly derives from an art. Whereas in the traditional esthetic, all literary effort consists in disguising the theme, in giving it unexpected variations, in *Mobile* there is no variation, but only variety, and this variety is purely combinatory. The units of discourse are, in short, essentially defined by their function (in the mathematical sense of the term), not by their rhetorical nature: a metaphor exists in itself; a structural unit exists only by distinction, *i.e.,* by relation to other units. These units are—and must be—beings so perfectly *mobile* that by shifting them throughout his poem the author engenders a kind of huge animate body whose movement is one of perpetual transmission, not of internal "growth": thus, the title of the object: *Mobile, i.e.*, a scrupulously articulated armature all of whose breaks, by shifting very slightly (which the delicacy of the combinatory method permits), produce paradoxically the most connected movements.

For there is, after all, a continuity of discourse in *Mobile* which is immediately perceptible, provided we forget the rhetorical model on which we are accustomed to pattern our reading. Rhetorical continuity develops, amplifies; it will agree to repeat only if it can transform. *Mobile's* continuity repeats, but combines differently what it repeats. Thus rhetorical continuity never returns to what it has set forth, while *Mobile's* continuity returns, recurs, recalls: the new is ceaselessly accompanied by the old; it is, one might say, a fugal continuity, in the course of which identifiable fragments ceaselessly reappear. The example of music is useful here, for the most connected of the arts actually possesses only the most discontinuous of raw materials: in music—at least, in our music—there are only thresholds, relations of differences, and constellations of these differences ("routines", one might say). *Mobile's* composition derives from this same dialectic of difference, which we also find in other forms of continuity: though who would dare say that Webern or Mondrian have produced an art "in crumbs"? Moreover, all these artists have in no way invented discontinuity merely in order to defeat it: discontinuity is the fundamental status of all communication: signs never exist unless they are discreet. The esthetic problem is simply how to mobilize this inevitable discontinuity, how to give it a rhythm, a tempo, a history. Classical rhetoric has given its answer, a masterly one for centuries, by erecting an esthetic of *variation* (of which the notion of "development" is merely the crude myth); but there is another possible rhetoric, a rhetoric of transmission: modern, no doubt, since we find it only in certain avant-garde works, and yet, elsewhere, how old! Is not every mythic narrative, according to Lévi-Strauss, produced by a *mobilization* of recurrent units, of autonomous *series* (the musicians would say), whose *infinitely possible* shifts afford the work the responsibility of its choice, *i.e.*, its singularity, *i.e.*, its meaning?

For *Mobile* has a meaning, and this meaning is perfectly *human* (since the *human* is what our stock criticism calls for here), *i.e.*, it refers on the one hand to the serious history of a man, who is the author, and on the other to the real nature of an object, which is America. *Mobile* occupies in Michel Butor's itinerary a place which is obviously not gratuitous. We know from the author himself that his *oeuvre* is *constructed;* this banal term covers a very precise project, one very different from the kind of "construction" recommended in the classroom; taken literally, it implies that the work reproduces an interior model assembled by the meticulous arrangement of parts: this model is, specifically, a *maquette:* the author works from a *maquette,* and we immediately see the structural signification of this art: the *maquette* is not, strictly speaking, a ready-made structure which the work must transform into an event; rather it is a structure to be realized starting from pieces of events, pieces which the author tries to bring together, to separate, to arrange, without altering their material figuration; this is why the *maquette* participates in that art of assemblage which Lévi-Strauss has just given its structural dignity (in *The Savage Mind*). It is possible that, starting from poetry—poetry, which is the exemplary art of literary assemblage (it is understood that the word has no pejorative nuance here), since in poetry word-events are transformed by mere arrangement into a system of meaning—Michel Butor has conceived his novels as a single structural investigation whose principle might be this: it is by *tieing* fragments of events together that meaning is generated, it is by tirelessly transforming these events into functions that the structure is erected: the writer (poet, novelist, chronicler) *sees* the meaning of the inert units in front of him only be *relating* them: thus the work has that simultaneously ludic and serious character which marks every great question: it is a masterly puzzle, *the puzzle of the best possibility.* We then see how much *Mobile* represents, in this direction, an urgent investigation (corroborated by *Vorte Faust,* which was written immediately afterwards, and in which the spectator himself is invited to organize the "routines" of the puzzle, to venture into the structural combination): art here serves a serious question, which we find throughout all of Michel Butor's *oeuvre,* a question which is that of the world's *possibility,* or to speak in a more Liebnitzian fashion, of its *compossibility.* And if the method is explicit in *Mobile,* it is because it has encountered in America (here we deliberately call the United States by its mythic name) a privileged object which art can account for only by an incessant *trial* of contiguities, of shifts, of returns, of entrances bearing on denominative enumerations, oneiric fragments, legends, flavors, colors, or simple toponymic noises, the sum of which *represents* this compossiblity of the New World. And here again, *Mobile* is at once very new and very old: this great catalogue of America has for distant ancestors those epic catalogues, gigantic and purely denominative enumerations of ships, of regiments and captains, which Homer and Aeschylus inserted in their narratives in order to testify to the infinite "compossibility" of war and of power.

Walter Benjamin,* or Nostalgia

BY FREDRIC JAMESON

Every feeling is attached to an a priori object, and the presentation of the latter is the phenomenology of the former.
—*Ursprung des deutschen Trauerspeils*

So the melancholy that speaks from the pages of Benjamin's essays—private depressions, professional discouragement, the dejection of the outsider, the distress in the face of a political and historical nightmare—searches the past for an adequate object, for some emblem or image at which, as in religious meditation, the mind can stare itself out, into which it can discharge its morbid humors and know momentary, if only an esthetic, relief. It finds it: in the Germany of the thirty years war, in the Paris of the late nineteenth century ("Paris—the capitol of the nineteenth century"). For they are both—the baroque and the modern—in their very essence allegorical, and they match the thought process of the theorist of allegory, which, disembodied intention searching for some external object in which to take shape, is itself already allegorical *avant la lettre*.

Indeed, it seems to me that Walter Benjamin's thought is best grasped as an allegorical one, as a set of parallel, discontinuous levels of meditation which is not without resemblance to that ultimate model of allegor-

Walter Benjamin was born in 1892 of a wealthy Jewish family in Berlin. Unfit for service in World War I, he studied for a time in Bern, and returning to Berlin in 1920 tried unsuccessfully to found a literary review there, before turning to academic life as a career. His *Origins of German Tragedy* was however refused as a Ph.D. thesis at the University of Frankfurt in 1925. Meanwhile, he had begun to translate Proust, and, under the influence of Lukacs' *History and Class Consciousness*, became a Marxist, visiting Moscow in 1926–27. After 1933, he emigrated to Paris and pursued work on his unfinished project *Paris: Capitol of the Nineteenth Century*. He committed suicide at the Spanish border after an unsuccessful attempt to flee occupied France in 1940. He numbered among close friends and intellectual acquaintances, at various moments of his life, Ernst Bloch, Gershom Scholem, T. W. Adorno, and Bert Brecht.

ical composition described by Dante in his letter to Can Grande della Scala, where he speaks of the four dimensions of his poem: the literal (his hero's earthly destinies), the allegorical (the fate of his soul), the moral (in which the encounters of the main character resume one aspect or another of the life of Christ), and the anagogical (where the individual drama of Dante foreshadows the progress of the human race towards the Last Judgement)*. It will not be hard to adapt this scheme to twentieth century reality, if for literal we read simply *psychological,* and for allegorical *ethical;* if for the dominant archetypal pattern of the life of Christ we substitute some more modern one (and for myself, replacing religion with the religion of art, this will be the coming into being of the work of art itself, the incarnation of meaning in Language); if finally we replace theology with politics, and make of Dante's eschatology an earthly one, where the human race finds its salvation, not in eternity, but in History itself.

Benjamin's work seems to me to be marked by a painful straining towards a wholeness or unity of experience which the historical situation threatens to shatter at every turn. A vision of a world of ruins and fragments, an ancient chaos of whatever nature on the point of overwhelming consciousness—these are some of the images that seem to recur, either in Benjamin himself or in your own mind as you read him. The idea of wholeness or of unity is of course not original with him: how many modern philosophers have described the "damaged existence" we lead in modern society, the psychological impairment of the division of labor and of specialization, the general alienation and dehumanization of modern life and the specific forms such alienation takes? Yet for the most part these analyses remain abstract; and through them speaks the resignation of the intellectual specialist to his own maimed present; the dream of wholeness, where it persists, attaches itself to someone else's future. Benjamin is unique among these thinkers in that he wants to save his own life as well: hence the peculiar fascination of his writings, incomparable not only for their dialectical intelligence, nor even for the poetic sensibility they express, but above all, perhaps, for the manner in which the autobiographical part of his mind finds symbolic satisfaction in the shape of ideas abstractly, in objective guises, expressed.

Psychologically, the drive towards unity takes the form of an obsession with the past and with memory. Genuine memory determines "whether the individual can have a picture of himself, whether he can master his own experience." "Every passion borders on chaos, but the

*It is, at least, a more familiar and less intimidating model than that proposed by Benjamin himself, in a letter to Max Rychner: "I have never been able to inquire and think otherwise than, if I may so put it, in a theological sense—namely in conformity with the Talmudic prescription regarding the forty-nine levels of meaning in every passage of the Torah."

passion of the collector borders on the chaos of memory" (and it was in the image of the collector that Benjamin found one of his most comfortable identities). "Memory forges the chain of tradition that passes events on from generation to generation." Strange reflexions, these—strange subjects of reflexion for a Marxist (one thinks of Sartre's acid comment on his orthodox Marxist contemporaries: "materialism is the subjectivity of those who are ashamed of their own subjectivity"). Yet Benjamin kept faith with Proust, whom he translated, long after his own discovery of communism; like Proust also, he saw in his favorite poet Baudelaire an analogous obsession with reminiscence and involuntary memory; and he followed his literary master in the fragmentary evocation of his own childhood called *Berliner Kindheit um 1900;* he also began the task of recovering his own existence with short essayistic sketches, records of dreams, of isolated impressions and experiences, which however he was unable to carry to the greater writer's ultimate narrative unity.

He was perhaps more conscious of what prevents us from assimilating our life experience than of the form such a perfected life would take: fascinated, for example, with Freud's distinction between unconscious memory and the conscious art of recollection, which was for Freud basically a way of destroying or eradicating what the former was designed to preserve: "consciousness appears in the system of perception *in place* of the memory traces . . . consciousness and the leaving behind of a memory trace are within the same system mutually incompatible." For Freud, the function of consciousness is the defense of the organism against shocks from the external environment: in this sense traumas, hysterical repetitions, dreams, are ways in which the incompletely assimilated shock attempts to make its way through to consciousness and hence to ultimate appeasement. In Benjamin's hands, this idea becomes an instrument of historical description, a way of showing how in modern society, perhaps on account of the increasing quantity of shocks of all kinds to which the organism is henceforth subjected, these defense mechanisms are no longer personal ones: a whole series of mechanical substitutes intervenes between consciousness and its objects shielding us perhaps, yet at the same time depriving us of any way of assimilating what happens to us or to any genuinely personal experience. Thus, to give only one example, the newspaper stands as a shock-absorber of novelty, numbing us to what might perhaps otherwise overwhelm us, but at the same time rendering its events neutral and impersonal, making of them what by definition has no common denominator with our private existences.

Experience is moreover socially conditioned in that it depends on a certain rhythm of recurrences and similarities, on certain categories of likeness in events which are properly cultural in origin. Thus even in

Proust and Baudelaire, who lived in relatively fragmented societies, ritualistic devices, often unconscious, are primary elements in the construction of form: we recognize them in the "vie anteriéure" and the correspondences of Baudelaire, in the ceremonies of salon life in Proust. And where the modern writer tries to create a perpetual present—as in Kafka—the mystery inherent in the events seems to result not so much from their novelty as from the feeling that they have merely been forgotten, that they are in some sense "familiar," in the haunting significance which Baudelaire lent that word. Yet as society increasingly decays, such rhythms of experience are less and less available.

At this point, however, psychological description seems to pass over insensibly into moral judgement, into a vision of the reconciliation of past and present which is somehow an ethical one. But for the western reader the whole ethical dimension of Benjamin's work is likely to be perplexing, incorporating as it does a kind of ethical psychology which, codified by Goethe, has become traditional in Germany and deeply rooted in the German language, but for which we have no equivalent. This *Lebensweisheit* is indeed a kind of halfway house between the classical idea of a fixed human nature, with its psychology of the humors, passions, sins or character types; and the modern idea of pure historicity, of the determining influence of the situation or environment. As a compromise in the domain of the individual personality, it is not unlike the compromise of Hegel in the realm of history itself: and where for the latter a general meaning was immanent to the particular moment of history, for Goethe in some sense the overall goal of the personality and of its development is built into the particular emotion in question, or latent in the particular stage in the individual's growth. For the system is based on a vision of the full development of the personality (a writer like Gide, deeply influenced by Goethe, gives but a pale and narcissistic reflexion of this ethic, which expressed middle class individualism at the moment of its historic triumph); it neither aims to bend the personality to some purely external standard of discipline, as is the case with Christianity, nor to abandon it to the meaningless accidents of empirical psychology, as is the case with most modern ethics, but rather sees the individual psychological experience as something which includes within itself seeds of development, something in which ethical growth is inherent as a kind of interiorized Providence. So, for example, the closing lines of *Wilhelm Meister:* "You make me think of Saul, the son of Kish, who went forth to seek his father's asses and found, instead, a kingdom!"

It is however characteristic of Benjamin that in his most complete expression of this Goethean ethic, the long essay on *Elective Affinities,* he should lay more stress on the dangers that menace the personality than on the picture of its ultimate development. For this essay, which speaks the language of Goethean life-psychology, is at the same time a critique of the reactionary forces in German society which made this psychology their own: working with the concept of myth, it is at the same time an attack on the obscurantist ideologies which made the notion of myth their rallying cry. In this, the polemic posture of Benjamin can be instructive for all those of us who, undialectically, are tempted simply to reject the concept of myth altogether, on account of the ideological uses to which it is ordinarily put; for whom this concept, like related ones of magic or charisma, seems not to aim at a rational analysis of the irrational but rather at a consecration of it through language.

But for Benjamin *Elective Affinities* may be considered a mythical work, on condition we understand myth as that element from which the work seeks to free itself: as some earlier chaos of instinctual forces, inchoate, natural, pre-individualistic, as that which is destructive of genuine individuality, that which consciousness must overcome if it is to attain any real autonomy of its own, if it is to accede to any properly human level of existence. Is it far-fetched to see in this opposition between mythical forces and the individual spirit a disguised expression of Benjamin's thoughts about past and present, an image of the way in which a remembering consciousness masters its past and brings to light what would otherwise be lost in the prehistory of the organism? Nor should we forget that the essay on *Elective Affinities* is itself a way of recovering the past, this time a cultural past, one given over to the dark mythical forces of a proto-fascist tradition.

Benjamin's dialectical skill can be seen in the way this idea of myth is expressed through attention to the form of Goethe's novel, no doubt one of the most eccentric of Western literature, in its combination of an eighteenth century ceremoniousness with symbols of a strangely artificial, allegorical quality: objects which appear in the blankness of the non-visual narrative style as though isolated against a void, as though fateful with a kind of geometrical meaning—cautiously selected detail of landscape, too symmetrical not to have significance, analogies, such as the chemical one that gives the novel its title, too amply developed not to be emblematic. The reader is of course familiar with symbolism everywhere in the modern novel; but in general the symbolism is built into the work, like a sheet of instructions supplied inside the box along with the puzzle pieces. Here we feel the burden of guilt laid upon us as readers, that we lack what strikes us almost as a culturally inherited mode of thinking, accessible only to those who are that culture's members: and no doubt the Goethean system does project itself in some such way, in its claim to universality.

The originality of Benjamin is to cut across the sterile opposition between the arbitrary interpretations of the symbol on the one hand,

and the blank failure to see what it means on the other: *Elective Affinities* is to be read, not as a novel by a symbolic writer, but as a novel *about* symbolism. If objects of a symbolic nature loom large in this work, it is not because they were chosen to underline the theme of adultery in some decorative manner, but rather because the real underlying subject is precisely the surrender over into the power of symbols of people who have lost their autonomy as human beings. "When people sink to this level, even the life of apparently lifeless things grows strong. Gundolf quite rightly underlined the crucial role of objects in this story. Yet the intrusion of the thing-like into human life is precisely a criterion of the mythical universe." We are required to read these symbolic objects to the second power: not so much directly to decipher a one-to-one meaning from them, as to sense that of which the very fact of symbolism is itself symptomatic.

And as with the objects, so also with the characters: it has for example often been remarked that the figure of Ottilie, the rather saintly young woman around whom the drama turns, is somehow different in its mode of characterization from the other, more realistically and psychologically drawn characters. For Benjamin however this is not so much a flaw, or an inconsistency, as a clue: Ottilie is not reality but appearance, and it is this which the rather external and visual mode of characterization conveys. "It is clear that these Goethean characters come before us not so much as figures shaped from external models, nor wholly imaginary in their invention, but rather entranced somehow, as though under a spell. Hence a kind of obscurity about them which is foreign to the purely visual, to painting for instance, and which is characteristic only of that whose very essence is pure appearance. For appearance is in this work not so much presented as a theme as it is rather implicit in the very nature and mode of the presentation itself."

This moral dimension of Benjamin's work, like Goethe's own, clearly represents an uneasy balance, a transitional moment between the psychological on the one hand, and the esthetic or the historical on the other. The mind cannot long be satisfied with this purely ethical description of the events of the book as the triumph of fateful, mythical forces; it strains for historical and social explanation, and at length Benjamin himself is forced to express the conclusion "that the writer shrouds in silence: namely, that passion loses all its rights, under the laws of genuine human morality, when it seeks to make a pact with wealthy middle-class security." But in Benjamin's work, this inevitable slippage of morality into history and politics, characteristic of all modern thought, is mediated by esthetics, is revealed by attention to the qualities of the work of art, just as the above conclusion was articulated by the analysis of those aspects of *Elective Affinities* that might best have been described as allegorical rather than symbolic.

For in one sense Benjamin's life work can be seen as a kind of vast museum, a passionate collection, of all shapes and varieties of allegorical objects; and his most substantial work centers on that enormous studio of allegorical decoration which is the Baroque.

The Origins—not so much of German *tragedy* ("Tragödie")—as of German *Trauerspiel:* the distinction, for which English has no equivalent, is crucial to Benjamin's interpretation. For "tragedy," which he limits to ancient Greece as a phenomenon, is a sacrificial drama in which the hero is offered up to the Gods for atonement. *Trauerspiel,* on the other hand, which encompasses the baroque generally, Elizabethans and Calderon as well as the 17th century German playwrights, is something that might best be initially characterized as a pageant: a funeral pageant—so might the word be most adequately rendered.

As a form it reflects the baroque vision of history as chronicle, as the relentless turning of the wheel of fortune, a ceaseless succession across the stage of the world's mighty, princes, popes, empresses in their splendid costumes, courtiers, masqueraders and poisoners—a dance of death produced with all the finery of a Renaissance triumph. For chronicle is not yet historicity in the modern sense: "No matter how deeply the baroque intention penetrates the detail of history, its microscopic analysis never ceases to search painstakingly for political calculation in a substance seen as pure intrigue. Baroque drama knows historical events only as the depraved activity of conspirators. Not a breath of genuine revolutionary conviction in any of the countless rebels who appear before the baroque sovereign, himself immobilized in the posture of a Christian martyr. Discontent—such is the classic motive for action." And such historical time, mere succession without development, is in reality secretly spatial, and takes the court (and the stage) as its privileged spatial embodiment.

At first glance, it would appear that this vision of life as chronicle is in *The Origins of German Tragedy,* a pre-Marxist work, accounted for in an idealistic manner: as Lutherans, Benjamin says, the German baroque playwrights knew a world in which belief was utterly separate from works, in which not even the Calvinistic preordained harmony intervenes to restore a little meaning to the succession of empty acts that make up human life, the world thus remaining as a body without a soul, as the shell of an object divested of any visible function. Yet it is at least ambiguous whether this intellectual and metaphysical position causes the psychological experience that is at the heart of baroque tragedy, or whether it is not itself merely one of the various expressions, relatively abstract, through which an acute and concrete emotion tries to manifest itself. For the key to the latter is the central enigmatic figure of the prince himself, halfway between a tyrant justly assassinated and a martyr suffering his passion: interpreted allegorically, he stands as the embodiment of Melancholy in a stricken world, and Hamlet is his most complete expression. This interpretation of the funereal pageant as a basic expression of pathological melancholy has the advantage of accounting both for form and content at the same time.

Content in the sense of the characters' motivations: "The indecision of the prince is nothing but saturnine *acedia*. The influence of Saturn makes people 'apathetic, indecisive, slow.' The tyrant falls on account of the sluggishness of his emotions. In the same fashion, the character of the courtier is marked by faithlessness—another trait of the predominance of Saturn. The courtier's mind, as portrayed in these tragedies, is fluctuation itself: betrayal is his very element. It is to be attributed neither to hastiness of composition nor to insufficient characterization that the parasites in these plays scarcely need any time for reflection at all before betraying their lords and going over to the enemy. Rather, the lack of character evident in their actions, partly conscious Machiavellianism to be sure, reflects an inconsolable, despondent surrender to an impenetrable conjunction of baleful constellations, a conjunction that seems to have taken on a massive, almost thing-like character. Crown, royal purple, scepter, all are in the last analysis the properties of the tragedy of fate, and they carry about them an aura of destiny to which the courtier is the first to submit as to some portent of disaster. His faithlessness to his fellow men corresponds to the deeper, more contemplative faith he keeps with these material emblems."

Once again Benjamin's sensitivity is for those moments in which human beings find themselves given over into the power of things; and the familiar content of baroque tragedy—that melancholy which we recognize from *Hamlet*—those vices of melancholy—lust, treason, sadism—so predominant in the lesser Elizabethans, in Webster for instance—veers about slowly into a question of form, into the problem of objects, which is to say of allegory itself. For allegory is precisely the dominant mode of expression of a world in which things have been for whatever reason utterly sundered from meanings, from spirit, from genuine human existence.

And in the light of this new examination of the baroque from the point of view of form rather than of content, little by little the brooding melancholy figure at the center of the play himself alters in focus, the hero of the funereal pageant little by little becomes transformed into the baroque playwright himself, the allegorist par excellence, in Benjamin's terminology the *Grübler:* that superstitious, overparticular reader of omens who returns in a more nervous, modern guise in the hysterical heroes of Poe and Baudelaire. "Allegories are in the realm of thoughts what ruins are in the realm of things"; and it is clear that Benjamin is himself first and foremost among these depressed and hyperconscious visionaries who people his pages. "Once the object has beneath the brooding look of Melancholy become allegorical, once life has flowed out of it, the object itself remains behind, dead, yet preserved for all eternity; it lies before the allegorist, given over to him utterly, for good or ill. In other words, the object itself is henceforth incapable of projecting any meaning on its own; it can only take on that meaning which the allegorist wishes to lend it. He instills it with his own meaning, himself descends to inhabit it: and this must be understood not psychologically but in an ontological sense. In his hands the thing in question becomes something else, speaks of something else, becomes for him the key to some realm of hidden knowledge, as whose emblem he honors it. This is what constitutes the nature of allegory as script."

Script rather than language, the letter rather than the spirit; into this the baroque world shatters, strangely legible signs and emblems nagging at the too curious mind, a procession moving slowly across a stage, laden with occult significance. In this sense, for the first time it seems to me that allegory is restored to us—not as a gothic monstrosity of purely historical interest, nor as in C. S. Lewis a sign of the medieval health of the (religious) spirit, but rather as a pathology with which in the modern world we are only too familiar. The tendency of our own criticism has been to exalt symbol at the expense of allegory (even though the privileged objects proposed by that criticism—English mannerism and Dante—are more properly allegorical in nature; in this, as in other aspects of his sensibility, Benjamin has much in common with a writer like T. S. Eliot). It is, perhaps, the expression of a value rather than a description of existing poetic phenomena: for the distinction between symbol and allegory is that between a complete reconciliation between object and spirit and a mere will to such reconciliation. The usefulness of Benjamin's analysis lies however in his insistence on a temporal distinction as well: the symbol is the instantaneous, the lyrical, the single moment in time; and this temporal limitation expresses perhaps the historical impossibility in the modern world for genuine reconciliation to last in time, to be anything more than a lyrical, accidental present. Allegory is on the contrary the privileged mode of our own life in time, a clumsy deciphering of meaning from moment to moment, the painful attempt to restore a continuity to heterogeneous, disconnected instants. "Where the symbol as it fades shows the face of Nature in the light of salvation, in allegory it is the *facies hippocratica* of history that lies like a frozen landscape before the eye of the beholder. History in everything that it has of the unseasonable, painful, abortive, expresses itself in that face—nay rather in that death's head. And as true as it may be that such an allegorical mode is utterly lacking in any 'symbolic' freedom of expression, in any classical harmony of feature, in anything human—what is expressed here portentously in the form of a riddle is not only the nature of human life in general, but also the biographical historicity of the individual in its most natural and organically corrupted form. This—the baroque, earthbound exposition of history as the story of the world's suffering—is the very essence of allegorical perception; history takes on meaning only in the stations of its agony and decay. The amount of meaning is in exact proportion to the presence of death and the power of decay, since death is that which traces the surest line between Physis and meaning."

And what marks baroque allegory holds for the allegory of modern times, for Baudelaire as well: only in the latter it is interiorized: "Baroque allegory saw the corpse from the outside only. Baudelaire sees it from within." Or again: "Commemoration [Andenken] is the secularized version of the adoration of holy relics . . . Commemoration is the complement to experience. In commemoration there finds expression the increasing alienation of human beings, who take inventories of their past as of lifeless merchandise. In the nineteenth century allegory abandons the outside world, only to colonize the inner. Relics come from the corpse, commemoration from the dead occurrences of the past which are euphemistically known as experience."

Yet in these late essays on modern literature a new preoccupation appears, which signals the passage in Benjamin from the predominantly esthetic to the historical and political dimension itself. This is the attention to machines, to mechanical inventions, which characteristically first appears in the realm of esthetics itself in the study of the movies ("The Reproduceable Work of Art") and only later is extended to the study of history in general (as in the essay "Paris—Capitol of the 19th Century," in which the feeling of life in this period is conveyed by a description of the new objects and inventions characteristic of it—the passageways, the use of cast iron, the Daguerrotype and panorama, the expositions, advertising). It is important to point out that however materialistic such an approach to history may seem, nothing is farther from Marxism than the stress on invention and technique as the primary cause of historical change. Indeed it seems to me that such theories (of the kind for which the steam engine is the cause of the industrial revolution, and which have recently been rehearsed yet again, in streamlined modernistic form in the works of Marshall McLuhan) function as a substitute for Marxist historiography in the way in which they offer a feeling of concreteness comparable to economic subject matter, at the same time that they dispense with any consideration of the human factors of classes and of the social organization of production.

Benjamin's fascination with the role of inventions in history seems to me most comprehensible in psychological or esthetic terms. If we follow, for instance, his meditation on the role of the passerby and the crowd in Baudelaire, we find that after the evocation of Baudelaire's physical and stylistic characteristics, after the discussion of shock and organic defenses outlined earlier in this essay, the inner logic of Benjamin's material leads him to material invention: "Comfort isolates. And at the same time it shifts its possessor closer to the power of physical mechanisms. With the invention of matches around the middle of the century, there begins a whole series of novelties which have this in common that they replace a complicated set of operations with a single stroke of the hand. This development goes on in many different spheres at the same time: it is evident among others in the telephone, where in place of the continuous movement with which the crank of the older model had to be turned a single lifting of the receiver now suffices. Among the various elaborate gestures required to prepare the photographic apparatus, that of 'snapping' the photograph was particularly consequential. Pressing the finger once is enough to freeze an event for unlimited time. The apparatus lends the instant a posthumous shock, so to speak. And beside tactile experiences of this kind we find optical ones as well, such as the classified ads in a newspaper, or the traffic in a big city. To move through the latter involves a whole series of shocks and collisions. At dangerous intersections, impulses crisscross the pedestrian like charges in a battery. Baudelaire describes the man who plunges into the crowd as a reservoir of electrical energy. Thereupon he calls him, thus singling out the experience of shock, 'a kaleidoscope endowed with consciousness'." And Benjamin goes on to complete this catalogue with a description of the worker and his psychological subjection to the operation of the machine in the factory. Yet it seems to me that alongside the value of this passage as an analysis of the psychological effect of machinery, it has for Benjamin a secondary intention, it satisfies a deeper psychological requirement perhaps in some ways even more important than the official intellectual one; and that is to serve as a concrete embodiment for the state of mind of Baudelaire. The essay indeed begins with a relatively disembodied psychological state: the poet faced with the new condition of language in modern times, faced with the debasement of journalism, the inhabitant of the great city faced with the increasing shocks and perceptual numbness of daily life. These phenomena are intensely familiar to Benjamin, but somehow he seems to feel them as insufficiently "rendered": he cannot possess them spiritually, he cannot express them adequately, until he finds some sharper and more concrete physical image in which to embody them. The machine, the list of inventions, is precisely such an image; and it will be clear to the reader that we consider such a passage, in appearance a historical analysis, as in reality an exercise in allegorical meditation, in the locating of some fitting emblem in which to anchor the peculiar and nervous modern state of mind which was his subject-matter.

For this reason the preoccupation with machines and inventions in Benjamin does not lead to a theory of historical causality; rather it finds its completion elsewhere, in a theory of the modern object, in the notion of "aura." Aura for Benjamin is the equivalent in the modern world, where it still persists, for what anthropologists call the "sacred" in primitive societies; it is in the world of things what "mystery" is in the world of human events, what "charisma" is in the world of human beings. In a secularized universe it is perhaps easier to locate at the moment of its disappearance, the cause of which is in general technical invention, the replacement of human perception with those substitutes for and mechanical extensions of perception which are machines. Thus it is easy to see how in the movies, in the "reproduceable work of art," that aura which originally resulted from the physical presence of actors in the here-and-now of the theater is short-circuited by the new technical advance (and then replaced, in genuine Freudian symptom-formation, by the attempt to endow the stars with a new kind of personal aura of their own off the screen).

Yet in the world of objects, this intensity of physical presence which constitutes the aura of something can perhaps best be expressed by the image of the look, the intelligence returned: "The experience of aura is based on the transposition of a social reaction onto the relationship of the lifeless or of nature to man. The person we look at, the person who believes himself looked at, looks back at us in return. To experience the aura of a phenomenon means to endow it with the power to look back in return."

And elsewhere he defines aura thus: "The single, unrepeatable experience of distance, no matter how close it may be. While resting on a summer afternoon, to follow the outline of a mountain against the horizon or of a branch that casts its shadow on the viewer, means to breathe the aura of the mountain, of the branch." Aura is thus in a sense the opposite of allegorical perception, in that in it a mysterious wholeness of objects becomes visible. And where the broken fragments of allegory represented a thing-world of destructive forces in which human autonomy was drowned, the objects of aura represent perhaps the setting of a kind of utopia, a utopian present, not shorn of the past but having absorbed it, a kind of plenitude of existence in the world of things, if only for the briefest instant. Yet this utopian component of Benjamin's thought, put to flight as it is by the mechanized present of history, is available to the thinker only in a simpler cultural past.

Thus it is his one evocation of a non-allegorical art, his essay on Nikolai Leskow, "The Teller of Tales," which is perhaps his masterpiece. As with actors faced with the technical advance of the reproduceable art-work, so also with the tale in the face of modern communications systems, and in particular of the newspaper. The function of the newspapers is to absorb the shocks of novelty, and by numbing the organism to them to sap their intensity. Yet the tale, always constructed around some novelty, was designed on the contrary to preserve its force; where the mechanical form "exhausts" ever increasing quantities of new material, the older word-of-mouth communication is that which recommends itself to memory. Its reproduceability is not mechanical, but natural to consciousness; indeed, that which allows the story to be remembered, to seem "memorable" is at the same time the means of its assimilation to the personal experience of the listeners as well.

It is instructive to compare this analysis by Benjamin of the tale (and its implied distinction from the novel) with that of Sartre, so similar in some ways, and yet so different in its ultimate emphasis. For both, the two forms are opposed not only in their social origins—the tale springing from collective life, the novel from solitude—and not only in their raw material—the tale using what everyone can recognize as common experience, the novel that which is uncommon and highly individualistic—but also and primarily in the relationship to death and to eternity. Benjamin quotes Valéry: "It is almost as though the disappearance of the idea of eternity were related to the increasing distaste for any kind of work of long duration in time." Concurrent with the disappearance of the genuine story is the increasing concealment of death and dying in our society: for the authority of the story ultimately derives from the authority of death, which lends every event a once-and-for-all uniqueness. "A man who died at the age of thirty-five is at every point in his life a man who is going to die at the age of thirty-five": so Benjamin describes our apprehension of characters in the tale, as the anti-psychological, the simplified representatives of their own destinies. But what appeals to his sensitivity to the archaic is precisely what Sartre condemns as inauthentic: namely the violence to genuine lived human experience, which never in the freedom of its own present feels itself as fate, for which fate and destiny are always characteristic of other people's experience, seen from the outside as something closed and thing-like. For this reason Sartre opposes the tale (it is true that he is thinking of the late-nineteenth century well-made story, which catered to a middle-class audience, rather than to the relatively anonymous folk product of which Benjamin speaks) to the novel, whose task is precisely to render this open experience of consciousness in the present, of freedom, rather than the optical illusion of fate.

There can be no doubt that this opposition corresponds to a historical experience: the older tale, indeed the classical nineteenth century novel as well, expressed a social life in which the individual faced single-shot, irreparable chances and opportunities, in which he had to play everything on a single roll of the dice, in which his life did therefore properly tend to take on the appearance of fate or destiny, of a story that can be told. Whereas in the modern world (which is to say, in Western Europe and the United States), economic prosperity is such that nothing is ever really irrevocable in this sense: hence the philosophy of freedom, hence the modernistic literature of consciousness of which Sartre is here a theorist: hence also, the decay of plot, for where nothing is irrevocable (in the absence of death in Benjamin's sense) there is no story to tell either, there is only a series of experiences of equal weight whose order is indiscriminately reversible.

Benjamin is as aware as Sartre of the way in which the tale, with its appearance of destiny, does violence to our lived experience in the present: but for him it does justice to our experience of the past. Its "inauthenticity" is to be seen as a mode of commemoration, so that it does not really matter any longer whether the young man dead in his prime was aware of his own lived experience as fate: for us, henceforth remembering him, we always think of him, at the various stages of his life, as one about to become this destiny, and the tale thus gives us "the hope of warming our own chilly existence upon a death about which we read."

The tale is not only a psychological mode of relating to the past, of commemorating it: it is for Benjamin also a mode of contact with a vanished form of social and historical existence as well; and it is in this correlation between the activity of story-telling and the concrete form of a certain historically determinate mode of production that Benjamin can serve as a model of Marxist literary criticism at its most revealing. The twin sources of story-telling find their archaic embodiment in "the settled cultivator on the one hand and the seafaring merchant on the other. Both forms of life have in fact produced their own characteristic type of story-teller . . . A genuine extension of the possibilities of story-telling to its greatest historical range is however not possible without the most thorough-going fusion of the two archaic types. Such a fusion was realized during the middle ages in the artisanal associations and guilds. The sedentary master and the wandering apprentices worked together in the same room; indeed, every master had himself been a wandering apprentice before settling down at home or in some foreign city. If peasants and sailors were the inventors of story-telling, the guild system proved to be the place of its highest development." The tale is thus the product of an artisan culture, a hand-made product, like a cobbler's shoe or a pot; and like such a hand-made object, "the touch of the story-teller clings to it like the trace of the potter's hand on the glazed surface."

In his ultimate statement of the relationship of literature to politics, Benjamin seems to have tried to bring to bear on the problems of the present this method, which had known success in dealing with the objects of the past. Yet the transposition is not without its difficulties, and Benjamin's conclusions remain problematical, particularly in his unresolved, ambiguous attitude towards modern industrial civilization, which fascinated him as much as it seems to have depressed him. The problem of propaganda in art can be solved, he maintains, by attention, not so much to the content of the work of art, as to its form: a progressive work of art is one which utilizes the most advanced artistic techniques, one in which therefore the artist lives his activity as a technician, and through this technical work finds a unity of purpose with the industrial worker. "The solidarity of the specialist with the proletariat . . . can never be anything but a mediated one." This communist "politicalisation of art," which he opposed to the fascist "estheticalisation of the machine," was designed to harness to the cause of revolution that modernism to which other Marxist critics (Lukacs, for instance) were hostile. And there can be no doubt that Benjamin first came to a radical politics through his experience as a specialist: through his growing awareness, within the domain of his own specialized artistic activity, of the crucial influence on the work of art of changes in the public, in technique, in short of History itself. But although in the realm of the history of art the historian can no doubt show a parallelism between specific technical advances in a given art and the general development of the economy as a whole, it is difficult to see how a technically advanced and difficult work of art can have anything but a "mediated" effect politically. Benjamin was of course lucky in the artistic example which lay before him: for he illustrates his thesis with the epic theater of Brecht, perhaps indeed the only modern artistic innovation that *has* had direct and revolutionary political impact. But even here the situation is ambiguous: an astute critic (Rolf Tiedemann) has pointed out the secret relationship between Benjamin's fondness for Brecht on the one hand and "his lifelong fascination with children's books" on the other (children's books: hieroglyphs: simplified allegorical emblems and riddles). Thus, where we thought to emerge into the historical present, in reality we plunge again into the distant past of psychological obsession.

But if nostalgia as a political motivation is most frequently associated with fascism, there is no reason why a nostalgia conscious of itself, a lucid and remorseless dissatisfaction with the present on the grounds of some remembered plenitude, cannot furnish as adequate a revolutionary stimulus as any other: the example of Benjamin is there to prove it. He himself, however, preferred to contemplate his destiny in religious imagery, as in the following paragraph, according to Gershom Scholem the last he ever wrote: "Surely Time was felt neither as empty nor as homogeneous by the soothsayers who inquired for what it hid in its womb. Whoever keeps this in mind is in a position to grasp just how past time is experienced in commemoration: in just exactly the same way. As is well known, the Jews were forbidden to search into the future. On the contrary, the Torah and the act of prayer instruct them in commemoration of the past. So for them, the future, to which the clientele of soothsayers remains in thrall, is divested of its sacred power. Yet it does not for all that become simply empty and homogeneous time in their eyes. For every second of the future bears within it that little door through which Messiah may enter."

Angelus novus: Benjamin's favorite image of the angel that exists only to sing its hymn of praise before the face of God, to give voice, and then at once to vanish back into uncreated nothingness. So at its most poignant Benjamin's experience of time: a pure present, on the threshold of the future honoring it by averted eyes in meditation on the past.

Steiner's Hitler*

BY ALVIN H. ROSENFELD

He is referred to in the poetry of Bertolt Brecht as *der Anstreicher* ("the house-painter"). His aggressive side is glimpsed in Shaw's *Geneva*, a minor play of 1938 which developed a "Mr. Battler," the pugnacity of the man indicated but also undercut by the touch of conventional stage comedy. Auden sought an image to explain the compelling hold he had over the millions and, in a famous poem, projected him as "a psychopathic god," a phrase later adopted by one of his biographers. Among the least compromised of his countrymen, Thomas Mann seems not to have known precisely how to understand so vexing and contradictory a figure, dismissing him as "our political medicine man" while acknowledging him as a "genius." Mann also denounced him as a "pitiable idler" and "fifth-rank visionary," a "sly sadist and plotter of revenge," but was moved to claim him as "an artist, a brother."

In Jewish writings, both during the period of the war and after, one finds no similar sense of fascination or fraternization. In fact, one finds almost no significant allusions to him at all. In Emmanuel Ringelblum's *Notes from the Warsaw Ghetto* he is called "Horowitz," an unexpected and uproariously bizarre appelation but one of a piece with other comic code names in the journal and explainable as part of the vengeance that Jewish wit exacts upon its enemies. Elsewhere one finds intermittent references to "the Beast" or to some latter-day Haman, but not much else. Leslie Epstein, in a recent novel that is as much a fictionalized cartoon as a piece of serious writing, alludes weakly to "the Big Man" in Berlin, and Alain Spiraux, in *Time Out*, another try at popular burlesque, uses the diminutive form of his name to refer, rather incredibly, to the child protagonist of his novel. Otherwise reference fades into still more oblique and abbreviated forms, as in the bare use of initials in Ernest Weiss's *The Eyewitness*, or, more typically, into silence, as if the very pronunciation of his name was a curse that would bring on untold calamities.

* Review of George Steiner, *The Portage to San Cristobal of A.H.* in *The Kenyon Review*, n.s. I, 2 (Spring 1979).

The sum of these occasional allusions, abstractions, and surprisingly minor references is a paradox of a startling kind, although one that seems to have gone generally unnoticed until now: the man who, more than any other, was responsible for bringing on the European catastrophe is virtually absent from the imaginative literature that has followed in its wake. That is not the case in other forms of documentation and representation, for the quantity of historical material about him and the destruction he unleashed is immense; he has occasioned more than a dozen biographies and innumerable specialized studies; has been the centerpiece of scores of films; was featured, in his lifetime, on stamps, coins, bills, posters, and the covers of popular magazines and, posthumously, has stimulated a small growth industry in picture books, records, medallions, toys, jewelry, and other assorted memorabilia. Clearly, the man has not lacked attention, yet with only few exceptions he has been almost entirely absent from contemporary literature.

Why is that so? What accounts for the fact that in that voluminous body of writings we have come to call Holocaust literature the principal perpetrator of the Holocaust is missing? Elsewhere, among historians, journalists, psychologists, sociologists, legal experts, political commentators, and others he has been of such preoccupying concern as to bring one of his recent biographers to predict "that more will be written about Adolf Hitler than about anyone else in history with the exception of Jesus Christ," yet among the serious run of poets, playwrights, and novelists he is hardly to be found.

What accounts for his absence? Surely not any lack of knowledge, for the man and his crimes have been among the most copiously recorded in history. On second thought, though, "knowledge" may be a misnomer in this instance, for while we do have an abundance of information, it does not seem to yield the kinds of insight and explanation that accompany an assured sense of knowing, of knowledge that is equivalent to mastery. As Alan Bullock, one of the most authoritative of the Hitler scholars has put it, there is in this case too large a gap between the explanation and the event, between our sense of the man and the size of the effects he brought on. An unsettling feeling of disproportion accompanies and seems to undermine whatever efforts at extended reflection we might make, a fact that by itself may account for at least part of his resistance to entering imaginative writing.

Consequently, for all we seem to know about him, and that is a very great deal, Hitler remains elusive and even now, thirty five years after the end of his Reich, tends to encourage a kind of wonder that does not easily enter language except in its most hyperbolic forms. In the opinion of a German scholar, for instance, "Hitler cannot be explained. He is a miracle. He is like a given in an equation that cannot be solved, he is like the will of destiny itself in whose path no one can stand." The phrasing here, awe-struck as it is, carries its own kind of appeal, but if one attempts to extend descriptive prose of this high blown nature, one ends up in fulsomeness and incredibility obfuscating rather than easing the epistemological problem referred to above.

I think, though, that there probably are deeper sources of impediment than those of rhetorical excess, particularly in the case of some of the Jewish writers, among whom the very name of Hitler seems to this day to carry an evil potency and is not to be casually invoked. When it is mentioned, as in the ghetto jokes recorded by Ringelblum and Chaim Kaplan, it is always in a vein of aggressive wit or within the context of a curse. Otherwise, Hitler's name is regarded by Jews in much the same way as Haman's name, as a stain upon language that is to be vigorously blotted out. In the case of Haman, the effacement is done at the Purim festival through a ritual enactment of uproar, the repeated waves of noise solicited by the public reading of the Scroll of Esther washing over the slightest mention of Haman's name in an effort literally to drown it out. No such ritual has yet been developed for the effacement of Hitler's name, which is still too recent a rent in the Jewish psyche and has not yet been exorcized by any similar act of the popular will. Rather, it is almost as if the name remains under a powerful word taboo and is referred to, if at all, most often in oblique and indirect ways or, as seems to be the preferred case, is simply rendered inaudible by a consensus of silence.

If this analysis is correct, then we may be able to understand a little better the general absence of Hitler from a literature that he more than anyone else has brought into being. His shadow and weight are everywhere to be detected in the writings of the Holocaust, but his presence, for reasons given above, hardly at all. As for his name, even Brecht and Mann, two of his most strong-willed antagonists, could not easily bring themselves to pronounce it, the former representing him in weak dramatic guise as Arturo Ui, the latter relegating him to the borders of society as a slick charlatan and magician.

Seen against this background of general literary proscription, George Steiner's *The Portage to San Cristobal of A.H.* astonishes in the way any breakthrough work must. The astonishment, it should be noted, has nothing to do with the fact of Steiner's authorship, for this is not the first work of fiction by Steiner to treat the war years. The three stories collected in *Anno Domini*,* published originally in 1964 and now newly reissued, all rehearse moments of personal crisis brought on by the infinitely larger crisis of the Hitler period. The latter, however, is intentionally backgrounded in the fiction of *Anno Domini* and consequently is felt less as overt subject than as informing context. In the essays of *Language and Silence* (1967) a far more explicit attention is given to the Holocaust, especially as seen from the standpoint of language and the erosions it has sustained in the aftermath of a time when words were made the servant of political barbarism. From at least the point of this important collection of essays, then, Steiner's work has been drawn to reflections on the ontological status of language, more specifically to linguistic devaluation and dehumanization, the compelling focus as well for much of the writing in *Extraterritorial* (1971) and *In Bluebeard's Castle* (1971). The author's recent study of *Martin Heidegger* (1979) likewise devotes itself to probing the connections between historical descent and a kind of moral and linguistic obliquity, in this case as represented by one of the foremost philosophers of language whose life and work were both troublingly implicated in Nazism. The implication strikes to the heart of Steiner's subject, and there is no reason to imagine he could move away from it in his fiction any more than in his analytic and essayistic work. The latter, in fact, might usefully be seen as preparation for the novel, itself an elaborate rehearsal of the resourcefulness and hellishness of human speech.

One merit of fiction, at least at its best, is that it puts flesh on these abstractions, endows them with far more of a physical sense than expository writing can ever hope to achieve. To make this acknowledgement is in no way to disparage the merits of exposition but simply to state a truism of writing. Steiner, as is well known, is an accomplished, even elegant essayist, but the art of the essay is characteristically one of reflection, discrimination, and evaluation, not of representation. The essayist makes distinctions, delineates, judges, but rarely attempts to show or to embody. Explanation is the essayist's art; incarnation, the novelist's.

* Woodstock, New York: The Overlook Press (1980).

As readers of Steiner's new book will quickly see, one of the striking features of *The Portage to San Cristobal of A.H.* is its immense feeling of physicality, a tangible quality of experience embodied in the dense jungle landscape that makes up the principal setting of the novel but also, and even more dramatically, in the book's unusually varied landscape of speech. Both are vividly rendered, the first as a Conradian "green hell," the second as an extension of Steiner's long-term attempts to get at human motivation and conduct from the inside of language, through a fine probing, as it were, of the signals transmitted by syntax, inflection, and innuendo. The territory of swamp land and jungle is densely, even brilliantly registered, but the truly breathtaking penetration in this fiction is into another kind of territory, that belonging to the dark underside of words and to those whose handling and mishandling of them may be as true a measure of character as any we possess.

In the realm of words and word power, one of the century's great wielders and corrupters of language, of course, was Adolf Hitler, the "A.H." of Steiner's title. He is brought into the novel slowly, even a bit cautiously, as befits the introduction into fiction of so momentous an historical figure. Since Hitler is not first and foremost a literary "character," a personality composed of words on a page, but already occupies a preponderant status within historical consciousness and the popular imagination, it becomes an open question whether he can be fictionalized at all. Given the anterior claims of factuality, the novelist cannot invent Hitler but only reinvent him, which is to say offer us a literary version of a figure about whom we already know and imagine a great deal. To think in these terms is not to say that the novelist has nothing left to do but that whatever he does do gets done against a world of historical and apocryphal reference that precedes his own efforts at image-making.

What, then, is the image of Hitler against which Steiner's image of him has to contend? It is, overwhelmingly, one of diabolism — in the words of a Yiddish poem, the image of "a devil who became a man,/ who lived with us here upon the earth,/lived and was seen, lived and was heard,/ and — incinerating, gassing—crucified/a people." Or, to vary the terms only slightly by quoting from someone recently involved commercially in what was purported to be Hitler's skull, "Hitler is the supreme criminal of all times. He out-Neroes Nero, he out-Caligulas Caligula. Therefore, he is a most fascinating man." Although it may be recalled by some that he built the Autobahn, was a vegetarian, and loved dogs, what we remember of Hitler above everything else is that he was the executioner of European Jewry. It is that staggering act of criminality that fascinates and repels and that keeps alive so many questions about the man's power and depravity.

A sizable part of that power, and one that holds a special fascination for George Steiner, was oratorical. It is difficult to think of Hitler, in fact, and not imagine the man *speaking*, an image reinforced by miles of film footage displaying him wielding his considerable histrionic skills over the mesmerized German citizenry massed somewhere below him. It is just this kind of image that introduces Hitler into the novel: "They say your voice could burn cities. They say that when you spoke. Leaves turning to ash and men weeping. They say that women, just to hear your voice, that women would tear their clothes off, just to hear your voice." As the narrative works itself out, Hitler's voice will remain a faint and enfeebled one until the very ending of *The Portage*; in fact, through sixteen of the book's seventeen chapters Hitler says hardly a word and has almost no distinctive presence in his own right. Nevertheless, although we hardly see or hear him, he is the focal point of all significant attention and directs the words and actions of every other character involved with him.

In plotting the novel and filling it with a multi-national array of characters, Steiner has sought to probe the nature of this involvement from half a dozen different points of view. His concern, in fact, is, until the very end of the narrative, less with Hitler than with the unsettling place he has assumed in consciousness, a place that remains for the most part still unacknowledged. The menace of the man may have run its course in history, but within the history of feeling he remains very much alive and influences attitudes that vary in nature and intensity from obsessive fantasies of revenge on the part of Jewish Holocaust survivors to the bland and evasive procedural gestures of jurists, politicians, and diplomats. Whatever the nature of the connection, though, the central fact of the novel is clear: Hitler is of consequence and will remain with us as the most profound of historical and metaphysical disturbances until the unprecedented destruction he brought on is confronted once and for all.

Steiner's way into this confrontation is via a Conradian descent into the heart of darkness, represented in this case by a team of Israeli agents who are intent on tracking Hitler to his hiding place deep in the jungles of South America. For this search to take place at all, of course, Steiner had to build into his fiction a lingering fictive account of Hitler's last days, one that claims the German Führer did not die by suicide but escaped his bunker at the last moment and successfully managed a flight out of Berlin to a prearranged haven abroad. One doubts that Steiner places much credence in this myth (H.R. Trevor-Roper examines it in great detail in the important introduction to the third edition of his definitive study, *The Last Days of Hitler*), but the story, apocryphal though it is, does allow the author a major narrative breakthrough, for it is a means to keep Hitler alive, not only in memory but in the flesh, and hence to make possible, and ultimately to force, an encounter with him. Imagine, so this novel asks of us, "What would you do if Adolf Hitler walked into the room?" Never mind that the man would now be past ninety, that his Reich crumbled into ruin almost four decades ago, that later dictators have also shown us the face of mass murder — if Hitler appeared before you, what would you do? Such a confrontation, so the novel insists, must take place, and while it would be unnerving, no other encounter would be more decisive, more revealing, more necessary. For Hitler was not just one murderer among many, one tyrant among other tyrants, but, in Steiner's view, the pivotal figure on whom the history of our time seems to turn, and hence the one above all with whom we have to come to grips.

But how is one to grapple with Hitler? Who, among his victims and survivors, stands ready to contend with him and to judge him? And what precisely would be the purpose of engaging him in trial? To put these questions in the language of the novel itself, "Exactly what is it he did to man?" and, after more than thirty-five years, "Who cares?" Who, even, wants to remember?

The novel raises these questions through a shifting point of view that brings into focus a many-sided interest in the person, career, and meaning of Hitler. Through a complex but neatly controlled progression of plot, the Israelis, British, Russians, Germans, French, and Americans all tune in to the Israeli tracking team, catching and interpreting the signals transmitted by their radio from the heart of the Brazilian jungles. After some hesitancy, a decoding of the messages brings the startling news: Hitler has been found by the Israeli trackers, who will attempt to bring him out alive. To British Intelligence, represented by a character whose scholarly passions recall Trevor-Roper, this information is received with the keenest interest, the nature of which is chiefly forensic. To the Russian, still intimidated by earlier Stalinist practices, the capture of Hitler is a challenge to a previous era of politically-motivated doctoring of the evidence about Hitler's last days, and especially about his suicide. The Germans are represented as taking an intense although abstract legal interest in the matter; the French want nothing so much as to prevent events from reviving too close an inquiry into the crimes of the Vichy Government; and the Americans manifest both a blatantly commercial and diplomatically opportunistic interest in the affair. None of these shorthand descriptions does justice to the novel's multiple and richly projected point of view, which not only brings into focus the national preoccupations of the various interested parties but does so in the peculiar syntax and with the distinctive feeling of the Israeli, British, Russian, German, French, and American sensibilities. Steiner's gifts as a polymath serve him well in these instances, and while there are moments where the portrayal of national characteristics begins to slide into caricature, for the most part the novel's international dimension is fully credible and bears out the notion that, with respect to Hitler, "No one wants him like anyone else. Each in his own little way."

As indicated above, Steiner has worked Hitler into his novel in such a way as to have him mirror back something deep in the national psyches of all who confront him. As such, he is a test of the strength and integrity of national will, of the truthfulness or evasiveness of individual stances toward history. Within these terms, the ultimate confrontation in the novel — ultimate for being most intimate, most intense, most obsessive — is, as it must be, with the Israelis. They, as representatives of the people Hitler wanted most, are the ones who most want him and who will see to it that they get him.

What keeps them on his track? In searching out Hitler, what precisely are they in quest of? The brilliance, and importance, of Steiner's novel is that these questions are raised in such a way as to bring to a climactic moment of clarification and justification the whole Jewish obsession with the Holocaust. This is achieved through a character whom we never see but whose voice directs the Israeli trackers to their quarry, drives them deeper and deeper into the dead air and fever-ridden swamps of the South American wastelands, scourges them with the most punishing claims of historical memory, and, by so doing, sustains them in their search. The voice belongs to Emmanuel Lieber.

> Emmanuel Lieber, whose fingers they were, often fumbling and ten thousand miles from arm's length, but his as surely as if he were now standing with them, dreaming the web, spinning and tightening it over the grid of the jungle, directing their racked, unbelieving bodies to the quarry, as he had for thirty years from London, then from Turin (where they had first, in worlds past it seemed, picked up the scent) and now from the small, unmarked office in Lavra Street in Tel Aviv. They were his creatures, the animate embers of his calm, just madness. Of a will so single, so inviolate to any other claim of life, that its thread went through Lieber's sleep producing one incessant dream. That of this capture.

If it is Lieber who drives on the Israeli hunters, it is the Holocaust that drives on Lieber. "The fires at Bialka, the children hung alive, the bird droppings glistening on the shorn heads of the dying," all this and more remains unforgettable to him, as it does to the Jews at large.

Following the Nazi immolation of European Jewry there are, in the words of one of the Israelis, only "two kinds of Jews left, the dead and those who are a bit crazy." Lieber is of the latter kind, a Jewish survivor of Hitler "who crawled out from under the burnt flesh in the death pits" and ever since has lived with a perception of life "so outside the focus of man's customary vision" as to mark him out as having "a piercing strangeness." If such strange vision constitutes craziness, then Lieber is indeed crazy, but no more so than Artur Sammler or Ernie Levy or the Elie Wiesel and Primo of *Night* and *Survival in Auschwitz.* The "craziness" in every one of these cases is owing to a heightened not a distorted vision, a chastened form of historical consciousness that knows from experience "exactly what it is that Hitler did to man." In this respect, all Jews are a bit crazy and Lieber, as a representative Jew, is only one among many.

Still, he is the one singled out by Steiner to represent Jewish consciousness at its most acute, which in the post-Holocaust period means a consciousness possessed by historical memory at its most lacerating. To bear the burden of such memory is to carry a weight of experience almost too heavy for words to express, and as a result Holocaust literature is often caught at a point of impasse between the imperatives of testimony and the infirmities of language. Confronted by so intractable a dilemma, writing frequently tends either to heighten into expostulation and apostrophe, raising the voice to sometimes uncontrolled levels of utterance, or to drift toward silence, extinguishing the voice in a dwindling sob of elegiac lament. One of Steiner's extraordinary achievements in *The Portage* is that he has found for Emmanuel Lieber a style that mediates between these two extremes, a precise register of exclamation and lamentation that simultaneously records and mourns, coldly enumerates yet carries an immense affect. André Schwarz-Bart achieved something similar in the memorable ending of *The Last of the Just*, as Paul Celan also did in the compelling rhythms of his famous "Todesfuge," but otherwise in the entire corpus of Holocaust literature one would be hard put to identify a passage of poetry or prose that surpasses the strength of Lieber's speech in the sixth chapter of this novel. This speech is too long and too much of a piece, unfortunately, to be cited here in excerpt, but it is no exaggeration to say that, had Steiner written nothing else, the power of Lieber's words would by themselves insure *The Portage* a permanent place in the literature of the Holocaust. Like Schwarz-Bart's intermingling of the words of the *Sh'ma* with the names of Nazi concentration camps, Lieber's discourse takes the form and carries the tones of sacred litany; it lists and counts, lists and counts, lifting name and number to the level of eloquence and consequence. Like Celan's stuttering and hallucinatory lyricism, it also drives language into and beyond ellipsis, finding in fragments of speech a literary form to encompass and express brokenness. Prose of this order is rare, and rarely sustained, yet Lieber's voice goes on and on, filling the pages of this chapter with a kind of preachment that stuns the mind with its punishing directness and clarity. One reads it in the same way that the Wedding Guest listened to the Ancient Mariner, spellbound, and comes away with the wisdom that accompanies deep suffering and deep eloquence.

At the heart of Lieber's speech is history, chronicled rather than imagined, hypostatized rather than transformed. It is important to note these emphases, for Jewish consciousness, at least that strain of it that comes to expression here, is involved not in the making of myths but in the creation of conscience. For that task one does not look to the more emblematical tropes of figuration but to the more disciplined resources of documentation. If, then, the Jews "are the people of the word," as one of the characters in the novel declaims, it is the word stripped of its magical potencies and dedicated to recording and vivifying factuality. Lieber's "craziness," one comes to understand, is a function of his literalness: he will not let go of the severe knowledge that experience has brought him or attempt in any way to turn it into symbolic meaning. It can have no such meaning, for it is beyond the transfiguring reach of metaphor and the modes of fictive imagining. For altogether different reasons, Hitler himself could not easily imagine it:

> Read what he said to his familiars, what he spoke in his dancing hours. He never alludes to the barracks or the gas, to the lime-pits or the whipping blocks. Never, as if the will to murder and the knowledge were so deep inside him that he had no more need to point to them. Our ruin was the air he moved in.

The description here is of a psyche that knows no distance between the wish and the deed, which in this case means between the imagination of murder and the bloody act itself. Hitler's mind as imagined by Lieber is one so infused by the passions of anti-Jewish obsessions as to leave no space for any sense of the Jew other than as deadly antagonist. In this respect, it, too, is a representative mind, exceptional only because it was endowed with the power to "make real the old dream of murder. Everyman's itch to clear his throat of us. Because we have lasted too long. Because we foisted Christ on them." Hitler, in this view of him, made a difference not so much because he espoused a new or different course of action toward the Jews but because his own kind of eloquence unlocked the passions that turned an age-old dream into day: "His words made the venom spill."

Although Lieber and Hitler never come face to face in the novel, then, the ultimate confrontation in *The Portage* is, as it must be, between them. Since Steiner keeps them physically apart, their encounter is represented as taking place on the level of language, or within language between two distinctly different attitudes toward the word, the one dedicated to representing the truths of history and the Lord of history, the other an apocalyptic assault against historical and theological thinking and the people who carry it forward into the world. I do not mean to suggest that Steiner reduces Hitler's war against the Jews to a language war, for that would be a trivialization and a distortion. However, inasmuch as Steiner looks to language as an establishing source of being and not only as its reflection, he is given to understanding radical semantic oppositions as being of the gravest historical consequence. If, as already noted, the Jews are the people of the word, they are so in a way very different from the way that Hitler was a master of words, a "word-spinner, mountebank":

> As it is written in the learned Nathaniel of Mainz: there shall come upon the earth in the time of night a man surpassing eloquent. All that is God's, hallowed by his name, must have its counterpart, its backside of evil and negation. So it is with the Word, with the gift of speech that is glory of man and distinguishes him everlastingly from the silence or animal noises of creation. When He made the Word, God made possible also its contrary. Silence is not the contrary of the Word but its guardian. No, He created on the nightside of language a speech for hell. Whose words mean hatred and vomit of life. Few men can learn that speech or speak it for long. It burns their mouths. It draws them into death. But there shall come a man whose mouth shall be as a furnace and whose tongue as a sword laying waste. He will know the grammar of hell and teach it to others. He will know the sounds of madness and loathing and make them seem music. Where God said, let there be, he will unsay.

The biblical voice here is Lieber's, describing the voice of one dedicated to negating the Bible and "banishing God from creation." In this view, the nihilism of Nazism is understood as being in a perverse way theological and Hitler a kind of counter-Messiah or reverse-Jew. Within the terms of some apocalyptic derangement, he is even imagined as being "the last Jew," one who has come to shut down history, or at least Jewish history, to throw off "the blackmail of transcendence" that Judaism has pressed on the world and hence return it to a pagan earthiness freed of any of the claims of conscience and the aspirations of the ideal.

These views come into the novel, and bring it to a climax, in Hitler's speech at the end of *The Portage.* Like Lieber's speech, this one also takes up a full chapter and unfortunately cannot be quoted easily here. The only significant utterance of Hitler in the book, it is spoken at an improvised trial before his Israeli captors and is meant to be taken, at least implicitly, as a reply to Lieber. It is, in fact, Hitler's self-defense, or at least the self-defense of a character in the book who is called by Hitler's name and charged with his crimes.

In its own way the speech is a grand performance, but a number of questions about it rush to mind and complicate one's final response to the novel. One such complication results from the inevitable juxtaposition of Steiner's Hitler with his historical prototype: try as one may to suspend disbelief and to allow a writer to indulge in full all the liberties of fiction, it is highly unlikely that Adolf Hitler, the Führer of the German Third Reich, would think or speak in the terms of this discourse. This judgement is made, I realize, through references that are external to the novel itself, but the name Hitler is not a literary fabrication and, at least at this point in history, cannot be reduced solely to the fictive. Steiner manages to avoid this vexing problem of representation until the end of his book by having people speak *about* Hitler but by having Hitler himself remain virtually silent. Ultimately, though, he must give him a voice, and one does not hear in it much that would have come from the mouth of the real A.H.

What one does hear, surprisingly, is a language that is recognizably Steiner's own, taken as it is from key sections of *In Bluebeard's Castle* and some of the author's other expository writings. The ideas set forth by the Hitler of *The Portage* — ideas that link Nazi doctrines of covenantal election, racial purity, historic destiny, and the like with biblical sources — have been presented by Steiner before in some of his non-fictional work. Now there is nothing wrong with returning to such work and mining it for a later novel, but to carry over not only the thinking but the distinctive idiom of one's earlier writing and ascribe it to Hitler is something else again, and something strongly unsettling. Steiner has argued speculatively in the past that Nazism was a travesty of Judaism, that the Jews as the embodiment of conscience became intolerable to a Christian Europe that remained pagan at heart, that by introducing God, Jesus, and Marx into the world the Jews pressed upon a reluctant mankind a "blackmail of transcendence" that it could not abide and finally threw over in the explosion that was the Holocaust. In making these formulations, Steiner boldly challenged earlier and weaker arguments of both historical positivists and psychohistorians in an effort to get at what may be some of the larger and deeper cultural and religious strains of Nazism. There are those who have criticized this aspect of the author's work as being too conjectural and others who have found it unusually bold and perceptive. What baffles in this instance, though, are not Steiner's ideas but their transference virtually verbatim into the mouth of Hitler, as if Steiner's understanding of Hitler were identical with the latter's self-understanding. A necessary distance between the author and his principal character seems to have collapsed here, with the result that the novel ends on a note that is improbable and jarring.

Why end it at all, in fact, with Hitler's speech? Why give Hitler the last word, a fairly triumphant word at that, one that aims not only to explain Nazism as a run-away Judaism but to vindicate the genocide of the Jews as the necessary historical spur to the establishment of the State of Israel? As the voice of Hitler is made to say, "would Palestine have become Israel . . . had it not been for the Holocaust?" To frame a complex historical question in this way is to solicit a simple answer, after which one is tempted to assent as well to Hitler's occult musing that follows: "Perhaps I *am* the Messiah," he declares, "the true Messiah, the new Sabbatai whose infamous deeds were allowed by God in order to bring His people home." According to this view of things, Hitler was as much the Jews' redeemer as their destroyer, a violent successor to Herzl who "made of the long, vacuous daydream of Zion a reality." As he himself arrogantly suggests to his Israeli captors, should you now "not be a comfort to my old age?"

Whatever one's understanding of Zionism and Israel, the reality that looms largest here is neither religious nor political but rhetorical. Steiner's Hitler is involved in the devil's game of language subversion, a game that his historical prototype brought to a kind of deadly perfection. The deadliness lies in appropriating a vocabulary of sacred terminology and inverting it so that words are evacuated of their customary meaning and made to take on a reverse signification. It is this process that characterizes the grammar of hell and makes the sounds of madness seem like music. To close the novel on this note is to succumb, rhetorically, to the seductive eloquence of negation, a closure that runs counter to the major thrust of George Steiner's whole career and the high standards of moral intelligence it has consistently upheld.

These reservations about the book's ending aside, *The Portage to San Cristobal of A.H.* must be counted among the most vigorous attempts to portray the presence and meaning of Hitler in our lives. As implied by the noun in the book's title, we have been "carrying" Hitler for a long time, for the most part unconsciously, as a burden of tragedy, guilt, shame, fear, and worry. While it is beyond the power of any single novel to unpack him all at once, Steiner's work goes far in revealing the staggering weight of the man within history, a history that to this day has not succeeded in comprehending him or even, in many instances, of truthfully confronting him. *The Portage to San Cristobal of A.H.* forces the confrontation upon us in a way hardly seen before in fiction, and for this we are hugely in Steiner's debt.

Games American Writers Play

Ceremony, Complicity, Contestation, and Carnival

BY TONY TANNER

> "But every now and then, players in a game will, lull or crisis, be reminded how it is, after all, really play — and be unable to continue in the same spirit. . . . Nor need it be anything sudden, spectacular — it may come in gentle — and regardless of the score, the number of watchers, their collective wish, penalties they or the Leagues may impose, the play will, walking deliberately . . . say *fuck it* and quit the game, quit it cold."
>
> (*Gravity's Rainbow*)

How do we read books which emerge from our own environment, which are part of our ongoing contemporaneity? If we address ourselves to works of the past, products of a different society, a different economy, a different historical matrix, we are not only reading those works but by implication the silent language of anticipations and expectations, permissions and prohibitions, which surround them and made up their context. Whatever else a book may do it records a series of choices from the available discourses at a particular time. It is a commonplace to say that the condition of meaning is exclusion, but it is worth remembering when reading a book from the past that we are indirectly reading or being exposed to the tacit social rules and conditions which governed the exclusions and inclusions which are as much a part of the book as any more ostensible subject-matter. To put it very simply, when we read a book from the past we are in fact reading a book and a context, but in reading a book from the present we *are* the context.

Reading a contemporary work we should be aware, or better, we should be *made* aware, of the discourses within us which we bring to the text. For example, a book which attempts to do this quite deliberately, and successfully to my mind, is Robert Pirsig's *Zen and the Art of*

Motorcycle Maintenance. The very title suggests the interaction or confrontation of discourses traditionally kept separate and the book is based on the idea of giving new visibility to contemporary discourses by just such confrontations and recontextualizations. They "interrogate" each other. One quotation from the book: the narrator gives what he calls a "classical" description of a motorcycle. Then comments: "There's certainly nothing strange about this description at first hearing. It sounds like something from a beginning text-book on the subject, or perhaps a first lesson in a vocational course. What is unusual about it is seen when it ceases to be a mode of discourse and becomes an object of discourse. Then certain things can be pointed to." A lot of contemporary American fiction, it seems to me, is working in this area of turning modes of discourse into objects of discourse, and a lot of its vitality is dependent on the reader's ability to recognize the shifting relation between discourse as mode and as object within the book and within himself. Then — "certain things can be pointed to." In the future different readers will point to different things — if only because they are inevitably reading through our readings.

What I want to point to in some recent American fiction can perhaps be most economically prepared for by the introduction of four words, each suggesting a different relationship between literature and society — thus we might consider literature as ceremony, complicity, contestation, or carnival. The first three words may be found in Sartre's *What Is Literature*? The first kind of writing is produced "when the power of the religious and political ideology is so strong and the interdictions so rigorous that in no case is there any question of discovering new countries of the mind, but only of putting into shape the *commonplaces* adopted by the elite in such a way that reading . . . is a ceremony of *recognition*." Whatever Sartre's intentions, ceremony suggests something positive, public and based on shared beliefs and values. Complicity suggests a more covert activity, involving a degree of conscious or unconscious bad faith on the part of the writer as he simply confirms the public in its own image and its own selective perspectives on the society of the time. Bourgeois society in particular "does not ask to be shown what it is, but it asks rather for a reflection of what it thinks it is." (This crucial distinction could be amplified by considering Freud's essay on Fetishism and the tension between knowledge and belief that he diagnoses as being present in a "fetishistic" relationship to reality; and by considering Lacan's notion of people who inhabit the realm of the "Imaginary", living lives based on "mirages and misconstructions".) The bourgeois audience did not ask the writer "to restore the strangeness and opacity of the world, but to dissolve it into elementary subjective impression which made it easier to digest." They wanted to "buy with their eyes closed." A writer attempting to resist this kind of complicity will find himself engaged in contestation, attempting to make society more aware of its own structuring. "If society sees itself and, in particular, sees itself as *seen*, there is by virtue of this very fact, a contesting of the established values of the regime. The writer presents it with its image; he calls upon it to assume it or change it. At any rate, it changes; it loses the equilibrium which its ignorance had given it; it wavers between shame and cynicism; it practises dishonesty: thus, the writer gives society *a guilty conscience*." Contestations become more radical as they increasingly refuse any complicity with what they are describing, just as the writer feels an increasing dissonance with his society as his own position becomes more problematical and his role in society has to be constantly re-invented. In such conditions, literature moves increasingly towards "negation" until finally it turns on itself. "In the end there was nothing left for literature to do but to contest itself. That is what it did in the name of surrealism." Generalising from Sartre's argument we can say that unless a writer overtly accepts and celebrates the value system and reality picture of the society in which he writes, he must inevitably move towards complicity or contestation. These activities can obviously take many forms and may occur together in the same work; the question I wish to consider is where contemporary American writers situate themselves in this tension between complicity and contestation, and whether they have found an alternative way of being-in-society at the present time.

One obvious problem is that writers and readers alike are over-exposed to language so that a gesture of revolt is easily transformed — by our present context — into a distraction for entertainment. Just what a writer might do in contemporary society is one of the problems implicit in Fredric Jameson's book *Marxism and Form*. He cites Marcuse and his contention that "the consumer society, the society of abundance, has lost the experience of the negative in all its forms, and that it is the negative alone which is ultimately fructifying from a cultural as well as an individual point of view." He describes Adorno's conception of the work of art and its relationship to its immediate historical situation, namely that it inevitably "reflects" society but it should also "refuse the social . . . the socio-economic is inscribed in the work, but as concave to convex, as positive to negative." And Jameson's own contention is this: "we begin to glimpse what is the profound vocation of the work of art in a commodity society: *not* to be a commodity, *not* to be consumed, to be *unpleasurable* in the commodity sense." Here then are three possible prescriptions for the contemporary writer — to attempt to discover significant ways of reintroducing the experience of negativity to the reader; to reflect society by refusing it; to produce works which are non-commodities and thus somehow to violate the pleasure principle of the purchaser-consumer. We may add Sartre's injunctions that a work of literature should be "a task to be discharged", one implication of this being that it should turn readers into active producers rather than passive consumers. In general it would seem that what is needed is what Zamyatin called "harmful literature" which is quite different from any specific didactic, polemical, or propagandist literature. "Harmful literature is more useful than useful literature, for it is antientropic, it is a means of combating calcification, sclerosis, crust, moss, acquiescence." ("On Literature, Revolution, Entropy, and other Matters") What we find when we turn to some recent American fiction are, I will contend, varying attempts to move beyond complicity and contestation into an area which I will designate as carnival. But let me start to be more specific.

Here are two quotations; the first is from Ishmael Reed's *Yellow Back Radio Broke Down*: "Whats your beef with me Schmo, what if I write circuses? No-one says a novel has to be one thing. It can be anything it wants to be, a vaudeville show, the six o'clock news, the mumblings of wild men saddled by demons." The second is from Jerome Charyn's *The Tar Baby*. In this novel the main character, Anatole, loses his "feel for mapping": "He wanted to clear his head of taxonomies, to quit being a reader of griddles and signs." My preceding comments all ultimately concerned the literary work as being some kind of mimesis — positive or negative. What the quotations point to is an impulse to move beyond the constraints of existing categories, so that in reading the work it is impossible to stabilise it within any one genre. If category *per se* can be seen as being connected to the different modes of discourse which "systematize" us then the impulse to confront, conflate, dissolve or even annul categories can be seen as part of an attempt to desystematize the reader. (As Nietzsche reminds us in *Will to Power* you can devalue categories without devaluing the universe. Indeed it may be necessary to devalue categories in order to revalue the universe.) Reed is euphoric; Charyn's Anatole is melancholic, and his exhaustion with "signs", his desire to rid himself of taxonomies altogether, point to a possible ambiguity in this thrust beyond contemporary modes of "mapping" experience. It may lead into an exhilarating circus of categories, or into a taxonomic void. Thus a deliberate dis-orientation may lead to a new re-orientation or a state of no-orientation; both are felt to open up the possibilities of a new freedom which is unavailable within the existing categories. This is why, I think, there is a very discernible increase in the emphasis on writing as a "game" among contemporary American writers and critics — Albert Guerard has written extensively of "the sense of fun writers take in the games they play"; Philip Stevick in his interesting inquiry, "Metaphors for the Novel" lists a collection of some fifty metaphors he has found being employed to describe the novel and concludes: "Fiction in the Seventies is dream, prayer, cri de coeur, and fingernails on a blackboard. But pre-eminently, as Fielding, Sterne, and Jane Austen knew, the novel is a game." Ronald Sukenick's idea of a New Tradition in the Novel is called, gamefully enough, Bossa Nova which "needless to say . . . has no plot, no story, no character, no chronological sequence, no verisimilitude, no imitation, no allegory, no symbolism, no subject matter, no 'meaning' . . . " The general consensus among such writers and critics is that contemporary fiction should be anti-realistic, non-representational, non-referential, and attempt to "present elements of its texture as devoid of value; new fiction . . . seeks this value-less quality not as an act of subtraction, or dehumanization, or metaphysical mystification, not as a gesture of despair or nihilism, but as a positive act in which the joy of the observer is allowed to prevail as the primary quality of the experience." (Stevick) John Barth's praise for Smollett's *Roderick Random* as "a novel of non-significant surfaces" is representative of this way of thinking about new fictional possibilities. I think that all these descriptions of, and prescriptions for, the novel are problematical if taken literally. Even the metaphor of fiction as "game" has its difficulties. As Stevick himself pointed out, it poses the question of whether the game is in the writing, the reading, or the book itself, or all three. Also games have rules in a way that improvised play does not, and in some contemporary American fiction it would be difficult to maintain a distinction between "game" and "play". Another problematical aspect of the metaphor is worth noting. As Lévi-Strauss points out in *The Savage Mind*, "Games thus appear to have a *disjunctive* effect: they end in the establishment of a difference between individual players or teams where originally there was no indication of inequality. And at the end of the game they are distinguished into winners and losers. Ritual, on the other hand, is the exact converse; it *conjoins* for it brings about a union (one might even say communion in this context) or in any case an organic relation between two initially separated groups". In a highly competitive western society, the word "game" is necessarily ambiguous, suggesting at once a temporary reprieve from work, and a disjunctive striving to establish winners and losers at all levels. Hence the use of such phrases as "the games people play" and even "war games". If society itself is seen as a series of more or less vicious and exploitative games, then what kind of "game" is the novel playing?

Perhaps a word which contains suggestions of play, game, and ritual would be useful here. It might therefore be helpful to invoke the word "carnival" as defined by Michael Bakhtin in his monumental work on *Rabelais and His World.* In his terms, during carnival life is lifted out of its routines, hierarchies are dissolved, fixed models are unstructured, the closed world enshrined in official concepts and formulae is broken open. In addition, in carnival the existing forms of coercive socio-economic and political organization are suspended, in particular by games; games are "extra-official" and "extra-territorial" and involve a liberation *from* (not argument *with*) officially sanctioned laws and regulations and beliefs. Carnival inverts and fractures and demystifies prevailing ideologies which are static, hierarchic, based on rigid categorical separations and constituting the reification of *one* organized and power-sanctioned view of reality. Bakhtin sees the Renaissance as, "so to speak, a direct 'carnivalization' of human consciousness, philosophy, and literature." And he notes a related phenomenon in the literature of the period—"the carnivalization of speech, which freed it from the gloomy seriousness of official philosophy as well as from truisms and commonplace ideas." Just such a "carnivalization" of consciousness and speech can, I think, be detected in some recent American fiction. There is one important point about the word "carnival": carnival is public, for all the people, originally connected with the market place as a central meeting place. Can the "public-ity" of the carnival be recreated on the privacy of the page? There is, certainly, one important possible similarity between a carnival and a novel. It might not make much sense to ask what is carnival "about" but you can ask—what is going on there? This is what Bakhtin did and in his opinion carnival is an enactment of life freeing itself from old rigidifying forms, experiencing its own boundless potentiality for ever more life in ever more forms, none of them final, and releasing an energy of regeneration. Many contemporary novelists and critics abhor the use of the word "about" in discussing contemporary fiction, one reason being that in asserting what a book is "about" a commentator may in effect reduce the novel to the very thematic simplifications and conventional formulations which it set out to escape from. (Criticising the "about" approach in the classification of folk tales Propp makes the crucial criticism of such an approach, namely that it offers "no single principle for the selection of decisive elements". However I think it remains an indispensable word and I will return to it at the end.) But if novels may be considered, metaphorically, as carnivals and games, we—the public—can at least ask, what is going on there? even if any one particular game wishes to maintain that it is only "about" itself, non-representational, against interpretation, and so on. And the claim that a particular work is disengaged from all considerations of meaning, referentiality, signification, etc., may *itself* be a game, a strategy to enable the writer to be free to explore new ways of meaning (not just new meanings) and new aspects of our unavoidable conditions of living among significations. (Significations can of course cease to be registered as 'significant' though it seems hard to maintain a stable distinction between the two; or significations may be felt to drown out significance. We are becoming very aware of the complex shifting relationships between signal, sign, signification, and significance, and it is hardly surprising that some contemporary novelists incorporate the problem into their work in a variety of ways. Joyce is obviously a key influence in all this, but Joyce's own work, with its almost totalitarian ruthlessness and fanatical efficiency of ordering, albeit on his own unique terms, lacks the "carnival" element which I am trying to identify in some contemporary American fiction.) That there are distinct possible advantages in this strategy of considering the novel as "game" may perhaps be thrown into sharper focus if we consider briefly an avowedly "serious" novel in which life itself, but not the book, is compared to a game, albeit a hard and mean one. I am referring to Joan Didion's *Play it as it Lays*, which has been compared to Eliot's *Wasteland* and the works of Nathanael West.

The problem with this novel, to put it very simply, is that it is too easy to read. It involves that kind of debasement of referentiality which other writers are trying to resist by asserting that their books are not "about" anything in the conventional manner. I am not referring to the vocabulary, or the syntax, or the economic brevity of the chapters in Didion's novel; it is the descriptive conventions operating in the text which are too familiar. Tentatively borrowing an over-used word from linguistics I would say that in its depth structure the book is almost completely cliché-ic. It offers a species of instant supermarket nihilism. What the words refer to is upsetting and disturbing enough—suicide, abortion, isolation, mental breakdown, etc. But the patterning of the words is ultimately undisturbing. To take two of Piaget's terms, the book does not require accommodation (which involves struggle or work); it can be assimilated, which is a comparatively effortless automatic process.* This is commodity nihilism which involves us in no new experience of negation, no real refusal of society, and in itself offers no evidence of struggle against being a commodity. The test is not in what the book appears to refer to (in which case every daily paper would be another *Wasteland*), but in what the book does to us as readers. It sets us no tasks, it does not drive us back into our own discourses to discover there the accumulating clichés and stereotypes which we mistake for thinking. It seems to imply that while life may be all problem, the language in which it is re-presented is no problem. But in a contemporary work of *fiction*, if language is not a problem *nothing else is*. ('Problem' is not meant here to be synonymous with 'the difficult'; it is intended simply to refer to that which makes of the reader an active participant rather than a passive consumer.) Didion's novel is a quick "wasteland" assembly kit (think by contrast of the *work* initially required to read Eliot's *Wasteland*, or the real sense of strangeness released by West's books which contemporaries also found hard to read), and as we automatically assemble it as we read we experience not "a strangeness and opacity" restored to the world, but a familiarity and transparency unrevoked from the words.

In this essay I wish to look at three recent American fictions which have been regarded as "games"** and try to answer the queston—what is going on there? Let me turn first to a work which visibily offers itself as a game, of a sustained piece of play, *Willie Masters' Lonesome Wife* by William Gass. We may note immediately that a lonesome wife is already a potential paradox suggesting both solitude and connection, a lapsed contract, a failed union, and the text concerns itself with those things which both join and separate us—lips, sexual organs, dances, words. There is a hovering parallel between semen given and taken away (in a

* This is perhaps a too simple adaptation of Piaget's terms which he applies to stages of sensory-motor development. This is how he makes the distinction: "Now all such behavior that has innate roots but becomes differentiated through functioning contains, we find, the same functional factors and structural elements. The functional factors are *assimilation*, the process whereby an action is actively reproduced and comes to incorporate new objects into itself (for example, thumb sucking as a case of sucking), and *accommodation*, the process whereby the schemes of assimilation themselves become modified in being applied to a diversity of object." (*Structuralism*) My contention would be that serious fiction in one way or another modifies our mental "schemes of assimilation" and it is this which Joan Didion's novel fails to do.

** Of course it would be possible to choose many other novels. In particular Robert Coover's *The Universal Baseball Association Inc.* not only explores games, and the instinct to create games; it also, as far as I can make out, brings the language of game theory into the text so that it too is changed from a mode to an object of discourse. But Coover's work would require a whole separate essay. My choice of these three works is necessarily arbitrary and I can only hope to justify it by the end of the paper.

contraceptive) and semantics, meaning which we own and lose. The pages seem to unite us to the writer; they even carry images of the stains of a coffee cup as if to put us in the position *vis a vis* the page which the writer was in while penning it. But it is an illusion of course, and tells us that we are *not* where the writer was. It is not our coffee cup, not our stain. The paper divides us where we seem to meet. In the middle of the book there is a reference to Bottom playing at being the wall (in *Midsummer Night's Dream*). The text is both the wall and the crack through which Pyramus and Thisbe have to try to make contact. But the wall and the crack are also illusory and we the readers are also left lonesome.

In attempting to describe the book it is impossible to invoke the usual categories. It is an assault on our customary orderings. Typographically it is a kind of game. The print varies constantly, lines inflate and grow smaller, tumesce and detumesce; footnotes crowd out the text and corner us; the text divides into two, into three, into more—it cannot be read in a linear way. Clusters of words murmur or shout at us from unexpected places in the margins; asterisks begin to proliferate like some rapidly reproducing organic life until they fall around the pages like stars. There are headlines and placards, even bursts of music. The pages change color. In every way the texture of the text is constantly transforming itself; it is chameleon, protean, metamorphosing—whatever else it does, it is constantly unstabilizing us as conventional readers. The book also pretends to be a body, with photographs of breasts on the cover and buttocks on the back. This is not incidental, for orifices, nourishment and excrement, are central concerns of the book. We are, it reminds us, constantly taking things in and as constantly secreting or excreting them, as excrement, saliva, dirt, semen, and words. There are intermittent allusions to pipes, tunnels, corridors, intestines—world and words flow through us: we swallow objects and disgorge signs. On the title there is a photograph of a hand reaching out—and we are after all always trying to "mancipate" things and people who in turn e-mancipate themselves from our grasp. There is also perhaps a cultural echo of Michaelangelo's Adam. But there is no answering hand of God, or anyone else. The wife is lonesome. The book begins with body and ends with words, or rather, they seem to come together—the text corporealised, the body verbalised. It is a monologue of a woman dreaming to herself; it is a monologue of language dreaming to itself.

As we read it seems to be the reverie of a woman, a former burlesque actress and stripper, thinking about the men who have entered her and left her. "Empty I began, and empty I remained." Just so, many voices have entered the language, used it, and departed, from Shakespeare to the crudest vernacular lout. By an unstated inversion or reciprocation, a woman becomes a language used for different occasions in different ways, and language is a woman used for different occasions in different ways. At one point the text announces: "A distinction is usually made between adherence and adhesion. The tendency prevails to confine adhesion to physical attachment, adherence to mental or moral attachment." Perhaps a fragment from philosophy? As the text has no one original author but is instead a nexus for fragments of a multiplicity of discourses, it doesn't matter where the words *come from*. What they *do* is remind us that we are creatures of ever-attempting, ever-failing modes of attachment. We try to adhede ourselves to other bodies through embraces and holdings and adhere to the world through words and concepts. Yet the text constantly touches on the dread involved in the sense of the failure of all our adhesions and adherences. Throughout there is a sense of loneliness, lovelessness, emptiness, fear, the coldness of frost, the dark Africa of the night sky. It is a recognizable American geography, perhaps the mid-West, but more generally a geography of intense solitude. It is also a lexical geography, language itself in a reverie over its past.

We start by hearing a woman musing over the growth of her own body, but soon the interplay between body and language starts. The voice in the text says, "I dream like Madame Bovary. Only I don't die, during endings. I never die." Men die, sexually and corporeally. Language does not. Thus she goes on: "Travel, dream. I feel sometimes as if I *were* imagination (that spider goddess and threadspinning muse)—imagination imagining itself imagine." The echoes are of Becket of course, and all those spiders of the American imagination, Walt Whitman and Emily Dickinson included. As she says: "I used to write the scripts myself. I stole from the best, from the classiest greats. . . . They laughed just the same." Then there is a sudden change in tone: "she felt the terror of terminology. Why aren't there any decent words." And the mind/voice turns to words, just words, turning them over, playing with them as a sort of non-epistemic pigment, sounds to cuddle up with—"catafalque", "crepuscular", "dirigibility"—"but catafalque is best". Catafalque, perhaps not entirely coincidentally, is the structure on which the coffin rests which holds the body. The body dies: language, which to a large extent sustains and constitutes the body throughout its life, remains. Like a catafalque. Dryden, Flaubert, Hardy, Joyce and many other dead writers linger on in fragments in her drowsy monologue. Similarly the voice is a woman, but also "I'm only a string of noises, after all, a column of air moving up and down." Noncorporeality is both death and a kind of immortality, like the literature which continues to move around inside this "string of noises". People die—how often we are reminded of it—but, "I, on the other hand, made so luckily of language—last..........even in a row of dots..........in silence..........in nothing..........I am. Back now, of course, composing myself again, full of liberty, creation and my claw." Thus we keep encountering in different forms the interminglings and separations of the wastings of the body and the preservations of the word. And one thing that does emerge as transcending the seedy middle-West existence bespoken at one level of the text is this: "the whole of literature lies before us . . . like a land we live in, once we've moved there, in the purest figure of our former life . . . only here in this sweet country of the word are rivers, streams, woods, gardens, houses, mountains, waterfalls and the crowding fountains of the trees eternal as it's right they should be. . . ."

After all kinds of mockery and teasings of the conventional reader—the crude "literalist" who, like a bad lover, can only think of plunging straight ahead in a crude monolinear manner—the text moves to a beautiful conclusion in which the woman and language speak together: "When a letter comes, if you will follow me, there is no author fastened to it like the stamp; the words which speak, they are the body of the speaker. It's just the same with me. These words are all I am. Believe me. Pity me. Not even the Dane is any more than that. Oh, I'm the girl upon this couch, all right, you needn't fear; the one who's waltzed you through these pages, clothed and bare, who's hated you for her humiliations, sought your love, just as the striptease dancer does. . . . Could you love me? Love me then . . . then love me . . . Yes. I know. I can't command it. Yet I should love, if ever you would let me, like a laser, burning through all foolish ceremonials of modesty and custom. . . . My dears, my dears . . . how I would brood upon you: you, the world; and I, the language. . . . . . I am that lady language chose to make her playhouse of. . . ."

The idea of the "playhouse" of language might be set beside Nietzsche's idea of "the prison house of language" to give some idea of the sense of release experienced by reading Gass's text.* Indeed the

* Although Derrida's famous essay on "Structure, Sign and Play in the Discourse of Human Sciences" was not consciously in my mind while I wrote this paper, it was probably an indirect influence and, as was pointed out to me by a student after a lecture, is of course very relevant to what I am trying to suggest might be going on in some contemporary American fiction.

transformation of that prison house into a playhouse through the use of all kinds of techniques of eruption, displacement, decategorization and everything implied in the word "carnivalisation" could be seen as the motive force behind the "games" American writers play. The ultimate aim may indeed be to escape from the prisonhouse altogether, just as a character in one of Gass's stories tries to "drive himself into wordlessness" and the speaker/writer of his present work in progress, "Tunnels", seems bent on burrowing out of language itself. But if we can never finally avoid being to some extent "creatures at the mercy of language" (Lacan) then at least—let the game go on. So Gass's text ends with the lady-language exhorting herself. . . . "Then let us have a language worthy of our world, a democratic style where rich and well-born nouns can roister with some sluttish verb yet find themselves content and uncomplained of. We want a diction which contains the quaint, the rare, the technical, the obsolete, the old, the lent, the nonce, the local slang and argot of the street, in neighbourly confinement. Our tone should suit our time: uncommon quiet dashed with common thunder. . . . Experimental and expansive . . . it will give new glasses to new eyes, and put those plots and patterns down we find our modern lot in. Metaphor must be its god now that gods are metaphors." It is as though language itself is seeking for the conditions of its own carnivalisation. Gass's text takes us into the heart of the heart of the desolations of our corporeal existence, but it also takes us into "the sweet country of the word"—writer and reader talking and dying alike, the lonesome self losing and recreating itself in language, the prisonhouse turning itself into the playhouse before our very eyes.

One of John Barth's most recent works was entitled *Lost in the Funhouse* and in his latest novel he continued to explore the problematical position of the writer in the playhouse. We are named before we name, spoken before we speak, told stories before we narrate; given a hyper-awareness of this condition what is a contemporary narrator to do? Barth's *Chimera* can best be read, I think, as his projection of various aspects of the situation of the American writer now.

Barth is a narrator; he has all of world literature available to him and to varying extents internalized within him, so that it is doubtful if he can ever tell an original story, for all the narrative structures and patternings have been explored. By the same token he is a voice, but is that voice his own? Thus the narrating voice on the page — and the subsuming of voice into page is an important aspect of the whole book — says/writes: "I wonder how many voices are telling my tale. . . . I'm full of voices, all mine, none me; I can't keep straight who's speaking as I used to. . . ." But if he cannot tell an original story in an individual voice he can attempt to explore the origins of story and try to lay bare all the ambiguities of using a narrative voice which both is and is not his own. The title itself points to both the structure and the ambiguity of the book. The Chimera is a three-fold monster — lion, goat, serpent — it is a taxonomic freak, an ironic challenge to orthodox taxonomy. It is also an apparition, an illusion. Within the book there are three contiguous but discontinuous stories, as in the parts of the beast. "Du yazdiad," which is effectively concerned with the position of the story teller, "Perseid," an authentic hero, and "Bellerophoniad," a 'phony' or inauthentic hero (Barth himself pointed out the pun in the name). In the original legends both these heroes killed monsters with the aid of magic and divinely-given aids. These aids include Pegasus, the winged horse now associated with poetry. Pegasus also defies taxonomy in being a magic synthesis but is a transcendence of natural forms and human categories, whereas the Chimera is an anomalous and counter-transcendent assortment — not a super-real synthesis but a sur-real, or unreal, botch. The opposition between these two is somewhere at the heart of Barth's book which is itself a kind of Pegasus/Chimerical entity.

The book itself engages the phenomenon of heroes, figures who through *action* created a distinct pattern in their own lives, then a distinct pattern in oral *legend*, and thence a distinct *narrative* pattern in printed words. This movement from life into words is an ambiguous one, and it is one which is confronted in the text as the heroes/voices/pages discuss how life is transformed into legend, reality into myth, archetype into stereotype, action into print — transformations which also involve a move from time into relative immortality. This points to another central preoccupation in the book — what lasts? An aspect of this is, what is the relationship between narrating and time? "Perseid" opens in this way: "Good evening. Stories last longer than men, stones than stars, stars than stones. But even our stars' nights are numbered, and with them will pass this patterned tale to a long-deceased earth." Perseus threatened with the Gorgon's head finally becomes a star and, putting it very simply, one problem the book keeps returning to is how to achieve the good immortality of estellation and avoid the bad immortality of petrification. Or as Barth himself put it in an interview — the thing is to find the narrative trick of turning stones into stars. And he also said that he likes the idea of himself as a writer using a pencil like a lance, "riding the horse of inspiration to kill the chimera which has become a synonym for fictions, illusions, and hallucinations." In this way he hopes to avoid the petrifaction which threatens him as a fiction writer, and he attempts to do this by piercing through all the layers of legend — text, voice, life — to confront and contest the very origin of the narrating impulse. To put it very simply — here is the question the modern writer asks himself: "What can I say that's new?" One answer: "I can say 'What can I say that's new'", thus putting the problem in a larger context in which it can be approached and probed from as many angles as the writer cares to explore. The old stories can only be retold as meta-stories, stories commenting on themselves in a variety of other languages including modern vernacular and computer programming terminology.

At this point let me give two quotations from the endings of the two tales about the ancient heroes. At the end of the "Perseid" Medusa asks Perseus if he is happy with the way this story ends. He answers: "My love, it's an epilogue, always ending, never ended . . . which winds through universal space and time . . . I'm content . . . to have become . . . these silent, visible signs; to *be* the tale I tell to those with eyes to see and understanding to interpret; to raise you up forever and know that our story will never be cut off, but nightly rehearsed as long as men and women read the stars. . . ." This is the satisfactory resolution of life into tale and print. Bellerophon on the other, who was thrown from Pegasus while trying to fly up to the gods directly and who wandered wounded and alone into utter obscurity, has a different conclusion. While falling he has a conversation with his teacher Polyeidus, and asks: "Can you turn me into this story?" to which Polyeidus answers in the emphatic negative, adding: "What I *might* manage . . . is to turn *myself* from this interview into you-in-Bellerophoniad-form: a certain number of printed pages in a language not untouched by Greek, to be read by a limited number of 'Americans,' not all of whom will finish or enjoy them." To which Bellerophon replies with a complaint to the world: "I hate this, World! It's not at all what I had in mind for Bellerophon. It's a beastly fiction, ill-proportioned, full of longueurs, lumps, lacunae, a kind of monstrous mixed metaphor. . . ." and he trails off into silence and we are left with the incomplete book in our hands. How will our modern fictions end — integration and synthesis at a higher level (Pegasus) or the collapse into a heterogeneous mess? What Barth is doing to us as readers is expose us to, and engage us in, the problematics of narrative utterance and writing in our present age. At one point he includes in the book an amusing account of someone who tries to program a computer to compose "not hypothetical fictions, but the 'Complete', the 'Final Fiction'." Everything from magic to myths to masterplot summaries is fed in, and out comes an alphabetical chaos. With so much available disparate data, what chance is there for an innocent fiction any longer? What Barth seems to be insisting is that if fiction seems to have exhausted its possibilities (and his text includes some weary enumerations of all the different devices used by novelists in the past either to mystify or demystify their readers), then it must find its future in the centre of that exhaustion. What is at stake is active survival amid over-abundance of inert material — or a new approach to estellation among increasingly threatening modes of petrification.

At one level this is a book which makes the critic or commentator completely redundant. Barth puts his sources into his text, he includes letters and statements revealing his ideas about the writings of the novel, he lists his pet motifs and favorite themes. There is very little for the critic to trace, interpret, or decipher. The only secret in the book is that it keeps no secrets. It gives them away at a rate which does indeed make the book difficult to read in any conventional way. All a commentator can do is to step back into a different frame of reference and, once again, ask, not what is the book about so much as, what is going on here? A certain amount of arbitrariness in the ordering of any comments offered by way of an answer is justified by such a text and I propose to isolate just three aspects of the book. The first concerns the false hero Bellerophon. As represented by Barth he is a figure obsessed with pattern, the heroic pattern in this case, which occurs in various forms and diagrams in his story. There is in this the idea of a man deliberately trying to sacrifice his self-hood to a pattern, which means that the pattern takes precedence over life, pre-forms it, indeed petrifies it in advance, since the individual with such an aspiration can only ever become an imitation, not the thing itself. As Bellerophon realizes near the end: "I saw the chimera of my life. By imitating perfectly the Pattern of Mythic Heroes, I'd become, not a mythic hero, but a perfect Reset . . . it's hardly to be imagined that those patterns we call 'Perseus,' 'Medusa,' 'Pegasus,' . . . are aware of their existence, any more than their lettered counterparts on the page." One problem being explored here is that of excessive self-consciousness, and the over-abundance of *schema* and models. Barth is fond of Borges' comment that God doesn't study theology, any more than saints study the lives of saints or (as Barth said in interview) birds study ornithology. But we are reading and encountering stories, forms, patterns all the time, so how can we *be* the original story of our life and not a simple retelling of one gone before, and how can a writer *tell* an original story rather than merely repeat one that has already been told? One answer is to be found in the second aspect of the book I wish to mention —

namely, what is going on in the first section of the book called "Dunzadiad"?

This is apparently a story told by the younger sister of Scheherezade and is obviously related to the situation of the novelist today, since Dunyazade has to listen to all the stories Scheherezade tells and then at the end has to face the problem of what story *she* will tell. *The Thousand and One Nights* would seem to be an abiding obsession for Barth, with its intimate connection between narration/copulation/and survival. In this tale, through the auditor Dunyazade, he images Scheherezade exploring the possibilities of story-telling, trying to get at its secret power so that she can prolong her life. She has given up expecting salvation by a genie, knowing that the only magic is in words. "The real magic is to understand which words work, and when, and for what: the trick is to learn the trick." Scheherezade refers to all the stories about treasure to which no one can find the key and adds that she has the key but can't find the treasure, the key being the pen and ink she doodles with. What she suddenly realizes is that "the key to the treasure *is* the treasure" at which point a genie does appear, the genie of her imagination. Between them they go into all the problems of fiction, its future and origins, as he remembers stories she has yet to tell. Two or three key points in this story are worth isolating. The genie — and now think of this as, say, the contemporary American novelist's imagination — explains the situation he was in until those words — "the key to the treasure is the treasure" — came to him. "There's a kind of snail in the Maryland marshes — perhaps I invented him — that makes his shell as he goes along out of whatever he comes across, cementing it with his own juices, and at the same time makes his path instinctively toward the best available material for his shell; he carries his history on his back, living in it, adding new and larger spirals to it from the present as he grows. That snail's pace has become my pace, but I'm going in circles, following my own trail." The shell is not a statement about the material it is made of, though without that material it could not exist. What it adds to the world is its own spiral shape. The spiral is an open-ended form; the circle is closed. This is important — the contrast between the circle and the spiral turns up repeatedly in this book and while the "Perseid" is based on the spiral, the "Bellerophoniad" is organized on the circle. It would seem that one way of putting the problem for some contemporary American novelists is how to break out of the circle into the spiral: in going round in a circle, narrative degenerates into cliché and language disintegrates into a purposeless jumble of letters and empty spaces, the remnants of a code no longer transformable into messages. The spiral shell is purposive, a thing assembled, an extension of the code which at the same time both permits and *is* a new kind of message. (Of course the spiral shell of Daedalus is somewhere behind this, but it touches on a much larger problem, namely that of the very idea of a 'new' piece of writing.) To put it in simple terms, there are two impossible extremes when it comes to writing a novel — total repetition and total innovation or novelty. The first is precluded by temporal considerations so that, as Borges has reminded us, *Don Quixote* written now using exactly the same words in the same order would be a different book. The second is precluded by conditions governing communication. No one can invent a completely new language which can also be used for purposes of communication, so any novelist must to some extent traffic in the familiar. In between these two impossible extremes there are varying degrees of what I will call here "imbrication." The extent to which a novel (say) overlaps with what is known and familiar can vary enormously and it would be impossible to establish any metric by which to measure degrees of imbrication. Yet we can clearly register works which seem to try to reduce the degree of imbrication to a minimum, and others which rely heavily on a high degree of imbrication, merely changing or modifying a little so that the reader is teased but not taxed. (These problems of imbrication and modification point to the basic problems of repetition and difference in language itself which have concerned French writers such as Deleuze. This is outside the sphere of my competence but for a very lucid and helpful assessment of the subject see Edward Said's article "An Ethics of Language" in *Diacritics* [Summer, 1974].) One example where a change in the degree of imbrication affected a writer's reception can be seen in the changing response to Melville's work. The earlier books were popular as they seemed to be recognizable as belonging to a familiar genre of travel writing. Imbrication was high. In *Moby Dick* the imbrication is drastically reduced as the familiar genre spirals out into new areas of fictional exploration. The result was that the book was much less popular than Melville's previous work, and from this point his career as a writer declined as far as readership was concerned. For the writer imbrication is involved with survival.

For the writer to go round in a circle is to engage in repetitions of increasing probability, which may be said to contribute to fictional entropy. To open the narrative circle to the spiral, then, would be to counteract this entropic tendency. And for Barth the way out of the circle into the spiral seems to lie in the realization that the key to the treasure is the treasure. We may think of that proposition applying to fiction in these terms. According to older epistemologies reality was the treasure and to get at it you had to find the right key - right representational mode, appropriate verbal procedure, etc. To say that the key *is* the treasure is to reject that kind of dualistic model; indeed in a way it rejects the idea of any pre-existent reality waiting to be opened. The key is language, and if the key is the treasure, language is the treasure of reality. This extreme conclusion does not, I think, imply some kind of complete solipsism, nor any idealist denial of material existence (though it may preclude the fictional engagement of historical, political and social problems). Barth's work is very aware of the body, of sexuality, of love and loss, of death. The emphasis, I think, is on the contention that the only reality we can do anything about is language, not how the world appears but how it reappears in words and how words reappear in new contexts. In every sphere man is a creature who engenders re-presentations, and interest in fiction has increasingly shifted from the 'what' of presentation to the 'how' of representation. This is the point of one exchange between Scheherezade and her genie in which they are discussing the relation between framed and framing tales, and Dunyazade comments: "This relation (which to me seemed less important than what the stories were *about*) interested the two of them no end, just as Sherry and Shahryar were fascinated by the pacing of their nightly pleasures or the refinement of their various positions, instead of the degree and quality of their love." The answer of Scheherezade is notable as it contains implicitly a whole theory of the aesthetics of the novel. "That other goes without saying . . . or it doesn't go at all. Making love and telling stories both take more than good technique — but it's only the technique that we can *talk* about." This is very different from an autotelic theory of art; it does not deny subject matter, but rather asserts that you can only talk about how you talk about it. Which is literally metalanguage — a statement about making statements. This conclusion is in line with William Gass's well-known observation that increasingly "the forms of fiction serve as the material upon which further forms can be imposed. Indeed, many of the so-called anti-novels are really metafictions."*

* The whole debate concerning whether fiction ought to be, or can be, "referential" or can only be "meta" is probably both too familiar and certainly too large to be addressed here. Some of the problems can be resolved by recognising that all usages of language involve both as Jacobson pointed out, but that will go almost no way towards explaining why Joyce Carol Oates writes the kinds of novels she does and William Gass writes the kind of novel he does. It is quite clear that they think that words within a fictional text are to be arranged in very different ways to very different ends. To see the issue from another angle, it is interesting to note some of the comments of Henri LeFebvre in *Everyday Life in the Modern World*, in which he diagnoses a "decline of

The final aspect of the book I wish to touch on concerns the figure who in many ways is a key to the whole enterprise, Polyeidus, the seer of many forms, the protean counselor whom Barth reminds us he has always been interested in. As a tutor to Bellerophon he speaks of "ontological metamorphosis" with a contemporary weariness with such over-familiar terminology. In Barth's terms he is a version of the figure who, as he becomes more aware of his art, loses his potency as an artist.

referentials" as part of the malaise of modern life, since it leads to an "uncoupling of signifiers and signified". "The decline of referentials had generalized the uncoupling; in the absence of a referential and a code providing *common places (topoi* and *koina*, social topics) the link between the two signs is insecure; we are already familiar with the floating stock of *meaningless signifiers*." One result of this is "the fascination of signs": "floating in swarms and clouds they are free for all, ever available and, taking the place of action, they appropriate the interest formerly involved in activity." Thus "language and linguistics relations become *denials* of everyday life." We live in the age of "metalanguage". Here is a very clear statement of his position. "There is *contradiction between referential and metalinguistic functions*, the latter eroding the former and supplanting them; the vaguer the referential the more distinct and significant grows metalanguage . . . metalanguage becomes a substitute for language by assuming the attributes of referential-endowed language; the disappearance of each referential liberates a signifier and makes it available, whereupon metalanguage promptly appropriates its, employing it for jobs 'at one remove', which contributes to the decline of referentials, while metalanguage reigns, detached and 'cool'." This is almost to hypostatise metalanguage, or to make of it an independent force taking over society in an almost Burroughs-like manner, yet one can see what Lefebvre is getting at. I have not, of course, done justice to his whole argument, but two comments on his position occur to me. If the situation is as he describes it, then can a writer still use language as though it still had the kind of referential function and potency which Lefebvre says has in fact been pre-empted by metalanguage? Or might he or she, recognizing that something has happened along the lines of Lefebvre's diagnosis, rather not confront this increasing predominance of metalanguage and, in one way and another "lay it bare" in their own texts in such a way as to make the reader more aware of this metalinguistic take-over, so that he will perhaps be less vulnerable to the manipulative and coercive abuse of signs in other metalinguistic areas of life (such as advertising) which is one of Lefebvre's concerns?

I only read Lefebvre after writing this paper but I was interested to note that he also writes about the "death of the ludic spirit" in contemporary everyday life and laments the decline of "festival, of which play and games are only one aspect." He hopes for a "resurrection of the Festival" but for him it must be social, actual. There can be no other form of festival. "Art can replace neither Style nor the Festival in a society dominated by the quotidien, and is an increasingly specialized activity that parodies the Festival, an ornament adorning everyday life but failing to transform it." I can respect this point of view, but would still want to propose that the parodies of festivals (and festivals of parodies) offered by some Art can have a positive "transforming" effect on everyday life. However I must record that my own experience of other peoples' readings of the works I am discussing in this paper does not do much to sustain my contention. Thus on the one hand I have heard a philosopher who is very aware of problems of language praise Didion's work very highly, and on the other, heard an expert in the field of cognitive development admit that after a few pages he couldn't be bothered to go on with *Gravity's Rainbow*. Outside of students, who are the readers I am referring to? This is also a problem too big to be engaged here, but I felt it appropriate to record it.

At first he could turn into other people, then places, but later he mainly turns into documents — a kind of précis of the writer's changing attitude to the power of his own words. On one memorable occasion he finds himself in prison and tries to turn into the cell itself so that the guards will think he has escaped and go away leaving him to go free. But he has lost his power in three dimensions and turns, not into his dungeon cell, but into a "magic message spelling out that objective: *I am a chamber.*" This does give him a kind of freedom, but he now finds himself a firebreathing monster with a lion's head, goat's body, and serpent's tail — a chimera. The idea of a writer turning himself into the prison he is in is already very suggestive. The further suggestion that, since this cannot be managed literally, he turns himself into a message which stands in lieu of the prison by naming it, is even more so. And the unexpected development whereby in his liberation he finds that he has turned into an enormous fiction, or a fictional enormity (the inversion is Barth's own), is a very telling piece of wit. At the very least it suggests some of the ambiguities involved in trying to break out of the prisonhouse of language (and all the patterning determinants it contains) through the playing of fictional games. As the book nears its end Polyeidus is plotting how to turn into the pages we are reading, finally permeating the whole work, the ultimate metamorphosis which will prolong his existence through pagination. Polyeidus becomes the book we are holding: there are no monsters, no heroes, not even any voices, for even they remind us that they are "all mere Polyeidic inklings, written words." There is a curious feeling here of the narrative plenitude which is our past suddenly dissolving into ink and paper, becoming apparitional, chimerical. We don't even actually have the novel. As Barth has said, what is a novel, where is it? Its ontological status is uncertain. What we hold is only one copy. Of a copy. Barth's quest for the origins of narrative, through the strategy of a continuous displacement of myth into modernity and vice versa, has brought him close to the point at which the quest discovers its own futility and the writer finds that there are no origins, only "inklings".

Perhaps there is a state of contemporary consciousness, felt with particular acuteness by a writer of fictions and stories, when a repletion of material and motif suddenly feels like an emptiness, and with all the stories of the world in his head he is suddenly thrown back into himself, alone, in an empty room, self-ejected from the fictions he may hitherto have played with, as all the narrational wonders of the world resolve themselves into mere arbitrary marks on the page. And if pages have their longevity they have their pathos too. It is perhaps at this point that the writer transforms himself into a statement about his cell in order to escape from it. But I think there is an even more central concern in everything I've mentioned. It emerges very directly once in the shortest possible sentence, when the author is characteristically discussing his main thematic concerns. One of these is "the mortal desire for immortality . . . and its ironically qualified fulfillment — especially by the mythic hero's transformation, in the latter stages of his career, into the sound of his own voice, of the story of his life. I am forty." I am forty. This suddenly brings before us the mortal narrator, half way into life, half way into death. What is going on here is, I think, a game of mid-passage, the very existence of narrator and narrativity alike in the balance. It shows signs at times of being a quite desperate game, and it is always a dangerous one, since at any moment the Pegasus flight may give way to the chimerical condition.

Of all the works of recent American fiction which have been referred to as "games" by one critic or another, the strangest would seem to be *Gravity's Rainbow*, yet there is no doubt that the book offers some sort of dark carnival of discourses which undermines all our habitual modes of apprehension as we confront it. Pynchon's concern has always been related to problems of decipherment and what Lukács described as "the incommensurability of . . . interiority and adventure — in the absence of a transcendental 'place' allotted to human endeavours, particularly as this incommensurability manifests itself in a permanent instability in the relationship between the interpreting mind and the varying fields of signification which it must negotiate." His first novel, *V*, can be seen as a modern repetition and distortion of the paradigm novel for Western fiction, *Don Quixote*. Stencil is the figure (also the copy) who attempts to apprehend and pattern reality according to his single "ideal" obsession with "V". In Lukács' terms his consciousness is much "narrower" than the world through which he moves and everything either has to be "translated" into terms consonant with his one interpretative scheme, or screened out. (His obsession with "V" is the clue with which he attempts to find his way through the labyrinth, but in the process he transforms the labyrinth into clues.) At the other extreme is Benny Profane whose consciousness seems to be so wide and unselective that he experiences no gestalt at all in his perceptions of the world around him. For Stencil everything signifies too much and taken to its logical extreme his mind would conflate the whole of existence into a single sign — "V"; all differences would finally vanish as the over-integrated world resolved itself into one undifferentiated clue. That it would be a clue to itself indicates the ultimate danger of such a quest, for if V can mean everything it means nothing. For Benny Profane there are more signals than significances; he detects no clues anywhere and is a motiveless wanderer up and down the generic street of the twentieth century, going nowhere and seeing only separate objects in a disintegrating world. The contrast is between a mind which sees everything as interconnected and over-determined and one which sees no connections and experiences only randomness, contingency and indeterminacy. Is Stencil a lunatic, or a man with creative vision? Is Benny Profane a realist, or a figure of dulled and impoverished perceptions? Between them these two figures point to the question which worries so many of Pynchon's characters. Are we surrounded by plots — social, natural, cosmic; or is there no plot, no hidden configuration of intent, only gratuitous matter and chance? This of course is the problem which takes hold of Oedipa Maas in *The Crying of Lot 49*. She is named the executrix of a will and in trying to discover its meaning she feels plots starting to take shape around her and clues starting to multiply, so that out of necessity she becomes a desperate cryptologist. The problem becomes a matter of where to look for meaning and of what to regard as significant. It is as if she were reading a book but whereas in a stable text the words stand out against the blank paper as figures against ground, in the book she is reading words and blanks, figure and ground, exist in a very unstable relationship to each other and at times seem to become interchangeable. If there is no significance in the word or the figure then the reading mind starts to search in the spaces around and between them. Putting it very simply, if the sign turns into a blank then, the feeling goes, perhaps the blank will turn into a sign. In the case of Oedipa Maas the book is called America and what she has to try to decide is whether there is a strange ambiguous system or conspiracy at work, a second America hidden but operating in the interstices of the visible social structure?* Or whether she is hallucinating, "in the orbiting ecstasy of a true paranoia"?

I am stressing this aspect of Pynchon's work because whatever else *Gravity's Rainbow* is, or does, it provides an exemplary experience in

* In defining the position in society of various minority groups or sub-cultures, sociology sometimes applies the idea of 'marginality' or 'peripherality'. The point about such metaphors is that they imply a stable and locatable area for the minority group — the margin is that clear demarcated area which is not part of the text, the periphery is that part or boundary furthest from the centre. It might be more appropriate to the times to introduce the notion of 'interstiality' as a mode of existence for all kinds of people and groups who do not feel themselves to be part of the established social structure but find their way of life in various gaps. Just as any language depends on spaces, pauses, intervals, so even the most monolithic society must contain some gaps. Between the paving stones, life persists in the crevices.

modern reading, so that you do not proceed from some ideal "emptiness" of meaning to a fullness, but instead find yourself involved in a process in which any perception can precipitate a new confusion and an apparent clarification turns into a prelude to further difficulties. The novel does indeed have a recognizable historical setting — unlike the other "games" I have discussed. It is engaged with Europe at the end of the Second World War and just after. In choosing to situate his novel at this point in time Pynchon is concentrating on a crucial moment when a new trans-political order began to emerge out of the ruins of old orders which could no longer maintain themselves. At one point he describes the movements of displaced people at the end of the war, "a great frontierless streaming". The sentences that follow mime out this "frontierless" condition in an extraordinary flow of objects and people and conclude, "so the populations move, across the open meadow, limping, marching, shuffling, carried, hauling along the detritus of an order, a European and bourgeois order they don't yet know is destroyed forever." A later passage suggests what is taking the place of this vanished order: "Oh, a State begins to take form in the stateless German night, a State that spans oceans and surface politics, sovereign as the International or the Church of Rome, and the Rocket is its soul." The Rocket is specifically the V-2 which was launched on London, and, because it travelled faster than sound, crashed before the sound of its flight could be heard — a frightening disruption of conventional sequence and cause-effect expectations. (Hence the famous opening sentence — "a screaming comes across the sky.") But it also becomes the paradigm product of modern technology, and in making it the central object of the book Pynchon is clearly addressing himself to the socio-political implications of contemporary trends in history. But he refuses to do this in a conventional narrative way because conventional narrative procedures were themselves products of that vanished bourgeois order and it is no longer possible to "read" what is going on in any conventional manner. Thus Pynchon's characters move in a world of both too many and too few signs, too much data and too little information, too many texts but no reliable editions, an extreme "overabundance of signifiers", to borrow another phrase from Lévi-Strauss. I stress this first because before attempting to indicate what the novel is "about" in any traditional sense, I think it is important to consider how to read it, for more than anything else this book provides an experience in modern reading. People who expect and demand the traditional narrative conventions will be immediately disoriented by this book.

There is one phantasmagoric episode in a "disquieting structure" which is a dream-version of some contemporary hell. We read: "It seems to be some very extensive museum, a place of many levels, and new signs that generate like living tissue — though if it all does grow toward some end shape, those who are here inside can't see it." Now this is not only applicable to all the dozens of characters in the book itself — drifting in and out of sections, participating in different spaces, finding themselves on different levels; it is both their *dream* and their *dread* to see an "end shape" to it all, though of course, being in the book they never will. But, and I think this is very important, nor do we as readers. One of the things Pynchon manages to do so brilliantly is to make us participate in the beset and bewildered consciousness which is the unavoidable affliction of his characters.

As you read the book you seem to pass through a bewildering variety of genres, behavioral modes, and types of discourse — at different times the text seems to partake of such different things as pantomime, burlesque, cinema, cabaret, card games, songs, comic strips, spy stories, serious history, encyclopaedic information, mystical and visionary meditations, and scrambled imagery of dreams, the cold cause-and-effect talk of the Behaviourists, and all the various ways that men try to control and coerce realities both seen and unseen — from magic to measurement, from sciences to séances. At one point, one character is reading a Plasticman comic; he is approached by a man of encyclopaedic erudition who engages him in a conversation about etymology. Here is a clue for us — we should imagine that we are reading a comic, but it is partly transparent, and through it we are also reading an encyclopaedia, a film script, a piece of science history, and so on. There is only one text but it contains a multiplicity of surfaces, modes of discourse are constantly turning into objects of discourse with no one stable discourse holding them together. This is not such a bizarre undertaking as it may sound. We can all read and decode the different languages and genres Pynchon has brought into his book. Modern man is above all an interpreter of different signs, a reader of differing discourses, a servant of signals, a compelled and often compulsive decipherer. In Henri Lefebvre's use of the word, we do live in a "pleonastic" society of "aimless signifiers and disconnected signifieds" on many levels, so that you can see evidence of hyper-redundancy in the realm of signs, objects, institutions, even human beings. Wherever we look there is too much to "read". But never before has there been such uncertainty about the reliability of the texts. One character in the novel, making his way across the wastelands of post-war Europe, wonders whether it does contain a "Real Text". He thinks that such a text may be connected with the secrets of the Rocket — but perhaps the "Real Text" is the desolate landscape he is traversing, or perhaps he missed the Real Text somewhere behind him in a ruined city. . . . Reading Pynchon's novel gives us a renewed sense of how we have to read the modern world. At times in his book it is not always clear whether we are in a bombed-out building, or a bombed-out mind, but that too is quite appropriate. For how many of those rockets that fell in London fell in the consciousness of the survivors, exploding in the modern mind? And, looking around and inside us, how can we be sure how much is Real Text, and how much ruined débris?

In all this it is impossible to say with confidence what the book is "about" but constantly you have the sense of many things that it seems to be about. We may take a phrase from Lévi Strauss, admittedly out of context, and say that for the reader there is an "overabundance of signifiers" in the book just as, for the characters, there is a comparable overabundance in the world they seem to inhabit. But the Rocket is always there. It is phallic and fatal, Eros transformed into Thanatos, invading "Gravity's grey eminence" only to succumb to it, curving through the sky like a lethal rainbow then crashing to the earth. Does it strike by "chance" or according to some hidden design, some "music" of annihilation which we will never hear but is always being played? Around the rocket and its production Pynchon builds up a version of war-time England and post-war Europe which is staggering both in its detail and its fantasy. In addition the novel, as if trying to reach out into wider and more comprehensive contexts, extends back into colonial and American history, down into the world of molecules, up into the stars, back even to Bethlehem when men saw another kind of burning light in the sky. In all this certain abiding preoccupations may be discerned. Pattern, plots, and paranoia — these are familiar in Pynchon's world; add to those paper, plastic, preterition, and Pavlovian conditioning, and some of the main themes have been listed (the alliteration is not of course accidental — Pynchon, as author, knows that he is engaged in an activity related to Stencil's search for V. Unlike Stencil, however, he is constantly breaking up the gathering pattern of echoes, clues, and similarities). What emerges from the book is a sense of a force and a system — something, someone, referred to simply as "They" — which is actively trying to bring everything to zero and beyond, trying to institute a world of non-being, an operative kingdom of death, covering the organic world with a world of paper and plastic and transforming all natural resources into destructive power and waste — the rocket and the débris around it. "They" are, precisely non-specific, unlocatable. There is always the possibility of a They behind the They, a plot behind the plot; the quest to identify "Them" sucks the would-be identifier into the possibility of an endless regression. But whatever Their source and origin, They are dedicated to annihilation — this is a vision of entropy as an extremely powerful world-wide, if not cosmos-wide, enterprise. From Their point of view, and in the world of insidious reversals and inversions They are instituting, the war was a great creative act, not the destruction but the "reconfiguration" of people and places. They are also indentified with "the System" which "removes from the rest of the World vast quantities of energy to keep its own tiny desperate fraction showing a profit. . . . The System may or may not understand that it's only buying time . . . (that it) sooner or later must crash to its death, when its addiction to energy has become more than the rest of the World can supply. . . . Living inside the System, is like riding across the country in a bus driven by a maniac bent on suicide." The ecological relevance of this is all too frighteningly obvious.

Inside the System everything is fixed and patterned but its organizing centre — its "soul" — is the Rocket. To the extent that the System, and everyone inside the System, in one way or another converge on the Rocket, they are converging on death. Outside the System, and one of its by-products as it were, is the Zone in which nothing is fixed and there are no patterns or points of convergence. There are "no zones but the Zone", says one voice. This is the area of "the new Uncertainty" — "in the Zone categories have been blurred badly". In the Zone everything and everyone is adrift for there are no taxonomies, and no narratives, to arrange them. If all the concepts are blurred, can the people in the Zone have any knowledge of reality, or are they perhaps nearer to reality by living in a deconceptualized state, fumbling around among the débris left when the prisonhouse of language itself seems to have been destroyed? In the Zone there are only "images of Uncertainty". This involves a release from feeling that one is living in a completely patterned and determinate world, but also a panic at being outside any containing and explaining "frame" (in his review Richard Poirier wrote at length on the significance of the "frame" throughout the book). Those outside the System seemed doomed to go on "kicking endlessly among the plastic trivia, finding in each Deeper Significance, and trying to string them all together . . . to bring them together, in their slick persistence and our preterition . . . to make sense out of, to find the meanest sharp sliver of truth in so much replication, so much waste. . . ." Figures in the book inhabit either the system or the Zone or move between them (or do not know whether they are in either or both, for of course System and Zone have no locational as well as no epistemological stability), and this in turn elicits two dominant states of mind. Paranoia and anti-paranoia. Paranoia is, in terms of the book, "nothing less than the onset, the leading edge, of the discovery that *everything is connected*, everything in the Creation, a secondary illumination — not yet blindingly One, but at least connected." Of course, everything depends on the nature of the connection, the intention revealed in the pattern, and just *what* it is that may connect everything in Pynchon's world is what worries his main characters, like Slothrop. The opposite state of mind is anti-paranoia, "where nothing is connected to anything, a condition not many of us can bear for long." And as figures move between System and Zone, so they oscillate between paranoia and anti-paranoia, shifting from a seething blank of unmeaning to the sinister apparent legibility of an unconsoling labyrinthine pattern or plot. "We are obsessed with building labyrinths, where before there was open plain and sky. To draw ever more complex patterns on the blank-sheet. We cannot abide that openness; it is terror to us." Those who do not accept the officially sanctioned "delusions" of the System as "truth", but cannot abide pure blankness, have to seek out other modes of interpretation. Thus "those like Slothrop, with the greatest interest in discovering the truth, were thrown back on dreams, psychic flashes, omens, cryptographies, drug-epistemologies, all dancing on a ground of terror, contradiction, absurdity." This is the carnival of modern consciousness which the book itself portrays.

All this is related to our situation as readers. To put it very crudely, the book dramatizes two related assemblings and disassemblings — of the rocket and of the character or figure named Slothrop. Slothrop is engaged in trying to find out the secret of how the Rocket is assembled but in the process he himself is disassembled. Similarly the book both assembles and disassembles itself as we try to read it. For just as many of the characters are trying to see whether there is a "text" within the "waste" and a "game behind the game"; that is what we are having to do with the book as it unfolds in our attention. There is deliberately too much evidence, partaking of too many orders of types of explanation and modes of experience for us to hold it all together. In seeing some possible connections we are missing others. Reading itself thus becomes a paranoid activity which is, however, constantly breaking down under the feeling that we will never arrive at a unitary reading, never hold the book in one "frame": the sense of indeterminateness is constantly encroaching on us. We fluctuate between System and Zone, paranoia and anti-paranoia, experiencing both the dread of reducing everything to one fixed explanation — an all-embracing plot of death — and the danger of succumbing to apparently random detritus. Behind all this is the process of nature itself, working by organization and disorganization. The rocket is described as "an entire system *won*, away from the feminine darkness, held against the entropies of lovable but scatter-brained Mother Nature." It engorges energy and information in its "fearful assembly", thus its "order" is obtained at the cost of an increase in disorder in the world around it, through which so many of the characters stumble. But in its fixity and metallic destructive inhumanity it is an order of death — a *negative* parallel of the process of nature, since its disintegration presages no consequent renewal and growth. That is one reason why at the end the rocket is envisaged as *containing* the living body of a young man (Gottfried), for this is the System *inside* which man is plotting his own annihilation. If we as readers try to win away one narrative "System" from the book we are in danger of repeating mentally what They are doing in building the rocket. To put it in its most extreme form, they are trying to reduce all of nature's self-renewing variety to one terminal rocket; we must avoid the temptation to reduce the book to one fixed meaning. That is why our reading should be paranoid and anti-paranoid, registering narrative order, and disorder, experiencing both the determinate and the indeterminate*, pattern and randomness, renewing our awareness of our acts and interpretations as being both conditioned and free, and of ourselves as synthesizing and disintegrating systems.

In this way we can to some extent be released from the System-Zone bind which besets Pynchon's main characters, in particular the figure of Slothrop. What happens to Slothrop is in every sense exemplary. One of the earliest events in his life is being experimented on in a Pavlovian laboratory (which is related to the obsession with all kinds of control and "conditioning" which the book also explores). He is last seen, if seen at all, on a record cover. In between he has been the Plasticman and Rocketman of the comics he reads, played a variety of roles for English and American intelligence, been involved in the distorted fantasies and plots of dozens of figures in post-war Europe all the time approaching the centre, the secret of the rocket, which is also the absolute zero at the

* I was sent a very interesting essay on 'indeterminacy' in *Gravity's Rainbow* by Melvin Ulm and David Holt at Ohio State University, in which they suggest the relevance of the work of W. V. Quine, in particular *Word and Object*, in considering what Pynchon is doing in the novel. To my knowledge the essay has not been published, but it does contain some fruitful ideas which merit attention and I wish to acknowledge that I profited from reading it.

heart of the System. He knows that he is involved in the evil games of other people, whether they are run by the army or blackmarketeers or whatever, but he cannot finally get out of these games. Indeed, leaving all the games is one of the hopes and dreams of the few people with any human feeling left in the book. But it remains a dream. Reality has been pre-empted by games, or it has been replaced by films so that people can be said to live "paracinematic lives". As he moves through different experience-spaces he suffers a loss of emotion, a "numbness", and a growing sense that he will never "get back". Along with this erosion of the capacity to feel, he begins to "scatter", his "sense of Now" or "temporal bandwith" gets narrower and narrower and there is a feeling that he is getting so lost and unconnected that he is vaporizing out of time and place altogether. Near the end of his travels Slothrop suddenly sees a rainbow, a real one, and he has a vision of it entering into sexual union with the green unpapered earth; it is the life-giving antithesis to the rocket's annihilating penetrations: "and he stands crying, not a thing in his head, just feeling natural . . ." After that he effectively vanishes. There is a story told about him. He "was sent into the Zone to be present at his own assembly — perhaps, heavily paranoid voices have whispered, *his time's assembly*, and there ought to be punch line to it, but there isn't. The plan went wrong. He is being broken down instead, and scattered." The disassembling of Slothrop is, as I have suggested, in some way related to the assembling of the Rocket — the plan that went right — and it has far-reaching and disturbing implications.

The last comment on the possible whereabouts of Slothrop is this: "we would expect to look among the Humility, among the gray and preterite souls, to look for him adrift in the hostile light of the sky, the darkness of the sea. . . ." This idea of "the preterite" is very important in this book and, I think, central to Pynchon's vision; as he uses it, it refers to those who have been "passed over", the abandoned, the neglected, the despised and the rejected, those for whom the System has no use, the human junk thrown overboard from the ship of state (a literal ship in this book, incidentally, named *Anubis* after the ancient Egyptian God of the Dead). Set against the Preterite are the Elite, the users and manipulators, those who regard the planet as solely for their satisfaction, the nameless and ubiquitous "They" who dominate the world of the book. It is one of the modern malaises which Pynchon has diagnosed that it is possible for a person to feel himself entering into a state of "preterition". But, and once again Pynchon's erudition and wit work admirably here, the idea of humanity being divided into a Preterite and an Elite or Elect is of course a basic Puritan belief. In theological terms the Preterite were precisely those who were not elected by God and, if I may quote from one of those chilling Puritan pronouncements, "the preterite are damned because they were never meant to be saved." In redeploying these terms, which after all were central to the thinking of the people who founded America, and applying them to cruelly divisive and oppositional modes of thought at work throughout the world today Pynchon once again shows how imaginatively he can bring the past and present together. One of Slothrop's ancestors wrote a book called *On Preterition* supporting the Preterite as being quite as important as the Elect, and Slothrop himself wonders whether this doesn't point to a fork in the road which America never took, and whether there might not be a "way back" even in the ruined spaces of post-war Europe? — "maybe for a little while all the fences are down, one road as good as another, the whole space of the Zone cleared, depolarized, and somewhere inside the waste of it a single set of coordinates from which to proceed, without elect, without preterite, without even nationality to fuck it up . . ." This then is the organising question of the book. Is there a way back? Out of the streets "now indifferently gray with commerce"; out of the City of Pain, which Pynchon has taken over from Rilke's Tenth Duino Elegy and offers as a reflection of the world we have made; a way back out of the cinemas, the laboratories, the asylums and all our architecture of mental drugging, coercion and disarray (derangement)? Out of a world in which emotions have been transferred from people to things, and images supplant realities? Where, ultimately, would the "way back" lead to, if not some lost Eden previous to all categories and taxonomies, election and preterition, divisions and oppositions, "griddles and signs"? Can we even struggle to regain such a mythic state? Of course the book offers no answers, though the possibility of a "counter force" is touched on. It moves to a climax which is deliberately a sort of terminal fusion of many of the key fantasies and obsessions in the book — the note is comic-apocalyptic, or, perhaps we can now simply say, Pynchonesque. The opening page evokes the evacuation of London, with a crucial comment — "but it's all theatre." On the last page we are suddenly back in a theatre. We're waiting for the show to start — as Pynchon comments we've "always been at the movies (haven't we?)." The film has broken down, though on the darkening screen there is something else — "a film we have not learned to see." The audience is invited to sing, while outside a Rocket "reaches its last unmeasurable gap above the roof of the old theatre." It is falling in absolute silence, and we know that it will demolish the old theatre — the old theatre of our civilization. But we don't see it because we are in the theatre trying to read the film behind the film; and we won't hear it because, under the new dispensation, the annihilation arrives first, and only after — "a screaming comes across the sky."

If these three books are "games" they are, I think, games trying to break the games which contemporary culture imposes on us at all levels. They are games to "quit the game" to the extent that this is possible. They are games, if you like, in line with the prescription laid down by the Russian critic Dobrolyubov when he wrote: "It is necessary to work out in our soul a firm belief in the need and possibility of a complete exit from the present order of this life, so as to find the strength to express it in poetic forms." Such exits can only be temporary and in this sense the books themselves are, and offer, limited periods of such an exit. Inasmuch as what Lacan calls the master-words of the city ("maitresmots de la cité") may tend to reify into a dominant "privileged" discourse, these games may challenge and disturb this mastery and simply make readers aware of new possible ways of being in language. But from another point of remove they are games very much *about* important matters, for one is about the future and survival of language, one is about the future and survival of the narrator, and one is about the future and survival of the planet itself. They are games in the sense intended by Adorno when he wrote that "The unreality of games gives notice that reality is not yet real. Unconsciously they rehearse the right life." (*Minima Moralia*).*

* In the context the translation seems to make no distinction between game and "play". Adorno is writing about how children use play as "a defence." "In his purposeless activity the child, by a subterfuge, sides with use value against exchange value. Just because he deprives the things with which he plays of their mediated usefulness, he seeks to rescue in them what is benign towards men and not what subserves the exchange relation that equally deforms men and things."